BELIEF, ATTITUDE, INTENTION AND BEHAVIOR:

An Introduction to Theory and Research

BELIEF, ATTITUDE, INTENTION AND BEHAVIOR:

An Introduction to Theory and Research

MARTIN FISHBEIN
University of Illinois at Urbana-Champaign

ICEK AJZEN
University of Massachusetts, Amherst

ADDISON-WESLEY PUBLISHING COMPANY

Reading, Massachusetts • Menlo Park, California
London • Amsterdam • Don Mills, Ontario • Sydney

This book is in the
ADDISON-WESLEY SERIES IN SOCIAL PSYCHOLOGY

ISBN 0-201-02089-0
DEFGHIJKLM-MA-89876543210

Preface

As Gordon Allport pointed out some forty years ago, ". . . attitude is probably the most distinctive and indispensable concept in contemporary American social psychology. No other term appears more frequently in experimental and theoretical literature." Allport's words are as true today as they were in 1935. The centrality of the attitude concept remains unchallenged and, if anything, its importance has increased. Nevertheless, conceptions of attitude have undergone many changes in the past four decades. Most of these changes were necessitated by the failure of attitudes to live up to their promise as the central device for explaining and predicting behavior. Unfortunately, despite the vast amount of research and the publication of countless books and articles on the topic, there is little agreement about what an attitude is, how it is formed or changed, and what role, if any, it plays in influencing or determining behavior. This state of affairs clearly presents a dilemma for students and teachers alike. How does one select a course of study from a truly overwhelming amount of literature on various attitude-related topics? To make matters worse, how does one select from a literature that, in almost every topic area, is characterized by a lack of integration, radically different approaches and definitions, and what appear to be nothing more than inconsistent, contradictory, and inconclusive findings? It should come as no surprise that some investigators are calling for the abolishment of the attitude concept by pointing to the lack of a systematic approach and the failure of the field to provide a cumulative body of knowledge.

It is our contention that these calls are premature and probably unwarranted. The purpose of this book is to present a coherent and systematic conceptual framework that can be applied to the diverse literature on attitudes. We hope to show that the attitude literature is neither as inconsistent nor as inconclusive as it first appears, and, more importantly, that we are, in fact, moving toward a cumulative body of knowledge. While there is much to be criticized in the attitude area (and we will be severe critics when this seems necessary), we hope to show that our knowledge of attitudes has progressed considerably in the past twenty years.

Our conceptual framework has grown out of our own research in the attitude area. It emphasizes the necessity of distinguishing among beliefs, attitudes, intentions and behavior; four distinct variables that have often been used interchangeably in the past. This distinction not only permits us to classify previous research into conceptually independent categories but it also serves to eliminate many of the apparent inconsistencies in the area. Further, the distinction among beliefs, attitudes, intentions, and behaviors is accompanied by a consideration of the relations among these variables. Research which on the surface appears to deal with a single problem can thus be shown to involve different issues. While some investigators have been concerned with relations among beliefs or among attitudes, others have studied relations between beliefs and attitudes, beliefs and behavior, attitudes and behavior, etc. Distinguishing among these different types of relations again serves to eliminate much of the apparent inconsistency in the literature.

One purpose of this book is to expose the reader to as much of the diverse theoretical and empirical literature in the area as possible. Our second major aim is to show that this literature can be incorporated and understood within a unified and systematic theoretical structure. Generally speaking, we view humans as rational animals who systematically utilize or process the information available to them. The theoretical structure or conceptual framework we have adopted assumes a causal chain linking beliefs, formed on the basis of available information, to the person's attitudes, beliefs, and attitudes to intentions, and intentions to behavior. Since the performance of behavior may provide the person with new information that again influences his or her beliefs, the causal chain starts all over again.

We attempted to write this book so that it could be understood by readers with little or no background in attitude theory and research. At the same time we wrote the book to provide a comprehensive overview of the attitude area. Our approach has had two consequences: First, it has led us to write a book in which each chapter builds on the preceding ones. While an advanced student should have relatively little trouble skipping certain chapters, a beginning student may find some of the later chapters difficult to comprehend without having first read the earlier chapters or at least the Conclusions of those chapters. Second, because we attempted to be comprehensive, we have covered many issues that may appear tangential to, or unnecessary for, an introductory student. Further, we have included in our discussions issues and problems that, by their very nature, may be complex and confusing. Consequently, we hope the book will be used differently by readers who are merely trying to gain an overview of the field and those who are trying to understand the field in depth. For example, some of the material in Chapter 3—*Attitude Measurement* (such as the discussion of unipolar versus bipolar belief measures), the later parts of Chapter 5—Belief Formation (particularly the sections on cue utilization, learning to make accurate inferences, probability models) and some parts of Chapter 6—*Attitude Formation* (particularly the discussions of adding versus averaging, the section on information integration, and the discussion concerning the importance of opinion items) are probably more detailed than necessary for an introductory overview. We hope that instructors using the book will emphasize some sections and merely skim or omit others, depending on their special interests and the level of their class.

One cannot write a book like the present one without the help, assistance, and encouragement of many people. Before acknowledging these contributions, however, we want to do something a bit unusual and express our indebtedness to each other. Neither of us could, or would, have written the book alone, and it represents, in the truest sense of the term, a joint effort. There is not a single word or sentence that we did not write together. When theoretical, organizational, or semantic differences arose (and they did arise with unexpected frequency), they were often resolved only after heated debate. Thus the book served as a valuable learning experience for both of us. It provided us with an opportunity to try out and defend new ideas, and forced us to think about new problems.

Many of our colleagues and associates provided invaluable help. We are indebted to Jerry Cohen, Alice Eagly, Sam Himmelfarb, Patrick Laughlin, George Levinger, Arie Kruglanski, Tino Trahiotis, Nancy Wiggins, and Robert Wyer for their comments and criticisms of selected chapters. We are particularly indebted to Kerry Thomas and Mary Tuck for their criticisms and reviews of several drafts of the entire manuscript. Many of our students also read and reacted to all or some of the chapters. While it is impossible to acknowledge each of these students, we feel we should pay special tribute to James Jaccard, Güliz Ger, Myron Glassman, Bill Holmes, and Rick Pomazal.

We also want to thank our departments for their continual encouragement and assistance throughout this project. Most importantly, they allowed us to arrange our teaching schedules so that we could commute between Champaign and Amherst for long weekends that enabled us to get the work done. We came back from these trips with pages of handwritten manuscript, and we are grateful to Esther Celnik and Carol Marsh who took the time to almost unerringly transcribe our unintelligible hieroglyphics into a legible typed manuscript. They, as well as Ken Carls, Linda Carter Baker, Deborah Filipkowski, and Elsie Osterbur performed yeoman service in typing and retyping various drafts of the manuscript. We are especially indebted to Elsie for obtaining all of the necessary permissions to cite from the works of other investigators.

Finally, and in keeping with tradition, we want to thank our wives, Deborah and Rachel. It is worth noting that this entire acknowledgment section is one of the few concessions to tradition or a traditional approach that we have made in this book. If we did not feel that all acknowledgments were deserved we would not have made them. Thus, it is really with deep affection and admiration that we acknowledge our wives. Not only did they have to put up with a book that took more of our time and energy than any mistress, but unlike most authors' wives, they were often physically abandoned for long periods of time. Despite some often deserved but usually untimely "bitching," our marriages have survived. While this book would definitely have been written sooner without them, our lives would not only be emptier, but a great deal less fun. We therefore dedicate this book to them.

London, England   M. F.
Amherst, Massachusetts   I. A.
February 1975

Contents

Chapter 1

Introduction

Considering that attitude is probably "the most distinctive and indispensable concept in contemporary American social psychology" (Allport, 1968, p. 59), it is characterized by an embarrassing degree of ambiguity and confusion. In part, this may be attributable to its use as an explanatory concept in diverse areas of investigation. Under the general rubric of attitude research, attempts to explain discriminatory behaviors have typically made reference to attitudes, stereotypes, prejudice, and ethnocentrism. Similarly, research on performance, absenteeism, and turnover in industry has frequently invoked concepts like attitude, job satisfaction, and morale. Attitudes, opinions, and voting intentions have appeared as central concepts in studies of voting and other political activities. Attempts to explain various aspects of consumer behavior have focused on attitudes toward products, brand loyalty, product attributes, and brand images. Finally, concepts such as attitude, attraction, attribution of dispositions, liking, and behavioral intentions have been used to account for a wide variety of interpersonal behaviors.

All concepts mentioned above, as well as many others, have been subsumed under (or incorporated within) the general label "attitude." This undoubtedly leads to some of the confusion and ambiguity surrounding the attitude concept, and it is hardly surprising that few investigators agree on an explicit definition of attitude (cf. McGuire, 1969; Elizur, 1970; Kiesler, Collins, and Miller, 1969). The great diversity of proposed definitions has often been made explicit in reviews of the attitude concept (e.g., Campbell, 1963; Greenwald, 1968), and reviewers have sometimes attempted to provide an integration of these different definitions (e.g., Allport, 1935; Nelson, 1939). More recently, however, they have tended to acknowledge "the diversity of attitude definitions and [despair] of finding consensus or justification for one definition as opposed to others" (Greenwald, 1968; p. 361). As McGuire (1969) has pointed out, most investigators intuitively select

1

a particular measurement procedure that seems to fit the purpose of their study. Support for this argument can be gained by reviewing the different measures of "attitude" that have been reported in the literature. In a review of research published between 1968 and 1970, Fishbein and Ajzen (1972) found more than 500 different operations designed to measure attitude. These operations include standard attitude scales (e.g., Likert, Guttman, Thurstone, and semantic differential scales); other indices across various verbal items; single statements of feelings, opinions, knowledge, or intentions; observations of one or more overt behaviors; and physiological measures.

Single-response measures illustrate most clearly the wide range of operations that have been employed. In all these measures, attitudes, opinions, values, intentions, or other "attitudinal" concepts are inferred from observation of a single response, whether it is a verbal form (e.g., a questionnaire response) or an overt act. Most single-response measures are verbal in nature; the subject is asked to make a judgment either about himself or about some other person, object, or event.

For instance, in a classic study of the relations between attitude and behavior, LaPiere (1939) sent letters to hotels and restaurants asking the following question: "Will you accept members of the Chinese race as guests in your establishment?" An attempt was made to relate this measure of "attitude" to actual acceptance of a Chinese couple that visited those establishments. In a more recent study, Ostrom (1969) measured three aspects of "attitude" toward the church on three 9-point scales labeled as follows: *I feel strong liking–disliking* (for the church); *I believe the church has extremely desirable–extremely undesirable qualities;* and *I act strongly supportive–strongly hostile* (toward the church). In a well-known study of attitude change, Cohen obtained judgments with respect to a confrontation between students and the police (Brehm and Cohen, 1962). The statement "Considering the circumstances, how justified do you think the New Haven police actions were in the recent riots?" was rated on a 31-point scale ranging from *completely justified* to *not justified at all*. Festinger and Carlsmith (1959) reported an experiment in which subjects performed some boring tasks. At the end of the experiment they rated the tasks on an 11-point scale ranging from *extremely interesting and enjoyable* through *neutral, neither interesting nor uninteresting*, to *extremely dull and boring*. Studying the influence of role playing on opinions, Janis and King (1954) asked subjects to make the following quantitative estimate: "How many years do you think it will be before a *completely effective* cure for the common cold is discovered?" In another classic study, Brehm and Cohen (1959) measured children's attitudes toward toys by asking the children to rate each toy on a 51-point scale ranging from *don't like it at all* to *really like very, very much*. Aronson and Cope (1968) measured positive feelings toward another person by asking subjects to volunteer to make phone calls. Specifically, subjects were asked, "Would you be willing to help Dr. Cope by making some phone calls and asking people to serve as subjects? Other people have volunteered to call anywhere from two to fifty people—would you be willing to help him out?"

The number of phone calls a subject volunteered to make served as a measure of attitude toward Dr. Cope. A final example is Fromkin's (1970) measurement of the degree to which a subject values a given environment. As an indirect measure of this "attitude," subjects were asked to indicate the amount of time they would be willing to spend in the environment.

As mentioned above, nonverbal behaviors have also been used to measure attitude. Various physiological measures, such as galvanic skin response, palmar sweating, pupillary dilation and contraction, and heart rate, have been employed. Overt behaviors as measures of attitude have included choice between alternatives; various learning, recall, and recognition tasks; eye contact; and physical distance.

Frequently an investigator will obtain two or more judgments or observations which are considered alternative measures of the same underlying concept (e.g., attitude, opinion, prejudice). Analyses are sometimes performed on each individual measure. Alternatively, an index may be computed on the basis of the different measures. Standard procedures are available that aid the investigator in determining whether different measures are indeed assessing the same underlying concept and, if so, how they can be combined to construct an overall index. The traditional attitude-scaling methods to be discussed in Chapter 3 are examples of some of these standard procedures.

All too often, however, no standard procedure is followed, and different measures are combined in arbitrary ways. The kinds of combinations that have been used are almost as numerous as the kinds of measures described above. They include such combinations as weighted or unweighted sums or averages, difference scores, similarity indices, squared differences, differences between differences, ratios, products, etc.

Although it would be desirable to have general laws that could be shown to hold across any kind of dependent measure of "attitude," the great diversity of such measures makes this goal highly unlikely. For example, changes in a person's judgment that a given action is justifiable may not be accompanied by any change in his judgment of how good or bad that action is, who should engage in the action, or any other evaluation of the behavior. Similarly, a manipulation that is shown to affect a person's judgment that an object has a given attribute (e.g., that a person is honest) may not have any effect on different judgments concerning the object, such as attributions of other characteristics (e.g., intelligence, physical attractiveness), liking for the object, willingness to perform various behaviors toward it, or the actual performance of such behaviors.

The use of different measurement procedures to assess a concept such as attitude may increase our confidence in a given empirical finding. When different measures of attitudes are found to be related to each other, to be influenced by the same factors, and to exert the same effects on other variables, the generality of our conclusions and thereby our confidence in these conclusions are increased. However, when different measures of attitude are unrelated to each other, when they are not influenced by the same factors, or when they have differential effects on other variables, it becomes difficult to maintain that they assess the same underlying concept, i.e., attitude. Anyone minimally familiar with the attitude literature is aware that different results are frequently obtained when different measures of "attitude" are employed. Of recent studies that have reported the use of more than one attitude measure, about 70 percent have found different results (Fishbein and Ajzen, 1972). It is noteworthy that since these different measures were viewed as assessing the same underlying variables (attitude, opinion, value, etc.), there was usually no expectation that different results would be obtained.

Carlsmith, Collins, and Helmreich (1966) reported results for six questions, each of which was designed to assess attitude toward an experimental task.

1. How pleasant did you find the test?
2. Was it an interesting test?
3. Did you learn anything from the test?
4. Would you recommend the test to a friend?
5. Would you describe the test as fun?
6. What is your general overall mood at the present time?

Subjects responded to each question on an 11-point scale ranging from −5 to +5. For example, on question 1, the subjects were asked to indicate the degree to which the experimental task had been pleasant or unpleasant, with a −5 standing for *very unpleasant* and a +5 for *very pleasant*. Identical statistical analyses were performed for each item. The experimenters' hypotheses were supported with respect to questions 2 and 5, but not with respect to the other questions.

Studying the effects of physical attractiveness on dating behavior, Walster *et al.* (1966) looked at the relation between a subject's own physical attractiveness and his or her evaluation of a computer-selected date. Subjects were asked several questions about their dating partners, and their answers resulted in seven attitudinal measures. (The response format employed is not made explicit in the report, and further, some of the measures appear to be indices based on more than one question.) Specifically, the following seven measures of attitude toward the date were obtained.

1. How much the subject liked his or her date
2. How socially desirable the date seemed to be ("How physically attractive is your date?" "How personally attractive is your date?")
3. How uncomfortable the subject was on this blind date
4. How much the date seemed to like the subject
5. How similar the date's values, attitudes, and beliefs seemed to the subject's own
6. How much effort the subject made to ensure that the date had a good time, and how much effort the date made on the subject's behalf
7. Whether or not the subject would like to date this partner again

For male subjects, a significant negative relation was found between their own physical attractiveness and their "attitudes" toward their partners, when attitude was assessed by measures 1, 2, or 7, but not by the other measures. For females, the expected relation was found only on measures 2 and 7.

Many other similar examples could be described. Frequently subjects are asked to rate an object on a set of bipolar adjective scales (e.g., the semantic differential; see Chapter 3), and each item is analyzed separately. Different results are usually obtained for different bipolar scales (e.g., Berkowitz, 1969; Landy and Aronson, 1968).[1] Other studies have used indices based on several items as their measures of attitude. For example, Nemeth (1970) measured liking of another person by summing over four highly intercorrelated responses to the following questions.

1. How much do you like the other person?
2. How much would you like to work with this other person?
3. How much would you like the other person as a neighbor?
4. How much would you like the other person as a personal friend?

In addition, as a second measure of liking, Nemeth measured the number of seconds the subject spent talking to the other person. No relation between these two measures of attitude was found, and different results were obtained with respect to each. Clearly, when the same label "attitude" is attached to these different measures, the results must appear contradictory and confusing.

DEFINITION OF ATTITUDE

The examples above demonstrate that the intuitive selection of measurement procedures that seem to fit the purpose of a study can easily lead to apparently conflicting results and different conclusions concerning the relations between attitude and other variables. An explicit definition of attitude appears to be a minimal prerequisite for the development of valid measurement procedures. According to current views in philosophy of science, the meaning of a concept is defined in terms of its relations to other constructs in a theoretical network. Thus two investigators may offer different explicit definitions of attitude. However, if their attitude theories revealed that they agreed on the relationships between attitude and other concepts, such as confidence, anxiety, intelligence, age, involvement, etc., it could be argued that the term "attitude" has the same meaning for the two investigators. Although the meaning of a concept such as attitude emerges only

---

1. Two methodological issues are raised by this practice of separately analyzing multiple measures of attitude. First, some of the apparent inconsistency in results may be avoided if the assumption that the different items are all measuring the same concept is tested prior to conducting the study. Second, since significant results are usually obtained for only some of the measures, it appears unjustified to take such results as evidence in support of the hypothesis.

within the framework of a general theory, an explicit conceptual definition of attitude may nevertheless be valuable since it suggests procedures for measuring (or manipulating) attitudes. Adequate conceptual definitions should lead to measurement procedures that most investigators would consider acceptable quantifications of the concept in question. It may thus be suggested that conceptual definitions will be most useful when they provide an adequate basis for the development of measurement procedures without trying to elaborate on the theoretical meaning of the concept.

However, as Kiesler, Collins, and Miller (1969) have pointed out, "all too often, social psychologists have tried to make their definition of attitude both a [conceptual] definition and a theory of the concept" (p. 4). For example, most investigators would probably agree that attitude can be described as *a learned predisposition to respond in a consistently favorable or unfavorable manner with respect to a given object*. Consensus on this description of attitude, however, does not eliminate the existing disagreements among attitude researchers. It merely serves to obscure the disagreements by providing a description with multiple interpretations. A closer examination of the description reveals some of the underlying ambiguity. There are three basic features: the notion that attitude is learned, that it predisposes action, and that such actions are consistently favorable or unfavorable toward the object.

Consistency

Perhaps the major source of conceptual ambiguity concerns the notion of response consistency. At least three types of consistency can be distinguished. First, a person may be observed to consistently perform the same response or set of responses in the presence of a given stimulus object. This *stimulus-response consistency* may be taken as reflecting an attitude toward the object (Campbell, 1963). A definition of this type, however, fails to distinguish attitude from other concepts, such as habit, trait, drive, or motive. One can alleviate this problem in part by requiring that each response express some degree of favorableness or unfavorableness toward the object in question.

A second interpretation involves the degree of consistency between different responses with respect to the same object. Instead of the requirement that the same responses be made with respect to an object, the requirement in this case is that, whatever the responses are that are elicited by the object, they should be consistent with one another. This *response-response consistency* has also been taken as indicative of an attitude toward the object (DeFleur and Westie, 1963). It is not clear, however, what is meant by consistency in this context. Consider, for example, a person who splits his ticket and votes for a Democratic governor but a Republican senator. His behavior appears inconsistent in terms of party preferences, but it would be considered consistent if he voted for the more liberal candidate for each office. Consistency of a person's behaviors must be judged along some dimension. Two behaviors are considered to be consistent if both are located on the same side of the dimension; they are inconsistent if they are located on opposite sides. Clearly, as in the example above, two behaviors may be consistent with respect to one dimension (liberal-conservative) but inconsistent with respect to another (Democrat-Republican).

Like stimulus-response consistency, the notion of response-response consistency fails to discriminate between attitude, trait, motive, and various other concepts. At this point let us recall that the proposed definition of attitude refers to behaviors that are consistently *favorable* or *unfavorable*. That is, response consistency should be judged with reference to an evaluative or affective dimension. Two or more behaviors are considered consistent in this sense when both are located on either the positive or negative side of the evaluative dimension. Observed consistencies of this type are taken as evidence for the existence of favorable or unfavorable attitudes.

The third type of response consistency is related to multiple behaviors at different points in time. Even in the absence of stimulus-response or response-response consistency, a set of behaviors may exhibit *evaluative consistency* over time. That is, on different occasions a person may perform different behaviors with respect to an object. The overall favorability expressed by these behaviors, however, may remain relatively constant, and in this sense they may be defined as consistent. Clearly, overall consistency of this kind could also be defined in terms of dimensions other than evaluation or affect, such as aggressiveness, liberalism-conservatism, dominance, authoritarianism, etc. Again, however, attitudes are evidenced by overall *evaluative* consistency (e.g., Thurstone, 1931; Doob, 1947). For example, canvassing for a political candidate, contributing money to his campaign fund, attending a rally in support of his candidacy, working in his campaign office, as well as voting for him, are some of the favorable behaviors with respect to the candidate that a person may perform. On a given occasion, the person may be observed to perform some of these behaviors and to refuse to perform others. Although the person may perform different behaviors on different occasions, and although these behaviors may not be consistent with one another, the degree of favorability toward the candidate expressed by his behaviors may remain constant. Thus, on a given day the person may attend a rally for the candidate and make a contribution to his campaign fund, but he may not canvass or work in the campaign office. On another occasion he may work in the campaign office during the day and canvass his neighborhood in the evening but not contribute money or attend a rally. The overall favorability expressed by these different patterns of behavior, however, remains relatively constant. It is assumed that the favorability of the person's attitude toward the candidate corresponds to the overall favorability expressed by his behavioral pattern.

This discussion of consistency points to the ambiguity inherent in the phrase "respond in a consistently favorable or unfavorable manner." Some of the confusion surrounding the attitude concept may have resulted from the failure of most investigators to specify what they mean by response consistency. Whatever an investigator's interpretation of response consistency, however, the notion of favorable and unfavorable behavior plays a central role in all definitions. Evaluative or affective consistency is what distinguishes between attitude and other concepts, and it is therefore hardly surprising that the evaluative dimension has frequently been regarded as the most distinctive feature of attitude (e.g., Thurstone, 1931; Osgood, Suci, and Tannenbaum, 1957; Fishbein, 1967c).

The different views of consistency discussed above imply different ways of measuring or assessing an attitude. As we shall see in Chapter 3, most attitude measurement relies on overall evaluative consistency although some measures are based on stimulus-response consistency. To the best of our knowledge, none of the common attitude-measurement techniques rely on the notion of response-response consistency.

Attitudes Are Predispositions

The second major feature of the description under consideration is the notion that attitude is a predisposition. Attitude is typically viewed as a latent or underlying variable that is assumed to guide or influence behavior. One immediate implication of this view is that attitudes are not identical with observed response consistency. Indeed, attitudes cannot be observed directly but have to be inferred from observed consistency in behavior.

We showed above that "response consistency" can be interpreted in at least three very different ways. Since predispositions must be inferred from such consistency, it follows that their interpretation depends on the definition of consistency. The stimulus-response interpretation of consistency implies that the individual is predisposed to make a particular response or set of responses in the presence of a given object. Knowledge of a person's attitude, therefore, permits prediction of one or more specific behaviors.

Adopting the response-response interpretation of consistency implies a more general predisposition. In this case, the individual is predisposed toward performing a class of behaviors, all of which are either favorable or unfavorable with respect to the object. Thus a person holding a favorable attitude toward the object would be expected to perform any favorable behavior and not to perform unfavorable behaviors, whereas the reverse would be true for a person holding an unfavorable attitude.

Defining consistency in terms of overall evaluation implies a predisposition of an even more general nature. Here a person is seen as predisposed to a certain degree of favorability in his behavior toward the object, which may be expressed in different behavioral ways. Thus the predisposition refers neither to a particular behavior nor to a class of behaviors, but rather to the overall favorability of a behavioral pattern. Knowledge of a person's attitude in this case does not permit prediction of any specific behavior on his part.

It is of interest to note that the early conceptions of attitude were largely restricted to specific predispositions or mental sets; the concept of attitude gained popularity only after it was viewed as a more general behavioral disposition (cf. Fleming, 1967). Of greater importance, the notion of predispositional specificity points to some additional ambiguities with respect to the attitude concept. In the first two interpretations discussed above (i.e., stimulus-response and response-response consistency), the predisposition is linked to one or more specific responses. Once a person's predisposition (i.e., attitude) has been established, it is expected that the person will (or will not) perform the behavior in question. The stimulus-response interpretation of consistency implies that a given attitude always elicits a given response or set of responses (in terms of which the attitude was defined). Response-response consistency implies that a positive attitude will lead to the performance of positive behaviors and a negative attitude to the performance of negative behaviors. In contrast, the third view of predisposition (i.e., overall evaluative consistency) makes no such assumption. Even though an individual may have a favorable attitude, there is no expectation that he will perform any particular behavior with respect to the object, favorable or unfavorable.

These problems are compounded when the level of dispositional specificity fails to correspond to the interpretation of response consistency. In a typical example, an investigator may infer attitude by observing overall evaluative consistency but assume a predisposition to perform a specific behavior. We will show in a later chapter that this problem may have caused some of the controversies concerning the attitude-behavior relation.

Many of the disagreements concerning the definition of attitude can be traced to the investigator's description of the nature of the predisposition. For example, Sarnoff (1960) defined attitude as "a disposition to react favorably or unfavorably to a class of objects." Thurstone (1931) and others have argued that attitude is an affective or evaluative predisposition. Although not discussing its nature per se, Chave (1928) provided a detailed description of the factors that influence a person's predisposition: "An attitude is a complex of feelings, desires, fears, convictions, prejudices, or other tendencies that have given a set or readiness to act to a person because of varied experiences." A direct description of the nature of a predisposition has been offered by Krech and Crutchfield (1948), who defined attitude as "an enduring organization of motivational, emotional, perceptual, and cognitive processes with respect to some aspect of the individual's world."

Attitudes Are Learned

The disagreements concerning the nature of the disposition lead to the final feature of attitudes to be considered, namely, the notion that attitudes are learned. Although virtually every attitude theorist would agree with this assumption, its importance is frequently not recognized. The social scientist confronts the formidable task of trying to explain the behavior of organisms with complex and unique past experiences. It is widely accepted that residues of this experience influence or modify behavior of the organism. Since a person's complete history is not available to the investigator, he often turns to variables that reflect residues of past experience. Attitudes are generally assumed to constitute such residues (Campbell, 1963), and hence attitudes are considered to be learned.

In other words, predispositions to respond in consistently favorable or unfavorable ways are assumed to be the result of past experience. Clearly, the level of predispositional specificity at which an investigator is working will tend to determine the kinds of past experiences that he considers relevant for attitude formation. For example, concern with predispositions to perform a particular response is likely to lead to considerations of past experiences directly related to performance and nonperformance of the behavioral response in the presence of the stimulus object. Thus investigation may focus on consequences of the behavior, such as monetary rewards, punishments, social approval or disapproval, and on the effort involved in performing the behavior, as well as on social pressures to perform or abstain from performing it.

In contrast, concern with general predispositions to behave in a favorable or unfavorable manner with respect to some object may direct attention to any kind of prior experience with the object. In a study of a person's predisposition toward Catholics, for example, it would be possible to consider consequences of different behaviors with respect to Catholics, social pressures concerning such behaviors, factual knowledge about Catholics, general feelings one had previously experienced in the presence of Catholics, etc. Indeed, almost any experience might be deemed relevant for the formation of a general predisposition toward Catholics.

In conclusion, most investigators would probably agree with a description (or definition) of attitude as a learned predisposition to respond in a consistently favorable or unfavorable manner with respect to a given object. In the discussion above we have attempted to reveal some of the disagreements concealed by the apparent consensus. Agreement with this description of attitude leaves five basic problems unanswered. First, different interpretations may be given to the phrase "respond in a consistently favorable or unfavorable manner." Second, the predisposition may be viewed as specific or general, and it may or may not be linked to particular behavior. Third, response consistency and level of dispositional specificity may or may not be coordinated. Fourth, disagreement exists concerning the nature of the predisposition. Finally, different kinds of past experiences may be considered relevant for the formation of the disposition.

Clearly, there exists a great diversity of viewpoints concerning the attitude concept, and this state of affairs is reflected in a multitude of definitions of attitude. Many of the disagreements among investigators are questions of theory rather than definition. For example, we saw above that many definitions of attitude make explicit reference to the nature of the disposition or to factors that influence it. Theorists usually have not made clear which aspects of an elaborate theoretical description of attitude are essential defining aspects of the concept and which are speculative arguments that require empirical verification. It follows that these definitions of attitude have no clear implications as to how attitudes are to be measured, and the result is the arbitrary selection of measurement procedures noted earlier. What is needed at the present time, therefore, is a conceptual definition of attitude which specifies only the essential characteristics of the attitude concept which must be assessed in order to obtain a valid measure of attitude.

CONCEPTUAL DISTINCTIONS

Attitude. In discussing the notion of response consistency, we noted that the major characteristic that distinguishes attitude from other concepts is its evaluative or affective nature. Indeed, there is widespread agreement that affect is the most essential part of the attitude concept. Further, in Chapter 3 we will see that most of the commonly accepted attitude-measurement procedures arrive at a single number designed to index this general evaluation or feeling of favorableness or unfavorableness toward the object in question. Consistent with Thurstone's (1931) position, attitude may be conceptualized as the amount of affect for or against some object. We therefore suggest that "attitude" should be measured by a procedure which locates the subject on a bipolar affective or evaluative dimension vis-à-vis a given object.[2]

Although one should recognize that this definition does not capture the full complexity that has come to be associated with the attitude concept, there seems to be widespread agreement that affect is the most essential part of attitude, and the proposed definition therefore appears to do justice to the concept of attitude.

Clearly, the proposed definition of attitude would invalidate many of the measures used in empirical investigations, since those measures often do not unambiguously locate an individual on a bipolar evaluative dimension. Conversely, such labels as opinion, satisfaction, prejudice, intention, value, belief, etc., have sometimes been applied to clear measures of evaluation. The result has been to confound the distinctions between attitude and other concepts. Distinctions between some of these terms have at times been suggested (e.g., Rokeach, 1968; Triandis, 1971; Harvey, Hunt, and Schroeder, 1961; Katz, 1960; Osgood, Suci, and Tannenbaum, 1957), but the prevailing view holds that such distinctions are not warranted at the present time, since it has not been demonstrated that these variables obey different scientific laws. According to this view, a distinction between belief and attitude, for example, would be justified only if research could demonstrate that different factors determine these two variables, and/or that a change in beliefs leads to different consequences than does a change in attitudes (McGuire, 1969). This book will attempt to demonstrate that some distinctions not only are justifiable but are necessary for an adequate understanding of the attitude area.

One distinction that has been repeatedly proposed is the age-old trilogy of

---

2. The terms "affect" and "evaluation" are used synonymously throughout this book. Although it might be argued that there is a difference between a person's judgment that an object makes him feel good and his evaluation that the object is good, there is little evidence to suggest that a reliable empirical distinction between these two variables can be made.

affect, cognition, and conation. Affect refers to a person's feelings toward and evaluation of some object, person, issue, or event; cognition denotes his knowledge, opinions, beliefs, and thoughts about the object; and conation refers to his behavioral intentions and his actions with respect to or in the presence of the object. Since, when dealing with attitudes, we are concerned with predispositions to behave rather than with the behavior itself, it seems desirable to make a distinction between behavioral intention and actual behavior. This suggests a classification consisting of four broad categories: affect (feelings, evaluations), cognition (opinions, beliefs), conation (behavioral intentions), and behavior (observed overt acts). Although many attitude theorists appear to agree with such a classification, they seldom make use of it in their research.

We have already reserved the term "attitude" for one of these categories, namely, affect. The term "belief" will be used for the second category, cognition, and the term "intention" for the third category, conation.

Belief. Whereas attitude refers to a person's favorable or unfavorable evaluation of an object, beliefs represent the information he has about the object. Specifically, a belief links an object to some attribute. Here and throughout this book, the terms "object" and "attribute" are used in a generic sense, and they refer to any discriminable aspect of the individual's world. For example, the belief "Russia is a totalitarian state" links the object "Russia" to the attribute "totalitarian state." Another belief may link "using birth control pills" (the object) to "preventing pregnancy" (the attribute). Thus the object of a belief may be a person, a group of people, an institution, a behavior, a policy, an event, etc., and the associated attribute may be any object, trait, property, quality, characteristic, outcome, or event.

With respect to any object-attribute association, people may differ in their *belief strength.* In other words, they may differ in terms of the perceived likelihood that the object has (or is associated with) the attribute in question. Thus we recommend that "belief strength," or more simply, "belief," be measured by a procedure which places the subject along a dimension of subjective probability involving an object and some related attribute. The use of subjective probability in relation to beliefs has increased in recent years, and several recent models of belief change have applied mathematical probability theory to make predictions about subjective probabilities, i.e., beliefs (cf. Cronkhite, 1969; Scheibe, 1970; Warr and Smith, 1970; Wyer, 1970a). Some of these models will be considered in a later chapter.

Behavioral intention. The third class of variables refers to a person's intentions to perform various behaviors. In many respects, intentions may be viewed as a special case of beliefs, in which the object is always the person himself and the attribute is always a behavior. As with a belief, the strength of an intention is indicated by the person's subjective probability that he will perform the behavior in question. It can thus be recommended that the strength of an intention, or more simply, "intention," be measured by a procedure which places the subject along a subjective-probability dimension involving a relation between himself and some action.

In sum, the concept "attitude" should be used only when there is strong evidence that the measure employed places an individual on a bipolar affective dimension. When the measure places the individual on a dimension of subjective probability relating an object to an attribute, the label "belief" should be applied. When the probability dimension links the person to a behavior, the concept "behavioral intention" should be used. Other concepts that have been employed in the attitude area appear to be subsumed under one or another of these three broad categories. For example, concepts like attraction, value, sentiment, valence, and utility all seem to imply bipolar evaluation and may thus be subsumed under the category of "attitude." Similarly, opinion, knowledge, information, stereotype, etc., may all be viewed as beliefs held by an individual. Other items, such as brand image, prejudice, and morale, are usually defined so broadly that they may relate to all three categories. Thus a person may hold prejudicial beliefs, attitudes, and intentions.

Behavior. At this point, a few comments about the fourth category, overt behavior, are in order. First, note that all questionnaire or verbal responses are also instances of overt behavior. That is, they are observable acts of the subject. Usually, however, such responses are not treated as records of behavior but are instead used to infer beliefs, attitudes, or intentions. In contrast, the behavioral category in our classification refers to overt behaviors that are studied in their own right. That is, an investigator obtains a measure of overt behavior because he is interested in that particular behavior and is trying to understand its determinants.

Note further, however, that any given behavior may either be studied in its own right or be used to infer beliefs, attitudes, or intentions. Thus, in Nemeth's (1970) study mentioned earlier, the number of seconds spent talking to another person was taken as a measure of liking. The same measure could have served as a record of verbal behavior. The results of this study indicate that time spent talking to another person should probably not be viewed as a measure of attitude or liking, since it was found to have no relation to an independent, more direct measure of the affective dimension.

To reiterate, the term "behavior" will be used to refer to observable acts that are studied in their own right. A more thorough discussion of some of the problems involved in measuring and predicting behaviors will be presented in Chapter 8.

A CONCEPTUAL FRAMEWORK

The purpose of this book is to organize and integrate research in the attitude area within the framework of a systematic theoretical orientation. Our aim is to expose the reader as much as possible to the wide range of theoretical viewpoints and empirical investigations conducted in this area, while at the same time providing a coherent framework that permits a systematic theoretical analysis. The foundation for our conceptual framework is provided by our distinction between beliefs, attitudes, intentions, and behaviors. The major concern of the conceptual framework, however, is with the relations between these variables.

Beliefs are the fundamental building blocks in our conceptual structure. On the basis of direct observation or information received from outside sources or by way of various inference processes, a person learns or forms a number of beliefs about an object. That is, he associates the object with various attributes. In this manner, he forms beliefs about himself, about other people, about institutions, behaviors, events, etc. The totality of a person's beliefs serves as the informational base that ultimately determines his attitudes, intentions, and behaviors. Our approach thus views man as an essentially rational organism, who uses the information at his disposal to make judgments, form evaluations, and arrive at decisions.

At the simplest level, beliefs formed on the basis of direct observation may lead to the formation of new beliefs. For example, on the basis of an observation (and consequent belief) that John is wearing a plain gold ring on his left hand, a person may infer that John is married. Although beliefs can be arrived at by a number of different inference processes, we assume that such inferences are usually made in an orderly fashion on the basis of the beliefs already held by the individual.

An information-processing approach is also viewed as underlying the formation of attitudes. Specifically, a person's attitude toward an object is based on his salient beliefs about *that* object. An individual's attitude toward the church, for example, is a function of his beliefs about the church. If those beliefs associate the object with primarily favorable attributes, his attitude will tend to be positive. Conversely, a negative attitude will result if the person associates the church with primarily unfavorable attributes. It can thus be seen that a person's attitude toward some object is determined by his beliefs that the object has certain attributes and by his evaluations of those attributes.

We have made it clear that attitude is viewed as affective or evaluative in nature, and that it is determined by the person's beliefs about the attitude object. Most people hold both positive and negative beliefs about an object, and attitude is viewed as corresponding to the total affect associated with their beliefs. In terms of the relation between beliefs and attitudes, our conceptual framework thus suggests that a person's attitude toward some object is related to the *set* of his beliefs about the object but not necessarily to any specific belief.

In a similar fashion, attitude toward an object is viewed as related to the person's intentions to perform a variety of behaviors with respect to that object. Again, however, the relation is between attitude and the set of intentions as a whole, and attitude toward an object will usually not be related to any specific intention with respect to the object.

To give a concrete example, a person may hold many beliefs about the Democratic Party, such as "the Democratic Party is disorganized," "the Democratic

Party is in favor of increased social security benefits," "the Democratic Party is against big business," etc. These beliefs may lead the person to hold a moderately favorable attitude toward the Democratic Party. This attitude leads to a set of intentions which, in their totality, are also moderately favorable. Thus the person may intend to vote for a Democratic candidate and to donate money to the party's campaign fund, but not to canvass his neighborhood to raise money for the party.

Each intention is viewed as being related to the corresponding behavior. Since we view most social behavior as being volitional, barring unforeseen events, a person should perform those behaviors he intends to perform. It follows that attitude toward an object will again be related only to the total behavioral pattern rather than to any specific behavior with respect to the attitude object.

Like most other investigators, we agree that an attitude can be *described* as a learned predisposition to respond in a consistently favorable or unfavorable manner with respect to a given object. It should be clear that since a person's attitude is assumed to be related to the total affect associated with his beliefs, intentions, and behaviors, we define response consistency in terms of overall evaluative consistency. Thus attitude is viewed as a *general* predisposition that does not predispose the person to perform any specific behavior. Rather, it leads to a set of intentions that indicate a certain amount of affect toward the object in question. Each of these intentions is related to a specific behavior, and thus the overall affect expressed by the pattern of a person's actions with respect to the object also corresponds to his attitude toward the object.

The description above is admittedly brief, and it omits feedback loops at various stages of the process. For example, once established, an attitude may influence the formation of new beliefs. Similarly, performance of a particular behavior may lead to new beliefs about the object, which may in turn influence the attitude. The notions discussed thus far are illustrated in Fig. 1.1.

It has usually been assumed that a person's attitude toward an object can be

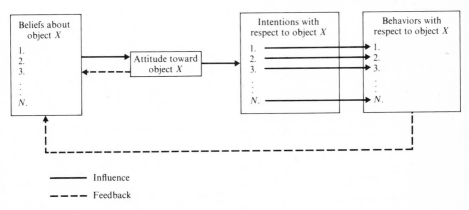

Fig. 1.1 Schematic presentation of conceptual framework relating beliefs, attitudes, intentions, and behaviors with respect to a given object.

used to predict his behavior with respect to the object. Our conceptual framework, however, suggests that the performance or nonperformance of a specific behavior with respect to some object usually cannot be predicted from knowledge of the person's attitude toward that object. Instead, a specific behavior is viewed as determined by the person's intention to perform that behavior. This raises the question of the factors that influence the formation of behavioral intentions.

According to our conceptual framework, a person's intentions, in the final analysis, are a function of certain beliefs. Rather than being beliefs about the object of the behavior, however, the relevant beliefs are concerned with the behavior itself. Some of these beliefs influence the person's attitude toward the behavior. Specifically, his attitude toward performing a given behavior is related to his beliefs that performing the behavior will lead to certain consequences and his evaluation of those consequences. This attitude is viewed as one major determinant of the person's intention to perform the behavior in question. Other beliefs relevant for a behavioral intention are beliefs of a normative nature, i.e., beliefs that certain referents think the person should or should not perform the behavior in question. The person may or may not be motivated to comply with any given referent. The normative beliefs and motivation to comply lead to normative pressures. The totality of these normative pressures may be termed "subjective norm." Like his attitude toward the behavior, a person's subjective norm is viewed as a major determinant of his intention to perform the behavior. Thus a person's behavioral intention is viewed as a function of two factors: his attitude toward the behavior and his subjective norm. As noted earlier, this intention is viewed as the immediate determinant of the corresponding behavior. The factors influencing intentions and behavior are illustrated in Fig. 1.2.

ORGANIZATION OF THIS BOOK

In the remainder of this book we will attempt to fill in the details of the conceptual framework outlined in the present chapter and to show how other approaches to

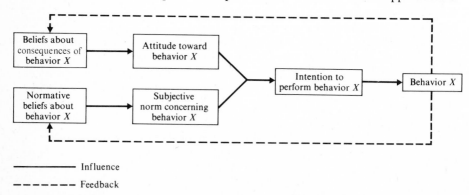

————————— Influence

— — — — — — Feedback

Fig. 1.2 Schematic presentation of conceptual framework for the prediction of specific intentions and behaviors.

attitude theory and research can be integrated within this conceptual framework. From our point of view, attitude theory and research deal with three major questions: (1) What are the determinants of beliefs, attitudes, intentions, and behavior? (2) How are these variables related to each other? (3) What are the ways in which these variables can be changed?

The first part of the book provides a general overview of attitude theory and measurement. Chapter 2 examines the ways in which current attitude theories deal with one or more of the three questions stated above. Several theoretical orientations are reviewed, including learning theories, expectancy-value theories, the congruity principle, balance theory, dissonance theory, and theories of attribution, and each theory is analyzed in terms of our conceptual framework. Chapter 3 discusses various techniques for the measurement of beliefs, attitudes, and intentions. The discussion deals not only with the standard attitude-scaling methods (Guttman, Thurstone, Likert, and semantic differential scales) but also with indirect attitude measures, measures of cognitive structure, and multidimensional scaling. An attempt will be made to show that different measurement procedures may imply different views of the nature of beliefs, attitudes, and intentions and of the relations between these concepts. The final chapter in Part I, Chapter 4, considers some more general methodological issues related to attitude measurement and research. Included in this chapter are discussions of reliability and validity of measurement; reactive effects, such as demand characteristics and experimenter bias in laboratory experiments; and internal and external validity of experiments.

Parts II and III turn to substantive research in the attitude area. Part II deals with the determinants of beliefs, attitudes, intentions, and behaviors and with the relations between these variables. Chapter 5 examines belief formation. Particular emphasis is placed on inference processes underlying the formation of beliefs. Theory and research in the attitude area, as well as in other areas of psychology, are brought to bear on the question of inferential belief formation. A number of inference processes are identified and discussed, including trait inferences, concept formation, cue utilization, syllogistic reasoning, subjective probability models, and attribution processes. The chapter will attempt to demonstrate that inferential beliefs are formed in accordance with orderly principles of information processing.

Chapter 6 attempts to demonstrate the importance of beliefs for attitude formation. Various approaches to attitude formation will be examined, including research on impression formation, interpersonal attraction, and classical conditioning of attitudes. We will show that all this research is compatible with the general notion that a person's attitude toward a given object is a function of his beliefs that the object has certain attributes and his evaluation of those attributes.

Chapter 7 turns to the formation of intentions. Traditional approaches to the prediction of intentions will be discussed, as well as an alternative model based on our conceptual framework outlined earlier. We will review research generated by this model and show that a person's intention to perform a given behavior is a function of his attitude toward that behavior and his subjective norm concerning the behavior.

The final chapter in Part II, Chapter 8, deals with the determinants of behavior and with behavioral prediction. We attempt to explain the failure of the traditional approach, which assumes a strong relation between attitude toward an object and specific behaviors with respect to that object. We suggest an alternative approach, in which a distinction is made between single-act and multiple-act behavioral criteria. We show that attitude toward an object is related to multiple-act criteria, whereas the best predictor of a single-act criterion is the person's corresponding intention. Factors influencing the intention-behavior relation are also discussed.

Clearly, Part II starts with a consideration of beliefs and describes their sequential relations to attitudes, intentions, and behaviors. Chapter 9 uses our conceptual model to analyze processes of change. We show that, in the final analysis, change in any variable is initiated by changes in beliefs. Such changes are brought about by exposing a person to new information. Exposure to such information may initiate a chain of effects, beginning with changes in beliefs, which may produce changes in attitudes. Changes in appropriate beliefs and attitudes influence intentions and corresponding behaviors. Research dealing with various links in the chain of effects is reviewed.

The next two chapters in Part III discuss the two major strategies of change employed in the attitude area. Chapter 10 examines research on active participation. We discuss effects of interpersonal contact, role-playing, forced compliance, and choice behaviors, and we attempt to reconcile conflicting findings within the framework developed in Chapter 9. Chapter 11 deals with the influence of persuasive communication. We discuss the nature of persuasive messages, and we present a theory of the persuasion process and contrast it with the traditional approach to communication and persuasion. The theory's major focus is on acceptance of information provided by an outside source, and it distinguishes between acceptance of information and changes in beliefs, attitudes, intentions, and behavior. We show how this theory can account for apparently inconsistent effects of traditional variables, such as discrepancy between the position advocated in the message and the subject's own position, communicator credibility, and type of appeal. Finally, Chapter 12 provides a general overview of attitude research, its problems and prospects.

Part 1

Attitude
Theory
and
Measurement

Chapter 2

Theories of Attitude

The preceding chapter provided conceptual definitions of belief, attitude, intention, and behavior, as well as a brief outline of a theoretical network linking these concepts. In the present chapter we will consider alternative formulations by reviewing some contemporary theories of attitude. We will provide a brief description of each theory, using its original terminology, and we will then attempt to identify its basic constructs and their interrelations in terms of the conceptual framework outlined in Chapter 1. We will thus examine the implications of each theory for an understanding of the relations between beliefs, attitudes, intentions, and behavior.

Most contemporary attitude theories have their origins in two major schools of thought that have shaped theory and research in social psychology. Whereas the various learning theories of attitude are based on the stimulus-response approach of behavior theory, most theories of cognitive consistency are influenced by the cognitive approach of field theory. A distinction is therefore usually made between behavior theories of attitude and cognitive consistency theories (e.g., Kiesler, Collins, and Miller, 1969; Fishbein, 1967a; Greenwald, Brock, and Ostrom, 1968). This classification into behavior-versus-consistency theories, however, blurs the distinction between a theory's theoretical origin and the phenomena it deals with. For example, Osgood and Tannenbaum's (1955) congruity principle is typically viewed as a consistency theory (since it deals with attitudinal consistency or congruity) although it originated within the behavior-theory tradition. The present review de-emphasizes the distinction between behavior and consistency theories in favor of a more unified presentation.

LEARNING THEORIES

Several investigators have used principles taken from the learning theories of Hull (1943, 1951), Spence (1956), and Tolman (1932) to study the acquisition of beliefs and attitudes. Generally speaking, these learning theories are concerned with the processes whereby a given response becomes associated with (or conditioned to) a given stimulus. Most learning is explained in terms of two basic conditioning paradigms: classical conditioning and operant or instrumental conditioning.

Conditioning Principles

An *unconditioned stimulus* (UCS) elicits automatically, without prior learning, one or more overt *unconditioned responses* (UCR). For example, an unexpected loud noise produces a startle response; a bottle in an infant's mouth produces sucking, salivation, and swallowing; an electric shock or other painful stimulus leads to various withdrawal responses. The classical conditioning paradigm starts with an unconditioned stimulus that is always followed by some characteristic unconditioned response. Now consider a new stimulus that does not initially elicit the unconditioned response although it may elicit some other response (R_x). When this new *conditioned stimulus* (CS) is consistently paired with the unconditioned stimulus, it ultimately comes to elicit some of the response characteristics previously produced only by the unconditioned stimulus. That is, the CS by itself now elicits the UCR. When an initially neutral stimulus (the CS) acquires the ability to elicit a response (the UCR) originally elicited only in the presence of another stimulus (the UCS), learning is said to have occurred.[1] Figure 2.1 provides a schematic representation of the classical conditioning paradigm.

The solid lines in Fig. 2.1 represent either innate, nonlearned associations or associations that have been previously learned. That is, once the CS comes to elicit the UCR consistently, it can serve as the UCS in another conditioning situation. This process is known as higher-order conditioning.

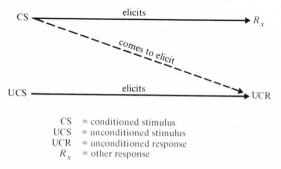

CS	= conditioned stimulus
UCS	= unconditioned stimulus
UCR	= unconditioned response
R_x	= other response

Fig. 2.1 The classical conditioning paradigm.

---

1. The decision to label a given event as a stimulus or a response is somewhat arbitrary, since any response can also serve as a stimulus for some other response.

As an example of classical conditioning, consider a child who always cries (UCR) at the sight of a spider (UCS). Classical conditioning occurs when the child hears the word "spider" (CS) being uttered consistently in the presence of the spider. After several such CS-UCS pairings, the child starts to cry whenever he hears the word "spider," even when no spider is actually present.

Various factors have been found to influence classical conditioning. Among the most important are the frequency with which the CS and UCS are paired (the greater the number of pairings, the more the response to the CS resembles the response to the UCS) and the temporal relation of the CS and UCS. When the UCS precedes the CS, little learning is evidenced; maximal learning seems to occur when the CS precedes the UCS by a short time interval, such as 0.5 second. (For a review of this research, see Kimble, 1961.)

In classical conditioning, then, the response to be learned is initially elicited by the unconditioned stimulus. In contrast, operant conditioning (or trial-and-error learning) involves a situation in which the organism initially emits a variety of different responses. One of these responses (R_r) is reinforced; i.e., the response R_r is *instrumental* to obtaining some reward or avoiding some punishment. The probability of the recurrence of the reinforced response increases with each reinforced trial, and the response is said to be learned when it occurs with high probability. The instrumental conditioning paradigm is illustrated in Fig. 2.2.

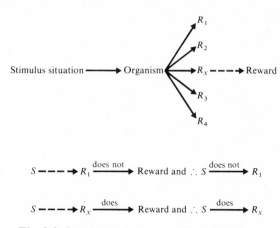

Fig. 2.2 Operant or instrumental conditioning.

As an example of instrumental conditioning, a mother gives her child a piece of chocolate every time he picks up his toys (R_x) but not when he cries, demands chocolate, or throws objects at his brother. The reinforcer (chocolate) will thus strengthen R_x, and the child will learn to pick up his toys.

Factors that have been found to influence instrumental conditioning include frequency of reinforcement (number of times the response is followed by reward), temporal relation between the response and the reinforcement, schedules of reinforcement, and magnitude of the reinforcer (cf. Kimble, 1961).

When a given response reduces the drive state by leading to appropriate reward or by enabling the organism to avoid punishment, the response is said to be reinforced, and the reward is known as a reinforcer. A distinction is made between *primary* and *secondary* (or learned) reinforcers. Primary reinforcers are rewards that are unlearned reducers of drive states (e.g., food, chocolate, water), and secondary reinforcers are previously neutral stimuli that acquire reinforcement properties because they have been associated with primary reinforcers. That is, just as a CS comes to elicit UCR, a stimulus that is consistently paired with a reward will take on some of the reinforcing properties of the reward itself.

Implicit versus explicit responses. In the discussion above, we have considered only observable stimuli and responses. The same processes are assumed to occur with implicit (nonobservable) responses or stimuli. For example, Hull (1951) referred to a "fractional antedating goal reaction," a (usually covert) portion of the overt goal response that antedates, anticipates, or mediates the overt reaction. Osgood, Suci, and Tannenbaum (1957) describe this process with reference to the classical conditioning of a buzzer (CS) to electric shock (UCS):

> Many experiments on the details of the conditioning process combine to support the following conclusion: Components of the total unconditioned reaction vary in their dependence on the unconditioned stimulus and hence in the ease with which they may become conditioned to another stimulus. Typically, the less energy-expending a reaction component (e.g., "light-weight" components like glandular changes and minimal postural adjustments) and the less interfering a reaction component with on-going overt behavior (e.g., components which do not hinder overt approaches, avoidances, manipulations, and the like), the more promptly it appears in the conditioned reaction, and hence the more readily available it is for the mediation function. The argument thus far may be summarized as follows: *Whenever some stimulus other than the [UCS] is contiguous with the [UCS], it will acquire an increment of association with some portion of the total behavior elicited by the [UCS] as a representational mediation process.* As diagrammed [in Fig. 2.3], this stimulus-producing process ($r_m \rightarrow s_m$) is *representational* because it is part of the same behavior (R_T) produced by the [UCS] itself—thus the buzzer becomes a sign [CS] of shock [UCS] rather than a sign of any of a multitude of other things. It is *mediational* because the self-stimulation (s_m) produced by making this short-circuited reaction can now become associated with a variety of instrumental acts (R_x) which "take account of" the [UCS]—the anxiety state generated by the buzzer may serve as a cue for leaping, running, turning a rachet, or some other response sequence which eliminates the signified shock. (Osgood, Suci, and Tannenbaum, 1957. p. 6).

Learning Theories of Attitudes

In one of the first applications of learning theory to the attitude area, Leonard Doob (1947) defined attitude as a learned, implicit anticipatory response. That is, he viewed attitude as an unobservable response to an object that occurs prior to, or in the absence of, any overt response. Osgood, Suci, and Tannenbaum

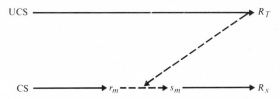

Fig. 2.3 Conditioning of an implicit meaning response. (Adapted from Osgood, Suci, and Tennenbaum, 1957.)

(1957) argued that the implicit mediating response represents the "meaning" of the object, and they suggested that attitude refers only to the *evaluative* part of the total meaning response. Osgood's view of attitude as a mediating evaluative response has met with general acceptance by theorists working within the behavior-theory tradition (e.g., Staats and Staats, 1958; Rhine, 1958; Fishbein, 1967c).

Most learning theories of attitude are concerned with the ways in which attitudes are acquired, i.e., how implicit (evaluative) responses become associated with a given stimulus object. For example, consider a child who has frequently eaten M & M candies. The stimulation involved produces overt responses, such as sucking, salivating, swallowing, etc. In addition, an implicit response with a positive evaluative component has occurred prior to, or in conjunction with, the overt responses. According to the mediational conditioning principle, there will be a tendency for this implicit response to become associated with the candies themselves; i.e., the child develops a favorable attitude toward M & M candies. Further, once this new association has been learned, any other stimulus frequently paired with the M & M candies will also tend to elicit the positive mediating response. Thus, according to the principle of higher-order conditioning, if the M & M's are always dispensed by the child's uncle, a positive attitude toward the uncle should develop.

Primary and higher-order classical conditioning are the basic paradigms in the approach taken by Staats (1968) and Staats and Staats (1958). In addition to classical conditioning, Lott and Lott (1968) have emphasized instrumental conditioning as a basis for attitude formation. That is, "a person who experiences reinforcement or reward for some behavior will react to the reward, i.e., will perform some observable or covert goal response" (p. 68). As indicated above, this covert goal response is often viewed as an attitude. Consistent with the principle of classical conditioning, this implicit response becomes conditioned to all discriminable stimuli present at the time of reinforcement.

Lott (1955) also made use of a second major principle, mediated generalization. According to this principle, once some overt response and the implicit reaction are associated with a given stimulus, any other stimulus that elicits the same mediating reaction will also come to produce the overt response. To return to our previous example, a child who has been rewarded for approaching M & M candies will also tend to approach his uncle, who in the past has given him M & M's.

Doob (1947) emphasized that a person first learns an implicit mediating response (i.e., attitude) to a given stimulus, and he must then also learn to make a specific overt response to the attitude. The first process can be accounted for by classical conditioning, the second by instrumental learning. For other similar stimuli to elicit the same response, principles of generalization are invoked. Thus, according to Doob, the entire mediating response is the attitude. He distinguished between this attitudinal response and other mediating responses (e.g., habit) by reserving the term "attitude" for those implicit responses that are elicited by socially relevant stimuli. In contrast, recall that Osgood, Suci, and Tannenbaum (1957) viewed the total mediating response as representing the meaning of a stimulus and that they defined attitude as only the evaluative part of meaning. Thus Doob argued that people with the same attitude may learn to behave differently, whereas Osgood *et al.* further accounted for low attitude-behavior relations by pointing out that attitude is only a part of the total implicit response, and thus two people with the same attitude toward a given stimulus may differ on other dimensions of meaning vis-à-vis the stimulus.

The discussion above has been concerned primarily with the conditioning of an implicit (evaluative) response to one or more stimuli. The next question to be raised concerns the effects of combining two or more stimuli, each of which elicits a *different* implicit reaction, into a stimulus complex. In fact, most stimulus objects can be considered as representing a complex array of stimuli, and different implicit evaluative reactions may have been conditioned to the different component stimuli. Imagine, for example, that for some person a favorable mediating response has been conditioned to *athlete* and an unfavorable mediating response to *lazy*. According to most learning approaches, the implicit evaluative response to the stimulus complex *lazy athlete* is some function of the evaluative reactions elicited by the component stimuli.

The Congruity Principle

Although learning theory does not specify the exact combinatorial principle involved, Osgood and Tannenbaum (1955) have proposed the congruity principle to describe this process. According to the congruity principle, whenever two stimuli are combined, the "mediating reaction characteristic of each shifts toward congruence with that characteristic of the other, the magnitude of the shift being inversely proportional to the intensities of the interacting reactions" (Osgood, Suci, and Tannenbaum, 1957, p. 201).

Assume that implicit evaluative reactions can be measured on a 7-point scale ranging from +3 (favorable) through 0 (neutral) to −3 (unfavorable). According to the congruity principle, the more intense or polarized the evaluative reaction (i.e., the greater its distance from the neutral point), the less that evaluation will shift toward the other. Indeed, the amount of shift is assumed to be inversely proportional to the degree of polarization. Algebraically, the point of resolution (i.e., the evaluative reaction to the complex stimulus) can be predicted from Eq. 2.1 (Osgood, Suci, and Tannenbaum, 1957, p. 207),

$$P_R = \frac{|p_1|}{|p_1| + |p_2|} \, p_1 + \frac{|p_2|}{|p_1| + |p_2|} \, p_2, \qquad (2.1)$$

where P_R is the point of resolution, p_1 and p_2 are the evaluations of the component stimuli and $|p_1|$ and $|p_2|$ are the absolute values of these evaluations, i.e., the polarities of the component stimuli.

For example, if *athlete* had a value of $+1$ and *lazy* a value of -2, the point of resolution for *lazy athlete* would be -1, as shown by the following computation.

$$P_R = \frac{1}{1+2} \, (1) + \frac{2}{1+2} \, (-2) = \frac{1}{3} + \frac{(-4)}{3} = -1.$$

We will show below that the congruity principle has also been applied to other attitudinal phenomena, and in such applications, the principle is quite similar to a number of so-called consistency theories.

Concept Formation

Theories of concept formation are also relevant for an understanding of the ways in which mediating responses become associated with complex stimulus objects. According to a learning-theory approach, concept formation involves the conditioning or learning of a common response to a set of discrete stimuli. For example, the response "vegetable" becomes conditioned to (associated with) a variety of stimuli, such as beets, spinach, carrots, etc. As mentioned above, the implicit evaluative reaction elicited by the concept "vegetable" should be some function of the evaluative reactions associated with the stimuli that elicit this concept, i.e., the evaluative reactions associated with beets, carrots, spinach, etc. Thus, as Fishbein (1967c) has argued, whenever a new concept is learned, an attitude toward that concept is acquired simultaneously. Once a concept has been learned, however, new stimuli may be associated with it, and the mediating evaluative reactions elicited by these new stimuli will also become conditioned to the concept and change the attitude toward it. At any point in time, a given stimulus object (i.e., a concept such as "vegetable") will elicit a large number of responses, some of which correspond to the stimuli that originally defined the concept (e.g., carrots, beets, spinach), and some of which may have been acquired at a later stage (e.g., edible, nourishing).

Recall that each of these associated objects (e.g., beets, nourishing) elicits an implicit evaluative reaction and that the final attitude toward the concept ("vegetable") is some function of all these evaluative reactions. Again, however, learning theory does not specify the exact combinatorial principle involved.

A Model of the Relationship between Beliefs and Attitudes

Fishbein (1963, 1967c) has proposed a model that deals with the ways in which evaluative mediating responses combine to produce the overall attitude. According to this model, a given stimulus object may elicit a variety of responses that refer to the characteristics, attributes, or qualities of the object. It is assumed that these stimulus-response associations are learned through conditioning processes; the strength of an association should thus be a function of the number of conditioning trials. The different responses to the object are viewed as constituting a "habit-family hierarchy," in which the responses are ordered in terms of the probability that they will be elicited by the stimulus object, i.e., in terms of the strength of their association with the stimulus object.

Further, an implicit evaluative reaction is associated with each of the responses in the hierarchy. It is assumed that each evaluative reaction is conditioned to the stimulus object in direct proportion to the strength of the association between the stimulus object and the corresponding responses in the hierarchy. Thus, the lower the position of a response in the habit-family hierarchy, the less the evaluative reaction associated with it will contribute to the overall attitude toward the object. A further assumption is that evaluative mediating responses combine in an additive manner, and the overall attitude toward the object is therefore viewed as a weighted sum of all implicit evaluative reactions conditioned to the object.

Analysis of Learning Theories

Let us now examine the ideas that have been discussed in terms of the conceptual framework presented in Chapter 1. Throughout the discussion above, attitude has been viewed as an implicit, mediating response. Although some investigators leave the exact nature of this implicit response unspecified (e.g., Doob, 1947; Lott and Lott, 1968), most theorists would agree that attitude can best be viewed as an evaluative mediating response. This conception, therefore, is very similar to our definition of attitude as a person's location on a bipolar evaluative or affective dimension with respect to some object. The implicit evaluative reaction, i.e., attitude, is viewed as predisposing the individual to perform various overt behaviors. Thus the individual may be said to hold various behavioral intentions. However, Doob (1947) has made it clear that any particular response will be performed only to the extent that it has been positively reinforced. Thus, consistent with our conceptual framework, two persons may hold the same attitude but learn to perform different responses.

In discussing the acquisition of attitudes, the various learning theories make reference to stimulus-response conditioning processes. It may be argued that stimulus-response bonds established in this manner correspond to what we have called beliefs. We defined beliefs in terms of the probability that a given object is related to some attribute, i.e., to some other object, concept, or goal. If the object is now viewed as a stimulus and the related attribute as a response, a belief about an object corresponds to the probability that the stimulus elicits the response, i.e., to the strength of the stimulus-response association. Indeed, Tolman (1932) explicitly viewed "cognitions" as "expectancies" or subjective probabilities that one event is associated with (or follows from) some other event.

One important implication of these considerations is that, according to a behavior-theory approach, belief formation should follow the laws of learning. Whenever a belief is formed, some of the implicit evaluation associated with the response becomes conditioned to the stimulus object. The implicit evaluation associated with a response constitutes an attitude which may have been formed as the result of prior conditioning. The implication of this conditioning paradigm is that attitude toward an object is related to beliefs about the object.

Fishbein (1963) has made this relationship an explicit part of his theory of attitude, which can be described as follows: (1) An individual holds many beliefs about a given object; i.e., the object may be seen as related to various attributes, such as other objects, characteristics, goals, etc. (2) Associated with each of the attributes is an implicit evaluative response, i.e., an attitude. (3) Through conditioning, the evaluative responses are associated with the attitude object. (4) The conditioned evaluative responses summate, and thus (5) on future occasions the attitude object will elicit this summated evaluative response, i.e., the overall attitude.

According to the theory, a person's attitude toward any object is a function of his beliefs about the object and the implicit evaluative responses associated with those beliefs. The central equation of the theory can be expressed as follows:

$$A_o = \sum_{i=1}^{n} b_i e_i, \tag{1.2}$$

where A_o is the attitude toward some object, O; b_i is the belief i about O, i.e., the subjective probability that O is related to attribute i; e_i is the evaluation of attribute i; and n is the number of beliefs.

Consider, for example, a person's attitude toward the supersonic transport (SST). Assume that he holds the following beliefs: (1) SST is an airplane; (2) SST is noisy; (3) SST is not economical; and (4) SST is a pollutant. According to Fishbein's model, his attitude toward the SST is a function of the strength with which he holds these beliefs (i.e., his subjective probability that the SST is related to the different attributes) and of his evaluations of each attribute. Table 2.1

Table 2.1 Hypothetical Attitude toward SST

Belief	b	e	be
Airplane	.90	+2	1.80
Noisy	.80	−2	−1.60
Not economical	.60	−1	−0.60
Pollutant	.50	−3	−1.50

$A_o = \sum b_i e_i = -1.90$

presents subjective probabilities and evaluations that might have been obtained.[2] Note that this person is predicted to hold a negative attitude toward the SST.

This analysis of the relations between beliefs and attitude is consistent with our conceptual framework, which also indicates that a person's attitude toward some object is a function of his beliefs about the object (see Chapter 1).

EXPECTANCY-VALUE THEORIES

Fishbein's model is concerned with the relations of beliefs to attitudes, and it is of interest to note that other theorists have arrived at similar formulations in attempts to account for overt behavior. The theories presented by Tolman (1932), Rotter (1954), Atkinson (1957), and others may be viewed in this light.[3] We have already seen that, according to Tolman (1932), people learn "expectations," i.e., beliefs that a given response will be followed by some event. Since these "events" could be either positive or negative "reinforcers" (i.e., could have positive or negative valence), his argument, essentially, was that people would learn to perform (or increase their probability of performing) behavior that they "expected" to lead to positively valenced events.[4]

Perhaps the best known expectancy-value model is the subjective expected utility (SEU) model of behavioral decision theory (Edwards, 1954). According to this theory, when a person has to make a behavioral choice, he will select that alternative which has the highest subjective expected utility, i.e., the alternative which is likely to lead to the most favorable outcomes. The subjective expected utility of a given alternative is defined in Eq. 2.3,

$$SEU = \sum_{i=1}^{n} SP_i U_i, \tag{2.3}$$

where SEU is the subjective expected utility associated with a given alternative; SP_i is the subjective probability that the choice of this alternative will lead to some outcome i; U_i is the subjective value or utility of outcome i; and n is the number of relevant outcomes.[5]

In our terminology, this model deals with beliefs about the consequences of performing a given behavior ($SP_i \sim b_i$) and with the evaluations associated with the different outcomes ($U_i \sim e_i$). Thus SEU can be reinterpreted as the per-

2. Discussions of appropriate measurement procedures will be found in Chapter 3.

3. See Feather (1959) for a comparison of some of these theories.

4. This is a grossly oversimplified statement of Tolman's position. For a complete discussion, see Tolman (1932).

5. Since n usually refers to a mutually exclusive and exhaustive set of outcomes, $\Sigma SP_i = 1.00$ in most behavioral-decision-theory analyses.

son's attitude toward the behavior (A_B), and Eq. 2.3 can be rewritten as follows:

$$A_B = \sum_{i=1}^{n} b_i e_i. \tag{2.4}$$

Note that, whereas the SEU model appears to assume a direct link between SEU and behavior, no direct relation between A_B and behavior is assumed. This question will be raised again in a later chapter dealing with the prediction of intentions.

An Instrumentality-Value Model

Rosenberg (1956) was perhaps the first to introduce an explicit expectancy-value model in the attitude area. He defined attitude as a *"relatively stable affective response to an object"* and argued that this attitude is "accompanied by a *cognitive structure* made up of beliefs about the potentialities of that object for attaining or blocking the realization of valued states" (p. 367). According to Rosenberg (1956), the more a given "object" (i.e., an action or policy) was *instrumental* to obtaining positively valued goals (or consequences) and to blocking (or preventing) negatively valued goals, the more favorable the person's attitude toward the object. This hypothesis is expressed in Eq. 2.5,

$$A_o = \sum_{i=1}^{n} I_i V_i, \tag{2.5}$$

where I_i is instrumentality, i.e., the probability that o would lead to or block the attainment of a goal or value i; V_i is value importance, i.e., the degree of satisfaction or dissatisfaction the person would experience if he obtained value i; and n is the number of goals or value states.

Note that this equation is very similar to Fishbein's (1963) model (see Eq. 2.2) and to the SEU model. That is, Rosenberg's model also deals with beliefs about the object and with associated evaluations or values.

It is interesting that, whereas Fishbein's model was developed within the framework of behavior theory, Rosenberg's formulation was influenced by what today is called a functional approach to attitudes. This approach suggests that attitude formation and change can be understood only in terms of the functions that attitudes serve for the individual. For example, Smith, Bruner, and White (1956) discussed three functions: object appraisal, social adjustment, and externalization. Katz (1960) mentioned the instrumental, adjustive, or utilitarian function, the ego-defensive function, the value-expressive function, and the knowledge function. According to this view, attitudes are necessary because they permit the individual to achieve certain goals or value states (e.g., they allow him to organize knowledge, to maintain his self-esteem, to express his views). Rosenberg's (1956) initial formulation can be viewed as being concerned with the extent to which an object facilitates or hinders the attainment of such valued goals.

In his later theorizing, Rosenberg (1960, 1965a) expanded his definition of attitude by including beliefs within the attitude concept. This expansion was accompanied by an explicit statement of affective-cognitive consistency. Specifically, he argued that "humans have a need to achieve and maintain affective-cognitive consistency" (Rosenberg, 1965a, pp. 123–124). It is worth noting that Fishbein's (1963) model accounts for the relation between beliefs and attitude in terms of conditioning processes, whereas Rosenberg's (1956) formulation relies on the assumption of a need for cognitive-affective consistency to account for the same relations. Nevertheless, the two models have considerable structural similarities, and the basic hypothesis of each can be described by the same algebraic expression, such as Eq. 2.2.

Rosenberg's (1960, 1965a) theory of cognitive-affective consistency is one of a number of theories dealing with the effects of inconsistencies among beliefs, attitudes, intentions, and behaviors. The origin of these consistency theories can in large part be traced to Fritz Heider's (1944, 1946, 1958) principle of balance.

BALANCE THEORY

Heider's concern with balanced configurations grew out of his interest in the factors that influence causal attribution of an event to a person. As we shall see below in our discussion of attribution theory, many factors may influence causal attributions. One conclusion arrived at by Heider is that "if the attitudes toward a person and event are similar, the event is easily ascribed to the person." He further argued that "a balanced configuration exists if the attitudes toward the parts of a causal unit are similar" (Heider, 1946, p. 107). That is, a balanced state exists when the two entities composing a unit have the same "dynamic character," in other words, when the person's attitudes or sentiments vis-à-vis the two entities are both positive or both negative.

Consider, for example, a person who attributes responsibility to the President for the fact that his son was drafted. A balanced state exists when the person likes the President and approves of the fact that his son was drafted, or when he dislikes the President and disapproves of this fact. When he has a positive attitude toward one element (e.g., the President) but a negative attitude toward the other (e.g., the drafting of his son), a state of imbalance is said to exist.

According to Heider's model, balance also exists if the person holds different attitudes toward the two elements and perceives that one element has not been caused by the other. Thus, if in the above example the person liked the President, disapproved of the fact that his son was drafted, but perceived that the President was not directly responsible for the drafting of his son, a balanced state would exist.

Note that Heider takes a phenomenological approach; that is, he is concerned with a person's *perceptions* of the relationships between elements. Three basic elements are usually involved: the focal person (p), another person (o), and an object or event (x). In the model discussed above, p likes (L), or dislikes ($\overline{L}$) o and x, and perceives a causal unit relation (U) between o and x. Heider was aware, however, that two elements may be perceived to form a unit on the basis of processes other than causal attribution. The Gestalt principles of perception suggested that o and x might also be perceived to form a unit on the basis of similarity, proximity, membership, possession, or belonging. The unit oUx can mean, for instance, o owns x or o made x. The segregation of o and x, that is, $o\overline{U}x$, can mean o does not own x, etc. Other examples of unit relations are: o is familiar with, used, or knows x.

Thus Heider (1946) was able to generalize his balance principle to all unit relations. A balanced state is said to exist if p has similar attitudes toward the two elements of the unit oUx (that is, pLo and pLx or $p\overline{L}o$ and $p\overline{L}x$) and if he holds different attitudes toward two segregated elements $o\overline{U}x$.

Heider (1946) further extended his theory to allow perceived liking relations between o and x (that is, oLx and $o\overline{L}x$). In addition, he included unit relations between p and o (for example, p and o are brothers) and between p and x (for example, p owns x). Finally, he pointed out that more than one relation may exist between two entities. For example, p may own and like x, or p may respect but dislike o.

The basic balance principle can now be stated as follows: "In the case of two entities, a balanced state exists if the relation between them is positive (or negative) in all respects, i.e., in regard to all meanings of L and U. . . . In the case of three entities, a balanced state exists if all three relations are positive in all respects, or if two are negative and one positive" (Heider, 1946, pp. 110–111). Balanced and imbalanced triadic configurations are illustrated in Fig. 2.4.

Although Heider presents the balance principle in this general form, he draws attention to some of the problems that may be involved in generalizing from causal

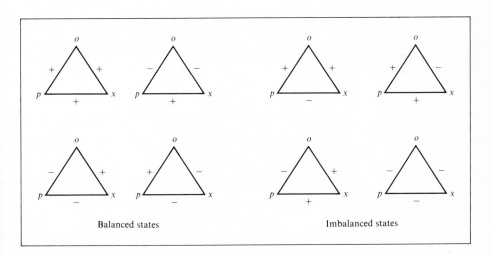

Balanced states   Imbalanced states

Fig. 2.4 Balanced and imbalanced triads. All triads reflect p's perspective: Lines between elements represent either unit or sentiment relations; the + and − signs stand for positive and negative relations, respectively.

units to other unit relations and to perceived liking relations. A case in point involves the unit relation of ownership. At first glance, the triad pLo, oUx, and pLx appears balanced. However, o owns x sometimes implies that p cannot own x. Since p likes x, the situation is imbalanced (i.e., in a dyad, $p\bar{U}x$ and pLx are imbalanced). Heider refers to this case as an example of envy and provides a similar explanation for jealousy.

A basic dynamic principle underlies balance theory, namely, that liking and unit relations tend toward a balanced state. By a balanced state is meant a situation in which the relations among the entities fit together harmoniously; there is no stress toward change. Further, if a balanced state does not exist, then forces toward such a state will arise. If a change is not possible, the state of imbalance will produce tension (Heider, 1958, p. 201).[6] When changes are possible, either the dynamic characters will change—that is, p's attitudes toward o or x may change—or the unit relations will be changed through action or through cognitive reorganization (Heider, 1946, pp. 107–108).

Analysis of Balance Theory

Having described balance theory using Heider's terminology, we will again examine the major ideas in terms of our conceptual framework. The primary concern of balance theory is with the dynamic interactions among beliefs and attitudes. A person's perception of a relation between o and x corresponds to our definition of a belief about o. Thus the person may believe that o likes movies, that o owns a typewriter, or that o is married to some other person. Unlike our probabilistic conception of belief, however, in Heider's system beliefs are dichotomous; i.e., the person either believes that o is related to x or that o is not related to x.[7]

In addition to dealing with beliefs about an object, balance theory considers a person's beliefs about himself. Thus the person may believe that he is engaged to

---

6. Although this notion of tension has often been interpreted as a "need" for balance, Zajonc (1968a) has argued that "the dynamic principle of change proposed by Heider does not involve psychological forces of overwhelming strength. They are more akin to *preferences* than to driving forces. There is no anxiety when structures are imbalanced; imbalanced states are not noxious; a compelling need to strive for balance is not assumed. Forces toward balance have the same character as Gestalt forces toward 'good figures' in the perception of forms." (p. 341)

7. Note further that negative associations (that is, $\bar{L}$ and $\bar{U}$) are not permissible in probabilistic or behavior theory terminology. That is, in these frameworks, one has only positive associations. Thus, whereas balance theory views the statement "o is not x" as $(o)\ \bar{U}\ (x)$, behavior theory and probability models view it as (o) is $(not\ x)$. As we shall see below, assigning a negative sign to the evaluation of (x) is not the same as obtaining an evaluation of $(not\ x)$, and thus expectancy-value models will lead to different predictions when a statement such as $(o$ is not $x)$ is treated as a negative association between (o) and (x) than when it is treated as a positive association between (o) and $(not\ x)$.

another person (pUo), that he performed some behavior (pUx), or that he is not responsible for some event ($p\overline{U}x$).

The balance model also deals with a person's attitudes. Heider's conception of an attitude or sentiment, like our own, concerns positive or negative evaluation. Again, however, whereas we consider a bipolar *dimension* of affect, balance theory is restricted to positive or negative attitudes. That is, a person either likes or dislikes some other entity.

It is of interest to note that when the perceived *o-x* relation is reinterpreted as a person's belief about *o*, his attitude toward *x* is equivalent to the evaluation of the attribute *x* associated with *o*. Thus one implication of the balance principle is that a person's attitude toward an object (that is, *p*'s attitude toward *o*) may be influenced by his belief about the object and by the evaluation of the related attribute. We saw above that the same conclusion [that is, $A_o = f(b,e)$] can be derived from a number of different theoretical approaches. However, balance theory has implications that go beyond this conclusion. For example, *p*'s belief about *o* may be a function of his attitudes toward *o* and *x*, and his attitude toward *x* may be influenced by his belief about *o* and his attitude toward *o*. Further, since all three relations in a triad may be unit relations, the theory has implications for the interactions among beliefs. For instance, consider the case in which *p* buys a car and then finds out that his wife hates it. This triad can be described as pUo, pUx, and $o\overline{L}x$. Since the configuration is imbalanced, there will be a tendency for at least one of the beliefs to change.

An important and frequently neglected aspect of Heider's balance model is that beliefs may change as a result of some action taken by the person. In the triad above, for example, *p* may sell his car; that action will lead to the belief that he no longer owns it and thereby restores balance. The notion that a person's actions are represented cognitively in the form of beliefs and may thus influence other beliefs or attitudes plays a crucial role in Festinger's (1957) dissonance theory, which will be discussed below.

In sum, then, balance theory is very rich in its implications. Not only does it deal with the relations between beliefs and attitudes; it has important implications for belief formation and the relations between beliefs. Further, since a person's behaviors may be represented as beliefs, the balance model suggests that a person's beliefs and attitudes may be influenced by his behavior.

One should realize, however, that Heider's original balance theory has certain limitations. As pointed out earlier, the theory deals only with qualitative relations between entities. Thus the relation between two entities is either positive or negative; beliefs and attitudes do not vary in degree. Another limitation is the fact that the theory deals with the relations between a maximum of three entities. A third limitation is that, although Heider discusses the possibility of multiple relations between two entities, he says nothing about the degree of balance that would exist in such complex dyadic or triadic configurations.

A number of theorists have attempted to overcome some of these limitations. For example, Cartwright and Harary (1956) employed principles of mathematical graph theory to deal with multiple entities and multiple relations between them. Although these relations are not quantified, graph theory provides a means for assessing the degree of balance in a given configuration. Cartwright and Harary applied their model to actual relations within social structures, thereby generalizing the balance principle beyond a given person's perceptions. Similarly, Newcomb (1953) applied Heider's balance model to actual structural relations between two persons. Finally, Abelson and Rosenberg (1958) used concepts of matrix algebra to extend the balance principle beyond three entities and, like Cartwright and Harary (1956), they suggested ways of estimating degrees of balance or imbalance within a given structure. For some other extensions of Heider's balance model, see Feather (1964a, 1971a).

None of these extensions of Heider's balance model has attempted to quantify beliefs or attitudes. Such quantifications, however, are part of other consistency theories. For example, Rosenberg's (1960, 1965a) affective-cognitive consistency model discussed earlier not only quantifies beliefs and attitudes but also deals with multiple beliefs about the attitude object. Similarly, the congruity principle mentioned above has been applied to situations of interest to the balance model. When this is done, the congruity formulation is structurally similar to the balance model, but in addition, it provides quantification of some of the relations involved.

THE CONGRUITY PRINCIPLE

Just as balance theory begins with a consideration of unit formation, Osgood and Tannenbaum's (1955) congruity principle has as its starting point an assertion that links two objects of judgment. The simplest assertion is merely a descriptive statement, such as "athletes are lazy" or "cigarettes contain nicotine." A more complex situation is that in which a source makes an assertion about a concept, e.g., "communists like strong labor unions" or "the President favors medicare" (Osgood and Tannenbaum, 1955). These assertions, or "coupling actions," may be either associative (*favors, are*) or dissociative (*opposes, are not*).[8]

Although positive or negative assertions may appear to be equivalent to positive or negative relations between o and x in the balance model, there is an important difference. An associative or dissociative assertion is treated as a given in the congruity model, whereas balance theory is concerned with p's *perception* of the relation between o and x. According to the congruity principle, if p encounters an assertion such as "the President favors medicare," then the President and medicare are positively related. In contrast, according to the balance model, even if such an assertion was made, a positive relation between the President and medicare would obtain only if p actually believed the assertion. If p disbelieved the assertion, i.e., if he believed the President to oppose medicare, a negative relation be-

---

8. Note again that within a behavior theory approach, dissociative assertions would not be permissible.

tween the President and medicare would be entered in the balance model. Thus, whereas balance theory is concerned with *perceived* relations between o and x, the congruity principle deals with "objective" or stated relations, i.e., assertions.

Osgood and Tannenbaum's (1955) congruity principle is similar to Heider's balance model in that its assertions are qualitative in nature; i.e., they are either associative or dissociative. In contrast, p's attitudes toward, or evaluations of, o and x are given quantitative values in the congruity principle. Recall that according to the congruity principle, whenever two objects of judgment are related by an assertion, the mediating reaction (i.e., evaluation) characteristic of each shifts toward congruence with the evaluation of the other, the magnitude of the shift being inversely proportional to intensities of the interacting evaluations. A state of congruence exists when the evaluations of two objects are equally intense (i.e., polarized) either in the same direction in the case of associative assertions, or in opposite directions in the case of dissociative assertions (see Osgood, Suci, and Tannenbaum, 1957, pp. 201–203). Thus, although a configuration may be balanced (according to balance theory), it will be incongruous (according to the congruity principle) unless the evaluations of both objects are equally polarized. Balance, therefore, is a necessary but not sufficient condition for congruence.

When a state of incongruity exists, the evaluations of the two objects will tend to change in the direction of congruity.[9] Consider, for example, a person whose evaluation of the President (on a scale ranging from -3 to $+3$) is $+2$ and whose evaluation of medicare is -1. Any assertion linking these two objects, whether associative or dissociative, would result in incongruity. With an associative assertion, congruity would exist if the two objects were evaluated identically. According to the principle of congruity (see Eq. 2.1), in this example both the President and medicare would come to have an evaluation of $+1$. With a dissociative assertion, the exemplified situation is balanced but incongruous. A state of congruence would exist if the evaluations of the two objects were equally polarized but differed in sign. In order to take the direction of the assertion into account, the congruity formula (see Eq. 2.1) can be rewritten as

$$P_R = \frac{|p_1|}{|p_1| + |p_2|} p_1 + \frac{|p_2|}{|p_1| + |p_2|} p_2 d,$$

where d is the direction of the assertion ($+1$ or -1), and all other terms are as given previously. The predicted values of p_1 and p_2 (that is, $\hat{p}_1$ and $\hat{p}_2$) are then given by Eq. 2.6 and 2.7.

$$\hat{p}_1 = P_R. \tag{2.6}$$

$$\hat{p}_2 = P_R d. \tag{2.7}$$

---

9. This tendency was mentioned in our discussion of congruity theory in the context of word combinations, and it may best be viewed as a compromise response when conflicting evaluations are linked by an assertion (see Osgood, Suci, and Tannenbaum, 1957).

In the present example, the congruity principle predicts that the evaluation of the President would shift to +1.67 and the evaluation of medicare to −1.67. That is,

$$P_R = \frac{2}{2+1}\,(2) + \frac{1}{2+1}\,(-1)(-1) = \frac{4}{3} + \frac{1}{3} = \frac{5}{3} = 1.67,$$

and $\widehat{p}_1 = 1.67, \quad \widehat{p}_2 = -1.67.$

Note that the magnitudes of the shifts in evaluations are again inversely proportional to their polarizations. That is, the +2 evaluation of the President shifts ⅓ of a unit, and the −1 evaluation of medicare shifts ⅔ of a unit.

One implication of viewing an assertion as a given is that incongruity can be resolved only by shifts in evaluations of the two objects and not by a change in the assertion itself. Consider, for example, a person who places a value of +2 on both the President and medicare and who receives a message asserting that the President opposes medicare. According to Heider's balance model, this dilemma is resolved if p rejects the assertion and perceives or believes that the President is in favor of medicare. This resolution is not possible in congruity theory, where the dilemma is resolved only when both evaluations shift to the neutral point.

In their research on the congruity principle, Osgood and Tannenbaum (1955) soon came to realize that a given assertion may not be believed. To enable their model to handle such cases, they introduced a "correction for incredulity." They assumed that some degree of incredulity exists when there is imbalance, that is, when two positively evaluated objects are dissociated or when one positively and one negatively evaluated object are associated. The greater the polarity of evaluations, the greater the degree of incredulity. Osgood and Tannenbaum argued that the congruity principle applies only to the degree that the assertion is perceived as credulous. In the extreme case of complete incredulity, no change is expected since it is assumed that no link between the two objects has been established.

An "assertion constant" was also added to the model in order to account for the finding that the object of an assertion (i.e., the x in the o-x link) tends to change more than would be predicted by the congruity formula.

Analysis of the Congruity Principle

Reconsidering the congruity principle in terms of our conceptual framework, we can see that its major concern is with attitudes toward two objects. Here again, attitude is defined in terms of an evaluative or affective dimension. Although the formal model deals with assertions linking one object to another, the concept of belief does not enter into the theory until the notion of incredulity is introduced. It is only at this stage that the person's belief in the assertion, i.e., his belief that o is related to x, is explicitly taken into account. Attitude change is expected to occur only to the extent that the assertion is believed. Unfortunately, Osgood and Tannenbaum's (1955) assessment of incredulity is problematic when it is viewed as a measure of belief. Not unlike Heider's (1944) notion that belief formation is influenced by the dynamic character of the elements comprising the belief (i.e., by p's attitudes toward o and x), incredulity is assessed by assuming that it varies directly with imbalance and incongruity. This implies that imbalanced assertions are not likely to be believed, but balanced ones are. That is, incredulity is assumed to occur only when imbalance is present; the greater the incongruity of these imbalanced states, the greater the degree of incredulity. Clearly, however, this assumption does not always hold. It is possible for p to believe that a liked o opposes a liked x (for example, p's preferred candidate opposes a policy favored by p), or to disbelieve that a liked o favors a policy approved by p.

To be sure, these configurations constitute imbalanced states, but from a balance-theory viewpoint, incredulity or disbelief need not result. Indeed, it is because p holds the belief that imbalance is present. Further, recall that it is only when the assertion is not rejected that attitude change is expected in congruity theory. Thus the congruity principle again implies that a person's attitude is influenced by his belief that the attitude object is related to some attribute and by the evaluation of that attribute. Although the original congruity principle dealt with only one belief about an object, it was later extended to handle several beliefs simultaneously (Triandis and Fishbein, 1963; Anderson and Fishbein, 1965).

It is worth noting that inconsistency within a triadic configuration may involve beliefs, attitudes, or both. Assume that o and x are perceived as a unit or, in Osgood and Tannenbaum's (1955) terminology, that the assertion is credulous; p is linked to each of the two elements constituting the unit. In balance theory, these links may be either beliefs or attitudes, but in congruity theory only p's attitudes toward o and x are considered. Consequently, in balance theory inconsistency may exist between two beliefs, two attitudes, or a belief and an attitude; in congruity theory, inconsistency always involves two attitudes. In contrast, the consistency theory that has attracted most attention, i.e., dissonance theory, may be viewed as dealing only with inconsistency between beliefs.

A THEORY OF COGNITIVE DISSONANCE

Festinger's (1957) theory of cognitive dissonance begins with a consideration of the relations between two cognitive elements. "These elements refer to . . . the things a person knows about himself, about his behavior, and about his surroundings" (Festinger, 1957, p. 9). The following are examples of cognitive elements: "I know I smoke," "I know that smoking causes cancer," "I know I enjoy smoking," and "I know that George is my brother."

The terms *dissonance, consonance,* and *irrelevance* are used to describe three kinds of relations that may exist between any two cognitive elements. *"Two elements are in a dissonant relation if, considering these two alone, the obverse of one element would follow from the other.* To state it a bit more formally, x and y are dissonant if not-x follows from y." (Festinger, 1957, p. 13) For example, the element "I know I smoke" would not follow from the element "I know smoking causes cancer," and hence these two cognitive elements are dissonant.

"If, considering a pair of elements, either one *does* follow from the other, then the relation between them is consonant" (Festinger, 1957, p. 15). For instance, since the element "I know I smoke" follows from the element "I know I enjoy smoking," this pair of cognitive elements is in a consonant relation.

Finally, "where one cognitive element implies nothing at all concerning some other element, these two elements are irrelevant to one another" (Festinger, 1957, p. 11). An irrelevant relation is exemplified by the two elements "I know I smoke" and "I know that George is my brother."

The basic hypothesis of dissonance theory was stated as follows:

> The existence of dissonance, being psychologically uncomfortable, will motivate the person to try to reduce the dissonance and achieve consonance. . . . The strength of the pressure to reduce the dissonance is a function of the magnitude of the dissonance. (Festinger, 1957, pp. 3, 18; italics omitted)

Considering a dissonant pair of cognitive elements, the magnitude of dissonance increases with the importance of the elements to the person. However, a given element may have relevant relations to more than one other element. Thus the cognitive element "I know I smoke" is consonant with "I know I enjoy smoking" and is dissonant with "I know that smoking causes cancer." The total amount of dissonance between any given cognitive element (e.g., "I know I smoke") and all other relevant elements is a function of the number of dissonant relations relative to the total number of relevant relations. The magnitude of dissonance will of course also depend on the importance of those relevant elements that exist in consonant or dissonant relations with the one in question.

It is possible to express these ideas more formally, as in Eq. 2.8,

$$D_k = \frac{\sum_{d=1}^{n} I_d}{\sum_{d=1}^{n} I_d + \sum_{c=1}^{m} I_c}, \tag{2.8}$$

where D_k is the magnitude of dissonance associated with cognitive element k; I_d is the importance of dissonant element d; I_c is the importance of consonant element c; n is the number of cognitive elements in a dissonant relation with element k; and m is the number of cognitive elements in a consonant relation with element k.[10]

When two cognitive elements exist in a dissonant relation, psychological tension or discomfort will motivate the person to reduce the dissonance and achieve

---

10. It has also been suggested that the magnitude of dissonance can be defined as a ratio of dissonant to consonant elements, each weighted by its importance (Kiesler, Collins, and Miller, 1969; Brehm and Cohen, 1962). Despite the difference between this definition and Eq. 2.8, where the ratio is computed in terms of the total number of relevant relations, the two formulations have sometimes been discussed as if they were interchangeable (e.g., Brehm and Cohen, 1962).

consonance. The only way to completely eliminate the existing dissonance is to change one of the two elements involved. For example, the dissonant relation between the two cognitive elements "I know I smoke" and "I know that smoking causes cancer" could be changed to a consonant relation in one of two ways. The person might change the first cognitive element to "I know I don't smoke," or he might change the second to "I know that smoking does not cause cancer."

Given that cognitive elements are responsive to "reality" (Festinger, 1957), it may sometimes be impossible to change either of the cognitive elements in a dissonant relation. However, the *magnitude* of dissonance associated with a cognitive element may be reduced in two ways. First, the person may add new cognitive elements that are consonant with the element in question. Thus, in the example above, the cognitive element "I know that I enjoy smoking" may be introduced. Indeed, a person may be expected to actively seek new consonant information and try to avoid exposure to dissonant information. Second, the person may reduce the importance of one or both elements in the dissonant relation.

Festinger (1957) described four basic situations that give rise to cognitive dissonance: decision making, forced compliance, voluntary and involuntary exposure to dissonant information, and disagreement with other persons. For example, whenever a person makes a choice between two or more alternatives, dissonance is assumed to exist. That is, his knowledge that the unchosen alternatives have favorable aspects and his knowledge that the chosen alternative has unfavorable aspects are both dissonant with his knowledge of his choice. In this situation, the theory predicts that dissonance may be reduced by increasing one's evaluation of the chosen alternative and/or decreasing one's evaluation of the unchosen alternatives. The amount of change will be related to the magnitude of dissonance involved. The magnitude of postdecision dissonance is an increasing function of the general importance of the decision and of the degree to which chosen and unchosen alternatives are similar in attractiveness.

In the forced-compliance situation, an individual is induced to perform a behavior that is inconsistent with his beliefs or attitudes. For example, a prisoner of war who believes that communism is a repressive system might be induced (through threat of punishment or promise of reward) to state publicly that communism is not a repressive system. Dissonance would exist between the two cognitive elements "I know that communism is a repressive system" and "I know I publicly said that communism is not a repressive system." The magnitude of dissonance in this situation is inversely related to the amount of threatened punishment or promised reward. That is, the greater the justification for the behavior, the less dissonance it arouses. Here dissonance theory predicts that the person can reduce dissonance by changing his belief about communism such that it becomes consonant with his behavior. The greater the magnitude of dissonance, the greater the expected change in belief.[11]

---

11. Note that dissonance will also arise when the person refuses to comply. Then the dissonance exists between "I know I refused to state publicly that communism

These examples point to another important assumption in dissonance theory, namely, that cognitive elements are responsive to reality; by and large they mirror or map reality. This does not mean, however, that cognitive elements will always correspond to reality. Rather, "the major point to be made is that the reality which impinges on a person will exert pressures in the direction of bringing the appropriate cognitive elements into correspondence with that reality" (Festinger, 1957, p. 11; italics omitted).

Analysis of Dissonance Theory

When dissonance theory is viewed in terms of our conceptual framework, a number of interesting implications can be derived. First, it may be argued that cognitive elements are equivalent to what we have defined as beliefs. That is, a cognitive element refers to a person's *knowledge* that he holds a certain attitude or a certain belief or that he performed a certain behavior and *not* to the attitude, belief, or behavior itself. For example, consider the following three cognitive elements.

1. I know I like Senator Kennedy.
2. I know I believe that Senator Kennedy participated in an antiwar demonstration.
3. I know I participated in an antiwar demonstration.

The first element constitutes a belief about an attitude; the second refers to a belief about a belief; and the third is the person's belief about his own behavior. Not unlike some of the consistency theories we have discussed earlier, dissonance theory deals only with qualitative beliefs. That is, a person either holds or does not hold the belief in question.

From our point of view, beliefs about attitudes are not equivalent to the attitudes themselves, nor are beliefs about behaviors equivalent to the behaviors themselves. It could be argued, however, and indeed Festinger (1957) has argued that beliefs about beliefs are psychologically equivalent to the beliefs themselves.

Similarly, it is possible that measures of beliefs about attitudes will sometimes yield results similar to those of direct measures of attitude. Thus a measure of "I like Kennedy" on a probability dimension may be highly correlated with a measure of the concept "Kennedy" on an evaluative or affective dimension. However, some psychodynamic theories might suggest that a person does not always know what his "true" belief or attitude is, i.e., that the cognitive element may not be a veridical representation of the belief or attitude. For example, according to psychoanalytic theory, defense mechanisms such as repression or reaction formation may affect veridicality by eliminating some threatening belief or attitude from consciousness or by replacing it with its opposite.

---

is a repressive system" and "I know I was punished for my refusal." The magnitude of dissonance in this situation is an *increasing* function of amount of punishment obtained or reward forgone.

It is worth noting that research on dissonance theory has usually obtained measures of beliefs and attitudes, rather than of their cognitive representations. Although this may appear problematic in view of the considerations above, the issue is really more theoretical than practical since beliefs and attitudes are usually assessed by direct self-reports in studies on dissonance theory. In some cases, however, a direct measure of attitude may not be the same as a measure of the belief about the attitude, and then the measure of attitude would be inappropriate for a test of dissonance theory. Further, indirect measures of attitude (see Chapter 3) may also be inappropriate since they may not correspond to the person's knowledge of his attitude.

Also noteworthy is the fact that Festinger's cognitive elements can be viewed as perceived relations in the balance-theory formulation. In the example above, the following triad emerges: "I admire Senator Kennedy" (pLo); "Senator Kennedy participated in an antiwar demonstration" (oUx); and "I participated in an antiwar demonstration" (pUx). However, Festinger's cognitive elements refer to the person's knowledge or belief about each relation in the triad. That is, "I believe (pLo)"; "I believe (oUx)"; and "I believe (pUx)."

Clearly, then, consonance and dissonance refer to relations between beliefs and only between beliefs. Other variables, i.e., attitudes, intentions, or behaviors, are relevant only to the extent that they are represented cognitively. However, relations between beliefs, i.e., between cognitive elements, may influence these other variables (as well as the beliefs themselves). Thus changes in beliefs, attitudes, intentions and behaviors are all viewed as influenced in a similar manner by dissonant relations between beliefs. Although Festinger regarded beliefs about one's own behavior as a special set of cognitive elements, he made little or no distinction between the cognitive representations of beliefs and attitudes. Thus dissonance theory makes no differential predictions about the effects of dissonance on changes in beliefs and attitudes. Moreover, in most applications of dissonance theory, distinctions are usually not made between beliefs, attitudes, and behaviors themselves on the one hand and their cognitive representations on the other.

A typical investigation examines the effects of behaviorally induced dissonance on beliefs and/or attitudes. In a later chapter we will suggest that some of the conflicting findings in research on dissonance phenomena may be due to the failure of dissonance theory to make a distinction between beliefs and attitudes, and to the assumption that a dissonant relation between cognitive elements will have similar effects on these two variables. Perhaps the most important contribution of dissonance theory has been to direct attention to the possibility that different amounts of dissonance may be created by the performance of a given behavior, and therefore that the performance of the behavior may sometimes lead to a considerable change and at other times to little change in any given belief, attitude, or intention. Unfortunately, the assumption of dissonance theory that these effects are mediated by beliefs and the relations between beliefs has often been neglected.

One problem that has arisen with respect to dissonance theory is related to the difficulty of specifying when two cognitive elements stand in a dissonant relation; that is, what is meant by "the obverse of one element follows from the other"? Aronson (1968) has suggested that "the major source of conceptual ambiguity rests upon the fact that Festinger has not clarified the meaning of the words 'follows from' " (Aronson, 1968, p. 9). He suggested a rule of thumb whereby "the obverse of one element follows from the other" would be defined in terms of the violation of an expectancy.

This interpretation implies a distinction between imbalance and dissonance. A person's knowledge that a liked friend has a negative trait is clearly imbalanced, but it is not necessarily dissonant. It would be dissonant only if the person did not expect his friend to have that negative trait. This distinction between imbalance and dissonance corresponds closely to the distinction between affective and cognitive inconsistency. As we pointed out earlier, balance theory deals with both types of inconsistency whereas dissonance theory, which is concerned with dissonance between cognitions or beliefs, can deal only with cognitive inconsistency.

A second and perhaps more important problem concerning dissonance theory is the specification of the amount of dissonance that is expected to result from the performance of a behavior in a given situation. Most elaborations and extensions of dissonance theory have centered on this problem. The most important factor relates to "volition," or freedom of choice, in performing the behavior. The basic argument is that dissonance is created only to the extent that the person feels he had freedom of choice (Brehm and Cohen, 1962). This notion is closely related to Festinger's (1957) discussion of the forced-compliance situation, where the amount of dissonance resulting from compliance is inversely related to the amount of pressure to comply (e.g., threatened punishment or promised reward). The person's perception of his freedom of choice may be expected to decrease with increased pressure. In other words, dissonance is likely to occur to the extent that there is insufficient justification for the performance of the behavior. It is assumed that promised rewards or threatened punishments, for example, will provide justification for performing the behavior and hence will add consonant elements to the dissonant relation. This should serve to reduce the magnitude of total dissonance.

Finally, one might question the necessity of postulating an aversive motivational state, i.e., dissonance, in order to account for the effects of behavior on beliefs and attitudes in situations such as forced compliance or decision making. Bem (1965, 1968a, 1972) has in fact argued that it is not necessary to make such an assumption, and he has proposed an alternative interpretation based on Skinner's (1957) analysis of verbal behavior. According to this position, beliefs and attitudes are simply self-descriptive, verbal responses. Such responses, like other responses, are under the control of internal or external stimuli. One important source of stimuli for "attitudinal" responses is the person's own behavior, together with the context in which it occurs. Thus "an individual's belief and attitude statements and the beliefs and attitudes that an outside observer would attribute to him are often functionally equivalent in that both sets of statements are 'inferences' from the same evidence" (Bem, 1965, p. 199).

To see how this might explain dissonance phenomena, consider a person who states publicly that America should cease to support Nationalist China. If he does so for a large reward (e.g., $5,000), other people as well as the person himself will perceive this behavior to be under the control of external stimuli, namely, the reward, and thus little information is provided about the person's stand on the issue. In contrast, when he makes the same statement for little reward (e.g., $1), his behavior will be attributed to internal stimuli, i.e., his personal belief. Thus, in the low-reward condition the inference drawn will be that the person really believes that America should cease to support Nationalist China; this inference will not be drawn in the high-reward condition. Note that this prediction is the same as that derived from dissonance theory (i.e., the smaller the reward, the greater the dissonance, and thus the more change).

Bem's analysis concerns the attribution of dispositions (i.e., beliefs, attitudes, etc.) to one's self and to others. Although Bem's analysis has been applied primarily to the explanation of dissonance phenomena, theories of attribution deal with questions of a more general nature, namely, with the formation and change of beliefs.

THEORIES OF ATTRIBUTION

Recall that Heider's (1946, 1958) development of the balance model grew out of his interest in causal attribution, i.e., the formation of causal units. His first question concerned the degree to which a given action or event would be attributed to some person or object. Imagine, for example, that a violent crime has been committed and that two persons were in the vicinity at the time of the crime. As we have seen earlier, according to Heider, a causal unit will easily be formed if the dynamic characters of two entities are similar. Thus, if one of the persons involved is perceived as brutal and the other as gentle, the violent crime is likely to be attributed to the first. If only the gentle person had been found in the vicinity of the crime, the event might still not have been attributed to him but to an external factor, e.g., a third person (Heider, 1944).

Heider (1958) distinguished five levels of causal attribution in reference to the attribution of responsibility for the outcomes of an action: association, commission, foreseeability, intentionality, and intentionality with justification. At the first level, the actor is held responsible for any effect that is in some way associated with him. At the second level, he is held responsible only when the effect is seen as a direct result of his behavior. Attribution of responsibility at the third level requires that the effect was foreseeable, even if not intended. Intentionality is the prerequisite for attribution of responsibility at the next level; that is, here the actor is held responsible only for effects that he foresaw and intended. Finally, if his action is perceived as justified, i.e., caused by factors beyond his control, he will be held less responsible, even though he may have intended to produce the observed effects.

Later, Heider (1958) went beyond the formation of causal units and considered attribution of stable dispositions to an actor. "Dispositional properties are the invariances that make possible a more or less stable, predictable, and controllable world. They refer to the relatively unchanging structures and processes that characterize or underlie phenomena" (Heider, 1958; p. 80). Indeed, for the most part, attribution theory is concerned with inferences about stable dispositions of people based on information about or direct observation of their actions. Specifically, attribution theory deals with specifying the conditions under which attributions to a person will or will not be made.

A distinction has been made between internal and external attribution; that is to say, a person's behavior may be attributed to some disposition of the person himself or to some external factor. In the latter case, no inferences can be made about the person's stable characteristics. For example, if a person is observed to succeed at some task, his performance may be attributed to his ability or motivation (i.e., internal attribution) or to an external cause, such as good luck or the low difficulty level of the task.

Heider (1958) distinguishes between personal and impersonal causality. By personal causality he refers to levels four and five in the attribution of responsibility, i.e., to instances in which a person is perceived to have caused a certain event intentionally. According to Heider, internal attributions are made only under conditions of personal causality, i.e., where the action is perceived to be purposive. Jones and Davis's (1965) analysis of attribution processes centers on such personal causality. According to this analysis, attribution of a disposition to an actor is based on the observation of his action and its consequences or effects. The perceiver's basic problem is to decide which of these effects, if any, were intended by the actor. Two factors are assumed to influence the degree to which the actor will be perceived to have intended a given action. The first condition in the inference process is the assumption of knowledge (or foreseeability) on the part of the actor; that is, "in order to perceive that at least some of the effects achieved by an action were intended, the perceiver must first believe that the actor was aware his actions would have the observed effects" (Jones and Davis, 1965, p. 220). The second condition in the inference process is the assumption of ability on the part of the actor; that is, the observed effects may have been achieved as a result of luck or chance rather than ability. Thus, for intention to be inferred, the actor must be perceived to have had (a) the knowledge that the effects would result from his action, and (b) the ability to produce the effects. These ideas are summarized in Fig. 2.5.

Two questions, then, are central to dispositional attribution: (1) What dispositions will be attributed to an actor? (2) What factors influence the confidence with which such attributions are made? Most theorizing on attribution processes is concerned with the latter question rather than the former.

Fig. 2.5 The action-attribute paradigm. (Reproduced from Jones and Davis, 1965, p. 222.)

According to Jones and Davis (1965) the certainty of attributions (or as they call it, correspondent inference) depends on two factors: the desirability of the effects produced by the action, and the degree to which these effects are common to other behavioral alternatives that were available to the actor. Assume that a person is observed to perform one of two possible behaviors, and that these behaviors would produce some common and some noncommon effects. The lower the perceived desirability of the effects produced by the behavior that is performed and the fewer the unique effects (i.e., noncommon effects) produced by that behavior, the more confident an observer will be in attributing a disposition to the actor. The particular disposition that is attributed will correspond to the unique effects produced by the behavior.

For example, consider a person who can take his date either to a party or to a movie, and assume that the relevant effects of these alternative behaviors are as follows:

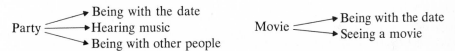

First, note that "being with the date" is common to both alternatives. The other effects are unique. If the person went to the party, two attributions could be made. According to the theory, the actor might be perceived to like music or to like being with other people. Thus the observer would not be certain as to the actor's disposition. If the actor went to the movie, however, the attribution would be made that he likes movies. Further, according to the theory, the less attractive or desirable that particular movie is perceived to be, the more certain the observer will be that the actor likes movies.

On the basis of Heider's (1958) analysis, Kelley (1967, 1971, 1972, 1973) has also discussed some of the ways in which effects produced by an action are attributed to the various factors present in the situation. He suggested two major principles of causal attribution. The first is the *principle of covariation,* which states, "The effect is attributed to that condition (factor) which is present when the effect is present and which is absent when the effect is absent" (Kelley, 1967,

p. 194). Not unlike a scientist, the naive observer is assumed to examine the presence or absence of effects under different conditions, at different points in time, and for different actors. One of Kelley's major concerns is with attributions to the actor (internal) as opposed to other factors (external). Internal attribution requires that the actor behave consistently under different conditions and at different times, and also that his behavior differ from that of other actors. For example, if a person always assists others in need of help, even under adverse conditions, and in this behavior he is not like other actors in similar situations, he is likely to be perceived as altruistic. When the actor's behavior varies across situations and is similar to the behaviors of others in those situations, some factor in the situation is assumed to be responsible for his behavior; that is, an external attribution is made.

Specifically, Kelley (1967, 1972) identified three major factors that influence attribution. (1) *Consistency*—the degree to which the actor performs the same behavior toward an object on different occasions. The more consistent his behavior, the more likely it is that an internal attribution will be made. (2) *Distinctiveness*—the degree to which the actor performs different behaviors with respect to different objects. The lower the distinctiveness (i.e., the more the actor performs the same behavior with respect to different objects) the more likely it is that an internal attribution will be made. (3) *Consensus*—the degree to which other actors perform the same behavior with respect to a given object. Internal attribution decreases with consensus.

The second principle refers to *multiple plausible causes* for a behavior performed at a given point in time. Clearly, the greater the number of plausible explanations, the lower the certainty of any given attribution.

Other factors, such as the actor's perceived decision freedom and the prior probability of his behavior, have also been suggested as determinants of the likelihood that an attribution will be made. For example, Steiner (1970) argued that confidence in an internal attribution should increase with the actor's perceived decision freedom. Steiner's notion of perceived decision freedom is related to the desirability of the effects associated with the actor's behavioral alternatives. According to Steiner (1970, p. 195) "whenever an individual must choose between two or more available alternatives, decision freedom should be a negative function of the discrepancies between the gains offered by the available options." Consider, for example, a person who performs a behavior that results in desirable consequences. If the other alternatives available to him would also have led to desirable consequences, the actor would be perceived to have had a high degree of decision freedom; since he was free to choose other attractive alternatives, his actual behavioral choice can be used to make inferences about his dispositions. However, if the other available alternatives would have led to undesirable consequences, he would be perceived to have had little decision freedom; thus little information about his dispositions would be gained.

It is worth noting that all the factors above that have been assumed to influence attribution involve the utilization of information obtained about an actor's behavior and about the circumstances under which it occurred. However, as Heider (1958) and others have noted, factors residing in the observer may also affect his attributions. Thus, as indicated earlier, a person's attitudes may influence his perception of causal units. Jones and Davis (1965) argued that when an actor's behavior directly affects the observer, attributions to the actor are made with greater confidence than when the same behavior is directed toward some other person. Another possibility that has been mentioned (e.g., Heider, 1944; Kelley, 1971; Jones and Nisbett, 1971) is that an observer may tend to underemphasize the importance of the environment and to exaggerate the importance of the personal factor.

Analysis of Attribution Theories

From the point of view of our conceptual framework, attribution theory deals with the formation and change of beliefs.[12] These beliefs are *inferences* about the causes of observed events or about an actor's stable dispositions. All the principles discussed above concern the degree to which observing a person's behavior influences beliefs about him or about the environment. Since a person also serves as an observer of his own behaviors, attribution theory has implications for the formation of beliefs about one's self. Although it has been argued that the principles governing attribution of dispositions to others are similar to those governing attributions of dispositions to one's self (e.g., Bem, 1965; Steiner, 1970), some theorists (e.g., Jones and Nisbett, 1971) have suggested that different processes are involved. This question will be discussed in Chapter 5.

Irrespective of whether self-attributions or attributions to others are considered, a central concern of attribution theory is with the subjective probability that a given trait or disposition is associated with a given actor. However, it must also be realized that, prior to observing the actor's behavior, the observer will have had some subjective probability that the actor has the disposition in question (even if that probability is .50, or complete uncertainty).[13] One may therefore argue that the degree to which an attribution has been made in a given situation is reflected in the *change* or shift in the belief (i.e., a change in subjective probability), rather than in the absolute level of the belief (see Ajzen, 1971).

This conceptualization of the attribution process as a revision in subjective probability suggests the possibility of applying Bayes's theorem as a model of the attribution process. Bayes's theorem and other probability models describing relations between beliefs (cf. McGuire, 1960a,b,c; Warr and Smith, 1970) will be discussed in Chapter 5, which considers the formation of beliefs.

---

12. As in dissonance theory, these may be beliefs about attitudes, intentions, or behaviors.

13. Such prior beliefs may be based on familiarity with the actor, with his social background, education, etc. Indeed, one difference between attributions to self and others may be due to differences in prior beliefs held by actor and observer.

CONCLUSION

This chapter has reviewed some of the contemporary theories in the attitude area. Although we have repeatedly pointed to similarities, we have also shown that these theories differ in many respects. They differ in terms of the variables that play a central role in the theory, in the ways that the variables are interrelated, and in terms of focusing on processes of formation and/or change of the variables. First, a distinction should be made between the constructs of a theory and the operations that have been employed to manipulate or assess those constructs. For instance, in our discussion of dissonance theory we pointed out that at the conceptual level the theory deals only with cognitions, i.e., beliefs. Operationally, however, these cognitions are often manipulated by changing behavior and assessed by measuring attitude.

From our point of view, most theories can be classified at the conceptual level as dealing either with beliefs or attitudes or with both beliefs and attitudes. With the exception of a few learning theories (e.g., Doob, 1947; Lott and Lott, 1968) and Edwards's (1954) decision theory, behavioral intentions and behavior are dealt with only at the operational level, not at the conceptual level. A simple classical conditioning model deals only with attitudes (e.g., Staats and Staats, 1958) whereas dissonance and attribution theories deal only with beliefs. The more sophisticated learning theories, most expectancy-value models, congruity theory, and balance theory deal with both beliefs and attitudes at the conceptual level.

It should be clear that since different variables are involved, the theories described also deal with different relationships. Thus some theories are concerned only with the relations between attitudes (e.g., Staats and Staats, 1958), but others are concerned with relations between beliefs (e.g., dissonance theory). Most theories, however, deal with the relations between beliefs and attitudes. Further, some theories specify causal relations (e.g., expectancy-value models, attribution theories), and others are concerned with the dynamic interrelations among variables (e.g., balance theory, dissonance theory). For example, according to expectancy-value models, beliefs and associated evaluations are the determinants of attitude. In contrast, balance theory is concerned with the effects of imbalance on the relationships in a given configuration.

Stated somewhat differently, some theories postulate what can best be described as an information-processing model; information about an object or issue or about one's self leads to the formation of beliefs or attitudes. Other theories postulate a dynamic process where information affects beliefs or attitudes only to the extent that it introduces some inconsistency or instability among these variables.

This discussion suggests that virtually every theory is in some way concerned with information. The information may be about an object or about one's own beliefs, attitudes, intentions, or behaviors with respect to the object. Both types of information may be gained either through direct observation or by means of some communication. Although all theories deal with information about the object, relatively few (e.g., balance theory, dissonance theory, attribution theory) also deal with information about the self.

Some theorists might argue with the use of the term "information" in this context. For example, classical conditioning is usually assumed to occur without awareness. In contrast, the present analysis assumes that pairing an object with an unconditioned stimulus provides information about the object; that is, the subject is aware of the contingency and thus forms a new belief. This information contributes to his attitude. The question of awareness in classical conditioning will be discussed more fully in Chapters 4 and 6.

At the operational level, many investigators fail to distinguish between beliefs, attitudes, and intentions. Thus, although the conceptual variable in a theory may be attitude, the operation utilized may be assessing beliefs, intentions, or even behavior. A second problem discussed previously regarding dissonance theory is the possibility that measures of beliefs, attitudes, intentions, or behaviors may not correspond directly to their cognitive representations. Thus, for example, a person's belief that he holds a certain attitude may not be adequately assessed by a direct measure of the attitude. It is interesting to note that although dissonance theory does suggest that beliefs about an attitude and the attitude per se may differ, at least one self-attribution theory (Bem, 1968a) holds that these two concepts are identical in that they are both self-descriptive responses. From our point of view, however, attribution theories deal only with beliefs, and tests of these theories should therefore employ only measures of beliefs.

Another difficulty of particular concern to dissonance theory is its failure to specify exactly the cognitive elements of relevance in a given situation. It is thus left to the investigator's intuition to select the relevant elements. Some investigators may employ measures of beliefs, and others may employ measures of attitude, etc.

Finally, the theories discussed in this chapter can be compared in terms of their focus on formation and/or change of beliefs and attitudes. Generally speaking, theories based on notions of information processing deal directly with processes of formation and therefore have immediate implications for change. Indeed, it is often difficult to tell whether some new information leads to the formation of a belief or attitude, or whether it changes an existing belief or attitude. The different learning theories, as well as expectancy-value models, are concerned with the effects of information on attitude whereas attribution theories are concerned with the effects of information on beliefs.

In contrast, theories postulating a dynamic process tend to focus on change, without great concern for the formation of beliefs or attitudes. Thus the congruity model is concerned with changes in attitudes produced by incongruity, and dissonance theory deals with the effects of inconsistent beliefs. Attempts to reduce dissonance may produce changes in beliefs, attitudes, intentions, or behaviors. Similarly, balance theory deals with changes in both beliefs and attitudes, and it can also be applied to changes in intentions and behaviors.

Our comparison of attitude theories discussed in this chapter is summarized in Table 2.2. One can see that theories may differ in terms of their conceptual variables and thus the kinds of relations they can deal with, in terms of the processes underlying these relations (informational or dynamic), and in terms of the operational variables that have been considered in empirical research. Finally—not shown in the table—information-processing theories focus on formation and change, whereas dynamic theories tend to deal with change only.

Table 2.2 Comparison of Contemporary Attitude Theories

	Conceptual variables	Type of theory	Operational variables
Learning theories			
Staats and Staats	A	Informational	A
Lott	b,A,B	Informational	b,A,I,B
Doob	b,A,B	Informational	—
Expectancy-value theories			
Fishbein	b,A	Informational	b,A
Edwards	b,A,B	Informational	B
Rosenberg	b,A	Dynamic	b,A
Consistency theories			
Balance (Heider)	b,A	Dynamic	b,A,I,B
Congruity (Osgood and Tannenbaum)	b,A	Dynamic	A
Dissonance (Festinger)	b	Dynamic	b,A,I,B
Attribution theories			
Self-attribution (Bem)	b	Informational	b,A,I
Attribution to others	b	Informational	b,A,I

Abbreviations: b = belief, A = attitude, I = intention, B = behavior

Chapter 3

Measurement Techniques

In Chapter 1 we provided conceptual definitions of belief, attitude, intention, and behavior. Attitude was defined as a person's location on a dimension of affect or evaluation. Belief was defined as his location on a probability dimension that links an object and an attribute. Intention was also defined as a dimension of probability, but the link here involves the person and some action with respect to the object. Finally, behavior was defined as a person's observable response when studied in its own right.

This chapter will discuss some of the techniques that have been used to assess beliefs, attitudes, and intentions. As noted in Chapter 1, an almost unlimited variety of measurement procedures have been employed in the attitude area. We will first try to show that most of these different procedures can readily be identified as measures of beliefs, attitudes, or intentions. There will then follow a discussion of the major attitude-scaling methods, namely, Guttman, Thurstone, Likert, and semantic differential scales. We will try to show that all of these standard scaling methods yield a single score that represents the person's location on an evaluative dimension, i.e., that they are all measures of attitude as here defined. Further, we will try to show that these attitude scores are always obtained by a consideration of beliefs or intentions and their associated evaluations. We will then consider some alternative attitude-measurement procedures, such as disguised and physiological measures. Finally, we will take up multidimensional scaling techniques and other measures of cognitive structure.

SINGLE-RESPONSE MEASURES

In the final analysis, all measurement involves observation of one or more responses made by a subject, whether they are verbal (e.g., a questionnaire response) or overt behavioral responses. Much research in the attitude area has relied on single-response measures to infer beliefs, attitudes, and intentions. Although more complex indices of beliefs, attitudes, and intentions can be obtained, these indices are always in some way derived from single-response measures. It may therefore be instructive to examine the nature of single-response measures employed in the attitude area.

Most single-response measures are verbal in nature; the subject is asked to make a judgment about himself or about some other person, object, or event. Any response of this kind involves three different aspects: the concept, the judgment, and the format. That is, using a certain response format, the subject makes some judgment about a given concept.

Response formats. Many different response formats have been used. Most frequently, some form of graphic scale is employed and the subject responds by placing a check mark on the scale, which may be a continuous line or a line divided into several categories. Different response categories may also be presented in a multiple-choice format. Other response formats are qualitative judgments and quantitative estimates. For example, the subject may be asked to indicate whether a person is intelligent or not intelligent (qualitative judgment) or he may be asked to estimate the person's I.Q. (quantitative estimate).[1]

Irrespective of the response format used, every judgment places some concept into one of several categories. The categories defined by the response format may be discrete, nominal categories (qualitative judgment), they may be discrete categories ordered along some dimension, or they may represent points along a continuous dimension.

Much more than by the response format, however, diversity of judgment is introduced by variations in the concept being judged and the nature or content of the judgment that is required.

The concept. Judgments can be made with respect to any concept whatsoever. The concept may be a physical object, an institution, a person, a trait, an attribute, a behavior, etc. Such concepts can be described in detail or in a more general fashion. For example, one concept might be "the church" (general) whereas another concept might be "the Church of the Latter-Day Saints." Different concepts are also involved when "Joe Namath as a quarterback" and "Joe Namath as a playboy" are rated. Similarly, "highly informative" and "moderately informative" constitute different concepts.

The concept may not consist of a single object, person, or attribute but may instead be a statement linking an object to an attribute. Examples: "Joe Namath is a quarterback." "I intend to donate money to the church." "Reading the *New York Times* is highly informative." Again, the latter concept is not the same as "Reading the *New York Times* is *moderately* informative."

---

1. Subjects are sometimes asked to describe a concept using their own words. Typically, more than one response is elicited. When the investigator singles out one of these responses, he must somehow quantify or categorize it.

Nature of the judgment. Just as there is no limit to the number of concepts that can be rated, there is no limit to the number of labels that can be associated with the judgmental categories or dimensions. The content of a judgment is defined by these labels. Sometimes only the dimension's endpoints are labeled, but at other times each category on the dimension is given a label. For example, endpoints of a scale might be labeled *intelligent–not intelligent,* or the dimension might be divided into four categories with the labels *extremely intelligent, quite intelligent, slightly intelligent,* and *not at all intelligent.* Other examples of endpoints used in attitude research are *justifiable–not justifiable, approve–disapprove, I will attend church–I will not attend church, strongly agree–strongly disagree,* and *good–bad.*

Depending on the labels associated with its endpoints, a scale may be unipolar or bipolar. For example, the scale ranging from *hot* to *cold* is a bipolar or bidirectional scale whereas scales such as *not at all hot–hot* and *not at all cold–cold* are unipolar or unidirectional. Note that judgments on a unipolar scale are not the same as judgments on a bipolar scale, and different results may be obtained. For example, consider the bipolar scale

clean	+3	+2	+1	0	−1	−2	−3	dirty
	extremely	quite	slightly	neither or both	slightly	quite	extremely	

and the following two unipolar scales.

0	+1	+2	+3
not at all clean	slightly clean	quite clean	extremely clean

0	−1	−2	−3
not at all dirty	slightly dirty	quite dirty	extremely dirty

There is considerable evidence that knowledge of a person's responses to the two unipolar scales allows specification of his response to the bipolar scale (e.g., K. J. Kaplan, 1972). However, a given bipolar response may be associated with very different unipolar responses. For example, the following three pairs of unipolar responses would all be associated with a bipolar response of −1: (1) quite clean and extremely dirty; (2) slightly clean and quite dirty; (3) not at all clean and slightly dirty. If only the first unipolar belief were used, some subjects would be classified as judging the concept to be slightly clean whereas on the bipolar measure they would be classified as judging the concept as slightly dirty. However, note that unipolar and bipolar scales often tend to be highly intercorrelated, and this problem may be of greater theoretical than practical significance.

By the variation of concepts, formats, and judgmental content, an infinite number of single response measures can be generated. It is amazing how many different measures have indeed appeared in the literature. What is more problematic, most of these measures have at one time or another been viewed as measures of "attitude." In the following sections we will try to show that most of the different measures can be classified as measures of attitudes, beliefs, or intentions.

Measures of attitude. Our definition of attitude requires a measurement procedure whereby a person assigns some concept to a position on a bipolar evaluative dimension. We noted earlier that many single-response measures ask the person to locate a concept along some bipolar dimension. The crucial question concerns the extent to which this dimension is evaluative in nature. Data concerning the evaluative nature of single bipolar scales are available (e.g., Osgood, Suci, & Tannenbaum, 1957). These data show that it cannot be assumed that such items will prove to measure affect under all circumstances. There is clear evidence that such scales may take on different meanings with respect to different concepts. For example, a scale ranging from *warm* to *cold* may have evaluative implications in reference to some concepts but not to others. If the concept rated is a person, a high correlation may be found between responses to the *warm–cold* scale and responses to a scale such as *good–bad*. That is, cold people are seen as being bad, and warm people as being good. On the other hand, in the judgment of an inanimate concept such as fire, the *warm–cold* scale may be used in a purely descriptive manner without any evaluative implications. Similar examples are scales such as *hard–soft, clean–dirty,* etc. A given scale may also be used differently by different subjects, even when the same concept is rated. Thus, in judging a person, one subject may use the *clean–dirty* scale in a descriptive manner, whereas another may use it evaluatively.

However, there are some scales that appear to be related to the evaluative dimension under most circumstances. Among these measures are a subject's self-rating of liking for the object (e.g., *like–dislike*), of his favorability with respect to the object (e.g., *favorable–unfavorable, approve–disapprove*), and his evaluation of the object on a single *good–bad* scale. Even these scales, however, may not always be perfect indicants of a person's attitude. Thus, in the absence of appropriate empirical evidence, single-response measures should not be taken as indicants of attitude, irrespective of the investigator's intuition regarding their affective nature. By the same token, unipolar scales, such as *not good–good* and other measures that involve only one pole of the evaluative dimension (e.g., rating of the concept "I like Joe Namath" on an *agree–disagree* scale), should not be viewed as measures of attitude. As noted earlier, unipolar scales may not yield the same results as bipolar scales, and thus they also require empirical evidence before they can be used as measures of attitude. Although many different scales may sometimes correlate with appropriate measures of attitude, they cannot be assumed to measure attitude under all conditions. The concept "attitude" should be employed only where there is clear evidence that the obtained measure places the concept on a bipolar affective dimension.

In sum, single-response measures often place a concept along some bipolar dimension. Whenever this bipolar dimension can be shown to be affective in nature, the judgment can be viewed as indicative of attitude. In all other instances, the judgment merely assigns the concept to a given content category or to a position on a unipolar or bipolar content dimension. According to our conceptual definitions, however, when the response scale is a measure of subjective probability—i.e., when it represents a probability dimension—the strength of a belief or of an intention is being assessed. Which of these two variables is being measured depends on the concept involved in the judgment.

Measures of belief. We have seen that a belief associates an object and an attribute. To measure beliefs about an object, it is therefore first necessary to identify the attribute that is linked to the object. One can do so by asking a person to place the object into one of several content categories. The label associated with the category selected defines the appropriate attribute. For example, a person might be asked to rate Humphrey Bogart on a seven-place scale ranging from *wise* to *foolish*. It is possible to assign numbers to these positions ranging from 1 (foolish) to 7 (wise) or from −3 to +3. Unfortunately, the interpretation of these numbers is not always clear.

Assume that the categories were defined such that −3 (or 1) meant it was *extremely probable* that Humphrey Bogart was *foolish,* −2 (or 2) meant *quite probable* that he was *foolish,* +1 (or 5) meant *slightly probable* that he was *wise,* +2 (or 6) meant *quite probable* that he was *wise,* etc. Here the endpoints of the scale define two attributes (*wise* and *foolish*), and the response indicates the *strength of the subject's belief* that Humphrey Bogart is associated with one of these two attributes.[2]

Alternatively, suppose that the categories were defined such that −3 (or 1) meant "extremely foolish," −2 (or 2) meant "quite foolish," −1 (or 3) meant "slightly foolish," etc., and that the respondent judged Humphrey Bogart to be "quite foolish" (i.e., rated him −2 on the seven-place *wise–foolish* scale). This judgment identifies the attribute the respondent associates with Humphrey Bogart but does not provide any indication of subjective probability or belief strength.[3]

---

2. Obviously, this is a *relative* rather than an *absolute* measure of belief strength. A judgment on this type of bipolar scale does not provide an unambiguous measure of either the strength of the subject's belief that Humphrey Bogart is wise or the strength of the belief that he is foolish. Rather, the bipolar judgment that Humphrey Bogart is *quite probably foolish* is best viewed as a function of the strength of the subject's two unipolar beliefs. For example, this bipolar response might reflect his beliefs that it is *extremely probable* that Bogart was *foolish* and *slightly probable* that he was *wise.*

3. Note again that a judgment on a bipolar content dimension such as *wise–foolish* does not permit an unambiguous identification of the attribute category. The rating on this scale may be viewed as a function of the ratings that would be made on the two unipolar scales it comprises, namely, *wise–not wise* and *foolish–not foolish.* For example, the bipolar judgment *quite foolish* may be a compromise response based on the unipolar judgments *extremely foolish* and *slightly wise.* Thus, in order to unambiguously identify the attribute associated with a given object, we would recommend use of a unipolar response measure.

Once the object-attribute link has been established, it is possible to measure *belief strength*. For example, the concept "Humphrey Bogart is quite foolish" could now be rated on a probabilistic scale such as *probable–improbable, true–false, yes–no, agree–disagree,* or *likely–unlikely.*

The discussion above should make it clear that, depending on the instructions provided to a subject (i.e., the labels attached to the various response categories), a response on a scale defined by the same endpoints (e.g., *wise–foolish, not clean–clean*) may provide a measure of *belief content* (i.e., only identify the *attribute* associated with the concept), or it may also provide a measure of *belief strength* (i.e., of the subjective probability that the object has, or is associated with, a given attribute).

Many single-response measures found in the literature ask a subject to locate an object along some attribute dimension or to place it into one of several discrete attribute categories. These judgments constitute measures of *belief content*. In a more general sense, they may also be viewed as measures of belief strength since they assign a value of 0 or 1 to the probability that the object has the attribute in question. A *quantitative* measure of belief strength, however, is obtained only when the subjective probability associated with a given object-attribute link is assessed.

In conclusion, any judgment linking an object to an attribute category or to a position on an attribute dimension constitutes a measure of belief content. To obtain a measure of belief strength, the subjective probability associated with the object-attribute link has to be assessed. In some instances a relationship may be found between belief content and belief strength. For example, the more intelligence a person is perceived to possess (e.g., if he is seen as *quite intelligent* rather than *slightly intelligent*) the higher should be the subjective probability that he is intelligent.[4]

Our discussion of single-response belief measures implies that the placement of a concept on any dimension constitutes a measure of belief content or belief strength. Thus, even when the concept is placed on a bipolar dimension, such as *good–bad* or *like–dislike*, these judgments, strictly speaking, must be treated as measures of belief. Our discussion of single-response attitude measures, however, indicated that these particular bipolar measures of belief, under most circumstances, are highly related to the evaluation of the concept. In a similar manner, some other measures of belief strength may also be related to evaluation. For example, when an object-attribute link such as "the church is good" is rated on a probability dimension, belief strength may be related to attitude toward the church. Strictly speaking, however, this measure must be interpreted as a measure of belief strength that happens to be related to evaluation.

Measures of intention. From our point of view, behavioral intentions constitute a special case of beliefs, where the object is the person and the attribute is a behav-

---

4. This relation is likely to be monotonic but not necessarily linear.

ior. As with beliefs, a distinction must be made between an intention's content and its strength. The content of an intention is determined by the behavior that is to be performed. Behaviors are sometimes quantified along some dimension, such as donating $10, $20, or $30 to the church or attending church never, sometimes, often, always. At other times, the subject is asked to indicate which of several behaviors he would perform in a given situation. The behavioral category selected defines the intention's content. The strength of the intention is assessed by asking the subject to rate a concept such as "I intend to donate $20 to the church" on a probability dimension.

Most frequently, subjects are presented with a single behavior and are asked to indicate whether or not they would perform it. When a single qualitative judgment is made (*yes* or *no, would* or *would not*), the response again defines the intention's content, and its strength is assessed by a measure of probability. Thus, if a person indicated that he would donate money to the church, the strength of his intention could be measured by a probabilistic rating of the concept "I would donate money to the church" on scales such as *probable–improbable* or *agree–disagree.*

Instead of obtaining qualitative judgments, many investigators have assessed intentions on seven-place or nine-place scales defined by the endpoints *would–would not, willing–unwilling, intend–not intend,* or *will try–will not try.* Although, strictly speaking, these scales may merely assess content of the intention, it appears that judgments on them are probabilistic in nature and can be used to measure strength of the intention to perform the behavior in question.

STANDARD ATTITUDE SCALING

We have seen that it may be possible to obtain a direct measure of attitude by asking the person to rate an object on a single bipolar scale, such as *good–bad* or *I like the object–I dislike the object.* In many instances, however, attitudes are assessed by computing an index over responses to a set of belief items or a set of intentional items. In Chapters 1 and 2 we discussed the relations between attitude on the one hand and beliefs and intentions on the other. Specifically, we argued that a person's attitude toward an object is related to his beliefs that the object possesses certain attributes and his evaluations of those attributes. Similarly, attitude is related to the set of a person's behavioral intentions with respect to an object, each intention weighted by its evaluative implications. For beliefs this relation was expressed symbolically as follows:

$$A = \Sigma b_i e_i.$$

When b is replaced by I (for intentions), the same formulation holds for the relation between attitude and intentions.

This formulation has interesting implications for attitude measurement. In order to measure a person's attitude toward an object, one can obtain measures of the strength of his beliefs (b) that the object has certain attributes and measures of his evaluation (e) of each attribute. The belief strength associated with a given object-attribute link is then multiplied by the person's evaluation of the attribute involved, and the resulting products are summed. This sum serves as an estimate of attitude toward the object under consideration. The same procedure would be followed for items of intention.

For example, if one is attempting to measure attitudes toward psychology, the first step involves identification of a set of attributes relevant for the subject population under investigation.[5] As a result of a pretest, the following statements might be constructed.

1. Psychology is not an exact science.
2. Psychology contributes to the solution of social problems.
3. Psychology is slightly interesting.
4. Psychology leads to control over man's mind.
5. Psychology is popular among students.
6. Psychology deals mainly with rats.
7. Psychology helps you to understand yourself.

Each of these statements associates the attitude object (psychology) with some other concept or attribute. In terms of our probabilistic definition of belief, an object and an attribute are perceived to be either associated to some degree or not to be associated at all; but there can be no negative association since probabilities cannot take on negative values.[6] Although some theorists (e.g., Heider, 1958; Osgood and Tannenbaum, 1955; Feather, 1971) have viewed object-concept links as either associative or dissociative, in the present conception all beliefs are of an associative nature. Thus, in the belief statements above, the attributes associated with psychology are as follows:

1. Not an exact science
2. Contributing to the solution of social problems
3. Slightly interesting
4. Leading to control over man's mind
5. Popular among students
6. Dealing mainly with rats
7. Helping you to understand yourself

Respondents are first asked to provide evaluations of these attributes (e). For example, each attribute could be rated on a seven-point *good–bad* scale or on a set of such evaluative scales. In keeping with the notion of a bipolar evaluative dimension, these ratings are scored from -3 (*bad*) to $+3$ (*good*). In order to obtain

---

5. Procedures for obtaining relevant attributes will be discussed in Chapter 6.

6. The same conclusion is derived from a stimulus-response definition of belief (Chapter 2).

measures of belief strength (b), each statement is rated on one or more probability scales. For example, a four-point scale ranging from *improbable* to *probable* could be used and could be scored from 0 to 3, allowing both beliefs and evaluation to carry equal weight in the prediction equation.[7] The $b \times e$ products can be computed for each item, and the attitude score is obtained by summing these products. (For a numerical example, see Table 2.1.)

The logic of this approach to attitude measurement underlies most standard attitude-scaling procedures. However, these standard procedures measure only the subject's belief strength (b) or the strength of his intentions. Attribute evaluations are not measured but are instead assumed to be the same for all subjects.

Beliefs as a Basis for Attitude Measurement

As in the procedure described above, standard attitude-scaling methods take an indirect approach by attempting to infer the person's location on the evaluative dimension on the basis of other responses. For example, Thurstone (1931) argued that "opinions" are verbal expressions of attitude and that they may therefore be used to measure attitude. Most attitude-scaling procedures arrive at an attitude score on the basis of a person's responses to a set of such opinion items. Specifically, these items are statements of belief or intention, and the person's response indicates his location along a probability dimension; i.e., it is a measure of the strength of his belief or intention. For example, the following items might be used to measure attitude toward Russia: (1) Russia is a totalitarian state, and (2) I would buy Russian products. The respondent usually is asked to indicate agreement or disagreement with each item. One major purpose of any scaling procedure is to select items that permit accurate inferences about the respondent's attitude.

To get a better understanding of how it is possible to use responses to items (i.e., the person's beliefs or intentions) to infer attitudes, it may be helpful to consider the balance model involving the focal person, p, another person, o, and an object, x, and the relations between these entities. Our present interest is in p's attitude toward o, and we will show how this attitude can be inferred from his beliefs about o.[8] Heider's (1958) theory assumed a tendency for triadic configura-

---

7. From a strict probability view, beliefs have to be measured on a scale that ranges from 0 to 1. However, our conceptual framework uses the notion of probability in a more general sense. For example, we do not assume that the beliefs about an object are mutually exclusive and exhaustive, and thus the probabilities are not expected to sum to 1. Although a probability scale ranging from 0 to 1 can be used, in the present example a four-point scale was used so that its range would be the same as that of the evaluative scale. Later in the chapter we shall see that use of a seven-point probability scale and bipolar scoring may be preferable in many practical applications.

8. A similar analysis would show how p's attitude toward o can be inferred from his intentions with respect to o. Here, only the $p\text{-}o$ dyad needs to be considered; the intention indicates a positive (U) or negative ($\overline{\text{U}}$) unit relationship between p and o. In a balanced dyad, $p\text{U}o$ implies a favorable attitude ($p\text{L}o$), and $p\overline{\text{U}}o$ implies an unfavorable attitude ($p\overline{\text{L}}o$).

tions to be balanced. Assuming that a balanced state exists, knowledge of any two relations provides information about the third. For example, in a balanced configuration, pLx and oUx imply pLo. Thus, p's attitude toward o can be inferred from knowledge concerning his belief about o (i.e., the perceived relation between o and x) and his evaluation of x. Although it is possible to assess both of these relations, the standard attitude-scaling methods assume a certain evaluation of x and then measure the o-x link. To make this assumption, it is necessary to eliminate items for which it is impossible to specify the evaluation of x. For example, consider the belief statement or item "The President is superstitious." If it is known that being superstitious is negatively evaluated by all respondents, it is possible to use this item in order to assess p's attitude toward the President. Specifically, p would be asked to indicate his agreement or disagreement with the item. If he agreed, a negative attitude toward the President would be inferred ($p\bar{L}x$ and oUx imply $p\bar{L}o$), but a positive attitude would be inferred if he disagreed with the item ($p\bar{L}x$ and $o\bar{U}x$ imply pLo). However, if different respondents had different evaluations of being superstitious, the item would have to be eliminated by the standard scaling procedures. This follows from the fact that when the liking relation between p and x is unknown, no inference about the p-o relation can be made, even when knowledge of the o-x relation is available. Thus one purpose of a scaling procedure is to identify items that will have the same attitudinal meaning for all respondents.

The assumption of a balanced configuration also implies that knowledge concerning p's attitude toward o and x specifies p's belief about o, that is, his agreement or disagreement with the item. For instance, in the example above it is assumed that if p has a positive attitude toward the President and a negative evaluation of being superstitious, he will disagree with the statement "The President is superstitious." Indeed, the standard attitude-scaling procedures are based on the assumption that since the item has been selected such that p's evaluation of x is given, his agreement or disagreement with the item must be a function of his attitude toward o, and thus p's agreement or disagreement with the item can be used as an indication of p's attitude. An attempt is made to eliminate items that fail to meet this expectation. For example, respondents will tend to agree with the statement "Kennedy is a Democrat" regardless of their attitudes toward Kennedy or their evaluation of being a Democrat. In this case responses are clearly determined by factors other than the person's attitude, and the item will be eliminated by standard scaling procedures.[9]

Since elimination of items on this basis presupposes knowledge about the person's attitude toward the object (and the assumption that his evaluation of x is fixed), the question arises as to how it is possible to have knowledge of the person's attitude if the item itself is being used to measure the attitude. One obvious solution to this problem is to use samples of respondents whose attitudes are as-

---

9. As we shall see below, items eliminated on this basis may still serve as valid indicants of attitude (Fishbein, 1967d).

sumed to be known. For example, in the construction of a scale for the measurement of attitudes toward "labor unions," company executives (with assumed negative attitudes) and union officials (with assumed positive attitudes) could be used. Given a statement that links o (labor unions) to some positively evaluated x (job security), union officials should agree with the statement (pLo and pLx imply oUx), company executives should disagree ($p\bar{L}o$ and pLx imply $o\bar{U}x$). This technique of "known group comparisons," however, is usually employed to "validate" the total attitude scale rather than to select items. We will see shortly that most scaling methods contain a procedure for obtaining a preliminary estimate of the person's attitude toward the object, and they use this estimate in their item analyses.

One additional point needs to be made before we turn to a consideration of attitude scaling. In the discussion above, attitude was inferred from a single belief. Clearly, such a procedure will usually not provide a satisfactory measure of attitude. According to classical test theory, a person's response to a given item is composed of a "true" score reflecting the underlying dimension (in this case, his attitude) and some measurement error. It is usually assumed that as the number of items increases, measurement errors cancel each other out, and the sum or average across all items is thus a more accurate reflection of the "true" attitude. Indeed, all standard attitude scales use multiple-item formats.

Bogardus's Measure of Social Distance

In an attempt to measure social distance or prejudice toward members of various national, religious, and racial groups, Bogardus (1925) developed an instrument composed of seven intentional items. For each stimulus group (e.g., Armenians, Germans, Jews) his respondents were asked to indicate whether or not they would willingly admit members of this group as follows:

1. To close kinship by marriage
2. To my club as personal chums
3. To my street as neighbors
4. To employment in my occupation in my country
5. To citizenship in my country
6. As visitors only to my country
7. Would exclude from my country

Bogardus found that responses to these items tended to follow a certain pattern. A person who would exclude members of a given stimulus group from his country would also exclude them from all other settings. Similarly, if he agreed with Item 6, he would disagree with Items 1 through 5. Conversely, a person who would admit members of a given group to close kinship by marriage also tended to agree with Items 2 through 5 and to disagree with Items 6 and 7. In other words, the order of these seven items "seems to constitute (further experimentation is needed) a gradation in social . . . distance" (Bogardus, 1925, p. 303). Thus, although no item analysis was conducted, Bogardus assumed that the seven items implied increasing degrees of social distance.

A social-distance score is obtained by simply counting the number of settings from which members of a given group would be excluded.[10] This score can range from 0 to 6. That is, a score of 6 is obtained when a respondent agrees only with Item 7 and thus excludes the given group from the other 6 settings; a score of 0 is obtained when he agrees with Items 1 through 5, disagrees with Items 6 and 7, and thus does not exclude members of the group from any setting. The higher the score, the greater the degree of social distance, i.e., the more negative the attitude. This score may be viewed as a function of the respondent's intentions (i.e., his agreements or disagreements) and of the evaluations of the behaviors in question. From our point of view, an attitude score could have been obtained by assigning values of 1 (agreement) or 0 (disagreement) to the probability of an intention, and values of +1 (Items 1 through 5), 0 (Item 6), or −1 (Item 7) to the evaluation associated with each intention. Consistent with an expectancy-value model, the products of these values are summed to obtain a measure of attitude. The higher the score, the *less* social distance, or the *more* favorable the attitude. The Bogardus social distance measure can be obtained by subtracting 5 from this attitude score.

Note that assigning an evaluation of +1 or −1 to each item ignores the assumption that the different items express different *degrees* of social distance. This would not constitute a problem if all items followed the general cumulative pattern described above. If all responses followed the pattern, a score of 3 could be obtained only when a subject agreed with Items 4 and 5 and disagreed with all others. In comparison, consider a person who agrees with Items 2 and 3 and disagrees with all others. He, too, would have a score of 3. However, one may argue that this person exhibits less social distance since he would be willing to admit members of the group in question to settings that are assumed to imply less social distance. If the assumed differential evaluations associated with each item are to be neglected in computing the attitude score, it is necessary to demonstrate that responses to the set of items employed do indeed fall into a cumulative pattern. This is a major objective of the Guttman scaling procedure.

Guttman's Scalogram Analysis

In order to clarify the properties or characteristics of a cumulative scale, consider an example from the area of ability testing. A test designed to measure some ability (e.g., mathematical reasoning) is composed of a number of items varying in difficulty level; that is, the items differ in terms of the number of respondents who solve the problem posed in the item. Such a set of items forms a perfect cumula-

---

10. In practice, this can be done by reversing the response to Item 7 (i.e., treat agreements as disagreements and vice versa), ignoring the response to Item 6, and counting the number of disagree responses.

tive scale (i.e., a perfect Guttman scale) under the following conditions: A person solves all items up to a certain difficulty level and no items beyond that level. Thus, the more items a person passes, the higher his level of ability, and the most difficult item passed corresponds to his ability level. It follows that the number of items passed can be taken as an index of his ability. Response patterns of a perfect cumulative ability scale are shown in Table 3.1 (cf. Guttman, 1944).

Table 3.1 Response Patterns in a Perfect Cumulative Scale

Response patterns		Item difficulty						Ability score
	Low	1	2	3	4	5	High	
A		0	0	0	0	0		0
B		1	0	0	0	0		1
C		1	1	0	0	0		2
D		1	1	1	0	0		3
E		1	1	1	1	0		4
F		1	1	1	1	1		5

Note: A zero indicates failure, a one success with respect to a given item.

As Table 3.1 shows, such a cumulative scale has two interesting properties. First, knowledge of a person's ability score allows one to reproduce his performance on each item of the scale. A person with a score of 3 must have response pattern D, indicating that he passed the three easiest items and failed the two most difficult items. Second, of two respondents, A and B, if A has a higher score than B, then A has passed all items that B has passed as well as at least one additional (more difficult) item.

These properties imply that items on a perfect cumulative scale are ordered along a single dimension—in our example, along an ability dimension. Note that items are merely *ordered* in terms of their difficulty levels, and no assumptions are made about their exact locations on the dimension. Thus only an ordinal and not an interval scale is implied; there is no assumption that the distances between items are of equal magnitude. In the same vein, a person's ability score is also ordinal in nature.

As pointed out above, the properties of a cumulative scale provide information about the relationship between ability scores and performance on items on the scale. This relationship is expressed graphically in Fig. 3.1. We can see that the relationship between the person's location on the ability dimension and the probability that he will pass a given item can be described as a step function. This relationship is usually referred to as the item *operating characteristic* or *traceline*

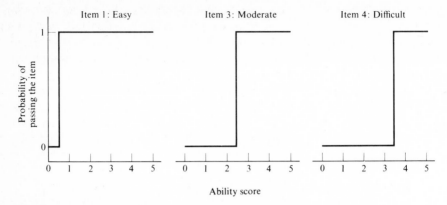

Fig. 3.1 Tracelines of Guttman items with varying difficulty levels.

(B. F. Green, 1954). Figure 3.1 shows that both persons and items can be located on the ability dimension. A basic property of a perfect Guttman scale is that when the person's location on the dimension is lower than that of a given item, the probability that he will pass the item is 0; conversely, when his location on the dimension is as high as or higher than that of the item, the probability that he will pass the item is 1.

Note that the relation between total score and the responses to any given item is not linear; rather, it is step-shaped. High correlations between total score and single-item responses should not be expected since a correlation coefficient is an index of the degree of *linear* relationship.

Thus far we have discussed cumulative scales designed to assess an ability dimension. The same considerations apply to items designed to measure an evaluative dimension, i.e., attitude. The investigator begins by obtaining a number of belief or intentional items that are related to the attitude object under consideration. Bogardus's measure of social distance might comprise such a set of items. As pointed out earlier, a given set of items may not form a perfect cumulative scale; the Guttman scaling procedure is designed to assess the degree to which a given set of items form a cumulative scale.

As a first step, responses are obtained from a sample of subjects, and the items are ordered in terms of their frequencies of endorsement. This step is analogous to ordering items on an ability test in terms of their difficulty levels. Although it appears reasonable to assume that more difficult items (i.e., items with low probabilities of passing) require greater ability, it is not clear what is implied by probabilities of endorsement of belief or intentional items. The usual assumption is that such probabilities reflect the degree of favorableness (or unfavorableness) that is implied by the different items. Therefore the scale is assumed to measure an evaluative dimension, i.e., attitude toward the object.[11]

11. However, probabilities of endorsement conceivably could reflect an evaluative dimension with respect to an object other than the one considered by the investigator,

Once the items have been ordered, the obtained response patterns of each subject can be examined. Usually the subjects are also ordered in terms of their total scores. Thus, if the set of items formed a perfect Guttman scale, the pattern of responses would be triangular in form and would correspond to the pattern depicted in Table 3.1.[12] However, perfect Guttman scales are seldom obtained, and the working assumption is that deviations from the expected response patterns are due to measurement error. Clearly, however, such deviations may also indicate that the items under consideration are not unidimensional, i.e., that more than one dimension is necessary to account for the observed responses. The question then revolves around the amount of deviation that can be tolerated under the assumption of unidimensionality.

To this end, the "errors" in the response patterns are counted. That is, for each respondent whose pattern deviates from the expected, the minimum number of changes necessary to produce a scale pattern is considered the number of errors. The total number of errors in the sample of respondents is taken as an indication of deviation from unidimensionality. More precisely, Guttman suggested the coefficient of reproducibility as an index of the degree to which an empirical scale approaches a perfect Guttman scale. This coefficient, R, is presented in Eq. 3.1,

$$R = 1 - \frac{\text{Number of errors}}{\text{Total number of responses}}, \tag{3.1}$$

where the total number of responses is equal to the number of subjects multiplied by the number of items to which they respond. Guttman (1944) suggested that when $R \geq .85$, the scale may be considered acceptable.

This criterion, however, does not take into account the degree to which responses can be reproduced simply on the basis of relative frequencies of item endorsement. As A. L. Edwards (1957) pointed out, "the reproducibility of any single statement can never be less than the frequency present in the modal category" (p. 191). For example, if 70 percent of the respondents disagreed with a given item, one could predict disagreement for every respondent and be right 70 percent of the time. It is possible to compute a coefficient of minimal marginal reproducibility, MMR, as in Eq. 3.2:

$$MMR = \frac{\text{Number of responses in modal categories}}{\text{Total number of responses}}. \tag{3.2}$$

---

or they may reflect some other dimension altogether. For example, instead of reflecting degree of favorableness toward war, probabilities of endorsement may reflect favorableness toward the military-industrial complex. Alternatively, they may reflect social constraints, social desirability, or degrees of implied aggressiveness. Thus, one must take care in interpreting a Guttman scale as a measure of attitude toward some object.

12. The scoring for negative items will usually be reversed prior to the analysis.

The coefficient of reproducibility must be compared with this index of minimal marginal reproducibility; only when R greatly exceeds MMR (and R ⩾ .85) is there an advantage in using the Guttman scale.

When the coefficient of reproducibility is relatively low, one should conclude that the items in question do not form a unidimensional scale.[13] Frequently investigators attempt to raise the coefficient of reproducibility by eliminating items that contribute a large number of errors. Since this practice amounts to a redefinition of the attitude domain under investigation, it is not clear that the remaining set of items will measure the attitude originally intended by the investigator.

Like Bogardus's social-distance measure, the Guttman scale can be viewed as arriving at an attitude score through a consideration of beliefs or intentions and their associated evaluations. Unlike the scaling procedures to be discussed below, Guttman scaling is primarily concerned with testing the assumption that a set of items forms a unidimensional cumulative scale, rather than with selecting appropriate items from a larger pool. To some degree, selection is involved when items are eliminated to increase the coefficient of reproducibility. This procedure eliminates items that cannot be ordered along the evaluative dimension under consideration. That is, they are eliminated because they may have ambiguous attitudinal meaning or because they may be responded to on the basis of one or more irrelevant underlying dimensions.

The remaining standard attitude-scaling procedures also try to locate respondents on an evaluative or affective dimension, but unlike the Guttman scale, they do not result in a cumulative set of items. In Thurstone as in Guttman scaling, an attempt is made to order items along the evaluative dimension. Thurstone scaling, however, goes beyond ordinal measurement and attempts to locate the position of items on an equal-interval scale.

Thurstone's Equal-Appearing Interval Scale

The first step in Thurstone scaling involves the collection of a large pool of belief or intentional items related to some attitude object. As mentioned earlier, Thurstone (1931) assumed that responses to such items (i.e., the person's beliefs or intentions) are expressions of the person's attitude. More specifically, he made the assumption that different items may express different degrees of favorableness or unfavorableness toward the attitude object. A major purpose of Thurstone scaling is to specify the location of each item on the evaluative dimension by assigning a scale value to the item. On the basis of his work in psychophysical scaling, Thurstone first applied the method of paired comparisons to achieve this aim. Since this procedure becomes unwieldy as the number of items increases,[14] he developed the method of equal-appearing intervals as an approximation to the more sophisti-

---

13. It is usually also assumed that the universe from which the items are sampled is not unidimensional.

14. The number of judgments required for n items is equal to $n(n-1)/2$.

cated paired-comparisons technique. Although these two methods tended to yield similar scale values, he noticed some lack of correspondence for items with extreme scale values. The method of successive intervals was developed to adjust for this effect. By far the most popular and most widely used Thurstone scaling procedure is the method of equal-appearing intervals, and this method will be discussed in the present chapter. Interested readers are referred to A. L. Edwards (1957) for detailed discussion of the other techniques.

The pool of items collected by the investigator is given to a sample of judges representative of the population of subjects whose attitudes are to be assessed. Instead of being asked to agree or disagree with these items, the judges are required to indicate the amount of favorableness or unfavorableness toward the attitude object implied by agreement with a given item. More specifically, the judges sort each item into one of eleven categories that they are to consider equal intervals along the evaluative dimension, ranging from "unfavorable" through "neutral" to "favorable" toward the attitude object. For example, if a judge felt that the belief "The President is superstitious" indicated an extremely favorable attitude toward the President, he should place this item in the eleventh category; if he felt that the belief indicated an extremely unfavorable attitude, he should place it in the first category; and if he felt that it indicated neither a favorable nor an unfavorable attitude, he should place it in the neutral category. The remaining categories express equally spaced degrees of intermediate favorableness or unfavorableness.

The basis for item placement by judges can again be viewed in terms of a balanced triangle. The belief or intentional statement determines a given link between o and x. The statement "The President is superstitious" exemplifies an oUx link, and the statement "The President opposes medicare" exemplifies an $o\overline{U}x$ link. The judge's perception of most people's (p's) evaluation of x determines the p-x link, thereby allowing the judge to make a direct inference about what p's attitude toward o would be if p agreed with the oUx link. For example, if a judge perceived that most people evaluate medicare favorably, he would assume that agreement with the statement "The President opposes medicare" implied a negative attitude toward the President (pLx and $o\overline{U}x$ imply $p\overline{L}x$). The more positive or negative the perceived evaluation of x, the more favorable or unfavorable is the implied attitude.

We can see that an item will express an unambiguous degree of favorableness only when judges agree as to how most people evaluate x. Thurstone proposed the *criterion of ambiguity* to eliminate items on which judges disagree. By this criterion, an item is eliminated if judges place the item into widely discrepant categories. More specifically, the interquartile range (i.e., the range that includes the middle 50 percent of categories into which the item was placed) or the standard deviation of the item placements is computed. These indices measure the degree of dispersion (i.e., disagreement among judges) in the placement of a given item. A large interquartile range or standard deviation leads to rejection of the item. The median or the mean is computed for each remaining item and this score is taken as the scale value of the item. A set of approximately 20 items representing more or less equally spaced scale values ranging along the entire continuum are then identified.

Most investigators employ this set of items as their attitude scale and give it to a new sample of subjects whose attitude scores are to be measured. In contrast to the instructions given to the judges, the instruction to these subjects is to check all items with which they agree. Each subject's attitude score is obtained by computing the median or mean scale value of all items endorsed. Thus a subject who endorsed three items with scale values of 2.6, 3.0, and 3.4, respectively, would have an attitude score of 3.0.

According to the Thurstone scaling procedure, however, identification of a set of equally spaced and nonambiguous items is not sufficient as a basis for constructing an adequate attitude scale. Thurstone argued that a second criterion, the *criterion of irrelevance,* must also be met by each item on the scale. As mentioned earlier, scaling procedures should eliminate not only items that are ambiguous but also items that elicit responses which are determined by factors other than the attitude that is being assessed, i.e., by irrelevant factors. The criterion of irrelevance is designed to achieve the latter purpose in Thurstone scaling. The basic assumption underlying the criterion of irrelevance is that an item with a given scale value is most likely to be endorsed by respondents whose attitudes are located at the same position on the attitude dimension. The greater the discrepancy between the person's location on the evaluative dimension (i.e., his attitude score) and the item's location on that dimension (i.e., the item's scale value), the lower the probability that the person will agree with the item. This relationship between attitude score and probability of endorsement for an item with a given scale value is shown in Fig. 3.2.

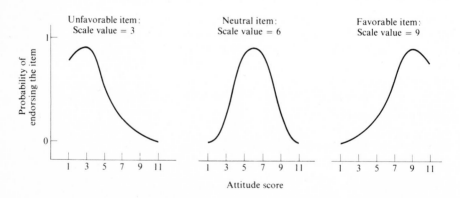

Fig. 3.2 Tracelines of Thurstone items with different scale values.

Note that the relation between the person's location on the evaluative dimension and the probability that he will endorse a given item, i.e., the item operating characteristic or traceline, takes the form of an inverted U. That is, the relation is nonmonotonic with a single maximum. This kind of traceline indicates first that the items constituting a Thurstone scale are not cumulative. Thus, knowledge of a person's attitude score does not provide information about his responses to all items on the scale. For example, a person with an attitude score of 8 may endorse some items that have higher scale values, and he will usually not have endorsed all items with lower scale values. In contrast to a Guttman scale, the more the item's scale value falls below 8, the less likely he is to endorse it.

Further, even more so than for a Guttman scale, a high correlation between attitude scores and endorsement of items cannot be expected for a Thurstone scale since the correlation coefficient measures linear rather than curvilinear, non-monotonic relations.

Inspection of Fig. 3.2 suggests that the criterion of irrelevance may be tested by plotting the subjects' responses to a given item against their attitudes. This, however, would require knowledge of the attitudes. A preliminary estimate can be obtained on the basis of the initially selected set of items, as described earlier. Thurstone and Chave (1929) developed an alternative procedure which does not require knowledge of attitudes but instead is based on the item's scale value and its probability of endorsement. Basically, the assumption is that items with similar scale values will exhibit similar patterns of endorsement.[15] Items failing to meet the criterion of irrelevance as assessed by either procedure are eliminated from the scale. The remaining items have passed both the criterion of ambiguity and the criterion of irrelevance, and they constitute the Thurstone scale. This set of items can now be used to assess attitudes in the manner described above. That is, an investigator administers the scale to a sample of subjects and computes their attitude scores by obtaining the median or mean scale value of all items endorsed.

One major criticism of the equal-appearing interval procedure has focused on Thurstone's assumption that the judges' own attitudes do not influence their judgments and thus have no influence on item scale values. Empirical evidence suggests that this assumption appears to be justified under most conditions. Later in this chapter, the issue will be considered in greater detail in the context of the "own categories" procedure. Partly in response to this criticism and partly to avoid the time and effort spent in obtaining item scale values, Likert (1932) suggested an alternative scaling procedure.

Likert's Method of Summated Ratings

Collecting a large pool of items is also the first step in constructing a Likert scale. As with Guttman and Thurstone scales, these items may be statements of either beliefs or intentions. For each item, the investigator first decides whether it indicates a favorable or unfavorable attitude toward the object in question. If the item is ambiguous or appears to indicate a neutral attitude, it is immediately

---

15. Interested readers are referred to Thurstone and Chave's (1929) discussion of the criterion of irrelevance.

eliminated. The investigator thus fulfills the function of a judge in Thurstone scaling, except that his task is simplified because items are merely placed into three categories: favorable, unfavorable, reject. The remaining items are administered directly to a sample of subjects representative of the target population. Typically, subjects are asked to respond to each item in terms of a five-point scale defined by the labels *agree strongly, agree, undecided, disagree,* and *disagree strongly.*

A preliminary estimate of each respondent's attitude is obtained as follows: First, responses to each item are scored from 1 to 5. Strong agreements with favorable items are given a score of 5, and strong disagreements with these items are given a score of 1. Scoring is reversed for unfavorable items, such that disagreement with an unfavorable item results in a high score. The person's preliminary attitude score is obtained by summing across all his item scores. For a set of 100 items, these attitude scores could range from 100 to 500; the higher the score, the more favorable the attitude.

Since constructing a Likert scale requires the elimination of items that do not reflect the attitude under consideration, an item analysis is performed. To be retained, an item must meet Likert's *criterion of internal consistency.* According to this criterion, the more favorable a person's attitude, the more likely he should be to endorse favorable items and the less likely he should be to endorse unfavorable items. This relationship between attitude score and probability of item endorsement is illustrated in Fig. 3.3.

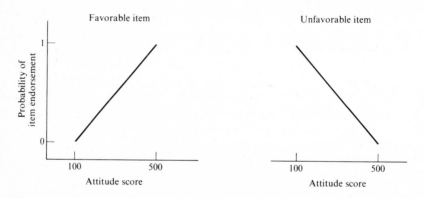

Fig. 3.3 Tracelines of favorable and unfavorable Likert items.

Note that in Likert scaling the item operating characteristic or traceline is assumed to be linear. Again, this traceline indicates that items on a Likert scale will not be cumulative. Here, however, a correlation between attitude score and item endorsement is not only expected but actually constitutes the criterion for inclusion of an item in the scale.

It follows that a given item meets the criterion of internal consistency if the item score correlates significantly with the attitude score. In practice, the preliminary attitude score is used and is correlated with the item score.[16] Prior to the introduction of computers, a simpler procedure was employed whereby the preliminary attitude score was used to select the top and bottom 25 percent of the sample, i.e., subjects assumed to have the most and least favorable attitudes, respectively. Mean item scores are computed within each group. An item meets the criterion of internal consistency if it discriminates between the two extreme groups, i.e., if the favorable group has a significantly higher mean score on the item than the unfavorable group.[17]

The twenty or so items with the highest correlations (or the most discriminating items) constitute the Likert scale. This scale can now be given to a new sample of subjects whose attitude scores are computed in the manner described earlier with reference to the preliminary attitude score. The Likert scaling procedure, then, ensures that ambiguous items as well as items that elicit responses based on factors other than the attitude under consideration are eliminated.

All scaling procedures discussed thus far place individuals along a single dimension of affect by considering their responses to a set of items assumed to reflect this underlying dimension. The derived attitude score represents the person's location on the evaluative dimension. Throughout our discussion, we have emphasized that items reflecting the respondent's location on other dimensions are eliminated by the scaling procedures. The fourth standard scaling procedure to be discussed, the semantic differential technique, permits the identification of items reflecting not only the evaluative dimension but also other dimensions.

Osgood's Semantic Differential Technique

Osgood's measurement technique was developed not for purposes of assessing attitudes but rather as an instrument for the measurement of meaning. The reader will recall that in Osgood's behavior theory the implicit anticipatory response to a stimulus object is viewed as the object's meaning. Since this implicit response cannot be directly observed, overt responses to the object have to be considered. In his search for overt responses that are "maximally dependent upon and sensitive to meaningful states, and minimally dependent upon other variables" (Osgood, Suci, and Tannenbaum, 1957, p. 11), Osgood (1952) settled on verbal responses to the object or concept. He argued that since the basic function of ordinary language was assumed to be the communication of meaning, ordinary language could be used to differentiate between concepts and measure their meaning. The semantic differential technique is based on this premise.

Osgood, Suci, and Tannenbaum argued that as a first step it was necessary to devise a "sample of alternative verbal responses which can be standardized across

---

16. A negative correlation indicates that the investigator's initial decision concerning the item's favorableness was in error, and the item score is reversed.

17. Alternatively, groups assumed to have positive or negative attitudes can be compared in terms of their responses to each item. This is the "known group comparison" technique mentioned earlier.

subjects . . . and [which would] be representative of the major ways in which meanings vary" (p. 19). Ascertaining an object's meaning was viewed as similar to playing the game of "Twenty Questions" with the respondent. Thus, to identify the meaning of a given object, the respondents might be asked questions such as: "Is it hard or soft?" "Is it pleasant or unpleasant?" "Is it fast or slow?" etc. "Just as in 'Twenty Questions' the selection of successive alternatives gradually eliminates uncertainty as to the object being thought about, so selection among successive pairs of common verbal opposites should gradually isolate the 'meaning' of the stimulus" (Osgood, Suci, and Tannenbaum, 1957, pp. 19–20). To increase the measuring instrument's sensitivity, a seven-point scale is inserted between the bipolar adjective pairs so that the subject can indicate both the direction and intensity of each judgment.

A large number of such bipolar adjective scales were constructed in an attempt to obtain a representative sample of the possible dimensions along which concepts can be judged. The semantic differential technique involves providing the respondent with one or more concepts to differentiate and a set of bipolar adjectives against which to do so. The respondent's task is to rate each concept on each scale. In this manner, a profile of ratings is obtained for each concept; it is assumed that two concepts are similar in meaning to the extent to which their profiles are similar. Hypothetical profiles for three concepts are illustrated in Fig. 3.4. The degree to which two profiles are similar, i.e., the degree to which two

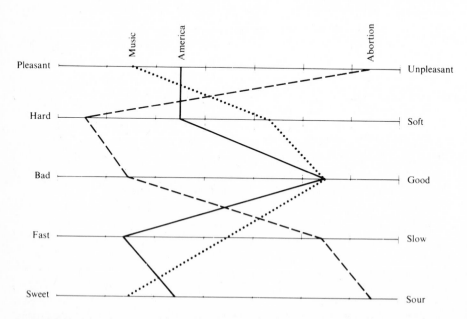

Fig. 3.4 Hypothetical profiles for three concepts rated on five bipolar adjective scales.

concepts have similar meanings, is measured by the generalized distance formula presented in Eq. 3.3,

$$D = \sum_{i=1}^{n} d_i^2, \qquad (3.3)$$

where D is the distance between two concepts (i.e., their dissimilarity) and d_i is the difference in ratings of the two concepts on the ith bipolar adjective scale. The squared differences are summed across the n scales on which the two concepts are rated.

Although the generalized distance formula provides an index of the degree to which two concepts are similar in meaning, it does not identify the meaning of any given concept. For such an identification to be made, the concept's position on each of the bipolar scales would have to be described. Not only is this highly impractical when the concept is rated on a large number of bipolar scales, but it should be possible to describe a concept's meaning in terms of a smaller number of basic dimensions since different scales may be reflecting the same aspect of meaning. Indeed, the major aim in developing the semantic differential was to identify the major dimensions of meaning. To do this, Osgood, Suci, and Tannenbaum applied the statistical procedure known as factor analysis.

The general idea behind factor analysis can be illustrated by considering responses to two bipolar adjective scales. When these responses are highly correlated, the scales may be said to be alternative measures of the same variable or dimension. To generalize this principle to a large set of scales: If all scales are highly intercorrelated, they are all considered to assess the same underlying dimension or factor. In the context of the semantic differential, they are all considered to measure the same basic aspect of meaning. The purpose of factor analysis is to identify the number of dimensions that are being assessed by a large set of scales. More precisely, it specifies the degree to which each scale is a measure of each of the underlying dimensions. The basic data matrix on which a factor analysis is usually performed consists of the set of correlations between all possible pairs of scales.[18] The resulting factor matrix can be conceptualized as representing the correlations between the scales and the underlying factors or dimensions. Bipolar adjective scales which are themselves highly intercorrelated should load on (i.e., correlate with) the same factor or factors. Factor analysis is one convenient method for summarizing the interrelationship among a large number of scales since, ideally, the number of factors should be considerably less than the number of scales (N. Wiggins, 1973).

In a large number of studies involving different scales and different concepts, Osgood and his associates have repeatedly found three basic factors or dimensions underlying semantic differential ratings. Based on inspection of the scales that had high loadings on (i.e., high correlations with) these factors, the three major di-

---

18. Note that factor analysis is a general procedure that can be applied to any intercorrelation matrix.

mensions were interpreted as *evaluation, potency,* and *activity.* For purposes of illustration, Table 3.2 shows some of the results of a factor analysis presented by Osgood, Suci, and Tannenbaum (1957, p. 39). For this analysis, 100 subjects rated 20 concepts on 50 bipolar adjective scales. Correlations were computed between all possible pairs of scales. Since each subject responded to each scale 20 times (once for each concept), each correlation was based on 2000 pairs of observations. The concepts were selected from different domains and included, for example, "lady," "symphony," "lake," and "America." Table 3.2 presents the obtained loadings of nine selected scales on the three major factors. As we can see, the evaluative factor is characterized by scales such as *good–bad, clean–dirty,* and *beautiful–ugly;* the potency factor is characterized by scales such as *large–small, strong–weak,* and *thick–thin;* and some of the scales loading on the activity factor are *fast–slow, active–passive,* and *hot–cold.*

Table 3.2 Selected Factor Loadings of Scales on the Three Major Dimensions (from Osgood, Suci, and Tannenbaum, 1957, p. 37)

Scale	Factor		
	Evaluation	Potency	Activity
good–bad	.88	.05	.09
clean–dirty	.82	−.05	.03
beautiful–ugly	.86	.09	.01
large–small	.06	.62	.34
strong–weak	.19	.62	.20
thick–thin	−.06	.44	−.06
fast–slow	.01	.00	.70
active–passive	.14	.04	.59
hot–cold	−.04	−.06	.46

Osgood argued that a person's attitude toward an object is equivalent to the object's evaluative meaning for the person. Consistent with the view expressed in this book, Osgood's definition of attitude was in terms of a bipolar evaluative dimension. He thus concluded that one could measure a person's attitude toward any object by having him rate that object on a set of scales known to have high loadings on the evaluative factor. Once a set of evaluative scales has been identified, it can be used to measure attitudes toward a large number of concepts. This apparent generality of the semantic differential has resulted in its being used in a variety of contexts, and indeed, it is probably today's most widely used attitude-measuring instrument. Typically, an investigator will select five to ten adjective scales that were found to have high loadings on the evaluative factor by Osgood, Suci, and Tannenbaum or by some other investigator. Sometimes activity and potency scales are also employed. Subjects are then asked to rate one or more concepts (i.e., attitude objects) on each scale. A measure of attitude toward each object is obtained in the following manner: Responses to each evaluative scale are scored from $+3$ to -3, with positive values assigned to the positive side of the scale. The scores are summed across all evaluative scales, and this value or the average score is taken as an index of attitude. Similarly, activity scores and potency scores can be calculated.

It is seldom realized, unfortunately, that this practice may not meet some of the requirements of the semantic differential technique. Investigators have found that the same bipolar adjective scale may load on different factors when it is used to measure different concepts (cf. Osgood, Suci, and Tannenbaum, 1957). For example, in studies of person perception, the *hard–soft* scale has often been found to correlate with the evaluative dimension. The same scale may not correlate highly with the evaluative dimension when the concept "war" is rated; instead, it will tend to load on the potency factor. And although the *hard–soft* scale tends to correlate with the evaluative dimension for person concepts, *soft* will be the positive end of the scale for feminine concepts (e.g., "mother") but the negative end for masculine concepts (e.g., "father"). Further, different factor structures tend to emerge when the analysis is based on the ratings of a single concept than when it is based on ratings of that concept and other concepts on the same set of scales. In the present example, the *hard–soft* scale correlates with the evaluative dimension when the ratings of either "father" or "mother" are analyzed. However, in an analysis based on the ratings of both concepts, the *hard–soft* scale would not correlate with the evaluative dimension, since that correlation takes on different signs for the concepts "mother" and "father." When both concepts are considered, therefore, the correlation of the *hard–soft* scale with the evaluative dimension will be close to 0. Thus, in this example, the potency dimension (as represented by the *hard–soft* scale) merges with the evaluative dimension when a single concept is considered, but the two dimensions emerge as separate factors when both concepts are included in the analysis.

This tendency for scales to load on different factors when different concepts are rated has been called "concept-scale interaction" (Osgood, Suci, and Tannenbaum, 1957). It follows from these considerations that scales found to load on a given factor in a multiconcept analysis cannot be assumed to load on the same factor for any given concept, even when that concept is part of the original set. These phenomena, therefore, preclude the notion of a generalized attitude-measuring instrument. Indeed, Osgood and his associates were unable to find sets of scales that would consistently load on a given factor across a wide variety of concepts. Thus, if the semantic differential is to be used as a measure of attitude, it (like all other standardized instruments) must be submitted to an item analysis. Since most attitude measurement is concerned with assessing attitudes toward a single concept, it would be desirable to identify a set of adjective scales that best reflect the evaluative dimension for that concept.

Use of factor analysis in the development of the semantic differential assumes a linear (or monotonic) traceline; that is to say, responses to evaluative scales correlate with the subject's attitude score, i.e., with the evaluative dimension. Thus the item operating characteristic of items on the semantic differential is the same as that for items on a Likert scale (see Fig. 3.3). This suggests that Likert's criterion of internal consistency could be used to analyze items on a semantic differential. To do so, one would consider only scales that appear to be evaluative in nature. If the investigator could not decide which side of the bipolar scale was positive and which negative, the scale would be immediately eliminated. Separate scale-total score correlations would be computed, and only scales with high correlations would be retained.

More in line with Osgood's approach, subjects would rate the concept in question on a heterogeneous set of scales, and their ratings would be submitted to a factor analysis. Scales with high loadings on the evaluative factor would be retained. This set of items constitutes a semantic differential scale for the measurement of attitude toward the concept in question.

Bipolar adjective scales, such as those constituting the semantic differential, have previously been described as measures of either belief content or belief strength. It is important to note that Osgood's original instructions for using the semantic differential defined the bipolar scales as measures of belief *strength*. More specifically, Osgood asked subjects to indicate the degree to which "the concept is . . . *related* to one or the other end of the scale" (Osgood, Suci, and Tannenbaum, 1957, p. 83; italics added). That is, Osgood asked subjects to indicate the strength of the relationship between the concept and one of the two bipolar adjectives. Given these instructions, the subject indicates by his response the likelihood that the concept is associated with one or the other attribute in the pair. That is, his response can be viewed as a probability judgment, and it constitutes a measure of belief *strength*.[19] Also recall, however, that the *good–bad* scale was viewed as a possible direct measure of attitude. We can now see that when Osgood's original instructions are given to subjects, a *good–bad* scale, like any other bipolar adjective scale, constitutes a measure of belief strength. Consider for example ratings of "war" on a *safe–dangerous* and on the *good–bad* scale. Each scale links the object "war" to an adjective pair. The subject's response indicates the degree to which he perceives the object to be associated with one or the other attribute in the pair, and his response can be viewed as a probability judgment. Unlike most other bipolar adjective scales, however, the *good–bad* scale is found to have a consistently high loading on the evaluative factor, irrespective of the concept under consideration. This particular belief, therefore, almost always tends to be

_____

19. Note again that when bipolar scales are used, *relative* rather than *absolute* belief strength is being measured. That is, one is assessing the probability that the concept is attribute A (e.g., fair) relative to attribute B (unfair) rather than the probability that the concept is, or is related to, attribute A independent of any other attribute. As we have seen, however, knowledge of the two absolute judgments should permit prediction of the relative judgment.

highly correlated with attitude, and thus, as suggested earlier in this chapter, it may be used as a direct measure of attitude.[20]

A Comparative Analysis of Standard Scaling Procedures

In this chapter we have discussed four standard attitude-scaling procedures, all of which arrive at single attitude scores based on responses to statements of beliefs or intentions. Of course, these scaling methods can also be based on behavioral observations, where performance or nonperformance of the behavior is treated as equivalent to agreement or disagreement with a belief or intentional statement. This notion plays an important role in Chapter 8, which deals with the relation between attitude and behavior.

Irrespective of scaling technique or item content, the resultant attitude score represents an individual's location on a bipolar evaluative dimension vis-à-vis a given object. Beyond this fundamental similarity, several important differences between the standard scaling procedures must be recognized. Table 3.3 indicates

Table 3.3 A Comparison of the Four Standard Attitude Scales

	Guttman	Thurstone	Likert	Semantic Differential
Properties of Items				
Quantification	ordinal	"interval"	qualitative	—
Neutral items retained	yes	yes	no	no
Tracelines	monotonic (step-shaped)	nonmonotonic (inverted U)	monotonic (linear)	monotonic (linear)
Cumulative scale	yes	no	no	no
Item selection	response-inferred	response-inferred and judgmental	response-inferred	response-inferred
Properties of Attitude Scores				
Values of b	$0, \pm 1$	$0, 1$	-2 to $+2$	0 to 3
Values of e	± 1	-5 to $+5$	$-1, +1$	$-1, +1$
Values of $b \times e$	$0, 1$	-5 to $+5$	-2 to $+2$	-3 to $+3$
Disbeliefs	yes	no	yes	no
Computational formulas	$\Sigma\, b_i e_i$	$\Sigma\, b_i e_i / \Sigma\, b_i$	$\Sigma\, b_i e_i$	$\Sigma\, b_i e_i$ or $\Sigma\, b_i e_i / n$
Quantification	ordinal	"interval"	ordinal	"interval"

20. As noted previously, the same may be true for certain other single bipolar scales, such as *I like–dislike* or *favorable–unfavorable*.

some of the differences between scales in terms of item characteristics and properties of attitude scores.

Properties of items. All scaling procedures locate individuals along an evaluative dimension (by assigning attitude scores), but Guttman and Thurstone scales also locate each item on the same evaluative dimension. By using judges, the Thurstone procedure assigns a scale value to each item, which represents the item's location on the evaluative dimension. It is assumed that these judgments are made on an equal-interval scale, and thus item scale values as well as attitude scores are assumed to have equal-interval properties. In contrast, Guttman scaling results in an ordering of items along the evaluative dimension without the assumption of equal intervals. Consequently, Guttman scores represent an ordinal scale.

Items on a Likert scale do not reflect different *degrees* of favorableness; instead, they are classified as either positive or negative. This categorical assignment of items also results in attitude scores with ordinal properties. Finally, since semantic differential items are bipolar, they can be assigned to neither a positive nor a negative category and are merely assumed to correlate with the evaluative dimension. The seven places on the bipolar scales are assumed to represent equal intervals, and thus semantic differential attitude scores, like those obtained from a Thurstone scale, are assumed to have equal-interval properties.

One interesting implication of these differences in item quantification concerns the utility of neutral statements in the assessment of attitude. In Thurstone scaling, since neutral items are viewed as valid indicants of attitude, they are part of the attitude scale. Neutral items may be included in a Guttman scale, but there is no way of distinguishing them from other items because Guttman scaling examines the degree to which a set of items can be ordered along a single dimension. Thus, it is possible for the items under consideration to be all favorable, to be all unfavorable, or to range from favorable through neutral to unfavorable.

In contrast, Likert scaling explicitly excludes items that cannot be classified as positive or negative, and the implicit assumption is therefore that neutral items are not valid indicants of attitude. Finally, the issue of item neutrality applies to the semantic differential in that it eliminates bipolar adjective scales (i.e., items) that are not clearly evaluative in nature. At the same time, however, a neutral response on a bipolar evaluative scale is permissible.

All scaling procedures are designed to identify items that are unambiguous indicants of a person's attitude. The different criteria employed result in the selection of items with different operating characteristics or tracelines. Thus Guttman, Likert, and semantic differential items have monotonic tracelines, whereas items on the Thurstone scale have nonmonotonic tracelines. A monotonic traceline indicates that as the attitude score increases, the probability of item endorsement increases or remains constant but never decreases. The Likert and semantic differential tracelines are assumed to approach linearity, but in the Guttman scale it has a step-shaped form. In Thurstone scaling, the probability of item endorsement is assumed to increase as the person's attitude score approaches the item's scale value (from either end of the bipolar dimension), resulting in an inverted U-shaped traceline.

A related difference between the scales is that items on the Guttman scale are cumulative whereas items on the other scales are not. Thus each attitude score obtained in Guttman scaling is associated with one—and only one—pattern of responses to the items on the scale. In contrast, many different response patterns may result in the same attitude score when any of the other techniques is used. Thus item responses can be predicted from the attitude score only with the Guttman scale.

Before we turn to a more detailed analysis of attitude scores, one other comment concerning item selection procedures is in order. Since only the Thurstone scale makes use of an independent sample of judges to obtain item scale values, it has often been called a "judgmental scale." In contrast, the other scales have been termed "response-inferred" since responses to the items (i.e., agreements or disagreements) are basic to their item-selection procedures. Recall, however, that in Thurstone scaling it is also necessary to obtain responses from subjects in order to test for the criterion of irrelevance. Thus, when properly constructed, the Thurstone scale is at least in part response-inferred.

Properties of attitude scores. Most remaining differences between the four attitude scaling methods are related to the computation of attitude scores. Generally speaking, in all procedures subjects agree or disagree with items that indicate some degree of favorableness or unfavorableness toward the attitude object. A score is obtained for each item by multiplying degree of agreement and item favorableness. It can be shown that this item score is equal to the product of belief about the object (b) and the evaluation of the object's attributes (e), discussed earlier.[21]

In all four standard scaling procedures, attitude scores are computed by taking the sum or average over all item scores or $b \times e$ products. Thus, as Table 3.3 shows, attitude scores are always obtained in accordance with an expectancy-value formulation. The difference between scaling procedures concerns the relative weights placed on beliefs and evaluations of associated attributes. More specifically, Table 3.3 shows that the semantic differential assigns a value of $+1$ to the positive adjective and a value of -1 to the negative adjective on a given scale, and the subject's response can be viewed as indicating the strength of his

---

21. More specifically, a person agrees or disagrees (b') with a favorable or unfavorable statement (e') which associates or dissociates (u) the attitude object and some attribute (in the case of a belief statement) or the person's behavior (in the case of an intentional statement). The following two equations show that b and e can be derived from b', e', and u.

$$b = b'u, \quad \text{and} \quad e = e'/u.$$

Despite the differences between b and b' on the one hand and e and e' on the other, the next equation shows that the $b \times e$ product is equivalent to the $b' \times e'$ product.

$$be = b'u \, (e'/u) = b'e'.$$

belief that the concept is associated with one or the other adjective; belief strength can vary from 0 to 3. In Likert scaling, each item is assumed to indicate either a favorable ($+1$) or unfavorable (-1) attitude, and responses are given on a five-point scale ranging from strong agreement ($+2$) to strong disagreement (-2). Thus belief strength varies from -2 to $+2$, and evaluations of associated attributes are either $+1$ or -1.

Both the semantic differential and Likert scales place greater weight on b than on e in computing attitude scores, but the opposite is true in Thurstone scaling. Here a subject either agrees ($+1$) or disagrees (0) with each item, and the item's favorableness can range from -5 to $+5$. Finally, a respondent either agrees or disagrees with items on a Guttman scale. For some items agreement is scored $+1$ and disagreement is scored 0; for other items scoring may be reversed in order to produce a cumulative response pattern. Although items may reflect different degrees of favorableness, they are all assigned a score of $+1$ in computing the attitude score. Thus, as in Likert scaling, the assumption is that disagreement (-1) with a negative item (-1) is equivalent to agreement ($+1$) with a positive item ($+1$). In terms of the $b \times e$ formulation, then, b may take on values of 0, $+1$, or -1, and e may be either $+1$ or -1.

These considerations suggest that the standard attitude-scaling procedures differ in the way they treat nonagreements and disagreements with belief or intentional items in the computation of attitude scores. In Likert scaling, disagreement with an item is assumed to be indicative of the person's attitude. Thus disagreement with a negative statement is taken as an indication of a positive attitude. By way of contrast, in Thurstone scaling, nonendorsement of an item is viewed to have no implications for attitude; only the scale values of endorsed items (i.e., items the subject agrees with) are considered in computing the attitude score. Nonendorsement may or may not contribute to attitude scores in Guttman scaling, depending on whether or not the item has been reversed. For items with reversed scoring, nonagreement with a statement is treated as equivalent to agreement with its opposite, and thus it contributes to the attitude score. With respect to the semantic differential, a "neutral" response is treated as nonagreement with either member of the adjective pair, and thus nonagreements enter the computation of attitude scores.

In sum, disagreements or nonagreements influence attitude scores in Guttman, Likert, and semantic differential scales, but not in the Thurstone scale. Further, Table 3.3 shows that only the Guttman and Likert scales can assign negative values to beliefs, thereby implying that a person may hold disbeliefs which contribute to his attitude. That is, in these two scales the respondent may actively disagree with a statement. In contrast, the semantic differential does not assign negative values to belief, and although neutral responses contribute to the attitude score, they indicate lack of belief rather than disbelief.

Unipolar versus bipolar belief measures. Recall that in our conceptual framework, belief strength was defined as a person's location on a probability dimension linking an attitude object and some other concept. Although it is easy to conceptualize lack of belief as a zero probability, the question of disbeliefs becomes problematic since probabilities cannot take on negative values. That is, the object is always linked to the concept with a probability that ranges from 0 to 1; a disbelief therefore has to be conceptualized as the probability that the object is linked to the negation of the concept. Thus, according to a probabilistic view of beliefs,

$$p(\bar{b}) = 1 - p(b), \tag{3.4}$$

where b is a given belief and $\bar{b}$ is the negation of b. This notion can be illustrated in a general way by representing a belief as $[(o) \text{ is } (x)]$ and its negation as $[(o) \text{ is } (\bar{x})]$.

For example, consider a person's disagreement with the belief statement "Chairman Mao is dead." Equation 3.4 suggests that this disagreement can be viewed as equivalent to an agreement with the statement "Chairman Mao is not dead." As a numerical example, imagine that the following measure of belief was obtained.

Communist China is aggressive

$$\text{disagree} \; \underline{\left| \; \frac{\text{X}}{-3} \; \right| \; \frac{}{-2} \; \left| \; \frac{}{-1} \; \right| \; 0 \; \left| \; +1 \; \right| \; +2 \; \left| \; +3 \; \right|} \; \text{agree}$$

Instead of treating this response as a disbelief, Eq. 3.4 suggests that within a probability formulation it should be viewed as an indication of the belief that Communist China is not aggressive, and the strength of this belief would be $+2$.[22]

This practice, however, may prove problematic within the context of an expectancy-value formulation. Clearly, the evaluation of an attribute that is related to the attitude object and the evaluation of its negation will not be the same. For example, assume that the concept "aggressive" is evaluated -3. In conjunction with the disbelief of -2 noted above, an expectancy-value formulation assigns an item score of $(-2)(-3) = 6$. However, this computation is not permissible in the framework of a probabilistic conception of beliefs, where beliefs cannot take on negative values. As shown earlier, within this framework the -2 disbelief would be treated as a $+2$ belief that "Communist China is not aggressive." To compute the $b \times e$ product, one would have to know the evaluation of "not aggressive," and one cannot assume that it is $+3$ (i.e., that it is merely the polar opposite of "aggressive").

The implications of these considerations for attitude measurement are as follows: All attitude scales derive a person's attitude from his beliefs about the attitude object and the evaluations of associated attributes. Each belief implies

---

22. Although on logical grounds a belief and its negation are mutually exclusive and exhaustive, and thus $p(\bar{b}) = 1 - p(b)$, psychologically this may not be true. For example, the concept "not aggressive" may not be perceived to cover everything that is the negation of "aggressive"; thus, psychologically, the concepts "passive," "peace loving," etc., may not be completely subsumed under the concept "not aggressive."

some degree of favorableness or unfavorableness toward the object. The most accurate inferences are likely to result when the following four pieces of information are available for each belief statement linking o to x.

1. $p(b_x)$ the probability that o is related to x
2. $p(b_{\bar{x}})$ the probability that o is related to $\bar{x}$, the negation of x
3. e_x the evaluation of x
4. $e_{\bar{x}}$ the evaluation of $\bar{x}$

As Table 3.4 shows, for each belief statement, products can be obtained of $p(b_x)e_x$ and $p(b_{\bar{x}})e_{\bar{x}}$. The sum of these two products is the best indicant of the subject's attitude implied by the statement in question. For example, Table 3.4 illustrates that a unipolar or probabilistic measure of the subject's belief that o is x and a measure of his evaluation of x lead to the inference of a negative attitude toward o in all three hypothetical cases. However, if the investigator also assessed the subject's belief that o is $\bar{x}$ and his evaluation of $\bar{x}$, and used both beliefs to infer the subject's attitude, he would have concluded that the subject had a positive attitude toward o. It is usually assumed that $p(b_x) = 1 - p(b_{\bar{x}})$, and that the evaluations of x and $\bar{x}$ are equally polarized with opposite signs (that is, $e_{\bar{x}} =$

Table 3.4 Computation of Item Scores

		Unipolar belief scale			Bipolar belief scale	
		p	e	pe	$p' = p - .5$	$p'e$
Case 1 Symmetric probabilities: $p(b_{\bar{x}}) = 1 - p(b_x)$ and Symmetric evaluations: $e_{\bar{x}} = -e_x$	x	.2	-3	$-.6$	$-.3$	.9
	$\bar{x}$	.8	$+3$	2.4	.3	.9
	Σ			1.8		1.8
Case 2 Symmetric probabilities: $p(b_{\bar{x}}) = 1 - p(b_x)$ and Asymmetric evaluations: $e_{\bar{x}} \neq -e_x$	x	.2	-3	$-.6$	$-.3$	.9
	$\bar{x}$	.8	$+1$	.8	.3	.3
	Σ			.2		1.2
Case 3 Asymmetric probabilities: $p(b_{\bar{x}}) \neq 1 - p(b_x)$ and Symmetric evaluations: $e_{\bar{x}} = -e_x$	x	.2	-3	$-.6$	$-.3$	.9
	$\bar{x}$	.9	$+3$	2.7	.4	1.2
	Σ			2.1		2.1

$-e_x$), and under these assumptions, all necessary information could be derived from one measure of probability and one measure of evaluation (Case 1).

Unfortunately, such assumptions of symmetric probabilities and evaluations are not always warranted, and Table 3.4 shows that when either assumption is not met (Cases 2 and 3), appropriate measures of the subject's belief that o is x and his evaluation of $\bar{x}$ would lead to very different estimates of attitude than that based on deriving these measures under the assumptions of symmetry.

One way to avoid at least some of these problems is to treat beliefs in a bipolar fashion. That is, a response scale measuring beliefs can be scored either from $-$ to $+$, indicating a range from disbelief to belief, or from 0 to $+$, implying a range from lack of belief to belief. Thus a unipolar probability scale ranging from 0 to $+1$ can be converted into a bipolar belief scale by subtracting the value of .5. The computations in Table 3.4 illustrate the effects of treating the probability measure in such a bipolar fashion. As we can see, when bipolar measures of beliefs are used, estimates based on both beliefs (o is x and o is $\bar{x}$) lead to the same inference about the direction of the subject's attitude toward o (positive) as estimates based on either belief considered alone. We can also see that when all four measures are available, using unipolar or bipolar belief scales will lead to the same results so long as the assumption of symmetric evaluations is met (Cases 1 and 3). When evaluations are asymmetric, however, different results are obtained by using unipolar and bipolar belief scales (Case 2).

Our comparison of standard attitude scales indicates that all procedures involve the multiplication of a belief and the evaluation of the associated attribute for each item. Since in all scaling methods only one b value and one e value are employed, it will clearly make a difference whether a unipolar or a bipolar belief scale is used.

Looking at Table 3.4, we can see that whenever a single belief is measured, use of a bipolar scale is preferable. Irrespective of the wording of the item, the same inference about the direction of attitude will be made. That is, one can usually assume that $p(b_{\bar{x}})$ and $p(b_x)$ will be negatively related (even if probabilistic symmetry cannot be assumed), and thus a respondent who has a high probability of endorsing a statement linking o and x will have a low probability of endorsing a statement linking o and $\bar{x}$. Since only one form of the statement will appear on a given scale, a unipolar scoring procedure will make very different inferences about the attitude, depending on the content of the particular item. For example, in Table 3.4 we can see that if x is evaluated -3 and $\bar{x}$ is evaluated $+3$, a .2 probability that o is x will be taken as an indication of a slightly unfavorable attitude $(-.6)$, whereas a .8 probability that o is $\bar{x}$ will be taken as an indication of a very favorable attitude $(+2.4)$. In contrast, with bipolar scoring, the response to either statement is indicative of the same attitude $(+.9)$. The same logic applies when there is reason to assume asymmetric evaluations or probabilities. That is, Cases 2 and 3 also show that when only a single belief is measured (for example, o is x or o is $\bar{x}$), bipolar scoring leads to the same directional inference, but unipolar scoring does not. However, Table 3.4 suggests that when there is reason to suspect that assumptions of symmetry are not met, both beliefs (b_x and $b_{\bar{x}}$) and their attribute evaluations (e_x and $e_{\bar{x}}$) should be obtained.[23]

Beliefs as indicants of attitude. Throughout the discussion above the argument has been that a person's attitude can be assessed by considering beliefs about the attitude object and evaluations of attributes associated with the object. All standard scaling methods obtain some measure of the person's beliefs about the object; a measure of attribute evaluation is not obtained from the person whose attitude is measured, but rather, it is assigned by the investigator, and it is assumed to be the same for all respondents. To meet this condition of uniform evaluations, many items are eliminated by the different scaling methods. Thus items that have positive attitudinal implications for one respondent but negative implications for another cannot be included on the standard scales. However, if the respondent's evaluation of each attribute were known, these items could be used to measure attitude.

Indeed, Fishbein (1967d) has argued that responses to any belief or intentional statement can serve as an indicant of a person's attitude, provided that his own evaluation associated with the statement and his belief or intention are known. Thus beliefs (b) and attribute evaluations (e) can be measured simultaneously for each respondent. It has been shown (e.g., Fishbein, 1963; 1967d) that, in accordance with an expectancy-value model, the summed products of b and e thus obtained can serve as a measure of attitude.

The considerations above point out that many beliefs that may serve as determinants of a person's attitude get eliminated from attitude scales by the standard scaling procedures. For example, it is often assumed that a person's attitude toward a political candidate is in part a function of the candidate's party affiliation. Thus the belief "Candidate X is a Democrat" should influence a person's attitude toward Candidate X. A belief statement of this kind, however, would be eliminated by the standard scaling methods since virtually everybody would agree with the statement, and thus its traceline would not meet scaling requirements. Nevertheless, the statement can be used to measure attitude, provided that the respondent's evaluation of "Democrat" is known. Thus a person who agreed with the statement and favorably evaluated "Democrat" would be assumed to hold a favorable attitude toward Candidate X. Similarly, a person who agreed with the statement but evaluated "Democrat" negatively would be viewed as having a negative attitude toward Candidate X.

Consistent with our discussion above, if the respondent assigned a low probability to the statement, or if he disagreed with it, inferences about his attitude

---

23. As Table 3.4 shows, when both beliefs are measured under conditions of evaluative symmetry (Cases 1 and 3), both forms of belief scoring will yield identical results. When evaluation is asymmetric (Case 3), however, unipolar measures do not yield the same results as bipolar measures. Since bipolar scoring is merely a convenience for dealing with the single-belief problem, we recommend the use of unipolar scales whenever both beliefs are assessed.

would require additional knowledge about his evaluation of "not a Democrat." In the absence of this information, evaluations of "Democrat" and "not a Democrat" are usually assumed to be symmetric, and therefore responses to the belief scale are scored in a bipolar fashion. However, the present example illustrates that the assumption of symmetric evaluations may not always be warranted. The possibility of asymmetric evaluations provides an additional reason for using several belief statements, rather than a single item, to measure attitude.

We argued earlier that responses to a single item can be viewed as consisting of a "true" score reflecting the attitude under consideration and some measurement error. Differences between the standard scaling procedures in terms of relative weights placed on beliefs and evaluations, inclusion or exclusion of disbeliefs and neutral items, etc. (see Table 3.3), can perhaps be regarded as measurement error. Across a large number of items, the errors will tend to cancel out, and the obtained attitude score will approximate the "true" attitude score. In fact, despite the existing differences, there is considerable evidence that the standard attitude scales tend to yield comparable results.

So far as obtaining a measure of attitude is concerned, therefore, the differences between the standard procedures are of relatively minor importance. These differences become relevant for an understanding of the formation of beliefs, attitudes, and intentions, for the study of changes in these variables, and for the prediction of overt behavior. For example, Likert and Guttman scaling arrive at the attitude score by *summing* $b \times e$ products, whereas an *average* is obtained in Thurstone scaling (see Table 3.3). Both a sum and an average have been used for semantic differential scales. Although the distinction between an averaging and an additive model has been of minor importance in attitude measurement, it has led to a theoretical controversy in research on attitude formation (see Chapter 6).

Response consistency. A final difference between the standard scaling procedures that is of theoretical significance concerns their implications for the notion of response consistency. In Chapter 1 we argued that attitudes are inferred from response consistency and that different interpretations can be given to this term. Item-selection procedures can be viewed as an attempt to examine responses to belief or intentional statements for a particular type of consistency. Thus Guttman scaling examines the degree to which cumulative response patterns are exhibited consistently by different individuals; that is, stimulus-response consistency is basic to the construction of Guttman scales.

In comparison, Likert and semantic differential scales examine the degree to which responses to one statement are consistent with responses to other statements. Use of a correlational selection procedure implies response-response consistency.

Finally, Thurstone scaling considers the degree to which a given individual responds consistently to items with the same scale value, as well as the degree to which he responds differently to items with different scale values. The consistency sought is between the evaluation associated with an item and responses to that item; this may be termed overall evaluative consistency.

The response consistency implied by the different item-selection procedures, however, is not necessarily the same as that implied by the final attitude scores. Specifically, with the exception of Guttman scores, the standard scaling procedures obtain attitude scores that reflect overall evaluative consistency. Two individuals with identical Thurstone, Likert, or semantic differential scores may exhibit completely different response patterns. Strictly speaking, the notion of response-response consistency implies that all of a person's responses indicate the same attitude toward the object in question. The absence of such consistency (e.g., if his response to one item indicated a favorable attitude and his response to another item indicated an unfavorable attitude), implies absence of an attitude. However, like Thurstone scaling, Likert and semantic differential scales result in attitude scores for all individuals, even when response-response inconsistency occurs.

In Guttman scaling, stimulus-response consistency is implied by the attitude score, just as it was implied by the item-selection procedure. That is, in a cumulative Guttman scale, attitude scores are associated with one—and only one—response pattern.

The lack of correspondence between the kinds of response consistency implied by item-selection procedures and by attitude scores in Likert and semantic differential scaling is reminiscent of a similar lack of correspondence discussed in Chapter 1. There we mentioned that investigators often obtain attitude scores that reflect overall evaluative consistency, but they assume that attitudes are predispositions to perform a particular response or a consistent set of responses; that is to say, the investigators assume stimulus-response or response-response consistency. The present discussion indicates that since most standard procedures result in overall evaluative attitude scores, those scores cannot be expected to predict individual responses.

In conclusion, although there are many important differences between standard attitude-scaling methods, they share two basic features. First, all four methods discussed infer attitude by considering a person's beliefs or intentions and their associated evaluations. Second, in all methods, those beliefs and associated evaluations are combined into an attitude score in accordance with an expectancy-value formulation. These conclusions support our conceptual framework, in which attitude is viewed as a function of an individual's beliefs and is expected to be related to his intentions. One criticism sometimes voiced with respect to the standard scaling procedures is that they frequently do not include belief items that are important determinants of the attitude in question. In fact, as we have indicated, the different item-selection procedures may eliminate just such belief statements. This problem can be overcome by obtaining independent measures of evaluations associated with a belief, as well as of belief strength. This more complete use of an expectancy-value notion obviates the need to eliminate any items in attitude measurement.

In the remainder of this chapter, we will see that other verbal attitude measures also appear to be based on an expectancy-value formulation involving beliefs and associated evaluations. Further, we will see that certain measures of cognitive structure can also be obtained by considering these beliefs and/or their associated evaluations.

ALTERNATIVE MEASUREMENT TECHNIQUES

All measurement procedures discussed so far, including the standard scaling methods, can be viewed as nondisguised techniques. That is, the respondent is usually aware that his attitude is being assessed; no attempt is made to conceal the purpose of the measurement. One possible exception is the semantic differential, which is sometimes presented to the respondent as a measure of meaning, and the inclusion of nonevaluative scales may disguise its purpose to some degree.

Disguised Techniques

Most other attitude-measurement procedures which have been developed make an explicit attempt to disguise the purpose of the measuring instrument. The underlying assumption is that when the purpose of the instrument is not apparent, respondents are less likely to "distort" or "falsify" their responses, and thus a more valid measure of attitude can be obtained. Usually the respondent is led to believe that his responses will be interpreted as indicants of some variable other than attitude.[24] (For an excellent comprehensive review of disguised measurement techniques, see Kidder and Campbell, 1970.) The present discussion will be concerned primarily with those techniques that have demonstrated some degree of utility for the measurement of attitude. Numerous attempts to measure attitudes have been based on projective personality tests, such as the Thematic Apperception Test (TAT), Rorschach, and doll play, but these techniques will not be reviewed here, because there is little evidence for their reliability or validity as attitude measures (cf. Sechrest, 1968).

Hammond's Error-Choice Technique

One way of disguising the purpose of an attitude-measuring instrument is to lead the respondent to believe that he is to make some objective judgment, i.e., that there is some "correct" response. An example of this kind of disguise is given by Hammond's (1948) error-choice technique, in which respondents are led to believe that their factual knowledge concerning some object is being assessed. The underlying assumption is that attitudes will bias responses in a consistent way and, therefore, that such biased responses can be used to infer attitude. "Under the guise of an 'information test' items [are] presented with alternate choices for an-

---

24. Recent concern with the ethics of psychological research has led to criticism of such deceptive practices. Some more general questions of deception will be considered in Chapter 4.

swers, both choices being incorrect, either equidistant from the truth or truth being indeterminable. The subject [is] forced into error. This method is termed the 'error-choice technique'." (Hammond, 1948; p. 43)

For example, the following item, which has response alternatives equidistant from the truth, appeared on Hammond's original scale measuring "labor-management" attitudes.

Average weekly wage of the war worker in 1945 was

1. $37

2. $57

The correct figure would have been $47. Hammond assumed that prolabor subjects would be biased toward the first response and promanagement subjects toward the second.

On a second scale measuring attitude toward Russia, the following item had no determinably correct response.

Russia's removal of heavy industry from Austria was

1. Legal

2. Illegal.

Note that this item is very similar to a dichotomous semantic differential scale. That is, agreement with the first alternative would be taken to imply a positive attitude toward Russia, and agreement with the second would be viewed as evidence for a negative attitude. The same argument can be made for the first item concerning labor-management attitudes; one response alternative would be viewed as indicating a favorable attitude $(e = +1)$, the other an unfavorable attitude $(e = -1)$.

For each item, the respondent indicates which of the two bipolar alternatives is associated with the attitude object $(b = 1)$. Consistent with an expectancy-value formulation, the $b \times e$ products are computed for each item, and the attitude score is a sum of those products. To test the validity of each item as an indicant of attitude, as well as the validity of the total score, Hammond used the "known group comparison" technique. His respondents were union employees and businessmen. Most item scores and the total attitude score were found to discriminate between these two groups. Use of known group comparisons indicates that, as in Likert scaling or the semantic differential technique, items are selected in terms of their internal consistency. That is, each item must be shown to discriminate between subjects with positive and negative attitudes; thus a linear traceline is assumed. This suggests that in constructing an error-choice scale, one could select items by computing the correlation between item scores and the preliminary total score in lieu of using known group comparisons. Items with low correlations would be eliminated.

Cook's Plausibility Technique

Another way of disguising the purpose of an attitude measure involves the following procedure. Instead of indicating his agreement with a series of statements, the respondent judges each statement in terms of its validity, effectiveness, evaluative implication, or plausibility. For example, the task of judges in Thurstone scaling is to rate the favorableness of each item on an 11-place scale. A disguised measure of attitude would be obtained if these ratings were used to infer the judges' attitudes. In fact, as will be seen below, such judgments are used to infer involvement and other indices by a technique known as the "own categories" procedure.

Perhaps the best example of such a disguised technique in attitude measurement is Cook's measure of plausibility (Waly and Cook, 1965; Brigham and Cook, 1970). The underlying assumption is that a person's attitude will bias his judgment of a statement's plausibility. Specifically, it is assumed that "a statement will be considered a more plausible or effective argument by subjects who agree with the position which the statement supports than by subjects who disagree with that position" (Waly and Cook, 1965, p. 746). In developing a plausibility measure of attitude toward racial integration, Waly and Cook had their subjects rate the effectiveness of each of a set of arguments labeled "prosegregation" or "prointegration" on an 11-point scale ranging from *very ineffective* (-5) to *very effective* ($+5$). The following two items were among the arguments rated.

1. *Prosegregation:* Immediate desegregation damages the Negro by giving him responsibilities for which he does not have the necessary background and preparation.

2. *Prointegration:* If integration is adopted, race hatred will quickly disappear in southern communities which are now torn apart by the issue.

"Subjects' ratings on the prosegregation items were assigned scores from $+5 = 0$ to $-5 = 10$; that is, the more *ineffective* the argument was considered to be by the subject, the higher his score. Scores for the prointegration items were reversed, that is, the more *effective* the argument was considered to be by the subject, the higher the score." (Waly and Cook, 1965, p. 746) The item scores are summed to obtain a measure of attitude. The higher the attitude score, the more favorable the attitude toward integration.

This scoring procedure is very much like that used in Likert scaling. A given item is assumed to indicate either a favorable ($+1$) or an unfavorable (-1) attitude, and judgments of effectiveness are given scores of -5 to $+5$. As noted above, the assumption is that judging a statement as effective indicates agreement with it and judging it as ineffective indicates disagreement. Under this assumption, judgments of effectiveness can be viewed as measures of belief strength. Consistent with an expectancy-value formulation, $b \times e$ products can be obtained for each statement and summed to yield a measure of attitude. Indeed, this procedure yields a score which is equivalent to the score obtained by Waly and Cook.

Just as the error-choice technique was shown to be similar to the semantic differential, the plausibility technique can be viewed as similar to a Likert scale. Items are assumed to discriminate between individuals with positive and negative attitudes; i.e., they are assumed to have linear tracelines. This suggests that a scale based on plausibility judgments should be constructed by applying Likert item-selection criteria. Only discriminating items should be retained.

Recall that disguised techniques were developed in part in an attempt to avoid distortions or falsifications of responses used to infer attitudes. The basic assumption underlying these techniques is that if the subject is unaware that his attitude is being assessed, his responses are more likely to be valid indicants of his "true" attitude. The error-choice and plausibility techniques attempt to achieve this aim by leading subjects to believe that their factual knowledge is being measured or that the investigator is interested in judgments of plausibility. These responses are assumed to be systematically biased by the respondent's attitude. Clearly, the validity of the error-choice and plausibility techniques rests on the validity of that assumption.

Estimation of Others' Responses

A similar assumption is made when subjects are told that their knowledge of other people's opinions is being measured. Subjects can be asked to respond to any question as they think some other person or group of persons would respond. Based on psychodynamic theory, the assumption is that subjects project their own beliefs, attitudes, or intentions onto those other persons and thus, when they respond "as they think others would," they actually respond the way they themselves would. Unlike the previous disguised techniques, this one does not require development of a specific instrument. That is, a subject can be asked to indicate the way that "most people" would respond to any of the standard attitude scales, to the error-choice technique, or to any other verbal measure. Since estimates of others' responses are assumed to be equivalent to the subject's own responses, the normal procedures for computing attitude scores can be employed.

It is worth noting, however, that the assumption of equivalence between projected and own responses may hold for some items but not for others. It follows that an item may not be a valid indicant of attitude when estimates of other people's responses are obtained, even though it may be valid when the subject's own responses are used. For example, if subjects with favorable attitudes agree with an item but subjects with unfavorable attitudes disagree with it, the item meets Likert criteria and is considered a valid indicant of attitude. The same item, however, may fail to discriminate between subjects with favorable and unfavorable attitudes when estimates of other people's responses are involved. All subjects, irrespective of their attitudes, may estimate that most other people would agree (or disagree) with the item. Such an item, therefore, should be eliminated from the scale when subjects are asked to make estimates of others' responses.

Recall that item analyses can be done in two ways: by comparing responses of subjects with presumed-known attitudes (known groups comparison) or by comparing responses of subjects whose preliminary attitude scores are high or low (internal consistency). Clearly, when the known groups comparison method is used, items are selected in terms of a single "objective" external criterion. In contrast, the internal consistency criterion may differ for the selection of items based on subjects' own responses as opposed to estimates of other people's responses. Thus attitude scores based on disguised items will be similar to attitude scores based on nondisguised items when the known groups comparison criterion is used in item selection. The similarity will not necessarily exist when the internal consistency criterion is employed. This implies that an independent item analysis must be performed to construct an attitude scale that employs estimates of other people's responses. The failure to perform such item analyses may explain the relatively low validity of scales that have used the estimation procedure.

The "Bogus Pipeline" Technique

Another general procedure designed to measure a subject's "true" beliefs, attitudes, or intention has been suggested by Jones and Sigall (1971). The basic assumption underlying the "bogus pipeline" procedure is that "no one wants to be second-guessed by a machine. If a person could be convinced that we *do* have a machine that precisely measures attitudinal direction and intensity, we assume that he would be motivated to predict accurately what the machine is saying about him." (Jones and Sigall, 1971, p. 349)

With this technique, the respondent is attached to some machine that purportedly can measure his true response to any item by recording his implicit reactions to the item. Needless to say, subjects must be convinced that the machine can indeed do so. Subjects can then be asked to guess or predict the machine's readings of their responses to any item. Thus, in a sense, the subject's task is to predict his own "true" implicit responses. On the assumption that he does not want to be outguessed by the machine, the subject is expected to respond as truthfully as possible.

Under this procedure, a subject can be asked to predict his responses to any item or set of items, including standard attitude scales. Note that if a set of belief statements is to be used to infer the respondent's attitude, the same problems discussed with respect to estimates of other people's responses apply to predictions or estimates of one's own responses. That is to say, an item analysis must be performed to construct an attitude scale where attitudes are inferred from estimates of own responses.

Frequently, however, the bogus pipeline technique will be used to obtain a "direct" measure of the subject's true attitude. For example, the subject may be asked to predict the machine's reading of his response to the attitude object "desegregation" on a seven-point bipolar scale ranging from *good* to *bad*. As pointed out at the beginning of this chapter, responses to this item may be viewed as relatively direct measures of attitude. Clearly, the bogus pipeline technique may elicit a different response from that which would be obtained if the subject were simply asked to rate "desegregation" on the seven-point *good–bad* scale.

The possibility of obtaining different results by using disguised and nondisguised techniques raises the question as to which type of instrument provides a more accurate measure of attitude. Proponents of disguised techniques argue that since these techniques are designed to avoid deliberate distortions and falsifications, they result in more valid measures of attitude. However, the question of validity is an empirical one and will be discussed in the following chapter.

Physiological Measures

In contrast to the disguised measurement techniques considered thus far, where an attempt is made to avoid distortion by concealing the instrument's purpose, physiological measures attempt to prevent distortion by assessing involuntary responses over which the individual has little or no control. A large number of physiological responses have been considered in the search for a valid, nonverbal indicant of attitude. Among them are the galvanic skin response (GSR) measuring electrical skin conductance, heart rate, palmar sweat, pupillary dilation and constriction, respiration, etc. Despite considerable research efforts, there is little evidence to indicate that any physiological measure can be used as a valid indicant of attitude. One problem is that most physiological measures appear to assess general arousal and therefore cannot be used to distinguish between positive and negative affective states. Since attitude has been defined in terms of an evaluative dimension ranging from favorableness to unfavorableness, these measures are by definition inadequate.

The pupillary response. One physiological measure, however, appeared for a time to be capable of distinguishing between positive and negative affective states, namely, the pupillary response. Specifically, Hess (1965) suggested that increase in pupil size (dilation) indicates a positive attitude toward the object viewed, whereas constriction in pupil size indicates a negative attitude. Further, he suggested that the amount of dilation or constriction corresponds to differences in attitudinal intensity. Unfortunately, the initial promise of this measure has not been fulfilled. In an excellent review of the pupillary response as a measure of attitude, Woodmansee (1970, p. 532) concluded that "studies which are relevant to the issue suggest that the pupil does not measure attitude or qualitatively different affective states. There is ample evidence, however, that the pupil, in its reflex dilation reaction, may be used to indicate arousal, attentiveness, interest, and perceptual orienting."

In conclusion, it would definitely be desirable to have a nonverbal measure of attitude not under the subject's control, but it appears unlikely that any known physiological reaction will serve this purpose.

Behavioral and Unobtrusive Measures

Various overt behaviors have been used to infer attitudes. For example, church attendance has been used to measure religiosity, choice behaviors are assumed to express preferences, and duration of eye contact has been assumed to reflect interpersonal attraction, as has amount of communication and volunteering to help. Unobtrusive measures have included return rate of ostensibly lost letters addressed to various persons or organizations, relative frequencies with which bumper stickers in support of various political candidates are displayed, and purchase frequencies of various brands of a given product.

As previously mentioned, when such behavioral observations are used to infer attitudes, they are comparable to verbal responses to items on an attitude scale. The implication of this notion is that overt responses must be submitted to the same scaling procedures that are applied to verbal items before they can be assumed to reflect attitude. It should be obvious that not all behaviors with respect to a given object are valid indicants of attitude toward that object. This issue will be considered again in Chapter 8 on the relation between attitude and behavior.

Multidimensional Scaling Procedures

All measurement techniques discussed thus far attempt to locate an individual on a single bipolar evaluative dimension with respect to some object. Although this approach is consistent with our definition of attitude, the reader should recall that other investigators have defined attitude as a complex multidimensional concept. Clearly, this multidimensional conception of attitude is incompatible with the measurement techniques we have discussed. Thus some investigators have turned to multidimensional scaling procedures, where an attempt is made to measure attitude in terms of the object's location in a multidimensional space.[25]

The major purpose of multidimensional techniques is to identify the relevant dimensions that underlie a person's judgments of a given object or set of objects. Thus, although one expects that different dimensions may be relevant for different subjects and for different objects, these dimensions should *not* vary as a function of the particular set of judgments the subject is asked to make.

The most frequently used multidimensional technique is factor analysis. We showed earlier in this chapter how factor analysis was used to construct the semantic differential measure of attitude. On the basis of Osgood's work on the semantic differential, Triandis (1964) developed the "behavioral differential" to investigate dimensions of interpersonal intentions. First, a large set of interpersonal behaviors was selected, such as "elect to political office," "go fishing with," "accept as an intimate friend," "work for," and "exclude from my neighborhood."

---

25. For example, some investigators have used the semantic differential and have argued that attitude toward a concept is defined by the person's location on all emerging dimensions, rather than only the evaluative dimension.

Subjects were asked to indicate on a nine-point scale whether they *would* or *would not* perform each behavior with respect to a variety of complex stimulus persons (e.g., a 50-year-old, Negro, Roman Catholic, male physician).

A factor analysis was performed on the matrix of correlations between behaviors, and five dimensions of interpersonal intentions were identified. These dimensions were interpreted as (1) formal social acceptance or respect; (2) marital acceptance; (3) friendship acceptance; (4) social distance; and (5) super-ordination-subordination. These results will be discussed in greater detail in Chapter 7, which deals with the formation of intentions. There we will see that different factors tend to emerge in different studies.[26]

Indeed, a major problem with the factor-analytic approach is that the emerging dimensions *are* dependent on the particular set of items used to elicit judgments. That is, factor analysis identifies the dimensions underlying a given set of judgments rather than all relevant dimensions; any dimension not represented by the particular set of judgments used cannot be identified. For example, if a semantic differential included only a set of evaluative scales, potency and activity dimensions would not emerge in a factor analysis of those scales. To avoid this difficulty, a number of context-free multidimensional scaling procedures have been developed. Most of these procedures are based on judgments of distance (or similarity) between objects. The basic principle involved can be exemplified as follows: Consider an investigator who is interested in identifying the relevant dimensions along which three objects, A, B, and C, are judged or compared. As a first step, he could ask subjects to judge the degree of similarity between the three possible pairs of objects (AB, AC, and BC) on a seven-point scale ranging from *similar* (0) to *dissimilar* (6). Figure 3.5 presents hypothetical responses of two subjects.

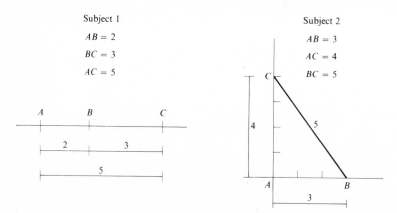

Fig. 3.5 Hypothetical similarity judgments and their use in multidimensional scaling.

---

26. It is worth noting, however, that irrespective of the label assigned to it, the first factor to emerge can usually be interpreted as an evaluative dimension.

The assumption is that the more similar a pair of objects, the closer their locations in multidimensional space. Thus similarity judgments can be interpreted as measures of the distance between objects in that space. The analytic problem of multidimensional scaling is the determination of the number of dimensions required to locate the objects' positions in the space in accordance with their distances from each other. In the example of Fig. 3.5, only one dimension is necessary to account for the first subject's distance estimates, but two dimensions are required for the second subject. This principle can be generalized to any number of objects, and the analytic procedure will determine the number of dimensions that are required.

The basic data used in multidimensional scaling are contained in a matrix of distances between a set of objects.[27] A procedure similar to factor analysis is employed, and as in factor analysis, a set of dimensions is identified. In addition, each object's location on these dimensions is obtained. Each dimension is given a psychological interpretation (i.e., it is named) by considering the kinds of objects that are located at opposite ends of the dimension. Figure 3.6 illustrates a hypothetical two-dimensional space for the judgment of politicians. The locations of

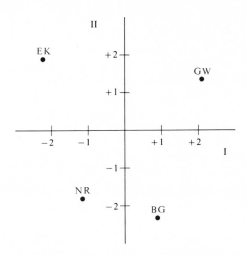

Fig. 3.6 Hypothetical two-dimensional space.

politicians in this space are determined by the values obtained in multidimensional scaling, shown in Table 3.5.

Since the two Democrats (Kennedy and Wallace) are located at one end of the second dimension and the two Republicans (Goldwater and Rockefeller) at the other, it seems reasonable to label this dimension "party affiliation." The first

27. In most applications, the entries in each cell of the matrix are mean distance ratings over a sample of subjects. If a given individual's set of dimensions is to be obtained, however, his own distance ratings must be analyzed.

Table 3.5 Hypothetical Results of
Multidimensional Scaling

	Dimension I	Dimension II
Barry Goldwater	+ .9	−2.3
Nelson Rockefeller	−1.1	−1.8
Edward Kennedy	−2.2	+1.9
George Wallace	+2.1	+1.3

dimension might be labeled "liberalism-conservatism" since Kennedy and Rocke-feller are located on one end and Goldwater and Wallace on the other. How-ever, this dimension could also have been interpreted as a geographic dimen-sion since Kennedy and Rockefeller are from the North while Goldwater and Wallace are from the South. Within our conceptual framework, all dimensions emerging in multidimensional scaling represent different beliefs about the ob-jects. Returning to our example in Fig. 3.5, we can interpret the second dimen-sion as beliefs about party affiliation. Similarly, the first dimension can be interpreted as beliefs about the politicians' liberalism or as beliefs about their regional origins. However, as in factor analysis, one of the emerging dimen-sions can usually be interpreted as evaluative. This is always the case when the analysis is performed at the level of the individual subject, but a clear evaluative dimension may not emerge when the analysis is based on data from a sample of respondents (see note 27). In our example, the first dimension can be interpreted as evaluative, since it could be argued that the politicians are ordered in terms of their attractiveness. This implies that some beliefs are related to the evaluative dimension while others are unrelated. However, as we pointed out in discussing factor analysis, for another set of politicians, liberalism-conservatism may not be related to the evaluative dimension (it might emerge as an independent dimen-sion), while beliefs about party affiliation may be related.[28]

In conclusion, multidimensional scaling can be used as a general measure of attitudes toward a set of objects since, at least at the individual level, it locates those objects on an evaluative dimension. Moreover, it identifies the number of underlying belief dimensions that are used by a person in making judgments about the objects.[29] This suggests that different respondents may be compared in terms of the number of belief dimensions they employ in judging a given set of objects.

---

28. The same considerations apply to interpreting the dimensions of interpersonal intentions that have been obtained in studies using the behavioral differential. That is, although all emerging dimensions can be viewed as representing different kinds of interpersonal intentions with respect to a given set of persons, one dimension is usually evaluative in nature and can thus be used as a measure of attitude.

29. All emerging dimensions should be considered beliefs; however, in all individual analyses, and in many group analyses, one of the dimensions can also be interpreted as an evaluative dimension.

A measure of "cognitive complexity" can be obtained in this fashion. It should be clear that two individuals with similar attitudes toward one or more objects can differ in their degree of cognitive complexity. Measures of this kind may be useful in explaining why people with similar attitudes behave in different ways or differ in their acceptance of new information. Indeed, many measures of cognitive structure have been employed in attitude research.

Measures of Cognitive Structure

Associated with a person's attitude is a set of beliefs about the object of the attitude. In our consideration of learning theory we have suggested that these beliefs form a hierarchy in terms of the strength with which they are held. This hierarchy may be viewed as a person's belief system with respect to a given object or issue. Various measures of cognitive structure can be based on this belief system. To do so, however, requires that an adequate procedure be available for eliciting the person's belief hierarchy. Clearly, the technique employed should permit any belief in the hierarchy to be elicited, and it should not elicit beliefs that are not part of the person's belief system. Unfortunately, none of the techniques that have been used to elicit beliefs seems to completely satisfy these requirements.[30]

Perhaps the simplest and most direct procedure involves asking the subject to describe the attitude object, using a free-response format. For example, he could be asked to list "the characteristics, qualities, and attributes" (Zajonc, 1954) of an object such as "organized religion," or he could be asked to list the consequences of performing some behavior.

The number of beliefs elicited in a free-response situation has been used as an index of cognitive differentiation. Clearly, once the person's belief hierarchy has been obtained, he can be asked to rate his own beliefs in a variety of ways. Within the framework of an expectancy-value notion, the probability of each belief and the evaluation of the associated attribute would be assessed. It has been shown how these measures can be used to compute an attitude score, but it is also possible to derive measures of cognitive structure from the same measures. For example, an index of the intensity with which beliefs are held would be obtained by computing the average belief strength (i.e., probability). Two persons with the same attitude can have cognitive structures varying in intensity, and they may be differentially resistant to attitude change. A measure of total affect within the belief system can be obtained by summing the absolute values of the $b \times e$ products. The difference between this index and the absolute value of attitude could be considered a measure of ambivalence with respect to the object (K. J. Kaplan, 1972). Consistency among beliefs can be assessed by computing the ratio between the number of beliefs with positive (or negative) associated evaluations and the total number of beliefs. Table 3.6 illustrates these indices with respect to two persons' beliefs about Toyotas. It should be clear that many other indices of cognitive struc-

---

30. These procedures include sentence completion, word association, adjective check lists, and the "repertory grid." A review of some of these techniques can be found in Triandis (1971).

Table 3.6 Indices for Two Hypothetical Belief Systems Concerning Toyotas

	Person 1				Person 2		
Beliefs elicited	b	e	$b \times e$	Beliefs elicited	b	e	$b \times e$
Reliable	+3	+2	6	Inexpensive	+3	+1	3
Inexpensive	+2	0	0	Small	+3	−1	−3
Inconvenient	+2	−3	−6	Made in Japan	+3	−2	−6
Small	+2	−1	−2	Economical	+1	+2	+2
Ugly	+1	−2	−2				

(1) Attitude $\Sigma\, b_i e_i$	−4	−4
(2) Differentiation: No. of beliefs	5	4
(3) Intensity $\lvert \Sigma\, b_i \rvert / (2)$	2	2.5
(4) Total affect $\Sigma \lvert b_i e_i \rvert$	16	14
(5) Ambivalence $(4) - \lvert (1) \rvert$	12	10
(6) Consistency $\dfrac{\text{No. of neg } (b \times e) \text{ products}}{(2)}$	0.6	0.5

ture can be obtained on the basis of the b and e values. Further, subjects could be asked to rate the importance of each belief or to estimate conditional probabilities between beliefs (e.g., subjects could indicate the probability that a car is inexpensive if it is made in Japan). These and other measures could then be used to compute additional indices of cognitive structure.[31]

Position Uncertainty, Belief Confidence, and Indifference

As we noted in our discussion of belief measures, subjects are often asked to place an object into one of several content categories. The categories may be ordered along some dimension, or they may be merely nominal categories. This procedure identifies the perceived object-attribute link. The indices of cognitive structure discussed above are based on subjective probabilities associated with the object-attribute link and on evaluations of the attribute category.

Position uncertainty. In addition to estimating the probability that the object has the indicated attribute, the subject can be asked to rate how confident or *certain* he is that the object has the attribute in question. There is considerable evidence that such certainty ratings are systematically related to probability estimates; the

---

31. Clearly, some of these indices can also be constructed without eliciting the respondent's own beliefs but rather by using some standard set of belief statements. Interested readers are referred to Zajonc (1960) and Scott (1969) for examples of indices of cognitive structure and their use in attitude research.

more polarized or extreme (either high or low) the person's probability estimate, the greater his certainty. Minimal certainty (or maximal uncertainty) is found when the probability estimate is at chance level (Beach and Wise, 1969; Wyer, 1973).

Assume a set of mutually exclusive and exhaustive attribute categories. The probabilities associated with these alternative categories must sum to 1.0. The probability defining the chance level is $1/n$, where n is the number of attribute categories. Maximal uncertainty with respect to a given object-attribute link thus occurs when the subjective probability of that link is $1/n$. With two response alternatives, maximal uncertainty is at the .50 level of probability ($\frac{1}{2}$). When four response categories are available, a probability of .25 represents chance level and thus maximal uncertainty.

Since position uncertainty decreases as subjective probabilities deviate from chance levels, there should be a U-shaped relation between probability and certainty. This relationship is shown in Fig. 3.7 for the dichotomous case. Support for this relationship has been reported by Beach and Wise (1969), who concluded that certainty ratings "are essentially another . . . version of the subjective probability estimates" (p. 441). Once an object has been assigned to a given attribute category, the subject's certainty in his judgment is essentially equivalent to his subjective probability that the object belongs in that category.

Thus far we have discussed an individual's uncertainty associated with his response category. It is also possible to consider uncertainty associated with the entire set of response categories. Clearly, this overall uncertainty will be re-

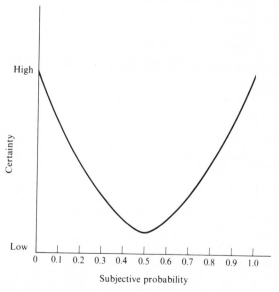

Fig. 3.7 Reaction between subjective probability and certainty.

lated to the subjective probabilities associated with each of the different response alternatives available to the subject. Consider, for example, a subject who rates "cornflakes" as *quite nutritious* on the following scale.

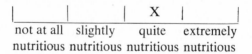

not at all   slightly   quite   extremely
nutritious nutritious nutritious nutritious

We saw previously that he can also be asked to indicate his subjective probability that "cornflakes are quite nutritious." The higher this probability, the more certain he should be that his judgment is correct.

In addition, the subject can also be asked to indicate his subjective probabilities that cornflakes are associated with each of the other three response categories, i.e., that cornflakes are not at all nutritious, slightly nutritious, and extremely nutritious. The subjective probabilities associated with the four attribute categories can now be used to compute an index of overall uncertainty with respect to this attribute dimension. Generally speaking, the lower the variability among these subjective probabilities (i.e., the more similar they are to each other), the higher is the person's overall uncertainty.[32] In our example, maximal uncertainty is expected when cornflakes are equally likely to be rated extremely, quite, slightly, or not at all nutritious. Minimal uncertainty is expected when the respondent's subjective probability that cornflakes belong in one of the four categories is 1.0 and that they belong in any of the other three categories is 0. Wyer (1973) has shown that overall uncertainty associated with an attribute dimension is related to the person's uncertainty with respect to his own position on the dimension. When a person believes that the object may be associated with any one of the attribute categories (high overall uncertainty), his certainty about his own preferred category tends to be low. However, this relation between overall uncertainty and position uncertainty may not hold for any position other than the person's own. For example, a person whose overall uncertainty is moderate may assign a low probability to one of the content categories. With respect to the latter category, his position certainty might be quite high.

Belief confidence. Two persons who assign the same subjective probability to a given position on the content dimension may vary in their confidence associated with this probability estimate. It is thus possible to distinguish between position

---

32. More specifically, it is possible to use the information theory index of average uncertainty,

$$u = - \sum_{i=1}^{n} P_i \log_2 P_i,$$

where u is uncertainty, P_i is the subjective probability of response category i, and n is the number of response categories (cf. Wyer, 1973).

certainty and belief confidence.[33] Unlike position certainty, belief confidence may be unrelated to the subjective probability; that is, a person's belief confidence may be high or low irrespective of his subjective probability. However, it seems likely that belief confidence is related to stable individual difference variables. Thus some persons tend to be more confident in their beliefs than others. Some evidence indicating stable individual differences in belief confidence was provided by Ewing (1942).

Indifference. In addition to obtaining probability estimates for each response category, one can obtain evaluations of each category. To return to our example, subjects could be asked to rate "extremely nutritious," "quite nutritious," "slightly nutritious," and "not at all nutritious" on a *good–bad* scale.

The variance of the individual evaluations could be taken as one possible index of the person's *indifference*. When the alternative response categories are evaluated equally, the respondent may be said to be maximally indifferent to the attribute dimension in question (i.e., "nutritiousness" in the present example). Minimal indifference (or maximal concern) is indicated by a large variance of evaluations. Two persons with similar evaluations of a given attribute category may vary in terms of their indifference toward the attribute dimension. One interesting implication of these considerations concerns the effect of changing a person's location on a content dimension on his attitude toward the object of the belief. When the person is indifferent toward the attribute dimension, a change in belief from one content category to another may have little effect on his attitude.[34]

In sum, measures of beliefs and their associated evaluations can be supplemented by indices of position uncertainty, belief confidence, and indifference. As with other measures of cognitive structure, these indices may prove useful for an understanding of the effects of persuasive communications and other factors on the formation and change of beliefs, attitudes, and intentions.

All indices of cognitive structure discussed so far are based on measures of belief strength and attribute evaluations. The "own categories procedure" has

---

33. In statistical terms, belief confidence may be viewed as analogous to the confidence interval around a parameter estimate. Thus position certainty is equivalent to a probability judgment, and belief confidence refers to the confidence interval around this judgment.

34. The possibility of obtaining probability and evaluation ratings for each category on a content dimension again suggests that more than one $b \times e$ product can be computed for each content dimension. Earlier we considered the simplest case of a dichotomous dimension, and we saw that it is often necessary to consider probabilities and evaluations associated with both response categories. This notion can now be generalized to any number of response alternatives. It seems doubtful, however, that consideration of multiple categories would greatly increase the accuracy of attitude measurement. Further, there are obvious practical limitations to such an extension.

been used to derive a number of cognitive structure measures that do not rely on either of these two variables.

The Own Categories Procedure

On the basis of their work in social judgment, Sherif and Hovland (1961) questioned Thurstone's assumption that a judge's own attitude toward some object does not influence his judgments of the favorableness of statements concerning the object. Their attempts to demonstrate effects of attitudes on judgments eventually led to the development of an instrument known as the own categories procedure. Consistent with their expectations, Sherif and Hovland found that judgments of the favorableness of some statements were influenced by the judge's attitude. Specifically, judges with extreme attitudes rated some statements differently than did a random sample of judges. The practical implications of this phenomenon for Thurstone scaling, however, are relatively minor since the scale values used for computing attitude scores are based on a sample of judges representative of the population to be studied. Further, even when shifts in scale values do occur, they are relatively small.

In analyzing the responses of judges with extreme attitudes, Sherif & Hovland found that these judges made differential use of the response categories. Although all extreme judges tended to place relatively few items into neutral categories, judges with extremely positive attitudes placed a disproportionate number of items into unfavorable categories, and judges with extremely negative attitudes placed a disproportionate number of items into favorable categories. It thus appeared that involved subjects (with extreme attitudes) tended to use fewer categories than noninvolved subjects. The own categories procedure is based on this premise and has been used primarily to measure involvement with some attitude object or issue.

Instead of being asked to sort statements into 11 categories, the respondent is simply asked to "sort the pool of items into any number of piles, or categories, that seem to him necessary, so that items within each category seem to him to 'belong together' . . . he is told to place the items into categories as objectively as possible in terms of how 'favorable' or 'unfavorable' they are toward the persons, events, issues, or objects in question" (Sherif and Sherif, 1967, pp. 190–191). The number of categories used is taken as a measure of involvement; the fewer the categories, the greater the involvement. According to Sherif and Sherif, the number of items in each category can be used as an index of category width.

After they have sorted items into piles, subjects can be asked to indicate (a) the pile which comes closest to their own view of the object or issue (most acceptable pile), (b) other piles containing acceptable statements, (c) the pile which is most objectionable from their point of view (most objectionable pile), and (d) other piles containing objectionable statements. The number of statements in all acceptable piles is taken as a measure of the subject's *latitude of acceptance;*

the number of statements in all objectionable piles constitutes a measure of *latitude of rejection;* and the number of remaining items defines the *latitude of noncommitment.*

When Thurstone scale values are available for items used in the own categories procedure, the person's attitude is usually determined by averaging the scale values of all items in the most acceptable category. For all practical purposes, this attitude score is the same as a traditional Thurstone attitude score. Latitudes of acceptance, rejection, and noncommitment can now be defined in terms of the range of scale values in these regions.

A more direct procedure for obtaining measures of a person's latitudes of acceptance, rejection, and noncommitment involves use of an ordered set of items or any other representation of an evaluative dimension (Sherif, Sherif, and Nebergall, 1965; Sereno and Mortensen, 1969). Subjects are asked to check the most acceptable item or position on the scale,[35] other acceptable positions, the most objectionable position, and other objectionable positions.

We can see, then, that the own categories procedure is primarily a measure of involvement but also provides various indices of cognitive structure. Although it can be used to measure attitude, its primary impact has been in the area of persuasive communications (see Chapter 11), where the notion of latitudes has been used to explain differential effects of communications on subjects with the same attitude scores.

CONCLUSION

This chapter has reviewed some of the techniques used to measure beliefs, attitudes, and intentions. We have tried to show that all measurement ultimately rests on responses to single statements of belief or intention. The standard attitude-scaling methods use such responses to infer the person's location on a bipolar affective dimension vis-à-vis the object in question. Consistent with our definition of attitude, all traditional measurement techniques—whether direct, disguised, or physiological—attempt to arrive at a single attitude score which represents the person's evaluation of the attitude object. Standard attitude scaling is designed to select a set of beliefs or intentional statements which can be used to measure a person's attitude. Responses to these statements indicate strength of beliefs or intentions, and certain assumptions are made about associated attribute evaluations. Consistent with our expectancy-value model of attitude, the attitude score is based on these two pieces of information.

Measures of belief strength and attribute evaluations can also be used to arrive at various indices of cognitive structure. However, only few attempts have been made to develop and validate such measures of cognitive structure. Most

---

35. This response can be used as a measure of the person's attitude.

work on measurement techniques has concentrated on attitude, and relatively little attention has been paid to beliefs or intentions. Nevertheless, we have seen that techniques are available for the measurement of all three concepts. The next chapter will show that these techniques provide reliable and valid measures of beliefs, attitudes, and intentions.

Chapter 4

Methodological Considerations

In the preceding chapters we have argued that, although interrelated, beliefs, attitudes, and intentions are conceptually distinct concepts which must be independently assessed. In the first part of this chapter we will try to show that available techniques for measuring each of these variables are reliable and have both convergent and discriminant validity. This discussion will be followed by a consideration of more general methodological problems of experimentation in the attitude area.

RELIABILITY AND VALIDITY OF MEASUREMENT

The concepts of reliability and validity concern the degree to which the measuring instrument is free of measurement error. In Chapter 3 we mentioned that an observed score can be viewed as composed of a "true" score and some measurement error. The error component can be further divided into two parts: variable or random error and constant error. This model is presented in Eq. 4.1,

$$x_i = t_i + e_r + e_c,$$ (4.1)

where x_i is the observed score; t_i is the "true" score; e_r is the variable error; and e_c is the constant error.

Reliability refers to the degree to which a measure is free of variable error. Thus, if we assume that the "true" score remains constant (e.g., that the person's "true" attitude has not changed), a perfectly reliable instrument will yield the same results on different occasions. Variable factors, such as the person's mood, the temperature or other weather factors, the testing situation, etc., may have different effects on responses on different occasions, thereby reducing the instrument's reliability. Needless to say, the lower the reliability of some measuring instrument, the less useful it is.

Validity refers to the degree to which an instrument measures the "true" score it was designed to measure—in the present context, the degree to which it measures a given belief, attitude, or intention rather than some other variable. Clearly, the presence of constant error will reduce a measure's validity since the observed score will be consistently contaminated by some irrelevant factor.

One potential source of constant errors is response biases and response sets (Cronbach, 1946, 1950; Guilford, 1954; Scott, 1968). For example, subjects may differ in the extent to which they tend to agree with statements (acquiesce), to give socially desirable responses, and to use extreme or moderate response categories. It should be obvious that when a subject's responses do not reflect his personal beliefs (i.e., the "true" score) but rather reflect his perception of what is socially desirable, the observed score will not be an adequate measure of the true score. Recall that one purpose of most standard scaling methods is to eliminate items to which subjects respond on the basis of variables other than their attitudes. However, these standard techniques may not always succeed in arriving at an instrument that is free of response biases. Guilford (1954), A. L. Edwards (1957), and Scott (1968) have discussed various means by which it is possible to reduce the effects of such biases.

Reliability

There is abundant evidence that standard attitude scales are highly reliable, yielding comparable results when administered on different occasions. Shaw and Wright (1967) and Robinson and Shaver (1969) have reported reliability coefficients for a large variety of Likert, Thurstone, Guttman, and semantic differential scales. Reliabilities are generally very high.

That disguised techniques and physiological measures have tended to be much less reliable (cf. Kidder and Campbell, 1970) may account in part for the fact that investigators have hesitated to employ such techniques in their research.

The reliability of single-response measures varies considerably, depending on the particular judgment required of the subject. Osgood, Suci, and Tannenbaum (1957) have reported relatively high reliabilities for single seven-point bipolar scales used in the semantic differential. Thus responses to probabilistic scales of the semantic-differential type, such as *probable–improbable, likely–unlikely* tend to yield highly reliable measures of the strength of beliefs or intentions. For example, Davidson (1973) reported test-retest reliabilities greater than .95 for the *likely–unlikely* scale.

Clearly, it is possible to locate subjects on evaluative and probabilistic dimensions with a high degree of reliability. The question of reliability, therefore, does not pose a major problem for the measurement of beliefs, attitudes, and intentions when appropriate instruments are employed.

Convergent and Discriminant Validity

Attempts to assess the validity of a measuring instrument can take several forms. If an instrument is a valid measure of attitude toward some object, it should correlate highly with another valid measure of attitude toward the same object; that is, the two measures should exhibit *convergent* validity. The same should be true for two measures of a given belief or two measures of a given intention.

Although many investigators are content with establishing convergent validity, Campbell and Fiske (1959) have argued that an instrument should also have *discriminant* validity. Clearly, two measures of the same concept may be highly correlated (i.e., have convergent validity), but the basis for the correlation may be the same constant error rather than the "true" score. To eliminate this possibility it must be shown that when the same method or instrument (e.g., the semantic differential or the Likert procedure) is used to measure different variables (e.g., attitudes toward different objects), different results are obtained.[1]

Convergent validity. One question to be raised is the degree to which different measures within a given conceptual category can be expected to yield equivalent results. As noted in Chapter 3, there is one and only one attitude toward a given object. In contrast, a multitude of beliefs and intentions can be specified with respect to the same object. Each belief about a given object links the object to a different concept and thus constitutes a different probability dimension. Similarly, each intention with respect to a given object also constitutes a different probability dimension. These probability dimensions link the individual to different actions with respect to the object. In terms of convergent validity, different measures of a given single dimension (evaluative or probabilistic) should yield comparable results. In contrast, convergent validity cannot be expected when two different probability dimensions or two different evaluative dimensions are assessed.

Consistent with these expectations, whenever investigators have obtained more than one measure of attitude toward the same object, the results were almost always identical. Evidence for the convergent validity of standard attitude scales has been available for some time. For example, Edwards and Kenney (1946) constructed Thurstone and Likert scales to measure attitudes toward the church. These different measures of the affective dimension were found to be highly correlated. Similarly, Osgood, Suci, and Tannenbaum (1957) compared their semantic differential measure of attitude toward crop rotation with a Guttman scale designed to measure attitudes toward the same object. Again, these two techniques yielded comparable results. In several studies, Byrne's (1966, 1971) two-item measure of interpersonal attraction was found to be related to standard attitude scales, such as the evaluative dimension of the semantic differential. Moreover, this index was also found to correlate with the seven-point *good–bad* scale. Ostrom

---

1. Of course, different results can be obtained only to the extent that the different "true" scores are unrelated or independent.

(1969) and Fishbein and Ajzen (1974) found that single self-report scales of attitude toward religiosity (e.g., "My attitude toward being religious is *extremely favorable–extremely unfavorable*") correlated highly with four traditional attitude scales (Thurstone, Guttman, Likert, and semantic differential scales).

There is abundant evidence, then, for the equivalence of different measures of attitude toward the same object. Recall that measures of beliefs and intentions locate an individual on dimensions of probability. The question must be raised whether different measures of a given probability dimension will also produce comparable results. Unfortunately, relatively few studies have obtained more than one measure of a given belief or a given intention. One reason for the relative lack of evidence for convergent validity of different measures of beliefs or intentions is that few attempts have been made to develop standard scaling procedures for these dimensions. Some findings of relevance come from studies by Fishbein and his associates. For example, Fishbein and Raven (1962) used semantic differential scales such as *probable–improbable, true–false, likely–unlikely, agree–disagree,* and *possible–impossible* to measure belief strength. Although most investigations have been concerned with the sum across such scales as a general index of belief, these scales have also proved to be highly intercorrelated. Thus ratings of a statement such as "Orientals are intelligent" on a *true–false* scale yields approximately the same results as ratings of the same statement on a *probable–improbable* scale.

Ajzen (1971a) obtained estimates of belief strength by asking such questions as "The chances are _____ in 100 that Student B is in favor of ending the nuclear arms race." In addition, such statements as "Student B is in favor of ending the nuclear arms race" were rated on four of Fishbein and Raven's (1962) probability scales mentioned above. The sum over the four scales was taken as one measure of belief and the quantitative estimate as a second. The two measures were found to correlate highly and to yield comparable results.

There is thus some evidence that different measures of the same belief are comparable. Since intentions also deal with probability dimensions, it is to be expected that this conclusion also holds for different measures of the same intention. Empirical support for the convergent validity of intentional measures was reported by Davidson (1973), who used *true–false* and *likely–unlikely* scales to assess a variety of family-planning intentions. For example, women's intentions to have two children in their completed families were measured first by one scale and later in the questionnaire by the second scale. The two measures yielded comparable results; convergent validity coefficients were approximately .90.

One may therefore conclude that different measures of a given dimension, whether it is evaluative or probabilistic, will tend to produce comparable results. However, different results may be obtained for measures of different dimensions. This is the problem of discriminant validity.

Discriminant validity. It seems hardly necessary to show that measures of *different* dimensions will tend to yield different results. As noted in Chapter 1, many studies have measured different beliefs, attitudes, and/or intentions and have obtained markedly different results for each measure. Responding in part to these inconsistent findings, we have suggested the distinctions between beliefs, attitudes, intentions, and behaviors. From our point of view, there is no reason to expect that measures of different dimensions, whether they are beliefs, attitudes, or intentions, will yield comparable results. To be sure, one dimension may be related to some other dimension, and thus similar results may sometimes be obtained. However, the relation between two different dimensions is an empirical question. It follows that one should usually be able to demonstrate a given instrument's discriminant validity by showing that it yields different results when applied to two or more different dimensions. For example, the Likert technique could be used to measure attitudes toward the *church* and toward *supersonic transports*. On the assumption that the "true" attitudes toward these two objects are unrelated, the instrument would have discriminant validity if the observed attitude scores were also found to be unrelated. However, different acquiescence tendencies (i.e., tendencies to agree with any statement) and other factors may result in a spurious correlation between the two attitudes.

The multitrait-multimethod matrix. Since the degree of reliability sets the upper limit for convergent validity, and since apparent discriminant validity may be merely the result of unreliability, Campbell and Fiske (1959) have suggested a procedure that allows simultaneous examination of reliability, convergent validity, and discriminant validity. This procedure is known as the *multitrait-multimethod matrix* analysis since it involves the measurement of at least two traits (or attitudes) by at least two methods. This analysis is based on the intercorrelation matrix of the different traits assessed by the different methods, as well as of the same traits measured by the same methods (i.e., reliabilities). A hypothetical multitrait-multimethod matrix is presented in Table 4.1, where perfect reliabilities and validities are assumed. The solid parallel lines are called the reliability diagonal since they contain correlations between the same measure of the same attitude taken on two different occasions.[2] The broken parallel lines are called the convergent validity diagonal; they contain correlations between two different measures of the same attitude. The solid triangles contain correlations between different attitudes measured by the same method, and the dotted triangles contain correlations between different attitudes measured by different methods.

Lack of perfect reliability would be indicated by coefficients below unity in the reliability diagonal. Similarly, lack of perfect convergent validity is shown by coefficients below unity in the convergent validity diagonal. Lack of perfect discriminant validity is indicated by correlations above 0 in the triangles of Table 4.1.[3]

---

2. Split-half or equivalent-forms reliability coefficients could also be entered in this diagonal.

3. The degree of discriminant validity has to be assessed on the basis of multiple comparisons between coefficients in the triangles and the diagonals. Interested readers are referred to Campbell and Fiske (1959).

Table 4.1 Hypothetical Multitrait-Multimethod Matrix with Perfect Reliabilities and Validities

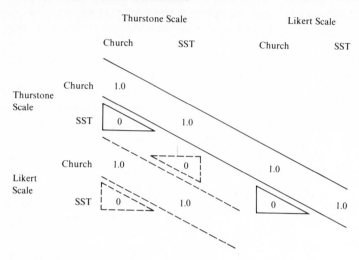

Note: Cell entries represent correlation coefficients.

Davidson (1973) has reported multitrait-multimethod analyses for measures of attitude and measures of intention. He demonstrated high reliabilities as well as considerable convergent and discriminant validities for his measures. Table 4.2 shows Davidson's multitrait-multimethod matrix for two measures of attitude, each assessing attitudes toward two different objects. The two methods were (1) a sum over three evaluative semantic differential scales and (2) a Guilford self-

Table 4.2 Multitrait-Multimethod Matrix for Attitude Measures (Adapted from Davidson, 1973)

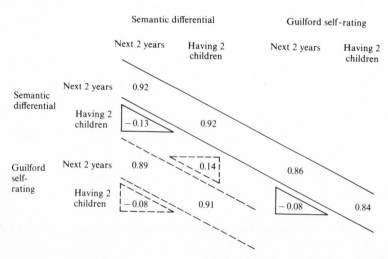

rating scale. The attitude objects were "having a child in the next two years" and "having two children in my completed family." A comparison of Table 4.2 with Table 4.1 shows the high reliabilities, convergent validities, and discriminant validities of the two attitude measures employed.[4]

Relation between Reliability and Validity

Equation 4.1 above indicates that a measure cannot be valid unless it is reliable; that is, in the presence of variable error, the observed score cannot be equivalent to the "true" score. The relationship between reliability and validity is expressed in Eq. 4.2, *Spearman's correction for attenuation*,

$$r_{xy} = r'_{xy} \sqrt{r_{xx'}} \sqrt{r_{yy'}}, \tag{4.2}$$

where r_{xy} is the observed convergent validity of measures x and y; r'_{xy} is the "true" convergent validity of measures x and y, assuming that these measures are perfectly reliable; $r_{xx'}$ is the observed reliability of measure x; and $r_{yy'}$ is the observed reliability of measure y.

With perfect reliabilities ($r_{xx'} = r_{yy'} = 1$), the observed convergent validity is equal to the "true" convergent validity ($r_{xy} = r'_{xy}$). As the reliability of either measure decreases, so does the observed convergent validity.

One factor that influences the reliability of a given attitude scale is the number of items on the scale. We mentioned in Chapter 3 that when the length of a scale is increased, random or variable errors will tend to cancel out across different items. This relationship between the number of items on a scale and its reliability is described by the *Spearman-Brown prophecy formula*, given in Eq. 4.3,

$$r'_{xx'} = \frac{mr_{xx'}}{1 + (m-1)r_{xx'}}, \tag{4.3}$$

where $r'_{xx'}$ is the estimate of the reliability of a scale m times as long as the original scale, and $r_{xx'}$ is the observed reliability of the original scale.

For example, consider a 20-item Likert scale with an observed reliability of .80. According to Eq. 4.3, if only one of these items was used as the measure of attitude, its reliability could be only .17 and the 20-item scale would still have a

---

4. Our discussion of convergent and discriminant validity has been concerned only with correlations between two or more measures of a given concept. Investigators have also attempted to validate attitude measures through known-group comparisons or by looking at the degree to which the measure is predictive of overt behavior. The known-group comparison method was described in Chapter 3. The problems involved in using a measure of attitude to predict overt behavior will be discussed in Chapter 8; at this point it is sufficient to note that both convergent and discriminant validities have to be assessed even when overt behavior is used as the criterion against which an attitude measure is to be validated.

reliability of .80.[5] Thus a single-item measure may be highly unreliable although a test made up of many such items may have considerable reliability.

This single-item measure of x could be correlated with some criterion y for purposes of validation. Assuming perfect "true" convergent validity (and perfect reliability of the criterion measure y), Eq. 4.2 indicates that the observed convergent validity would be equal to $\sqrt{r_{xx'}}$, the square root of the observed reliability of x. Since $\sqrt{.17} = .412$, the single-item measure would not be a good predictor of the criterion. In contrast, the 20-item scale would result in an observed convergent validity of $\sqrt{.80} = .894$.

These considerations point to some of the problems inherent in the widespread use of single-response measures in the attitude area, without independent evidence for their reliability. Clearly, many apparently conflicting findings may be due in part to the use of such unreliable and invalid measures. Conflicting findings, however, may be due not only to unreliable and invalid measurement but also to other methodological problems, including low validity of the experimental situation and improper data analyses. Some of these problems will be considered in the remainder of this chapter.

INTERNAL AND EXTERNAL VALIDITY OF RESEARCH DESIGNS

The basic purpose of an empirical investigation is to further our understanding of some phenomenon. Ideally, an investigator starts out with a theoretical network of interrelated constructs from which several hypotheses concerning a given phenomenon can be deduced. He then attempts to test these hypotheses empirically in order to support his theory. When a given hypothesis is repeatedly disconfirmed, he modifies his theory to take account of the data.

Two primary research methods can be distinguished: the *correlational* method and the *experimental* method (Cronbach, 1957). The former approach is largely descriptive; investigators examine the covariation of different variables, compare different groups with respect to one or more variables, look for dimensions underlying sets of responses, etc. For example, the correlational approach could be used to further our understanding of religious behavior. It would be possible to correlate church attendance with various demographic variables, such as age, sex, religious preference, and social status, or with attitudes toward the church, toward God, toward the Bible, etc. Similar information could be obtained by comparing persons who attend church with those who do not on each of these variables.

Alternatively, it would be possible to observe a large number of religious behaviors (e.g., church attendance, donation of money to a religious institution, tak-

---

5. This can be seen in the following computation:

$$r'_{xx'} = \frac{1/20(.80)}{1 + (1/20 - 1).80} = \frac{.04}{1 - .76} = .17.$$

ing Bible classes, etc.) and to perform a factor analysis in an attempt to determine the dimensions that underlie these behaviors.

The most characteristic feature of the correlational approach, therefore, is its reliance on existing variation. In contrast, the experimental approach creates variation by manipulating one or more variables and examines the effect of the manipulation (the independent variable) on some response measure (the dependent variable). In the correlational approach one merely obtains an index of the relationship between attitude toward the church and church attendance; the correlation between these variables is based on preexisting individual differences in attitudes and in church attendance. Clearly, a causal effect of attitude on church attendance could not be inferred since an observed relationship between these variables could also be the result of church attendance causing the attitude. Moreover, the relationship may also be a function of a third variable (e.g., belief in God) to which both attitude and church attendance are related.[6]

Internal Validity

Causal inferences, however, are the main objective in the experimental method. For example, one could manipulate attitude toward the church and observe the effects of this manipulation on church attendance. The most characteristic feature of the experimental method, therefore, is the experimenter's control over the independent variable or variables. However, the demonstration that a manipulation of attitude is accompanied by a change in church attendance is not sufficient evidence for inferring a causal relation. Care must be taken to ensure that the observed effects on church attendance are indeed attributable to the manipulation of attitude and not to some other uncontrolled variable. The term *internal validity* has been used for the degree to which an experimental design is free from such uncontrolled factors—that is, the degree to which changes in the dependent variable can be confidently attributed to the experimental manipulations and only to the experimental manipulations. High internal validity, therefore, eliminates possible alternative explanations of the observed effects (D. T. Campbell, 1957).

Indeed, in the design of an experiment, emphasis has usually been placed on ensuring a high degree of internal validity in order to eliminate alternative explanations and to allow causal inferences to be made. Campbell (1957) and Campbell and Stanley (1963) have discussed a number of factors that may impair the internal validity of an experimental design and have suggested ways to avoid these difficulties.

Consider, for example, an experiment in which attitude toward some product x is measured five weeks before and immediately after exposure to a commercial advertising the product. Imagine that the mean attitude of subjects after exposure is significantly more positive than before exposure. Clearly, this effect may be

---

6. It is a well-known fact that the amount of damage observed at a fire increases with the number of firemen present. Clearly, this relationship is not a causal one; rather, it is the result of a third variable, the size of the fire.

attributable to factors other than the experimental manipulation (i.e., exposure to the commercial). One uncontrolled factor is the possible effect that taking the pretest may have on posttest responses; the pretest itself may have provided new information about product x, it may have made the subjects familiar with the brand name, etc. Another possibility is the occurrence of uncontrolled events in the interval between pretest and posttest. Some subjects may have used the product in the meantime (perhaps because the pretest made them aware of it) and they may have liked it; they may have been exposed to other ads in the interval or obtained additional information about the product, etc. Obviously, each of these factors constitutes a potential alternative to the explanation that the change in attitude was produced by the commercial.

The simplest way to deal with these uncontrolled factors is to add a group of subjects who are not exposed to the commercial but whose attitudes are measured at the same points in time. Subjects should be assigned at random into experimental and control groups. This procedure reduces the likelihood of systematic differences between the groups. The uncontrolled factors discussed above should therefore be as likely to occur in the control group as in the experimental group. One can conclude that the commercial had an effect on attitudes toward product x only if the change (from pretest to posttest) in the experimental group is significantly greater than the change in the control group.

Internal validity requires that an observed effect be attributed *solely* to a given manipulation. That is, it must also be shown that the effect cannot be attributed to any factor other than the manipulation. In the example above, use of a control group does not eliminate the possibility that the commercial had an effect only because subjects were pretested. Even though the experimental group may have changed significantly more than the control group, the pretest may have interacted with the commercial to produce the change in attitude, and if a pretest had not been given, the commercial might not have led to a more favorable attitude in the experimental group than in the control group. For example, the pretest may have sensitized subjects to the subsequent commercial, increased their attention, and thereby enabled the commercial to produce a significant change in attitudes.[7]

This pretest-manipulation interaction can be avoided by eliminating the pretest in the experimental and control groups; effects of the manipulation are then assessed by comparing the posttest scores of the two groups. Assuming initial equivalence in attitudes produced by random assignment, a significant difference between experimental and control groups is attributable to the manipulation.

If it is desirable to assess the degree to which a pretest-manipulation interaction is operative in a given experiment, the Solomon Four-Group Design can be used. In this design, all four groups mentioned above are employed, i.e., two experimental groups (one with a pretest and one without it) and two control

---

7. Campbell and Stanley (1963) discussed this effect in the context of external validity, which will be considered below.

groups (with and without pretest). The interaction effect is tested by considering the posttest scores of the four groups. For a more complete discussion of this and other designs, see Campbell and Stanley (1963).

The notion of pretest-manipulation interactions suggests that the experimental manipulation might not have produced the observed effect in the absence of a pretest. Similarly, it has been argued that the observed effects of manipulations in any experimental setting are partly a function of the experimental setting itself. That is, the manipulation may interact with the experimental setting in producing the observed effect. For example, knowledge of taking part in an experiment may increase attention to the commercial or any other manipulation. Furthermore, the subjects may form beliefs about the purpose of the experiment or about the experimenter's expectations; their responses may then be in part a function of these beliefs rather than of the manipulation itself.

Phenomena of this kind, called *reactive effects,* have attracted increasing attention in recent years.[8] Whereas the pretest-manipulation interaction can be controlled for by an appropriate experimental design, little can be done to reduce reactive effects in most experimental settings. Indeed, most research on reactivity has attempted to *demonstrate* the operation of these effects in various experimental settings (e.g., Orne, 1962; Rosenthal, 1966; Rosenthal and Rosnow, 1969; Page, 1969, 1970a) rather than to eliminate them.

We shall consider these reactive effects in greater detail below. First, however, the reader should realize that the hypothetical experiment discussed earlier (even if internally valid) would permit only the conclusion that the commercial had an effect on attitudes. Little could be said as to which aspects of the commercial produced the change. Thus, the investigator might assume that the *information* about product x provided in the commercial was responsible for the effect, but in reality the change might have been brought about by *any* commercial irrespective of the kind or amount of information it contained. To test the hypothesis concerning effects of information about product x would require a different experiment involving additional manipulations. Specifically, the kind and amount of information about product x contained in the commercial would have to be systematically manipulated.

Laboratory versus field studies. It has often been argued that field studies provide mainly descriptive data and laboratory studies are more analytical and yield data about causal relationships. Generally speaking, this has indeed been true since most field studies have used the correlational method whereas the majority of laboratory studies have used the experimental method. However, there is no necessary relationship between a research setting and a research method. Thus the correlational method has frequently been employed in laboratory studies, and there is a growing interest in using the experimental method in field research.

---

8. Reactive effects were also treated in the context of external validity by Campbell and Stanley (1963).

Campbell and Stanley (1963) have discussed a number of "quasi-experimental" designs that ensure maximal internal validity in a variety of field settings.

It has also been argued that although field studies have lower internal validity than laboratory studies, their findings are more generalizable than findings obtained in the laboratory. Again, however, there is no necessary relation between generalizability and research setting. Campbell and Stanley have discussed the problem of generalizing experimental (as opposed to correlational) findings under the heading of external validity of experimental designs.

External Validity

Campbell (1957) has argued that an experiment must have not only internal validity but also generalizability or external validity. That is, "to what populations, settings, treatment variables, and measurement variables can this effect be generalized?" (Campbell and Stanley, 1963, p. 5). Clearly, these questions can be asked of any research, whether correlational or experimental, conducted in the field or in the laboratory.

Generalizing across populations. The prevalent use of college students in social-psychological research has always been a major focus of criticism on the grounds that college students are not representative of the general population. Similarly, it may be argued that research findings cannot be generalized from one culture or subculture to another.

Lack of generalizability constitutes a serious problem when the purpose of the research is primarily descriptive. Thus permissive attitudes toward use of marijuana found among college students may not be generalizable to other populations. However, when psychological processes, theories, or lawful relationships are under investigation, generalization across populations may be less problematic (cf. Kruglanski, 1973; in press). For example, although college students may have more favorable attitudes toward using marijuana than, say, law enforcement officers or union members, one may argue that the formation and change of these attitudes obey the same laws for all subject populations. Specifically, attitude toward marijuana use may always be found to be a function of beliefs about the consequences of using marijuana and the evaluation of those consequences.

Since the major purpose of most experimental investigations that use college students is to discover lawful processes (rather than to provide descriptive accounts of the research population), the concerns with problems of generalization across populations may have been exaggerated. This is not to say that the problem can be ignored in experimental investigations, since different psychological processes may be operating in different populations or cultures. Empirical evidence to date, however, indicates that most psychological processes are generalizable across different subject populations (Byrne, 1971; Triandis, Malpass, and Davidson, 1972).

Problems of generalizing to different populations also arise when manipulations interact with other aspects of the experimental situation. One possibility is the pretest-manipulation interaction previously discussed under the heading of internal validity. Campbell (1957) has treated this interaction effect in the context of external validity since he interpreted it as preventing generalization of a finding from a pretested population to a nonpretested population.

Another possibility, also mentioned above, is reactive effects which may be interpreted as reducing the generalizability of findings from experimental subjects (aware that their responses are being observed) to nonexperimental populations. Reactive effects, however, are often viewed as impairing generalizability from an experimental *setting* to a nonexperimental setting (Campbell, 1957).

Generalizing across settings: Reactive effects. Specific research findings may not be generalizable from one setting to another. For example, Minard (1952) examined discriminatory behavior of white coal miners in Pocahontas County, Pennsylvania. He found that although 80 percent of the white miners were friendly toward blacks in the mine, only 20 percent were friendly in town. The conclusion that whites discriminate against blacks, therefore, cannot be generalized from the town to the mine.[9] Again, however, the processes underlying discriminatory or nondiscriminatory behavior may be the same in both settings, and hence the problem of generalizing across settings may be less severe in studies investigating psychological processes.

A more important problem arises when the research setting interacts with the experimental manipulation to produce the observed effects, i.e., when reactive effects are present.[10] Reactive effects have been discussed under the labels of *demand characteristics* (Orne, 1962, 1969), *experimenter bias* (Rosenthal, 1966), and *evaluation apprehension* (M. J. Rosenberg, 1965b, 1969). Orne (1962, p. 778) described reactive effects as follows: "At some level [the subject] sees it as his task to ascertain the true purpose of the experiment and respond in a manner which will support the hypotheses being tested. Viewed in this light, the totality of cues which convey an experimental hypothesis to the subject becomes significant determinants of subjects' behavior." Orne called the sum total of these cues the "demand characteristics of the experimental situation."

For example, subjects may come to believe that one purpose of the experiment is to evaluate their emotional stability, intelligence, or mental health. Rosenberg (1965b) has argued that subjects who form such beliefs will try to behave in the experiment in a manner they think will win the experimenter's approval. He called this phenomenon "evaluation apprehension."

Cues that may allow the subject to form beliefs about the purpose of the ex-

---

9. The same problem exists when attempts are made to generalize specific findings over time; attitudes or behavioral patterns will tend to change over time.

10. Reactive effects are usually viewed as responses to the total experimental situation, including the experimental manipulation. Alternative explanations attributing the observed effects to aspects other than the experimental manipulation, however, can be ruled out by using an appropriate control group. The crucial reactive effects, therefore, are those produced by the manipulation-setting interaction.

periment, as well as beliefs about the experimenter's expectations, may be provided by the experimenter's behavior; Rosenthal (1966) has called this phenomenon "experimenter bias" effects. Other cues are provided by the situation itself. "For example, if a test is given twice with some intervening treatment, even the dullest college student is aware that some change is expected, particularly if the test is in some obvious way related to the treatment" (Orne, 1962, p. 779). The situational cues may be more subtle; Glinski, Glinski, and Slatin (1970), for example, found that a subject was more likely to believe that the experiment was concerned with persuasion when he was faced with unanimous opposition from a group than when at least one member of the group agreed with his position.

The social psychology of the psychological experiment. The various reactive effects are related to three broad processes: (a) The subject forms hypotheses to explain the sequence of experimental events that he observes. The hypotheses may be related to the purpose of the experiment or to contingencies between his own behavior and other events. (b) He forms beliefs that the experimenter expects or would like him to behave in certain ways. (c) He is or is not willing to meet the perceived expectations of the experimenter.

There seems to be little doubt that experimental manipulations may affect hypotheses that are being formed about the purpose of the experiment (Page, 1969, 1970; Silverman and Regula, 1968). For example, as mentioned above, variations in the unanimity of disagreeing majorities in a conformity situation were found to influence subjects' beliefs that the experiment was concerned with persuasion (Glinski, Glinski, and Slatin, 1970).

Evidence from verbal conditioning experiments indicates that subjects also form hypotheses about the contingencies between their own behavior and reinforcing events (Dulany, 1968; Page, 1969). Thus subjects may form the hypothesis that whenever they start a sentence with "I" or "We," a certain event occurs (e.g., a light appears or the experimenter says "good").

There is also abundant evidence for experimenter bias effects (e.g., Barber and Silver, 1968a, 1968b; Rosenthal, 1968; Rosenthal and Rosnow, 1969). In a series of experiments by Rosenthal and his associates, subjects were shown ten photographs of faces and were asked to rate the degree of success or failure shown in the face of each person. The task was administered by student experimenters, who were told either that subjects tend to rate the faces as expressing success or that subjects tend to rate them as expressing failure. The students were further told that the experiment's purpose was to "see how well they could duplicate experimental results which were already well established" (Rosenthal, 1969, pp. 223–225). Rosenthal found that experimenters tend to get results consistent with their expectations.

It can thus be argued that the experimenter's bias provides the subject with cues as to what is expected of him. A controversy has developed around the ease with which these biases can be communicated to the subject. Available evidence indicates that they are not likely to occur unless there is an intentional influence attempt by the experimenter (Barber and Silver, 1968a, 1968b; Gallo and Dale, 1968). Such intentional influence attempts are likely to occur in Rosenthal's experimental paradigm described above.

Finally, evidence suggests that the experimental setting itself can influence a subject's willingness to perform what he perceives is expected of him. For example, when evaluation apprehension is produced by the experiment, subjects will tend to respond in a direction of favorable self-presentation, whether this is consistent or inconsistent with their perceptions of the experimenter's expectations (e.g., Silverman and Shulman, 1970).

A number of factors have been found to influence the effects above. Volunteering may increase the likelihood of belief formation and of motivation to meet the experimenter's perceived expectations (Horowitz, 1969; Rosnow and Suls, 1970). Differences in overall suspicion may affect reactions to the experiment (Stricker, Messick, and Jackson, 1969), as may use of a pretest (Rosnow and Suls, 1970). Similarly, variables that may be related to the subjects' sophistication (e.g., previous experience in experiments, knowledge of psychology, time of semester at which the experiment is conducted) have influenced obtained results (Holmes and Appelbaum, 1970). None of the factors discussed, however, has consistently produced significant results; contradictory findings are to be expected since different experimental settings may vary in the extent to which they allow beliefs and hypotheses to be formed. (Extensive reviews of this literature can be found in Rosenthal and Rosnow, 1969; Weber and Cook, 1972; A. G. Miller, 1972; and Kruglanski, in press.)

Demand characteristics, evaluation apprehension, experimenter bias, etc., have typically been viewed as variables that affect behavior only in research settings. It has therefore been argued that research findings cannot be generalized to other settings. However, we mentioned earlier that reactive effects involve the formation of beliefs about the situation, about the consequences of behavior, and about the expectations of other people, and further that they may be related to the subject's willingness or motivation to meet those expectations. Since the same processes are likely to operate in any situation, reactive effects in an experiment can be viewed as specific instances of the kinds of variables that influence behavior in general. In contrast to the notion that experimental settings are atypical, therefore, one could argue that they are actually quite representative of most real-life situations.

These considerations suggest that subjects, like other human beings, are conscious, active, intelligent organisms who react to the total situation in which they find themselves. It is therefore virtually impossible to study the effects of some manipulation in isolation from the beliefs and hypotheses that subjects form about the situation. To return to the question of internal validity, perfect internal validity appears to be an unobtainable goal in research on human subjects, since it is impossible to ascertain the pure or "true" effect of the experimental manipulation on some dependent variable. The subject's perception and interpretation of the total situation may always interact with the manipulation and thus "contaminate" the effect of the latter.

Acceptance of the conclusion that "reactive effects" are an inevitable part of experimental settings and, for that matter, of any other setting suggests that an alternative research strategy is called for. Research to date has attempted either to demonstrate the operation of reactive effects (e.g., Orne, 1962; Page, 1969, 1970; Page and Scheidt, 1971; Rosenthal, 1966) or to minimize their "detrimental" impacts (Rosenberg, 1965b). It appears that little can be gained from this line of research on reactive effects. In order to increase our understanding of the ways in which an experimental manipulation affects some dependent variable, it seems necessary to consider the manipulation within a broader frame of reference. Specifically, research should be directed at investigating the formation of beliefs about behavioral contingencies, about the purpose of the experiment, and about expectations of other people, and at the determinants of the person's motivation to meet those expectations, etc. In the context of an experimental setting, these variables may be influenced by many factors, including the experimental manipulation; differences between experimental and control groups are expected only when the manipulation influences one or more of the variables.

Consistent with this reasoning, Page's (1969, 1970) attempts to demonstrate the operation of demand characteristics have shown that in many studies, experimental manipulations affect the dependent variables by influencing one or more of the following (intervening) variables: *contingency awareness, demand awareness,* and *motivation to comply.* The first variable is the subject's awareness of the relationships between his own behavior in the experiment and the occurrence of certain (reinforcing) events. This kind of awareness has been investigated primarily in studies of verbal conditioning. Demand awareness is the subject's awareness of the experimenter's hypothesis and expectations. The third variable is the subject's motivation to behave in accordance with the experimenter's hypothesis.

Although Page has not employed his analysis beyond attempts to demonstrate the operation of demand characteristics, Dulany (1961, 1968) had previously employed similar constructs to deal with questions of awareness in studies of verbal conditioning. More important, these variables were developed as part of a more general theory that can be used to predict behavior in experimental as well as nonexperimental settings. This theory and some of its implications for the attitude area will be discussed in Chapter 7.

In conclusion, although there is little doubt that various reactive effects are operating in experimental settings, it appears that these effects need not seriously impair generalizability of experimental findings to nonexperimental settings, since similar "reactive effects" influence behavior in the latter settings. So long as the investigation is concerned with psychological processes (rather than with descriptive accounts of phenomena), it appears possible to generalize from one setting to another.

Generalizing across measurement variables. There is little disagreement that the effect of a manipulation on a dependent measure x may not be generalizable to a totally different dependent measure y. For example, manipulation of physical effort expended during a 15-minute period may influence consumption of milk, but the effect would hardly be generalizable to consumption of a bitter quinine solution.

In Chapter 1 we showed that one serious problem in attitude research is the practice of unwarranted generalization across different measurement variables. For example, the generalization that "communicator credibility affects attitude change" is comparable to the generalization that "physical effort influences consumption of liquids." Just as a distinction has to be made between milk, quinine solutions, and other liquids, a distinction has to be made between different attitudes, such as attitude toward the church, toward marijuana, toward a political candidate, etc. Further, just as the effects of physical effort on consumption of milk cannot be generalized to consumption of horse meat, the effects of communicator credibility on attitude toward marijuana cannot be generalized to the belief that marijuana is produced in South America or to the intention to sell marijuana.

In contrast, it should be possible to generalize across different measures of the *same* belief, the *same* attitude, or the *same* intention. One major problem in attitude research, then, is not so much the question of generalizing across different measurement variables as the failure to distinguish between different variables and the concomitant view that experimental effects should hold for any measure that is labeled "attitude."

Generalizing across treatment variables. Up to this point we have focused attention on the problems of measuring and distinguishing between different dependent variables relevant to attitude research. Similar problems can be identified with respect to experimental manipulations or treatments, i.e., the independent variables. Different noncorrelated operationalizations can be found for the same concept, and the identical operation is often given different conceptual labels. For example, "distraction" has often been manipulated by delayed voice feedback, performance of an irrelevant task, noise, visual displays, anticipation of a noxious experience, etc. At other times, the same manipulations have been labeled effort, fear, stress, and arousal. Such practices are likely to result in what appear to be inconsistent findings. For example, two studies (Friedman, Buck, and Allen, 1970; Hendrick and Shaffer, 1970) investigated the effects of "arousal" in a communication and persuasion paradigm and reported contradictory results. Closer inspection reveals, however, that one study was concerned with the effects of a drug (epinephrin), and the other considered the volume of a recorded persuasive message. Although it is true that multiple operations of a given concept may increase the generality of a conclusion beyond the specific details of any one experiment, frequent reports of inconsistencies point to the possibility that the different manipulations (even when given the same label) are far from equivalent. It follows that different manipulations may constitute operationalizations of different independent variables. Thus, as with dependent measures, the problem is not so much a question of generalizing across different manipulations of the same variable as the failure to distinguish between different kinds of independent variables.

Recapitulation

The experimental method has typically been viewed as characteristic of laboratory research whereas field research has generally been considered correlational in nature. We have pointed out, however, that there is no necessary relation between research method and research setting. The question of internal validity is relevant only in the context of the experimental method, since it is here that causal inferences are being made; the question of external validity, however, applies equally to experimental and correlational methods. It has frequently been argued that laboratory research has higher internal but lower external validity than field research. We have noted, however, that the experimental method can be applied in field research, thus increasing internal validity.

With respect to external validity, a distinction has to be made between generalization of specific descriptive research findings and generalization of psychological laws or processes. There is little doubt that descriptive research findings may not be generalizable across different populations or across different settings. Since field studies tend to employ more representative populations and settings, descriptive results obtained in such studies will have greater external validity than will descriptive laboratory findings. However, when the investigation is concerned with psychological processes rather than description, generalizations across populations or settings are possible to the same extent in laboratory and field research. We have argued that such generalizations will frequently be justifiable.

Finally, we have tried to show that attitude research is characterized by overgeneralization across and failure to distinguish between different treatment variables and different measurement variables. Thus widely different operations are used to manipulate a given conceptual independent variable. Clearly, this practice is desirable only if different operations produce the same results; unfortunately, investigators have continued to use the same conceptual labels for different operations, even when these operations have led to contradictory results. As we have shown in previous chapters, the same conclusion can be reached with respect to conceptual dependent variables, since a wide variety of different measures have all been given the same label, "attitude." Clearly, then, in order to resolve apparent inconsistencies in the attitude area, greater attention must be paid to the labels that are associated with different manipulations and with different measures.

Data Analysis and Interpretation

Another problem that may be responsible for some of the conflicting findings is related to the analysis and interpretation of data. One cannot fail to be impressed by the widespread mistreatment of data, abuse of statistical procedures, and the frequency with which invalid conclusions are drawn in attitude research. A complete discussion of these problems is beyond the scope of this book, but some general comments are in order. For an excellent discussion and some examples of problems of data analysis and interpretation in one area of investigation, the reader is directed to the exchange between Barber and Silver (1968a, 1968b) and Rosenthal (1968).

Let us return to the hypothetical attitude-change experiment in which an experimenter pretests two groups of subjects, exposes one to a commercial, and posttests both groups. Assume that the attitude measure is always a single seven-point evaluative *good–bad* scale. First, note that the obtained data can be scored in a variety of ways. It is possible to compute pretest means and posttest means for each group; to compute pre- to posttest change scores for each subject and obtain the average change score for each group; to simply count the number of subjects changing in a positive or negative direction in each group; to compute the proportion of subjects changing in a positive direction in each group; to rank-order the subjects in each group in terms of their pretest, posttest or change scores; etc. Clearly, statistical analyses based on these different scores may yield different results. For example, a significant difference may be found between experimental and control groups in terms of proportion of subjects changing their attitudes in a positive direction, but the average amount of change may not differ significantly. Thus, just as it is important to pay attention to differences in manipulations and measuring instruments, so it is important to realize that different indices (e.g., of attitude change) based on the same data may not be comparable.

Different tests of significance applied to a given set of data may also yield different results. In part, this circumstance may be attributable to the fact that different significance tests often require different indices. (For example, some tests are based on means, others on ranks or proportions.)

Another problem is that many studies published in the attitude literature are presented as supporting the researcher's hypotheses when either the results obtained fail to reach acceptable levels of statistical significance by some small margin or they are not significant in one statistical analysis but are shown to be significant in another. When the findings of a study are close to being significant, the investigator may simply discuss the effects as if they were significant, pointing to differences between groups that are in the expected directions. The American Psychological Association *Publication Manual* specifically cautions against "inferring trends from data which fail by a small margin to meet the level of significance adopted. Such results are most economically interpreted as a function of chance and should be reported as non-significant." Although we are aware that the five percent significance level is an arbitrary convention, its utility is evidenced by the literature. Much contradiction and controversy might have been avoided if findings not reaching this criterion had been rejected.[11]

---

11. In addition to observing the requirement of a minimum level of significance, research reports would be more useful if they also included estimates of the percent of variance accounted for by the experimental effects.

A similar suggestion is that significant results obtained on the same set of data by one statistical analysis but not another should also be interpreted as a function of chance and should lead to the rejection of the hypothesis unless the different analyses were initially predicted to yield different results.[12]

CONCLUSION

This chapter has dealt with a number of methodological issues that are of importance in attitude research. We have discussed reliability and validity of measurement techniques as well as problems of internal and external validity of research designs; we have pointed out that attention must be paid to the exact nature of independent and dependent variables; and we have considered some of the problems in data analysis and their interpretation. We have seen that beliefs, attitudes, and intentions can be empirically distinguished and that reliable and valid techniques for measuring these concepts are available. Results obtained with respect to a given dependent variable may not generalize to some other variable, and different manipulations of a given independent variable may also lead to apparently conflicting findings, since they may actually be operationalizations of different variables. The question of generalization across populations or settings was seen to be of greater relevance to descriptive research than to theory- or process-oriented investigations.

To justify the proposed distinction between beliefs, attitudes, intentions, and behaviors, it is necessary to demonstrate that different laws apply to these concepts. That is, it must be shown that different factors influence these variables or that they are differentially related to other variables. In Chapter 1 we outlined a conceptual framework of the relationships between beliefs, attitudes, intentions, and behaviors. The remainder of this book examines empirical research in the attitude area. We shall see that much of the research deals with the relations between beliefs, attitudes, intentions, and behaviors and with the effects of various factors on these variables.

Earlier in this chapter we suggested that the effects of a given event or manipulation on a given dependent measure can be understood only in terms of a larger frame of reference involving the person's interpretation of the event. In the

---

12. Unfortunately, for the purpose of salvaging a nonsignificant experiment, data are often manipulated until a significant result is obtained. In addition to shifting to another (and usually weaker) statistical test or transforming the dependent variables, the investigator can often accomplish this goal post hoc by combining conditions, subdividing the sample and performing internal analyses, shifting from a two-tailed to a one-tailed test of significance, etc. Although some of these practices may serve an exploratory purpose and provide ideas for future research, they do not provide conclusive evidence for a hypothesis, and the obtained results are best interpreted as a function of chance. For an excellent discussion of the use of many of these techniques, the reader is directed to the exchange between Barber and Silver (1968a, 1968b) and Rosenthal (1968) on experimenter bias effects.

framework of our conceptual system, this implies that a person exposed to some stimulus situation will form beliefs about it. The beliefs themselves can serve as a focus of research. For example, an investigator may vary the frequency with which he rewards different subjects for producing response x. He can then obtain a measure of the subjective probability (i.e., belief) that response x leads to obtaining the reward. Thus the subject forms beliefs that are descriptive of the stimulus situation to which he is exposed.

Usually, however, an investigator is less interested in these descriptive beliefs than in the effects of the stimulus situation and particularly his manipulation on some other belief, attitude, intention, or behavior. For example, he may be interested in the effects of the reinforcement schedule on the subject's belief that the experimenter expects him to perform response x; he may be interested in the subject's attitude toward the person who administered the rewards; in the subject's intention to help the experimenter in a future study; or in the actual frequency with which behavior x is performed by the subject.

Our conceptual framework suggests that all these effects are mediated by the different descriptive beliefs formed in the situation. Specifically, given the belief that behavior x leads to reward, the subject may infer that the experimenter expects him to perform the behavior. He may also infer that the experimenter is honest; in conjunction with other descriptive and inferential beliefs about the experimenter, the belief concerning honesty may influence the subject's attitude toward the experimenter. In a similar fashion, the different descriptive beliefs can mediate intentions and behaviors.

Thus, according to our conceptual framework, the effects of any given stimulus variable on a response are mediated by processes within the organism. In studying the effects of a commercial about product x, for example, the investigator may be interested in changing beliefs about product x, changing attitudes toward the product, changing intentions to buy the product, or influencing actual purchasing behavior. Our conceptual system deals with the different kinds of intervening processes that must be studied in order to understand the effects of a stimulus (the commercial), on the different dependent measures. Conflicting findings are to be expected when these intervening processes are not taken into account.

Part II

Foundations
of
Beliefs,
Attitudes,
Intentions,
and
Behaviors

Chapter 5

Belief
Formation

The centrality of the belief concept has been emphasized in previous chapters. Within our conceptual framework, beliefs about an object provide the basis for the formation of attitude toward the object, and we have shown that attitudes are usually measured by assessing a person's beliefs. Although the importance of beliefs has frequently been acknowledged (Thurstone, 1931; Cronkhite, 1969; Ostrom, 1968; Rokeach, 1968; Scheibe, 1970), surprisingly little research in the attitude area has focused on the acquisition or formation of beliefs. Clearly, in order to account for the formation and change of attitudes and intentions, the processes of belief formation have to be investigated. Generally speaking, beliefs refer to a person's subjective probability judgments concerning some discriminable aspect of his world; they deal with the person's understanding of himself and his environment. Specifically, we have defined belief as the subjective probability of a relation between the object of the belief and some other object, value, concept, or attribute.[1] Thus a person may believe that he possesses certain attributes (e.g., that he is intelligent, honest, punctual, etc.), that a given behavior will lead to certain consequences, that certain events occur contiguously, etc.

This definition implies that belief formation involves the establishment of a link between any two aspects of an individual's world. One obvious source of

1. A distinction can be made between beliefs in the existence of an object (e.g., belief *in* God) and beliefs in the existence of a relationship linking the object to some attribute (e.g., a belief *about* God, such as "God is omnipotent"). However, beliefs *in* the existence of an object can also be viewed as beliefs *about* the object, i.e., as beliefs linking the object to the concept of existence (e.g., "God exists"). Thus, without any loss in generality, beliefs in an object may be viewed as a special case of beliefs about the object, and the remainder of this book will be concerned only with beliefs about an object.

information about such a relationship is direct observation; that is, a person may perceive (via any of his sense modalities) that a given object has a certain attribute. For example, he may see or feel that a given table is round, he may taste or smell that a given glass of milk is sour, or he may see that a given person has dark skin. These direct experiences with a given object result in the formation of *descriptive beliefs* about that object. Since the validity of one's own senses is rarely questioned, these descriptive beliefs are, at least initially, held with maximal certainty. (Over time, forgetting may reduce belief strength.)

Clearly, however, an individual forms beliefs that go beyond directly observable relationships. For example, interaction with another person may lead to the formation of beliefs about such unobservable characteristics or dispositions as the person's honesty, friendliness, introversion, or intelligence. Bruner (1957) has suggested two ways in which an individual can go beyond observable events. First, he may make use of previously learned relationships. For instance, obese people are often assumed to be jolly; a person who is crying is assumed to be sad; and observation of smoke leads to the assumption of fire. A second way of going beyond observables involves the use of "formal coding systems." On the basis of the observations that Joe is taller than Ralph and Ralph is taller than Harry, a person may form the belief that Joe is taller than Harry—even though he has never observed Joe and Harry together. Formal coding systems thus refer to various rules of logic that allow the formation of beliefs about unobserved events.

Beliefs that go beyond directly observable events may be called *inferential beliefs*. The inferential beliefs in the examples above were based on prior descriptive beliefs. Thus the descriptive belief formed on the basis of the observation that "*O* is obese" produced the inference "*O* is jolly." Similarly, the descriptive beliefs "Joe is taller than Ralph" and "Ralph is taller than Harry" provided the basis for the inference that "Joe is taller than Harry." It should be clear, however, that inferential beliefs need not be based on descriptive beliefs but may instead be formed on the basis of prior inferences. For example, the inferential belief that *O* is jolly may lead to the further inference that *O* is happy. Although an inferential belief can thus be based on a prior inference, in the final analysis most inferences can be traced to descriptive beliefs.

It is worth noting that the distinction between descriptive and inferential beliefs is somewhat arbitrary. Many attributes of an object that appear to be direct observations cannot be directly perceived. For example, attributes such as round, sour, obese, happy, and dark are themselves concepts that have been acquired in the past. In Chapter 2 we pointed out that concept formation involves the conditioning of a common response or label to a set of discrete stimuli. The label "obese," for instance, is associated with certain physical dimensions of a person or animal. "Obesity" may be viewed as an attribute that is inferred from observation of certain characteristics of the object. Once such attributes or concepts have been well learned, however, a person tends to perceive the attribute or concept directly instead of perceiving a set of discrete stimuli. Thus one perceives trees, dogs, roundness, obesity, etc., and directly associates these concepts and attributes in the formation of what were previously called descriptive beliefs. It is thus possible to view beliefs as representing a continuum from descriptive to inferential. At the descriptive end of the continuum, a person's beliefs are directly tied to the stimulus situation, and at the inferential end, beliefs are formed on the basis of these stimuli as well as residues of the person's past experiences; the continuum may be seen as involving minimal to maximal use of such experiential residues. For instance, a subject in an experiment is usually found to form beliefs about the race and sex of other participants, about the number of members in his group, about whether another person agreed or disagreed with him, etc. These are examples of relatively pure descriptive beliefs. Further along toward the inferential end of the continuum, McEwen and Greenberg (1969, 1970) varied the intensity of modifiers and verbs included in a communication. In one study, subjects were asked to rate the potency of the speaker's language and in another, the extremity of his position; in both cases, the appropriate inference was made. At the extreme inferential end of the continuum, beliefs may be almost entirely self-generated. For example, Miller's (1970) subjects were asked to "record their impressions" of a stranger by checking one member of each of 170 adjective pairs. The only information they had about the stranger was his or her photograph.

Many of our beliefs are formed neither on the basis of direct experience with the object of the belief nor by way of some inference process. Instead, we often accept information about some object provided by an outside source. Such sources include newspapers, books, magazines, radio and television, lecturers, friends, relatives, coworkers, etc. For example, we may read in the magazine *Time* that Paul Newman wears elevator shoes. On the basis of this information we may indeed form the belief that Paul Newman wears elevator shoes. Beliefs formed by accepting the information provided by an outside source may be termed *informational beliefs*. Although direct observations of an object-attribute relation will usually lead to the formation of a descriptive belief, outside information that links an object (e.g., Paul Newman) to an attribute (e.g., wears elevator shoes) may or may not lead to the formation of an informational belief. Many factors determine the degree to which information provided by an outside source will be accepted (see Chapter 11).

Whether or not the person forms an informational belief, exposure to information provided by an outside source will usually lead to the formation of a descriptive belief. That is, the person will come to believe that the source provided information concerning the relation between an object and some attribute. In the example above, he would have directly observed and formed the descriptive belief that "Time Magazine said that Paul Newman wears elevator shoes."

Later chapters will show the importance of this distinction between believing that an object (O) has an attribute (X) and believing that a source (S) provided information that O has the attribute X. The following schematic representation illustrates these two beliefs.

$$(O) \text{ is } (X).$$
$$(S) \text{ said } (O \text{ is } X).$$

In the first case, belief formation involves the establishment of a link between O and X. In the second case, a source S makes the assertion that O *is* X; the O-X link itself is established by the source. In some instances formation of the descriptive belief "(S) said (O is X)" may lead to the informational belief "(O) is (X)" and in other instances it may not. Clearly, then, evidence that a person believes or "knows" that a given source asserted a relation between O and X cannot be taken as evidence that the person accepts the assertion itself, i.e., believes that O is related to X.

To summarize briefly, three different processes may underlie belief formation. First, a link between O and X may be actively established on the basis of direct observation (descriptive belief). Second, a link between O and X may be actively established through a process of inference from some other belief about O (inferential belief). Finally, a link between O and X may be established by some source, and this link may be accepted (informational belief).

We noted in Chapter 3 that a belief involves a link between an object and a content category (an attribute) and that belief strength refers to the subjective probability that the object is associated with the category in question. Strictly speaking, therefore, a belief is formed as soon as an object is linked to an attribute, irrespective of the subjective probability associated with the link. In theory, an individual may be viewed as having some subjective probability between 0 and 1 for all conceivable object-attribute links. Of course, he will be aware of only a limited number of such associations; that is, a person usually has a relatively small number of beliefs about any given object. Nevertheless, when presented with a novel object-attribute combination, he can indicate his subjective probability that the object has the attribute. Clearly, his response must in this case be an inference based on his prior beliefs. It follows that the mere presentation of an object and an attribute in combination (as in an opinion questionnaire) may result in the formation of inferential beliefs. To be sure, when the person has little information on which to base the inference, his subjective probability may be at chance level, indicating a high degree of uncertainty.

In this chapter we will discuss empirical research dealing with the formation of descriptive and inferential beliefs. Most research on the formation (and change) of informational beliefs has been conducted in investigations of persuasive communication and will be discussed in Chapter 11. Since the formation of descriptive beliefs has received relatively little attention, the present chapter will deal primarily with processes of inferential belief formation. Following a brief discussion of descriptive beliefs, we will turn to an examination of research related to the two bases of inferential belief formation identified by Bruner (1957). Thus we will first consider inferences based on perceived or learned relations between beliefs and then review research dealing with more formal models of the inference process. We will show that many different lines of investigation fall within one or the other of these two broad categories. For the most part, these investigations have not been viewed as falling within the attitude area. From our point of view, however, research on belief formation is of essential importance, both in its own right and as the basis for an understanding of processes underlying the formation and change of attitudes, intentions, and behaviors. Our approach is essentially based on an information processing model, and a person's beliefs represent the information he has about himself and his social and physical environment. The first question of interest concerns the extent to which a person's descriptive beliefs formed on the basis of personal experience correspond to reality. Whether descriptive beliefs are veridical or inaccurate, we assume that inferences based on such beliefs are made in a systematic and predictable manner. That is, the information available to an individual is assumed to be processed in an internally consistent and orderly fashion, relatively uninfluenced by nonrational or dynamic forces.

DESCRIPTIVE BELIEFS

Manipulation Checks

Much of the information about the formation of descriptive beliefs in the attitude area comes to us in the form of incidental data collection or manipulation checks. In a typical experiment, subjects are exposed to a complex situation containing physical objects, persons, instruments, instructions, etc. Independent variables are manipulated by systematic variation in some of these stimuli. For example, some subjects may interact with a male experimenter, some with a female; the experimenter may reward or punish the subject; another person may agree with the subject's judgments; different subjects may be exposed to different communications, etc. Information about the formation of descriptive beliefs is obtained when the experimenter attempts to check the effectiveness of such manipulations by asking his subjects some direct questions about the manipulations. Subjects have been asked to indicate whether they had been rewarded or punished by the experimenter, whether another person had agreed or disagreed with their judgments, who the source of a communication was, etc.

Not only are subjects found to form beliefs on the basis of their observations; the bulk of the evidence indicates that the beliefs formed tend to accurately reflect what occurred in the situation—i.e., they tend to be *veridical*. Basically, beliefs assessed by manipulation checks represent tests of the subject's ability to recognize or recall events that occurred during the experiment. This question of memory has been investigated most intensively in studies on verbal learning.

Verbal Learning and Memory

Although research on verbal learning is probably as problematic as research in the attitude area (cf. Tulving and Madigan, 1970), some of the phenomena investigated by learning theorists have interesting implications for an understanding of belief formation. In Chapter 2 we showed that within the framework of learning theory, beliefs can be viewed as stimulus-response bonds. Any information concerning the establishment of stimulus-response bonds may therefore have implications for belief formation. Thus interval between observation of object and attribute, number of object-attribute presentations, reinforcement of object-attribute associations, etc., may all influence belief strength.

It may prove useful, then, to examine some of the phenomena being investigated in the area of verbal learning and memory. Most investigators in the area (Bahrick, 1965; Postman, Jenkins, and Postman, 1948) have tended to view recognition and recall as indicants of the same learned stimulus-response relationship, although recognition is assumed to be a more sensitive measure in that it tends to show effects of learning where recall would not. After some practice in memorizing a list of words, for example, a person will usually be able to recognize more of them (when they are presented among other words) than he will be able to recall freely.[2] This implies that measures of recognition may lead to different conclusions concerning belief formation than will measures of recall. For example, Osterhouse and Brock (1970) found that distraction during a persuasive communication reduced recognition of persuasive arguments but had no significant effect on a measure of recall. Different results for recognition and recall were also reported by Zimbardo *et al.* (1970).

A phenomenon of considerable interest to the attitude area is the *serial position effect,* or the finding that recall of stimuli presented serially to the subject depends in part on their position in the sequence. Specifically, stimuli presented at the beginning and end of a list tend to be recalled better than stimuli appearing in the middle. Figure 5.1 illustrates the serial position effect in a typical learning

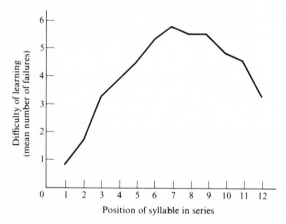

Fig. 5.1 Number of failures for each syllable position in the Hovland (1938) experiment. (Adapted from Hovland, Janis, and Kelley, p. 118.)

2. Recently, Adams and his associates (e.g., Adams and Bray, 1970; Adams, McIntyre, and Thorsheim, 1969; Adams, 1967) have suggested that different processes may underlie recall and recognition; the former is assumed to be based on a memory trace and the latter on a stimulus or response trace.

experiment, in which subjects were read a list of 12 three-letter syllables (Hovland, 1938). The implications of this phenomenon for the attitude area becomes apparent when a communication such as a persuasive message is viewed as a sequence of arguments to which a subject is exposed. The serial order effect suggests that subjects should be better able to recall what the communicator said at the beginning and end of his communication than what he said in the middle. A study by Jersild (1929) provided support for this argument (see Fig. 5.2). In that study, subjects read a series of 70 narrative biographical statements, and the pattern of recall exhibited the serial position effect.

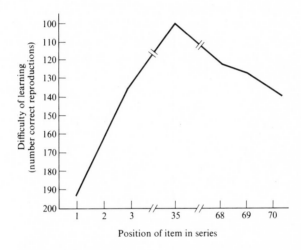

Fig. 5.2 Recall scores as a function of serial position of narrative items in the Jersild (1929) experiment. (Adapted from Hovland, Janis, and Kelley, p. 118.)

The serial position effect is found consistently for an ordered sequence of *homogeneous* verbal stimuli—nonsense syllables, meaningful words, or belief statements. However, the probability that stimuli in the middle of a sequence will be recalled can be increased by various manipulations. For example, when unfamiliar, novel, or unique stimuli that contrast with the remaining stimuli are inserted in the middle portion of a sequence, they are likely to be recalled.[3] A similar phenomenon occurs in short-term memory when subjects are asked to recall each individual stimulus in a list 10 or 20 seconds after its presentation. When homogeneous sets of stimuli are used, the percentage of subjects who correctly recall each succeeding stimulus tends to decline. As soon as stimuli of a

3. This is an example of the Von Restorff phenomenon. For a review, see Wallace (1965).

different kind are introduced, however, short-term memory tends to improve.[4] For example, Wickens (1970) has shown that shifting from words on one pole of the evaluative dimension (e.g., religious, success, nice, knowledge) to words on the opposite pole (e.g., hill, danger, lose, disease) results in a marked improvement in short-term memory. This effect can be seen in Fig. 5.3, which illustrates introduction of the novel evaluative stimulus on the fifth trial. Wickens obtained similar results with shifts along the activity and potency dimensions, shifts from high- to low-frequency words, and shifts from one class of nouns (e.g., birds) to another (e.g., occupations).

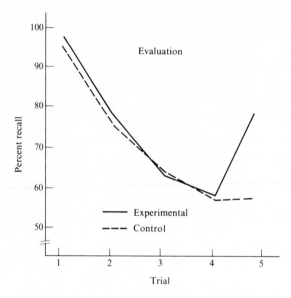

Fig. 5.3 The effect of shifting from one end to the other end of the Evaluative dimension. (Adapted from Wickens, 1970, p. 5.)

This phenomenon has potential implications for the *recency-primacy* issue in studies of impression formation and persuasive communication. A recency effect is obtained when information presented last has a stronger impact than information presented first, and the reverse is true for a primacy effect. In the context of the present discussion, the question is whether information presented first or last will be better recalled.[5] In a typical study, one side of an issue is presented and

---

4. These effects have been attributed to the operation of proactive inhibition and its release (Wickens, 1970) although increased rehearsal has been offered as an alternative explanation.

5. The recency-primacy issue is usually studied with respect to persuasion, i.e., *acceptance* of belief statements rather than their recall.

followed by a presentation of the opposite side, or a person is first described negatively and then positively (or vice versa). The research discussed above indicates that serial order position may be relatively unimportant for recall since the shifts from pro to con arguments or from positive to negative descriptions will tend to prevent deterioration of recall for information that occupies an intermediate position in the sequence of events.

Studies on verbal learning have also shown that meaningful, familiar stimuli are better recalled than meaningless, unfamiliar stimuli and that positively or negatively evaluated stimuli are better recalled than stimuli that are neutrally evaluated. The latter effect has also been found in the attitude area. McLaughlin (1970) described three persons in terms of 20 pieces of information; subjects were better able to recall information about the persons they liked and disliked than about the person for whom they had intermediate liking. Similar results were reported by Lott, Lott, and Walsh (1970), and somewhat related to these findings, Johnson, Middleton, and Tajfel (1970) found that children had more factual knowledge about liked and disliked than about neutral countries.

Other phenomena related to verbal learning and memory are potentially relevant to belief formation and change. A complete discussion of this research, however, is beyond the scope of this book. The primary aim of the discussion above is to draw the reader's attention to a relevant body of literature that has often been ignored by researchers in the attitude area.[6] The main interest of attitude researchers has been in the recognition or recall of the contents of a persuasive message.

Recall of Message Content

Whenever a subject is exposed to a communication from some source S which links an object O to an attribute or concept X, he is likely to form the belief that S said O is X. That is, the subject will usually be able to recognize or recall what the communication said. However, he may or may not accept (i.e., believe) the communication's content. For present purposes we are interested only in the subject's ability to recognize or recall events that occurred during an experiment, i.e., in his belief that S said O is X. Many studies have attempted to assess these beliefs by giving tests of recognition, recall, reception, or learning. Each of these methods involves one of two procedures: Either the subjects are asked to reproduce the content of the communication (*recall*), or they are given a set of statements and are asked to indicate which of the statements were part of the message (*recognition*). Since most recognition tests are presented in a multiple-choice or true-false format, the subject may respond by selecting either a statement that he believes was part of the communication (i.e., recognition) or a statement that represents his own belief (i.e., acceptance). Unfortunately, many research reports

---

6. Interested readers are directed to Adams (1967) and Tulving and Madigan (1970) for reviews of some of the literature in verbal learning and memory.

describe the measure of reception or learning that was used without an explicit indication as to the judgment the subjects were required to make. If subjects are given no specific instructions, their responses may reflect either recognition or acceptance.

Thus it is quite possible that many studies employing some measure of reception or learning have confounded recognition and acceptance; this may in part account for some of the conflicting findings about effects of different variables on recognition of message content. When only studies with measures of recall or clear measures of recognition are considered, however, results appear to be consistent with findings concerning verbal learning and memory.

One issue that has attracted repeated attention is the degree to which a person's own beliefs or attitudes affect his recall or recognition of belief statements contained in a communication. Perhaps on the basis of psychodynamic theory, it has often been assumed that, as a defensive reaction, individuals will reduce their attention to or comprehension of unpleasant, inconsistent, or threatening material. Thus it has been hypothesized that a person will be better able to recall information consistent with his own beliefs or attitudes than inconsistent information.

One of the first studies to clearly demonstrate this effect was conducted by Levine and Murphy (1943) who used five pro- and five anti-Communist college students as their subjects. Each subject participated in 10 sessions; in each of the first five sessions (learning phase) the subject read two prose passages, one of which was strongly anti-Communist, the other moderately pro-Communist. Subjects were asked to read the first passage twice and 15 minutes later to reproduce it as accurately as possible. The procedure was then repeated for the second passage. In the last five sessions (forgetting phase), only the recall task was performed. The results indicated that in all 10 sessions, exact reproduction of "idea groups" in a given passage was greater for subjects whose attitudes were consistent with that passage than for subjects whose attitudes were inconsistent with it. That is, pro-Communist subjects correctly recalled more of the pro-Communist passage than did anti-Communist subjects, and the reverse was true with respect to the anti-Communist passage.[7]

These findings have frequently been cited as evidence that a person's own attitude influences his recall of belief statements contained in a communication. However, many other studies performed before and after the Levine and Murphy experiment did not support this hypothesis (Watson and Hartman, 1939; A. L. Edwards, 1941; Jones and Aneshansel, 1956; Brigham and Cook, 1969; Malpass, 1969). In fact, most investigations have found little or no effect of a person's own beliefs or attitudes on his recall of belief statements to which he has been exposed. Other variables are usually found to play a more important role in deter-

---

7. However, all subjects recalled more of the pro-Communist than of the anti-Communist passage, a result that is perhaps attributable to the different contents and styles (e.g., use of extreme or unusual words, etc.) of the passages.

mining recall of message content. Brigham and Cook (1969), for example, failed to replicate the Levine and Murphy study. Subjects were exposed to a "transcript" of a discussion on integration that contained eight prointegration and eight antiintegration statements. Four statements in each set were considered plausible, the other four implausible. Subjects were selected on the basis of a multifactor racial attitude inventory (Woodmansee and Cook, 1967); data for subjects with the 22 highest and 22 lowest racial attitude scores were analyzed. Measures of free recall and recognition were obtained. There was no evidence that subjects recalled or recognized more statements consistent with their own attitudes than inconsistent statements. Jones and Kohler (1958), however, had found some support for the argument that the Levine and Murphy finding obtains only with plausible statements and that subjects recall more inconsistent than consistent statements when they are implausible. Although Brigham and Cook found better recall for implausible than for plausible statements, the Jones and Kohler findings were not replicated; that is to say, implausible statements were better recalled irrespective of the subject's own attitude or the position expressed in the statements.

In conclusion, there appears to be little evidence for the hypothesis that belief statements consistent with a person's own position are recalled or recognized better than belief statements inconsistent with his position. Indeed, as the research on verbal learning and memory suggests, many factors other than supportiveness tend to affect the degree to which information is recalled. Thus arguments differing in their supportiveness may also vary in terms of their plausibility, evaluative polarity, novelty, or familiarity, and such factors are likely to influence recognition and recall. Further, it may sometimes be to the person's advantage to recall certain arguments regardless of their supportiveness. For example, Jones and Aneshansel (1956) found that recall for nonsupportive arguments could be increased by telling subjects that they would be able to use those arguments in a later task. Such factors, therefore, have to be taken into consideration when selective recall is investigated.

Factors of this type are less likely to be involved in investigations of the effects of beliefs about the source or attitudes toward the source on recall of a communication from the source. In these studies, all subjects are exposed to the same communication. A typical experiment manipulates the expertise, trustworthiness, or attractiveness of the source, and the effects of these manipulations on recognition and recall of message content can be studied. The evidence overwhelmingly indicates that neither beliefs about the communicator's credibility nor attitudes toward the communicator have any appreciable effects on a subject's recognition or recall of the contents of his communication (Hovland, Janis, and Kelley, 1953; Johnson and Scileppi, 1969; Singer, 1969). For example, Johnson and Scileppi's subjects read a communication atttributed to one of two sources. One source was described as "a medical authority who is recognized as an expert on the issue of chest X-rays and tuberculosis" and the other source as "a medical quack who had served a prison term for medical fraud and who knew nothing substantial about the issue, but had written the communication for a magazine catering to sensationalism"

(p. 32). This extreme manipulation of source credibility had no significant effects on a measure of recall of message content.

A third question concerns the effects on recognition or recall of stable individual-difference variables, such as sex, self-esteem, intelligence, chronic anxiety, dogmatism, authoritarianism, etc. The limited evidence available on this question suggests that variables of this type have little or no systematic effect on recognition or recall of the contents of a communication.[8] There is little evidence, then, that a person's beliefs about or attitude toward a source or the topic of his communication influence recognition or recall of message content or that stable individual-difference variables have any consistent effects. Studies in verbal learning and memory suggest, however, that several other factors may influence such recall. For instance, interference during the learning stage and motivation have been found to affect recognition and recall. Similarly, in the attitude area recall has been influenced by drug-produced arousal (Friedman, Buck, and Allen, 1970) and by some but not all types of distractors or manipulations of acute fear or anxiety (e.g., Haaland and Venkatesan, 1968; Zimbardo *et al.,* 1970; McArdle, 1972). Some of these factors will be considered in our discussion of communication and persuasion in Chapter 11.

Recall of Contingencies

We have tried to show that descriptive beliefs are formed on the basis of direct observation. A final line of research providing support for this notion comes from studies dealing with the role of awareness in verbal conditioning. In our discussion of reactive effects (Chapter 4) we pointed out that subjects tend to form beliefs about the experimental situation, including beliefs about the consequences of their own behavior and about contingencies between other events. In fact, it has been found that verbal "conditioning" does not occur unless subjects are aware of these contingencies (Dulany, 1961, 1968; DeNike and Leibovitz, 1969; Uleman, 1971; Page, 1969). Some studies have employed a classical conditioning paradigm in which neutral stimuli are consistently paired either with positively or negatively evaluated stimuli. Changes in evaluation of the neutral stimuli are found only when subjects are aware of these consistent pairings. Other studies have used an operant conditioning paradigm in which certain responses made by the subject are reinforced by the experimenter. Again, increments in response strength are observed only for subjects aware of the reinforcement contingencies. A more detailed discussion of research on the conditioning of attitudes will be presented in Chapter 6; at present we note only that observation of events occurring in some situation leads to the formation of beliefs.

Most research has been satisfied with demonstrating that such beliefs are

---

8. Effects of some of these variables (e.g., intelligence) may be somewhat obscured because of the relatively narrow range of scores among subjects sampled from a student population.

indeed formed, but some studies have also examined factors that may influence the formation of beliefs about contingencies. For example, Uleman and Vanden-Bos (1971) reported that the formation of the correct contingency hypotheses in an operant conditioning paradigm was more likely to occur with a short than a long delay of reinforcement. The reinforcer in this study was a buzzer, and the duration of buzzing was also manipulated. The effect of this manipulation interacted with delay of reinforcement in influencing the formation of correct contingency hypotheses. Thus, with a three-second delay, contingency awareness increased with duration of buzzing, but with a five-second delay, variations in duration had no effect on contingency awareness. Finally, in this study as well as in a study by Dulany (1968), instructions as to the meaning of the reinforcing event were found to influence the formation of beliefs about contingencies.

Schedules of reinforcement may also be expected to have some effect on the formation of beliefs about contingencies. For example, subjects reinforced on a 100 percent schedule should be more likely to form the hypothesis in question than subjects on a 50 percent or random schedule. Some indirect evidence comes from studies which show that subjects' predictions of the occurrence of future events tend to correspond to the relative frequency with which such events have previously occurred (e.g., Humphreys, 1939; Estes, 1964).

To summarize, it is evident that people tend to form beliefs that reflect the things they experience, and under most circumstances, the beliefs formed tend to be fairly veridical. Nevertheless beliefs are sometimes found to be nonveridical. This is especially likely when events occur unexpectedly or when the person does not have sufficient time to observe the event carefully. For example, witnesses of a crime or an accident often form different beliefs about the events that occurred. Other evidence for occasional nonveridicality in descriptive belief formation comes from studies on optical illusions. The illusions occur in situations where stimuli are arranged in such a way as to produce incorrect perception.

With the exception of illusions, however, there appears to be little systematic bias in descriptive belief formation. That is, there is practically no evidence to support the notion that a person's own beliefs, attitudes, or personality characteristics have any systematic effects on descriptive beliefs based on direct observation. This should not be taken to mean that all types of beliefs are unaffected by such variables; on the contrary, some of them play an important role in the formation of beliefs that go beyond direct observation; i.e., they will tend to affect the inference process.

INFERENTIAL BELIEFS

The most characteristic feature of inferences is that in addition to the stimulus situation, the individual uses residues of past experience to make his judgments. Consider, for example, a person who has a negative attitude toward the People's Republic of China and who positively values freedom of religion. Imagine further that this person has never received any direct information about the degree of religious freedom in China and that he has in fact never considered the link between these two concepts. If he were now asked to indicate his subjective probability that China has religious freedom, he would probably have little difficulty in making a judgment. Clearly, his judgment would represent an inference rather than a descriptive belief. This part of the present chapter deals with the processes underlying such inferential belief formation.

One possible basis for the formation of inferential beliefs was discussed in Chapter 2, namely, Heider's (1944, 1958) notions concerning causal attribution and balance. Heider suggested that two elements will be perceived as forming a unit relation when both elements have the same dynamic character, i.e., when both are positively or negatively evaluated. When one element is evaluated positively and the other negatively, the person will perceive no relation between the elements; i.e., they will tend to be segregated. Similarly, the reader should recall that in a triadic configuration, pLo and pLx imply oUx, and $p\bar{L}o$ and pLx imply $o\bar{U}x$. The latter configuration is a balanced triad that is applicable to our example above. Since the person in question has a negative attitude toward China and a positive attitude toward freedom of religion, he should, according to Heider's theorizing, form the inferential belief that China does not have freedom of religion. His subjective probability that China has religious freedom should therefore be low.

This judgment is representative of the kinds of judgments that subjects are typically asked to make when they respond to standard attitude scales. As mentioned in Chapter 3, most standard scaling methods are designed to select items that have a given p-x link; agreement or disagreement with the item is then assumed to be primarily a function of the p-o link, i.e., of the person's attitude toward the object under consideration. In fact, many indirect and almost all disguised measures of attitude are based on the assumption that responses to certain statements are primarily determined by the subject's own attitude.

These considerations imply that evaluation may provide one basis for inferential belief formation. In its most general form, this principle suggests that inferences follow along the lines of *evaluative consistency*. A person is expected to infer that liked objects have positive attributes and that disliked objects have negative attributes. Conversely, he is not expected to infer that liked objects have negative attributes or that disliked objects have positive attributes.

Clearly, however, the person may form inferential beliefs as a result of other processes. In the example above, the subjective probability judgment may be the conclusion based on syllogistic reasoning. Thus the person might hold the following two beliefs.

1. The People's Republic of China is a Communist country.
2. Communist countries do not have religious freedom.

On the basis of these beliefs he might form the following inference.

3. China does not have religious freedom.

Note that although the person has formed the same inferential belief, the underlying process did not involve evaluative consistency; instead, it was based on considerations of relations between different beliefs. Although the inference process need not follow the rules of *formal* logic, it tends to be internally consistent. The consistency in this case refers to relations between cognitions or beliefs. To contrast this type of consistency with evaluative consistency as a basis for inferential belief formation, we will refer to it as *probabilistic consistency*.

These considerations suggest that an inferential belief linking an object and an attribute in an evaluatively consistent manner may actually be based on probabilistic rather than evaluative consistency. A simple example is given by the inferential belief that "hypochondriacs are anxious." Since both "hypochondriac" and "anxious" are negatively evaluated, the belief exhibits evaluative consistency, and it is possible that this evaluative consistency led to the inference. More likely, however, this belief is formed in a more direct probabilistic fashion since hypochondria is usually viewed as related to anxiety. (That is, on the basis of prior learning, the conditional probability that a person is anxious if he is a hypochondriac will tend to be high.)

A more interesting example is given by a person's inferential belief that "Khrushchev was immature." In terms of evaluative consistency this inference would be made by individuals who disliked Khrushchev as well as immaturity; in terms of probabilistic consistency, this inference could be a function of the belief that Khrushchev took off his shoe and banged it on the table in the United Nations and the belief that people who behave in this way are immature.[9]

Inferences Based on Relations between Beliefs

The examples above should make clear that it will often be impossible to distinguish between inferences based on evaluative consistency and inferences based on probabilistic consistency. The confounding between evaluative and probabilistic consistency was recognized in research on trait inferences (Peabody, 1967). Although much of this research has been conducted outside the attitude area, it is obviously relevant for our present discussion of inferential belief formation.

Trait Inferences

Initial impetus to much of the work on trait inferences came from Asch's (1946) studies of impression formation. In one experiment, subjects were read one of two lists of seven personality traits that were supposedly descriptions of a real person; the lists were identical except for the fourth trait in the list, which was either *warm* or *cold*. The two lists used were: intelligent, skillful, industrious,

---

9. Incidentally, the belief about Khrushchev's behavior may be in part responsible for a person's negative attitude toward Khrushchev as well as for the inference that Khrushchev was immature. This newly formed inferential belief will also contribute negatively to the person's attitude toward Khrushchev.

(warm or cold), determined, practical, cautious. After hearing the list, subjects were asked to write brief descriptions of the person the traits brought to mind, and to indicate for each of 18 pairs of different bipolar traits the term that best fitted the impression they had formed. The positive member of each trait pair is shown in Table 5.1.

Not only did the two lists of traits produce qualitatively different written impressions, but there were huge quantitative differences with respect to some of the items on the checklist. For example, when the description included the trait *warm,* most subjects perceived the person involved to be generous, humorous, sociable, popular, and good-natured. Inclusion of the trait *cold* in the stimulus list led not to these generally favorable impressions but to their bipolar opposites.

In a second experiment, Asch used the same stimulus lists, except that the traits *polite* and *blunt* were substituted for *warm* and *cold.* Differences in impressions produced by the two new lists were relatively minor, and Asch concluded that in the context of the stimulus lists employed, the *warm-cold* variable was more central to impression formation than the *polite-blunt* variable. The results of these two experiments are given in Table 5.1. In still other experiments, the traits *warm* and *cold* were embedded within new sets of stimulus traits, and their effects in some of these lists tended to be relatively small; that is, *warm* and *cold,* like *polite* and *blunt* in the previous study, operated as peripheral rather than central traits.

In another series of experiments, Asch varied the order of traits describing a stimulus person. Specifically, a given set of traits was read to the subjects in one of two orders. For example, in one experiment the lists were read in the following orders.

Order A: intelligent-industrious-impulsive-critical-stubborn-envious

Order B: envious-stubborn-critical-impulsive-industrious-intelligent

As Table 5.1 shows (Experiment 3), subjects receiving Order A were more likely than those receiving Order B to infer that the stimulus person was happy, good-natured, good-looking, and restrained. Asch reported somewhat weaker order effects when he used another set of traits in the following two orders (Experiment 4).

Order A: intelligent-skillful-industrious-determined-practical-cautious-evasive

Order B: evasive-cautious-practical-determined-industrious-skillful-intelligent

Asch concluded that these studies demonstrated a primacy effect in impression formation. In Experiment 3, the traits on the list were ordered in terms of their evaluation such that Order A gradually shifted from positive to negative traits, and the reverse was true for Order B. In Experiment 4, "unlike the preceding series, there is no gradual change in the merit of the given characteristics, but

Table 5.1 Results of Asch's Impression Formation Experiments

| | Centrality effects | | | | Order effects | | | |
| | Experiment 1 | | Experiment 2 | | Experiment 3 | | Experiment 4 | |
	Warm (N = 90)	Cold (N = 76)	Polite (N = 20)	Blunt (N = 26)	Order A (N = 34)	Order B (N = 24)	Order A (N = 46)	Order B (N = 53)
1. generous	91[a]	8†	56	58	24	10	42	23
2. wise	65	25†	30	50	18	17	35	19
3. happy	90	34†	75	65	32	5*	51	49
4. good-natured	94	17†	87	56	18	0*	54	37
5. humorous	77	13†	71	48	52	21*	53	29
6. sociable	91	38†	83	68	56	27	50	48
7. popular	84	28†	94	56	35	14	44	39
8. reliable	94	99	95	100	84	91	96	94
9. important	88	99	94	96	85	90	77	89
10. humane	86	31†	59	77	36	21	49	46
11. good-looking	77	69	93	79	74	35*	59	53
12. persistent	100	97	100	100	82	87	94	100
13. serious	100	99	100	100	97	100	44	100*
14. restrained	77	89	82	77	64	9†	91	91
15. altruistic	69	18†	29	46	6	5	32	25
16. imaginative	51	19†	33	31	26	14	37	16
17. strong	98	95	100	100	94	73	74	96
18. honest	98	94	87	100	80	79	66	81

[a] Percentage of subjects attributing positive trait to the stimulus person
* $p < .05$
† $p < .01$

rather the abrupt introduction at the end (or at the beginning) of a highly dubious trait" (Asch, 1946, p. 272). The primacy effect refers to the finding that the lists starting with favorable traits (Order A) led to a greater number of favorable inferences (see Table 5.1). Thus, in Experiment 3, Order A led to more favorable inferences than Order B on 14 of the 18 response traits; in Experiment 4, this difference was observed on 12 of the 18 response traits. However, the order effect is usually quite small when any given inference is considered. Indeed, a statistical analysis of Asch's data reveals only five significant differences in Experiment 3 and one significant difference in Experiment 4. Further, the latter difference indicates a recency rather than a primacy effect.[10]

More on the basis of the subjects' qualitative descriptions of the stimulus person than on these quantitative data, Asch suggested a "change in meaning" explanation for both the centrality and order effects. He argued that within a given set, some traits play a more central role than others. "The whole system of relations determines which will become central. These [central traits] set the direction for the further view of the person and for the concretization of the dependent traits." (Asch, 1946, p. 284) Thus traits appearing first in a list often become central and direct the overall impression by influencing the meaning of the subsequent traits. However, Asch pointed out that "it is not the sheer temporal position of the item which is important. . . . The effects of primacy should be abolished —or reversed—if it does not stand in a fitting relation to the succeeding qualities, or if a certain quality stands out as central despite its position. The latter was clearly the case for the quality 'warm-cold' in Experiment 1 [see Table 5.1] which, though occupying a middle position ranked comparatively high." (Asch, 1946, p. 272) Further, when placed in a different context, the *warm-cold* variable appeared to occupy a less central position, and according to Asch, its meaning had changed.

Focusing on either the order effect or the centrality effect, other investigators have offered alternatives to Asch's directed impression or change in meaning explanation. To account for order effects in impression formation, it has been suggested (e.g., N. H. Anderson, 1968a; Anderson and Hubert, 1963; Anderson and Barrios, 1961) that the weight or importance of a given trait varies according to its position while its meaning remains constant. Specifically, a primacy effect would result if smaller weights were placed on each succeeding trait in the process of impression formation. Research concerning this question will be reviewed in Chapter 6 since this research has dealt almost exclusively with the formation of attitudes rather than beliefs. Indeed, Asch's experiments may be the

---

10. It is noteworthy that in the context of impression formation, primacy and recency effects must be considered with reference to some dimension common to stimulus and response traits. Asch defined his primacy effect in terms of an evaluative dimension. Although other dimensions could be considered, we shall see that virtually all research on order effects in impression formation has been concerned with the evaluative dimension or liking for the stimulus person.

only investigation of order effects in belief formation. As indicated earlier, a secondary analysis of his data showed few significant effects of order on inferential beliefs, and further, those results which were significant indicated both primacy and recency effects.

With respect to the question of centrality, several investigators (e.g., Wishner, 1960; Rosenberg, Nelson, and Vivekananthan, 1968) have proposed an explanation which revolves around the perceived relations between traits. Consider, for example, any set of 20 traits. For any pair in the set, subjects can be asked to indicate the likelihood that a person will have trait x if he has trait y. These conditional probabilities (that is, $P(x|y)$, the probability of having trait x, given trait y) can be obtained for all possible pairs of traits, and the matrix of 20×20 conditional probabilities represents a complete description of the perceived relations between traits. Alternatively, it is possible to have subjects rate one or more stimulus persons on the 20 traits. (For example, they could be asked to indicate the probability that the stimulus person has each trait.) These ratings can be used to compute an intercorrelation matrix between all possible pairs of traits, which would again represent a complete description of the perceived relations among traits; the higher the correlation, the greater the perceived relationship.

It may be argued that the introduction of a given trait into a stimulus list will affect responses to an adjective checklist to the extent that the trait in question (1) is *not* related to the other traits in the stimulus list and (2) *is* related to the traits in the response list. An early study by Bruner, Shapiro, and Tagiuri (1958) showed that perceived relations among individual traits could be used to make predictions concerning inferences based on two or three traits in combination. For example, one group of subjects indicated the degree to which an *intelligent* person would be likely to have 59 other traits, such as *aggressive, unreliable, submissive,* etc. A second group of subjects made the same inferences for a person who was *inconsiderate,* and a third group for a person who was both *intelligent* and *inconsiderate.* Generally speaking, the judgments made by subjects in the third group could be predicted from the judgments made by subjects in the first two groups.[11]

This finding suggests that in the Asch studies, impression formation may have been a function of the perceived relations among the stimulus traits and the response traits. Wishner (1960) obtained a matrix of intercorrelations for all stimulus and response traits used in the Asch study. The results provided considerable support for the argument that Asch's findings could be interpreted in terms of the relations within stimulus traits as well as between stimulus and response traits. That is, when *warm* and *cold* were "central" traits, they tended to have low cor-

---

11. Unfortunately, the investigators did not take full advantage of the available probabilistic data, relying instead on a rather gross distinction as to whether or not the majority of subjects in a given group perceived some degree of likelihood that one trait implied another. Thus no firm conclusions can be drawn on the basis of this study; it is mentioned here primarily for its pioneering role in using conditional probability measures.

relations with the other traits in the stimulus list and to correlate highly with those traits in the response list that were most influenced by the manipulation. Rosenberg, Nelson, and Vivekananthan (1968) also reported evidence in support of this argument. Using a multidimensional scaling procedure, these authors found that two or three factors could account for the relationships among the traits used in Asch's study, and they argued that Asch's results could be predicted from a knowledge of the loadings of the traits on these dimensions.

Much of the research on trait inferences has been concerned with describing the interrelationships among traits. Perhaps in response to Bruner and Tagiuri's (1954) argument that perceived interrelations among traits represent naive or common-sense "theories of personality," investigators turned their attention to the dimensions underlying perceived trait relations in order to identify the basic structure of these *implicit theories of personality*. Factor analysis and multidimensional scaling procedures have been employed in these investigations (e.g., Cattell, 1946; Tupes and Christal, 1961; Norman, 1963). An excellent review of this body of literature can be found in J. S. Wiggins (1973, Chapter 8).

Many of these studies are concerned with five major orthogonal dimensions that appear to account for much of the variance in trait inferences. Table 5.2 presents the results of a factor analysis based on intercorrelations of 20 bipolar adjective scales. These data are based on ratings of fraternity members by their peers (i.e., other fraternity members) on the 20 bipolar scales (Norman, 1963). The scales were selected to represent the five factors identified by Tupes and Christal (1961) in a study based on Cattell's (1946) pioneering work in this area. The same factor structure emerged in Norman's analysis (see Table 5.2). Many additional studies using the same set of scales have replicated the basic factor structure. The same factor structure emerged whether the factor analysis was performed on ratings of the stimulus persons on the 20 scales (Norman, 1963), on judgments of similarity between pairs of traits (D'Andrade, 1965), or on ratings of conditional probabilities between pairs of traits (Hakel, 1969). Further, the factor structure was replicated for ratings of complete strangers (Passini and Norman, 1966) as well as close acquaintances (Norman, 1963).[12]

It appears, then, that in the natural usage of trait descriptions, certain traits tend to form a consistent pattern, and the implicit structure of trait relations closely parallels the structure obtained when real persons are judged. Thus, once a given trait has been assigned to a person on any basis, "the remaining ratings

---

12. However, there was greater consensus among subjects rating a common acquaintance than among subjects rating a stranger. It has been argued (J. S. Wiggins, 1973) that when a subject rates a stranger, he is forced to rely on "superficial characteristics," such as dress, demeanor, physical size, etc., to infer some personality trait. Once a given rating has been made on this basis, the remaining traits are relatively fixed by the existing implicative structure among trait terms. Since subjects may make different initial inferences, there will be relatively little agreement in their descriptions of a stranger. For a common acquaintance, however, inferences and overall descriptions are likely to coincide.

Table 5.2 Factor Matrix of Peer Ratings in a Fraternity Sample
(from Norman, 1963, p. 579)

Scales	Factors				
	I	II	III	IV	V
Extraversion					
Talkative–Silent	**90**	02	−02	04	−00
Frank, Open–Secretive	**78**	−08	07	−03	07
Adventurous–Cautious	**78**	15	−20	32	01
Sociable–Reclusive	**86**	01	−18	−01	−02
Agreeableness					
Goodnatured–Irritable	17	**80**	17	12	07
Not jealous–Jealous	−10	**64**	20	49	07
Mild, Gentle–Headstrong	−20	**80**	27	19	10
Cooperative–Negativistic	33	**74**	28	13	11
Conscientiousness					
Fussy, Tidy–Careless	−33	−08	**66**	−35	20
Responsible–Undependable	−03	32	**86**	08	18
Scrupulous–Unscrupulous	−30	44	**68**	−02	20
Persevering–Quitting, Fickle	−05	28	**74**	12	27
Emotional stability					
Poised–Nervous, Tense	01	56	15	**61**	05
Calm–Anxious	06	21	−10	**82**	−07
Composed–Excitable	13	06	16	**71**	24
Not hypochondriacal–Hypochondriacal	21	27	−00	**65**	−09
Culture					
Artistically Sensitive–Insensitive	−04	08	39	−10	**75**
Intellectual–Unreflective, Narrow	−04	05	47	04	**74**
Polished, Refined–Crude, Boorish	15	25	53	16	**46**
Imaginative–Simple, Direct	12	19	03	10	**68**

are relatively 'fixed' by the implicative structure that exists among trait terms"
(J. S. Wiggins, 1973). As Table 5.2 shows, if a stimulus person is perceived as
sociable, he is also likely to be seen as *talkative, frank, open,* and *adventurous.* If
he is considered *calm,* he is also likely to be perceived as *poised, composed,* and
not hypochondriacal. These consistently emerging factors are generally viewed as
representing perceived dimensions of personality.

Note, however, that the procedure whereby these factors were identified
strongly resembles the procedure used by Osgood and his associates (Osgood, Suci
and Tannenbaum, 1957) to identify the basic dimensions of meaning. That is to
say, in both lines of research the investigator starts with a large number of adjec-

tives or bipolar adjective scales against which various stimuli are judged. Osgood's subjects rated stimuli from various domains (e.g., persons, animals, values, inanimate objects, etc.), whereas investigators studying "implicit theories of personality" used only persons as stimulus concepts. In both approaches, however, dimensions underlying these ratings were identified by factor analysis or multidimensional scaling. Perhaps it is not surprising, therefore, that many investigators (e.g., D. R. Peterson, 1965; Hallworth, 1965; Becker, 1960; Burke and Bennis, 1961) began to argue that the perceived dimensions of personality identified in research on trait inferences are "nothing but" general dimensions of meaning as applied to judgments of people. Thus Peterson (1965) argued that

> The invariant "personality" dimensions discussed above [neuroticism and extraversion] are rather easily construed as topical variants of more general ways of attributing meaning to objects, in this case human objects. "Adjustment" is good, "neuroticism" is bad. Extraversion "means" strong and active. (p. 57)

The diverging interpretations of the factors emerging in studies of trait inferences have led to the distinction made earlier between evaluative and probabilistic consistency in inferential belief formation. The central question is whether two traits that are perceived to be related are seen as related because they are evaluatively similar to each other or because they share descriptive or semantic similarity. For example, when a person who is judged to be *trustworthy* is also judged to be *cooperative,* the perceived relation between the two traits may be due to their common positive evaluative meaning or to their descriptive similarity in terms of dependability or stability.

As stated by Peabody (1967, p. 2),

> The problem is that a judgment is commonly at the same time both an estimate of the factual situation and an evaluation. For example, consider such contrasts as "kind-cruel" or "cautious-rash." The judgment that a person or action is "kind" or "rash" combines a descriptive aspect (e.g., that the action helps others, or involves very large risks) and an evaluative aspect (e.g., that the action is desirable or undesirable). In a single trait term (and its opposite) the two aspects are confounded since they always combine in the same way (e.g., helping as desirable, hurting as undesirable).

Thus Peabody argued that evaluative and descriptive similarity have been confounded in studies on trait inferences. In other words, it is not clear whether the formation of inferential beliefs is based on evaluative or probabilistic consistency.

To investigate this problem, Peabody devised a paradigm that attempts to separate evaluative and probabilistic consistency by orthogonally manipulating the evaluative and descriptive similarity of adjective pairs. Consider, for example, the positively evaluated trait *cautious* and an inference to the dimension defined by the endpoints *bold* (positive) and *timid* (negative). Peabody argued that if trait inferences were based on evaluative similarity, a person who was described as *cautious* should also be judged as *bold*. But if inferences followed descriptive similarity, he should be judged as *timid.*

Peabody constructed sets of four adjectives that varied in terms of evaluative and descriptive similarity. Table 5.3 presents four of the sets used by Peabody. The numbers in front of each trait represent the mean evaluation of the trait based on evaluative semantic differential ratings. Note that within each set of traits, two are positively evaluated (e.g., *cautious* and *bold*) and two are negatively evaluated (e.g., *timid* and *rash*). Further, each positive trait is descriptively similar to a negative trait (e.g., *cautious* is descriptively similar to *timid,* and *bold* is descriptively similar to *rash*). After constructing these sets, Peabody obtained judgments using items such as:

CAUTIOUS

bold |———|———|———|———|———|———|———| timid

Subjects were instructed to "assume a person with the characteristic given in capital letters. On the scale immediately beneath, you are to judge how likely it is that this person has one or the other of the traits given by the scale" (Peabody, 1967, p. 5).

Within each set of traits, four critical judgments of this kind are possible. For the first set in Table 5.3, the following *critical* judgments were obtained.

CAUTIOUS: bold–timid
TIMID: cautious–rash
BOLD: cautious–rash
RASH: bold–timid

In each item, the capitalized trait is descriptively similar to one member of the associated adjective pair and evaluatively similar to the other member of the pair.

In addition, each trait (e.g., CAUTIOUS) was rated on bipolar scales formed from traits in the other sets (e.g., on *thrifty–extravagant*). These *"unselected"* ratings are considered to represent typical trait inferences where evaluative and

Table 5.3 Sets of Trait Terms Differing in Evaluative Meaning (from Peabody, 1967)

+ .9	Cautious	+1.1	Bold
−1.1	Timid	−1.2	Rash
+1.7	Self-controlled	+1.1	Uninhibited
−1.4	Inhibited	− .3	Impulsive
+ .9	Thrifty	+1.8	Generous
−2.0	Stingy	− .8	Extravagant
+ .5	Skeptical	+1.8	Generous
−1.4	Distrustful	−1.4	Gullible

descriptive similarity are confounded. That is, it could be argued that the trait *cautious* is both descriptively and evaluatively similar to the trait *thrifty.* In most cases, however, the problem is not one of confounding evaluative and descriptive similarity but rather the fact that descriptive similarity may be involved but cannot be readily identified. For instance, when the trait CAUTIOUS is judged against *tense–relaxed,* it is not clear which, if either, of the two adjectives is descriptively more similar to cautious. Thus the critical judgments constituted attempts to separate evaluative and descriptive similarity, whereas these two aspects were confounded in the unselected judgments. Peabody's subjects rated 90 traits on 40 scales, thus making 3600 judgments. Of these judgments, 80 involved rating a trait that was also one of the bipolar adjectives of the scale; these judgments were excluded from the analyses. Of the remaining 3520 judgments, 70 were critical and 3450 were unselected.

With respect to unselected judgments, 67 percent followed evaluative similarity. Thus, when descriptive similarity is either ambiguous or confounded with evaluative similarity, the majority of judgments may be viewed as exhibiting evaluative similarity. In contrast, all 70 critical judgments followed descriptive similarity. Peabody therefore concluded that when evaluative and descriptive similarity are separated, inferences tend to follow lines of descriptive similarity.[13]

Using Peabody's procedure, Felipe (1970) replicated these findings. Of the 136 unselected judgments in this replication, 73 percent exhibited evaluative similarity. Of 32 critical judgments, however, 75 percent followed descriptive similarity. In addition, Felipe constructed two different types of response scales from the basic sets of four personality traits. The first type contrasted traits that were descriptively similar but differed in evaluation (e.g., *stingy–thrifty; extravagant–generous*). The second type contrasted traits that had the same evaluation but differed descriptively (e.g., *stingy–extravagant; thrifty–generous*). As expected, Felipe found that almost all inferences exhibited evaluative similarity for the first type of scales and descriptive similarity for the second type. Thus, like Peabody, he concluded that trait inferences are likely to follow descriptive similarity when possible; that is, descriptive similarity will be exhibited when the

---

13. Peabody also performed a factor analysis on the interscale correlations obtained from the 90×40 matrix of average trait inferences. He concluded that none of the major factors could be clearly identified as evaluative. Rosenberg and Olshan (1970), however, pointed out that this factor analysis did not provide a crucial test of Peabody's hypothesis (even if an evaluative factor had been found) since it was based primarily on unselected judgments. Moreover, Peabody (1970) agreed with Rosenberg and Olshan's argument that a factor analysis of these intercorrelations was inappropriate for his data. Using multidimensional scaling on similarity indices among Peabody's traits, Rosenberg and Olshan found a clear evaluative dimension. Similarly, A. L. Edwards (1969) also found an evaluative dimension when responses to an adjective checklist based on all of Peabody's traits were factor analyzed. However, as indicated above, the emergence of evaluative factors in these analyses do not contradict the notion that inferences are based on descriptive similarity.

traits share some degree of denotative or descriptive meaning. In the absence of descriptive similarity, inferences are likely to be based on evaluative similarity.

To summarize briefly, our discussion of research on trait inferences has revealed some important implications for an understanding of inferential belief formation. Much of the research in this area has attempted to provide systematic descriptions of the perceived relationships among traits. The most prominent finding has been that inferences from one trait to another follow a consistent pattern. Asch's findings concerning the effect on trait inferences produced by using *warm* or *cold* among a set of stimulus traits can be understood in terms of the dimensions underlying stimulus and response traits (Rosenberg, Nelson, and Vivekananthan, 1968). This stable factor structure was often interpreted as representing perceived personality dimensions. It was recognized, however, that the emerging factor structure could be interpreted as nothing more than instances of Osgood's general dimensions of meaning, and it became important to know whether the perceived trait relations (that produced the factor structure) were the result of evaluative or descriptive similarity. This issue in part led to the more general question raised earlier, namely, the extent to which inferential beliefs are formed on the basis of evaluative or probabilistic consistency. In contrast to the assumption of evaluative consistency that underlies much of attitude measurement as well as the notions of balance, congruity, affective-cognitive consistency, etc., research on trait inferences suggests that probabilistic rather than evaluative consistency plays a predominant role in inferential belief formation. Indeed, only in the absence of probabilistic consistency does evaluative consistency appear to determine the formation of inferential beliefs—at least so far as trait inferences are concerned.

Studies of interpersonal attraction. To further illustrate this point, it may be instructive to examine some experiments on interpersonal attraction which, although not directly concerned with belief formation, have obtained measures of belief in addition to measures of attitude. Generally speaking, subjects in these studies are given information about another person that is expected to influence their attraction to that person. On the assumption that individuals operate on the basis of evaluative consistency, a manipulation which is found to increase attraction toward the other person should also increase the belief that he has favorable attributes. This prediction follows from the assumption of an evaluatively consistent link between attitude and beliefs. In contrast, the assumption of probabilistic consistency implies that although certain information about another person may influence attraction, it will affect some but not all beliefs about that person. Specifically, its major impact should be on beliefs that are probabilistically related to the information provided.

Byrne (1969, 1971) and his associates have studied the relationship between similarity and interpersonal attraction. Subjects are given descriptions of a stranger's opinions or personality characteristics that differ in the extent to which they are similar to the subject's own opinions or personality traits. Subjects are then asked to rate the stranger on Byrne's interpersonal judgment scale, which consists of two items designed to measure attraction and four "filler items." The latter items are measures of the subject's beliefs about the stranger's *intelligence, knowledge of current events, morality,* and *adjustment.* In a limited number of studies data concerning these filler items are reported, and the findings suggest a probabilistic inference process (see Fishbein and Ajzen, 1972). That is, inferences were made consistently only when the information provided about the stranger was descriptively similar to the judgment required. For example, beliefs about the other's knowledge of current events were affected only when the information dealt with political issues (Byrne, Bond, and Diamond, 1969) or a variety of opinions about social issues (Byrne and Ervin, 1969; Mascaro and Lopez, 1970). Beliefs about the other's adjustment were affected by similarity only in a study that provided information about the stranger's responses to a repression-sensitization test (Byrne and Griffitt, 1969). Finally, judgments of morality were affected by information about a candidate's stand on six social issues (Byrne, Bond, and Diamond, 1969).

Similar conclusions emerge from other experiments dealing with interpersonal attraction. For example, in two studies subjects provided information about themselves. A confederate then gave positive or negative personality evaluations of the subject, ostensibly on the basis of the information provided by the subject. The confederate who made positive evaluations was rated as higher in social sensitivity (Lowe and Goldstein, 1970) and as more intelligent and doing a better job (Sigall and Aronson, 1969). In contrast, when the subject merely overheard the confederate saying that he did or did not like the subject (Landy and Aronson, 1968), the confederate who expressed liking received higher ratings of kindness and friendliness, but no differential inferences were made with respect to eight other traits, including intelligence and sensitivity. Thus there is again little evidence that the subject's responses follow evaluative consistency. The generalizability of this conclusion to other processes of inferential belief formation will be examined below.

Cue Utilization

The basic research paradigm in studies of trait inferences is as follows: A stimulus person is described as possessing Trait A, and the subject is asked to indicate how likely it is that the stimulus person has Trait B. For example, the stimulus person might be described as *rich,* and the subject could be asked to indicate his subjective probability that the person is *intelligent.* An alternative strategy would be to provide information that the stimulus person earns a specified amount of money ($10,000, $15,000, or $20,000), and the subject could be asked to estimate how intelligent the person is (in terms of I.Q. scores). In this case, both the information provided and the subject's responses represent positions on different content dimensions. The subject's task is to infer the position of a stimulus person on one content dimension on the basis of information about his position on some other content dimension. It seems reasonable to assume that this inference will be determined by the perceived relation between the two content dimensions. One possible way of estimating this relationship is to compute the correlation between the amount of money earned by the stimulus person and the subject's judgment of his I.Q.

This procedure can be extended by providing the subject with more than one item of information or *cue* about the stimulus person. In fact, in everyday life, people are often confronted with situations in which they must make some prediction or inference on the basis of several items of information or cues. For example, in hiring a job applicant, a personnel director may have to predict the applicant's probability of success on the job on the basis of information about the applicant's intelligence, previous experience, letters of reference, and amount of education. Similarly, stockbrokers make predictions about stock market behavior on the basis of such information as volume of trade, Dow Jones averages, etc.; doctors diagnose the probability that a tumor is malignant on the basis of X-rays, blood samples, size of tumor, etc. Indeed, most human judgments involve utilization of various items of information presumed relevant to the judgment in question.

When more than one cue is provided, it becomes possible to study a number of factors that may affect the inference process. For example, it is possible to examine the ways in which different cues are combined to arrive at the criterion judgment, to assess the effects of redundancy and inconsistency among cues, and to consider the extent to which cues are used efficiently to arrive at accurate inferences.

Multiple Regression Approach

For the purpose of studying such inference processes, a typical experiment on cue utilization might ask a subject to predict (infer) the intelligence quotients (I.Q. scores) for each of a group of college students on the basis of information about their grade point averages, aptitude test scores, credit hours attempted, and number of hours studied per week. The subject receives several quantified pieces of information (i.e., cues) about each stimulus person and is asked to infer that person's I.Q. score. As in natural situations, the cues take on different values for each college student.[14] Table 5.4 illustrates hypothetical profiles for 10 college students whose intelligence scores are to be inferred. Typically, a large number of such profiles are to be judged by each subject.

Once the subject has made his inferences, correlations can be computed between each cue dimension and the subject's predictions of intelligence. These correlations provide an indication of the extent to which a given cue dimension affects the inferential judgment. One major issue in research on cue utilization concerns

---

14. The cue values can be selected such that different cues are either independent, redundant, or inconsistent (i.e., uncorrelated, positively correlated, or negatively correlated) with each other.

Table 5.4 Hypothetical Cue Profiles for 10 College Students

		Cues		
Hypothetical student	Grade point average	Aptitude test score	Credit hours attempted	Hours studied per week
1	3.2	465	9	17
2	1.3	379	9	5
3	4.0	631	12	21
4	3.9	375	10	12
5	2.5	440	9	12
6	2.7	391	12	13
7	1.9	412	12	8
8	3.2	676	9	35
9	4.0	820	14	10
10	2.6	429	9	15

the process whereby different cues are combined to arrive at the inference. The simplest process is a linear combination of cues in which cue values are combined in an additive fashion. It is usually assumed that cue dimensions are given different weights, depending on their relevance for (or relation to) the criterion dimension. Much research on cue utilization has attempted to test the validity of this weighted linear model. Multiple regression analysis has served as the primary tool for this test since it provides estimates of cue weights as well as an index of the predictive accuracy of the weighted linear model.

To state it simply, the purpose of a multiple regression analysis is to provide an index of the degree of correlation between a *set* of independent variables (in this case the cues) and a given dependent variable (in this case the inference or criterion). That is, a multiple correlation coefficient is obtained which expresses the degree to which simultaneous consideration of the cues permits prediction of the inference. More specifically, each cue is given a weight (its *regression weight*) which represents its independent contribution to the prediction of the inference. The multiple regression analysis identifies optimal regression weights, that is, weights which lead to the most accurate prediction.[15] Further, multiple regression analysis combines the weighted cues in an additive fashion to arrive at the prediction. It follows that the multiple correlation is an indication of maximal predictability under the assumption of a linear (additive) model.

The correlations between cues and inference are used to compute regression weights. When the cues themselves are uncorrelated, the regression weight of each cue is identical to the cue's correlation with the inference. When the cues are correlated, these correlations are taken into account such that a given cue's regression

---

15. The optimization procedure is based on the least-squares criterion; that is, it minimizes the squared differences between predicted and obtained scores.

weight expresses the contribution this cue makes toward the prediction independent of all other cues. These regression weights are often assumed to indicate the
relative weight placed on a given cue by the individual in making his inferences.
Thus regression weights have been taken as indices of the relative *importance* of
cues for a given inference.

Slovic and Lichtenstein (1971) have reviewed a large number of studies in
which subjects were asked to use cues to make judgments about such things as
personality characteristics, performance in college or on the job, physical and
mental pathology, and legal matters. These studies demonstrate that inferential
beliefs are predicted with considerable accuracy on the basis of a weighted linear
combination of cues. Indeed, Slovic and Lichtenstein (1971, p. 678) concluded,
"In all of these situations the linear model has done a fairly good job of predicting
the judgments, as indicated by [multiple correlations] in the 80's and 90's for the
artificial tasks and in the 70's for the more complex real-world situations."

Prediction versus description of the inference process. Despite the predictive success of the linear model, one cannot necessarily conclude that respondents actually
combine cues in a linear fashion when forming inferential beliefs. In fact, there is
some evidence that information may be combined in nonlinear or configural ways
(e.g., Wiggins and Hoffman, 1968; Tversky, 1969; Einhorn, 1970).[16] However,
research on configurality has repeatedly shown that even when there is evidence
for configural processes, the linear model accounts for most of the variance in
inferential beliefs (cf. Slovic and Lichtenstein, 1971; Goldberg, 1968). This
suggests that accurate prediction by the linear model may not always provide a
valid description of the inference process.

Other evidence suggesting that the linear model may not, in fact, accurately
describe the actual inference process comes from studies in which subjects are
asked to estimate the relative weight they placed on each cue in making their
judgments. For example, Summers, Taliaferro, and Fletcher (1970) had subjects
infer the level of socioeconomic development of 175 nations on the basis of four
cues (amount of foreign investment in the country, amount of government influence over private enterprise, foreign aid received from United States, and number of socialist deputies or representatives in the nation's congress). After making
these 175 judgments, subjects indicated the subjective weight they thought they
placed on each cue by distributing 100 points among the four cues. The subjective
weights were then compared with regression weights obtained in a multiple regression analysis. Large discrepancies were found between subjective and obtained
weights. Moreover, although the multiple regression analysis indicated that approximately 75 percent of all subjects utilized three cues or fewer in making their

---

16. Wiggins and Hoffman (1968) found that in comparison with a simple linear
model, a configural model improved predictions for many respondents. However, the
increment in predictability was minimal.

judgments, almost every subject reported using all four cues. Thus the linear regression model and subjective reports suggest different combinations of cues in making the inferences. Such discrepancies between subjective and obtained weights have been found in many other studies (e.g., Hoffman, 1960; Hoepfl and Huber, 1970; Oskamp, 1962; Pollack, 1964). In comparison with the weights provided by the linear regression model, respondents tend to overestimate the importance they place on minor cues (i.e., on cues with low regression weights), and they underestimate their reliance on a few major cue dimensions.

Interestingly, there is some evidence (Slovic, Fleissner, and Bauman, 1972) that the correspondence between subjective and obtained weights decreases as the respondent becomes more experienced. Slovic and Lichtenstein (1971) have suggested that judgments become more automatic with experience and that experienced judges, therefore, may be less able to report the ways in which they utilize cues. This account implies that obtained weights represent the respondent's actual weights more accurately than his own subjective weights, but other investigators have argued that discrepancies between obtained and subjective weights reflect inadequacies of the linear model. Although the predictive accuracy of the linear model is not questioned, there is considerable doubt concerning its ability to provide an accurate *description* of the inference process. Indeed, there is a growing concern among investigators that the linear model may not provide an accurate descriptive account of inferential belief formation, despite its predictive success. As Slovic and Lichtenstein (1971, p. 683) have pointed out, "notions about nonlinear processes are likely to play an increasing role in our understanding of judgment despite their limited ability to outpredict linear models."

Whatever the descriptive utility of the linear model, the multiple regression approach to cue utilization has provided information concerning a number of important issues. One major focus of research in this area has been the systematic investigation of individual differences. There seems to be little doubt that respondents vary considerably in terms of the weights they place on given cues. That is, respondents tend to use the same information in very different ways, and thus the same information may lead to the formation of different inferential beliefs. Moreover, Wiggins, Hoffman, and Taber (1969) found that the weights placed on different cues were related to various personological characteristics of the judges. Subjects in this study inferred the intelligence of stimulus persons on the basis of nine cues, such as high school ratings, mother's education, emotional anxiety, and study habits. A factor-analytic procedure was used to identify types of judges who had made similar inferences; eight different groups or types of judges were thus isolated. Multiple regression analyses were performed for each group of judges by correlating the nine cue values associated with a given stimulus person with the group's mean judgment of the stimulus person's intelligence. As Table 5.5 shows, the different types of judges placed different weights on the nine cues, and the number of significant cues varied from one (Judge 7) to eight (Judge 6). Thus, for example, judges of Type 1 appeared to consider only high school rating and

Table 5.5 Multiple Correlations between Nine Input Cues and Mean Intelligence Judgments of 75 Profiles for Eight Discrete Subject Groups (From Wiggins, Hoffman, and Taber, 1969)

Profile cues	Zero-order correlations by groups							
	I (n=45)	II (n=28)	III (n=53)	IV (n=10)	V (n=5)	VI (n=2)	VII (n=1)	VIII (n=1)
1. High school rating	.97‡	.34†	.45‡	.61‡	.38‡	.43‡	.05	.70‡
2. Status	.08	.08	.20	.05	.81‡	.35†	.01	.10
3. Self-support	−.03	−.09	.07	.08	.03	.25*	.10	.17
4. English effectiveness	.16	.90‡	.42‡	.24*	.32†	.27*	.02	.07
5. Responsibility	−.10	.04	.46‡	−.01	.20	.18	.01	−.32†
6. Mother's education	.05	.07	.15	.26*	.12	.39‡	−.06	−.06
7. Study habits	.00	.03	.46‡	−.08	−.09	.24*	.00	.08
8. Emotional anxiety	.08	.09	.11	.05	.11	.29*	.99‡	.07
9. Credit hours	.23*	.27*	.24*	.75‡	.17	.44‡	−.09	.04
Multiple correlation	.99‡	.99‡	.98‡	.95‡	.97‡	.93‡	.99‡	.80‡

* $p < .05$.
† $p < .01$.
‡ $p < .001$.

number of credit hours attempted, whereas judges of Type 5 placed primary emphasis on status, high school rating, and English effectiveness.[17]

We can gain some understanding of the basis for these differences by examining certain personological characteristics of the different types of judges. Types 1 and 2, who were found to place most weight on seemingly relevant cues (high school rating, English effectiveness, credit hours attempted), tended to be intelligent and low in ethnocentrism. In contrast, judges of Type 5, who placed heavy emphasis on the "character" variables of responsibility and study habits (cues which are seemingly irrelevant to the judgment of intelligence), were high on authoritarianism and religious conventionalism. These results support our earlier argument that the formation of inferential beliefs involves factors other than those in the immediate stimulus situation.

In addition to showing that different individuals place different weights on the various cues, research using the multiple regression approach has also made it clear that the weights of cues may vary with the judgment being made. Thus, for example, if Wiggins, Hoffman, and Taber had asked their subjects to judge each stimulus person's grade point average or motivation (rather than his intelligence),

---

17. One additional aspect of these results is worth noting. All nine cues as well as the criterion can be placed along an evaluative dimension. Nevertheless, there is little evidence for the notion of evaluative consistency since evaluative consistency implies that all cues should contribute to the inferences.

the weights of the cues would have shifted considerably for each type of judgment. Such effects are to be expected since, as we saw in our discussion of trait inferences, a given stimulus trait (or cue) tends to exhibit different degrees of relationship with different response traits (or criteria). This supports our argument in Chapter 4 that the effect of a given independent variable on a measure of belief cannot be generalized to measures of other beliefs or to measures of attitudes or intentions.

Analysis of Variance Approach

A second major approach to the investigation of the ways in which cues are combined or integrated has relied on the analysis of variance (ANOVA). For example, N. H. Anderson (1970, 1971a) has relied on the ANOVA model in developing his theory of information integration. This theory is concerned with two interrelated problems. First, Anderson has used the ANOVA model to obtain scale values of the various cues as well as to assign appropriate weights. Second, integration theory uses the ANOVA approach to test certain models of information integration.

Basically, an analysis of variance partitions the total variance in the dependent variable (the judgments) and provides estimates of the amount of this variance due to each of the stimulus dimensions or factors (main effects) and their interactions. Further, the analysis of variance tests the statistical significance of these main effects and interactions. If a simple additive or linear combination of cue values determined judgments (as is suggested by a linear regression model), only the main effects should be significant. Findings of significant interactions constitute evidence for configurality in judgments.

In the multiple regression approach to cue utilization discussed above, investigators have typically selected cue profiles that were descriptive of real persons or objects. Indeed, they have frequently employed available cue profiles. Thus many studies employing the multiple regression approach have used the personality profiles of 861 psychiatric patients analyzed by Meehl (1959). In contrast, when the analysis of variance (ANOVA) paradigm is used, investigators must construct all possible combinations of cue values. Use of such an orthogonal factorial ANOVA design ensures that the cue dimensions are unrelated since every cue value is paired with every other cue value.

Most research on Anderson's integration theory has focused on attitudes rather than beliefs, and this research will be reviewed in Chapter 6 on attitude formation. In one of the few studies applying integration theory to inferential beliefs, Himmelfarb and Senn (1969) had subjects infer the social class of stimulus persons on the basis of three cues: income, education, and occupation. Using four values for each cue, they constructed the 64 possible cue profiles shown in Table 5.6. For example, the cell in the upper left-hand corner represents a stimulus person who is a tobacco laborer with fourth-grade education and a yearly income of $2,500. The cell in the bottom row of the third column represents a jeweler with a professional degree and a yearly income of $20,000. Note that some of the profiles in

Table 5.6 ANOVA Design Used by Himmelfarb and Senn (1969)

Education	Yearly income	Occupation			
		Tobacco laborer	Taxicab driver	Jeweler	Banker
Fourth grade	$ 2,500				
	4,500				
	10,000				
	20,000				
Ninth grade	2,500				
	4,500				
	10,000				
	20,000				
College degree	2,500				
	4,500				
	10,000				
	20,000				
Professional degree	2,500				
	4,500				
	10,000				
	20,000				

Table 5.6 are highly unlikely and would usually not have been included in a multiple regression analysis.[18] Among such unlikely stimuli are a "banker with a professional degree making $2,500 a year" and a "tobacco laborer with a fourth-grade education and a yearly income of $20,000."

The 70 subjects in Himmelfarb and Senn's experiment judged each of the 64 stimulus profiles twice. Separate analyses of variance performed for each of the 70 subjects revealed significant interactions for 22 subjects, indicating that the simple linear model was inadequate for at least some respondents. Himmelfarb and Senn also computed an analysis of variance over all subjects and found that all main effects as well as the pooled interaction[19] were significant. Thus each

18. Indeed, Brunswik (1952) has argued that judgments should be studied in realistic settings, and the inclusion of unrealistic profiles may be disruptive of the very process they were meant to disclose.

19. The pooled interaction is the amount of variance associated with all four interaction terms in the analysis (i.e., occupation × income, occupation × education, income × education, and occupation × education × income).

dimension made a significant contribution to judgments of social status, but prediction could be improved by taking interactions into account. This finding again indicates that a simple linear model is not an accurate description of the way in which some of the subjects utilized information to make judgments about social status.

Himmelfarb and Senn attempted to explain the deviations from linearity. In accordance with Anderson's integration theory, they used row and column means as estimates of each cue's scale value. For example, the mean judgment of social status for all stimulus persons who are tobacco laborers (i.e., all stimuli in the first column of Table 5.6) is used as an estimate of the scale value of the cue "tobacco laborer." Similarly, the mean judgment of social status for all persons earning $10,000 is used as an estimate of the value placed on the cue "$10,000." Assuming equal weights, they combined these scale values in a linear fashion to compute predicted judgments for each stimulus person. By examining those profiles that exhibited the greatest discrepancies between predicted and obtained judgments, Himmelfarb and Senn discovered a "contrast effect." When one cue value was high and the other two low (or when one was low and two high), the obtained judgment was higher (or lower) than the judgment predicted by a linear model with equal weights.[20] Thus the judgments indicated that more weight was placed on the inconsistent cue.

There is clearly some evidence for nonlinear combinations of cues in the analysis of variance paradigm, but here, as in studies using multiple regression analyses, much of the variance can be accounted for by a linear combination rule.

In conclusion, research on cue utilization suggests that a person's inferences are derived in a consistent and predictable manner from the information available to him. When either a multiple regression or an analysis of variance approach is used, integration of diverse items of information is found to be consistent with a weighted linear model. That is, by making the assumption that each cue dimension is given a weight and that the weighted cue values are combined in an additive fashion, one can make highly accurate predictions of the individual's inferences. However, there is considerable doubt whether the weighted linear model is an accurate description of the actual inference process. Empirical evidence suggests that people often combine information in nonlinear ways to arrive at their judgments, in spite of the fact that a weighted linear model accounts for much of the variance in these judgments. A more detailed comparison of linear and non-

---

20. This contrast effect contradicts the findings of an earlier study by Anderson and Jacobson (1965), in which the inconsistent cue was found to be "discounted"; that is, it was given less (not more) weight than expected on the basis of a linear model. However, in contrast to the judgments of belief content required of subjects in the Himmelfarb and Senn experiment, subjects in the earlier study made evaluative judgments. Thus, again, a given finding with respect to attitudinal responses may not be generalizable to a belief dimension. Moreover, in a second study reported by Himmelfarb and Senn (1969) neither a contrast nor a discounting effect was found.

linear models will be found in our discussion of attitude formation in Chapter 6.

Irrespective of the descriptive validity of a linear model, research on cue utilization, like research on trait relations, suggests that an individual's inferences are based on fairly stable and internally consistent patterns of relations among beliefs. Since studies on cue utilization have often obtained judgments about objects other than persons, subjects may be viewed as holding not only implicit theories of personality but also implicit theories about the attributes of objects, institutions, or events. By focusing on individual differences, cue utilization research has demonstrated that the perceived relations among attribute dimensions vary across individuals. This raises the question as to how a person learns the relations between beliefs.

Learning to Make Accurate Inferences

Thus far, we have been concerned primarily with descriptive accounts of inferential belief formation, and we have not paid much attention to the accuracy of the inferences. Festinger (1954) has suggested that people strive to hold correct opinions or beliefs about the world. Indeed he "posited the existence of a drive to determine whether or not one's opinions were 'correct'" (p. 118). He further argued that when objective, nonsocial means are not available, people test the accuracy of their opinions by comparing them with the opinions of others. It follows that individuals will tend to revise their beliefs as a function of the positive and negative feedback they receive from the social or nonsocial environment. For example, a person may believe that a certain politician favors increased military spending. He can attempt to assess the accuracy of this belief by discussing the candidate's position with his friends, coworkers, etc., who will agree or disagree with him. Depending on the nature of this feedback, he may revise his belief. Alternatively, he can examine the politician's voting record or attend a lecture given by the politician, thus receiving direct information concerning the degree to which his belief is correct. Festinger (1954) has argued that a person will compare his beliefs with those of others primarily when objective criteria are not available. As a result of this feedback and revision process, a person will tend to hold beliefs that reflect physical realities or, when objective physical criteria are unavailable, beliefs that tend to agree with those of certain relevant others.[21]

Two lines of research have been concerned with the effects of feedback on inferential beliefs: multiple cue learning and concept formation.

Multiple Cue Learning

We have seen that multiple regression analyses have been used to estimate the relative weights that an individual places on different cues in arriving at an inference. These weights were found to permit accurate prediction of the individual's

---

21. Among other things, Festinger's theory of social comparison processes attempts to identify the relevant others who are used for comparison purposes.

inferences on the basis of a weighted linear model. We can now ask whether it is possible to provide the individual with information that will change these weights such that he will make more accurate judgments of the criterion.[22]

In multiple cue learning, a subject is shown a set of cues describing some object and is asked to make an inferential judgment about the object. After each judgment he is given feedback as to the accuracy of his judgments. Sometimes subjects are simply told whether their inferences were correct or incorrect. Alternatively, they may be given information about the degree to which they have placed appropriate weights on the various cues (Hammond and Summers, 1972).

Brunswik's lens model. Clearly, multiple cue learning requires that some "objective" criteria or "distal variables," such as the stimulus person's actual I.Q. score or grade point average, be available. The correlation between a given cue dimension and this objective criterion is taken as an index of the cue's relevance with respect to the criterion; it has been called the cue's *ecological validity.* In addition, it is possible to compute the correlation between the individual's prediction and the actual criterion. This correlation, called the *achievement index,* reflects the accuracy of the individual's judgment. The relations between cue values, judgments, and criterion scores are part of a more complex set of relations defined by Brunswik's lens model (cf. Brunswik, 1955, 1956; Dudycha and Naylor, 1966). Figure 5.4 illustrates Hammond, Hursch, and Todd's (1964) conceptualization of

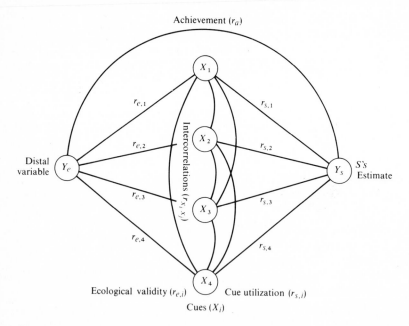

Fig. 5.4 The Lens Model. (From Hammond, Hirsch, and Todd, 1964.)

---

22. Such changes may occur, whether or not the person can accurately report the regression weights.

Brunswik's model. The model deals with relations among cues, with relations of cues to the subject's estimates (cue utilization) and to the criterion (ecological validity), and with the relation between estimates and criterion (achievement).

Early studies examined the degree to which subjects can learn to form more accurate inferential beliefs. Several studies have shown that accuracy increases as the subject's weights (i.e., his cue utilizations) come to approximate the ecological validity of cues. When subjects are given feedback as to the accuracy of their judgments, they progressively learn to place more appropriate weights on the various cues (e.g., Azuma and Cronbach, 1966; Lee and Tucker, 1962; Summers, 1962). With respect to the type of feedback given, Hammond and Summers (1972) found that telling subjects whether their inferences were correct or incorrect is not so effective as giving them information about the degree to which they placed appropriate weights on the various cues.[23]

Hammond and Summers (1972) have also shown that accuracy is influenced not only by appropriate weighting of cues but also by the degree to which these weights are used in a systematic fashion. Even after a person has learned to assign appropriate weights to the cues, such random factors as boredom, mood, and inattention can result in inconsistent application of cue weights, thus adding error to the judgment and reducing accuracy. Consistent with this notion, Goldberg (1970) showed that the multiple regression equation (which uses the subject's regression weights in a systematic fashion) enabled predictions of the criterion which were more accurate than the subject's own predictions. Hence the "model of man" (i.e., use of a linear regression model) tends to be more consistent and accurate than man himself.[24]

According to Hammond and Summers (1972), a distinction must be made between *obtaining* "knowledge" or information and *using* that knowledge appropriately. A similar distinction has been made in research on concept formation between learning the *attributes* of a concept (i.e., learning the relevant cues) and learning the *rule for combining* these attributes.

Concept Formation

The basic research paradigm in studies on concept formation is very similar to multiple cue learning. The subject is shown a multidimensional stimulus, such as

---

23. Studies of multiple cue learning have manipulated various aspects of ecological validity to examine effects on accuracy. For example, the relevance of cues, the nature of the cue-criterion relation, redundancy and inconsistency among cues, etc., have been found to influence accuracy of inferences and the number of trials or time required to achieve a given level of accuracy. For a review of this literature, see Slovic and Lichtenstein (1971) and D. M. Johnson (1972).

24. This finding led Goldberg to suggest a "bootstrapping" strategy to systematize prediction by using expert judges to obtain regression weights and then use the regression equation to make predictions. This procedure is similar to an approach taken by W. Edwards (1962) and others in attempts to systematize use of information in Bayesian decision making, to be discussed below.

a card containing three large blue circles. The dimensions along which stimuli vary in studies of concept formation (e.g., color, size, shape, numerosity) are comparable to cues (such as grade point average, number of credit hours attempted, etc.) in studies of multiple cue learning. The subject is then asked to associate a concept label with the stimulus or to indicate whether the stimulus is or is not an instance of a particular concept class. For example, the investigator might define the concept YAF as "three blue objects." Any stimulus displaying three blue objects—whether large or small, circles or squares—is considered a member of the concept class (is a positive instance of YAF); any stimulus that fails to display the two attributes "three" *and* "blue" is a negative instance. The investigator may define his concept in terms of any number of attributes under a variety of combination rules. In our example, the combination rule was *conjunctive* (i.e., three *and* blue). The disjunction "three" *or* "blue" would be an alternative combination rule defining a different concept. In this case, any stimulus displaying either all blue objects or any three objects would be a positive instance of the concept class. Following each judgment, the subject is told whether his judgment was correct or incorrect.

This research paradigm allows systematic investigation of the ways in which a person acquires a concept in many real-life situations. For example, a child is exposed to various moving objects, and he is told that some of these moving objects are positive instances of the concept BUS and that others are negative instances. He somehow uses this information to identify the defining attributes of BUS.

The subject's task in a concept formation study, then, is to discover the attributes and the combination rule that define a given concept. In this framework, belief formation can be viewed as a problem-solving process. Individuals use information to revise their beliefs or hypotheses concerning relevant attributes and combination rules. We can now see that multiple cue learning is also a problem-solving situation in which subjects revise their hypotheses about the relevance of cue dimensions for the criterion (i.e., about each cue's ecological validity).

As in multiple cue learning, feedback leads to successive revisions in hypotheses until the concept is correctly identified. For example, a subject might be told that the concept is defined by a conjunctive rule and that the stimulus complex "two large green squares" is a positive instance of the concept in question. At this stage, he knows that all other attributes (e.g., one, small, red, or circle) are not part of the concept. He may at this stage form the hypothesis that the concept is "square and green." If he now learns that the stimulus "two large *red* squares" is also a positive instance of the concept, he will tend to eliminate color as a relevant attribute. On the other hand, if he learned that "two large red squares" was a negative instance, he would know that "green" *is* a relevant attribute. Investigations using positive and negative instances of this kind have shown that both types of information permit subjects to form the appropriate concept. Depending on the combination rule, positive instances may be more or less informative than negative instances. Specifically, positive instances tend to be superior when the concept involves a conjunctive rule (e.g., red *and* square) whereas negative instances are superior with disjunctive rules (e.g., red *or* square). In either case, however, subjects can learn to use both types of instances with equal effectiveness (see Hovland and Weiss, 1953; Freibergs and Tulving, 1961; Chlebek and Dominowski, 1970).

Not surprisingly, studies of concept formation have manipulated many of the same stimulus variables considered in studies of multiple cue learning. Thus stimulus attributes have been manipulated in terms of redundancy, consistency, number of relevant and irrelevant attributes, the rules relating attributes to concepts, etc. To a large extent, emphasis has been placed on the effects of these factors on speed of concept acquisition (e.g., number of trials required to identify the concept) or number of errors. (For reviews of this literature, see D. M. Johnson, 1972, and Bourne, Ekstrand, and Dominowski, 1971.) Although speed of learning and number of errors are relevant in a problem-solving context, these measures provide little direct information concerning processes underlying formation of inferential beliefs. These measures deal with the accuracy of beliefs rather than with the ways in which inferences are made, whether the inferences are accurate or not.

Some aspects of research on concept formation, however, are more directly relevant for an understanding of inferential belief formation. Concept formation is often viewed as involving a process of logical reasoning whereby alternative hypotheses are successively eliminated (cf. Levine, 1966; Huttenlocker, 1967; Bourne, 1963). Much of the concept formation research has attempted to identify and describe the kinds of strategies that subjects use in their attempts to discover the "correct" concept [25] (e.g., Bruner, Goodnow, and Austin, 1956; Levine, 1966; Laughlin and Jordan, 1967; Laughlin, 1965, 1966; Bourne, 1963). These strategies or logical reasoning processes employed by persons when they acquire a concept are examples of formal coding systems (Bruner, 1957) that may provide the basis for inferential belief formation.

Formal Inference Models

We have seen that inferences are often based on perceived relations among beliefs. These lawful relations among beliefs tend to be based on probabilistic consistency. Various models derived from probability theory deal explicitly with the relations between subjective probabilities (i.e., beliefs). Only recently, however, have models of this type attracted the attention of investigators in the attitude area. Prior to the development of mathematical probability theory, philosophers concerned with logic and syllogistic reasoning also attempted to formalize the inference process, and we therefore turn first to a brief discussion of syllogistic reasoning.

---

25. Sometimes subjects are asked to provide verbal reports of their hypotheses at various stages of the concept formation process.

Syllogistic Reasoning

Logical syllogisms. In our discussion of concept formation, we emphasized the processes whereby a person solves the problem of identifying a given concept. One possible interpretation of the person's behavior in concept formation or problem-solving situations is that he attempts to eliminate alternative hypotheses by some process of logical reasoning. The approach to an understanding of such processes has been for the experimenter to specify a logical analysis of the necessary and sufficient steps or operations for solving the problem. "The logical sequence then serves as a normative model of the subject's behavior and the experimenter looks for evidence of this logic in the subject's actual behavior." (Bourne, Ekstrand, and Dominowski, 1971, p. 230)

The problem of drawing valid conclusions from certain premises has occupied philosophers for a long time, and their efforts have resulted in a set of formal rules for making such inferences. Research concerning the degree to which individuals draw valid conclusions as prescribed by these formal models has centered around the logical syllogism. A syllogism consists of three belief statements or propositions, two of which serve as premises and the third as a conclusion. For instance, consider the following three propositions.

Premise 1:   Communists are atheists.

Premise 2:   Russians are Communists.

Conclusion: Russians are atheists.

Belief statements of this kind link an object (O) to an attribute (X). Within the syllogistic framework, four forms of belief statements have been considered.

1. Universal affirmative: All O is X.
2. Universal negative: No O is X.
3. Particular affirmative: Some O is X.
4. Particular negative: Some O is not X.

One standard syllogistic figure involving the conclusion O is X consists of a minor premise linking O to some middle term M, a major premise linking M to X, and the conclusion O is X. Indeed, the example above concerning Russians and atheism can be stated symbolically as follows:

Major premise: M is X (Communists are atheists).

Minor premise: O is M (Russians are Communists).

Conclusion: O is X (Russians are atheists).

One difficulty with this example is its failure to specify whether its affirmative propositions are universal or particular, thus making impossible the determination of the conclusion's validity. The conclusion "All Russians are Communists" would be valid only if both major and minor premises were stated in universal affirmative form. Clearly, by varying the forms of belief statements (i.e., their universality and affirmativeness), one can construct many different syllogisms, only some of which have valid conclusions.

Similarly, it is possible to construct different types of syllogisms by varying the position of the middle term in major and minor premises. Four basic configurations, or types, can be identified.

	Type 1	Type 2	Type 3	Type 4
Major premise:	M is X.	X is M.	M is X.	X is M.
Minor premise:	O is M.	O is M.	M is O.	M is O.
Conclusion:	O is X.	O is X.	O is X.	O is X.

Stated in universal affirmative form, only the first type of syllogism is valid. When forms other than the universal affirmative are used, the different types of syllogisms lead to some valid and some invalid conclusions. Further, it can be impossible to determine whether the conclusion is valid or invalid.

Syllogistic reasoning has often been investigated by varying the type of syllogism and the form of the propositions. A judgment is typically elicited in one of two ways. First, the complete syllogism is presented, and the subject is asked to indicate whether the conclusion is valid or invalid (true-false format). Alternatively, the two premises are presented together with the set of four forms of the conclusion, and the subject is asked to judge which form is valid (in a multiple-choice format); he is usually given the additional alternative "No valid conclusion is possible." Experimental research indicates that more invalid conclusions are reached with some types of syllogisms and proposition forms than with others (Woodworth and Sells, 1935; Morgan and Morton, 1944; Chapman and Chapman, 1959; Roberge, 1970). Further, with the multiple-choice format, different subjects tend to make similar systematic errors. For example, given a syllogism where no valid conclusion is possible, there is usually strong agreement among subjects that one of the incorrect alternatives is valid (Roberge, 1970). Another factor that has influenced judgments of conclusion validity is the content of the propositions. Syllogisms have been presented in terms of abstract symbols (e.g., "All x are y"), in terms of nonsense syllables (e.g., "All DAB are ZIG"), or in terms of meaningful statements (e.g., "All Russians are Communists"). Although the same type of errors tends to be found with the different formats, the introduction of meaningful propositions results in certain unique aspects. For example, the desirability or controversiality of the conclusion has been found to affect judgments of validity (e.g., Janis and Frick, 1943; Lefford, 1946).

Like studies of multiple cue learning and concept formation, studies of syllogistic reasoning have dealt with problem-solving situations, and they are only indirectly relevant for an understanding of the processes underlying inferential belief formation. However, by carefully examining the kinds of errors that subjects typically make, one can gain some information concerning their reasoning processes. Note that within a problem-solving situation, a person may agree that a given conclusion can be validly derived from the premises, even though he may not *agree* with either the premises or the conclusion. Indeed, as noted above, some investigators have examined the degree to which a person's own beliefs or attitudes affect his judgments of validity. Although such effects have sometimes been found, there is evidence that subjects who score high on an ordinary test of reasoning ability (i.e., one using abstract symbols or noncontroversial material) are most able to discount their own biases when judging the validity of controversial conclusions (Feather, 1964b). This finding, like others noted above, suggests that subjects tend to make inferences along lines of probabilistic consistency and will make judgments along evaluative lines only when there is no basis for probabilistic consistency or when they fail to perceive such a basis.

This question concerning effects of beliefs and attitudes on reasoning emphasizes the distinction between a problem-solving approach and our interest in inferential belief formation. To study the formation of inferential beliefs, one would be concerned not with the effects of various factors on a subject's ability to judge the *validity* of a given conclusion, but rather with their effects on the degree to which he *agrees* with the conclusion. Thus one would be interested in knowing whether the type of syllogism or form of propositions influences acceptance of the conclusion. Similarly, one would investigate the extent to which acceptance of the conclusion is influenced by the degree to which a person agrees with (or believes) the major and minor premises or by his judgment of the conclusion's desirability.

Verbal generalizations. Abelson and his associates (Gilson and Abelson, 1965; Abelson and Kanouse, 1966; Kanouse, 1971) have investigated the likelihood that subjects will *accept* some general conclusion on the basis of limited information. "In these studies respondents were presented with simple assertions (i.e., propositions) containing a subject, verb, and object. In addition they were given mixed evidence bearing on the truth of the assertion; that is, some of the evidence supported the assertion while some contradicted it. The respondent's task was to indicate whether he felt that the assertion was true or false in the light of the given evidence." (Kanouse, 1971, p. 2) The evidence consisted of three propositions pertaining either to the subject or the object of the conclusion. Further, the information was selected such that subjects could either make an induction by inferring the conclusion from specific instances or make a deduction by inferring the conclusion from more general qualities. Examples of the four kinds of quasi-syllogisms used by Abelson and Kanouse (1966) are presented in Table 5.7. Respondents were given a large number of such items, with subjects, verbs, and objects systematically varied from item to item. "Instructions emphasized that the task should not be regarded as a test of logic but that the subjects' answers should be based on their intuitive reactions to the evidence." (Kanouse, 1971; p. 2) Nevertheless, it appears that a certain degree of problem solving is involved in this task; that is, subjects are asked to judge whether the conclusion appears reasonable in light of the evidence presented.

Results of several studies indicated that these judgments were influenced primarily by three factors: whether the item involved induction or deduction,

Table 5.7 Quasi-Syllogisms (from Abelson and Kanouse, 1966)

Form I.   Altogether there are three kinds of tribes:
           Southern, Northern, Central

       Southern tribes do not have sports magazines
       Northern tribes have sports magazines
       Central tribes do not have sports magazines

       Do tribes have sports magazines?

Form II.   Altogether there are three kinds of magazines:
           Sports, News, Fashions

       Southern tribes do not have sports magazines
       Southern tribes do not have news magazines
       Southern tribes have fashion magazines

       Do Southern tribes have magazines?

Form III. All candidates are ambitious, long-winded, outgoing individuals

       Ambitious individuals produce choral music
       Long-winded individuals produce choral music
       Outgoing individuals do not produce choral music

       Do candidates produce choral music?

Form IV.   All choral music is agreeable, rhythmic, noninstrumental sound

       Candidates produce agreeable sound
       Candidates do not produce rhythmic sound
       Candidates produce noninstrumental sound

       Do candidates produce choral music?

whether the evidence was subject-specific or object-specific, and the kind of verb used. For inductive items, object-specific evidence produced greater agreement than subject-specific evidence, whereas the opposite was true for deductive items. Further, the amount of agreement produced by inductive or deductive items depended on the nature of the verb in the conclusion. Attempts to explain the unanticipated strong effect of the verb have focused on the universality of propositions. We have shown earlier that statements such as "candidates produce choral music" are ambiguous in that they do not specify whether the proposition is universal or particular. Clearly, a given set of evidence may be sufficient for a person to agree that "*some* candidates produce choral music" but not that "*all* candidates produce choral music." Abelson and Kanouse (1966) found that different verbs influence the amount of evidence required to produce agreement with the ambiguous conclusion.[26]

---

26. Kanouse (1971) has suggested an alternative explanation, according to which different verbs lead respondents to assign different "implicit quantifiers" (i.e., all, some, a few, etc.) to subjects and objects.

Although these studies are suggestive of the ways in which relations among propositions can be investigated, and although they have produced some interesting results, the processes of probabilistic inferences have not been formalized. In our opinion, research concerning these questions could profit from an application of some more formal probabilistic models which provide precise statements of the relations between premises and conclusions. Such models make explicit the central question asked in the studies by Abelson and his associates: What is the probability of accepting a conclusion, given certain types of evidence? Let us thus consider some probabilistic formulations that have been applied in research on inferential belief formation.

Probability Models

Based on mathematical probability theory, various models have been employed to account for relationships between subjective probabilities.[27] These models are *normative* rather than *descriptive;* that is to say, they prescribe what relations should exist between probabilities or how beliefs ought to change in light of new information. Thus probability models describe the belief structures of "rational" or "logically consistent" persons rather than those of actual persons. Nevertheless, it is possible to use probability models as first approximations for a psychological theory of inferential belief formation (Peterson and Beach, 1967). Probabilistic consistency, therefore, refers to the degree to which a person's inferences correspond to the relationships specified by probability theory; deviations from the normative model indicate that such "nonrational" factors as the person's attitudes or personality characteristics may influence his probabilistic judgments or beliefs.

Several investigators have attempted to test the general hypothesis that relations among subjective probabilities obey objective-probability laws. For example, according to probability theory the conjunctive probability that both A and B are true is represented by Eq. 5.1,

$$p(A \cap B) = p(A|B)p(B), \qquad (5.1)$$

where $p(A \cap B)$ is the conjunctive probability of A and B; $p(A|B)$ is the conditional probability of A, given that B is true; and $p(B)$ is the probability of B.

The conjunction $p(A \cap B)$ can also be written

$$p(A \cap B) = p(B|A)p(A). \qquad (5.2)$$

Equations 5.1 and 5.2 imply that

$$p(A|B)p(B) = p(B|A)p(A). \qquad (5.3)$$

27. Following Savage (1954) it has usually been assumed that subjective probabilities have the same mathematical properties as the objective probabilities of mathematical probability theory. Thus, it is usually assumed that subjective probabilities range from 0 to 1 and that the subjective probabilities of a set of mutually exclusive and exhaustive events sum to 1.

According to probability theory, the disjunctive probability that either A or B is true is given by Eq. 5.4,

$$p(A \cup B) = p(A) + p(B) - p(A \cap B), \qquad (5.4)$$

where $p(A \cup B)$ is the disjunctive probability of A or B.

Wyer (1970a) investigated the descriptive accuracy of Eqs. 5.2 and 5.4. He obtained measures of subjective probabilities for each term in these equations on a scale ranging from 0 (*extremely unlikely*) to 10 (*extremely likely*). The estimates were divided by 10 so that the subjective-probability measures could range from 0 to 1. Subjects read nine hypothetical situations, and their subjective-probability estimates were based on these descriptions. For example, one situation dealt with the reelection of a political candidate (Governor Smith). Two belief statements were of central importance.

A: Governor Smith will be reelected.

B: State aid to education will be increased.

Subjects were asked to estimate the following probabilities.

$p(A)$	The probability that Governor Smith will be reelected
$p(B)$	The probability that state aid to education will be increased
$p(B\|A)$	The probability that if Governer Smith is reelected, state aid to education will be increased
$p(B\|\overline{A})$	The probability that if Governor Smith is not reelected, state aid to education will be increased
$p(A \cap B)$	The probability both that Governor Smith will be reelected *and* that state aid to education will be increased
$p(A \cup B)$	The probability either that Governor Smith will be reelected *or* that state aid to education will be increased *or* that both events will occur

Wyer's results supported the notion that subjective probabilities follow the laws of objective probabilities. A correlation was computed between $p(A \cap B)$ and $p(B|A)p(A)$ in each of the hypothetical situations; the average correlation was .61. Further, there was considerable correspondence between $p(A \cup B)$ and $p(A) + p(B) - p(A \cap B)$, as suggested by Eq. 5.4. Similar results were reported by Wyer and Goldberg (1970).

The descriptive accuracy of Eq. 5.3 was examined by Peterson *et al.* (1965). These investigators looked at inferences among a set of 20 personality traits, such as dishonest, brave, witty, weak. For each trait, subjects provided estimates of unconditional or prior probabilities by indicating the number of people in 100 that could be described correctly by the trait. Further, estimates of conditional probabilities for all 190 possible trait pairs were also obtained by asking the following question: 100 persons are known to be *Trait A* (e.g., weak). How many of them would you expect to be *Trait B* (e.g., witty)? Thus, for each subject

95 estimates of $p(A|B)$ and 95 estimates of $p(B|A)$ were available. A correlation was computed for each subject across the 95 values of $p(A|B)p(B)$ and $p(B|A)p(A)$; the mean correlation for the total sample of 12 subjects was .67. In a second study, a correlation of .92 was reported for a different estimation task.

It thus appears that probability formulations of this kind provide fairly accurate descriptions of the relations among subjective probabilities. Reviewing the literature on intuitive statistical inferences, Peterson and Beach (1967) concluded that "probability theory and statistics can be used as the basis for psychological models that integrate and account for human performance in a wide range of inferential tasks. . . . Experiments that have compared human inferences with those of statistical man show that the normative model provides a good first approximation for a psychological theory of inference." (pp. 29 and 42)

Wyer (1970b) has shown that probability notions can be used to provide explicit quantitative definitions of several concepts discussed previously. Thus *redundancy* of two pieces of information A and B is defined by the degree to which $p(A \cap B)$ is greater than $p(A)p(B)$. Conversely, *inconsistency* of two pieces of information is defined by the degree to which $p(A \cap B)$ is smaller than $p(A)p(B)$. These definitions can be derived from Eq. 5.1. When A and B are independent pieces of information, that is, when they are neither redundant nor inconsistent,

$$p(A|B) = p(A). \qquad (5.5)$$

Thus, if we assume independence, Eq. 5.1 can be rewritten

$$p(A \cap B) = p(A)p(B). \qquad (5.6)$$

According to Wyer, when $p(A \cap B) > p(A)p(B)$, the two pieces of information are redundant since their joint probability exceeds the probability that would be expected if they were independent. Similarly, when $p(A \cap B) < p(A)p(B)$, the two pieces of information must be inconsistent. Wyer also used probability notions to define *novelty;* specifically, he defined novelty of two pieces of information A and B as the probability of their disjunction, that is, $p(A \cup B)$. Looking at Eq. 5.4, we can see that novelty of two events is thus defined as the sum of the information provided by each event in isolation minus the information common to the two events. The utility of these definitions will be discussed in later chapters.

A Model of Logical Consistency

One of the first applications of probability notions in the attitude area was McGuire's (1960a, b, c) attempt to provide a quantitative definition of consistency among beliefs by developing a model that combined formal logic and probability theory. The model was developed and applied in the context of logical syllogisms. McGuire used syllogisms of Type 1 and argued as follows: "Consider three issues so interrelated that a person taking Stands a and b on two of these issues would, if he were to be consistent, be logically required to take Stand c on the third. That is, the three stands are in a syllogistic relationship, with c following as a valid conclusion from the conjunction of *a* and *b*. If the person's opinions on these issues are obtained by having him indicate his adherence to each of the Stands, *a*, *b*, and *c*, on a probabilistic scale, we can specify that to be completely consistent, these probabilistically scaled opinions must be interrelated in the form

$$p(c) = p(a \cap b) + p(k)(1 - p(a \cap b)), \qquad (5.7)$$

where $p(k)$ is his opinion of the probability of *c* on bases other than the conjunction of *a* and *b*." (McGuire, 1960b, p. 346) If we assume that *a*, *b*, and *k* are independent of each other [that is, $p(a \cap b \cap k) = p(a)p(b)p(k)$], and that $p(a \cap b)$ and $p(k)$ are mutually exclusive [that is, $p[(a \cap b) \cap k] = 0$], Eq. 5.7 simplifies to Eq. 5.8: [28]

$$p(c) = p(a)p(b) + p(k). \qquad (5.8)$$

McGuire (1960a, b) constructed 16 syllogisms, one of which read as follows:

Major premise: Any form of recreation that constitutes a serious health menace will be outlawed by the City Health Authority.

Minor premise: The increasing water pollution in this area will make swimming at the local beaches a serious health menace.

Conclusion: Swimming at the local beaches will be outlawed by the City Health Authority.

The 48 propositions constituting the syllogisms were presented in random order, and subjects were asked to "indicate in probabilistic terms the extent of their adherence to the stand taken in each proposition" (McGuire, 1960b, p. 346). These estimates were obtained on graphic scales ranging from *very improbable* (0) to *very probable* (100).

By assuming that $p(k)$ is equal across syllogisms or at least uncorrelated with the conclusion, one may disregard $p(k)$ in a correlational analysis.[29] McGuire's model then implies that the degree of a person's logical consistency is indexed by the correlation between $p(c)$ and $p(a)p(b)$.[30] The results in two of McGuire's (1960a, c) experiments indicated a considerable degree of logical consistency.

---

28. McGuire's basic model states that
$$p(c) = p[(a \cap b) \cup k].$$
Expanding the right-hand side, we get
$$p[(a \cap b) \cup k] = p(a \cap b) + p(k) - p(a \cap b \cap k).$$
Assuming that *a*, *b*, and *k* are mutually exclusive reduces this expression to
$$p(a \cap b) + p(k)$$
and after the assumption is made that *a* and *b* are independent,
$$p(c) = p(a)p(b) + p(k).$$
29. Adding a constant to a variable will not alter that variable's correlation with some other variable.
30. Because of the indeterminacy of $p(k)$, exact point predictions of $p(c)$ from $p(a)p(b)$ cannot be made; it can only be stated that $p(c) \geqslant p(a)p(b)$.

McGuire obtained group means for $p(a)$, $p(b)$, and $p(c)$ within each syllogism and computed the correlation between $p(a)p(b)$ and $p(c)$ across syllogisms. In one study (1960a), in which 16 syllogisms were used, the obtained correlation was .48, and in another study (1960c), with eight syllogisms, the correlation was .74.

Similar results were reported by Holt and Watts (1969) and Watts and Holt (1970), who used eight of McGuire's syllogisms in further tests of the model. Correlations were reported by Holt and Watts; the average correlation between predicted and obtained probabilities of the conclusion was .53. Similarly, Dillehay, Insko, and Smith (1966) used all 16 of McGuire's syllogisms and obtained an average correlation of .74 in one study and .54 in a second study.

McGuire (1960a, c) also attempted to investigate the notion that a person's attitudes toward the propositions (i.e., his ratings of their desirability) may influence the degree to which he is logically consistent. His subjects indicated their feelings regarding the desirability of each of the propositions on a five-place scale ranging from *very desirable* to *very undesirable*. A correlation of .40 was found between the mean desirability and probability ratings across 48 propositions (McGuire, 1960a). Other investigators (e.g., Holt and Watts, 1969; Watts and Holt, 1970; Dillehay, Insko, and Smith, 1966) have also found a tendency for subjects to agree more with desirable than with undesirable belief statements. However, as McGuire (1960a) has pointed out, this correlation between perceived likelihood and desires does not necessarily represent cognitive distortion or "wishful thinking." It may simply reflect the (plausible) view that desirable events are indeed more likely to occur than undesirable events.

Therefore, in order to examine the extent to which the desirability of propositions affects logical consistency, McGuire recomputed the correlation between $p(c)$ and $p(a)p(b)$ while statistically controlling for desirability. Specifically, he computed the partial correlation between mean $p(c)$ and mean $p(a)p(b)$ scores across all syllogisms, with the rated desirability of the conclusion and the mean of the desirability ratings of the two premises partialed out. These analyses increased the correlation from .48 to .85 in the study with 16 syllogisms (McGuire, 1960a) and from .74 to .96 in the eight-syllogism study (McGuire, 1960c). Unfortunately, this type of analysis has not been reported in other studies.[31]

McGuire's findings suggest that although there is considerable evidence for probabilistic consistency, inferences may be partially determined by evaluative

---

31. It has often been argued that wishful thinking is indicated when the discrepancy between predicted and obtained probabilities of the conclusion $[p(c) - p(a)p(b)]$ is larger for syllogisms with desirable conclusions than for those with undesirable conclusions. This argument assumes that $p(k)$ is constant across syllogisms (see note 29). However, the work of Abelson and his associates discussed above (Abelson and Kanouse, 1966; Kanouse, 1971) suggests that this assumption may be misleading. On the basis of their findings it could be argued that different amounts of evidence are required for acceptance of desirable and undesirable conclusions, and thus $p(k)$ would vary across syllogisms.

consistency. As in syllogistic reasoning, however, it has been found (Watts and Holt, 1970) that the relation between probability and desirability is stronger for low-intelligence subjects than for those of high intelligence. A similar result was found by Dillehay, Insko, and Smith (1966) in that the correlation was higher for freshmen and sophomores than for juniors and seniors. Thus it appears that intelligent and more educated individuals are likely to be logically consistent and are less likely to exhibit "wishful thinking."

A Conditional Consistency Model

In addition to the *categorical* statements of logical syllogisms (that is, *O* is *X*) it is possible to consider *conditional* statements of the form: If *A* then *B*. When such a conditional statement is taken as a major premise, a minor premise can be added and a conclusion can be deduced (cf. D. M. Johnson, 1972, p. 258). Consider, for example, the following propositions.

Major premise: If *A* is a fish, then *A* can swim.

Minor premise: *A* is a fish.

Conclusion: *A* can swim.

This formulation can be seen as representative of the situations employed by Wyer (1970a) and Wyer and Goldberg (1970). The situation involving reelection of Governor Smith can again serve as an illustration.

Major premise: If Governor Smith is reelected, then state aid to education will be increased—$p(B|A)$.

Minor premise: Governor Smith will be reelected—$p(A)$.

Conclusion: State aid to education will be increased—$p(B)$.

Wyer and Goldberg used the following probability model to describe inferential belief formation in such situations.

$$p(B) = p(B|A)\, p(A) + p(B|\overline{A})p(\overline{A}). \qquad (5.9)$$

The terms $p(B)$, $p(A)$, $p(B|A)$, and $p(B|\overline{A})$ were previously defined; $p(\overline{A})$ refers to the prior probability that A is not true and $p(\overline{A}) = 1 - p(A)$.[32] Wyer (1970a) and Wyer and Goldberg (1970) found considerable support for this model. Note that in contrast to McGuire's model of logical consistency, all terms in Eq. 5.9 can be directly estimated. Indeed, the reader will recall that subjects in these studies provided probability estimates for each term in the equation.

---

32. This model is a special case of the more general expression

$$p(B) = \sum_{i=1}^{n} p(B|X_i)p(X_i).$$

With two mutually exclusive and exhaustive events in X (that is, A and $\overline{A}$) this expression reduces to Eq. 5.9.

Predicted and obtained values of $p(B)$ should directly correspond if subjects make inferences as prescribed by the normative model. In support of this hypothesis, Wyer (1970a) and Wyer and Goldberg (1970) found that predicted and obtained probabilities corresponded very closely (see Fig. 5.5).

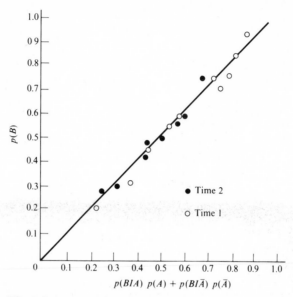

Fig. 5.5 Relation between predicted and obtained probabilities. (Reprinted from Wyer, 1970.)

Wyer and Goldberg further tried to show the correspondence between their model and McGuire's model of logical consistency (see Eq. 5.8). Basically, the $p(a)$, $p(b)$, and $p(c)$ terms in McGuire's model were considered equivalent to $p(A)$, $p(B|A)$, and $p(B)$, respectively, by Wyer and Goldberg. If McGuire's terms are substituted in Eq. 5.9, the following expression results.

$$p(c) = p(a)p(b) + p(c|\bar{a})p(\bar{a}). \qquad (5.10)$$

Comparing this expression with McGuire's model in Eq. 5.8, we can see that the two models are identical if $p(k)$ is set equal to $p(c|\bar{a})p(\bar{a})$. Although recognizing that $p(k)$ is not equivalent to $p(c|\bar{a})p(\bar{a})$, Wyer and Goldberg (1970) argued that the latter term can provide an estimate of $p(k)$, thus permitting a more precise test of McGuire's model.

In conclusion, it is apparent that subjective probabilities or beliefs are related to one another in systematic ways and that various normative probability models can provide fairly adequate descriptions of actual inference processes. McGuire (1960a) and Wyer and Goldberg (1970) also attempted to use their models to predict change in beliefs produced by persuasive communications. Clearly, according to these models, a change in one probability or belief is likely to produce changes in related beliefs, and these changes can be predicted from the model. However, the amount of change will depend on the particular interrelations existing among the various beliefs. These issues will be discussed at length in Chapter 9, which deals with principles of change.

It is important to note that, depending on the assumptions made, different models can be developed to deal with the same issues. We have already seen how the introduction of conditional probabilities by Wyer and Goldberg produced a model that, although similar to McGuire's, did not require an unspecified $p(k)$ term. Similarly, Warr and Smith (1970) compared the predictive power of six different probability models dealing with trait inferences. These models were designed to predict the conditional probability that a person has Trait A, given that he has Traits B and C. Although these models involved somewhat different assumptions, they were all found to predict inferences with considerable accuracy —another indication that trait inferences are based on probabilistic consistency. Note that any of the models used by Warr and Smith (1970) could be applied to an analysis of syllogistic reasoning since they deal with the effect of two pieces of information (e.g., two premises) on a third (e.g., a conclusion).

Bayes's Theorem

The probability models discussed thus far deal primarily with the interrelations among beliefs; when applied to belief change, they deal with the effect of change in one belief on changes in related beliefs. These models, however, do not address themselves to the question as to how the initial change is brought about. Bayes's theorem deals specifically with this problem; that is, it is concerned with the formation or revision of beliefs in light of new information. Again note that Bayes's theorem is a normative model in that it describes optimal revisions in probabilities; that is, it describes how probabilities should change if the available information is properly utilized. The theorem deals with revision of beliefs or hypotheses (H) on the basis of new information or data (D). In its simplest form, Bayes's theorem is expressed in Eq. 5.11.[33]

$$p(H|D) = \frac{p(D|H)p(H)}{p(D)}.$$ (5.11)

Consider a person who sees a stranger at a cocktail party. Without any further information, he might believe that there is a .30 probability that the stranger is a liberal. That is, on the basis of his past experience he might believe that approximately 30 out of 100 people are liberals. He now has a short conversation with the stranger, in the course of which he learns that the stranger voted for Goldwater in 1964. Bayes's theorem specifies how this new information should influence the person's belief that the stranger is a liberal—that is, what the posterior

---

33. The reader may note that this formulation can be derived from Eq. 5.3 by dividing both sides of the equation by $p(B)$. A discussion of Bayes's theorem and its implications can be found in W. Edwards, Lindman, and Savage (1963).

probability concerning the stranger's liberalness should be, given the new information that he voted for Goldwater. According to Eq. 5.11, three probabilities must be known to answer this question.

1. $p(D|H)$ The probability that a person voted for Goldwater, given that he was a liberal

2. $p(H)$ The prior probability that a person is a liberal

3. $p(D)$ The prior probability that a person voted for Goldwater

Let us assume that $p(D|H) = .10$ and that $p(D) = .40$; since we already know that $p(H) = .30$, we can compute $p(H|D)$, as follows:

$$p(H|D) = \frac{.10\ (.40)}{.30} = .13.$$

Thus, according to Bayes's theorem, the new information should reduce the person's subjective probability that the stranger is a liberal from .30 to .13. This predicted revision in subjective probability could now be compared with the person's actual revision to assess the degree to which the normative model is descriptive of actual inferences.

Bayes's theorem can also be written

$$p(H|D) = \frac{p(D|H)p(H)}{p(D|H)p(H) + p(D|\overline{H})p(\overline{H})}, \tag{5.12}$$

since $p(D) = p(D|H)p(H) + p(D|\overline{H})p(\overline{H})$. [This equation was adopted by Wyer and Goldberg (1970) as their model of conditional consistency; see Eq. 5.9.] One interesting implication of Bayes's theorem as presented in Eq. 5.12 is that no revision in belief should occur when $p(D|H) = p(D|\overline{H})$. That is, when the datum is equally likely whether or not the hypothesis is true, it should have no effect on the hypothesis. To return to our earlier example, if liberals and non-liberals were equally likely to have voted for Goldwater, the datum that the stranger voted for Goldwater would provide no information as to how liberal he is. In fact, when $p(D|H) = p(D|\overline{H})$, these terms drop out of Eq. 5.12, which then becomes

$$p(H|D) = \frac{p(H)}{p(H) + p(\overline{H})}.$$

However, $p(H) + p(\overline{H}) = 1$, so that $p(H|D) = p(H)$, and H and D are thus by definition independent (see Eq. 5.5). It follows that the datum D should have no effect on H when $p(D|H) = p(D|\overline{H})$.

When the difference between these two conditional probabilities is positive, i.e., when $p(D|H) - p(D|\overline{H}) > 0$, an upward revision in probability is expected. Conversely, when $p(D|H) - p(D|\overline{H}) < 0$, a downward revision should result. The greater the difference between $p(D|H)$ and $p(D|\overline{H})$, the more impact the datum in question should have on the posterior probability.

Clearly, a person may have several alternative hypotheses concerning a given situation. To return to our previous example, the stranger might be a liberal, moderate, or conservative, and the observer might believe that the corresponding probabilities of these hypotheses are .30, .50, and .20, respectively. The information that the stranger voted for Goldwater might lead to revisions in all these probabilities. Eq. 5.12 assumes two alternative hypotheses, $p(H)$ and $p(\overline{H})$. With reference to our example, $p(H)$ is the probability that the stranger is a liberal and $p(\overline{H})$ that he is not a liberal (i.e., a moderate or a conservative).

In many situations it is useful to consider two alternative hypotheses, $p(H)$ and $p(\overline{H})$, and Bayes's theorem can be stated with respect to each, as follows:

1. $p(H|D) = \dfrac{p(D|H)p(H)}{p(D)}.$

2. $p(\overline{H}|D) = \dfrac{p(D|\overline{H})p(\overline{H})}{p(D)}.$

A computationally convenient form of Bayes's theorem for two hypotheses is provided when the first of these equations is divided by the second:

$$\frac{p(H|D)}{p(\overline{H}|D)} = \frac{p(D|H)}{p(D|\overline{H})} \cdot \frac{p(H)}{p(\overline{H})} \tag{5.13}$$

In Eq. 5.13

$$\frac{p(H|D)}{p(\overline{H}|D)}$$

is the posterior odds with respect to Hypothesis H, that is, the extent to which Hypothesis H is more or less likely than Hypothesis $\overline{H}$. (Odds are interpreted as in betting situations.) Similarly,

$$\frac{p(H)}{p(\overline{H})}$$

is the prior odds with respect to Hypothesis H. Finally,

$$\frac{p(D|H)}{p(D|\overline{H})}$$

is known as the *likelihood ratio,* which is an index of the *diagnosticity* of the datum in question; that is, it indicates the degree to which the datum favors one hypothesis over the other. Equation 5.13 is often written more simply as

$$\Omega_1 = \text{LR } \Omega_0 \tag{5.14}$$

where Ω_1 is the posterior odds, Ω_0 is the prior odds, and LR is the likelihood ratio.

As Eq. 5.13 shows, the likelihood ratio comprises the two conditional probabilities considered earlier with respect to Eq. 5.12, that is, $p(D|H)$ and $p(D|\overline{H})$. Again, when these two terms are equal, LR = 1 and $\Omega_1 = \Omega_0$, and thus no revision in probability takes place. When $p(D|H)$ exceeds $p(D|\overline{H})$, the likelihood ratio becomes greater than 1, and the odds are expected to be revised in favor of Hypothesis H. Conversely, when $p(D|H) < p(D|\overline{H})$, LR < 1, and the odds are expected to be revised in favor of Hypothesis $\overline{H}$.

Suppose that prior to receipt of any information about the stranger in our previous example, the odds were 4:6 that he was a Republican rather than a Democrat. Further, assume that LR $= 20:1$; that is, the chances are 20 to 1 that a person who is a Republican rather than a Democrat would have voted for Goldwater. According to Bayes's theorem, the posterior odds should be 40 to 1 that the stranger is a Republican rather than a Democrat. Since the likelihood ratio greatly exceeded unity, the revision from Ω_0 to Ω_1 was considerable and in the positive direction.

Bayes's theorem can be applied sequentially for understanding the impact of several data. The posterior probability resulting from the first item of information is used as the prior probability for the second item of information, etc. Depending on the particular assumptions made, Bayes's theorem specifies whether the final posterior belief is influenced by the order in which these new items of information are received. When conditional independence between items of information is assumed, Bayes's theorem predicts that order does not affect the final posterior belief. When conditional independence is not assumed, Bayes's theorem suggests that order effects can strongly influence the final posterior odds. Thus, Bayes's theorem prescribes optimal aggregation of several items of information.[34]

A large number of studies have shown that Bayes's theorem is a reasonably good descriptive model of human information processing (see Peterson and Beach, 1967, for a good review of this literature). Revisions in beliefs tend to be probabilistically consistent and to correspond quite well to the prescriptions of Bayes's theorem.[35] In other words, there is a strong tendency not only for beliefs to be internally consistent but also for people to revise their beliefs in an orderly fashion as a result of new information. Despite this internal consistency of belief structures, however, many studies have found a tendency for subjects to be "conservative" information processors. That is to say, although "opinion change is very orderly, and usually proportional to numbers calculated from Bayes' theorem, . . . it is insufficient in amount" (Edwards, 1968, p. 18). Indeed, this tendency toward conservatism has been the focus of much of the research related to Bayes's theorem (see Edwards, 1968, and Slovic and Lichtenstein, 1971, for reviews of this literature).

The most common Bayesian experiment examines revision of beliefs about the characteristics of a population in light of a sample taken from that population.

---

34. The final posterior odds, given n items of conditionally independent information, are

$$\Omega_n = \prod_{i=1}^{n} \text{LR}_i \, \Omega_0.$$

35. However, see Kahneman and Tversky (1972) for a review of some evidence indicating that individuals may not be Bayesian information processors.

Thus a subject may be told that a bag contains either 70 percent blue and 30 percent red poker chips, or 30 percent blue and 70 percent red chips. He may then be shown a sample of, say, six blue and four red poker chips, taken at random (with replacement) from the bag. The subject estimates (either after each poker chip is drawn from the bag or at the end) the likelihood that the sample was taken from the predominantly blue bag. Since the prior probability of this event is .50, and since the likelihood ratio can be objectively determined in this situation, it is possible to compute the posterior probability by using Bayes's theorem. In this example, the posterior probability is approximately .845.[36] In comparison with this prediction, subjects tend to exhibit conservatism by estimating a somewhat lower probability.

It has been argued that this effect may be due either to the subject's *misperception* of the diagnostic value of a given datum [i.e., of the likelihood ratio $p(D|H)/p(D|\overline{H})$] or to his *misaggregation* of the data. That is, a person's subjective probabilities prior to receiving a new item of information may not be accurate, and hence his inference will not correspond to that prescribed by Bayes's theorem. Alternatively, even though the person's subjective probabilities concerning the impact of any given item of information may be accurate, he may fail to aggregate several such items in accordance with the normative model. We can see that this distinction is essentially the same as our earlier distinction between *obtaining* knowledge or information and *using* that knowledge appropriately.

The question of conservatism is concerned with the degree to which a person's inferences are *accurate,* rather than the degree to which they follow consistently from his perception of prior and conditional probabilities. As we have noted earlier, there is abundant evidence to indicate that an individual's belief structure is internally consistent and that it tends to be compatible with Bayes's theorem. Thus a person may misperceive the objective probabilities, but when his subjective probabilities are considered, Bayes's theorem allows quite accurate predictions. However, some evidence appears to indicate that subjects tend to misaggregate information; that is, their estimates of posterior probabilities tend to be conservative even in comparison with Bayesian predictions based on subjective probabilities provided by the subjects themselves (e.g., Peterson and Miller, 1965; Phillips, 1966). This apparent tendency for subjects to misaggregate data seems to be attributable to a subject's reluctance to give an extreme response early in the stimulus sequence for fear of arriving at the end of the probability scale before the last datum is presented. Indeed, investigators have found that the "misaggregation" effect disappears and conservatism is reduced when subjects are asked to

---

36. The equations are
$$\Omega_{10} = \Pi \, \text{LR} \, \Omega_0 = (7/3)^6 \cdot (3/7)^4 \cdot 1 = 5.44,$$
and
$$p(H|D) = \frac{5.44}{6.44} = .845.$$
(See note 33.)

provide estimates of odds rather than probabilities (DuCharme, 1970; Phillips and Edwards, 1966).

W. Edwards (1962) attempted to develop a strategy for aiding the decision maker such that conservatism would be eliminated. Since he assumed that conservatism was largely due to misaggregation, he proposed that experts provide estimates of likelihood ratios (and prior probabilities), and that Bayes's theorem be used to generate predictions of posterior probabilities. This procedure is quite similar to Goldberg's (1970) "bootstrapping" strategy based on research in cue utilization, which we mentioned previously. Although our discussion above suggests that misaggregation may not be a major contributor to conservatism, Edwards's strategy would nevertheless outpredict man. That is, as Goldberg suggested, the normative model operates more consistently than man and thus eliminates various sources of human error or response bias.

Very few applications of Bayes's theorem can be found in attitude research. Nevertheless, the few studies reported have dealt with such diverse areas as trait inferences (C. R. Peterson et al., 1965), impression formation (Cohen, 1973), perception of interpersonal relations (McNeel and Messick, 1970), attribution processes (Ajzen, 1971a), attitude-behavior relations (Fishbein and Ajzen, 1974), and reactions to disconfirmed expectancies (Brickman, 1972). One study of relevance to our discussion of inferential belief formation is Brickman's (1972) attempt to show that apparently irrational reactions to disconfirmed expectations may actually be quite rational revisions in beliefs; i.e., the reactions may be consistent with prescriptions of Bayes's theorem. Suppose that a person expected to get an A on an exam and received a hint that he had actually obtained a C. In comparison with a person who expected to get a C, the person who expected an A would be reluctant to accept this information; that is, his posterior probability of having a C would be relatively low. Although the apparent reluctance to accept disconfirming or unexpected information may appear to be an irrational attempt to avoid inconsistency or tension, Bayes's theorem suggests that the observed differences in posterior probabilities may merely reflect different prior probabilities. That is, a person will require more evidence to conclude with confidence that his grade is a C when he expected an A than when he expected a C.

Although Brickman's data analysis is open to criticism, his results appear to provide tentative support for these notions. Following an examination, students volunteered to learn their grades in the context of an experiment. Each student received a set of cards. All students were told that each card contained the letter A, B, C, or D and that the letter appearing most frequently in the set represented the grade for that student. They provided estimates of prior probabilities by distributing 100 points among the four letter grades. After viewing each card, each student revised his estimate by redistributing the 100 points. Each of the letters A, B, and C appeared most frequently for one third of the subjects selected at random. Thus the information was consistent with some subjects' prior probabilities and inconsistent with others'. Subjects could view as many cards as they desired. At the end of the experiment they indicated their certainty about their grades on an 11-point scale.

Consistent with expectations, subjects who received discrepant information were less certain about their grades than were subjects who received information consistent with their expectations. Since certainty can be viewed as a measure of subjective probability (see Chapter 3), this finding supports the notion that unexpected information leads to lower posterior probabilities than does expected information. However, comparing trial-by-trial *revisions* in subjective probabilities with optimal revisions prescribed by Bayes's theorem, Brickman found that unexpected information produced, on the average, smaller deviations than did expected information (but always in the direction of conservatism). Thus there was no evidence that disconfirmation of expectancies resulted in reluctance to accept the information; on the contrary, it appeared that unexpected information was used more rationally than was expected information. Unfortunately, the latter conclusion is open to question since alternative interpretations cannot be ruled out.[37] This study nevertheless provides an interesting application of Bayes's theorem, and the results suggest again that inferential belief formation tends to follow laws of probabilistic rather than evaluative consistency or tendencies toward wishful thinking.

In conclusion, Bayes's theorem specifies optimal revision of beliefs in light of new information, and it thus constitutes a model of a "rational" person whose inferences are unaffected by his desires or by other extraneous considerations. Available evidence indicates that the model provides a fairly accurate description of actual inference processes. Bear in mind, however, that at the present time Bayes's theorem has been applied only in a limited range of situations, and it is possible that greater deviations from the model will be observed in other situations.

Bayes's theorem deals with the impact of a new item of information on one or more beliefs or hypotheses. With two hypotheses (e.g., O is X versus O is not X) the likelihood ratio described earlier represents the information's *diagnosticity* with respect to the two alternative hypotheses. That is, the likelihood ratio indexes the datum's relative probability of occurrence under the two alternative hypotheses; the more the likelihood ratio deviates from unity (in either direction), the greater the information's diagnosticity. According to the model, the amount of change in a given belief is a function of the diagnostic value of the new item of information.[38]

---

37. Despite the author's claim to the contrary, the observed discrepancies between predicted and obtained revisions may be influenced by prior probabilities and may correlate with number of trials. Either of these factors could explain the greater conservatism obtained with consistent than with inconsistent information.

38. This can be seen most clearly when Bayes's theorem is stated in logarithmic form: $\log \Omega_1 - \log \Omega_0 = \log LR$ (see Eq. 5.14). In this form, the amount of revision is equivalent to $\log LR$, and it is independent of the prior odds.

The theorem itself, however, has little to say about the degree to which some new item of information has diagnostic value for a given inference. This value has to be determined on the basis of other considerations. In some situations, such as the poker-chip guessing task or in Brickman's (1972) study described above, it is possible to compute objective likelihood ratios; but in most situations of interest to the social psychologist, this cannot be done. When making an inference about a person's religiosity, for example, one would find it very difficult to determine the exact (objective) diagnosticity of the fact that the person in question was married in church. At best, we could ask our respondent to make a *subjective* estimate of the likelihood ratio under consideration and use it to predict his inference.

This is not to say, however, that it is impossible to develop some general ideas or theories about the factors that influence diagnosticity of certain kinds of information. Indeed, the different theories of attribution discussed in Chapter 2 can be viewed as attempts to specify some of those factors with respect to one kind of information, namely, information about a person's behavior. In the following section we will try to show that most of the factors which have been stipulated to influence causal attributions would also be expected to affect the diagnosticity of information on which attributions are based.

ATTRIBUTION PROCESSES

A person who observes the behavior of an actor can usually find many alternative explanations to account for the behavior; that is, he can attribute the observed behavior to different causal factors. Consider, for example, an actress who laughs at her husband's joke. In an attempt to explain this behavior, an observer might consider several hypotheses, such as: the joke is funny; the actress wants to please her husband; the husband knows how to tell jokes, etc. Unlike the poker-chip guessing task in a typical Bayesian experiment, the attribution situation involves a variety of possible hypotheses that need not be mutually exclusive. For each hypothesis the observer must determine how likely it is that the behavior in question would have been produced by, or could have been attributed to, the hypothesized causal factor.

Let B stand for the observed behavior (the datum) and H for the belief or hypothesis invoked to explain the behavior. The extent to which the behavior is viewed as produced by a given factor is represented by the likelihood ratio: $p(B|H)/p(B|\overline{H})$. The greater this ratio, the more likely it is that the behavior would have been performed if the hypothesized causal factor was present, i.e., if the hypothesis was correct. To return to our example, when the actress is viewed as likely to have laughed at her husband's joke if she wanted to please him but not otherwise, her desire to please her husband constitutes a likely explanation for her behavior.

We can see that causal attribution is here interpreted as corresponding to the likelihood ratio in Bayes's theorem. This interpretation has important implications for the effects of causal attributions on the observer's beliefs. Each alternative hypothesis constitutes at once a possible causal explanation for the behavioral event and a belief about one aspect of the total situation. For instance, the hypothesis that the joke is funny can be invoked to explain why the actress laughed at her husband's joke; at the same time it constitutes a belief about a property of the joke. The observer's posterior probability that the joke is funny has frequently been used as a measure of attribution. However, Bayes's theorem suggests that causal attribution (i.e., the likelihood ratio) corresponds to a *revision* in the belief that a given factor is present, rather than to the posterior odds in favor of that belief.

That causal attribution involves revisions from prior to posterior odds can be seen most clearly in the case of an irrelevant hypothesis. Consider the rather unlikely hypothesis that the actress laughed at her husband's joke *because* she was a brunette. Clearly, this search for a causal explanation cannot be equated with the posterior probability that the actress is a brunette. Let us assume that she indeed has brown hair. Following observation of her behavior, the observer will have a high subjective probability that the actress is a brunette (and a low subjective probability that she is not). This does not mean, however, that he will view her hair color as a satisfactory explanation for her behavior. According to Bayes's theorem, this explanation will be invoked only to the extent that the observer has *raised* his odds that the actress is a brunette *as a result* of observing her behavior. In our example, the observer's belief about the color of the actress's hair is not likely to have been influenced by the fact that she laughed at her husband's joke. It follows that this belief will not be viewed as a likely explanation for the behavior.

Most research on attribution processes has examined the effects of variations in experimental conditions on causal attributions. In terms of Bayes's theorem, one can argue that these experimental variations influence the diagnostic value of the observed behavior. Many studies have obtained direct estimates of the extent to which certain hypotheses were invoked as causal explanations for an observed behavioral event (e.g., Feather, 1969; Feather and Simon, 1971a,b; Weiner and Kukla, 1970; Frieze and Weiner, 1971; McArthur, 1972). Other studies have measured one or more of the observer's beliefs—usually about the actor's dispositions (e.g., Steiner and Field, 1960; Jones, Davis, and Gergen, 1961; Jones and Harris, 1967; Jones, Worchel, Goethals, and Grumet, 1971; Ajzen, 1971a). Most of the latter studies, however, have assessed only posterior probabilities, rather than revisions from prior to posterior odds. On the assumption that the prior odds (or probabilities) are the same in all experimental conditions, obtained differences in posterior odds should also be a direct function of the likelihood ratio, and the posterior odds or probabilities can be used as a measure of attribution. Unfortunately, posterior probabilities have sometimes been used as a measure of attribution even when prior probabilities could not be expected to be the same across experimental conditions, and from our point of view, such posterior-probability measures provide little information about attribution processes.

In conclusion, attribution theory deals with the perceived likelihood of alternative causal factors as *explanations* of observed behavior. The extent to which a potential causal factor is viewed as responsible for the behavior corresponds to the likelihood ratio in Bayes's theorem, where the behavior serves as the datum and the proposed explanation as the hypothesis. According to the Bayesian model, such causal attribution is equivalent to revisions in the hypotheses or beliefs under consideration.

Causal Attribution

An actor's behavior can usually be attributed to a large number of causal factors. If the only information available to the observer is the fact that the actor has performed the behavior in question, causal attribution may prove quite difficult. Frequently, however, the observer will have some additional information about the actor, the behavior, the conditions under which the behavior was performed, and the effects it produced. We shall now examine the effects of such additional information on the perceived likelihood of alternative causal explanations.

Effects of Consistency

In Chapter 2 we discussed several factors that are assumed to influence causal attribution. On the basis of Heider's (1958) theorizing, Kelley (1967, 1973) proposed two principles to account for causal attribution of an observed effect (or behavior). According to the *covariation principle,* "An effect is attributed to the one of its possible causes with which, over time, it covaries" (Kelley, 1973, p. 108). The *discounting principle* states that "the role of a given cause in producing a given effect is discounted if other plausible causes are also present" (Kelley, 1973, p. 113).

Consistency across occasions, objects, and actors. The covariation principle is closely tied to the notion of consistency. Kelley's analysis deals with the degree to which the behavior in question is displayed consistently on *different occasions* ("consistency"), toward *different objects* ("distinctiveness"), and by *different actors* ("consensus").

   McArthur's (1972) study illustrates these three aspects of consistency. In a direct test of Kelley's theory, McArthur described 16 hypothetical responses of different actors, such as "Ralph trips over Joan's feet while dancing," "Sue is afraid of the dog," and "Bill thinks his teacher is unfair." Consistency was manipulated by providing additional items of information. For example, to create high (or low) consistency across occasions, subjects were told that "In the past, Ralph has almost always (never) tripped over Joan's feet." High and low consistency across objects are illustrated, respectively, by "Ralph also trips over almost every other partner's feet" and "Ralph does not trip over almost any other partner's feet." Finally, high and low consistency across actors took the form of "Almost everyone (hardly anyone) else who dances with Joan trips over her feet." For each of the 16 hypothetical situations, the three kinds of consistency were varied in a 2 × 2 × 2 analysis of variance design.

Subjects indicated which of four alternatives had caused the actor's behavior: (1) something about the actor; (2) something about the object; (3) something about the particular circumstances; or (4) some combination of the first three alternatives. Note that the dependent measure of attribution in this study was a direct indication of the causal factor held responsible for the actor's behavior. A subject's response can be viewed essentially as an indication of the behavior's likelihood in the presence of a given causal factor (e.g., something about the object) relative to its likelihood under the alternative hypotheses. The response can therefore be interpreted as roughly corresponding to the likelihood ratio, $p(B|H)/p(B|\overline{H})$.

A Bayesian analysis of the expected effects is consistent with Kelley's (1973) theorizing. Consider the hypothesis that something about the actor is responsible for his behavior. The likelihood ratio for this hypothesis should increase with consistency across occasions and objects, and it should decrease with consistency across actors. To illustrate, Ralph is more likely to trip over Joan's feet when he possesses an appropriate disposition (such as clumsiness) than when he does not; that is, $p(B|H) > p(B|\overline{H})$. Each additional occasion on which Ralph trips over Joan's feet serves to increase the likelihood ratio. A similar argument can be made for repeated performance of the behavior with different partners. In contrast, information that other actors also trip over Joan's feet should increase $p(B|\overline{H})$, the probability that Ralph will trip over her feet even if he possesses no attribute that would predispose him to do so; the likelihood ratio should therefore decrease with consistency across actors.

Similar analyses with respect to the hypotheses that Ralph's behavior is due to something about Joan (the object) or about the particular circumstances lead to the following predictions: The likelihood ratio and hence causal attribution to the object should increase with consistency across occasions and actors but decrease with consistency across objects. For attribution to circumstances, the likelihood ratio should decrease as a function of consistency across actors, objects, and occasions.

McArthur (1972) tested these expectations by analyzing the frequencies with which the behavior was attributed to actor, object, and circumstances. Generally speaking, her results lent support to the predictions above. Additional empirical evidence for the predicted effects of consistency has been reported by Kelley and Stahelski (1970) and by Frieze and Weiner (1971).

Attributions to actor, object, or circumstances, however, do not provide the only possible explanations for the actor's behavior. As noted, McArthur's subjects could also attribute the behavior to some combination of those factors. By far the most frequent combinational hypothesis concerned the interaction between actor and object. Certain types of information led subjects to hypothesize that the behavior must have been caused by something peculiar to the particular combination of actor and object. This hypothesis was invoked, for instance, when there was high consistency across occasions but low consistency across objects and actors.

To see how such information would influence the likelihood ratio for the actor-object interaction, let us again consider Ralph, who trips over Joan's feet. When few other people trip over Joan's feet, when Ralph trips over few other partners' feet, but when he trips over Joan's feet time and time again, no single factor can account for the behavior. However, the probability of the behavior should be high if one assumes that the particular actor-object combination is at fault, leading to a high likelihood ratio for the combinational hypothesis.

Consistency across behaviors. We have seen that variations in consistency across occasions, objects, and actors are expected to influence the likelihood ratio in a manner compatible with Kelley's (1967, 1973) analysis of causal attribution. However, a Bayesian analysis suggests that the likelihood ratio may also be affected by the degree of consistency along other dimensions. Of particular importance is the consistency among *different behaviors* performed by the actor. It has often been argued that a person's attitudes (and other dispositions) are evidenced by consistency in his responses toward the attitude object (response-response consistency). In a similar manner it can be proposed that an observer attributes an actor's behavior to a given causal factor to the extent that other behaviors performed by the same actor are consistent with the proposed explanation.

Consider, for example, the hypothesis that Ralph tripped over Joan's feet because he is clumsy. The perceived likelihood of this explanation should increase if Ralph was also observed to spill his coffee, to drop his books, to burn his fingers while lighting a cigarette, etc. In terms of the likelihood ratio, the subjective probability of the totality of these behavioral events will be higher under the hypothesis that Ralph is clumsy than under the hypothesis that he is not. The total set of behaviors, including the tripping over a dance partner's feet, is therefore likely to be attributed to the actor's clumsiness.

Effects of sample size. The notion of consistency discussed so far refers to the *proportion* of consistent events. Specifically, we have dealt with the proportion of occasions on which a given behavior is performed, the proportion of objects toward which it is displayed, the proportion of actors who perform the same behavior, and the proportion of behaviors that are consistent with the hypothesis. The notion of consistency corresponds closely to the proportion of red and blue poker chips in a typical Bayesian experiment. The greater the proportion of red chips, the more likely it is that the sample was taken from the predominantly red bag and the less likely it is that it was taken from the predominantly blue bag. That is, the greater the proportion of red chips, the more the likelihood ratio will differ from unity. However, when the sample of chips is inconsistent (i.e., when an equal number of red and blue chips are sampled), it is about as likely that the sample was drawn from the red bag as from the blue bag and the likelihood ratio will be close to unity.

Work on Bayes's theorem suggests that when proportion is held constant, diagnosticity and hence causal attribution should increase with sample size, i.e., with the *number* of events that have been observed. Suppose that a student of average ability would pass about 50 percent of a series of tests. Information that a certain student has passed three out of four tests has considerably lower diagnostic value for inferring his ability than information that he has passed 30 out of 40 tests, although his performance is 75 percent consistent in both instances. Stated differently, it is not unlikely that a student of average ability would pass one more test than would be expected by chance (i.e., 3 out of 4) but a student who passes 10 more tests than expected (i.e., 30 out of 40) is likely to be perceived as having above average ability. Research in the poker-chip guessing situation has shown that the perceived likelihood ratio (and revision in subjective probabilities) increases with sample size (e.g., DuCharme and Peterson, 1969). Kahneman and Tversky (1972), however, have reported data suggesting that subjects may disregard sample size and base their posterior-probability judgments on the most salient characteristics of the sample, such as its proportion or mean. These conflicting findings have yet to be reconciled.

Attributions based on success and failure. In his treatment of attribution processes, Heider (1958) presented a rather detailed analysis of the factors that may be invoked to explain success or failure on a task. Adopting Heider's notions, Weiner and his associates (Weiner and Kukla, 1970; Weiner *et al.,* 1971; Frieze and Weiner, 1971) proposed four factors that may serve to explain success or failure on a task: ability, effort, task difficulty, and luck. The first two factors are internal, the last two external. Further, ability and task difficulty are relatively stable factors, and effort and luck are relatively unstable factors. This classification can be seen in Table 5.8.

Table 5.8 Perceived Determinants of Success and Failure (from Weiner *et al.,* 1971)

	Internal	External
Stable	Ability	Task difficulty
Unstable	Effort	Luck

A systematic investigation of the effects of consistency and other variables on causal explanation of success and failure has been reported by Frieze and Weiner (1971). They found that in comparison with failure, success on a task tended to be attributed to greater ability, effort, luck, and easiness of the task.[39] Obviously, these findings are quite consistent with a Bayesian analysis since success is more likely when these factors are present than when they are absent.

39. The dependent measure in this study constitutes a relatively direct measure of the likelihood ratio since subjects were asked to rate the likelihood of success or failure, given each of the four alternative hypotheses.

Of greater interest, causal attribution was also affected by consistency of an actor's present success or failure with his past performance on the same task, with his performance on similar tasks, and with the performance of other actors. The results were again in line with a Bayesian analysis. Consistent performance on the same or similar tasks increased attribution to stable factors whereas inconsistent performance increased attribution to unstable factors. Thus the success of an actor who in the past had always performed the same task successfully was attributed mainly to his ability and to the easiness of the task whereas the success of an actor who had always failed on the task was attributed to good luck. In terms of likelihood ratios, an actor's consistent success is more likely, given ability or an easy task than given lack of ability or a difficult task. However, success following failure is more likely, given good than bad luck. A Bayesian analysis also accounts for the finding that consistent performance across *actors* increased attribution to the task and reduced attribution to ability, effort, and luck.

In sum, the effects on causal attribution predicted on the basis of Kelley's (1967, 1973) covariation or consistency principle can also be derived from a consideration of the likelihood ratio in Bayes's theorem. The Bayesian analysis, moreover, suggests a number of related factors of potential importance, such as behavioral consistency and sample size.

Effects of Multiple Plausible Causes

Kelley's *discounting principle* deals with the effects of multiple plausible causes on the likelihood that a given causal factor will be invoked to explain the actor's behavior. A Bayesian analysis suggests that alternative plausible hypotheses will tend to reduce any given explanation's likelihood ratio by raising $p(B|\overline{H})$, the probability of the behavior in the absence of the causal factor under consideration.

A case in point is Bem's (1965, 1967) attributional analysis of dissonance phenomena, particularly with respect to counterattitudinal behavior under insufficient justification. Bem used the "interpersonal replication procedure," in which observers are given descriptions of one or another condition in a dissonance experiment and are asked to infer the actual subject's responses. In one study, for example, this procedure was applied to the Festinger and Carlsmith (1959) experiment on forced compliance. Observers were told that the actor who had just participated in an experiment agreed to tell and actually did tell a waiting subject that the experiment had been interesting. In one condition, the actor was said to have been offered $20, in another condition $1, for performance of this behavior. The observer's task was to infer the original subject's attitude toward the experiment. Bem found that his observers attributed a more favorable attitude to the subject in the low ($1) than in the high ($20) reward condition.

The dependent variable in this study can be viewed as the observer's posterior probability that the actor had a favorable attitude toward the experiment, given that he said the experiment was interesting. Since it seems reasonable to assume that the actor's perceived attitude prior to his telling the waiting subject that the experiment was interesting did not differ between conditions, this posterior probability can serve as a measure of attribution.

To account for Bem's findings, consider the likelihood ratio $p(B|A+)/p(B|\overline{A+})$, where B is the behavior of telling a waiting subject that the experiment was interesting, and $A+$ is the hypothesis that the actor had a favorable attitude toward the experiment. With other things equal, if the actor had a favorable attitude, he should be more likely to perform the behavior than if he did not. However, $p(B|\overline{A+})$ should increase with monetary reward offered for the behavior, producing a lower likelihood ratio under high-reward conditions. It follows that the actor's behavior should be attributed to a favorable attitude in the $1 condition but less so in the $20 condition. The same argument can be made for any other factor that serves to justify and hence to provide an alternative explanation for the actor's behavior, such as social pressure or threat of punishment for noncompliance.

Attribution of Dispositions

Internal Versus External Attributions

We have discussed variables that influence the extent to which an actor's behavior is attributed to alternative causal factors. It is often convenient to distinguish between factors *internal* to the actor, such as his stable dispositions or temporary moods and desires, and *external* factors residing in the object of his behavior or the environment. Inspired by Jones and Davis's (1965) monograph on attribution processes in person perception, much recent research has dealt with the conditions under which an observed behavior will provide the basis for a dispositional attribution. The question of interest is whether observation of a behavior will lead to the inference that the actor possesses a certain disposition (an internal factor) or to the inference that some external factor must have been present. To simplify exposition, assume that the observed behavior (B) can be attributed either to a dispositional internal factor (D) or to a nondispositional external factor ($\overline{D}$); that is, $p(\overline{D}) = 1 - p(D)$. Bayes's theorem with respect to these two alternative hypotheses can then be written as follows:

$$\frac{p(D|B)}{p(\overline{D}|B)} = \frac{p(B|D)}{p(B|\overline{D})} \cdot \frac{p(D)}{p(\overline{D})}. \tag{5.15}$$

Any factor influencing the likelihood ratio $p(B|D)/p(B|\overline{D})$ should have an effect on dispositional attribution; the greater this likelihood ratio, the more likely it is that a dispositional attribution will be made.

Based on Heider's (1958) analysis of personal causality, Jones and Davis (1965) proposed that a disposition can be attributed to an actor with confidence to the extent that the actor is perceived to have behaved intentionally. Jones and Davis therefore concentrated their analysis on the factors that influence *attribution of intention*. Following Heider, they suggested that the effects or outcomes produced by the actor's behavior are powerful determinants of dispositional attribution. An observer will attribute intentionality if he believes that the actor was aware that his actions would produce the observed effects and if he believes the effects were due to the actor's ability rather than chance factors.

Two major variables have been investigated in this context: the actor's perceived decision freedom and the perceived desirability or utility of his behavior. Generally speaking, dispositional attribution is expected to increase with perceived freedom of choice and to decrease with behavioral utility.

Perceived decision freedom. Several investigators have proposed that dispositional attribution will increase to the extent that the actor is perceived to have behaved under high freedom of choice. In an early study, Steiner and Field (1960) led subjects to believe that a confederate took a pro-segregation stand in a group discussion either under assignment to that role by the experimenter (low decision freedom) or of his own free choice (high decision freedom). Subjects were more confident in attributing a pro-segregation stand to the confederate under high than under low freedom of choice.[40]

The prediction of stronger attribution under high decision freedom also follows from a Bayesian analysis. It stands to reason that a behavior performed under low freedom of choice has little diagnostic value; that is, the behavior (B) is as likely to be performed with or without the disposition (D) in question. Under high freedom of choice, however, the behavior is more likely to be performed when the actor has the appropriate disposition than when he does not. To put this more formally, the likelihood ratio $p(B|D)/p(B|\overline{D})$ should be close to unity in the case of low decision freedom, whereas it should exceed unity under high freedom of choice.

Perceived behavioral desirability. According to Jones and Davis (1965), given the assumption that the actor intended to produce the observed behavior, the lower its apparent attractiveness or desirability, the more likely it is that a dispositional attribution will be made. For example, celebrating a religious holiday is usually considered more pleasant or desirable than driving to church in a snowstorm. The desirability hypothesis suggests that an actor will be seen as more religious when he has been observed driving to church in a snowstorm than when he has been observed celebrating a religious holiday. From a Bayesian point of view, a desirable behavior is likely to be performed whether or not the actor has the disposition in question [that is, $p(B|D) \approx p(B|\overline{D})$]. In contrast, an unattractive behavior is more likely to be performed by a person having the appropriate disposition than by a person who does not [that is, $p(B|D) > p(B|\overline{D})$]. It follows that an undesirable behavior will tend to be more diagnostic than a desirable behavior.

---

40. Contrary to expectations, however, the attributed positions themselves did not differ in the two conditions. This demonstrates that a probabilistic measure of belief strength may show different results than will a measure of belief position.

In an experimental test of the desirability hypothesis, Jones, Davis, and Gergen (1961) had subjects listen to a tape recording of a role-playing situation in which an actor was applying to become either an astronaut or a submariner. The instructions given to the actor (which were also recorded on the tape) made it clear that in the forthcoming job interview it would be desirable for the actor to respond in an inner-directed fashion (in the astronaut condition) or in an other-directed fashion (in the submariner condition). In the interview, the actor was heard to respond either in an inner- or in an other-directed fashion. After listening to the interview, subjects were asked to rate the actor's "true" other- or inner-directedness.[41]

The manipulations of this study resulted in a 2×2 analysis of variance design, which is shown in Table 5.9—together with the obtained results (high scores indicate attributed other-directedness). Note that undesirable behaviors, i.e., behaviors inappropriate for the job sought, had greater impact on posterior probabilities than did desirable behaviors. The actor who behaved in an other-directed manner was more likely to be viewed as truly other-directed when he applied to become an astronaut (for which his behavior was inappropriate) than when he applied to become a submariner. Similarly, for the actor who behaved in an inner-directed fashion, attributions of inner-directedness were more likely in the submariner than in the astronaut condition.

Table 5.9 Perception of Actor's Other- or Inner-Directedness (Adapted from Jones, Davis, and Gergen, 1961)

Interview condition	Desirable behavior	Actor's behavior	
		Other-directed	Inner-directed
Astronaut	Inner-directed	91.12	69.15
Submariner	Other-directed	69.26	43.92

Direct support for a Bayesian interpretation of these results has been provided by Trope and Burnstein (1973). These investigators used two job-interview situations in a manner similar to that of the Jones, Davis, and Gergen study. In one condition, for example, subjects received information about two applicants for a job "teaching current affairs in a Jewish Sunday School in Detroit." One applicant expressed a pro-Israeli position in the job interview (desirable behavior), the other an anti-Israeli position (undesirable behavior). As in the Jones, Davis, and Gergen study, subjects revised their estimates of the applicant's true position to a greater extent when the applicant performed the undesirable be-

41. It appears reasonable to assume that in this study prior probabilities that the actor was inner- or other-directed did not differ across conditions, and hence the posterior probabilities can serve as an index of attribution.

havior. Further, Trope and Burnstein obtained measures of the likelihood ratios for desirable and undesirable behaviors by asking subjects to indicate the probability that a person would take the position advocated by the job applicant if he had a pro-Israeli attitude $[p(B|D)]$ and if he had an anti-Israeli attitude $[p(B|\overline{D})]$. As expected, the subjective likelihood ratio $p(B|D)/p(B|\overline{D})$ was higher for the undesirable than for the desirable behavior.

Freedom versus desirability. Jones and Harris (1967) attempted to examine the simultaneous effects of perceived decision freedom and behavioral desirability. Subjects read a short essay on Castro's Cuba which was either pro-Castro (with assumed low desirability) or anti-Castro (high desirability), and its author (the actor) was alleged to have written it either under conditions of free choice (high decision freedom) or by assignment of a course instructor (low decision freedom). On the basis of this essay, subjects were asked to infer the actor's attitude toward Castro's Cuba. Unfortunately, this posterior estimate that the actor is in favor of (or against) Castro's Cuba cannot be directly used as a measure of attribution. Although Jones and Harris recognized that attribution must be defined as information *gained,* i.e., as a revision in beliefs, no estimates of prior probabilities were obtained. Without a prior-probability estimate, it is not clear whether the posterior attribution of a pro-Castro attitude represents a greater, the same, or a smaller revision in subjective probability than attribution of an anti-Castro attitude.[42] To obtain a rough measure of revision, it is possible to use the subject's own attitude toward Castro's Cuba as an estimate of the actor's perceived attitude prior to obtaining information about his behavior. On the average, the subjects' attitudes were somewhat negative toward Castro's Cuba (a score of approximately 32 on a scale ranging from 0 to 70). Estimates of revisions are obtained by subtracting this score from the attributed posterior attitudes in the different experimental conditions.

The results indicate that perceived attitudes were revised in the direction of the position adopted by the actor in writing his essay. The anti-Castro essay led to downward revisions, the pro-Castro essay to upward revisions. Interestingly, even when the actor was described as having had no freedom of choice, subjects tended to attribute his behavior to his attitude. The greatest revision, however, occurred in the condition where the actor performed an undesirable behavior under high decision freedom. Revisions in the remaining experimental conditions were lower and approximately equal.

Prior behavior probabilities. In an interesting monograph, Steiner (1970) linked perceived decision freedom to the perceived desirability of behavioral alternatives. According to Steiner, a person will be perceived to have had high decision freedom to the extent that his available options were equally desirable.

---

42. An even more serious confounding effect due to neglect of prior probabilities can be found in a study by Jones, Worchel, Goethals, and Grumet (1971) dealing with similar issues.

It can also be argued that a behavior's perceived desirability is related to its perceived probability of occurrence. That is to say, the probability that an actor will perform a given behavior will tend to increase with the behavior's desirability. As with desirability, therefore, a negative relation between prior probability and dispositional attribution may be expected. That is, dispositional attribution will be made with greater confidence as the behavior's prior probability decreases (Jones and Gerard, 1967; Jones and Harris, 1967, Ajzen, 1971a).[43]

To test these notions, Ajzen (1971a) manipulated desirability of chosen alternatives and perceived decision freedom in four hypothetical situations. Under high decision freedom, the actor had to make a choice from three desirable and one undesirable alternative; under low decision freedom, his choice was from three undesirable and one desirable alternative. Subjects were told that the actor had chosen either a desirable or an undesirable option.

For example, in one situation the actor could perform one of four behaviors on a Friday night.

High decision freedom		*Low decision freedom*	
1. Have dinner with a date	(+)	1. Have dinner with a date	(+)
2. Go to a party	(+)	2. Read assignments for next week's classes	(−)
3. Listen to some new record albums at a friend's place	(+)	3. Attend an optional evening quiz section	(−)
4. Inspect a friend's stamp collection	(−)	4. Inspect a friend's stamp collection	(−)

In both conditions of decision freedom, half the subjects were told the actor had chosen alternative 1 (desirable), the other half that he had chosen alternative 4 (undesirable).

Subjects indicated the probability that the actor had a particular disposition (e.g., that he enjoys eating out) after his choice was disclosed [$p(D|B)$]. Further, measures were obtained of $p(B)$—the prior probability of the behavior; of $p(D)$ —the prior probability of the disposition; and of $p(B|D)$. Consistent with ex-pectations, the chosen behavior's desirability as well as perceived decision freedom strongly affected the strength of dispositional attributions. Revisions from prior to posterior probabilities, that is, $p(D|B) - p(D)$, increased with perceived deci-sion freedom and decreased with the chosen alternative's desirability.

Ajzen also found that desirable behaviors were perceived to have higher prob-abilities of occurrence than did undesirable behaviors. Further, an average corre-lation of −.62 across the four situations supported the prediction of a negative

---

43. A negative relation between prior probability of an event (p) and its informa-tional value (h) or diagnosticity is also postulated in information theory where $h = - \log_2 p$.

relation between a behavior's prior probability and its diagnostic value. That is, the higher the behavior's prior probability, the lower was the revision in attribution of a disposition. Finally, posterior probabilities predicted on the basis of Bayes's theorem were found to correlate significantly with obtained posterior-probability judgments. The average correlation over the four situations was .52.

Multiple Dispositions

So far we have considered the conditions under which an observed behavior will be attributed to a given disposition of the actor, rather than to some external factor. Frequently, however, it may be possible to invoke more than one disposition to account for the behavior. The analysis presented by Jones and Davis (1965) assumes that any outcome or effect produced by the behavior can provide the basis for a dispositional attribution. One important factor is the extent to which the action leads to *unique* outcomes, i.e., to outcomes that would not be produced by alternative behaviors. The greater the extent to which a given effect is uniquely associated with the actor's chosen alternative, the more likely it is that a dispositional attribution will be made on the basis of that effect.[44]

Suppose that a person is planning a trip to Europe and that there are four package tours available within an acceptable price range. Each tour visits four major European cities. Assume that the actor is observed to select Tour A, which includes Berlin. According to the uniqueness principle, if Berlin is a unique outcome of Tour A, an observer would be more likely to infer that the actor is interested in visiting Berlin than if all four tours visited Berlin.

In terms of a Bayesian analysis, uniqueness of outcomes should affect the diagnostic value of the behavior. Let D stand for the actor's disposition (e.g., his desire to visit Berlin) and B for his behavior (e.g., his choice of Tour A). Now consider the situation in which Berlin is uniquely associated with Tour A. If the actor desires to visit Berlin, the probability that he will choose Tour A, that is, $p(B|D)$, should be relatively high. Conversely, if he does not desire to visit Berlin, the probability of his choosing Tour A, that is, $p(B|\overline{D})$, should be relatively low. The likelihood ratio $p(B|D)/p(B|\overline{D})$ would in this case be greatly above unity. In contrast, when Berlin is a common outcome of all tours, the probability that the actor will select Tour A should be the same, whether he desires to visit Berlin or not. In this case, the likelihood ratio will be close to unity. It follows that a behavior with a unique outcome is more diagnostic than one with an outcome common to other behavioral alternatives, and Bayes's theorem would predict stronger dispositional attribution in the former case.

---

44. The confidence with which such an attribution will be made should increase as the number of effects uniquely associated with the chosen alternative decreases (see Chapter 2).

To test this hypothesis, Ajzen [45] constructed four hypothetical situations similar to the touring example discussed above. In each situation, an actor was said to have chosen one of four alternatives. To manipulate uniqueness, Ajzen created four conditions such that one outcome was unique to the chosen alternative in Condition 1 and appeared in two, three, or all four alternatives in Conditions 2, 3, and 4. A condition with intermediate uniqueness is shown in Table 5.10 for a situation dealing with choice of a political candidate. The other three situations involved choice of a tour (described on p. 200), choice among four pro-

---

Table 5.10 A Condition of Intermediate Uniqueness in Ajzen's Study

---

Four candidates compete for a seat in the United States Senate. Mr. K must decide who to vote for. In their campaigns the candidates have expressed their positions on several issues, as follows:

Candidate A

Favors universal free medical services

Favors a guaranteed annual income

Favors immediate troop withdrawal from Vietnam

Opposes wage and price controls

Candidate B

Favors legalization of marijuana

Opposes wage and price controls

Favors universal free medical services

Favors immediate troop withdrawal from Vietnam

Candidate C

Favors universal free medical services

Favors immediate troop withdrawal from Vietnam

Favors increased military spending

→ Opposes busing of school children

Candidate D

Favors immediate troop withdrawal from Vietnam

→ Opposes busing of school children

Favors guaranteed annual income

Favors legalization of marijuana

Arrow signifies crucial aspect.

---

grams of study, and choice of an accurate personality description.

For each situation, subjects were asked to estimate $p(D|B)$, the probability that the actor had a particular disposition (e.g., that he was against busing of school children or that he was interested in visiting Berlin), given that he had chosen a certain alternative. In addition, measures were obtained of $p(D)$, $p(B|D)$, and $p(B|\overline{D})$. The results provided support both for the uniqueness hypothesis and for a Bayesian interpretation of the attribution process. Consistent with expectations, revisions in beliefs were found to increase with the outcome's uniqueness. In a similar fashion, the likelihood ratio $p(B|D)/p(B|\overline{D})$ also increased significantly with the extent of uniqueness.

---

45. Unpublished study. See also Ajzen and Holmes (1974).

Attribution to Self and Other

So far we have not made a distinction between attributions to another person as opposed to self-attributions. Since an actor may serve as an observer of his own behavior, an attributional analysis appears appropriate in both instances.

Beginning with Schachter's (1964) work on the determinants of emotional states, investigators have applied the notion of self-attribution to such areas as obesity (Schachter, 1971), insomnia (Storms and Nisbett, 1970), and psycho-therapy (Valins and Nisbett, 1971). For example, Storms and Nisbett asked insomnia volunteers to take a pill on two consecutive nights. In one condition the pill was described as a drug that would *increase* arousal whereas in a second condition it was described as a drug that would *decrease* arousal. (Actually the pill was a placebo with no physiological effects.) The assumption was that arousal is one reason for the insomniac's difficulty in falling asleep. In the first experimental condition, subjects could now attribute their arousal to an external factor (the pill), but in the second condition they had to attribute it to themselves. As expected, after taking the pill, subjects who could attribute their arousal to an external factor took less time to fall asleep than did subjects who attributed the arousal to themselves.

Thus there is evidence that people can attribute dispositional states to themselves on the basis of their own behaviors. However, disagreement exists as to the extent to which processes of self-attribution resemble those of attribution to another person.

The primary controversy revolves around the amount and kind of information available to actor versus observer and around the relative importance placed on different items of information. Bem (1965, 1967, 1968b) has argued that the behavior and its effects constitute, in most cases, the major cues for making an attribution to the actor. Since these cues are available to both the observer and the actor, the two should make the same attributions. In contrast, others (R. A. Jones *et al.,* 1968; E. E. Jones and Nisbett, 1971) have proposed that different information is available to actor and observer, and even when they have the same information, they tend to focus on different aspects of the behavioral situation. Specifically, Jones and Nisbett argued for a unidirectional difference such that "there is a pervasive tendency for actors to attribute their actions to situational requirements, whereas observers tend to attribute the same actions to stable personal dispositions" (1971, p. 2). According to Jones and Nisbett, this difference will obtain not only because the actor has more detailed knowledge of the circumstances but also because different aspects of the available information are salient for actor and observer. Specifically, the actor's behavior is assumed to be most salient for an observer, whereas situational factors take on greater salience for the actor himself.

A Bayesian analysis also leads to the expectation that actor and observer may sometimes differ in their attributions. From a Bayesian standpoint it is not unreasonable to expect that actor and observer will sometimes differ in their perceptions of a behavior's diagnosticity. As a result, they may not revise their beliefs about the presence of certain causal factors to the same extent. For example, when an actor is aware that he has little freedom of choice, his behavior has low diagnostic value for a dispositional self-attribution. However, an observer may be unaware of the actor's restricted freedom and may thus view the same behavior as highly diagnostic. In other situations the opposite may be true, such that the actor will view his own behavior as more diagnostic for a dispositional attribution than will the observer.

Several investigations have found significant differences between judgments of own versus other's ability following success or failure on a task (E. E. Jones *et al.*, 1968; Feather and Simon, 1971a; Jones and Nisbett, 1971). Frieze and Weiner (1971), however, have reported no significant differences between actor and observer in terms of causal attributions for successful or unsuccessful task performance. More important, Feather and Simon (1971a) showed that differences between actor and observer depend on the circumstances. Consistent with the Jones-Nisbett hypothesis, subjects were found to attribute another person's success more than their own success to ability. However, contrary to that hypothesis, another person's failure was judged to be due to external factors (such as bad luck) more so than was own failure.[46]

Bem's (1965, 1967) findings using the interpersonal replication procedure described earlier also appear to be inconsistent with the hypothesis advanced by Jones and Nisbett. In a number of studies Bem found that his observers were able to infer with considerable accuracy the original subject's responses in a dissonance experiment. He thus concluded that results obtained in dissonance experiments could be explained in terms of the subject's self-attribution without recourse to assumptions about a motivational state such as dissonance.[47] It may therefore be argued that actors and observers appear to make very similar causal attributions.

One difficulty with this argument is the fact that Bem (1965, 1967) dealt only with posterior-probability estimates. In terms of posterior probabilities, differences may obviously be expected whenever actor and observer hold different prior probabilities or beliefs. In fact, because of the actor's greater knowledge of his own past behaviors, feelings, and experiences, actor and observer are quite likely to hold different prior beliefs about the actor's dispositions. For example, after performing the experimental task (but prior to the counterattitudinal behavior), subjects in the Festinger and Carlsmith (1959) study described earlier tended to believe that the task was somewhat boring. An observer, however, may

---

46. The means in the direction of external attribution for success were 5.5 (self) and 4.8 (other); for failure 4.1 (self) and 5.8 (other). Unfortunately, no direct test of the relevant interaction was reported.

47. Other investigators, however, have not always been able to replicate Bem's findings (Dillehay and Clayton, 1970; Piliavin *et al.*, 1969; R. A. Jones *et al.*, 1968). A Bayesian analysis of dissonance research will be found in Chapter 10.

at this stage assume that the actor believed the task to be quite interesting. It is thus not clear that the posterior estimates made by actor and observer after performance of the counterattitudinal behavior represent the same amount of *revision* in beliefs, i.e., that they reflect the same attributions. Thus the subject's judgment of the task as quite interesting in the $1 condition of the Festinger and Carlsmith study may represent a considerable revision from his prior belief that it was somewhat boring. An observer's posterior belief that the actor found the task quite interesting, however, may reflect relatively little change in his judgment.

Dissonance theorists have criticized Bem's analysis precisely for this reason (e.g., R. A. Jones *et al.,* 1968). To demonstrate the importance of prior beliefs, observers were given information about the original subject's initial (i.e., prior) judgment. Not surprisingly, this information influenced the observers' inferences, and more important, the observers could no longer infer the actual subject's responses.

In an interesting refutation of these arguments, Bem (1968b) insisted that observers in the interpersonal replication procedure should *not* be given information about the subject's initial judgments since Bem assumed that the subject himself is not aware of his initial position at the time that he provides his posterior responses. In support of this claim, Bem and McConnell (1970) found that only few subjects in a dissonance experiment could accurately recall their initial beliefs.

To summarize, it appears that actors and observers may form different inferential beliefs on the basis of the actor's behavior. However, evidence to date does not indicate that different inference processes need to be invoked in order to explain the observed differences in inferential beliefs. Attributions to both self and other can be accounted for in a Bayesian framework. Observed differences in posterior beliefs can easily be explained in terms of differential availability of information affecting prior beliefs. Differences in causal attributions (or revisions in beliefs) will be found when information available to actor and observer lead to differences in the behavior's perceived diagnostic value.

Error and Bias in Attribution

The application of Bayes's theorem to causal attribution implies an observer who processes information about an actor's behavior in a rather rational and objective manner. Yet it should be obvious that his causal explanations do not always correspond to reality. For one thing, the information on which his inferences are based may be misleading. That inaccurate information will produce erroneous attributions was demonstrated by Valins (1966), whose subjects were given false feedback about changes in their heart rates while viewing slides of seminude females; pictures associated with heart-rate changes were judged to be more attractive.

Misperception of relevant information may occur without actual deception. We have noted a tendency for probability judgments to be conservative (W. Edwards, 1968) and to take insufficient account of sample size (Kahneman and Tversky, 1972). In many attribution situations it is impossible to tell what the correct inference would have been. A case in point is the study by Jones and Harris (1967) mentioned earlier, in which subjects tended to infer attitudes from expressed positions under no-choice conditions. It may be argued that even when the actor is assigned a given position, he exercises a certain degree of freedom in accepting the assignment and in the way he executes it. Subjects may thus be quite correct when they infer that the actor's attitude corresponds to some extent to the position he has advocated.

The attributional errors discussed thus far follow consistently from the observer's reasonable, albeit incorrect, beliefs about the situation. His misjudgment of a given behavior's diagnosticity may be construed as an "honest mistake." By way of contrast, attribution theorists have sometimes postulated certain more irrational tendencies on the part of the observer. The general idea is that a person's needs, values, and desires may influence his attributions.

Maintaining a Positive Self-Image

One kind of bias assumes a desire on the part of the observer to maintain a positive self-image. According to this view, ego-defensive biases will become operative whenever explanation of an observed event has positive or negative implications for the observer.

A study by T. J. Johnson, Feigenbaum, and Weiby (1964) has sometimes been taken to demonstrate defensive attribution. Subjects served as arithmetic teachers on two consecutive trials. The simulated student did poorly on the first trial. On the second trial the student continued to perform poorly for some teachers, and he improved for others. Teachers tended to attribute continued failure to the student whereas they attributed improved performance to themselves. Although these findings are consistent with a tendency toward ego-defensive attribution, alternative interpretations are available. For example, Kelley (1967) suggested that insofar as the teacher made a special effort on the second trial, the covariation of effort and success in the improvement condition would favor internal attribution, and lack of such covariation in the continued failure condition would favor external attribution. Alternatively, Kelley's notion of consistency suggests that consistent behavior across occasions is attributed to some factor internal to the actor whereas inconsistent behavior is attributed to an external factor. It follows that the student's consistent failure on the task should be attributed to an internal factor, such as his lack of ability. When he first fails and then succeeds (inconsistent performance), an external attribution to the teacher is likely. As noted earlier, these explanations are consistent with a Bayesian analysis, and they suggest a rational rather than defensive attribution process.

A related finding reported by Streufert and Streufert (1969) is that subjects tend to attribute their own success on a task to internal factors and failure to external factors. At first glance this finding also appears to indicate a defensive inference process in that subjects seem reluctant to accept blame for failure while accepting praise for success. It should be clear, however, that the hypothesis of defensive attribution is applicable only in the case of self-attribution. The finding that the same difference in causal attribution obtains when subjects are asked to account for some other person's performance (Frieze and Weiner, 1971) must therefore be interpreted as inconsistent with the notion of ego-defensive attribution.

If an ego-defensive bias appears untenable, Bayes's theorem suggests two alternative explanations of the obtained results. The first assumes that subjects perceive the experimental task as relatively difficult, with the effect that success has greater diagnostic value for the actor's ability than failure has for his lack of ability. As a result, success would be attributed to ability more than would failure to lack of ability.[48]

The second explanation would hold if subjects expected to succeed on the task. Feather (1969; Feather and Simon, 1971b) has either measured or manipulated the subject's prior expectation that he would succeed or fail on an anagram task. Actual performance consistent with expectations was attributed to stable internal factors (skill and ability), but performance inconsistent with expectations was attributed to unstable external factors (luck). Thus, when subjects expected success, they displayed the tendency found by Streufert and Streufert to attribute actual success to their own ability more than actual failure to their lack of ability. However, contrary to an ego-defensive bias but consistent with a Bayesian analysis, when subjects expected to fail, they attributed actual failure to their own lack of ability more than they attributed actual success to their ability.

Bayes's theorem thus accounts for the observed difference between inferences based on success and failure in terms of information processing without reference to irrationality or defensiveness.

Hedonic Relevance

A second type of bias is assumed to be elicited by factors that increase the observer's need to explain the event he has witnessed. An actor's behavior may sometimes have important rewarding or punishing implications for the observer. According to Jones and Davis (1965), such "hedonic relevance" increases dispositional attribution; the observer will tend to attribute the behavior to some dispositional factor internal to the actor.

Jones and deCharms (1957) investigated the effects of hedonic relevance in two experiments. A confederate working with four or five subjects always failed on a series of problem-solving tasks. In the low-relevance condition, a $1 reward was dependent simply on the subject's own success whereas in the high-relevance

---

48. Let S stand for success, F for failure, and A for ability. Given a difficult task, this argument assumes the following relation between the likelihood ratios:

$$p(S|A) / p(S|\overline{A}) > p(F|\overline{A}) / p(F|A).$$

condition, the reward was given only when all group members succeeded. The results provided only partial support for the predicted effects of hedonic relevance on dispositional attribution. In the first experiment, hedonic relevance decreased the perceived competence and dependability of the confederate, but it did not affect his perceived motivation. The second experiment provided even less support in that the predicted effect was significant only for attribution of dependability. This investigation therefore provides little support for motivational biases in attribution.

Attribution of Responsibility

A different motivational bias was postulated by Walster (1966) with respect to attribution of responsibility for an accident. According to Walster, a person's need to assign responsibility for an accident to the actor who has caused it increases with the severity of its consequences. Using descriptions of a hypothetical car accident, she manipulated severity of damage to a car and injuries to others.

Subjects listened to one of four tape recordings describing Lennie, a high school student, whose car rolled off a hill because of a brake failure. Walster manipulated mild and severe consequences in four experimental conditions: (1) The car's fender was only mildly damaged, but the car could have been completely destroyed; (2) the car was completely destroyed; (3) the car's fender was only mildly damaged, but bystanders could have been severely injured; and (4) bystanders were severely injured.

Consistent with predictions, the finding was that more responsibility was attributed to Lennie in Conditions 2 and 4 (severe consequences) than in Conditions 1 and 3 (mild consequences). The results, however, were not unequivocal; the difference between Conditions 3 and 4 only approached significance for the total sample and was not significant for female subjects. Further, it was found that injury to bystanders (severe consequence) did *not* lead to more attribution of responsibility than damage to the car (mild consequence). Most important, in subsequent studies, Walster (1967) as well as other investigators (Shaver, 1970a, 1970b; J. I. Shaw and Skolnik, 1971) failed to replicate the effect of severity on attribution of responsibility.

Perhaps because of the obvious implications for the judicial process, investigators have shown considerable interest in factors influencing attribution of responsibility. Much of the research in this area has been based less on systematic theoretical analyses of attribution processes than on intuitive hypotheses and speculations. Perhaps for this reason, studies on attribution of responsibility have yielded contradictory and inconclusive results.

According to the analysis by Jones and Davis (1965) discussed earlier, the severity or desirability of an act's outcomes will result in dispositional attribution only when the observer assumes intentionality on the part of the actor. Since the situations used in studies on attribution of responsibility for an accident clearly imply lack of intentionality on the part of the actor, Jones and Davis's analysis suggests that variations in outcome severity should *not* influence attribution of responsibility.

A number of other variables that might influence attribution of responsibility have been investigated: attractiveness of actor and victim (Landy and Aronson, 1969; Shepherd and Bagley, 1970), similarity of actor and subject (Shaver, 1970a; Shaw and Skolnik, 1971), whether or not the actor had insurance (Shaver, 1970b), etc. Generally speaking, results of these studies have been highly inconsistent and have not led to any firm conclusions. Partly in an attempt to understand these conflicting findings, investigators have obtained additional measures designed to assess the subject's perceptions of the hypothetical situations. Thus subjects have been asked whether the actor had been careless, whether he was conscientious, whether he could have foreseen the consequences, etc. Unfortunately, these questions have shed little light on attributions of responsibility.

A number of points need to be made with respect to these investigations. First, the term "attribution of responsibility" is somewhat misleading since responsibility can be described neither as a disposition of a person nor as a property of an object. Attribution of responsibility can perhaps best be viewed as a moral judgment. Moreover, Heider (1958) has made it clear that the term "responsibility" can be interpreted in different ways. As mentioned in Chapter 2, Heider distinguished five levels of responsibility that correspond in part to Piaget's (1932) developmental stages in moral judgment.

1. *Association.*[49] At the first and most primitive level, the actor is held responsible for any effects that are in any way associated with him.

2. *Commission.* At the next level, the actor is held responsible if he was instrumental in producing the observed effects (even if he could not have foreseen them).

3. *Foreseeability.* At this level, the actor is held responsible only if he could have foreseen the effects even though he might not have intended to produce them.

4. *Intentionality.* At the fourth level, the actor is held responsible only for effects he foresaw and intended.

5. *Justification.* Finally, at the fifth level, he is held responsible only to the extent that his intended behavior was not justifiable, i.e., not caused by factors beyond the actor's control.

At each successive level, attribution to the person becomes less likely, attribution to the environment more likely. One immediate implication of Heider's analysis is that general measures of responsibility will tend to be ambiguous. A question such as "Is the actor responsible for the accident?" could be interpreted in different ways: (1) Was the actor associated with the accident? (2) Was he

---

49. The labels used here for the five levels of responsibility were introduced by Shaw and Sulzer (1964).

instrumental in producing the accident, i.e., did he cause it? (3) Is he responsible in the sense that he could have foreseen the accident? (4) Did he intend to cause the accident? (5) To what extent was his behavior justified? Since subjects are usually not told at what level they are to respond, judgments of responsibility may take on different meanings in different conditions of an experiment, in different investigations, and for different subjects.

Shaw and his associates (Shaw and Sulzer, 1964; Shaw and Reitan, 1969) have used Heider's levels of responsibility in a somewhat different way. Their analysis suggests that not only can a *subject's responses* vary along these five levels but so can the *behavioral context*. That is, the context itself may suggest that the actor was merely associated with the event, that he committed (caused) the event, etc. If the fourth and fifth contextual levels are reversed, a two-way classification scheme can be constructed; [50] this scheme is presented in Table 5.11.

Table 5.11 Attributions of Responsibility in Terms of Heider's Levels of Causality

Developmental or response level	Contextual level				
	Association	Commission	Foreseeability	Justification	Intentionality
Association	X	X	X	X	X
Commission		X	X	X	X
Foreseeability			X	X	X
Intentionality				X	X
Justification					X

An X indicates that a judgment of responsibility would be made.

The X's in Table 5.11 indicate the combinations of developmental and contextual levels that should lead to attributions of responsibility. For example, a subject at the development level of commission (or a subject who believed that he was to interpret responsibility in terms of commission or instrumentality) would not attribute responsibility when the context merely associated the actor and the event, but he would attribute responsibility at the remaining contextual levels. In contrast, a subject at the fourth developmental level (intentionality) would attribute responsibility if the context suggested that the actor behaved intentionally, whether his behavior was justifiable or not. At the highest developmental level of justification, attribution of responsibility would occur only when the context suggested that the actor behaved intentionally without justification. It can thus be seen that the proposed classification scheme represents the pattern of a perfect

---

50. Actually, it is not clear that the contextual level of justification should be placed between foreseeability and intentionality. It is possible that justification leads to a level of attribution that stands between commission and foreseeability. Shaw and Reitan (1969) reported data that appear to support the latter order.

Guttman scale, suggesting that Heider's levels of causality form a single dimension of perceived responsibility.

This analysis implies that, unlike attributions of dispositions, attributions of responsibility can be made even when the actor is not perceived to have behaved intentionally. For example, at the developmental or response level of commission, an actor will be held responsible if he was instrumental in bringing about the observed effect, even though he may not have intended to produce it. More important, our analysis makes it clear that attribution of responsibility is a function of two factors: the observer's developmental or response level and the contextual level. When the level of one factor is held constant, attribution of responsibility should depend on the level of the other factor.

We can illustrate this principle in terms of the judicial system, where response level is determined by law and assignment of responsibility or guilt is determined by the contextual level. Thus, in a murder trial, the judge will carefully instruct the jury as to the response level they are to adopt. A guilty verdict requires intentionality when the charge is murder but not when the charge is manslaughter. Further, the law allows for justified homicide under certain circumstances. In an accident case, instrumentality or commission may be the response level specified by law for a judgment that the actor is guilty.

In these situations, then, the response level is clearly specified, and the observer must judge the contextual level in order to attribute responsibility. Alternatively, it is possible to specify the contextual level and let the response level be determined by the observer. This procedure was followed by Shaw and his associates (Shaw and Sulzer, 1964; Shaw and Reitan, 1969). Shaw and Sulzer used 20 short behavioral situations varying along the five contextual levels. For example, one description at the level of association read as follows: "A boy hit another child with Perry's toy gun. Is Perry responsible for the child being hit?" A description at the intentional level stated: "Perry opened the door so that the wind would blow the children's papers all over the room. Is Perry responsible for the scattered papers?" Attributions of responsibility were made on a six-point scale.

On the assumption that subjects work at a *given* developmental or response level, attribution of responsibility should increase with the contextual level (see Table 5.11). The results of two experiments support this prediction (Shaw and Sulzer, 1964; Shaw and Reitan, 1969). Further, for subjects working at *different* developmental or response levels, different profiles of responsibility assignment should be obtained. In support of the classification scheme shown in Table 5.11, Shaw and Sulzer (1964) reported different response profiles for second-grade children than for college students. The former appeared to work at the level of commission, the latter at the level of intentionality. Evidence that adults work at the level of justification was found by Shaw and Reitan (1969). Second-grade children were found to assign responsibility in situations that involved at least commission, and as expected, their attributions did not increase at the higher contextual levels. On the other hand, adults tended to attribute more responsibility at each successive contextual level. These findings are summarized in Fig. 5.6.

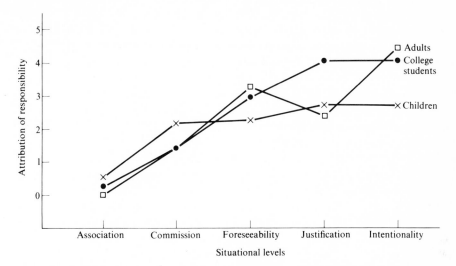

Fig. 5.6 Attribution of responsibility as a function of situational levels. (Adapted from Shaw and Sulzer (1964) and Shaw and Reitan, 1969.)

Shaw and Sulzer also varied outcome desirability (positive or negative), and consistent with expectations based on attribution theories, outcome desirability had its largest effect on attribution of responsibility when the action was intentional and a somewhat weaker effect when the outcome was foreseeable. At the other three contextual levels, outcome desirability had no effects on attribution of responsibility. These results are shown in Fig. 5.7. Similar results were found by Shaw and Reitan (1969), who varied not only outcome desirability but also intensity of outcomes (mild versus severe). The latter variable interacted with contextual levels, indicating that effects of severity on attribution of responsibility are greatest at the level of foreseeability.

As is apparent, when contextual levels are specified, assignment of responsibility follows predictable patterns. Further, as the comparison between children and adults shows, when developmental or response levels are specified, attribution of responsibility will also be made in a meaningful way. The conflicting and inconclusive results of most studies dealing with attribution of responsibility can now perhaps be appreciated since these studies have specified neither response levels nor contextual levels. For example, several studies have used Walster's (1966) description of an accident in which a car rolled down a hill. In this situation it is made quite clear that the effects were not *intended;* however, the contextual level may still involve either foreseeability, commission (instrumentality), or association. Furthermore, since subjects are given no instructions concerning response level, any of the five response levels may be involved. Judg-

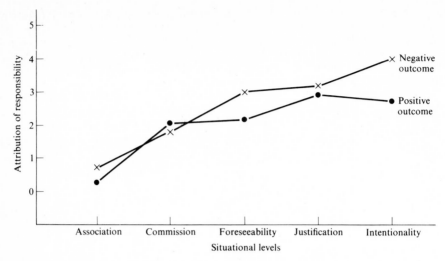

Fig. 5.7 Attribution of responsibility for acts with desirable and undesirable outcomes. (Adapted from Shaw and Sulzer, 1964.)

ments of responsibility in these studies are obviously uninterpretable, and conflicting findings are hardly surprising.

Summary of Attribution Research

Attribution theory deals with the ways in which a person arrives at an explanation for observed behavior. This attribution process is accompanied by and corresponds to revisions in the observer's beliefs about the actor and his environment. We showed that causal attribution and corresponding revisions in beliefs can be described in terms of Bayes's theorem. As one might expect from a Bayesian analysis, the observer's inferences generally tend to be quite realistic and to follow consistently from his prior beliefs about the situation. Although attribution theorists have often postulated certain more irrational dynamic processes, few studies have demonstrated these biasing effects convincingly.

Just as the observer makes causal attributions to explain the behavior of an actor, he can make self-attributions on the basis of his own behavior. To be sure, actor and observer may differ in their perception of a given behavior's diagnosticity, and they may therefore arrive at diverging causal attributions. However, attribution to both self and others can be accounted for in a Bayesian framework, and evidence to date does not indicate that different inference processes need to be invoked in order to explain differences in attribution between actor and observer.

Various factors have been proposed to affect causal attribution, including consistency across occasions, objects, and actors, uniqueness of behavioral effects, perceived desirability and probability of the behavior, and perceived decision freedom. We have reviewed some of the available evidence and shown that each of these factors tends to influence attribution as predicted. The different variables can all be viewed as influencing the likelihood ratio in Bayes's theorem; that is, the variables treated by attribution theories suggest some of the conditions under which an observed behavior will have high or low diagnostic value for causal inferences. Bayes's theorem can therefore serve as a framework that permits a unified and integrated approach to the study of attribution processes.

CONCLUSION

In this chapter we have sought to identify and review various areas of research relevant to belief formation. Many of these lines of research have not received a great deal of attention from investigators in the attitude area. Owing to the wealth of material associated with each of these areas and to our own limited acquaintance with some of them, we have of necessity not provided an in-depth analysis of each line of research. Our main purpose in reviewing the different approaches is to acquaint the reader with some of the available information and to demonstrate its relevance for an understanding of belief formation. We will now attempt to summarize some of the major conclusions we have drawn in our review of the literature.

First, a distinction must be made between *descriptive* and *inferential* beliefs. Relatively little information is currently available about the formation of descriptive beliefs. What little evidence there is suggests that descriptive beliefs are formed on the basis of direct observation and tend to be fairly veridical; there is little evidence that personal factors such as beliefs, desires, attitudes, or personality characteristics have any systematic effects on the formation of descriptive beliefs. This conclusion appears to hold for beliefs about statements made by other people (i.e., beliefs that "S said O is X") as well as beliefs about attributes of objects or actions (i.e., beliefs that "O is X").

The distinction between descriptive and inferential beliefs is in many ways analogous to the distinction between *acquisition* of new information and using or *processing* that information. The latter distinction is found in research on multiple cue learning, where subjects must first learn the ecological validity of cues and then learn to use these cues consistently in making their judgments. Similarly, research on Bayes's theorem has distinguished between misperception (incorrect beliefs about a datum's diagnosticity) and misaggregation (inappropriate processing of new information). In the area of concept formation, a similar distinction was made between learning a concept's attributes and learning the appropriate combination rules.

In contrast to descriptive beliefs, personal factors do play a major role in the formation of inferential beliefs. Generally speaking, on the basis of one or more items of information—i.e., beliefs about an object, person, or action—individuals are found to form new beliefs through some inference process. A question of considerable importance is the extent to which inferences are made along an *evaluative* or *probabilistic* dimension. Although much attitude research assumes that inferences are based on evaluative consistency (i.e., that individuals attempt to achieve evaluative consistency), our review of the literature provides little support for this assumption and suggests instead that the inference process is based primarily on probabilistic relations among beliefs. Although it is true that evaluative and probabilistic consistency are frequently indistinguishable, whenever it is possible to separate these two dimensions, inferences tend to follow lines of probabilistic reasoning.

This conclusion follows most directly from research on trait inferences, but it is also supported by findings in the areas of cue utilization and syllogistic reasoning. Perhaps most impressive, however, is the finding that various quantitative probability models provide fairly accurate descriptions and predictions of inferential belief formation. Research concerned with these models again provides little evidence that evaluative consistency has any direct effects on inference processes.[51]

It appears, then, that individuals acquire relatively stable conceptions of probabilistic relationships among sets of beliefs. This probabilistic structure serves as the basis for inferential belief formation. A new item of information about a given object or event will thus have implications for many other beliefs about the object or event. The most direct demonstration of this process is given by research on trait inferences and "implicit theories of personality." Similarly, observation of a given behavioral event was shown to have probabilistic implications for causal attribution; observation of an actor's behavior takes on differential diagnostic value with respect to different attributions.

It is worth emphasizing that inferential belief formation involves *revision* in subjective probabilities rather than subjective probabilities at a given point in time. Although it may be of interest to study the beliefs of a person at a given moment, attempts to understand the effects of a new item of information on those beliefs, i.e., attempts to understand inference processes, demands consideration of change in the beliefs produced by the new information. Clearly, unless one can assume that prior beliefs are equivalent across different experimental conditions, measures of posterior beliefs are insufficient for an understanding of the inference process.

Despite the apparently overwhelming evidence in favor of a probabilistic rather than evaluative basis for inferential belief formation, a cautionary note is in order. The experimental situations in which inferences have been studied have typically not dealt with highly involving or emotional issues. In many experiments the subjects are intelligent and educated college students who are capable of adopting a problem-solving approach and thus may attempt to provide logical or

---

51. Although not reviewed in this chapter, some indirect support for the relative weakness of evaluative inferences comes from studies that have used balance theory to predict inferences about interpersonal relations (Wyer and Lyon, 1970) or learning of them (Lewit and Shanley, 1969; Press, Crockett, and Rosenkrantz, 1970; Rubin and Zajonc, 1969). These studies found only weak support for predictions based on notions of affective balance.

rational responses. These conditions will favor probabilistically oriented inference processes.

Although emotional or affective factors may play a more important role in inferences about involving issues, evidence to date does not support this view, and we take the position that the inference process is based primarily on probabilistic consistency. Thus man may be viewed as a fairly rational processor of information available to him. His descriptive and inferential beliefs are not capricious, nor are they systematically distorted by motivational or emotional biases.

Chapter 6

Attitude
Formation

We are employing the term "attitude" to refer solely to a person's location on a bipolar evaluative or affective dimension with respect to some object, action, or event. An attitude represents a person's general feeling of favorableness or unfavorableness toward some stimulus object. In our conceptual framework, as a person forms beliefs about an object, he automatically and simultaneously acquires an attitude toward that object. Each belief links the object to some attribute; the person's attitude toward the object is a function of his evaluations of these attributes.

Suppose that a new product is introduced on the market and that a person's only information concerning this product is that it is a bedtime drink. On the assumption that he has a neutral evaluation of bedtime drinks, the person would be expected to hold a neutral attitude toward the product in question. Now imagine that through an advertising campaign he learns that the product is good for digestion. Since he positively evaluates things that are good for digestion, his attitude toward the product may shift in a positive direction. Note, however, that this new positive belief will not necessarily lead to the formation of a positive attitude. Because of the existing relationships among beliefs discussed in the preceding chapter, the belief that the product is good for digestion may lead to the formation of various inferential beliefs. For example, the person may infer that the product is a medicine for old people. A negative evaluation of medicine for old people may produce an overall attitude toward the product that is neutral or even negative.

As with beliefs, the distinction between attitude formation and attitude change is somewhat arbitrary. The example above implied that a positive attitude was formed when the person learned that the product was good for digestion. It could be argued, however, that a neutral attitude was *formed* as soon as the person

216

learned that the product was a bedtime drink and that this attitude *changed* as a result of the subsequent information.

It may be instructive to consider another example, where these processes are more readily apparent. Consider a person who holds a neutral attitude toward a stranger since he has no information about him. The person now learns that the stranger is a member of the Republican Party. Assuming that the person positively evaluates members of the Republican Party, we may expect formation of an initially positive attitude toward the stranger. This positive attitude may be further reinforced by the person's inferences that the stranger favors a balanced budget and less federal control (positions that are positively evaluated by the person himself). We can see that instead of producing a neutral attitude, as in the previous example, the initial item of information concerning the stranger's party affiliation led to the formation of a favorable attitude toward him. Clearly, any additional items of information may or may not produce changes in the attitude toward the stranger.

At the most general level, then, we learn to like (or have favorable attitudes toward) objects we associate with "good" things, and we acquire unfavorable feelings toward objects we associate with "bad" things. On a day-to-day basis we automatically acquire an attitude toward some new object when we learn its associations with other objects, attributes, or qualities toward which we already have attitudes. These attitudes (i.e., attribute evaluations) are themselves a function of beliefs linking the attribute to other characteristics and evaluations of those characteristics. The latter evaluations are again based on beliefs and evaluations, etc. It is possible to continue such an analysis indefinitely. Ultimately, however, one must probably fall back on hedonism, pleasure-pain principles, or other primary motives to account for the initial acquisition of affect. For example, for a newborn infant ingestion of milk satisfies hunger and may be viewed as giving pleasure or eliminating pain. Milk thus takes on some of the pleasurable (positive) qualities associated with hunger reduction. In this way, a positive attitude toward milk has been acquired. The evaluation of milk can now account in part for the development of attitudes toward other objects which come to be associated with milk (e.g., mother or breast).

Although it is possible in principle to trace through the development of a person's attitudes beginning with his early childhood, it will usually be sufficient to assess the evaluations of the attributes associated with the attitude object at a given point in time. Since an individual may be viewed as holding attitudes toward all discriminable aspects of his environment (even if the attitudes are neutral), whenever he learns that an object is linked to a given attribute, some of the evaluation of the attribute becomes associated with the object.

DETERMINANTS OF ATTITUDES

In the course of a person's life, his experiences lead to the formation of many different beliefs about various objects, actions, and events. These beliefs may be the result of direct observation or of inference processes. Some beliefs may persist over time, others may be forgotten, and new beliefs may be formed. Beliefs about such institutions as the church, democracy, and capitalism or beliefs about national and racial groups tend to be relatively stable. Beliefs about the consequences of a behavior or beliefs about a given person, however, can vary considerably. For example, beliefs about attending church on a particular occasion may differ from beliefs about that behavior on a different occasion. It is obvious, therefore, that a person's attitude may also change as a function of variations in his belief system. Some attitudes may be relatively stable over time, and others may exhibit frequent shifts. At any point in time, however, a person's attitude toward an object may be viewed as determined by his *salient* set of beliefs about the object.

Salience of Beliefs

Although a person may hold a large number of beliefs about any given object, it appears that only a relatively small number of beliefs serve as determinants of his attitude at any given moment. Research on attention span, apprehension, and information processing suggests that an individual is capable of attending to or processing only five to nine items of information at a time (e.g., G. A. Miller, 1956; Woodworth and Schlosberg, 1954; Mandler, 1967). It can therefore be argued that a person's attitude toward an object is primarily determined by no more than five to nine beliefs about the object; these are the beliefs that are *salient* at a given point in time. It is of course possible for more than nine beliefs to be salient and to determine a person's attitude; given time and incentive, a person may take a much larger set of beliefs into account. We are here merely suggesting that under most circumstances, a small number of beliefs serve as the determinants of a person's attitude. Clearly, salient beliefs are also subject to change; they may be strengthened or weakened or replaced by new beliefs.

An important question concerns identification of salient beliefs; that is, given that a person may hold a large number of beliefs, our task is to identify the five to nine salient beliefs that determine his attitude. We mentioned in Chapter 3 that a person's beliefs about a given object or action can be elicited in a free-response format by asking him to list the characteristics, qualities, and attributes of the object or the consequences of performing the behavior. It has been argued that salient beliefs are elicited first, and thus, consistent with the considerations above, beliefs elicited beyond the first nine or ten are probably not salient for the individual (Fishbein, 1967c; Kaplan and Fishbein, 1969). It is possible, however, that only the first two or three beliefs are salient for a given individual and that additional beliefs elicited beyond this point are not primary determinants of his attitude (i.e., are not salient). Unfortunately, it is impossible to determine the point at which a person starts eliciting nonsalient beliefs. Recommending the use of the first five to nine beliefs is therefore merely a rule of thumb.

Another problem is that the elicitation procedure itself may produce changes in a person's belief hierarchy. That is, previously nonsalient beliefs may become salient once they have been elicited. This implies that mere elicitation of beliefs may change a person's attitude. In other words, while listing his beliefs about an object, the person may recall some information he had forgotten or make a new inference on the basis of existing beliefs. The previously nonsalient beliefs may now become important determinants of his attitude. It follows that under these circumstances, the first few beliefs elicited will be highly related to the person's attitude as it existed prior to the elicitation of beliefs, but they may have a somewhat lower relationship to his attitude following elicitation. Similar problems emerge when a person responds to a standard set of belief statements, such as an attitude scale.[1] This experience may change his salient beliefs and thus affect his attitude. As with many other phenomena, attempts to assess salient beliefs may influence the phenomenon under investigation.

In conclusion, it appears impossible to obtain a precise measure of the beliefs that determine an individual's attitude since the number of salient beliefs may vary from person to person. However, a rough approximation can be obtained by considering the first few beliefs (five to nine) as the basic determinants of attitude. In many situations it may be desirable to have information about the salient beliefs in a given population (*modal salient beliefs*). For example, marketing research frequently attempts to identify the determinants of attitudes toward some product. To ascertain the modal salient beliefs within a given population, a representative sample of the population could be asked to elicit their beliefs about the product; the most frequently elicited beliefs could be considered the modal salient beliefs for the population.[2]

Salience and belief strength. In the preceding paragraphs we have suggested that salient beliefs can be identified by examining an individual's or a group's belief hierarchy. The first n beliefs elicited by a person are said to be his salient beliefs, and the n beliefs occurring with the greatest frequency are taken as the modal salient beliefs in a population. We noted previously that probability of elicitation can be viewed as analogous to the perceived probability of an association between object and attribute, i.e., that position in the hierarchy is related to belief strength. Thus it may appear that measures of belief strength can serve as indicants of salience. Unfortunately, this is not so. Although a high correspondence is expected between belief strength and position in the hierarchy for *salient* beliefs, the strength of nonsalient beliefs may be unrelated to their position in the hierarchy.

---

1. Although salient beliefs are viewed as the primary determinants of attitude, nonsalient beliefs can nevertheless be used to measure attitude. In fact, standard attitude scales comprise in large part statements concerning nonsalient beliefs. Responses to these statements are largely inferences consistent with the beliefs held by the person, and thus they, too, are likely to be predictive of his attitude.

2. One possibility is to take the 10 or 12 most frequently mentioned beliefs; this would allow for imperfect correspondence in the salient beliefs of different components of the population. Another possibility is to use those beliefs that exceed a certain frequency or to use as many beliefs as necessary to account for a certain percentage of all beliefs elicited.

As mentioned previously, a person is likely to elicit more than his salient beliefs about an object; some of the nonsalient beliefs (produced by remembering some item of information or by making an inference) may be assigned high probabilities. Further, when asked to respond to a belief statement, a person may strongly agree with the statement even though the belief involved is not salient and would not have been among the first few beliefs elicited. For example, suppose that a person is asked whether he believes that Italians have two legs. Clearly, he is likely to assign a high probability to this belief, but he would probably not have elicited it spontaneously. Thus, although one would expect to obtain a high rank-order correlation between belief strength and the position of salient beliefs (the position of the first five to nine beliefs a person elicits), one would not expect belief strength to correlate with the position of all beliefs elicited by the individual. Similarly, if one considered *only* the modal salient beliefs for a given population (the 10 or 12 most frequently elicited beliefs), a high correlation should be obtained between average belief strength and frequency of elicitation.

Considerable evidence supporting these hypotheses has been presented by Fishbein (1963) and Kaplan and Fishbein (1969). Fishbein obtained a rank-order correlation of .94 between the frequency with which a given salient attribute (e.g., dark skin) was elicited by the concept "Negro" and the average strength of the belief (e.g., the average rating of "Negroes have dark skin" on a probability scale). Similarly, Kaplan and Fishbein obtained a rank-order correlation of .90 between position and average belief strength when only the first six beliefs were considered. This correlation was reduced to .72 when the first nine beliefs were considered. Similar results were obtained when correlations were computed for single individuals. Further, when only the first six beliefs were considered, over 60 percent of the sample had perfect or near-perfect relations between hierarchical position and belief strength, and only 8 percent of the sample showed marked deviations from expectancies.

One interesting implication of these findings is that a measure of belief strength can aid the investigator in determining the number of salient beliefs in a hierarchy. So long as belief strength decreases with each successively elicited belief, it is reasonable to assume that one is dealing with salient beliefs. When the correspondence breaks down (i.e., when a high probability is assigned to a belief that is elicited late in the sequence or to a belief that has a low frequency of occurrence in a given population), one is likely to be dealing with nonsalient beliefs. However, information about belief strength alone, without information about the belief's position in the belief hierarchy, cannot be used to determine whether a belief is salient or not. As mentioned above, a nonsalient belief may be assigned a high probability; further, a salient belief may sometimes have a relatively low probability.

Importance of beliefs. In a way that is similar to our distinction between salient and nonsalient beliefs, it has sometimes been argued that some beliefs are more important than others in determining a person's attitude. This raises the question whether it is possible to use subjective estimates of importance to identify salient beliefs. To answer this question, it is necessary to distinguish between several possible interpretations of "belief importance." We have already encountered Rosenberg's (1956) concept of "value importance," which refers to the amount of satisfaction or dissatisfaction derived from an attribute that is associated with a given object (see Chapter 2). Clearly, this definition equates importance with the evaluation of the associated attribute, and there is considerable evidence that this evaluation is not related to belief salience (e.g., Zajonc, 1954; Fishbein and Kaplan, 1969; Fishbein, 1963).

Most frequently, the term "importance" has been used to refer to (1) the perceived importance of an attribute for the person, or (2) its perceived importance as a defining characteristic of the object, or (3) its perceived importance as a determinant of the person's attitude. The first of these usages is highly related to the polarity of the attribute's evaluation; that is, highly positive and highly negative attributes will tend to be perceived as important (Feldman and Fishbein, 1963a). The perceived importance of an attribute as a defining characteristic of an object is closely related to the subjective probability of an association between object and attribute. Thus, if a person has a high probability (i.e., strongly believes) that the Republican Party is conservative, he is also likely to believe that conservatism is an important characteristic of the Republican Party.[3] As was true with belief strength, this measure of importance cannot be used to determine whether a belief is salient or not.

In contrast to the interpretations of importance discussed so far, the last interpretation deals with the perceived importance of an attribute as a determinant of the person's attitude: The person is asked to estimate the relative importance of each belief as a determinant of his attitude. We saw in Chapter 5 that such subjective estimates of relative weights bear little resemblance to empirically derived weights. Specifically, studies of cue utilization have found that subjective estimates of each cue's relative importance as a determinant of a given judgment do not correspond to weights obtained in a multiple regression analysis. Of greater relevance to the present discussion, Kaplan and Fishbein (1969) found that subjective estimates of the importance of different attributes as determinants of attitude were unrelated to the positions of the beliefs in question in the belief hierarchy. Thus it appears that none of the different interpretations of belief importance can be used to derive measures that will identify salient and nonsalient beliefs.

One other method of attempting to estimate importance or salience of attributes as determinants of attitude has been to correlate each belief (taking

---

3. Zajonc (1954) has used the term "prominence" to refer to this view of importance. Clearly, a measure of prominence can be obtained only when dealing with attributes that refer to properties of an object but not with other types of attributes, such as outcomes of an act.

evaluation of the attribute into account) with the attitude. As in any multiple regression approach, these correlations (or the regression weights) are viewed as objective indices of importance. However, it is clear that correlations (or regression weights) provide no evidence as to causality, and it is therefore inappropriate to assume that a high correlation indicates an important *determinant* of attitude or that a low correlation is evidence that the belief is *not* an important determinant of attitude. Further, there is no evidence that these empirical weights or correlations can be used to identify salient and nonsalient beliefs (i.e., that these "objective" weights are related to a belief's position in the belief hierarchy).

INFORMATIONAL BASIS OF ATTITUDE

We have argued that a person's attitude is a function of his salient beliefs at a given point in time. In previous chapters we have shown that attitude can be measured by considering a person's responses to a set of belief statements even when they involve nonsalient beliefs. The relation between a set of beliefs and attitude was described in terms of an expectancy-value model. In Chapter 2 we showed that such a model is consistent with many theoretical approaches to attitude formation and change.

Each belief associates a given object with some attribute. According to an expectancy-value model, a person's evaluation of the attribute contributes to his attitude in proportion to the strength of his belief. It is clear that this approach postulates an informational basis for the formation of attitude; a person is viewed as processing the information he has about an object in arriving at his evaluation of the object.[4] In the remainder of this chapter we will discuss some of the evidence in support of an informational basis of attitude, and we will try to show that although other bases for attitude formation have been suggested, most can be interpreted in terms of an expectancy-value model.

Expectancy-Value Model

The model we have proposed deals with the relation between beliefs about an object and attitude toward that object. It is a descriptive model that is applicable to any set of beliefs, whether they are salient or nonsalient, new or old. Although we have argued that a person's salient beliefs *determine* his attitude, the model itself is not predicated on an assumption of causality but deals merely with the relation between beliefs and attitude. Specifically, it provides a description of the

---

4. This viewpoint is consistent with the notion that a person's attitude is determined by a limited number of beliefs since research has shown (e.g., G. A. Miller, 1956; Mandler, 1967) that a person is limited in his capacity to process information at a given point in time.

way in which different beliefs (and the evaluations of the associated attributes) are combined or integrated to arrive at an evaluation of the object. As we have suggested in previous chapters, the integration process is described by Eq. 6.1, in which A is the attitude toward an object, action, or event; b is the beliefs about the object's attributes or about the act's consequences; and e is the evaluations of

$$A = \sum_{i=1}^{n} b_i e_i, \qquad (6.1)$$

the attributes or consequences. Thus, according to the model, a person's attitude toward an object can be estimated by multiplying his evaluation of each attribute associated with the object by his subjective probability that the object has that attribute and then summing the products for the total set of beliefs. Similarly, a person's attitude toward a behavior can be estimated by multiplying his evaluation of each of the behavior's consequences by his subjective probability that performing the behavior will lead to that consequence and then summing the products for the total set of beliefs. The terms "attribute" and "consequence" are used in a very general sense to refer to any aspect of an object or behavior, respectively—that is, to any characteristic, quality, object, concept, value, or goal associated with the object or behavior.[5]

It is apparent that persons holding the same beliefs may have very different attitudes and that persons holding different beliefs may have the same attitudes. Attitudes are based on the total set of the person's salient beliefs and the evaluations associated with those beliefs. When the same beliefs are held with different strength or when evaluations of associated attributes differ, attitudes will also be different. Conversely, when different beliefs are held with equal strength and when they have identical evaluative implications, the same attitudes will result. It follows that knowledge of a person's attitude provides little information about the particular beliefs he holds or about his evaluations of attributes associated with the attitude object.

One other question concerning the expectancy-value model is worth considering. Looking at Eq. 6.1, one may think that attitudes would increase indefinitely with the addition of new positive beliefs since each new $b \times e$ product is added to the existing total. However, recall that a person's attitude is determined by a limited number of *salient* beliefs that are arranged hierarchically in terms of their probabilities. Within this hierarchy, then, each additional belief contributes successively less to the total attitude, and thus the total evaluation tends to level off after five to nine beliefs. Consider, for example, a person who holds

---

5. Measurement procedures for beliefs and evaluations were discussed in Chapter 3. There it was also mentioned that, strictly speaking, the model deals only with associative relations between object and attribute, and thus a belief such as "O is not X" is viewed as an association between the object O and the attribute *not X*.

seven positive beliefs about some object. With the assumption that evaluation of the attributes is constant (+2), his belief hierarchy might be as follows:

Belief	b	e	$b \times e$
1	.95	+2	1.90
2	.90	+2	1.80
3	.90	+2	1.80
4	.85	+2	1.70
5	.75	+2	1.50
6	.70	+2	1.40
7	.65	+2	1.30

Column 4 shows that each additional belief contributes less to the total attitude. Generally speaking, then, the theoretical relationship between number of positive beliefs and attitude (with evaluation of attributes held constant) is described by Fig. 6.1.

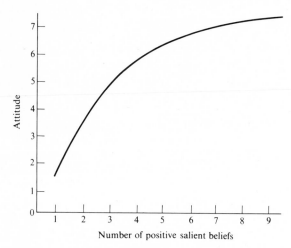

Fig. 6.1 Attitude as a function of positive number of beliefs, with attribute evaluation held constant.

Considerable evidence in support of the expectancy-value model can be found throughout the attitude area. We mentioned in previous chapters that virtually all standard attitude measures can be viewed in terms of an expectancy-value formulation, and research has repeatedly demonstrated the validity of these measures. More direct attempts to test the model have also been reported. For example, Fishbein (1963) first stated his formulation of an expectancy-value model with reference to attitudes toward Negroes. He constructed a set of 10 modal salient beliefs for his subject population by taking the 10 attributes that were elicited most frequently in response to the question: "What do you believe to be the characteristics of Negroes?" The 10 attributes, ordered in terms of frequency of elicita-

tion, were dark skin, curly (kinky) hair, musical, athletic, friendly, tall, uneducated, unintelligent, hard workers, and lazy. A new sample of subjects then evaluated each attribute on five evaluative semantic differential scales; the sum over the
five scales provided a measure of e in Eq. in 6.1. To provide a measure of belief
strength (b), subjects rated the probability that "Negroes have dark skin," "Negroes
are uneducated," etc., on a set of five probability scales in a semantic differential
format (e.g., *probable–improbable, likely–unlikely*); again a sum over the five
scales was obtained. The e and b measures could both range from -15 to $+15$,
with high scores indicating positive evaluation or high probability of association.
An estimate of each subject's attitude toward Negroes was obtained by multiplying each e by the corresponding b and summing the products. Finally, each subject's attitude toward Negroes was assessed directly by asking him to rate the concept "Negro" on five evaluative semantic differential scales. The sum over the
responses to these five scales served as an index of attitude. A correlation of .80
was obtained between the estimate and the direct measure of attitude, providing
support for the theoretical model.[6]

It may be instructive to examine two more recent experiments dealing with
attitudes toward political candidates and toward behaviors (e.g., using birth control pills). In a continuing series of studies, Fishbein and his associates (e.g.,
Fishbein and Feldman, 1963; Feldman and Fishbein, 1963a,b; Fishbein and
Coombs, 1974) have investigated the relation between beliefs about political candidates and attitudes toward those candidates. In the month prior to the 1964
presidential election, for example, over 600 residents of a small midwestern com-
munity were interviewed. The respondents, who were of voting age, expressed
their agreement or disagreement with a set of 24 belief statements concerning each
of the two presidential candidates, Johnson and Goldwater. In addition, they
evaluated each attribute in the 24 belief statements and provided direct measures
of their attitudes toward the two candidates.

The 24 belief statements were constructed on the basis of attributes elicited
from an independent sample of subjects in response to the following two questions: (1) What are the characteristics, qualities, and attributes of each candidate? (2) What do you think are the relevant issues in this campaign? The 24 belief statements used in the study are shown in Table 6.1. Each belief statement
was rated on a seven-point *probable–improbable* scale, and each attribute or issue
was rated on a seven-point *good–bad* scale. The products of these two measures, summed over the 24 beliefs, served as estimates of attitude toward the two
candidates. The estimates correlated .69 and .87 with the direct measures of attitudes toward Johnson and Goldwater, respectively. Similar results were found in
several other studies dealing with attitudes toward other presidential candidates as
well as candidates for the House of Representatives and the Senate; all these
studies provided strong support for the expectancy-value model presented in
Eq. 6.1.

---

6. A rank-order correlation was computed in this study ($N = 50$, $p < .001$).

Table 6.1 Belief Statements Used in Study of Attitudes Toward Presidential Candidates in the 1964 Election (from Fishbein and Coombs, 1974)

Lyndon B. Johnson (Barry Goldwater)

1. is a Republican
2. is a Democrat
3. is consistent in his views
4. is a conservative
5. is a moderate
6. is a liberal
7. is physically healthy
8. is mentally healthy
9. is a political opportunist
10. is in favor of our present foreign policy in Vietnam
11. is in favor of the antipoverty bill
12. is in favor of reducing the power of the Supreme Court
13. is in favor of allowing military personnel to make decisions about the use of nuclear weapons
14. is in favor of medicare
15. selected a well-qualified running mate for Vice President
16. is in favor of political extremism
17. is in favor of price supports for farm products
18. is in favor of using nuclear weapons in Vietnam
19. is in favor of swift enforcement of the Civil Rights Law
20. is in favor of increased social security benefits
21. is in favor of reducing the power of the federal government
22. approves of the John Birch Society
23. is in favor of the Nuclear Test Ban Treaty
24. approves of the Americans for Democratic Action

The final example extends the expectancy-value model to attitudes toward specific behaviors, as opposed to attitudes toward a class of people (Negroes) or a given individual (e.g., Goldwater). In a study by Jaccard and Davidson (1972), attitudes of women toward using birth control pills were considered. Beliefs about this behavior were elicited in private interviews with a sample of 22 women. In the course of the interviews these respondents were asked to indicate their beliefs about the consequences of using the pill, and to describe other advantages and disadvantages of using the pill. They were then asked to report if there was anything else they associated with using the pill. The 15 beliefs mentioned most frequently were used to construct a questionnaire that was given to a new sample of 73 women. The 15 consequences associated with using the pill are presented in Table 6.2. In a manner similar to the study on political candidates, measures were obtained of belief strength and evaluations of consequences; these measures were used to compute an estimate of attitude toward using birth control pills. In support of the model, the estimate was found to correlate .73 with a direct semantic differential measure of the same attitude.

Table 6.2 Consequences of Using Birth Control Pills (from Jaccard and Davidson, 1972)

1. leads to major side effects (e.g., blood clots)
2. leads to minor side effects (e.g., weight gain)
3. would affect my sexual morals
4. is immoral
5. is using a method of birth control that is unreliable
6. would give me guilt feelings
7. produces children who are born with something wrong with them
8. would increase my sexual pleasure
9. would enable me to regulate the size of my family
10. would enable me to regulate time intervals between pregnancies
11. would regulate my menstrual cycle
12. is using a method of birth control that is convenient
13. is using the best method available
14. would remove the worry of becoming pregnant
15. is using a method of birth control that is expensive

Many other studies have produced results in support of the expectancy-value model. They have dealt with attitudes toward persons, issues, institutions, concepts, behaviors, etc. (e.g., Rosenberg, 1956; E. R. Carlson, 1956; Fishbein, Landy, and Hatch, 1969; Ajzen and Fishbein, 1970, 1972; Insko *et al.,* 1970). For example, Rosenberg found a significant relation between a person's attitude toward the policy of allowing members of the Communist Party to address the public and beliefs as to whether that policy would facilitate or prevent the attainment of 35 values, such as "America having high prestige in other countries," "People being well educated," and "Keeping promises made to others." Several of these studies have also shown that attitudes can be estimated more accurately by considering both belief strength and evaluation of associated attributes (i.e., from $\Sigma b_i e_i$) than by using only the sum of the beliefs (Σb_i) or the sum of the evaluations (Σe_i).[7]

---

7. One exception occurs when the e's are either all positive or all negative. In this case, Σb_i alone will tend to be highly correlated with the attitude.

Although virtually all studies designed to test the expectancy-value model have obtained significant results, the correlation between estimated and observed attitudes has varied considerably. Generally speaking, it may be suggested that when attitudes are estimated on the basis of salient beliefs elicited by the subjects or on the basis of belief statements that have been selected by some standard scaling procedure, the correlation tends to be high (e.g., Fishbein, 1963; Jaccard and Davidson, 1972; Ostrom, 1969). When belief statements are selected in an intuitive fashion, many beliefs will tend to be nonsalient, and they may also be unrelated to the underlying attitude. Studies using such belief statements have generally obtained lower correlations (e.g., Insko *et al.*, 1970). Most studies that have obtained low correlations, however, have usually had some methodological problem concerning the measures of beliefs, evaluations, or the attitudinal criterion (e.g., Mascaro, 1970; L. R. Anderson, 1970; Szalay, Windle, and Lysne, 1970; Kaplan and Fishbein, 1969; Bass and Talarzyk, 1972; Sheth and Talarzyk, 1972). For example, measures of perceived importance of an attribute have sometimes been substituted for evaluation of the attributes (e.g., Bass and Talarzyk, 1972; Sheth and Talarzyk, 1972; Hansen, 1969). As mentioned in our earlier discussion, this measure of importance is not equivalent to evaluation; rather, it will tend to be related to *polarity* of evaluation.

Parenthetically, it has sometimes been argued that each item of information should also be given a weight for its importance, salience, or relevance (e.g., Hackman and Anderson, 1968; Wyer, 1970c). Thus it has been suggested that in addition to obtaining measures of probability and evaluation, investigators should obtain ratings of each attribute in terms of its importance; that is,

$$A = \sum_{i=1}^{n} I_i \, b_i e_i,$$

where I is perceived importance. Despite the intuitive plausibility of this position, recent studies have consistently found that including importance as an additional factor in the expectancy-value model tends to attenuate the prediction of attitude (e.g., L. R. Anderson, 1970; Hackman and Anderson, 1968; Kaplan and Fishbein, 1969; Wyer, 1970c). In light of our discussion of importance, these results are not surprising. Attributes that are important are typically evaluated more positively or negatively (i.e., are more polarized) than attributes that are unimportant. Similarly, people usually tend to have more information about things that are important to them, and thus they tend to be more certain and to have stronger beliefs about important than about unimportant attributes. Although there is no one-to-one relation between importance, evaluation, and belief strength, there is some recent evidence suggesting a high correlation between absolute $b_i e_i$ scores and judgments of importance. Indeed, the $\Sigma b_i e_i$ formulation appears to take enough of importance into account that the addition of an independent measure of importance to the $\Sigma b_i e_i$ formulation (i.e., when the model is changed to $\Sigma b_i e_i I_i$) merely provides redundant information that tends to attenuate prediction.

Adding Versus Averaging

So far we have assumed that an estimate of attitude is obtained by summing the $b \times e$ products (that is, $A = \Sigma b_i e_i$). It is possible, however, that some other combinatorial process, such as the average or mean of the $b \times e$ products [that is, $A_o = \Sigma b_i e_i / n$] might provide a better estimate of attitude. In most of the studies discussed thus far, the distinction between adding and averaging has no bearing on the results. In these studies a set of modal salient belief statements was constructed, and subjects were asked to indicate the strength of their beliefs (b) and their attribute evaluations (e). Estimates of attitude obtained by summing and averaging the $b \times e$ products will be perfectly correlated. That is, dividing a variable by a constant (the number of beliefs in this case) produces a new variable that has a perfect correlation with the original variable.[8] It follows that these two variables will have the same relation to any third variable (e.g., a direct measure of attitude).

However, when the number of beliefs is not constant, adding and averaging may produce different estimates of attitude. This notion has provided the basis for experimental tests comparing summation and averaging models of attitude formation. Consider a person who holds a number of positive beliefs. Typically the prediction is that if the summation model is correct, attitude will increase with additional favorable beliefs, but that no increase will occur if the averaging model is correct. Similarly, with the assumption of an initial set of unfavorable beliefs, the addition of other unfavorable beliefs is usually expected to decrease attitude when the summation model is applied, and no change is expected under the averaging model. Note, however, that these expectations are justified only when all beliefs are held with equal strength and when all attributes have equal evaluations. For example, if all probabilities are 1.0 and all evaluations are $+2$, a sum of the $b \times e$ products across two beliefs results in an estimated attitude of $+4$, and a sum of the $b \times e$ products across four beliefs results in an estimate of $+8$. An averaging model would predict an attitude of $+2$ in both cases. Thus, under the stated assumptions, the summation model predicts a more favorable attitude as number of positive beliefs increases whereas no difference is predicted by the averaging model.

Alternatively, it has been argued that the addition of mildly favorable beliefs to highly favorable beliefs should raise attitudes according to the summation model and lower attitudes according to the averaging model. Similarly, adding mildly unfavorable beliefs to highly unfavorable beliefs should lower attitudes according to the summation model and raise attitudes according to the averaging model. These expectations are justified only when all beliefs are held with equal strength and when subjects actually evaluate the attributes in accordance with

8. Dividing a variable by a constant is a linear transformation, and linear transformations do not affect correlation coefficients.

the experimenter's design. For example, suppose that all beliefs again have a probability of 1.0 and that subjects actually evaluate two attributes as +3 and two as +1. According to a summation model, a person holding the first two beliefs should have an attitude of +6, and a person holding all four beliefs should have an attitude of +8. In contrast, computing an average would predict attitudes of +3 and +2, respectively. Thus, under the specified assumptions, adding mildly favorable beliefs will raise attitudes according to the summation model and lower attitudes according to the averaging model.

In an experimental investigation, N. H. Anderson (1965a) attempted to "get a relative test of the additive and averaging formulations based on qualitative comparisons" (p. 395). Descriptions of hypothetical persons were provided in terms of either two adjectives or four adjectives. These adjectives had previously been rated for their likability by an independent sample of 100 subjects; some adjectives were highly favorable (H), some moderately favorable (M+), some moderately unfavorable (M-), and some low in favorability (L). The subjects rated each hypothetical person by assigning a score of 50 to a person he would neither like nor dislike, lower numbers to persons he would dislike, and higher numbers to persons he would like.

Consistent with our discussion above, Anderson constructed sets of adjectives that allowed for two types of "crucial" tests between the averaging and adding formulations. First he compared sets of two highly favorable adjectives with sets of four highly favorable adjectives (HH versus HHHH), and sets of two versus four adjectives of low favorability (LL versus LLLL). The second type of comparison was concerned with the effects of adding mildly favorable or unfavorable adjectives to highly favorable or unfavorable ones, respectively (that is, HH versus HHM+M+ and LL versus LLM-M-). Examples of these different sets of adjectives might be as follows:[9]

HH	intelligent, good-natured
HHHH	intelligent, good-natured, wise, friendly
HHM+M+	intelligent, good-natured, reserved, obedient
LL	hostile, conceited
LLLL	hostile, conceited, belligerent, self-centered
LLM-M-	hostile, conceited, meek, withdrawing

The results of this study were rather inconclusive. According to Anderson (1965a), the additive model appeared to be supported by the first type of comparison: Four highly favorable adjectives produced a more positive attitude than two highly favorable ones, and four highly unfavorable adjectives produced a

---

9. These examples were constructed on the basis of Anderson's (1968b) list of 555 personality trait words; they may or may not have been part of his study. The particular examples given have been constructed for the purpose of our subsequent discussion.

more negative attitude than two highly unfavorable ones (that is, HHHH > HH and LLLL < LL).[10] In contrast, the second type of comparison appeared to favor the averaging model since adding two mildly favorable adjectives to two highly favorable ones reduced evaluation of the hypothetical person whereas adding two mildly unfavorable adjectives to two highly unfavorable ones increased evaluation (that is, HH > HHM$^+$M$^+$ and LL < LLM$^-$M$^-$).[11]

The experimental paradigm used in this study and most others on the summation-averaging controversy varies the number of informational items used to describe a stimulus person and compares the resulting attitudes toward that person. This paradigm does not allow a crucial test between the summation and averaging models unless the two assumptions mentioned above are met: (1) All information about the stimulus person must be accepted (i.e., believed) to the same degree. (2) The adjectives used to describe the stimulus person must be evaluated in accordance with the experimental design (e.g., all H adjectives must be given the same evaluation, as must all M$^+$ adjectives, and the former must be more positive than the latter).

When either of these assumptions is not met, it is impossible to use the summation or averaging models to make predictions of attitudes in the experimental paradigm above. Table 6.3 illustrates predictions of the two models for attitudes based on two favorable adjectives (Set 1) versus four favorable adjectives (Set 2). Case 1 in Table 6.3 applies when both assumptions are met: All beliefs have a strength of 1.0, and all adjective evaluations are +2. As we can see, the summation model predicts that four positive adjectives produce a more favorable attitude than do two positive adjectives. In contrast, the averaging model predicts no difference.

When belief strength and/or evaluations are allowed to vary, both models can account for any obtained result. Case 2 and Case 3 in Table 6.3 show what could happen if belief strength varied (and adjective evaluations remained constant). Depending on the belief strength associated with adjectives in Sets 1 and 2, both models can predict that the four-adjective set will lead to more favorable or less favorable attitudes than will the two-adjective set. In Case 4, both belief

---

10. As will be seen below, Anderson (1965a) argued that this "set-size effect" could be accounted for by an averaging model.

11. With the assumption of equal belief strength and the evaluations specified by Anderson, the following predictions can be made with respect to attitudes based on the different descriptions:

Summation model:
    (HHHH) > (HHM$^+$M$^+$) > (HH) > (LL) > (LLM$^-$M$^-$) > (LLLL).
Averaging model:
    (HHHH) = (HH) > (HHM$^+$M$^+$) > (LLM$^-$M$^-$) > (LL) = (LLLL).
The actual findings were as follows:
    (HHHH) > (HH) > (HHM$^+$M$^+$) > (LLM$^-$M$^-$) > (LL) > (LLLL).

Note that these results support neither the summation model nor the averaging model.

Table 6.3 Averaging versus Summation: A Hypothetical Example

	Case 1			Case 2			Case 3			Case 4		
Set 1	b	e	$b \times e$	b	e	$b \times e$	b	e	$b \times e$	b	e	$b \times e$
Intelligent	1.0	+2	2.00	.60	+2	1.20	.60	+2	1.20	.60	+2	1.20
Good-natured	1.0	+2	2.00	.75	+2	1.50	.75	+2	1.50	.75	+2	1.50
$A = \Sigma b_i e_i$			4.00			2.70			2.70			2.70
$A = \frac{1}{2} \Sigma b_i e_i$			2.00			1.35			1.35			1.35
Set 2												
Intelligent	1.0	+2	2.00	.65	+2	1.30	.35	+2	.70	.30	+2	.60
Good-natured	1.0	+2	2.00	.75	+2	1.50	.40	+2	.80	.40	+3	1.20
Wise	1.0	+2	2.00	.90	+2	1.80	.15	+2	.30	.45	+2	.90
Friendly	1.0	+2	2.00	.95	+2	1.90	.25	+2	.50	.60	+1	.60
$A = \Sigma b_i e_i$			8.00			6.50			2.30			3.30
$A = \frac{1}{4} \Sigma b_i e_i$			2.00			1.63			.58			.83
Summation model	Set 1 < Set 2			Set 1 < Set 2			Set 1 > Set 2			Set 1 < Set 2		
Averaging model	Set 1 = Set 2			Set 1 < Set 2			Set 1 > Set 2			Set 1 > Set 2		

strength and evaluations vary; in the particular example provided, the summation model predicts an increase in attitude, and the averaging model predicts a decrease.

These examples should make it clear that there is no systematic relation between number of beliefs and attitude. Depending on the effects of new information on prior beliefs, the formation of new beliefs on the basis of this information may raise, lower, or have no appreciable effect on a person's attitude. This is true irrespective of whether a summation or an averaging model is employed. Unfortunately, this simple fact has usually not been recognized, and most studies on the summation-averaging controversy have employed the experimental paradigm described earlier without testing the assumptions that must be met before this paradigm can be used to provide a test between the competing models.

The examples in Table 6.3 demonstrate that by speculating about belief strength and evaluations one can account for any finding both in terms of an averaging model and in terms of a summation model. Table 6.3 also suggests, however, that it is possible to provide a more adequate test between averaging and summation by obtaining measures of belief strength and attribute evaluations. When this is done, it may often be found that means and sums over the $b \times e$ products make conflicting predictions about the effects of adding new items of information (for example, see Case 4 in Table 6.3). Unfortunately, most investigations concerning the adding-averaging controversy have obtained no measures of belief strength and have usually assumed that mean evaluations of attributes provided by an independent sample can serve as estimates of the subjects' actual evaluations of the attributes.

Perhaps the most basic problem with the research paradigm used in this area is that the subject's salient beliefs about the hypothetical person are not assessed. Instead it is assumed that the subject accepts the information he receives about the hypothetical person (i.e., that all beliefs are held with equal strength) and that his attitude toward the person is a function of these beliefs, and only these beliefs. From our perspective, however, a person's attitude is determined by his salient beliefs. It follows that a subject's attitude toward a hypothetical stranger described by a set of adjectives may or may not be based on the particular items of information he was given. The subject may believe that some but not all of the adjectives are descriptive of the person in question, and he may hold these beliefs with different strengths. Further, because of the implicative structure among trait adjectives discussed in the preceding chapter, he may form inferential beliefs about the hypothetical person on the basis of the description provided by the experimenter. Thus, in order to predict a person's attitude, it is not sufficient to know what information he has been given; rather, it is necessary to assess the beliefs he actually holds, i.e., his salient beliefs.

Redundancy and inconsistency. We can use the sets of two and four adjectives given above to illustrate this problem. Suppose that a hypothetical person has been described as *intelligent* and *good-natured* and that the subject has accepted this information. If he was asked to describe the person, he would elicit the beliefs that the person is *intelligent* and *good-natured*. On the basis of an inference process, however, he might also report that the hypothetical person has various other characteristics, perhaps that he is *wise* and *friendly*. Thus, even though he was given only two items of information, his attitude would be a function of four beliefs. (The inferential beliefs are perhaps held with less certainty.) Clearly, if the subject was given additional information indicating that the hypothetical person is *wise* and *friendly,* this information would be *redundant* with the earlier information and might merely strengthen the inferential beliefs. As a consequence, adding the two new adjectives would be expected to produce only a small increment in attitude.

Consistent with this argument, a number of studies have shown that addition of nonredundant information leads to a greater shift in attitude than addition of redundant information (Dustin and Baldwin, 1966; Wyer, 1968, 1970b; Schmidt, 1969). For example, Wyer (1968) described a hypothetical person in terms of two adjectives that were either the same (maximal redundancy), highly redundant (i.e., the conditional probability of Adjective A_2, given Adjective A_1, was high), or low in redundancy [that is, $p(A_2|A_1)$ was low]. It was found that for two favorable adjectives, the lower the redundancy the more positive the attitude. Similarly, given two unfavorable adjectives, the lower the redundancy, the more unfavorable the attitude.

Rather than being redundant, new information may sometimes be *inconsistent* with prior beliefs. Suppose that after accepting the information that a hypothetical person is *hostile* and *conceited,* a subject is told that the person is also *meek* and *withdrawing.* Since the subject may perceive that it is inconsistent for a person to be both *hostile* and *meek,* he may lower his confidence that the person is hostile, he may be unwilling to completely accept that the person is meek, or both effects may occur to some degree. In addition, the new information may affect inferential beliefs formed on the basis of the initial information (e.g., that the person is *belligerent* and *self-centered*). Again, we cannot assume that attitude is simply a function of the information provided. In fact, the present example shows how the addition of two moderately unfavorable items of information (meek and withdrawing) might actually increase attitude (in apparent contradiction to a summation model). Some evidence for effects of inconsistency has been provided by Wyer (1970b), Anderson and Jacobson (1965), and Hendrick and Costantini (1970) in studies of "discounting" of information. These studies will be discussed below.

In conclusion, most research comparing the summation and averaging models has used the research paradigm described previously, and results have therefore been inconsistent and inconclusive. Indeed, we know of only one study in which the expectancy-value model was used to set up situations in which the averaging and summation formulations would actually make differential predictions (Fishbein and Hunter, 1964). Unfortunately, even this study did not provide an adequate test since only limited information about a subject's beliefs was obtained and belief strength was not measured. Fishbein and Hunter described a hypothetical person in terms of one, two, four, or eight favorable adjectives and obtained a measure of attitude toward the person on five evaluative semantic differential scales. The following descriptions were used.[12]

---

12. These descriptions were part of a more complex design in which each subject received information about four different hypothetical persons (described by one, two, four, and eight adjectives). They represent the descriptions of the first stimulus described in four different experimental conditions.

1. honest

2. honest, loyal

3. honest, loyal, determined, successful

4. honest, loyal, determined, successful, kind, protective, friendly, helpful

Prior to receiving the description of the stimulus person, each subject rated each of 25 adjectives (including the traits used to describe the stimulus person) on the same five evaluative semantic differential scales. These ratings provided measures of attribute evaluations (e). Following his evaluation of the stimulus person, the subject was asked to write down the characteristics that had been attributed to the person. Fishbein and Hunter assumed a belief strength of 1.0 for each characteristic listed. Note, however, that an adequate measure of salient beliefs would require each subject to list *his beliefs* about the hypothetical person (not to *recall* the adjectives attributed to the person) and to indicate the strength of those beliefs. Despite these inadequacies in the belief measure used by Fishbein and Hunter, their study provided interesting data concerning the adding-averaging controversy.

Each subject's evaluation of the adjectives he reported as having been attributed to a given hypothetical person (whether or not they appeared in the actual description provided to him) were used to compute two predictions of his attitude toward that person. One predicted score was computed by taking the sum of the evaluations, a second score by averaging the evaluations. The investigators found that the averaging and adding formulations made conflicting predictions: The summation model predicted an increase in attitude with number of adjectives presented whereas the averaging model predicted a slight decrease (see Fig. 6.2). The obtained attitudes toward the hypothetical persons could therefore be used to test the two formulations. As Fig. 6.2 shows, the obtained results were very close to the predictions made on the basis of the summation model; attitudes increased with number of adjectives presented. These results in support of the additive model, however, are restricted to a situation in which beliefs are assumed to be held with equal strength; they may not be generalizable to an expectancy-value model which allows belief strength to vary.

Information Integration

We have discussed the expectancy-value formulation as a model of information integration. According to this model, a person's attitude toward some object is a function of the information (beliefs) he has about the object. The model describes how this information is integrated or combined in the formation of attitude. In the preceding chapter we discussed the multiple regression approach to inferential belief formation, which assumes a linear model of information integration. Although there are some similarities between an expectancy-value model and a simple linear model, one important difference has sometimes been overlooked. Let c

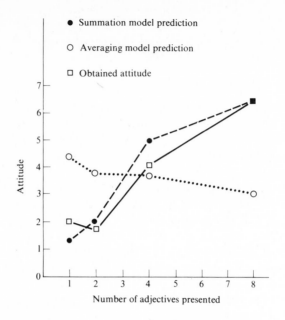

Fig. 6.2 Predicted and obtained attitudes as a function of number of adjectives presented. (Adapted from Fishbein and Hunter, 1964.)

be a constant and x, y, and z variables that can take on different values. The linear model in this case can be expressed as follows:

$$A = c_1x + c_2y + c_3z.$$

Each variable is given a constant weight in the linear model. For example, suppose that different stimulus persons are described in terms of three variables: physical attractiveness, intelligence, and conservatism. These variables will take on different values for different stimulus persons. However, for a given subject, the weight of a given variable remains constant across stimulus persons. Thus, in studies on cue utilization, each variable or cue is given a constant weight such that maximally accurate predictions of a subject's judgments can be made.

For any number of variables (v), the linear model can be written in the form

$$A = \sum_{i=1}^{n} c_iv_i, \qquad (6.2)$$

where c_i is the weight associated with variable v_i and the sum is taken over n variables. Although this formula appears to be similar to the expectancy-value model, the latter is not a simple linear model since both b and e are considered to be variables. Letting x and v stand for two variables, the expectancy-value model can be expressed in the form

$$A = \sum_{i=1}^{n} x_i v_i, \tag{6.3}$$

where x is the expectancy that the object has some attribute, v is the value of that attribute, and n is the number of attributes.[13]

According to Eq. 6.2, attitude is a *linear* function of v whereas according to the expectancy-value model (Eq. 6.3), attitude is a *nonlinear* function of v. A numerical example may help clarify this distinction. Suppose that stimulus persons are described in terms of three variables. Table 6.4 illustrates the distinction between the linear and the expectancy-value models for this situation. For example, stimulus person A may have been described as *slightly attractive, extremely intelligent,* and *quite liberal,* and the subject may place evaluations of 4, 7, and 5 on these traits, respectively. Similarly, Person C may have been described as *extremely unattractive, slightly intelligent,* and *extremely conservative,* with respective evaluations of 1, 5, and 1. According to a linear model, the weight placed on each variable is constant across stimulus persons. In our hypothetical example, the subject placed most weight on the third variable (liberalism), less on the first (attractiveness), and least on the second variable (intelligence) in forming his attitudes toward the stimulus persons. According to the expectancy-value model, however, the "weights" (i.e., expectancies) can vary across stimulus persons. For example, the subject strongly believed the information about B's attractiveness and intelligence, but not the information about his liberalism. With respect to Stimulus Person D, he accepted the information about D's liberalism but tended not to accept the information about his attractiveness or intelligence.

Figure 6.3 depicts the difference between the linear model and the nonlinear expectancy-value model for this example. Note that for the linear model the pre-

Table 6.4 Comparison of Linear and Expectancy-Value Models

Stimulus person	Linear model								Expectancy-value model							
	c_1	c_2	c_3	v_1	v_2	v_3	Σv_i	$\Sigma c_i v_i$	x_1	x_2	x_3	v_1	v_2	v_3	Σv_i	$\Sigma x_i v_i$
A	2	1	3	4	7	5	16	30	1	3	5	4	7	5	16	50
B	2	1	3	7	3	2	12	23	7	7	1	7	3	2	12	72
C	2	1	3	1	5	1	7	10	6	4	2	1	5	1	7	28
D	2	1	3	7	6	6	19	38	2	3	7	7	6	6	19	74

13. The expectancy-value model may be classified as a bilinear model when the $b \times e$ products are viewed as the variable and the weights are assumed to be equal across all of its values.

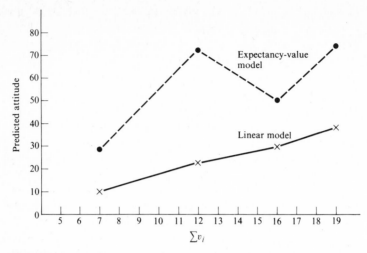

Fig. 6.3 Predicted attitude as a function of Σv_i according to linear and expectancy-value models for hypothetical values in Table 4.1.

dicted attitude ($\Sigma c_i v_i$) is linearly related to the evaluations of the attributes (that is, to Σv_i) but that no linear relation exists between $\Sigma x_i v_i$ and the evaluations of the attributes (Σv_i) according to the expectancy-value model. Clearly, then, although on the surface Eqs. 6.2 and 6.3 appear very similar, they do not represent the same model, and a linear model may make quite different predictions than the expectancy-value model.[14]

Anderson's Weighted Averaging Model

N. H. Anderson and his associates have made extensive use of a weighted linear model in their research on information integration and impression formation (for reviews, see Anderson 1970, 1971a). Anderson has been a vigorous proponent of this weighted averaging formulation, as opposed to a weighted sum, and he has claimed considerable empirical support for the averaging model. In its most general form, Anderson's weighted averaging model has been expressed as follows:

$$R = \frac{\Sigma w_i s_i}{\Sigma w_i}, \tag{6.4}$$

where R is a response on any judgmental dimension, s is the scale value of a given item of information on the same dimension, and w is the weight or importance

---

14. In light of this discussion, one may argue that the Fishbein and Hunter (1964) study discussed above represents a comparison of *linear* adding versus averaging formulations (where equal weights are assumed for each item of information) rather than a comparison in terms of the expectancy-value model. That is, the two predicted attitudes Σx and $\Sigma x/n$ both describe a linear relation between the predicted attitude and the evaluations of the attributes.

placed on that item of information. It is usually assumed that the weight associated with a given variable remains constant over all values of that variable (cf. Anderson, 1970). Thus, in most of its applications, the weighted averaging formulation is a linear model.[15] The weights in this linear model serve the same function as, and are comparable with, the regression weights obtained in a multiple regression analysis. When the weighted averaging model is applied to the attitude area, the response refers to the attitude toward an object, the scale value refers to the evaluation of a given attribute ascribed to the object, and w is the weight or importance of that attribute in the judgment.

In Chapter 5 we saw that a linear model has been found to lead to quite accurate predictions of a variety of inferential judgments. That is, the linear model accounts for much of the variance in these judgments even when there is evidence for a nonlinear or configural combinatorial process. Similar results have been obtained with respect to attitudinal judgments. In contrast to most work on cue utilization and inferential belief formation which has used a multiple regression approach, research in attitude formation has usually employed the analysis of variance approach. For example, in an early attempt to test his linear model, Anderson (1962) used sets of three adjectives to describe 27 hypothetical persons. A basic set of nine adjectives was used to describe all 27 persons; the nine adjectives were split into three subgroups containing one adjective each of low, medium, and high evaluation (as established by an independent sample of subjects). The 27 descriptions were created by forming all possible combinations in a $3 \times 3 \times 3$ analysis of variance design. Thus, one hypothetical person was described by three highly favorable adjectives, another by two highly favorable adjectives and one moderately favorable adjective, etc.[16] Twelve subjects rated the likeableness of each of the 27 stimulus persons on five different occasions and a separate analysis of variance was computed for each subject.[17]

In terms of the linear model, each subgroup of adjectives constitutes a variable with a set of scale values (high, medium, and low) and this variable is given a constant weight. In support of the linear model, most of the variance in each subject's attitudes was accounted for by the main effects of the three variables;

---

15. Parenthetically we note that Eq. 6.4 is equivalent to Eq. 6.2 when the weights sum to unity (i.e., when $\Sigma w_i = 1$).

16. When the subgroups of adjectives are viewed as cues and their high, medium, or low favorableness as the cue values, this design is similar to that used by Himmelfarb and Senn (1969), which was discussed in Chapter 5.

17. This application of Anderson's weighted averaging model "rests on two independence assumptions. First, it is assumed that there are no contextual effects; that is, the subjective value of any stimulus is assumed independent of what other stimulus it is paired with. Second, it is assumed that w_1 is the same for each row stimulus and w_2 is the same for each column stimulus" (Anderson, 1970; p. 155). Thus the weighted averaging model is a linear model in this application as in most of its applications.

that is, the more favorable an adjective describing a given person, the more like-able that person tended to be. Further, as would be predicted by the linear model (see Chapter 5), the interaction between the three variables was not significant for nine of the twelve subjects in the study. However, deviations from linearity did reach statistical significance for the remaining three subjects. Thus, although the linear model provided a reasonably good fit to the data, it could not account for all the obtained results.

Functional measurement. Anderson (1970, 1971a) has argued that the analysis of variance approach can be used not only to provide a test of the linear model but also to estimate weights and scale values. For example, once it has been shown that the linear model holds (i.e., that there are no significant interactions), the marginal means can serve as estimates of scale values if one assumes that each variable has a constant weight.

   To illustrate, consider a 2×2 design in which four hypothetical persons are described in terms of two sets of two adjectives. Further, suppose that each set is associated with a different source, as shown below:

		Source A		
		Adjective 1	Adjective 2	
Source B	Adjective 3	4	6	5
	Adjective 4	3	5	4
		3.5	5.5	

Thus a given hypothetical person is described in terms of two traits, one coming from Source A, the other from Source B. The values in the cells of the design represent attitudes toward the four hypothetical persons measured on a seven-point scale. Now assume that each source is given a constant weight, i.e., that the weight placed on Adjective 1 is equal to that placed on Adjective 2 and that Adjectives 3 and 4 also have equal weights. The marginal means can then serve as estimates of the scale values of the corresponding adjectives. Adjective 1 would have an estimated scale value of 3.5, Adjective 3 a scale value of 5, etc.[18]

   Anderson (1970, Weiss and Anderson, 1969) has shown that when certain additional assumptions are made, weights can also be estimated, once estimates of scale values are available.[19] However, when the levels of a variable can take on different weights as well as different values (i.e., when w and s can vary from row to row, from column to column, or from cell to cell in the ANOVA design), neither the weights nor the scale values can be estimated on the basis of the analysis of variance procedure.

---

18. Actually, the marginal means should be viewed as linear transformations of the subjective scale values.

19. For the ANOVA design above, weights can be estimated if it is assumed that $(s_1 - s_2) = (s_3 - s_4)$. An obtained inequality must then reflect differences in weights.

Comparing his weighted averaging model to the expectancy-value formulation, Anderson (1971a) has treated his scale values as the equivalent of attribute evaluation, and he has suggested that his weights may be analogous to subjective probabilities. That analogy seems unwarranted since in most applications of the weighted averaging formulation a linear model is used and the weights in a linear model are constants whereas the subjective probabilities in the expectancy-value model are variables. Although it may be reasonable to assume that different values of a given variable may be equally important in describing a person's attitude, there is no reason to assume that these different values are equally believable. For example, it is possible that information about a person's intelligence will be weighted in the same manner whether he is described as high or low in intelligence, but one cannot assume that these items of information will always be accepted to the same degree.

Similarly, it is not clear that scale values established in an analysis of variance design are equivalent to attribute evaluations. In terms of an expectancy-value model, attitude toward a stimulus person is determined by the products of belief strength and attribute evaluation (that is, $A = \Sigma b_i e_i$). If this model is correct, the marginal means that serve as estimates of scale values may actually represent estimates of $b \times e$ (for the different levels of a variable) rather than estimates of e. The analysis of variance can be used to test the accuracy of a linear model; in itself, however, it provides no information about the nature of the scale values. The expectancy-value formulation may also be viewed as a linear model (see note 13) in which the $b \times e$ products are the variable, and this variable is given a constant weight (w):

$$A = \sum_{i=1}^{n} w_i \, (b_i e_i).$$

In our discussions of the expectancy-value model, we have essentially assumed that the weight is 1.0 and can thus be neglected. We have further mentioned that adding a measure of importance, that is, adding a weight to the $b \times e$ products, has usually impaired rather than improved prediction. Nevertheless, when an expectancy-value model is viewed in this linear fashion, it can be seen that the scale value in Anderson's linear model may actually be equivalent to the $b \times e$ product.

Set-size effect. Just as an analysis of variance is insensitive to the nature of the scale values, it usually does not distinguish between a linear averaging model $[A = (1/n)\Sigma c_i v_i]$ versus a linear summation model ($A = \Sigma c_i v_i$). In the experiment described above, the prediction of nonsignificant interactions would be made on the basis of both models and could be taken as evidence in favor of either an additive or an averaging process.

The research paradigm employed in most studies of the summation-averaging controversy uses adjectives that have previously been scaled for their likableness. Even if one assumes that these ratings are accurate estimates of the subjects' actual scale values, and if measures of the subjective weights are *not* available, almost any obtained result can be interpreted as supporting either an additive or an averaging model by making appropriate post hoc assumptions about these weights (see Table 6.3). For example, we saw above that four highly favorable adjectives led to a more positive attitude than two highly favorable ones, and that four highly unfavorable adjectives led to a more negative attitude than two highly unfavorable ones (Anderson, 1965a). Under the assumption of equal weights, these findings provide evidence in favor of the summation model. However, Anderson (1965a, 1967, 1968a) has argued that this *set-size effect* can be accounted for by an averaging model. In order to explain the set-size effect, Anderson argued that prior to receiving information about a hypothetical person, subjects have an initial impression of that person which is usually assumed to be neutral.

To see how this notion might account for the set-size effect, consider the predicted difference in attitudes based on two versus four favorable adjectives with scale values of $+2$. With equal weights assumed, an averaging model would predict equal attitudes (that is, $(2 + 2)/2 = (2 + 2 + 2 + 2)/4 = 2$). However, when a neutral impression (with a scale value of 0) is taken into consideration, the larger set would result in a higher attitude (that is, $(2 + 2 + 0)/3 = 1.33 < (2 + 2 + 2 + 2 + 0)/5 = 1.60$). The qualitative prediction that is now derived from the averaging model is consistent with obtained results. A fairly precise quantitative fit to the data can be obtained by assuming that the initial impression is given a different weight than are the adjectives; the greater the weight placed on the initial impression, the stronger the set-size effect that would be predicted. Thus a set-size effect of almost any magnitude can be explained by making post hoc assumptions about differential weights. Clearly, the demonstration that weights *can* be found which will provide a reasonable fit between the data and a linear averaging model does not provide evidence for that model over some other model. Indeed, as we have shown earlier, it is possible to find weights that will make the data appear to support a linear summation model, or to find subjective probabilities that will fit the expectancy-value model. Without a clear a priori demonstration that averaging and summation models, whether they are linear or nonlinear (expectancy-value) models, make different qualitative predictions in a given situation, no crucial test of the two competing combination rules is possible.

Discounting effects. In the studies discussed so far, Anderson has claimed support for the averaging model on the assumption that different variables are given constant weights. In several studies, however, he has claimed support for the averaging model by assuming *unequal* weights (e.g., Weiss and Anderson, 1969; Anderson and Jacobson, 1965; Anderson, 1959; Anderson and Barrios, 1961). The basis for assuming equal or unequal weights is often not clear. For example, in the context of comparing linear adding and averaging models, Anderson (1965a) predicted that under the assumption of equal weights, attitudes toward a person described by two highly and two mildly favorable adjectives (HHM$^+$M$^+$) should be equal to the average of the two attitudes produced by four highly favorable adjectives (HHHH) and four mildly favorable ones (M$^+$M$^+$M$^+$M$^+$). Similarly, he predicted that the attitude toward a person described as LLM⁻M⁻ is equal to the average of the two attitudes toward persons described as LLLL and M⁻M⁻M⁻M⁻.[20] Although the results supported the first hypothesis, attitudes based on the (LLM⁻M⁻) set were significantly lower than predicted.

In contrast to his initial assumption of equal weights, Anderson suggested that "the discrepancy is in the direction that would be predicted by [the weighted averaging model] if the M⁻ adjectives had lower weights than the L adjectives" (Anderson, 1965a, p. 399). Note, however, that this assumption about unequal weights is merely a post hoc attempt to explain a finding inconsistent with the hypothesis. In a later study, Anderson and Alexander (1971) attempted to demonstrate that L adjectives are indeed given greater weight than M⁻ adjectives by asking subjects to rate the importance of these adjectives. Consistent with expectations, subjects reported that L adjectives were more important than M⁻ adjectives in determining their attitudes. However, an additional finding that H adjectives were rated as more important than M⁺ adjectives was inconsistent with Anderson's (1965a) earlier assumption that these adjectives are given equal weights. Thus, even if ratings of importance can be taken as estimates of weights, the findings do not fully support Anderson's interpretation.

Further, the assumption that L adjectives are given greater weight than M⁻ adjectives is also inconsistent with Anderson's (1962) test of the linear model (see p. 239), in which he assumed that H, M, and L adjectives are given equal weights. In fact, in a later study Anderson and Jacobson (1965) argued that adjectives varying in evaluative implications should not always be given equal weights. They described stimulus persons by three adjectives that were either highly favorable or highly unfavorable. Each adjective may be viewed as a variable that can take on a positive or negative scale value. Using a 2 x 2 x 2 analysis of variance design, they described eight stimulus persons. They hypothesized that an adjective inconsistent with the other two would be *discounted*, i.e., would be given lower weight. Thus, since an H adjective tends to be inconsistent with two L adjectives, it should be discounted. In one condition of the experiment, subjects were told that "one of the adjectives did not actually apply, that they should decide which one was inapplicable, and base their impression on the other two" (p. 534). In this condition, a significant interaction was obtained. Since a linear model that assumes equal weights would predict no interaction, this finding was taken to mean that different weights must have been applied to the adjectives, i.e., that discounting must have taken place.

It is interesting to note that in another experimental condition subjects were given Anderson's standard instructions, which emphasize that "all three words are accurate and each word is equally important" (Anderson and Jacobson, 1965, p. 534). Even under these instructions, which had previously been assumed to

---

20. Under the assumption of equal weights, the same predictions are made by linear averaging and summation models. These predictions do not follow when weights are unequal, as in the expectancy-value model, for example.

ensure equal weights, a significant interaction was obtained. Thus it appears that even under standard instructions, the assumption of equal weights may not be warranted.

More important, note that a significant interaction does not necessarily provide evidence for different weights or discounting. Instead, the interaction may be produced by interacting scale values. That is to say, when two or more adjectives are paired, one adjective may influence not only the weight of the other but also its scale value. Either effect would lead to an interaction. Unfortunately, the experiment reported by Anderson and Jacobson (as well as other experiments on the discounting effect) does not permit a distinction between change in weights and change in scale values. This distinction has become a major focus of investigation in research on order effects in impression formation.

Order Effects

In Chapter 5 we discussed Asch's (1946) work on impression formation. Among other things, Asch examined the effects of order of presentation and found evidence for a *primacy effect*. That is, adjectives appearing early in a list were found to exert a stronger influence on the formation of beliefs about the person described than adjectives presented later in the list. The same paradigm has been employed in research on order effects in attitude formation. In an early study, Anderson and Barrios (1961) used several lists of six adjectives each to describe different stimulus persons. Among the lists was that used by Asch (1946), in which adjectives were arranged in terms of their favorability: *intelligent, industrious, impulsive, critical, stubborn,* and *envious.* The order of presentation was reversed for half the subjects. Attitudes toward the stimulus person were measured on an eight-place scale ranging from *highly favorable* to *highly unfavorable.* Consistent with results reported by Asch, a primacy effect was obtained such that attitudes were more positive when favorable adjectives appeared at the beginning of the list than when the list was presented in reverse order.[21]

Similar results have been reported in several subsequent investigations that have used a variety of stimulus lists (e.g., Anderson and Hubert, 1963; Stewart, 1965; Hendrick and Costantini, 1970). Although the primacy effect is not always significant (e.g., Anderson and Norman, 1964), whenever a stimulus person is described by several adjectives and subjects are asked for their evaluation of the person following complete presentation of the list, adjectives presented early tend to have a stronger effect on attitudes than do adjectives presented late in the list.[22] Much of the recent research has attempted to test proposed explanations for this primacy effect.

---

21. The study used 61 different lists of adjectives; Asch's list was presented either first or last. The primacy effect was obtained only when the list was presented first.

22. The primacy effect is not found with very short lists of adjectives (e.g., Anderson and Barrios, 1961), and it tends to disappear with practice (Anderson and Barrios, 1961; Anderson and Hubert, 1963).

Change in meaning. One explanation was offered by Asch (1946) in terms of "directed impression" or "change in meaning." Asch suggested that adjectives presented early in a list may set up an initial impression that influences interpretation of later adjectives. However, Asch also pointed out that a primacy effect will not always be found, because an adjective in any position may for some reason play a "central" role and thus direct the overall impression. This explanation has been interpreted as suggesting that the meaning of a word in isolation may change when the word is placed in a certain context. With respect to the primacy effect, this implies that early adjectives influence the "meaning" of later ones, i.e., that the evaluations placed on later adjectives depend in part on the adjectives that have appeared earlier in the list.

Indirect evidence for a change in meaning interpretation has been obtained in studies of context effects. For example, Osgood and Tannenbaum's (1955) *congruity principle* was developed to explain the emergent meaning of a stimulus complex. In Chapter 2 we described the model for two items of information. In its more general form, the congruity principle can be expressed as follows:

$$A = \frac{|e_{n-1}|e_{n-1} + |e_n|e_n}{|e_{n-1}| + |e_n|} \tag{6.5}$$

In Eq. 6.5, e_{n-1} is the evaluation of a stimulus complex comprising $n-1$ items of information, e_n is the evaluation of the nth item of information, and $|e_{n-1}|$ and $|e_n|$ are the absolute values or polarities of these evaluations. As each new item of information is provided, it is essentially averaged with the attitude based on the preceding information. The congruity principle predicts how evaluations of words in isolation should change when combined in a stimulus complex. The predicted point of resolution is the person's attitude toward the stimulus complex, and according to the congruity principle, the evaluation of each word in the complex is the same as the overall attitude. Depending on the evaluations of prior and new information, either a primacy or a recency effect may be obtained.

Although most research on the congruity principle has been conducted in the area of communication and persuasion, the model has also been used in research on impression formation by predicting attitudes toward a person on the basis of information provided about the person (e.g., Osgood and Ferguson, 1957; Triandis and Fishbein, 1963; L. R. Anderson and Fishbein, 1965). Two of these studies compared the predictive accuracy of the congruity principle and other information integration models. Triandis and Fishbein compared the congruity principle with a simple sum of evaluations (that is, Σe_i), and Anderson and Fishbein compared it against the expectancy-value model.[23] Both alternative models were found to make more accurate predictions than the congruity principle

---

23. Triandis and Fishbein's study was designed to test the expectancy-value model under the assumption that subjects accept each item of information (that is, *b* was assumed to be 1.0). However, this assumption may not have been warranted.

made. It thus appears that the congruity model is not a very effective formulation in the context of impression formation.

Several investigators have attempted to provide an explicit test of the notion that a word changes its meaning when it is placed in different contexts. For example, Heise (1969, 1970) and Gollob (1968) found that evaluations of words in isolation differed from their evaluations in the context of a sentence. More directly relevant to impression formation, several investigators (Anderson and Lampel, 1965; Anderson, 1966; Wyer and Dermer, 1968; Wyer and Watson, 1969; M. F. Kaplan, 1971) have shown that evaluation of an adjective in the context of a stimulus list differs from the evaluation of that adjective in isolation. The general finding is that evaluation of an adjective in context is displaced toward the evaluations of the other adjectives in the list. To illustrate, Anderson (1966) placed H, M⁺, M⁻, and L adjectives in HH, M⁺M⁺, M⁻M⁻, and LL contexts. Evaluations of the test adjectives are shown in Fig. 6.4.

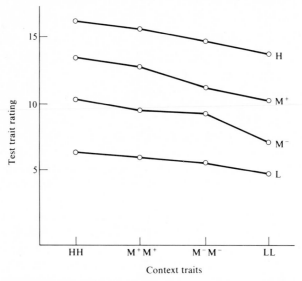

Fig. 6.4 Evaluations of adjectives in different contexts. (Adapted from Anderson, 1966.)

Although these context effects appear to support the hypothesis regarding change in meaning, Anderson (1966) challenged that interpretation. He argued in effect that an attitude toward a stimulus person who is described by several adjectives is based on the evaluation of each adjective in isolation. Once the attitude has been formed, however, the evaluation of a given adjective in the list may be influenced by the overall impression. Thus, "if this view is correct, the positive context effect would be a generalized halo effect rather than change of meaning" (Anderson, 1971b, p. 76). In keeping with his general integration theory, Anderson suggested that the evaluation of an adjective in context is a weighted average of its evaluation in isolation and of the overall attitude toward the stimulus person. Although several studies have been conducted to test some of these notions (e.g., Anderson, 1966; 1971b; M. F. Kaplan, 1971), the weighted averaging model has not been directly tested with respect to context effects, and the research generated to date by Anderson's interpretation cannot be taken as evidence for or against a change-in-meaning hypothesis.

Chalmers (1969) has proposed a change-in-meaning explanation of order effects which relies on changes in weights rather than changes in scale values. According to Chalmers, the weight of a given adjective in a trait set is determined by the affective value of the preceding adjectives. Thus the weight of a given adjective will be greater when it is preceded by similar adjectives than when it is preceded by different adjectives.[24] Therefore a shift from positive to negative adjectives, or vice versa, will lead to a reduction in weights and will thus result in a primacy effect. Chalmers showed that this hypothesis could account for data which had previously been interpreted as supporting an attention-decrement explanation of primary effects.

Attention decrement. Explanations of the primacy effect centering on change in weights have usually proposed that early adjectives are given more weight than later ones. One account of this process is based on the notion of an *attention decrement* (e.g., Anderson and Hubert, 1963; Anderson, 1965b; Stewart, 1965; Anderson and Norman, 1964; Hendrick and Costantini, 1970). According to this notion, subjects pay less attention to later adjectives; that is, they place lower weights on each successive adjective. Specifically, the hypothesis is that weights are a linear decreasing function of an adjective's serial position in a stimulus list.

To test this hypothesis, Anderson (1965b) systematically varied the serial order position of three highly unfavorable adjectives relative to a set of highly favorable adjectives. Similarly, a set of three highly favorable adjectives were interpolated within a set of highly unfavorable adjectives. The design for one experimental condition is illustrated in Table 6.5. The adjectives were read in the order illustrated, and subjects evaluated each stimulus person on an eight-point scale. As Table 6.5 shows, a primacy effect was obtained: The attitude formed was increasingly more positive as the unfavorable adjectives moved into later positions. Results were parallel for the interpolation of favorable adjectives among unfavorable ones. That is, the impression became less favorable as the serial position of the favorable adjectives decreased. Anderson argued that these results are consistent with the attention-decrement hypothesis if one assumes that weights decrease with serial order positions.[25]

---

24. This hypothesis, as well as Anderson's (1971b) weighted average explanation of context effects mentioned above, are conceptually related to the congruity-principle interpretation of context effects discussed above.

25. Anderson also argued that these results are consistent with his weighted averaging model. However, recall that Chalmers (1969) similarly argued that these results are consistent with his "change in meaning" model, which assumes that the weights are a function of the evaluation of previous adjectives, rather than a decreasing function of serial position.

Table 6.5 Adjective
Arrangements and Obtained
Attitudes (Adapted from
Anderson, 1965b)

Arrangement of adjectives	Obtained attitudes
LLLHHHHHH	5.10
HLLLHHHHH	5.20
HHLLLHHHH	5.25
HHHLLLHHH	5.40
HHHHLLLHH	5.50
HHHHHLLLH	5.55
HHHHHHLLL	5.60

However, Anderson did not provide a direct test of the attention-decrement hypothesis. For a direct test, it would be necessary to obtain estimates of each adjective's weight and to show that weights decrease with serial position. Most other studies also provide only an indirect test of the attention-decrement hypothesis by creating conditions which should induce subjects to pay attention to all adjectives in the list. This tactic is expected to eliminate attention decrement and thus reduce or eliminate the primacy effect. For example, subjects have been instructed that they would have to recall the adjectives presented (Anderson and Hubert, 1963), they have been asked to evaluate the stimulus person after each successive adjective (Stewart, 1965; and they have been asked to pronounce each adjective as it is presented (Anderson, 1968a; Hendrick and Costantini, 1970).

All these studies appear to support the attention-decrement hypothesis in that the usual primacy effect disappears when subjects are induced to pay attention to each adjective. In fact, some of the studies (e.g., Anderson and Hubert, 1963) reported a *recency* effect; i.e., later adjectives had a greater impact on the final evaluation than earlier adjectives. Note that the attention-decrement hypothesis cannot explain the emergence of these recency effects. If subjects pay equal attention to all adjectives, no order effect should be obtained. To account for a recency effect, one would have to assume that attention *increases* with serial position, although the psychological basis for such an assumption is not readily apparent.

Strong evidence against the attention-decrement hypothesis was reported by Anderson and Hubert (1963). In addition to obtaining evaluations of the stimulus person, these investigators asked subjects to recall the adjectives used to describe that person. Some subjects were told in advance that they would have to recall the adjectives, but others were not so informed. Attention decrement was expected for subjects who were not told that they would be asked to recall the adjectives. Those subjects should therefore have paid less attention to later adjectives and should have been less likely to recall them. Contrary to this hypothesis, recall increased (rather than decreased) with serial position.

Discounting. Another possible explanation is the previously discussed notion that inconsistent information will be *discounted* (i.e., given lower weight). Under the assumption that negative adjectives appearing late in the list are inconsistent with positive adjectives appearing early in the list, or vice versa, a primacy effect is expected if the later adjectives are discounted (e.g., Anderson and Jacobson, 1965; Anderson, 1968a).

On purely logical grounds, inconsistency resolution could be achieved equally well by discounting either the early or the late adjectives. It has been argued, however, that it is easier to discount the later information than to change the impression created by the initial information (Hendrick and Costantini, 1970). If this assumption holds, discounting would lead to a primacy effect.

Studies that have been viewed as supporting the attention-decrement hypothesis can also be viewed as supporting the discounting hypothesis if it is assumed that discounting of inconsistent information is less likely when subjects are induced to pay attention to all adjectives in a stimulus list (Anderson and Jacobson, 1965).

Attempts to provide tests between the competing hypotheses have yielded inconclusive results. For example, Anderson (1968a) constructed lists including H and M^+ adjectives or L and M^- adjectives. He argued that attention decrement could occur with these lists, but little discounting would be expected since the adjectives in a given list were not affectively inconsistent. Anderson thus proposed that a primacy effect should be observed if the attention-decrement hypothesis holds whereas no primacy effect would be expected under the discounting hypothesis. The data showed no effect of order of presentation for favorable adjectives and a recency effect for unfavorable adjectives. These findings were taken as support of the discounting principle.

Hendrick and Costantini (1970) noted, however, that Anderson's subjects had been asked to pronounce each adjective as it was presented, a procedure that tends to eliminate the primacy effect (see our earlier discussion), and they argued that Anderson's results were therefore consistent with both the attention-decrement and the discounting hypothesis. In their test of the discounting principle, Hendrick and Costantini used different lists of six (three H and three L) adjectives varying in consistency. (The lists varied in terms of perceived likelihood that a person possessing the H traits could also possess the L traits.) Subjects simply listened to the list of adjectives and then evaluated the stimulus person on an eight-point scale. Under the discounting hypothesis the prediction would be that the greater the inconsistency between H and L adjectives in a given list, the more discounting should occur and hence the stronger the primacy effect should be. Contrary to the discounting hypothesis, all adjective lists produced primacy effects, and the effect was no greater for highly inconsistent than for highly consistent lists. Thus they argued that their results supported an attention-decrement explanation.

To summarize briefly, research on order effects indicates that when a stimulus person is described in terms of a set of adjectives and subjects evaluate the person after all adjectives have been presented, a primacy effect is usually obtained. Various explanations have been offered to account for this effect, including change in meaning, attention decrement, and discounting. Studies designed to test the explanations have found that when subjects are induced to pay attention to all adjectives in the list, the primacy effect tends to disappear and is sometimes replaced by a recency effect. This finding, however, does not appear to provide clear evidence in favor of one explanation as opposed to another.[26]

Expectancy-Value Analysis of Order Effects

From our point of view, the finding that order of presentation influences attitude implies that when a given list of adjectives is presented in different orders, different belief systems are formed. In other words, order of presentation may result in the formation of different beliefs, may influence belief strength, or may affect evaluations of the adjectives. Which of these processes is responsible for a given order effect can be determined only when measures of beliefs and attribute evaluations are available. One possible interpretation of order effects from the point of view of an expectancy-value formulation is related to the recall of information presented. In most research in impression formation, subjects have no prior beliefs about the hypothetical stimulus person, and it seems reasonable to assume that the beliefs they come to hold are primarily determined by the information they can recall about the person. This does not mean that they will believe everything they recall or that the beliefs they do form will be held with equal strength. Moreover, subjects may form additional inferential beliefs about the stimulus person on the basis of these initial beliefs.

In our discussion of serial order learning in Chapter 5 we noted that items appearing at different positions in a list are not equally likely to be recalled. Now assume that for some reason subjects are better able to recall adjectives appearing early in the list. If the informational and inferential beliefs they actually form are based on the adjectives they can recall, a primacy effect will obtain. A similar argument can be made for a recency effect. When early and late adjectives are recalled equally well, neither primacy nor recency are expected. Research on serial order learning has shown that words at the beginning and end of a list tend to be better recalled than words in the middle. Further, there is usually a slight tendency for words at the beginning to be recalled better than words at the end, suggesting

---

26. Results supporting the attention-decrement or discounting principles have often been taken to rule out the change-in-meaning explanation. This conclusion does not necessarily follow, since increased attention to later information may influence the degree to which a change in meaning takes place. When subjects are induced to pay attention to all information, the items received first may no longer direct the overall impression; in fact, it is possible that an item appearing toward the end of the list will now become central and thus produce a recency effect.

that a primacy effect may often be obtained. However, it is also found that many other factors may influence serial order learning, such as transition from positive to negative adjectives or vice versa, the uniqueness or novelty of a word, its familiarity, etc. Thus no general predictions concerning recency or primacy effects can be made.

These considerations, based on findings in the area of serial order learning, should not be accepted uncritically, because research in this area has been concerned primarily with *accuracy* of recall; reports of information not contained in the list are usually treated as errors and are excluded from the analysis. (For an example in impression formation research, see Anderson and Hubert, 1963). Within our conceptual framework, these "errors" may constitute beliefs about the stimulus person that influence the subject's attitude.[27]

That order of presentation can influence inferential belief formation is shown by Asch's (1946) findings concerning order effects, which were reported in Chapter 5. Recall that Asch presented a list of adjectives in ascending or descending order of favorability and asked his subjects to indicate their beliefs about the stimulus person on 18 bipolar adjective scales. The inferential beliefs formed on the basis of the two orders of presentation differed greatly, and the expectancy-value formulation suggests that attitudes should differ accordingly. Specifically, presenting the list in a descending order of favorability led to the formation of more positive inferential beliefs than did presenting it in ascending order. Thus the former presentation should produce a more favorable attitude toward the stimulus person than the latter; i.e., a primacy effect is expected. This expectation was confirmed in a study by Anderson and Barrios (1961), in which Asch's original list was employed.

More direct support for these notions was obtained in a study by Jaccard and Fishbein (1975), who used six positive and six negative adjectives to construct the four lists shown in Table 6.6. Each list was read to a different group of subjects, who indicated their attitudes toward the stimulus person on a seven-point scale ranging from *like* to *dislike*. By comparing the effects of List 1 versus List 2 and List 3 versus List 4, one can see that this measure of attitude revealed a strong primacy effect.

To account for order effects in the framework of the expectancy-value formulation, Jaccard and Fishbein obtained serval additional measures. Each subject was asked to recall the adjectives used to describe the stimulus person, as well as to list any other adjectives (i.e., infer traits) that "you think might characterize the person described." The subject then indicated how certain he was that each adjective listed was in fact an attribute of the stimulus person (on a four-point *not at all certain–extremely certain* scale), and evaluated each adjective on a seven-

---

27. Support for this argument was provided by Fishbein and Hunter (1964), who showed that subjects "recalled" many adjectives that were not included in the stimulus list and that it was possible to predict attitudes toward the stimulus person by considering all adjectives reported. Unfortunately, no direct comparisons were made between predictions based on total and correct adjectives recalled.

Table 6.6 Descriptive Adjectives and Order of
Presentation (from Jaccard and Fishbein, 1975)

List 1	List 2	List 3	List 4
Loving	Critical	Ugly	Quiet
Sincere	Stout	Rude	Rich
Ambitious	Nervous	Boring	Musical
Musical	Boring	Nervous	Ambitious
Rich	Rude	Stout	Sincere
Quiet	Ugly	Critical	Loving
Ugly	Quiet	Loving	Critical
Rude	Rich	Sincere	Stout
Boring	Musical	Ambitious	Nervous
Nervous	Ambitious	Musical	Boring
Stout	Sincere	Rich	Rude
Critical	Loving	Quiet	Ugly
A 4.55	3.45	3.43	3.90
$\Sigma b_i e_i$ 14.72	6.16	−1.53	8.70

point *good–bad* scale. Finally, embedded within a longer list of traits, the 12 adjectives originally used to describe the stimulus person were each rated on the certainty and evaluative scales.

The measures of certainty (b) and evaluation (e) were used to compute $b \times e$ products, and three different estimates of attitude (that is, three $\Sigma b_i e_i$ scores) were derived for each subject: (1) based only on traits correctly recalled; (2) based on all traits recalled plus traits inferred (i.e., on all traits listed); (3) based on the 12 traits used to describe the stimulus person (whether recalled or not).

From our point of view, the second index, that based on *all* of the subject's salient beliefs about the stimulus person (whether provided by the experimenter or not), should serve as the best estimate of attitude. As Table 6.6 indicates, this estimate showed a primacy effect, just as did the direct measure of attitude. Further, consistent with expectations, this estimate had a significantly higher correlation with the direct measure of attitude ($r = .67$) than did either the first estimate based on recall ($r = .47$) or the third estimate based on adjectives provided ($r = .48$).

Since Jaccard and Fishbein obtained independent measures of belief strength, attribute evaluations, and recall with respect to each of the 12 adjectives presented, they could test the different explanations of the primacy effect discussed above. Specifically, the attention-decrement hypothesis suggests that recall should decline gradually with the adjective's serial position in the list. A discounting effect would be observed if adjectives in the second half of the list (which were inconsistent with those in the first half) were believed less than adjectives in the first half. Finally, the directed impression-hypothesis predicts that positive adjectives appearing first in the list should be evaluated more favorably than the same positive adjectives presented after a set of negative adjectives. The reverse effect should hold for negative adjectives appearing before and after a set of positive adjectives.

The results gave partial support to the discounting hypothesis, but there was no evidence for attention decrement or a directed impression. Although adjectives presented in the first quarter of a list were recalled better than later adjectives, there was no gradual decline. In fact, in some conditions the recall again increased toward the end of the list, as might be expected on the basis of the serial order effect in learning. With respect to discounting, there was an overall tendency to accept adjectives in the first half of the list more than those that followed. The tendency was not consistent across lists, however, and for at least two lists there was little evidence of discounting.

Conclusions Concerning the Informational Basis of Attitude

We have discussed theories and research based on the notion that attitudes are determined by information about the attitude object. Evidence was reviewed in support of an expectancy-value model according to which a person's attitude toward an object is a function of his beliefs about the object's attributes and his evaluation of those attributes. We noted that the expectancy-value formulation is not a linear model of information integration, despite its apparent similarity to such a model in terms of its algebraic expression. Although not necessarily a linear model at the conceptual level, Anderson's weighted averaging model assumes linearity in most of its research applications. Anderson's integration theory and, in particular, his linear weighted averaging model have stimulated many interesting lines of research, and attempts have been made to explain various research findings in terms of variations in weights and scale values (see Anderson, 1971a).

Since our conceptual framework assumes that the expectancy-value model is descriptive of attitude formation, it is instructive to reexamine research based on the linear model from the perspective of our conceptual framework. One major difference between these two approaches concerns the information that is assumed to determine attitudes. In research in impression formation the general assumption is that subjects form their attitudes toward a stimulus person on the basis of the adjectives attributed to that person. According to the linear model, each item of information is given some weight (which may be zero), and attitude toward the stimulus person is a function of the weighted scale values of these items of information and the initial impression (i.e., the initial attitude, which is often assumed to be neutral). In contrast, from our point of view, attitudes are determined by the salient beliefs that a subject comes to hold about the stimulus person as a result of the information presented to him. Clearly, he may not believe all the information he is given, and at the same time he may form additional inferential beliefs that can also influence his attitude. Thus the salient beliefs that a subject actually comes to hold about the stimulus person may not directly correspond to the information provided.

This distinction between information provided and formation of salient beliefs may help explain some of the inconsistent findings in research on impression formation. For example, we have noted that adding a new item of positive information about a person can produce either an increment, a decrement, or no change in the attitude toward that person. These apparently conflicting findings can be understood when one realizes that a new item of information may have several effects. (1) It may lead to the formation of an informational belief (i.e., it may be accepted to varying degrees). The strength of the informational belief may depend in part on the subject's prior beliefs about the stimulus person. (2) It may lead to the formation of inferential beliefs. (3) It may influence some of the prior beliefs. (4) It may affect evaluations of attributes associated with any of these beliefs. The standard research paradigm used to test between adding and averaging models has not been concerned with these possible effects. We have therefore argued that this paradigm is inappropriate and can yield only inconsistent and inconclusive results.

Similar considerations apply to an analysis of order effects. We have seen that different orders of presentation may influence the beliefs that are formed and hence may produce primacy or recency effects. Experimental variations are expected to influence attitudes to the extent that they have an effect on these beliefs or on the evaluations of the associated attributes. For example, manipulations designed to induce subjects to pay equal attention to all adjectives presented are likely to influence recall and hence to have an effect on the beliefs formed by the subjects. Thus, much of the research on order effects can be understood in terms of an expectancy-value formulation. Note, however, that many of the considerations above are ad hoc explanations of phenomena investigated in research on impression formation. By the same token, Anderson's (1971a) attempt to account for findings in this area in terms of his weighted averaging model and Chalmers's (1969) attempt to acount for the data in terms of his "change in meaning" model are also ad hoc explanations that have to be substantiated in future research. We have repeatedly noted that conclusive evidence for any model can be provided only when estimates of its parameters are available. Despite the elegance of Anderson's analysis of variance approach, and despite the fact that his integration theory has generated a considerable number of interesting studies, the absence in most studies of direct estimates of the weight and scale value parameters makes it impossible to reach unequivocal conclusions.[28]

In contrast, our conceptual framework provides clear definitions of beliefs and evaluations, and it suggests how these variables can be measured. This feature makes it relatively easy to test the expectancy-value model in various con-

---

28. Further, even when estimates of weights have been obtained, they have not usually been cross-validated. Since these weights are least-squares estimates, cross-validation is required to demonstrate their reliability.

texts by computing estimated attitudes that can be compared with obtained results. Evidence to date tends to support the expectancy-value formulation as a model of the attitude-formation process.

INTERPERSONAL ATTRACTION

Up to this point we have made no distinction between the formation of attitudes toward objects, persons, issues, actions, or events. We have suggested that attitudes toward any stimulus are based on information about that stimulus, and that the expectancy-value model describes the information integration process whereby attitudes are formed. Most research on attitude formation, however, has dealt with attitudes toward other persons, and several noninformational bases of interpersonal attraction have been suggested: similarity of beliefs, interests, or personality traits; complementarity of need systems; reciprocity of liking; high ability, competence, etc. In this section we will review some of the research on these noninformational bases of attitude formation. We shall see, however, that all research findings in this area are compatible with an information-processing approach.

Similarity and Attraction

Perhaps the most systematic program of research on interpersonal attraction is the work of Byrne and his associates on the relationship between similarity and attraction (for reviews of this literature see Byrne, 1969, 1971). The original hypothesis underlying this research can be summarized as follows: The more similar another person's opinions, interests, or personality characteristics to those of a perceiver, the more will the perceiver come to be attracted to the person. This hypothesis has been investigated in numerous studies using a standard research paradigm involving several steps. The subject is first asked to respond to a standard questionnaire, which may be an opinion survey, a personality inventory, a self-rating scale, an interest inventory, etc. At a later point in time the subject is shown the same questionnaire ostensibly completed by another person, who is a stranger to the subject. The stranger's responses are varied systematically in terms of the degree to which they are similar to the subject's own responses. After receiving this information, the subject rates the stranger's attractiveness on a standard instrument, the Interpersonal Judgment Scale (IJS).

In his initial experiment using this paradigm, Byrne (1961) gave college students a 26-item opinion survey early in the semester. All items were bipolar and presented in a six-alternative multiple-choice format. The following two items may serve as examples.

1. One true religion (check one)

_____ I strongly believe that my church represents the one true religion.

_____ I believe that my church represents the one true religion.

_____ I feel that probably my church represents the one true religion.

_____I feel that probably no church represents the one true religion.

_____I believe that no church represents the one true religion.

_____I strongly believe that no church represents the one true religion.

2. Situation comedies (check one)

_____I dislike situation comedies very much.

_____I dislike situation comedies.

_____I dislike situation comedies to a slight degree.

_____I enjoy situation comedies to a slight degree.

_____I enjoy situation comedies.

_____I enjoy situation comedies very much.

In a later session, each subject was given a questionnaire and was told that it had been filled out by another student of the same sex, who was not in their psychology class and whom the subject did not know. For half the subjects, the questionnaires were prepared in such a way that the stranger responded to all 26 of the issues exactly as the subject had done. Each of the remaining subjects received a questionnaire prepared in such a manner that it was a mirror image of his own responses. "For example, if the subject was strongly against integration and mildly in favor of smoking, the stranger was strongly in favor of integration and mildly against smoking." (Byrne, 1971, p. 51)

After reading the questionnaire, subjects were asked to respond to the Interpersonal Judgment Scale. The IJS consists of six seven-point bipolar items in multiple-choice format. The first four items deal with the stranger's intelligence, knowledge of current events, morality, and adjustment. These items have usually been treated as filler items, and responses to the remaining two questions have served as the dependent measure of interpersonal attraction.[29] Specifically, the sum over the following two items has been used as an index of attraction; this index can vary from 2 to 14.

1. Personal feelings (check one)

_____I feel that I would probably like this person very much.

_____I feel that I would probably like this person.

_____I feel that I would probably like this person to a slight degree.

_____I feel that I would probably neither particularly like nor particularly dislike this person.

_____I feel that I would probably dislike this person to a slight degree.

_____I feel that I would probably dislike this person.

_____I feel that I would probably dislike this person very much.

---

29. Responses to the four filler items were viewed as inferential beliefs in Chapter 5, where results concerning these items were discussed.

2. Working together in an experiment (check one)

_____I believe that I would very much dislike working with this person in an experiment.

_____I believe that I would dislike working with this person in an experiment.

_____I believe that I would dislike working with this person in an experiment to a slight degree.

_____I believe that I would neither particularly dislike nor particularly enjoy working with this person in an experiment.

_____I believe that I would enjoy working with this person in an experiment to a slight degree.

_____I believe that I would enjoy working with this person in an experiment.

_____I believe that I would very much enjoy working with this person in an experiment.

Consistent with expectations, the mean attraction toward the similar stranger (13.00) was significantly greater than the mean attraction toward the dissimilar stranger (4.41). This positive relation between similarity and attraction has been repeatedly replicated in a large number of subsequent investigations.

Although Byrne and Nelson (1965a) reported a high correlation ($r = .85$) between the two items that constitute the IJS attraction measure, our conceptual framework suggests that these items measure two different attitudes: The first question serves as a general measure of attitude toward the stranger and the second as a measure of attitude toward working with him in an experiment. Consistent with this argument, Mascaro and Lopez (1970) reported somewhat different results for these two items. Similarly, Ajzen (1974) found that although the two items correlated significantly ($r = .69$), results obtained with one item were not identical to results obtained with the other. Further, Ajzen (1974) as well as others (e.g., Gormly, Gormly, and Johnson, 1971) have reported different results for the IJS and a semantic differential measure of attraction. Despite these problems, it appears reasonable in many situations to regard Byrne's interpersonal-attraction measure as an index of attitude toward the stimulus person.

Degree of similarity. In Byrne's (1961) initial experiments, descriptions of the stranger were either in complete agreement or complete disagreement with the subject's opinions. In subsequent studies the *degree* of similarity was also manipulated. For example, Byrne (1962) constructed eight descriptions of a stranger using seven opinion items. The extent to which the stranger agreed with the subject was systematically manipulated (see Table 6.7, which also presents the obtained results). Consistent with expectations, attraction increased with degree of similarity. However, Byrne and Nelson (1965a) noted that these results could be due either to the *number* of similar items, the *number* of dissimilar items, or the

Table 6.7 Degree of Similarity
and Attraction (Adapted
from Byrne, 1962)

Experimental condition	Attraction
7 Similar, 0 dissimilar	12.15
6 Similar, 1 dissimilar	11.15
5 Similar, 2 dissimilar	11.43
4 Similar, 3 dissimilar	9.07
3 Similar, 4 dissimilar	8.69
2 Similar, 5 dissimilar	8.47
1 Similar, 6 dissimilar	7.71
0 Similar, 7 dissimilar	7.00

proportion of similar to dissimilar items since these two variables (i.e., number and proportion) are confounded.

In order to clarify this issue, Byrne and Nelson conducted an experiment in which they attempted to separate number and proportion of similar items. The design for this experiment is shown in Table 6.8. If the similarity-attraction relation were attributable to the number of similar or dissimilar opinions, a significant difference between column means should be obtained. Since the only significant effect in this study was the difference between row means (see Table 6.9), Byrne and Nelson concluded that attraction is a function of the *proportion* of similar items, regardless of the total number of items involved.[30]

In a later study, Rosenblood (cited in Byrne, 1971) presented subjects with sets of one, two, three, four, and six opinion items describing different strangers.

Table 6.8 Byrne and Nelson's Experimental
Design (Adapted from Byrne and Nelson,
1965a)

Proportion of similar opinions	Number of similar opinions		
	4	8	16
1.00	4–0*	8–0	16–0
.67	4–2	8–4	16–8
.50	4–4	8–8	16–16
.33	4–8	8–16	16–32

* The first value refers to the number of similar opinions, the second to the number of dissimilar opinions.

30. Byrne (1971) noted that these findings appeared inconsistent with Anderson's (1965a) notion of a set-size effect. If the set-size effect had been operative, a significant interaction between number and proportion of similar opinions should have been obtained.

Table 6.9 Attraction Toward Strangers with Varying
Numbers and Varying Proportions of Similar Opinions
(Adapted from Byrne and Nelson, 1965a)

Proportion of similar opinions	Number of similar opinions			
	4	8	16	Total
1.00	11.14	12.79	10.93	11.62
.67	10.79	9.36	9.50	9.88
.50	9.36	9.57	7.93	8.75
.33	8.14	6.64	6.57	7.12
Total	9.86	9.59	8.73	

Each set was either completely similar to or completely dissimilar from the subject. Thus proportion was held constant while the number of similar opinions varied. In contrast to the Byrne and Nelson study, the Rosenblood study found a relation between attraction and number of similar opinions.[31]

The findings concerning degree of similarity thus suggest that both proportion and number of similar items influence attraction. Although the proportion of similar items appears to be of primary importance, the number of similar items also plays a significant role, at least up to six or eight items.

Order effects. As in the area of impression formation, the possibility has been raised that different orders of sequential presentation of similar and dissimilar opinions may influence interpersonal attraction in the Byrne paradigm. To study this problem, Byrne and London (1966) prepared tape recordings in which a stranger verbalized his response to each of 56 opinion items. Four experimental conditions were created.

1. *Similar condition:* Stranger agrees with subject on all 56 opinion items.

2. *Similar-dissimilar condition:* Stranger agrees with subject on 28 opinion items in the following descending order: 8/8, 7/8, 6/8, 4/8, 2/8, 1/8, 0/8. Thus the stranger's responses progressed from complete agreement (8/8) to complete disagreement (0/8).

3. *Dissimilar-similar condition:* Stranger agrees with subject on 28 opinion items in an ascending order, the reverse of Condition 2. Here the stranger's responses progress from complete disagreement to complete agreement.

4. *Dissimilar condition:* Stranger disagrees with subject on all 56 items.

Mean attraction scores obtained in each condition can be seen in Table 6.10. Attraction decreased from the similar to the dissimilar condition. The key com-

---

31. Although Byrne (1971) argued that this difference in results was due to Rosenblood's use of a within-subjects design, Rosenblood's data also permit a between-subjects analysis which again shows the relation between attraction and number of similar opinions.

parison, however, is between Conditions 2 and 3. The results indicate a primacy effect since the similar-dissimilar order produced greater attraction than the reverse order, but the difference was not significant.

Table 6.10 Order Effects on Attraction (Adapted from Byrne and London, 1966)

Condition	Attraction
Similar	11.90
Similar-dissimilar	8.20
Dissimilar-similar	7.30
Dissimilar	5.50

The tendency toward a primacy effect when subjects are asked to evaluate the stimulus person only after all information has been presented is consistent with research on impression formation. In a later study, Byrne, Lamberth, Palmer, and London (1969) found that a recency effect is obtained when subjects are asked to evaluate the stranger either after each opinion item is presented or after every fourth opinion item. The findings of Byrne and his associates on order effects, therefore, are quite consistent with the work on impression formation discussed above.

Importance of opinion items. Byrne and Nelson (1964) proposed that topic importance was likely to be a major determinant of an item's effect on attraction. It stands to reason that a stranger's agreement or disagreement with respect to an important issue should have a greater impact on attitudes toward him than would his response on an issue of little importance. To test this hypothesis, four sets of 14 opinion items each were constructed on the basis of importance ratings supplied by an independent sample of subjects. The first list comprised the 14 items that had been rated as most important, the second list the 14 next most important items, etc. Each subject responded to one of these lists and was later given the responses of a stranger on the same list; the stranger either agreed or disagreed completely with the subject. Contrary to predictions, topic importance had no effect on attraction. Although the similar stranger was always evaluated more favorably than the dissimilar stranger, the difference was not greater for similarity of important opinions than it was for similarity of unimportant opinions.

In a second study, Byrne and Nelson (1965b) had each subject rate four strangers, each of whom was described by one of the four lists used in the previous study. The results again showed no significant effect of importance. A third study was then designed (Byrne, London, and Griffitt, 1968) in which opinions varying in importance were attributed to the same stranger, rather than to different strangers. Four experimental conditions were employed. In the first two conditions, the stranger agreed with the subject on 32 out of 56 opinion items (75 percent); in the remaining two conditions he agreed with 14 out of 56 items (25 percent). Within the 75 percent similarity groups, the stranger agreed on either the 32 most important or the 32 least important opinions. Similarly, within the 25 percent similarity groups, the stranger agreed on either the 14 most or the 14 least important opinions. Thus, in this "intra-stranger" design, the stranger agrees with the subject on the important items and disagrees with him on the unimportant ones or vice versa. The results of this study showed a significant effect of importance: In addition to the usual effect of degree of similarity, the stranger's agreement on important items (and disagreement on unimportant ones) led to greater attraction than did his agreement on unimportant opinions (and disagreement on important ones).

Similar findings were reported by Clore & Baldridge (1968), who varied interest value of opinion items instead of importance. Using a similar intra-stranger design, they found that subjects were more attracted to strangers who agreed with them on interesting issues and disagreed on uninteresting ones than to strangers who exhibited the reverse pattern. In a later study, Clore and Baldridge (1970) found the same pattern of results when opinion statements attributed to a stranger were treated as unimportant items of information and personal evaluations of the subjects, ostensibly made by the stranger, were treated as important items.

Byrne's attraction model. Based on the research above (and many other studies), Byrne and his associates (Byrne and Nelson, 1965a; Byrne and Rhamey, 1965; Byrne, 1971) have proposed a model of the similarity-attraction relationship. In its simplest form, the model states that attraction is a linear function of the proportion of similar opinion items,

$$A = cX + b, \tag{6.6}$$

where A is attraction, X is the proportion of similar opinions, and c and b are constants. If S and D stand for number of similar and dissimilar opinions, respectively, X can be written as $S/(S + D)$, and

$$A = c \left[\frac{S}{S + D} \right] + b. \tag{6.7}$$

Since agreement or disagreement on some opinion items may carry more weight in the determination of interpersonal attraction than agreement or disagreement on others, this model could be extended by including weighting parameters. The weighted formulation may then be written as follows:

$$A = c \left[\frac{\sum\limits_{i=1}^{S} W_i}{\sum\limits_{i=1}^{S} W_i + \sum\limits_{j=1}^{D} W_j} \right] + b. \tag{6.8}$$

In Eq. 6.8, W_i is the weight of the similar opinion i, and W_j is the weight of the dissimilar opinion j. The other terms are defined as in Eq. 6.7.

Although Eq. 6.8 implies that each opinion expressed by the stranger can be given differential weight, the model has not been applied in this fashion. Instead, Byrne and Rhamey (1965) proposed that one weight be given to similar opinions and another to dissimilar ones. With the weight for similar opinions denoted by W_S and that for dissimilar opinions by W_D, Eq. 6.8 then takes on the following form.[32]

$$A = c \left[\frac{W_s S}{W_s S + W_D D} \right] + b. \qquad (6.9)$$

Note that when similar and dissimilar opinions are given equal weights (that is, $W_S = W_D$), the weights cancel and Eq. 6.9 reduces to Eq. 6.7. In that case, the weights placed on similar and dissimilar opinions will have no effect on attraction.

Clore and Baldridge (1968, 1970) noted that Eq. 6.9 can explain the findings concerning effects of importance on attraction. Although important items may be given more weight than unimportant items, importance will influence attraction only when similar and dissimilar opinions are not equally important, i.e., when they are not given equal weights. In the first two studies dealing with this issue (Byrne and Nelson, 1964, 1965b), a given stranger was described in terms of opinion items that had been rated as equally important. By way of contrast, in the three studies that obtained a significant effect of importance (Byrne, London, and Griffitt, 1968; Clore and Baldridge, 1968, 1970), all similar opin-

---

32. In many studies, similar items vary in degree of similarity, and dissimilar items vary in degree of dissimilarity. For example, on similar opinions the stranger's positions could be removed 0, 1, or 2 scale points from the subject's own positions whereas on dissimilar items the distance could be 3, 4, or 5 scale points. To take degree of similarity or dissimilarity into account, Eqs. 6.7, 6.8, and 6.9 could be written as follows:

$$6.7 \colon A = c \left[\sum_{i=1}^{n} S_i \Big/ \left(\sum_{i=1}^{n} S_i + \sum_{j=1}^{m} D_j \right) \right] + b.$$

$$6.8 \colon A = c \left[\sum_{i=1}^{n} W_i S_i \Big/ \left(\sum_{i=1}^{n} W_i S_i + \sum_{j=1}^{m} W_j D_j \right) \right] + b.$$

$$6.9 \colon A = c \left[W_s \sum_{i=1}^{n} S_i \Big/ \left(W_s \sum_{i=1}^{n} S_i + W_D \sum_{j=1}^{m} D_j \right) \right] + b.$$

In these equations, S and D stand for the degree of an opinion's similarity or dissimilarity, respectively (in the example above, S and D might be scored from 1 to 3), and W is the weight of a similar or dissimilar opinion.

ions were important and dissimilar ones unimportant, or vice versa. This intra-stranger design allows weights of similar and dissimilar opinions to vary, and hence importance becomes a relevant variable.

In sum, Byrne's research program has conclusively demonstrated a positive relation between similarity and attraction. Although our discussion has been primarily concerned with the degree of similarity between *opinions* held by two persons, Byrne, Clore, and Worchel (1966) proposed that any aspect of similarity-dissimilarity affects attraction in the same manner. In search of support for this contention, Byrne and his associates have asked subjects to complete a large variety of questionnaires and have provided feedback concerning a hypothetical stranger's responses to the same questionnaires. As expected, manipulations of similarity on the basis of these questionnaires have consistently shown a positive relation between similarity and attraction. Among other things, attraction was found to be influenced by similarity with respect to personality inventories, such as a repression-sensitization scale, masculinity-femininity scale, dominance-submissiveness scale, and an introversion-extroversion scale; ability and intelligence tests; information about spending habits; and various self-descriptions in terms of personality characteristics or behavioral patterns. (For a review of this literature, see Byrne, 1971.) Thus there seems to be little question about the empirical relationship between similarity and attraction. The following sections will be concerned with the basis for this relationship.

Expectancy-Value Analysis of the Similarity-Attraction Relation

The reader has probably noted some obvious similarities between Byrne's research paradigm and studies of impression formation. In both areas of research, subjects receive information about a stimulus person, and their attitudes toward that person are measured. This parallel is most apparent when responses to a self-descriptive personality inventory are used in the Byrne paradigm. As in impression formation, subjects in these studies are shown a number of adjectives describing the stimulus person. The major difference between the two approaches involves the basis for selecting the descriptive adjectives: In the Byrne paradigm, the adjectives are selected such that the stimulus person appears similar or dissimilar to the subject whereas in studies of impression formation they are usually selected on the basis of their affective values.

From our point of view, however, the basis for selecting particular items of information about another person is largely irrelevant for an understanding of attitude formation in these situations. As in research on impression formation, subjects in Byrne's paradigm are provided with information about a hypothetical stranger (in the form of his opinions, personality traits, abilities, etc.) which is likely to lead to the formation of beliefs about the stranger's attributes. According to the expectancy-value formulation, the subject's attitude toward the stranger will be a function of those beliefs and the evaluation of the attributes. Consider, for example, a subject's attitude toward a political candidate. At the beginning of this chapter we described some of the research on political attitudes conducted by Fishbein and his associates, and we noted that beliefs about a political candidate, including beliefs about his positions on various issues, strongly influenced attitudes toward the candidate. That is, the attitudes could be predicted with great accuracy by considering the subject's beliefs about the candidate's positions on various issues and the subject's evaluations of those positions (i.e., by estimating $\Sigma b_i e_i$). These estimates of attitude are obtained without reference to the degree to which the candidate's positions are similar to those of the subject. Clearly, however, a measure of similarity of political opinions could be obtained, and Byrne's research suggests that such a measure of similarity would correlate with attitude toward the candidate. Indeed, Byrne, Bond, and Diamond (1969) reported a positive relation between similarity and attraction toward a political candidate when the candidate's positions on six issues varied in their degree of similarity to the subject's positions.

Two interpretations can be offered for the observed relation between similarity and attraction. In the first, similarity as such is an important determinant of attitude. According to this position, attraction toward another person is directly determined by the degree to which he is similar to the perceiver. This point of view has been characteristic of most research on the similarity-attraction relation. Another interpretation, one that is consistent with our conceptual framework, focuses on the information about the other person that is available to the subject. According to this view, favorably evaluated items of information lead to the formation of a favorable attitude. Similarity enters the picture only indirectly, and without causal effects on attraction. To return to attitudes toward a political candidate, it stands to reason that a subject will have favorable evaluations of positions with which he agrees and will negatively evaluate positions with which he disagrees.[33]

The same argument can be made for other types of information about a person, such as his opinions concerning nonpolitical issues or his personality characteristics. With respect to the latter, Stalling (1970) asked subjects to rate 121 personality traits (e.g., aggressive, honest, introverted) as "pleasant" or "unpleasant" and as "like me" or "unlike me." Most subjects perceived traits to be both positive and similar or negative and dissimilar; the correlation between perceived similarity and evaluation was .88. It can thus be argued that similarity may not have a direct effect on attraction. Instead, it is possible that attribute similarity is related to attraction only indirectly as a result of its association with attribute evaluation. That is, similarity may be related to attribute evaluation, which influences attraction.

These arguments suggest that if it were possible to separate attribute similarity and attribute evaluation, the former would have little or no effect on attraction.

---

33. A similar interpretation of attraction in the Byrne paradigm has been offered by Kaplan and Anderson (1973) in the framework of Anderson's theory of information integration. However, see the rejoinder by Byrne *et al.* (1973).

Several attempts have been made to separate these two factors (e.g., Tesser, 1969; McLaughlin, 1970, 1971; Stalling, 1970). In a recent study, Ajzen (1974) gave subjects a 100-item personality inventory and then provided them with "feedback" in the form of their personality profiles. These profiles consisted of 12 bipolar traits presented at opposite ends of six-point scales; the degree to which a subject possessed each of the traits was indicated by check marks on the scales. Examples of the traits used are: *selfish–unselfish, imaginative–unimaginative, cooperative–uncooperative,* and *tolerant–intolerant.* All subjects were given profiles placing them on the positive side of six scales and on the negative side of the remaining six scales. In addition, subjects were shown the profile of another person who was said to have taken the same personality inventory. The stranger was described either in a favorable manner (his profile placed him on the positive side of the scale for 9 of the 12 trait pairs) or in an unfavorable manner (3 out of 12 positive traits). Descriptions of subject and stranger were similar either on 9 of the 12 traits (75 percent similarity) or on 3 of the 12 traits (25 percent similarity). Thus four conditions were created in a 2 × 2 factorial design; they are given in Table 6.11, together with mean evaluations of the stranger on the IJS.

Table 6.11 Means of IJS Attraction Measure (Adapted from Ajzen, 1974)

Attribute similarity	Attribute evaluation Positive	Negative	Total
75%	10.57	7.25	8.91
25%	8.40	6.33	7.37
Total	9.49	6.79	

Although there was a tendency to evaluate the similar stranger more favorably than the dissimilar stranger, this effect of attribute similarity was not significant. In contrast, a positive description led to significantly greater attraction toward the stranger than did a negative description. (The interaction between similarity and affective value was not significant.) Thus, consistent with an information processing approach, attitudes were determined primarily by attribute evaluation, and attribute similarity had relatively little effect.

Ajzen (1974) also asked his subjects to evaluate each of the 12 traits (selfishness, imagination, cooperativeness, tolerance, etc.) on a seven-point scale ranging from *desirable* to *undesirable.* In order to permit the computation of an estimate of attitude toward the stranger, the subject's rating of each trait was multiplied by the position attributed to the stranger on the same trait. For example, if the stranger was described as *quite selfish*—i.e., if his position on the *selfish–unselfish* scale was

selfish | ___ | X | ___ | ___ | ___ | ___ | unselfish

a score of $+2$ was assigned. This value was multiplied by the subject's evaluation of selfishness. The products for all 12 traits were summed to provide the estimate of attitude. The correlation between this estimate and the direct measure of the subject's attitude was .48 when the IJS attraction measure was used and .57 for a semantic differential measure of attitude toward the stranger. Although these correlations are statistically significant, they are of relatively low magnitude. This finding should not be too surprising since no measure of the subject's own beliefs about the stranger were available. That is, attitudes were estimated by assuming that subjects believed the information provided. An adequate application of the expectancy-value model would require that subjects indicate their subjective probabilities that the stranger had each of the traits in question. Further, subjects may form inferential beliefs about the stranger, and these beliefs would also have to be assessed.

We have repeatedly made reference to research showing that information about another person's personality traits often leads to the formation of inferential beliefs about the stranger's personality. By the same token, information about another person's opinions may also produce inferential beliefs. Knowing that a person holds certain opinions may lead to the inference that he holds other opinions as well. Further, such knowledge may also lead to inferences about the person's personality attributes. For example, if a subject is told that a stranger believes in God, he is likely to infer that the stranger is religious. Similarly, if a subject is told that a stranger is opposed to racial integration in public schools and opposed to birth control, he may infer that the stranger is prejudiced and conservative. Attitudes toward a stranger may be based in part on such inferential beliefs.

Support for this notion was provided in a second study in which Ajzen (1974) described a stranger in terms of his responses to 12 opinion items similar to those used by Byrne and his associates; these items dealt with various social and political issues. The responses attributed to the stranger were randomized across subjects; that is, each subject received a different response profile, which had been constructed by placing check marks on the response scales at random. Thus no attempt was made to manipulate the similarity between opinions of stranger and subject. After viewing the stranger's responses, subjects were asked to rate him on the IJS and on a semantic differential scale. In addition, they were given a list of 100 adjectives for which Anderson (1968b) had previously reported mean likability ratings. Subjects indicated whether each of the 100 personality traits was descriptive of the stranger ($+1$) or not descriptive (-1), or whether they were undecided (0). The ratings for each trait were multiplied by Anderson's likability ratings for the same trait; the resulting products were summed as an estimate of the subject's attitude toward the other person.[34] This

---

34. Again, this estimate does not meet all the requirements of the expectancy-value model; measures of the subject's own evaluations and the strength of his beliefs would be required.

estimate correlated significantly with the IJS measure of attraction ($r = .68$) as well as with the semantic differential measure ($r = .66$).

In sum, Ajzen's (1974) study indicated that attraction toward a stranger is determined in large part by beliefs about the stranger's attributes and by evaluations of those attributes. Descriptions of a stranger in terms of his opinions or personality characteristics provide information which can serve as the basis for the formation of those beliefs. Further the study showed that attraction was determined by the evaluation of another person's attributes rather than by their similarity to the subject's own attributes. Our discussion above suggests, however, that similarity may be related not only to evaluations of attributes contained in the description of the stranger, but also to the evaluations of attributes assigned to the stranger on the basis of inference processes. Without measures of inferential beliefs, it may be impossible to completely separate attribute similarity from attribute evaluation, and even in studies that attempt to provide an experimental separation, a relation between similarity and attraction may sometimes be found—although the relation should be weak. In support of this argument, McLaughlin (1970) found no significant relation between similarity and attraction when he statistically controlled for attribute evaluation, and Tesser (1969) found a low, though significant, relation using the same procedure.[35] In a more recent study, McLaughlin (1971) obtained a significant effect of similarity when he experimentally separated attribute similarity and evaluation. In contrast to these inconsistent findings concerning the effects of similarity, attribute evaluations were always found to have a strong effect on attraction.

Evidence that inferential beliefs are formed about the stranger's personality characteristics on the basis of information about his opinions may provide an explanation for the finding that beyond approximately six opinion items, the number of items has no effect on attraction (see p. 259). We have argued that attitude is determined by a small number of a person's salient beliefs. When a subject is given information about one or two opinions held by a stranger, he is likely to make only a few inferences about his personality characteristics and perhaps to hold these inferential beliefs with low certainty. By the time he has received information on the stranger's responses to four or five opinion items, a larger set of salient beliefs will have been formed, and these beliefs are likely to be held with greater confidence. Information about additional opinions, so long as it does not lead to inferences inconsistent with prior beliefs, will not have much effect on the belief system and hence will not be expected to influence attraction.

Similarity and Reinforcement

We have argued that the frequently observed relation between similarity and attraction is not due to the direct effects of similarity on attraction but rather to the

---

35. These investigations examined the relation between similarity and attraction when attribute evaluation was held constant by computing a partial correlation (Tesser, 1969) or by conducting an analysis of covariance (McLaughlin, 1970).

tendency for similar opinions or personality characteristics to be favorably evaluated. For different reasons, Byrne and his associates (Byrne, 1969, 1971; Byrne and Lamberth, 1971; Clore and Byrne, 1974; Byrne and Clore, 1970) have also taken the position that similarity in and by itself does not determine attraction. Consistent with other theorists (e.g., Newcomb, 1956), Byrne suggested that people are attracted to others who reward them and dislike those who punish them. Byrne and Nelson (1965a) proposed a "law of attraction" according to which "attraction toward x is a positive linear function of the proportion of positive reinforcements received from x" (p. 662). The Byrne paradigm was developed on the assumption that agreement concerning some issue is positively reinforcing and disagreement has negative reinforcement value. To explain these effects of opinion similarity, Byrne borrowed from Festinger (1950, 1954), Newcomb (1953, 1956), and other theorists and suggested that

> the expression of similar attitudes by a stranger serves as a positive reinforcement because consensual validation for an individual's attitudes and opinions and beliefs is a major source of reward for the drive to be logical, consistent, and accurate in interpreting the stimulus world. In an analogous way, the expression of dissimilar attitudes by a stranger provides consensual invalidation, is therefore frustrating, and acts as a negative reinforcement. (Byrne, 1971, p. 338)

This notion that opinion similarity is reinforcing was generalized to similarity of any kind, including personality characteristics, abilities, etc. (Byrne, Clore, and Worchel, 1966). Further, Byrne and Clore (1970) and Clore and Byrne (1974) attempted to account for the development of interpersonal attraction within a more general learning theory framework. They suggested that reinforcing events elicit positive implicit responses whereas punishing events elicit negative affect. These implicit affective reactions become conditioned to the stimuli with which they are associated. "Thus, one likes others who reward him because they are associated with one's good feelings." (Clore and Byrne, 1974) It follows that each time a stranger agrees with the subject or exhibits traits or abilities that correspond to those of the subject, a positive implicit reaction may be elicited which becomes conditioned to the stranger. The more similar the stranger, the more he will tend to be liked. However, similarity may not always be positively reinforcing. For example, being similar to someone who is described in a negative fashion may not be particularly rewarding, and similarity will not be expected to produce attraction. These considerations are consistent with the finding that attribute similarity does not have a strong effect on attraction when attribute evaluation is held constant.

Unfortunately, as with most reinforcement notions, these arguments lead to circular reasoning since it is difficult to arrive at an independent definition of reinforcement (see Levinger, 1972). Specifically, similarity is said to lead to attraction because of its reinforcement value, and we know that it has reinforcement value when it produces attraction. Reinforcement value is therefore solely defined in terms of observed attraction, and it is impossible to know in advance whether similarity should or should not lead to attraction. Despite this limitation, the reinforcement explanation places the study of attraction in a broader theoretical framework that provides specific testable implications. For example, learning theory specifies that the amount of attraction should be a function of the *number* of reinforced trials. Byrne's (1971) conclusion that attraction is only a function of proportion and not of number of similar opinions is in direct opposition to most reinforcement theories.[36]

A second major implication is that some events are more reinforcing than others and hence should produce greater attraction. We have seen above that under appropriate experimental conditions, agreement on important issues led to greater attraction than agreement on unimportant issues. Similarly, personal evaluations received from a stranger had a greater effect on attraction than did his agreement or disagreement on opinion items. Byrne and his associates have interpreted these results as supporting the notion that more important items of information have greater reinforcement value. It is equally plausible, however, that agreement on an important issue is evaluated more favorably than agreement on an unimportant issue. Similarly, evaluations of praise may be more favorable than evaluations of a person's position on an issue. This interpretation is consistent with an expectancy-value formulation.

In a similar fashion, the reinforcement position implies that a given event (e.g., agreement on an issue) may be more reinforcing for some subjects than for others. Specifically, the reinforcement value of a given event should depend in part on the motivational state of the subject. For example, food is likely to be more reinforcing to a hungry person than to a person who has just eaten. Of greater relevance to attraction, agreement on opinion items should have greatest reinforcement value for persons with a high need for consensual validation or with a high need for approval. Thus the effect of similarity on attraction should interact with personality variables of this kind: The difference in attraction toward similar and dissimilar strangers should be greater for subjects on one side of the personality dimension (e.g., high need for approval) than for subjects on the other side of the dimension (low need for approval). Byrne (1971) reviewed studies that have attempted to test this hypothesis by examining personality variables such as authoritarianism, dogmatism, repression-sensitization, self-ideal discrepancy, cognitive complexity, test anxiety, manifest anxiety, need for approval, and need for affiliation. He concluded that "not only have perfectly reasonable personality variables failed to show any relationship to attraction responses but those variables for which positive results are obtained often show no effects in subsequent experiments or only in seemingly random subsequent experiments" (Byrne, 1971,

---

36. In defense of a reinforcement interpretation, it might be argued that conditioning of affect to the stranger reaches an asymptote after five or six reinforced trials. The finding that number of similar opinions has an effect on attraction up to about six opinion items is consistent with this argument. However, it appears unlikely that an asymptote is reached after so few reinforced trials.

p. 213). The evidence concerning personality variables, therefore, seems to argue against a reinforcement interpretation of the similarity-attraction relation.

A third implication of the reinforcement position can be stated as follows: If similar opinion items, personality traits, or abilities have positive reinforcement value and elicit positive affect, it should be possible to use such information as unconditioned stimuli in classical conditioning experiments or as reinforcers in operant conditioning (see Chapter 2). Byrne and his associates have tested these implications in a number of investigations (e.g., Golightly and Byrne, 1964; Byrne, Young, and Griffitt, 1966; Sachs and Byrne, 1970). This research will be reviewed below in the context of our discussion of conditioning as a basis for attitude formation. Suffice it to note here that although there is abundant evidence that similar and dissimilar opinion items can be used successfully in learning situations, our discussion in Chapter 4 has made it clear that such learning does not occur without awareness. As we shall see below, this implies an informational rather than a reinforcement basis for attitude formation.

A final implication of the reinforcement position is that any event that has reinforcement properties should influence attraction. Thus situations have been created in which another person behaves favorably or unfavorably toward the subject, evaluates him positively or negatively, rewards or punishes him by using bonus points or shocks, etc. Consistent with a general reinforcement hypothesis, these manipulations have usually been found to influence interpersonal attraction. However, these results do not provide direct evidence that *similarity* has reinforcement value.

In conclusion, there is little support for the reinforcement interpretation of the observed similarity-attraction relation. It appears more reasonable to suggest that this relation is due to the differential evaluations of similar and dissimilar items of information rather than to the reinforcement value of such information. This implies that attitude formation in the Byrne paradigm, as in other studies of impression formation, is based on information about the other person. This information enables the subject to form beliefs about the person, and these beliefs determine the subject's attitude, as described by an expectancy-value model.

Minitheories of Attraction

Many studies on interpersonal attraction have been isolated attempts to investigate the effects of one or more variables on the formation of attitude toward another person. For the most part, variables have been selected for study on the basis of some vague intuitive notion. Thus it has been hypothesized that another person will be liked if he is competent, if he praises the subject, if he performs a favor for the subject, if he maintains eye contact with the subject, if he commits a blunder, if he asks for help, etc. (see Aronson, 1970). Aronson, Willerman, and Floyd (1966), for example, conducted an experiment on the effects on attraction of competence and a pratfall. Subjects listened to a tape recording purportedly of a student who was a candidate for a university team in an intelligence competition. The candidate responded to a series of knowledge questions. In one condition, he exhibited great competence but in another condition he failed to answer even simple questions. For half the subjects in each condition, the tape ended with the candidate sipping a cup of coffee. For the other half, he spilled the coffee and exclaimed, "Oh my goodness, I've spilled coffee all over my new suit!" According to Aronson, Willerman, and Floyd (1966, p. 227)

> A near perfect or superior individual who shows that he is capable of an occasional blunder or pratfall may come to be regarded as more human and more approachable; consequently he will be liked better *because* of this pratfall. On the other hand, if a mediocre or average person commits an identical blunder, he will not undergo an increase in attractiveness. Indeed, since it would suggest only that he is *very* mediocre, it should lower his attractiveness.

Before one considers the results of this study, it is important to examine the implications of an intuitive hypothesis of this kind. Although this particular hypothesis may be of substantive interest, its theoretical import is negligible. This can best be seen by considering the implication of a failure to find support for the hypothesis. If the blunder did not raise attraction toward the superior person, the conclusion would simply be that this variable does not influence attraction. Disconfirmation of the hypothesis would have no theoretical importance and would merely suggest that the experimenters' intuition had been mistaken. Nobody would be particularly surprised or upset by the disconfirmation.

Suppose, on the other hand, that the blunder did increase attraction toward the superior individual. The experimenters might then conclude that "humanization" is an important determinant of attraction. Additional studies could be conducted to test this "minitheory" of attraction by looking for other variables that might serve to humanize a person. Thus the concept of humanization becomes a major focus of research. Note, however, that these research efforts are unlikely to appreciably advance our understanding of processes underlying interpersonal attraction or attitude formation. At best we might learn that humanization constitutes one of the myriad of factors that may be related to attraction, and we would still be left with a notion of little theoretical import. Such an approach is not likely to provide a cumulative body of knowledge concerning the formation of interpersonal attitudes.

Perhaps more damaging to such an approach is the fact that more often than not our intuition tends to be misleading, and no firm conclusions can be reached concerning the effects of a given variable on attraction. In the study by Aronson, Willerman, and Floyd (1966) the results provided only tentative support for the humanizing effect of a pratfall. As Table 6.12 shows, spilling the coffee tended to increase the attractiveness of the competent candidate, but it reduced attraction toward the incompetent candidate. Although the interaction between pratfall and competence was significant, the effect of the pratfall was

Table 6.12 Effects of a Pratfall on Attraction (Adapted from Aronson, Willerman, and Floyd, 1966)

	Pratfall	No pratfall
Competent candidate	30.2	20.8
Incompetent candidate	−2.5	17.8

significant only for the incompetent candidate. Thus, there seemed to be a tendency for the pratfall to humanize the competent individual, but the tendency was not significant.

Despite this lack of significance, a number of subsequent investigations have attempted to demonstrate that spilling a cup of coffee serves to humanize a competent person and to increase attraction toward that person. None of the subsequent investigations have found support for the predicted effect of humanization. Kiesler and Goldberg (1968) found that a pratfall had no effect on attraction toward a competent other. Helmreich, Aronson, and LeFan (1970) found that a pratfall tended to lower attraction toward another person irrespective of his competence. Finally, contrary to the humanization hypothesis, Mettee and Wilkins (1972) reported that in at least one condition a pratfall lowered attraction toward a *competent* person whereas it had no effect on liking for an incompetent person. Taken as a whole, these studies fail to provide support for the intuitive hypothesis that a blunder may serve to humanize a superior individual. In fact, despite a concentrated effort at investigating this "minitheory," we are left with no viable conclusion and little information concerning the factors that determine interpersonal attraction.

This series of studies on the effects of a pratfall exemplifies much recent research on interpersonal attraction. Although the research is based on intuitive notions and is conducted in a largely unsystematic manner, the basic research paradigm employed is in many ways similar to the more systematic investigations of impression formation and interpersonal attraction discussed earlier. As in studies on impression formation, subjects are exposed to a situation that provides information about another person, and their attitudes toward that person are measured. Usually, a factorial analysis of variance design is employed. In the studies on effects of a pratfall, for example, subjects listened to tape-recorded interviews that were designed to provide two items of information: (1) that the candidate has either high or low competence and (2) that he did or did not commit a blunder. In contrast to an impression-formation experiment in which a subject might simply be told that the candidate is competent and spilled his coffee, these items of information were conveyed to subjects in the context of a complex situational manipulation. An attempt is usually made to construct situations that will lead subjects to form appropriate inferences about the other person. To test the success of their competence manipulation, Aronson, Willerman, and Floyd

(1966) included a measure of the candidate's intelligence which confirmed that the competent individual was perceived as more intelligent than the incompetent one.

Within the framework of this approach, then, the assumption is that, with the exception of the two items of information concerning the person's competence and pratfall, everything is constant across conditions. Differences in attraction are therefore expected to be solely a function of these two items of information. One pervasive feature of much of this research is worth noting. Almost without exception, the basic hypotheses in these studies concern interaction effects. That is, the effect on attraction of one item of information is expected to depend on the other items of information that have been provided.

An investigator usually selects some variable that should clearly have an effect on attraction. For example, a similar person is usually liked better than a dissimilar person, praise usually leads to greater attraction than derogation, an individual who succeeds on a task is usually more attractive than one who fails or commits a blunder, etc. The investigator then speculates about the conditions under which these effects might not be found or even reversed. He might argue that opinion similarity will *not* produce attraction toward a stimulus person who is emotionally disturbed (Novak and Lerner, 1968) or that a pratfall will *increase* attraction for a highly competent individual (Aronson, Willerman, and Floyd, 1966). Essentially, then, these studies are designed to show that the information conveyed by a given manipulation or event takes on different *meaning* under different conditions. Similarity with respect to a normal person is supposed to be reinforcing whereas it may change its meaning and become punishing with respect to an emotionally disturbed person (Byrne and Lamberth, 1971). Similarly, a pratfall may take on different meaning when committed by competent and incompetent individuals.

Expectancy-Value Analysis of Factorial Experiments on Attraction

The research paradigm described above is readily interpretable within our conceptual framework. After exposure to the experimental situation, a subject will have formed a number of beliefs about the stimulus person. In fact, the complex experimental manipulations provide an array of information that is likely to lead to the formation of diverse descriptive and inferential beliefs. An expectancy-value formulation would suggest that the subject's attitude toward the stimulus person is determined by those beliefs about the person's attributes and by the subject's evaluations of the attributes. In contrast, investigators performing these experiments on attraction have singled out a small number of beliefs (e.g., *O* is competent, *O* spilled his coffee) and have assumed that differences in attitudes are determined only by differences in those beliefs.

Our discussions of research on impression formation and on the similarity-attraction relation have made it clear that the formation of attitudes in a given situation can be understood only by considering all of the subject's salient beliefs about the stimulus person. An experimental manipulation can be expected to have an effect on attraction only when it influences belief strength or attribute evaluations. For example, in the Aronson, Willerman, and Floyd (1966) experiment, subjects listened to a tape recording of a candidate responding to a series of questions. Inferences were probably made about the candidate's intelligence, competence, and ability, and perhaps about other attributes, such as his confidence, poise, pleasantness, etc. These inferences should differ for the competent and incompetent candidates. Introduction of a pratfall toward the end of the recording can have many different effects. First, it may itself lead to the formation of certain beliefs, such as that the candidate is clumsy, nervous, etc. The nature of these inferences based on the blunder may depend on the prior beliefs about the candidate. If he is believed to be competent and poised, the subjective probability that he is clumsy may be lower than if he is believed to be incompetent. Further, the evaluation of spilling a cup of coffee may differ when that blunder is committed by persons of high and low competence. That is, a blunder may take on different meaning in different contexts. Second, the pratfall may influence the strength of beliefs formed prior to the pratfall: Information that the candidate spilled his coffee may lower the subjective probability that he is poised or that he is competent. All these effects would contribute to the final evaluation of the candidate.

Without knowing which of these effects actually occurred, one cannot predict the attitudes that will be formed in the different experimental conditions. In order to understand the effects of a given manipulation on attraction, it is necessary to specify its locus of effect: whether it leads to the formation of new beliefs, whether it changes existing beliefs, or whether it influences evaluations associated with those beliefs. Clearly, without such information it is impossible to make accurate predictions about the effects of a given variable on attraction, and inconsistent findings are to be expected.

Gain-Loss Effect

It may be instructive to examine another series of studies which exemplify some of these problems. Aronson and Linder (1965) proposed a minitheory of attraction according to which "a gain in esteem is a more potent reward than invariant esteem and similarly a loss of esteem is a more potent 'punishment' than invariant negative esteem" (p. 156). In order to test this gain-loss theory of attraction, Aronson and Linder created a situation in which the subject was evaluated by a confederate seven times during the experiment. Subjects participated in one of four experimental conditions:

1. *Invariant high esteem.* The successive evaluations of the subject made by the confederate were all highly positive. On each occasion, the confederate described the subject in terms of positive attributes such as "a good conversationalist," "very intelligent," "probably having a lot of friends," etc.

2. *Invariant low esteem.* The successive evaluations of the subject made by the confederate were all very negative (e.g., "dull conversationalist," "rather ordinary person," "not very intelligent," etc.)

3. *Gain in esteem.* The evaluations in the first three periods were very negative (as in Condition 2) but then became gradually more positive such that in the seventh period they were equal to the evaluations in Condition 1.

4. *Loss in esteem.* The first few evaluations were positive but gradually became negative, leveling off at a point equal to the evaluations in Condition 2.

After the last period, subjects were asked to evaluate the confederate on a 21-point scale ranging from *like her extremely* to *dislike her extremely.* The results of the study showed a significant gain effect. That is, a gain in esteem led to greater attraction toward the confederate than invariant high esteem. However, the loss effect was not significant. There was only a tendency for loss in esteem to produce less liking than invariant low esteem. These findings in partial support of the gain-loss model are shown in Table 6.13.

Table 6.13 Attraction Toward Confederate (Adapted from Aronson & Linder, 1965)

Condition	Attraction
Gain in esteem	7.67
Invariant high esteem	6.42
Invariant low esteem	2.52
Loss in esteem	.87

Despite these inconclusive results, Aronson and Linder (1965) suggested several possible bases for the gain-loss effect, and several studies have been designed to test the proposed explanations (e.g., Landy and Aronson, 1968; Sigall and Aronson, 1969; Sigall, 1970). Overall, results of these studies have not been very consistent, nor have they identified the basis for the gain-loss effect (cf. Fishbein and Ajzen, 1972). This should not be surprising since, as we saw above, the original Aronson and Linder (1965) experiment provided only limited support for the existence of a gain-loss phenomenon. More important, a number of subsequent investigations have failed to find any support for the gain-loss hypothesis. For example, in a second study Sigall and Aronson (1967) reported neither a gain nor a loss effect on attraction, thus failing to replicate the earlier Aronson and Linder study. Further, in discussing research on the similarity-attraction relation, we noted a study by Byrne and London (1966) which can also be viewed as a direct test of the gain-loss hypothesis (see Table 6.10). In that study, a hypothetical stranger agreed continuously (invariant reward), disagreed continuously (invariant punishment), or gradually shifted from complete agreement to complete disagreement (loss) or from complete disagreement to complete agreement (gain). As Table 6.10 shows, neither a gain nor a loss effect was obtained. Similar results were recently reported by Hewitt (1972). At least three additional studies have also failed to support the gain-loss hypothesis (Taylor, Altman, and Sorrentino, 1969; Mettee, 1971; Chaikin, 1971).

Interestingly, one of the few studies providing clear evidence for any kind of gain-loss phenomenon examined the effects of gain and loss on the running speeds of rats. Giving rats one trial a day under constant drive conditions (22 hours' food deprivation), Crespi (1942) measured the running times for traversing a straight runway. A *constant-reward group* always received 16 units of food at the end of each trial, whereas in four other groups incentive magnitude was changed after the rats reached a specified performance level. In two *gain groups,* incentives were shifted upward from low reward (1 or 4 units) to the same level as the constant reward group (16 units). In the *loss groups,* incentives were shifted downward from high reward (256 or 64 units) to the constant reward level (16 units). Consistent with a gain-loss hypothesis, the finding was that after the shift, the gain groups traversed the runway at significantly higher speeds and the loss group ran at significantly lower speeds than did the constant-reward group. However, even with rats, this gain-loss effect appears to be unreliable. Zeaman (1949), reporting a study similar to Crespi's, found only a significant gain effect. As in the Aronson and Linder (1965) study, the loss was not significant.

In conclusion, a considerable number of studies have failed to demonstrate the gain-loss effect in interpersonal attraction. There is no evidence at all for a loss effect, and there is only very limited evidence for a gain effect. This research makes it clear once more that we cannot expect consistent and theoretically meaningful findings to be obtained when studies are designed merely to test intuitive propositions about the factors influencing attraction. In order to understand the effects on attraction of variations in evaluations received from another person, it is necessary to examine how those variations influence beliefs about the evaluator. Once the effects on beliefs are known, an expectancy-value model can be used to predict attitudes toward the evaluator in the various conditions of the experiment. Our conceptual framework, then, provides the foundation for identifying factors which may influence the formation of interpersonal attitudes. Only factors that have systematic effects on beliefs about another person are expected to influence attitudes toward that person.

Although our conceptual framework does not explicitly state what those factors are, it allows the investigator to understand why a given manipulation has an effect on attraction in some situations but not in others. Further, it explains why minor variations in procedures from experiment to experiment may produce different results: These procedural variations are likely to lead to the formation of somewhat different beliefs. For example, subjects in the Aronson, Willerman, and Floyd (1966) experiment listened to a tape recording of a person being interviewed, whereas in the study by Helmreich, Aronson, and LeFan (1970) they watched a videotape. Although the experimenters assumed that the crucial variables manipulated by both procedures were the candidate's competence and whether or not he committed a blunder, it should be obvious that a videotape provides different information about the candidate than does a tape recording. At the very least, a videotape allows beliefs to be formed about the candidate's physical attractiveness, his way of dressing, his mannerisms, etc. These beliefs may influence the effects of the competence and pratfall manipulations.

In recent years, a great deal of time and energy has been devoted to explorations of the bases for interpersonal attraction. Much of this research has tested isolated hypotheses based on the investigator's intuition. A review of the voluminous literature shows that the results have been no more consistent or illuminating than have those obtained in the research described above on the effects of a pratfall and on the gain-loss phenomenon. Indeed, these efforts have provided little in the way of a consistent and integrated body of knowledge concerning interpersonal attraction.

CONDITIONING OF ATTITUDE

We have tried to show that all the research discussed up to this point can be interpreted in the framework of an expectancy-value model. One implication of this conclusion is that information provides the basis for attitude formation. In our discussion of Byrne's explanation for the observed similarity-attraction relation, however, we encountered a different approach, which suggests that affect is directly conditioned to a stimulus object. Since it has been assumed that conditioning of affect to a stimulus object can occur without acquisition of information about the object, this process appears to contradict an informational basis of attitude formation. In order to illustrate the differences between these approaches, let us consider some of the research on conditioning of affect.

Classical Conditioning of Attitude

Most behavior theory accounts of attitude formation ultimately rely on the classical conditioning process. In our discussion of the development of attribute evaluations at the beginning of this chapter, we noted that in the final analysis such evaluations must be accounted for by assuming that affect somehow comes to be associated with the attribute. The classical conditioning paradigm describes this process. (See also Chapter 2.)

Perhaps the best-known study attempting to demonstrate classical conditioning of attitude was performed by Staats and Staats (1958). Subjects were told that they were to learn two lists of words simultaneously. One list containing six national names (German, Swedish, Italian, Dutch, French, and Greek) was projected on a screen. As each national name appeared on the screen, the experimenter read a word from the second list, and the subject was asked to pronounce it aloud. The second list consisted of 108 words such as gift, bitter, chair, happy, and twelve. Each national name was presented visually 18 times in random order, and each time it was paired with a different word from the second list. Of the 108 words in the second list, 18 had positive evaluations (e.g., gift, sacred, happy), 18 had negative evaluations (e.g., bitter, ugly, failure), and the remainder had "no systematic meaning" (e.g., chair, with, twelve). In one condition, the national name *Swedish* was paired with the 18 positive words, and *Dutch* was paired with the 18 negative words. In a second condition, *Dutch* was paired with the positive and *Swedish* with the negative words. The other four national names were paired with the neutral words on the second list. In behavior theory terminology, *Swedish* and *Dutch* served as conditioned stimuli (CS) and the positive and negative words as unconditioned stimuli (UCS). In a second experiment, six proper names (Harry, Tom, Jim, Ralph, Bill, and Bob) were substituted for the national names; *Tom* and *Bill* served as CS. The assumption is that on the basis of prior learning, a given UCS elicits an implicit positive or negative reaction (i.e., an attitude), which becomes conditioned to the CS with which it is paired (see Chapter 2).

At the end of the conditioning procedure, subjects were asked to evaluate each national or proper name on a seven-point scale ranging from *pleasant* to *unpleasant*. Consistent with expectations, the national and proper names that had been paired with positive words were evaluated more positively than the names that had been paired with negative words.

Many other studies using this paradigm have consistently obtained evidence for the "conditioning of attitudes." These studies have shown that attitudes can be conditioned not only to names but also to nonsense syllables (Staats and Staats, 1957), photographs of persons (Byrne and Clore, 1970), geometrical nonsense figures (Sachs and Byrne, 1970), and other stimuli. The paradigm has also been used to test other hypotheses derived from principles of learning theory. For example, Staats, Staats, and Heard (1960) explored the effects of partial reinforcement on conditioning of attitudes. They paired nonsense syllables with positive or negative words. One condition replicated the Staats and Staats (1958) procedure described above in that each CS was consistently paired either with positive or negative UCS words (100 percent reinforcement). In a 50 percent reinforcement condition, each nonsense syllable was paired with either positive or negative words on half of the trials, and on the other half it was paired with neutral words; the *number* of reinforced trials, however, was the same as in the 100 percent reinforcement group. A third condition paired nonsense syllables only with neutral words (0 percent reinforcement). The results showed that attitudes toward the nonsense syllables became more polarized as the percentage of reinforcement increased. These findings are consistent with Byrne's (1969, 1971) argument that attraction is a linear function of the *proportion* of positive reinforcements.

In another study, however, Staats and Staats (1959) found that *number* of reinforcements (i.e., conditioning trials) also had a significant effect on attitudes. In this study, subjects received either 0, 2, 4, 6, 8, 10, 12, 14, 16, or 18 conditioning trials. A significant linear relation between number of trials and attitudes was found for pairings with positive UCS words, and the relation approached significance for pairings with negative UCS words. Evidence for effects of number of trials on conditioning of positive and negative attitudes was also reported by Burgess and Sales (1971). These findings are inconsistent with Byrne's (1969, 1971) position that attraction is a function of the proportion of positive reinforcements and not of the number of reinforcements.

Byrne and Clore (1970) used the Staats and Staats paradigm in an attempt to demonstrate that similar and dissimilar opinion statements have positive and negative reinforcement value. They paired photographs of strangers with tape recordings of opinion statements that were either similar to or different from the subject's own views. Following the conditioning trials, attitudes toward the stranger were measured on six evaluative semantic differential scales. The stranger whose photograph had been paired with similar opinion statements was found to be more attractive than the stranger whose photograph had been paired with dissimilar statements. Recognizing the fact that these findings may have been obtained because subjects attributed the opinion statements to the strangers, Sachs and Byrne (1970) replicated the study pairing opinion statements with geometrical figures as well as photographs. Results comparable to the Byrne and Clore study were obtained for both types of conditioned stimuli.

The question of awareness. Although there seems to be little doubt that attitudes toward a stimulus object can be influenced by pairing that object with other stimuli of known positive or negative evaluation, the assumption of an automatic conditioning process is open to question.

If, as is implied by the classical conditioning paradigm, conditioning occurred without awareness, a noncognitive or noninformational basis for attitude formation would be identified. On the other hand, the presence of awareness would indicate that subjects had knowledge of the systematic pairings between the stimulus object and various attributes. Specifically, subjects could realize that the object was paired either with positive or with negative attributes. This contingency awareness could have one of two consequences. First, subjects might come to actually *believe* that the object in question has some of the attributes with which it was paired. Depending on the evaluation of those attributes, the subject could form a positive, negative, or neutral attitude toward the object. Second, contingency awareness might allow subjects to make inferences about the experiment's purposes or the experimenter's expectations. Thus, they might become aware that the experimenter was trying to establish a positive or negative attitude toward the stimulus object ("demand awareness"). Under the assumption that the subject wanted to please the experimenter or was otherwise motivated to comply with the perceived demands, his responses to the attitude measure would exhibit the expected "conditioning" effects.

The question of awareness has therefore been a major focus of concern in studies of conditioning. For example, in their first study, Staats and Staats (1958) asked their subjects to "write down anything they had thought about the experiment, especially the purpose of it, and so on, or anything they had thought of during the experiment" (p. 38). Of the 93 subjects who participated in the two experiments, 17 reported awareness of the systematic name-word relationship and were excluded from the analysis. "This was done to prevent the interpretation that the conditioning of attitudes depended upon awareness" (p. 38). Staats and Staats thus concluded that it was possible to condition the implicit evaluative responses elicited by the UCS words to the CS names without subjects' awareness. However, as we have repeatedly noted in previous chapters, a considerable number of studies have shown that verbal conditioning (classical or operant) is not obtained without awareness (e.g., Dulany, 1961, 1964; Page, 1969, 1970b; DeNike and Leibovitz, 1969; Lichtenstein and Craine, 1969). For example, Page (1969) used the Staats and Staats classical conditioning paradigm. In addition to going through the usual procedure, subjects were given at the end of the experiment a detailed questionnaire attempting to assess contingency and demand awareness.[37] It should first be noted that a detailed post-experimental inquiry (such as that used by Dulany or Page) reveals many more aware subjects than does a simple question about the purpose of the experiment. For example, although Staats and Staats (1958) reported that only 18 percent of their subjects showed awareness, Page (1969) reported 36 percent aware subjects. Page found no conditioning effects for subjects without awareness. Further, the amount of "conditioning" increased with the degree of awareness ($r = .67$ with contingency awareness and .81 with demand awareness).

We can thus conclude that there is little support for the notion that classical conditioning provides a noninformational basis for attitude formation. Instead, the findings of classical conditioning studies can readily be interpreted within an information processing framework. Although attitudes may be formed in a classical conditioning situation, they do not seem to be the result of automatic conditioning processes; rather, they appear to be determined by beliefs that are formed about the attitude object.

When subjects form beliefs about the attributes of some object, or when they form the belief that some person has rewarded or punished them, their attitudes toward that object or person will be influenced. However, we have also seen that responses to an attitude scale can be influenced by demand awareness. Although such changes are informationally based, they occur without the formation of beliefs about the attitude object. For example, a number of studies have demonstrated that responses to items on an attitude scale can also be influenced by conditioning (e.g., Singer, 1961; Insko, 1965; Insko and Cialdini, 1969). These studies have used an operant conditioning paradigm in which subjects may be rewarded for agreeing with favorable and disagreeing with unfavorable statements on an attitude scale. Rewards are usually administered in the form of verbal comments, such as "good," "um-hum," "right," "OK," etc. Such studies have

---

37. The questionnaire used is reproduced in Page (1969, p. 181).

consistently shown an increase in the reinforced response, but the effect is not obtained without awareness that a given class of responses is being reinforced by the experimenter. That is, subjects may indicate favorable or unfavorable attitudes simply because they perceive such a response to be desirable or correct in the situation. The role of demand awareness as a factor influencing a person's responses will be considered in subsequent chapters.

FREQUENCY OF EXPOSURE AND ATTITUDE FORMATION

One final area of research on attitude formation seems worth considering since it has attracted increased interest in recent years. In an impressive monograph, Zajonc (1968b) proposed that "mere repeated exposure of the individual to a stimulus is a sufficient condition for the enhancement of his attitude toward it. By 'mere exposure' is meant a condition which just makes the given stimulus accessible to the individual's perception" (p. 1). A similar hypothesis has played a major role in research on the effects of interracial contact on prejudice toward minority group members. However, Zajonc noted that in studies concerning the attitudinal effects of social contact and interaction, "mere exposure" is confounded with a multitude of other variables, and the results of these studies therefore provide little information about the frequency of *mere* exposure on attitude formation.

In order to isolate the effects of mere exposure, Zajonc and his associates employed a procedure first reported by R. C. Johnson, Thomas, and Frincke (1960). Subjects are exposed to novel stimuli, such as nonsense words, Chinese characters, facial photographs, or nonsense syllables. The frequency with which the stimuli are presented is varied systematically, and order of presentation is randomized. Thus each subject is exposed to several novel stimuli, each of which appears a different number of times. Following exposure, subjects are asked to evaluate each stimulus on a seven-point *good–bad* scale. Initial studies demonstrated that these evaluations become more favorable as frequency of exposure increases (e.g., Johnson, Thomas, and Frincke, 1960; Zajonc, 1968b; Matlin, 1970). The effect of exposure, however, becomes less with successive trials. Although a small number of exposures may greatly increase evaluation of a *novel* stimulus, the more familiar the stimulus, the greater the number of additional exposures necessary to produce the same increase in evaluation.[38] This relation between frequency of exposure and attitude is shown in Fig. 6.5 for two studies reported by Zajonc (1968b).

One implication of this relationship is that frequency of exposure will have little effect on meaningful English words since subjects are likely to have been exposed to the words on innumerable occasions in the past. Consistent with this notion, Amster and Glasman (1966) found no significant effect of exposure frequency on evaluation of meaningful words. The same general conclusion follows

---

38. According to Zajonc (1968b), attitude is a linear function of the logarithm of frequency.

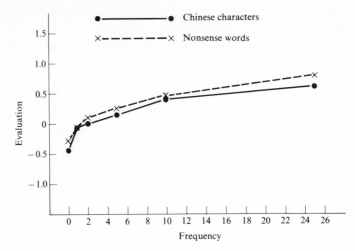

Fig. 6.5 Relation between frequency of mere exposure and attitude. (Adapted from Zajonc, 1968.)

from a series of early studies on music appreciation. Exposure to familiar works of music tends to have no effect on liking for the works, but exposure to unfamiliar works tends to enhance the listener's appreciation of them (e.g., Meyer, 1903; Moore and Gilliland, 1924; Downey and Knapp, 1927).

To account for the relationship between attitude and frequency of exposure found in the initial experiments, Harrison (1968) suggested a *response competition* hypothesis. According to this hypothesis, a novel stimulus elicits a variety of responses, many of which are incompatible. This response competition is assumed to be unpleasant. Repeated exposure to the stimulus eliminates some of the competing responses, thus reducing unpleasantness and leading to more favorable ratings of the stimulus. Several studies have attempted to support this hypothesis by showing that response competition decreases with frequency of exposure and that this decrease in response competition is accompanied by an increase in attitude (Harrison, 1968; Matlin, 1970). Following the exposure procedure, Harrison asked his subjects to give the first association that came to mind for each stimulus. Using latency of associations as an index of response competition, he found that response competition decreased with frequency of exposure. Matlin (1970) replicated this finding and, in another part of her study, asked subjects to give their first association to a list of 60 words that varied in their frequency of usage in the English language. She again found that response latency was greater for low-frequency words than for high-frequency words and, further, that the number of different responses to a given stimulus word decreased with the word's frequency of usage. These findings were again interpreted as evidence that there is more response competition with unfamiliar stimuli. As expected, both Harrison and Matlin also found a negative relation between evaluations of stimulus words and the various measures of response competition.

Although these data appear to support the response competition hypothesis, more recent studies (e.g., Zajonc *et al.,* 1971, 1972; Brickman *et al.,* 1972; Suedfeld *et al.,* 1971; Burgess and Sales, 1971) have reported findings that not only question this hypothesis but also the frequency-affect relation itself. Zajonc *et al.* (1971, 1972) have demonstrated that the positive relation between frequency and affect seems to hold only in a within-subjects design (i.e., when the *same* subjects experience different frequencies of exposure) and only for some novel stimuli but not for others. Perhaps most problematic is a study by Brickman *et al.* (1972) in which subjects first rated 20 abstract paintings on a seven-point evaluative scale. On the basis of these evaluations, three conditions were established such that subjects in one condition were exposed to the four paintings they had rated most favorably, in the second condition to four neutral paintings, and in the third condition to the four most negative paintings. In each condition, one painting was presented once and the others were presented two, five, and ten times. A significant interaction between initial evaluations and frequency of exposure indicated that attitudes *increased* with exposure in the first two conditions but *decreased* with exposure in the third. The latter finding is clearly inconsistent with the response competition hypothesis since, according to that hypothesis, evaluation of a stimulus should increase with frequency of exposure even when the stimulus has an initially negative evaluation.

In conclusion, early research on the relation between mere exposure and affect appeared to demonstrate that evaluation of novel stimuli increased with frequency of exposure. Later studies, however, have imposed severe limitations on the generality of this effect. More than that, they have shown that evaluations may be unaffected by or may even decrease with frequency of exposure. It appears that no single explanation has been offered to account for these inconsistent findings.

Within our conceptual framework, such inconsistent findings are not altogether unexpected. One should first realize that in terms of attitude formation, mere exposure constitutes a relatively minor factor. Zajonc (1968b) has noted that in most situations mere exposure is confounded with a variety of other variables, which are clearly more important determinants of attitude. Research on conditioning of attitudes, for example, has shown that when exposure to an object is accompanied by positive or negative stimuli, attitudes toward that object will be determined primarily by the evaluations of the accompanying stimuli, and frequency of exposure will not always have a positive effect on attitude. However, even when mere exposure can be isolated and separated from other variables, our conceptual framework suggests that inconsistent findings may be obtained. Frequency of mere exposure is really no different from any other manipulation of an independent variable. In order to understand its effects on attitude, one must first examine the ways in which it affects a person's salient beliefs about the attitude object. Perhaps a novel stimulus initially elicits few strong beliefs. As a result of repeated exposures, a person may form various associations and make inferences about the stimulus object. It is thus possible that his attitude toward the object will be influenced by frequency of mere exposure. Whether his attitude will change at all, and if so, whether it will change in a positive or negative direction depends on the nature of the beliefs he forms. If most beliefs associate the object with positively evaluated attributes, the person's attitude will become more positive. If most beliefs associate the object with negative attributes, his attitude will shift in a negative direction. In contrast, mere exposure to a *familiar* object should have little effect on attitudes toward that object since it is unlikely to change the person's prior beliefs.[39]

CONCLUSION

This chapter has reviewed several lines of research dealing with processes of attitude formation. We have discussed research based on expectancy-value models, on linear information-integration models, on reinforcement principles, as well as on more specific hypotheses. We have tried to show that all this research is consistent with the notion of an informational basis for attitude formation. In Chapter 5 we showed that a person forms descriptive and inferential beliefs about objects in his environment. These beliefs represent the information he has about the objects. An informational basis for attitude simply implies that the person's attitude toward any given object is determined by this information. In a typical experiment, a subject is exposed to a variety of objects, and he may form many beliefs about them. His attitude toward only one or two of them is of focal concern to the investigator. Usually, different experimental conditions are created by manipulating some of the observable stimuli in the situation. The manipulations are expected to influence the subject's attitude. However, throughout this chapter we have noted that the effects of a given manipulation on attitude can be understood only if its effects on the person's beliefs are known.

Our conceptual framework suggests that upon entering the experimental situation, a subject may hold certain prior beliefs about the particular object in question. Exposure to the experimental manipulations may lead to the formation of new descriptive and inferential beliefs about the object. By the time that attitudes are assessed, the subject will have considerable information about the attitude object. Since this information will determine his attitude, we have argued that attitude formation cannot be understood when its informational base is ignored.

A schematic illustration of these notions is presented in Figure 6.6. The broken arrow between stimulus conditions and the informational base indicates that the effects of a given stimulus manipulation are not invariant. That is, its effects on beliefs depend on the context in which it appears and on other manipulations with which it is combined. The solid arrow indicates that attitudes are determined by the person's information about the stimulus object. Inconsistent findings in the literature on attitude formation reflect the lack of a constant relation between a given manipulation and the informational base.

---

39. Support for some of these arguments has been reported by Grush (1974).

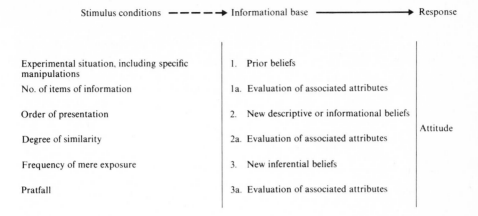

Fig. 6.6 Schematic representation of effects of stimulus variables on attitudes.

In contrast to the approach suggested by our conceptual framework, most research on attitude formation has examined the effects of a given manipulation on attitudes without examining its effects on beliefs. We have seen, however, that some of this research has been based on a systematic conception of intervening processes. N. H. Anderson's (1970, 1971a) work on impression formation, for example, assumes that each item of information presented by the experimenter has a certain scale value and weight; attitudes are affected by manipulations that influence these variables. Similarly, Byrne (1969, 1971) and others have suggested that various stimulus manipulations influence interpersonal attraction and attitudes by influencing the magnitude or proportion of reinforcements associated with an attitude object.

The majority of studies on interpersonal attraction, however, have not proposed any systematic intervening process. Instead, they have usually postulated different hypothetical processes to account for the effects of different manipulations. We have considered only two of these "minitheories": those dealing with effects of a pratfall and of gain and loss in esteem. We have not attempted to provide a full review of this literature since it deals with studies that have tested isolated and intuitive hypotheses and that have made little contribution to our understanding of attitude formation. Most of the studies have produced inconsistent and inconclusive results.

Although the systematic research programs generated by Anderson, Byrne, and their associates have at least been able to identify some stable phenomena, inconsistent findings here, too, have frequently been obtained. We have suggested that these apparent inconsistencies are attributable to the lack of concern for those variables that we believe to be the primary determinants of attitude, namely, a person's salient beliefs linking the stimulus object to various attributes and his evaluations of those attributes. We have tried to show how consideration of these variables would allow an investigator to determine why a given manipulation has different effects on attitude under different conditions. Since it is possible to obtain direct measures of beliefs and attribute evaluations, the explanations we have offered (as well as additional hypotheses) can easily be verified.

Anderson (1970, 1971a) has argued that his integration theory can also account for the disparate findings concerning attitude formation. Relying on his weighted averaging model, he has repeatedly demonstrated that a subject's attitude can be predicted with considerable accuracy by assigning appropriate weights to the different items of information provided by the experimenter. Similarly, it would probably be possible to account for attitudes toward a person who committed a blunder or pratfall by assigning appropriate weights to the two variables manipulated in experimental investigations, namely, the pratfall itself and the person's competence. For that matter, almost any phenomenon can be explained by a weighted linear model.[40]

The mere fact that appropriate weights can be found, however, provides little in the way of understanding a phenomenon. It is only when these weights can be given a meaningful psychological interpretation—and when they can be shown to be replicable—that they provide a mechanism for explaining observed relationships. Unfortunately, these conditions have often not been met in research on attitude formation. We have seen that Anderson's weighted averaging model has been used primarily in conjunction with an analysis of variance approach in studies of impression formation. In these studies, weights have usually not been estimated; instead, certain assumptions are made about the weights in order to account for a given phenomenon. For example, to explain primacy effects it has been assumed that words appearing in sequence have successively smaller weights. The analysis of variance design is then used to test these assumptions. Results conforming to expectations are taken as evidence for the linear model, as well as for the assumptions about the weights. We have seen, however, that different assumptions about the weights (or about the scale values) can account for the results equally well. Further, when results do not conform to expectations, it is always possible to make post hoc revisions in the assumption about the weights in order to account for the obtained results. It follows that, used in this manner, the analysis of variance approach does not provide conclusive evidence about weights and thus contributes little to our understanding of the processes underlying attitude formation. This problem could be overcome if the analysis of variance approach, like multiple regression, were used to obtain estimates of weights and if it could be shown that the weights were consistent with the assumptions and that they were replicable.

We have suggested an alternative approach based on the expectancy-value formulation. According to the expectancy-value model, a person's attitude toward

---

40. A good illustration of the way in which appropriate weights can be found for a given set of data is provided by Lopes (1972). Recall also that a weighted linear model can accurately predict almost any judgment based on a set of cues (see Chapter 5).

an object is related to the strength of his beliefs linking the object to various attributes multiplied by his evaluations of the attributes. Attitudes are predictable from the sum of the resulting products ($A = \Sigma b_i e_i$). Since it is possible to obtain measures of beliefs and attribute evaluations, it is possible to provide a direct test of the effects of any given manipulation on these mediating variables. Further, if one obtains a direct measure of attitude, it is also possible to test the predictive accuracy of the expectancy-value model. We have presented and discussed considerable evidence in support of this model and shown that the different lines of research on attitude formation can be interpreted within an expectancy-value framework. We have tried to show not only that this model is consistent with the findings in impression formation, interpersonal attraction, and conditioning, but that it can also account for some of the apparently inconsistent results in these and other areas of investigation. Whereas the expectancy-value model merely describes the *relations* between beliefs and attitudes, our conceptual framework suggests a causal link. Throughout this chapter we have emphasized that a person's attitude is determined by his salient beliefs about the object's attributes and by his evaluations of those attributes. At any point in time, a person holds a limited number of salient beliefs about any given object, action, or event, and those beliefs serve as the primary determinants of his attitude toward that object, action, or event.

Chapter 7

Formation
of
Intentions

In the preceding two chapters we examined factors influencing the formation of beliefs and attitudes and showed that attitudes are determined by a person's salient beliefs. The present chapter is concerned with the formation of intentions. We have defined intention as a person's location on a subjective probability dimension involving a relation between himself and some action. A behavioral intention, therefore, refers to a person's subjective probability that he will perform some behavior.

In Chapter 2 we noted that intentions have frequently been subsumed under the concept of attitude and that no distinction between attitude and intention has usually been made. This point of view implies a strong relation between attitudes and intentions. The usual assumption is that the more favorable a person's attitude toward some object, the more he will intend to perform positive behaviors (and the less he will intend to perform negative behaviors) with respect to that object.

The present chapter will first review some of the research that has dealt with the relation between a person's attitude and his intention to perform some behavior. We shall see that there is little evidence in support of such a relation. This is not unexpected from the point of view of our conceptional framework. Although we view a person's attitude toward an object to be related to the totality of his intentions with respect to the object, there is no necessary relation between his attitude and any given intention.

To gain a better understanding of the relation between attitude and intention, we shall then examine the concept of intention in greater detail. We shall see that intentions vary in specificity and that there are systematic patterns of relations among intentions. Following this analysis, we shall discuss a theoretical model for the prediction of intentions. The broad outline of our conceptual framework in Chapter 1 indicated that according to this model, a person's intention to per-

288

form a behavior is determined by two factors: his attitude toward the behavior and his subjective norm concerning that behavior. Following exposition of the model, we shall review some of the relevant empirical evidence.

The chapter will conclude with a discussion of research dealing with the effects of other variables on intentions. We shall try to show how the findings obtained in the research can be interpreted within our conceptual framework.

ATTITUDES AND INTENTIONS

Intentions have often been viewed as the "conative component of attitude," and it has usually been assumed that this conative component is related to the attitude's affective component. This conceptualization has led to the assumption of a strong relation between attitudes and intentions. Until recently, the conative component of attitude has been submitted to little empirical investigation, and the relation between attitude and intention has been largely neglected. However, many investigations designed to study the relation between attitude and behavior have actually not observed behavior but have instead used measures of behavioral intentions as their criteria. These studies provide some information about the attitude-intention relation.

Evidence concerning the attitude-intention relation. A series of investigations have obtained measures of subjects' attitudes toward blacks and have asked the subjects to indicate their willingness to be photographed with a black person and to sign release forms for the photographs. Although the signing of a release form has usually been viewed as an overt behavior, to regard it as an intention seems more appropriate since the photographs are not taken and the releases are therefore hypothetical (see Ajzen *et al.,* 1970).

In the first study of this series (DeFleur and Westie, 1958), subjects high and low in prejudice toward blacks were asked to indicate their willingness to pose for a photograph with a Negro person of the opposite sex. Irrespective of their response, they were then shown seven "standard photographic release agreements" which consisted of a graded series of situations in which the photographs might be used. Subjects could sign as many of the agreements as they saw fit. The complete form used is presented in Table 7.1. Note that the release agreements represent situational variations in terms of the amount of publicity the photograph would receive. DeFleur and Westie found a low but significant relation between attitudes toward blacks and the number of photographic releases that subjects signed.

Several subsequent investigations have also used the picture-release technique. In an attempt to replicate and extend the DeFleur and Westie study, Linn (1965) found no significant relation between attitudes and intentions. Similarly, studies by Darroch (1971) and J. A. Green (1972) have also revealed nonsigni-

Table 7.1 Photographic Release Agreements (Adapted from DeFleur and Westie, 1958)

I will pose for a photograph (of the same type as in the experiment) with a Negro person of the opposite sex with the following restrictions on its use:

1. I will allow this photograph to be used in laboratory experiments where it will be seen only by professional sociologists.

Signed _____

2. I will allow this photograph to be published in a technical journal read only by professional sociologists.

Signed _____

3. I will allow this photograph to be shown to a few dozen university students in a laboratory situation.

Signed _____

4. I will allow this photograph to be shown to hundreds of university students as a teaching aid in sociology classes.

Signed _____

5. I will allow this photograph to be published in the student newspaper as part of a publicity report on this research.

Signed _____

6. I will allow this photograph to be published in my hometown newspaper as part of a publicity report on this research.

Signed _____

7. I will allow this photograph to be used in a nationwide publicity campaign *advocating racial integration*.

Signed _____

ficant or low relations between attitudes toward blacks and intentions to release photographs with a black person.

Many other investigators have reported low and nonsignificant relations between attitudes and intentions. For example, Nemeth (1970) reported a correlation of .008 between liking for a person and volunteering to distribute questionnaires for him. Similarly, Fishbein and Ajzen (1974) correlated different measures of attitude toward religion with each of 100 intentions to perform various religious behaviors (e.g., donate money to a religious institution, pray before or after meals, take a religious course for credit). The average correlation between attitude and intentions was found to be .17. Novak and Lerner (1968) manipulated perceived similarity with another person and either indicated or did not indicate that the other person was emotionally disturbed. Although subjects always had a more favorable attitude toward the similar than the dissimilar person, they were more willing to interact with the dissimilar normal than with the similar disturbed. It should thus be clear that a person's attitude toward an object is not necessarily related to his intention to perform a given behavior with respect to, or in the presence of, that object.

Specific intentions versus sets of intentions. In Chapter 3 we showed that a person's attitude toward an object can be measured by considering a large set of his intentions with respect to that object. As with beliefs, statements of intentions can be used to construct an attitude scale by applying some standard scaling procedure. The resulting attitude score represents the person's general favorableness toward the attitude object. For example, there is considerable evidence that the Bogardus Social Distance Scale and Guttman scales based on intentional items correlate highly with other measures of attitude. Similarly, several studies have found that attitudes correlate highly with indices based on responses to Triandis's behavioral differential (e.g., Fishbein, 1964, 1967b).

Indeed, the relation between attitude and a set of intentions can be expressed in terms of an equation similar to the expectancy-value model for the relation between attitude and beliefs.

$$A = \sum_{i=1}^{n} I_i e_i. \tag{7.1}$$

In Eq. 7.1, A is the attitude toward some object; I_i is the intention to perform behavior i; e_i is the evaluation of behavior i; and n is the number of intentions. In contrast to our assumption of a causal link between beliefs and attitude, intentions are not assumed to determine attitudes. However, it is possible to view attitude as the determinant of the overall favorability of a person's intentions. Attitude is not assumed to determine any given intention, but it should influence the general level of favorability expressed by the person's intentions, whatever those intentions might be. Thus two persons may have the same attitude toward religion, but they may hold different intentions concerning religious behaviors. One person might intend to attend church regularly and to pray before meals, but not to donate money to his church or to sing in the church choir. The other person might intend to attend church regularly and to donate money to his church, but not to pray before meals or to sing in the church choir. The overall favorability expressed by their respective sets of intentions is approximately the same and corresponds to their attitudes.

In an attempt to test the relation between attitude and specific intentions on the one hand and sets of intentions on the other, Fishbein and Ajzen (1974) asked subjects to indicate whether they would or would not perform each of 100 behaviors that had previously been judged as indicating either a favorable or an unfavorable religious attitude. Taking this evaluation of the behavior into account, they computed an index by summing across responses to all 100 intentions. In addition, subjects filled out five traditional verbal measures of attitude toward religiosity (a self-report scale, a semantic differential, and Likert, Guttman, and Thurstone scales). The correlations between these measures of attitude and the index based on the 100 intentions ranged from .60 to .75. In marked contrast, the average correlation between attitude and single intentions ranged from .16 to .20 for the different attitude scales.

In conclusion, there appears to be no systematic relation between attitudes and intentions. Although attitudes tend to correlate highly with indices based on sets of intentions, the relation between attitude and single intentions is usually low and nonsignificant. To gain a better understanding of the relation between attitudes and intentions, it may be necessary to examine the nature of intentions in greater detail.

Specificity of Intentions

Intentions involve four different elements: the *behavior,* the *target* object at which the behavior is directed, the *situation* in which the behavior is to be performed, and the *time* at which the behavior is to be performed. Each of these elements varies along a dimension of specificity. At the most specific level, a person intends to perform a particular act with respect to a given object in a specified situation at a given point in time. For example, a person may intend to *have a drink* (behavior) with *George* (target) in *Harry's Pub* (situation) at *5 o'clock this afternoon* (time). At the most general level the person may simply intend to be gregarious (without reference to any specific behavior, target, situation, or time). It is relatively easy to identify the levels of specificity on the target, situation, and time dimensions, but the behavioral dimension poses greater difficulty.

Specificity of Target, Situation, and Time.

Intentions can be held with respect to a particular object (Ted Kennedy), a class of objects (politicians, Democrats), or any object (people in general). Similarly, with respect to situations, a person may intend to perform a behavior in a given situation or location (Henry's Pub), a class of locations (bars) or any location. Finally, intentions can be held with respect to a particular point in time (Tuesday, June 30, at 6:30 p.m.), a specified time period (August), or an unlimited time period (some time in the future). It should be clear that these factors are not unrelated. Certain objects never appear in a given location or at a given point in time; certain locations or situations are accessible only at specified time periods, etc.

Behavioral Specificity

It is usually possible to distinguish between specific and general behavioral intentions. A person's intentions to be gregarious, cooperative, or cautious are clearly very general since many different specific intentions may fall under these categories. Thus intentions to go to a party, to join a social club, and to invite a friend to dinner are possible instances of the intention to be gregarious. It is more difficult, however, to determine whether a given intention is a specific instance of some more general intention. For example, intention to invite a friend to dinner may be an instance of the intention to be gregarious, but it may also represent general intentions to be friendly, to be ingratiating, to seduce, etc. Thus, although it seems possible to say that one intention is more behaviorally specific than another, it may be difficult to determine whether some specific intention is an instance of a more general intention.

Relations among intentions. It is possible, however, to determine whether two or more intentions represent a common underlying dimension. In Chapter 3 we saw that factor analysis can be used to identify the dimensions underlying a large set of behavioral intentions. When the intentions are found to load on the same factor, they can be viewed as instances of a more general intention. Working from a multi-component definition of attitude, Triandis (1964) attempted to identify the basic dimensions of the conative component. Since the number of intentions that could be studied is almost unlimited, he restricted his investigation to *interpersonal* intentions. Triandis initially selected close to 700 interpersonal behaviors on the basis of a content analysis of American novels. Using various techniques to eliminate socially unimportant or very similar behaviors, he reduced the list to a final sample of 61 heterogeneous behaviors. Subjects were asked to indicate their intentions to perform these behaviors with respect to 34 complex stimulus persons. A "behavioral differential" of the following format was used.

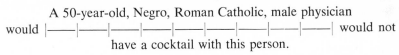

A 50-year-old, Negro, Roman Catholic, male physician
would |——|——|——|——|——|——|——|——|——| would not
have a cocktail with this person.

The intentions selected represented different levels of behavioral specificity and included behaviors such as the following.

Smile at
Vote for
Go out on a date with
Give dinner party in the honor of
Be partners with in an athletic game
Work for
Be commanded by
Praise suggestions of
Teach
Accept as an intimate friend
Admire the character of

Since neither time nor situation was specified, the intentions represent the most general levels of these two dimensions.

A factor analysis was performed on the matrix of correlations between behavioral intentions, and five dimensions of interpersonal intentions were identified. Some of the intentions with high loadings on these five dimensions can be inspected in Table 7.2.

Table 7.2 Dimensions of Interpersonal Intentions (Adapted from Triandis, 1964)

Intention	Factor loading	Intention	Factor loading
Factor I: Formal Social Acceptance with Subordination versus Rejection with Superordination			
Admire character of	.83	Praise suggestions of	.75
Obey	.88	Work for	.57
Ask for opinion of	.88	Be commended by	.58
Believe	.85	Admire ideas of	.62
Elect to political office	.85	Accept as an intimate friend	.53
Factor II: Marital Acceptance versus Rejection			
Marry	.97	Fall in love with	.94
Physically love	.96	Kiss the hand of	.93
Go on a date with	.95	Love even after his death	.91
Factor III: Friendship Acceptance versus Rejection			
Eat with	.80	Be partners with in an athletic game	.76
Go fishing with	.73	Accept as an intimate friend	.68
Factor IV: Hostile Acceptance versus Social Distance			
Exclude from my neighborhood	.79	Work with	−.63
Accept as close kin by marriage	−.72	Prohibit from voting	.77
Factor V: Interaction with Superiors-Subordinates			
Treat as a subordinate	−.71	Be commanded by	.43
Command	−.55	Admire ideas of	.61

Triandis and his associates (e.g., Triandis *et al.,* 1968; Triandis, Tanaka, and Shanmugam, 1966) have subsequently performed a number of additional factor analyses of interpersonal intentions. Although there is some stability in factor structure, the number and nature of the emerging factors are found to depend in part on the target persons considered, on the intentions included in the analyses, and on the subjects who are making the ratings. A given intention may load on a certain factor in one analysis and on another factor in a different analysis. Further, as Table 7.2 shows, a given intention may load on more than one factor. Thus "admire ideas of" loads on Factors I and V, and "accept as an intimate friend" loads on Factors I and III. Generally speaking, however, five clusters of intentions appear to emerge in most analyses; intentions tend to form the relatively stable patterns of interrelations shown in Table 7.3.

Table 7.3 Item Clusters Emerging in Factor Analyses of Intentions (Adapted from Fishbein, 1967b)

Cluster	Typical items
1. Admiration	Admire the character of Believe Admire ideas of Praise suggestions of
2. Subordination- Superordination	Be commanded by Elect to political office Treat as a subordinate Work for
3. Friendship	Accept as an intimate friend Treat as equal Eat with
4. Social distance	Invite to my club Exclude from my neighborhood Accept as a close kin by marriage
5. Marital	Go on a date with Fall in love with Marry

Depending largely on the types of stimulus persons that are rated, these different clusters tend to go together in different ways (i.e., they may load on the same or different dimensions in any given factor analysis). For example, in one study, admiration and friendship items may load on one factor, and social distance and subordination items may load on a second factor. In another study, admiration and subordination items may load on one factor, and friendship and social distance items may load on a second factor. Thus, although five relatively stable types of interpersonal intentions can be identified, these five general intentions are usually not independent. Relationships between the different types of behavioral intentions may vary from situation to situation, and one cannot assume that a given general intention will always be representative of the same factor.

A factor analysis, however, does serve to identify the dimensions underlying a given set of behavioral intentions with respect to a given set of target objects. This information can be used to obtain indices of general intentions in the context of a given study. For example, in Triandis's (1964) study it would have been possible to obtain a measure of intention to show "friendship acceptance" by selecting the four intentions with the highest loadings on this factor (i.e., Factor III in Table 7.2). The sum of the subject's responses to these four scales with respect to a given stimulus person would represent the subject's intention to show friendship acceptance toward that stimulus person.[1] Similar indices could be obtained for each of the other factors, and thus, each subject's general intentions with respect to a given stimulus person would be available.

Just as it is possible to obtain indices of general intentions or clusters of intentions, it is possible to combine these general intentions to arrive at the most global intention, namely, the person's intention to exhibit favorableness or unfavorableness in his behavior with respect to an object. Note that such an index of global intention is based on a large set of heterogeneous intentions to perform various behaviors at different levels of specificity. By the same token, each specific intention in a given cluster (e.g., intention to eat with the stimulus person—see Table 7.3) may itself be viewed as based on a variety of even more specific intentions to perform that behavior in different situations and at different points in time. These considerations suggest that intentions may be viewed as ordered in terms of the five levels of specificity shown in Fig. 7.1.

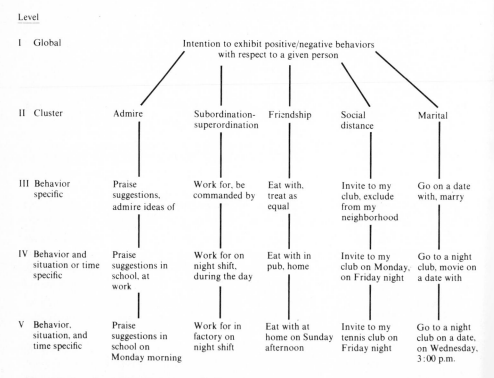

Fig. 7.1 Levels of intentional specificity.

---

1. A more sophisticated technique is to obtain factor scores that are based on all intentions and that weight each intention in terms of its loading on a given factor (for example, see Triandis, 1964).

Our discussion of the relation between attitude and intention suggested that a strong relation can be expected only when a global measure of intention (Level I) is used. We have noted that global intentions obtained by computing an index across all the intentions on Triandis's behavioral differential correlated highly with a measure of attitude. In the Fishbein and Ajzen (1974) study cited earlier, the index over 100 intentions also constituted a measure of global intention with respect to religiosity; this measure was found to correlate highly with various measures of attitude toward religiosity.

Global intentions can also be measured directly by asking a subject to indicate whether he intends to behave favorably or unfavorably with respect to some target.[2] For example, Ostrom (1969) measured global intentions with respect to the church on the following nine-point scale: *I act strongly supportive–strongly hostile* (toward the church). As might be expected, this global intention also correlated highly with various measures of attitude toward the church.

The second level in Fig. 7.1 represents the five basic clusters of intentions discussed earlier. These are still fairly general intentions to show admiration, to subordinate oneself, etc. Measures of these types of intentions can be obtained by asking a general question (e.g., "Do you intend to admire Person X?") or by computing an index across a set of intentions such as "praise suggestions," "admire ideas of," etc. The latter intentions are presented in Level III of Fig. 7.1. Greater specificity is introduced by considering situation or time (Level IV). The most specific intentions appear at Level V; these are intentions to perform a given behavior, with respect to the stimulus person, in a given situation, at a given point in time.

The intention at any given level can be estimated on the basis of a set of more specific intentions at the lower levels. For example, intention to "praise the suggestions of Person X in school" could be measured by considering intentions to praise his suggestions in school at various points in time. Clearly, as the intention becomes more and more specific, its relation to a general measure of attitude will tend to decrease. Even at Level II, the relation between attitude and intentions is somewhat unclear. It should be recalled that intentions at Level III (which define the clusters at Level II) tend to load on different factors in different analyses.

In Chapter 3 we noted that the first factor to emerge in a factor analysis is usually evaluative in nature. A given intention or cluster of intentions that loads highly on the first factor should therefore be related to attitude whereas intentions loading on the remaining factors may show little relation with attitude. Evidence for these notions is reported by Triandis and his associates (e.g., Triandis *et al.,* 1968; Triandis, Tanaka, and Shanmugam, 1966). Triandis *et al.* (1968) performed a factor analysis on 16 interpersonal intentions, and three factors emerged. Scores based on the first factor correlated .45 with a semantic differential mea-

---

2. It appears that an index based on a heterogeneous set of intentions is preferable to a single-item measure of global intention because the single-item measure may be affected by the exact wording used.

sure of attitude, and the correlations for the remaining two factors were .34 and .28, respectively. Generally speaking, at Level II the results of several studies seem to indicate that attitudes are most highly correlated with admiration and friendship intentions ($r \sim .55$), are moderately correlated with subordination and social distance intentions ($r \sim .35$), and are least correlated with marital intentions ($r \sim .15$).

In conclusion, there is little evidence for a systematic relation between attitudes and intentions. A measure based on a heterogeneous set of intentions, or a very general measure of intention to perform positive or negative behaviors with respect to some object, will be found to correlate with attitudes toward the object in question. As the measure of intention becomes more specific (in terms of the behavior, situation, or time), its relation to attitude will tend to decrease. Thus far we have assumed that attitudes and intentions are measured with respect to the same target object. Clearly, when different targets are involved, the attitude-intention relation will tend to be low, irrespective of the intention's specificity. For example, attitude toward blacks (a class of people) would not necessarily be expected to correlate highly even with a global intention to perform positive or negative behaviors with respect to Shirley Chisholm (a specific black woman, candidate for the Democratic Party's nomination for President of the United States in 1972) or Muhammed Ali. In other words, when attitudes and intentions are measured at different levels of target specificity, a high correlation cannot be expected.

DETERMINANTS OF INTENTIONS

From a practical point of view, intentions at Levels III, IV, and V are of most interest to an investigator. That is, the investigator usually attempts to understand and predict a person's intention to perform some particular behavior. The discussion above indicates that a measure of the person's attitude toward the target of the behavior will not allow accurate prediction. We must therefore turn to an examination of the determinants of such intentions.

Dulany's Theory of Propositional Control

One approach to this problem has been suggested by Dulany (1961, 1968). Investigating the role of awareness in studies of verbal conditioning, Dulany argued that subjects' responses in these studies are under volitional control; barring physical impediments, a person should do what he intends or tries to do. In a typical verbal conditioning experiment, subjects are reinforced for eliciting a certain class of verbal response (e.g., plural nouns). An increase in the frequency with which these responses are elicited is taken as evidence for conditioning. According to Dulany (1961) subjects form "self-instructional sets (or 'intentions') and ... these in turn lead to selection of the corresponding response class" (p. 252). Consequently, Dulany turned his attention to the determinants of behavioral intentions.

In previous chapters we have encountered many of the elements contained in Dulany's theory, which deals with the determinants of behavioral intentions. The theory can be described most easily in the context of a verbal operant conditioning experiment. In such an experiment, certain responses on the part of the subject are positively or negatively reinforced by the experimenter. According to Dulany, the subject forms a *hypothesis of the distribution of reinforcement* (*RHd*); i.e., he forms the hypothesis that the reinforcement follows a particular response or class of responses. This hypothesis about the contingencies between a subject's own responses and the reinforcement has previously been termed "contingency awareness." The effect of *RHd* on intentions depends on the subject's evaluation of the reinforcement. A positively evaluated reinforcer should increase the subject's intention to elicit the reinforced response, and a negatively evaluated reinforcer should decrease this intention.

In addition to being positively or negatively evaluated, the reinforcing event may also be perceived to signify that the reinforced response was "correct" or "incorrect." Dulany thus distinguishes between the *subjective value of a reinforcer* (*RSv*) and the subject's *hypothesis of the significance of a reinforcer* (*RHs*). In conjunction with *RHd*, the hypothesis of the distribution of reinforcement, *RHs* allows the subject to form a *behavioral hypothesis* (*BH*). For example, if the subject believes that Response *R* is followed by a reinforcer, and if he believes the reinforcer to signify that he has made a correct response, then he should form the behavioral hypothesis that he is supposed to elicit Response *R*. On the other hand, if he believes the reinforcer to signify an incorrect response, he should form the behavioral hypothesis that he is not supposed to elicit Response *R*. This hypothesis concerning the experimenter's behavioral expectations has previously been referred to as "demand awareness." The effect of *BH* on the subject's behavioral intention depends on his *motivation to comply* (*MC*) with the perceived expectations. A subject may believe that the experimenter wants him to elicit Response *R*, but he may or may not want to comply with the perceived expectation of the experimenter.

Letting *R* stand for the reinforced response and *BI* for the subject's behavioral intention to elicit that response, the central equation of Dulany's theory of propositional control can be expressed as follows:

$$R \sim BI = [(RHd)\ (RSv)]w_1 + [(BH)\ (MC)]w_2. \qquad (7.2)$$

In Eq. 7.2, *RHd* is the hypothesis of the distribution of reinforcement; *RSv* is the subjective value of the reinforcer; *BH* is the behavioral hypothesis; *MC* is the motivation to comply; and w_1 and w_2 are weights indicating the relative importance of the two components in determining behavioral intentions. Further, *BH* is defined as the product of *RHd* and *RHs*; i.e., $BH = (RHd)\ (RHs)$, where *RHs* is the hypothesis of the significance of the reinforcer.

Looking at Eq. 7.2 we can see that a subject's performance of the reinforced response is closely related to his intention to perform that response. The intention's level of specificity is determined by the response in question; that is, the intention corresponds directly to the behavior that is to be predicted. In the context of a verbal conditioning experiment, the subject's intention to elicit plural nouns might be measured.[3] The central determinant of this intention is *RHd*, the hypothesis of the distribution of reinforcement. As was true with intentions, *RHd* corresponds directly to the response that is to be predicted; its level of specificity is thus again determined by the response in question. In our example, *RHd* would be the subject's belief that elicitation of plural nouns produces ($+1$) or does not produce (-1) the reinforcer. The subject's positive ($+1$) or negative (-1) evaluation of the reinforcer (*RSv*) is multiplied with *RHd*, resulting in the first component of the theory $[(RHd)(RSv)]$. For example, if a subject did not believe that plural nouns produced the reinforcer (-1), and if he positively evaluated the reinforcer ($+1$), his score for the first component would be -1; that is, he should intend not to elicit plural nouns. However, if he negatively evaluated the reinforcer (-1), his score for the first component would be $+1$, and he should intend to elicit plural nouns.

In a similar fashion, *RHd* is multiplied by *RHs*, the subject's hypothesis that the reinforcer signifies he was correct ($+1$) or incorrect (-1), resulting in the behavioral hypothesis (*BH*). The central term *RHd* thus enters both components of the theory. Returning to our example, *BH* is the subject's hypothesis that he is supposed to ($+1$) or is not supposed to (-1) elicit plural nouns. Multiplying this behavioral hypothesis by his motivation to comply ($+1$) or not to comply (-1) with his perception of what he is supposed to do produces the theory's second component $[(BH)(MC)]$. If a subject formed the hypothesis that he is supposed to elicit plural nouns ($+1$), and if he were motivated to ($+1$), his score for the second component would be $+1$ and he should intend to elicit plural nouns.

Thus we can see that two components serve as the basic determinants of intentions in Dulany's theory. The first component is similar to an expectancy-value formulation in that it refers to the subject's expectation that a given response (e.g., elicitation of plural nouns) will lead to a certain event (e.g., the experimenter's saying "good"), and the subject's evaluation of the event. The second component essentially represents perceived "demands" and motivation to comply with these demands. Each of the two components is assumed to contribute to the determination of intentions, but their relative importance may vary from situation to situation. Dulany (1961, 1964, 1968) and his associates (Dulany and O'Connell, 1963; Dulany, Schwartz, and Walker, 1965; Schwartz, 1966) have used multiple regression analysis to estimate these weights and to predict behavioral intentions from the two components. They have reported considerable evidence supporting the theory in the context of verbal-conditioning experiments. The multiple correlation between behavioral intention and the two components of the theory has been approximately .85. Of greater relevance to the attitude area, however, is the work

---

3. Dulany has developed a fairly complex measurement procedure for indirectly assessing *BI, RHd, RHs,* and *BH* and for directly assessing *RSv* and *MC*. Interested readers should see Dulany (1968, Appendix).

of Fishbein (1967b) and his associates (see Ajzen and Fishbein, 1973), who have extended Dulany's theorizing to an analysis of social behavior.

Fishbein's Model for the Prediction of Intentions

Realizing that the first component of Dulany's theory had a certain resemblance to an expectancy-value formulation, and that the second component could be viewed as involving the concept of social norms, Fishbein (1967b) proposed an alternative formulation of the theory. In the modified version, the theory's constructs have been reinterpreted and relabeled in an attempt to reveal their relations to more familiar social psychological concepts. As in the original formulation, the modified version of the theory deals with the prediction of a specific behavioral act. In a given situation, a person is assumed to hold or to form a specific behavioral intention which influences his subsequent overt behavior. The intention in the present theory refers to performance of a given action in a given situation; it is the intention to perform the particular overt response that is to be predicted.

According to the theory, there are two major factors that determine behavioral intentions: a personal or "attitudinal" factor and a social or "normative" factor. These two components in the theory are given empirical weights. Symbolically, the central equation of the theory can be presented as follows:

$$B \sim I = (A_B)\mathrm{w}_1 + (SN)\mathrm{w}_2. \qquad (7.3)$$

In Eq. 7.3, B is the behavior; I is the intention to perform behavior B; A_B is the attitude toward performing behavior B; SN is the subjective norm; and w_1 and w_2 are empirically determined weights.

Behavioral intentions are a function of the weighted sum of two variables. The first, A_B, is the actor's attitude toward performing the behavior in question under a given set of circumstances. As we saw in Chapter 6, a person's attitude toward a specific behavior is proposed to be a function of the perceived consequences of performing that behavior and of the person's evaluation of those consequences. Thus

$$A_B = \sum_{i=1}^{n} b_i e_i, \qquad (7.4)$$

where b is the belief that performing behavior B leads to consequence or outcome i; e is the person's evaluation of outcome i; and n is the number of beliefs the person holds about performing behavior B.[4]

---

4. All of a person's salient beliefs about performing the behavior in question determine his attitude toward the behavior. The terms "consequences" and "outcomes" in this context are generic terms referring to any belief about the behavior, including its perceived consequences, effort to perform the behavior, cost, and other attributes.

The parallel between A_B and the first component in Dulany's theory is apparent. Whereas Dulany's first component dealt with the subject's belief that a given behavior led to some specified reinforcing event, Fishbein has generalized this notion to all of the subject's beliefs about performing the act. Consistent with the expectancy-value theory of attitudes, this generalization suggested that the first component of Dulany's theory could be viewed as an attitude. In contrast to a traditional attitudinal approach, however, the attitude in question is the person's attitude toward performing a given behavior rather than his attitude toward the object or target of the behavior.

The second or normative component of the theory, SN, deals with the influence of the social environment on behavior. The subjective norm is the person's perception that most people who are important to him think he should or should not perform the behavior in question. According to the theory, the general subjective norm is determined by the perceived expectations of specific referent individuals or groups, and by the person's motivation to comply with those expectations. This formulation is presented symbolically in Eq. 7.5,

$$SN = \sum_{i=1}^{n} b_i m_i, \tag{7.5}$$

where b_i is the normative belief (i.e., the person's belief that reference group or individual i thinks he should or should not perform behavior B); m_i is the motivation to comply with referent i; and n is the number of relevant referents. Of course, the potential reference groups or individuals whose expectations are perceived to be relevant will vary with the behavioral situation. In some instances the expectations of a person's family or friends may be most relevant, but in others it may be the expectations of his supervisors or the society at large which are most influential. Frequently, the expectations of more than one reference group will have to be considered. Then, of course, it is also necessary to measure the individual's motivation to comply with each of the relevant reference groups. According to Eq. 7.5, the $b \times m$ products are computed for each relevant reference group and summed. This sum is viewed as equivalent to a "generalized normative belief," i.e., the subjective norm (SN).

The parallel between SN and Dulany's second component is again apparent. In both cases, this component refers to perceived pressures to perform a given behavior and the subject's motivation to comply with those pressures. Although Dulany did not specify any particular referent for his second component, Fishbein interpreted this component in Dulany's theory as representing perceived expectations of the experimenter and the subject's motivation to comply with those expectations. Again, he generalized this notion by defining an overall subjective norm which includes all relevant reference groups and individuals.

The two major determinants, then, of behavioral intentions are the attitude toward the behavior and the subjective norm. As indicated in Eq. 7.3, the attitudinal and the normative components are given empirical weights in the prediction equation, proportional to their relative importance in the prediction of behavioral intentions. These empirical weights (w_1 and w_2) are expected to vary with the kind of behavior that is being predicted, with the conditions under which the behavior is to be performed, and with the person who is to perform the behavior. For some behaviors, normative considerations (expectations of friends, family, etc.) may be more important in determining behavioral intentions than are attitudinal considerations (the expected outcomes of the act). For other behaviors, the reverse may be true. In a similar fashion we may expect that the relative importance of the two components will be influenced by situational variables, such as the behavior's observability, and by personal characteristics and preferences.

Ideally, the weights for the attitudinal and normative components would be available for each individual with respect to each behavior in a given situation. Since adequate estimates of this kind are not presently available, the practice has been to use multiple regression techniques, and standardized regression coefficients have served as estimates of the weights for the theory's components. The present version of the theory, then, is a multiple regression equation where there are two predictors, A_B and SN, and the criterion is I, the behavioral intention under consideration.

It is worth noting that the theory can deal with behavioral intentions at any level of specificity. The criterion might be a general intention to cooperate or to be gregarious, or it might be a very specific intention to, say, have a drink with Bill in Henry's Pub at 5 p.m. this afternoon. Once the intentional criterion has been selected, however, it is important to make sure that measures of the attitudinal and normative components are calibrated at the same level of specificity. In the case of the specific intention, for example, the attitude toward "having a drink with Bill in Henry's Pub at 5 p.m. this afternoon" would have to be measured, and the appropriate subjective norm would be the subject's belief that most people who are important to him think "I should (or should not) have a drink with Bill in Henry's Pub at 5 p.m. this afternoon." With respect to the global intention to be cooperative, the subject's attitude and subjective norm with respect to "being cooperative" would have to be measured. Clearly, the ability of the model to predict behavioral intentions depends in large part on the degree of correspondence between the levels of specificity associated with the intention on the one hand and the two components of the model on the other.

The formation of the theory's attitudinal and normative components has to some extent been discussed in previous chapters. The nature of attitudes and the factors influencing attitude formation were reviewed in Chapter 6, where we also showed that attitude toward a behavior is determined by the person's salient beliefs about the behavior's consequences and his evaluation of those consequences. Although we have not encountered subjective norms or *normative* beliefs before, we discussed in Chapter 5 the formation of beliefs in general. It may be argued that the processes underlying belief formation discussed in that chapter are also relevant for the formation of normative beliefs. This argument implies that normative beliefs can be formed in two ways. First, a given referent or some other individual may tell the person what the referent thinks he should do, and the person may or may not accept this information. Second, the person may observe some event or receive some information that allows him to make an inference about a given referent's expectations. Very little research, however, has dealt directly with the formation of normative beliefs. Moreover, our discussion thus far has not touched on the nature of motivation to comply or on the factors that influence this variable. It therefore seems appropriate to consider the normative component in greater detail.

Nature of the Normative Component

One important question concerns the necessity for introducing a normative component in addition to attitude toward the behavior. It can be argued that normative beliefs may be considered a proper part of A_B as conceptualized in Eq. 7.4. That is, some of the consequences of performing a given act are that the act may please or displease relevant reference individuals or groups, and that it may lead to reward or punishment from a given referent. Depending on the person's evaluation of these consequences, his attitude toward the behavior should become favorable or unfavorable. The present theory is actually not incompatible with this view. In fact, beliefs of this type may be part of the person's salient beliefs about performing the behavior and may thus influence the first component in the model, i.e., the person's attitude toward performing the behavior.

Although it would be possible to reinterpret the normative component in terms of an expectancy-value formulation, the theory suggests that it is useful to maintain the distinction between beliefs about the consequences of performing a behavior and beliefs about expectations of relevant referents. Consider, for example, the normative belief that "my doctor thinks I should take medicine X." Clearly, a person can hold this belief without necessarily holding beliefs about the behavior, such as "taking medicine X will please my doctor" or "taking medicine X will lead to a reward from my doctor." Further, a given belief about a referent's reactions may have different effects on the attitudinal and normative components. Consider the belief that "buying Sugar Puffs will please my child." This belief, together with other salient beliefs about buying Sugar Puffs, may influence the attitude toward the behavior. At the same time, it may also be one of the factors leading to the inferential normative belief that "my child thinks I should buy Sugar Puffs." As we have seen in previous chapters, different processes underlie the formation of the attitude toward the behavior and of the normative belief. It follows that a given factor may have different effects on the attitudinal and the normative components of the theory. If one maintains the distinction between these two components, it becomes possible to gain a better understanding of the ways in which behavioral intentions are formed.

Moreover, this distinction emphasizes the importance of two basic social psychological concepts that have traditionally been treated independently. Psychologists and sociologists interested in individual behavior have frequently made use of the attitude concept whereas theorists dealing with groups and societies have often relied on the concept of social norm. By including an attitudinal and a normative component, the present theory emphasizes the importance of both concepts and provides a bridge between the two approaches to the study of human behavior.

We have seen above that normative beliefs may be formed as the result of an inference process. The argument was that if a person believes that a given referent would be pleased if he performed the behavior, the person may infer that the referent thinks he should perform the behavior. In Chapter 5 we discussed a number of different inference processes, and some of these processes may also be operative in the formation of normative beliefs. Some normative beliefs are perhaps formed as a result of syllogistic reasoning. For example, a person may believe that a given referent thinks he should cooperate (minor premise). He may further believe that behavior X is a form of cooperation (major premise) and may thus conclude that the referent thinks he should perform behavior X. The formation of other normative beliefs may involve an attribution process along the lines of Bayes's theorem. Consider a person who is given $5 by referent R for performing behavior X. Depending on the diagnostic value of this item of information, the person may or may not infer that referent R thinks he should perform behavior X. The normative belief that "R thinks I should perform behavior X" will be formed only if the conditional probability of receiving $5 from R, given that R thinks the person should perform behavior X, is perceived to be greater than the conditional probability of receiving $5 from R, given that R thinks the person should not perform behavior X. A similar attribution process may result when the person observes referent R perform behavior X.

Finally, normative beliefs may perhaps also be inferred from the referent's perceived attitude toward performing a given behavior. If the referent is perceived to have a favorable attitude toward performing the behavior, or more specifically, toward the person's performing the behavior, the normative belief may be formed that the referent thinks the person should perform the behavior in question.[5]

So far we have considered beliefs about the normative expectations of specific referent groups or of a generalized other. However, it is possible to conceive of a different interpretation of Dulany's (1968) behavioral hypothesis (BH). Specifically, BH could be viewed as a *personal* normative belief, i.e., as the person's own belief about what he should or ought to do. Indeed, in his original formulation, Fishbein (1967b) included a component dealing with personal normative beliefs. However, empirical findings have repeatedly indicated that a subject's report of his personal normative belief serves mainly as an alternative measure of his behavioral intention. Inclusion of personal normative beliefs in the theory therefore tended to confound, rather than clarify, the problem of understanding

---

5. In terms of a Bayesian analysis, the referent's perceived attitude toward performing a behavior has high diagnostic value in terms of the corresponding normative belief.

the determinants of behavioral intentions. For this reason, personal normative beliefs have been deleted from the present version of the theory.[6]

Motivation to comply. Turning to the last, and perhaps least understood, term in the theory, we can at the present time make only some tentative suggestions concerning the nature and determinants of motivation to comply. One problem is that this concept can be interpreted in different ways. In Eq. 7.5, m_i was defined as the respondent's general motivation to comply with referent i, regardless of the referent's particular demands. Alternatively, m_i could refer to the person's motivation to comply with referent i concerning the particular behavior or behavioral domain under consideration. When the measure of motivation to comply is specific to the behavior in question, m plays a role similar to the weight w_2, which is also behavior-specific. On both theoretical and empirical grounds it appears that motivation to comply is best conceived as the person's general tendency to accept the directives of a given reference group or individual.

As to the factors influencing motivation to comply, French and Raven's (1959) discussion of the bases of social power may be of relevance in this context. It stands to reason that a person's motivation to comply with a given referent would increase with that referent's power over the person. Thus motivation to comply may increase with the referent's power to reward or punish the person, with the person's liking for the referent, with the referent's perceived expertise, and with the extent to which it is legitimate for the referent to make demands of the person.

A person's motivation to comply with various reference groups may also be related to certain personality characteristics, such as his need for approval or affiliation, his self-esteem, or authoritarianism. However, previous work on personality variables of this kind in various areas of social psychology leads us to be rather pessimistic about the utility of this approach.

Perhaps of greater promise is an approach suggesting that motivation to comply can be interpreted as the person's *intention* to comply with the referent in question. The determinants of this intention are the same determinants discussed earlier with respect to any behavioral intention, and the following equation can be written to express these notions.

$$m \sim I_c = (A_c)w_1 + (SN_c)w_2. \qquad (7.6)$$

---

6. Although there is a clear conceptual distinction between personal normative beliefs and behavioral intentions, the high relation between obtained measures of these variables suggests that it may be difficult to develop a satisfactory operationalization of personal normative beliefs. Recently, Schwartz and Tessler (1972) have used a measure of personal normative beliefs that emphasizes moral considerations. Although this measure was highly related to intention, it did not account for all the variance in the criterion.

In this equation, m is the motivation to comply with referent R; I_c is the intention to comply with referent R; A_c is the attitude toward complying with referent R; and SN_c is the subjective norm concerning compliance with referent R.

Other Factors Influencing Intentions

According to Fishbein's theory, then, a person's intention to perform any behavior is determined by his attitude toward performing the behavior (A_B) and by his subjective norm (SN). The theory suggests that additional variables external to the model can influence intentions only indirectly by influencing either of the two components or their relative weights. A given variable will thus have an effect on intentions if it meets one or more of the following conditions. (1) It influences the attitudinal component, and that component carries a significant amount of weight in determining the intention. (2) It influences the normative component, and that component carries a significant amount of weight in determining the intention. (3) It influences the relative weights of the two components. Even though a given variable may affect one of the two components, it will not necessarily influence intention unless that component carries a significant weight in determining the intention.

For example, one variable external to the model that has received special attention is the subject's attitude toward the target object or target person. As we noted earlier, the usual assumption is that subjects will intend to perform positive behaviors with respect to persons and objects they like, and to perform negative behaviors with respect to persons and objects they dislike. Like any other variable, however, an individual's attitude toward some person or group of people (e.g., his attitude toward blacks) may be related neither to the attitudinal nor to the normative component, and it will then also be unrelated to his intentions with respect to the person or group. Furthermore, even when a traditional measure of attitude is correlated with one of the two components, it will still be unrelated to intention if that component carries little or no weight in the determination of the behavioral intentions in question.

There is no necessary relation between traditional measures of attitude toward an object and the model's predictors. For example, the perceived consequences of performing a certain behavior toward a liked person may, in some situations, differ from those of performing the same behavior toward a disliked person. In such a situation the attitude toward the person is expected to be related to A_B, the attitude toward the behavior, and hence to influence intention if A_B carries a significant weight in the prediction equation. In other situations a given behavior will be perceived to lead to the same consequences, irrespective of the actor's liking for the stimulus person. No influence of liking on A_B or on intention would be expected. Similarly, there are situations in which one is expected to behave differently toward a liked than toward a disliked person, whereas in others, subjective norms regarding behavior toward liked and disliked persons are identical. In the former case, some relation between attitude and intention might be obtained because of the influence of liking on subjective norm. Such a relation is unlikely in the latter case.

The theory thus can provide an explanation for the lack of consistent relations between traditional measures of attitude and specific behavioral intentions. The considerations above indicate that traditional attitude measures (e.g., toward people, groups, institutions) will be related to intentions under some conditions but not under others. Like any other variable external to the theory, the effects of attitudes on intentions can be understood only in terms of their influence on the two components (and their weights), which, according to the theory, are the immediate antecedents of behavioral intentions. Let us now consider some of the research that has been conducted in an attempt to find empirical support for the theory.

Empirical Support

Over the last few years, Fishbein and his associates have conducted a number of investigations based on the intentional model described above (Fishbein, 1966; Ajzen and Fishbein, 1969, 1970, 1972; Fishbein *et al.*, 1970; Ajzen, 1971b; Hornik, 1970; DeVries and Ajzen, 1971; A. R. Carlson, 1968; McArdle, 1972; Darroch, 1971; Glassman, 1971; Jaccard and Davidson, 1972). A review of some of this research can be found in Ajzen and Fishbein (1973). These studies have attempted to predict various intentions, including intentions to cooperate or compete, to buy certain products, to sign up for an alcoholic treatment program, to perform various leisure-time activities, to use certain types of contraceptives, to cheat on an exam, and to engage in premarital sexual intercourse.[7]

Predicting behavioral intentions. In Chapter 6 we described how attitudes toward a behavior can be measured and gave Jaccard and Davidson's (1972) study of women's attitudes toward using birth control pills as an example. Subjects were asked to rate the concept "using birth control pills" on a set of evaluative semantic differential scales. This measure of attitude was found to be highly related to the subjects' beliefs about the consequences of using birth control pills and their evaluations of those consequences. These were the 15 beliefs that had been elicited most frequently in interviews with an independent sample of women. In the same interviews, the respondents were also asked questions designed to elicit referents relevant to the use of birth control pills. For example, they were asked where they would go for more information about birth control pills and whether there were any particular individuals or groups who would approve or disapprove if they used birth control pills. The 12 most frequently mentioned referents were included in the questionnaire used in the subsequent study; among them were

---

7. Most of these studies were conducted before the development of the notion of a general subjective norm. The investigators therefore assessed the normative component by measuring normative belief (and motivation to comply) with respect to one or more specific referents.

mother, father, husband/boyfriend, Zero Population Growth, women's magazines, and "the religion I was brought up in." Normative beliefs concerning each referent were assessed by a statement, such as:

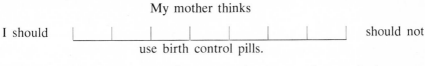

My mother thinks

I should |___|___|___|___|___|___|___| should not

use birth control pills.

Motivation to comply with each referent was also measured on a single seven-point scale, such as:

In general

I want to |___|___|___|___|___|___|___| I want not to

do what my mother thinks I should do.

These two measures were scored from $+3$ (I should, I want to) to -3 (I should not, I want not to) and multiplied by each other. The resulting products for the 12 referents were summed to provide a measure of the normative component ($\Sigma\ b_i m_i$). Finally, subjects also indicated their intentions to use birth control pills on the following seven-point scale:

I intend to use birth control pills.

probable |___|___|___|___|___|___|___| improbable

The investigators performed a multiple regression analysis and found a multiple correlation of .835 for the prediction of intention to use birth control pills from the attitudinal and normative components of the theory.

This high correlation is representative of the results obtained in most investigations. For example, two experiments (Ajzen and Fishbein, 1970; Ajzen, 1971b) have measured subjects' intentions to choose cooperative or competitive strategies in a two-person experimental game known as the Prisoner's Dilemma. In this game the two players make repeated choices between two alternatives (X and Y) which are assumed to serve the motives of cooperation and competition, respectively. The combined choices of the two players determine the payoff to each. A typical payoff matrix for a Prisoner's Dilemma game is as follows:

		Your partner	
		X	Y
You	X	$+6, +6$	$-8, +8$
	Y	$+8, -8$	$-2, -2$

The first entry in each cell of the matrix is the payoff to the subject, and the second is the payoff to his partner. Thus, if both players cooperate (i.e., both select X on a given trial), both gain 6 points; if both compete (i.e., both select Y), both lose 2 points; if one cooperates and the other competes, the person who cooperates loses 8 points, and the person who competes gains 8 points.

In both studies, measures were obtained of the subject's intention to choose X and Y, his attitude toward choosing X and Y, his belief that his partner thought he should choose X and Y, and his motivation to comply with his partner. Three games with different payoff matrices were played in the two experiments. The multiple correlations for predicting intentions from the attitudinal and normative components of the theory were .888, .899, and .818 for the three Prisoner's Dilemma games.

In another study, McArdle (1972) assessed intentions of alcoholics to sign up for the alcoholic treatment unit (ATU) in a V.A. Hospital. She also obtained measures of her subjects' attitudes toward "signing up for the ATU," their normative beliefs that their wife/ex-wife, doctor, parents, minister/priest, and close friends thought they should or should not sign up for the ATU, and their motivation to comply with each of these five referents. An index of subjective norms was again obtained by summing over the five $b_i m_i$ products. The multiple correlation of A_B and $\Sigma\, b_i m_i$ on intentions was found to be .740.

The evidence thus strongly supports the present theory by showing that the two predictors, A_B and SN, offer high multiple correlations with behavioral intentions. The relevant results obtained in 13 studies are shown in Table 7.4, along with the intentions that were predicted. Note that the multiple correlations are generally very high; the average correlation over all studies is .746.

Table 7.4 Multiple Correlation Coefficients for the Prediction of Intentions to Perform Various Behaviors

Study	Intention	Multiple correlation
Fishbein (1966)	Engage in premarital sexual intercourse.	.849
Carlson (1968)	Perform 30 behaviors toward an African Negro.	.839 *
Ajzen and Fishbein (1969)	Perform 8 leisure-time activities.	.766 *
Fishbein et al. (1970)	Send communications to coworkers.	.704
	Follow the instructions of coworkers.	.608
Hornik (1970)	Maintain missiles in an experimental game.	.806
Ajzen and Fishbein (1970)	Choose alternative X or Y in 2 PD games.	.714
Ajzen (1971b)	Choose alternative X or Y in PD game.	.716 *
DeVries and Ajzen (1971)	Cheat in college. Copy from other students' test papers. Allow other students to copy from one's own test paper.	.869 * .818 .566
Darroch (1971)	Sign 2 interracial photographic releases.	.647
Ajzen and Fishbein (1972)	Perform 4 behaviors involving risk.	.793 *
Jaccard and Davidson (1972)	Use birth control pills.	.836
McArdle (1972)	Sign up for alcoholic treatment unit.	.740
Glassman (1971)	Buy 8 products.	.665 *

* Average multiple correlation coefficients.

Relative weights of attitudinal and normative components. Perhaps of greater importance than the high multiple correlations are the relative weights of the two components in the prediction of behavioral intentions. According to the theory, these weights should vary with the behavior, with the situation, and with individual differences between actors. Over all studies conducted and across conditions within them, there is a slight tendency for the attitudinal component to take on a somewhat greater weight than does the normative component. However, such a comparison is theoretically meaningless. Different behaviors, different situations, and different individuals have to be compared.

The relative weights of the two components are estimated by standardized regression coefficients obtained in the multiple regression analyses. These coefficients represent empirical estimates of optimal weights for a given group of subjects and thus provide "objective" indices of the relative importance of the two components. As we noted in Chapter 5, however, such regression weights need not correspond to the subject's own judgment of the relative importance of the two components.

Table 7.5 Correlations, Regression Coefficients, and Multiple Correlations of A_B and $\Sigma b_i m_i$ on Intentions to Engage in Premarital Sexual Intercourse (From Fishbein, 1966)

	Correlation coefficients		Regression coefficients		Multiple correlation
Subjects	A_B	$\Sigma b_i m_i$	w_1	w_2	
Males	.518 *	.843 †	−.148	.947 †	.850 †
Females	.918 †	.759 †	.757 †	.232 *	.935 †

* $p < .05$
† $p < .01$

Fishbein (1966) found evidence for individual differences in regression weights in a study concerned with intentions to engage in premarital sexual intercourse (PSI) among undergraduates. At the beginning of the semester, subjects rated their intentions to "engage in PSI this semester" on a seven-point bipolar scale. In addition, measures were obtained of the subjects' attitudes toward "engaging in PSI this semester" and of their normative beliefs that their families and their closest friends thought they should engage in PSI this semester. The results of the study are presented in Table 7.5. Both components correlated significantly with intentions, and the multiple correlations were also high and significant for both male and female subjects. The relative weights of the two components differed, however, for the two sexes. For female subjects, the standardized regression coefficients in the prediction of intentions were .757 ($p < .01$) for the attitudinal component and .232 ($p < .05$) for the normative component. The strength of the regression weights was reversed for the male sample: The attitudinal component had a regression weight of $-.148$ (nonsignificant), and the regression coefficient of the normative component was $.947$ ($p < .01$). Thus it appears that attitudinal considerations of engaging in premarital sexual behavior were more important than normative considerations for female students. Subjective norms, however, were the primary determinants of behavioral intentions for males.

Carlson (1968) observed differences in regression weights as a function of the kind of behavior under consideration. He attempted to predict responses to a 30-item form of Triandis's (1964) behavioral differential. Using Triandis's standard procedure, Carlson first asked his female subjects to indicate their intentions to perform 30 different behaviors with respect to a "21-year-old, male, African Negro student." In addition, the subjects supplied measures of their attitudes toward performing each of these behaviors with respect to the target person, their beliefs that they should or should not engage in each of the behaviors with respect to the target person,[8] and their motivation to do what they thought they should do.

As in the work by Triandis, a factor analysis of the 30 behavioral intentions yielded five major factors that were labeled "formal social acceptance, informal social acceptance, marital acceptance, cooperation, and subordination-superordination." The loadings of the 30 intentions on these factors were found to correlate significantly with the regression coefficients of the attitudinal and normative components for each of the behaviors. For example, the regression coefficients of the normative component correlated .60 with the loadings of the behavioral intentions on the marital acceptance factor. That is, the more a given behavior involved marital acceptance, the greater was the importance of normative considerations. Similarly, there was a positive correlation ($r = .54$) between the regression weights of the attitudinal component and the formal social acceptance factor. The more a behavior involved formal social acceptance, the greater became the importance of attitudinal considerations.

Glassman (1971) obtained evidence that the weights of the attitudinal and normative components varied with the target of the intention under consideration. Women customers at a supermarket were asked to indicate their intentions to buy two different named brands in each of four product classes (coffee, detergents, potato chips, and gasoline). In addition, measures were obtained of their attitudes toward buying each of the eight brands, their normative beliefs that each of five referents (mother, friends, husband, consumer reports, advertising) thought they should buy each of the eight brands, and their motivation to comply with each of the five referents. Although attitudinal considerations were the more important determinants of all eight buying intentions, normative considerations significantly influenced intentions to buy two kinds of products, coffee and gasoline. With respect to these two targets, the perceived expectations of the women's husbands were of particular importance.

---

8. Personal, rather than social, normative beliefs were used in this study.

Situational characteristics can also be shown to influence the relative weights of the attitudinal and normative components. For example, these weights may take on different values in cooperative and competitive situations. It stands to reason that perceived expectations of others with whom a person is trying to cooperate will be more important than expectations of others with whom he competes. Conversely, considerations of an act's consequences (i.e., attitudinal considerations) should carry a greater weight under competition than under cooperation. These expectations were borne out in the studies by Ajzen and Fishbein (1970) and Ajzen (1971b) using the Prisoner's Dilemma game. In the first study, two subjects played two games with different payoff matrices under one of three motivational orientations: cooperation, individualism, or competition. In the cooperative condition the subjects were instructed to consider themselves partners; in the competitive condition they were told to do better than the other person; players in the individualistic condition were told to have no interest whatever in the fate of the other person. The regression coefficients of the attitudinal and normative components on behavioral intentions showed the expected patterns. Under cooperation, the regression coefficients of the normative component were .707 ($p < .01$) and .573 ($p < .01$) in the two games played. The corresponding weights of the attitudinal component were .229 and .239 (both nonsignificant). In the competitive conditions, the regression coefficients were .327 ($p < .01$) and .298 ($p < .01$) for the normative component and .691 ($p < .01$) and .669 ($p < .01$) for the attitudinal component. Clearly, subjective norms were more important under cooperation, and attitude toward the behavior was more important under competition. There were no appreciable differences between the weights of the components in the individualistic conditions. The results for one of the two Prisoner's Dilemma games played in this study are summarized in Table 7.6.

Table 7.6 Correlations, Regression Coefficients, and Multiple Correlations of A_B and $b_i m_i$ on Intentions to Choose the Cooperative Alternative in a Prisoner's Dilemma Game (Adapted from Ajzen and Fishbein, 1970)

Condition	Correlation Coefficients		Regression Coefficients		Multiple correlation
	A_B	$b_i m_i$ ‡	w_1	w_2	
Cooperation	.370 *	.752 †	.229	.707 †	.785 †
Individualism	.710 †	.780 †	.353 *	.552 †	.852 †
Competition	.883 †	.733 †	.691 †	.327 †	.922 †

* $p < .05$
† $p < .01$
‡ Only the perceived expectations of the other player were considered.

These findings were corroborated in an experiment where a different Prisoner's Dilemma game was played either under cooperative or competitive instructions (Ajzen, 1971b). The regression coefficient of the normative component was

.768 ($p < .01$) under cooperation but only .225 (not significant) under competition. The attitudinal component carried a significant ($p < .01$) regression weight under competition ($w_1 = .541$) but not under cooperation ($w_2 = .112$).

In conclusion, there is considerable evidence that behavioral intentions are predictable from the theory's attitudinal and normative components. Furthermore, the relative importance of these two components in the prediction of intentions varies with the type of behavior under consideration, with the situation in which the behavior is to be performed, with the target, and with individual differences between actors.

Determinants of the attitudinal and normative components. The determinants of beliefs and attitudes were considered in previous chapters. We have reviewed considerable evidence supporting the notion that attitudes are a function of beliefs about the attitude object's attributes multiplied by evaluations of those attributes. In Chapter 6 we showed that this expectancy-value formulation also held with respect to attitude toward performing a behavior. Thus A_B, the attitudinal component, is determined by beliefs about the consequences of performing the behavior in question and the person's evaluation of those consequences. Many of the studies discussed above have provided additional evidence for this notion (e.g., Fishbein, 1966; Ajzen and Fishbein, 1970, 1972; McArdle, 1972; Glassman and Fishbein, 1973; Jaccard and Davidson, 1972).

According to our theory, subjective norms are determined by normative beliefs and motivation to comply (that is, $SN = \Sigma\ b_i m_i$). Empirical evidence for the relation between SN and $\Sigma\ b_i m_i$ has been reported by King and Jaccard, (1973) and Glassman and Birchmore (1974). These studies obtained measures of subjective norms on the following scale.

Most people who are important to me think

I should | | | | | | | | I should not

perform behavior X.

This measure was correlated with $\Sigma\ b_i m_i$; correlations ranging from .625 to .910 were obtained.

Most studies conducted to date have not used measures of subjective norms (SN) but have measured normative belief and motivation to comply with one or more referents. Although the research on belief formation discussed in Chapter 5 is relevant for an understanding of the factors that influence the formation of normative beliefs, relatively little research has dealt directly with the determinants of such beliefs. As we noted earlier, normative beliefs are likely to be the product of certain inference processes. One possibility mentioned was that normative beliefs are inferred in part on the basis of beliefs about the referent's attitude toward the behavior in question.

Ajzen and Fishbein (1972) tested this notion by using four hypothetical decision situations involving a certain amount of risk. One situation, for example, was described as follows:

Over the last few years you have done some part-time work and you have saved the amount of $1,000. You would now like to invest this money profitably. It has come to your attention that a plot of real estate in a developing residential area is available for the amount of money in your possession. If a planned building project proves successful, the plot of land might double its present value. However, if the project fails, you would lose your entire investment.

The remaining three situations involved undergoing a delicate medical operation, renting your house to a Negro family, and undergoing a kidney transplant for your brother. An attempt was made to manipulate normative beliefs by telling the subject that a given referent believed there was either a high (.70) or a low (.30) probability that the risky behavior would lead to success. That is, the referents (close family and friends) were said to have low or high confidence in the risky behavior's chances of success. A direct measure of the referent's perceived attitude toward the behavior was obtained using four evaluative semantic differential scales. In addition, a measure of normative beliefs was taken. Over the four hypothetical situations, the average correlation between normative beliefs and perceived attitude of the referent was .635. Thus there is some empirical evidence that normative beliefs are related to the subject's perception of the referent's attitude toward the behavior in question. However, the correlations between the referents' perceived attitudes and normative beliefs varied across the four situations (ranging from .354 to .773). Such variations should not be surprising since the magnitude of this correlation should be related to the perceived attitudes' diagnostic value, which may differ from situation to situation.

Also in support of the notion that normative beliefs may be inferred from the referent's perceived attitude, the experimental manipulation of the referent's estimate that the risky behavior would lead to success (.70 versus .30) had a significant influence on both variables. When the subject was told that the referent's estimate of success was high, he inferred that the referent had a favorable attitude toward the risky behavior and that the referent thought he should engage in the risky behavior. The measures of normative beliefs and perceived attitudes were significantly lower when the referent was said to have a low estimate of success. Clearly, then, the perceived attitude of a relevant referent exerts a significant influence on normative beliefs.

It has been argued that motivation to comply with the referent's expectations may be related, among other things, to the referent's power over the actor. Limited support comes from Ajzen's (1971b) study using the Prisoner's Dilemma game. In this study, a measure was obtained of the subject's desire to please his partner. It is possible to argue that this measure is an indication of the other person's referent power (i.e., the subject's attitude toward the referent; cf. French and Raven, 1959). Consistent with expectations, the correlation of this measure with motivation to comply was found to be .661 ($p < .01$).

Effects of "external" variables. According to the theory, any variable other than A_B or *SN* can influence behavioral intentions only indirectly. Thus, "external" factors, such as demographic or personality characteristics of the actor, the nature of the particular behavior under investigation, or situational variables can affect intentions only if they influence the attitudinal or normative components, or their relative weights.

Many of the studies previously discussed have provided support for this prediction. The conclusion emerging from them is that any variable found to be related to behavioral intentions is also related to at least one of the two predictors in the theory. External variables unrelated to intentions are also unrelated to either the attitudinal or normative component. Moreover, whenever an external variable is related to intentions, this relation is considerably attenuated when A_B and SN are statistically held constant. For example, Ajzen and Fishbein (1970) studied the effects of the players' authoritarianism and sex on strategy choices in the Prisoner's Dilemma. Further, two games differing in their payoff matrices were played under one of three motivational orientations: cooperation, competition, and individualism. The results indicated that intentions were affected significantly by the payoff matrix and by motivational orientation. There were no significant relations between intentions and either sex or authoritarianism. Examination of findings with respect to normative beliefs and attitude toward the act showed the same pattern: significant effects of payoff matrix and motivational orientation; no significant effects of sex and authoritarianism on either of the theory's two predictors. A statistical technique known as analysis of covariance (in which attitude toward the behavior and normative beliefs were held constant) reduced the effect of the payoff matrix on intentions to nonsignificance. The effect of motivational orientation, though significant at the .05 level, was greatly attenuated.

These results demonstrate the intervening role played by the theory's two components. The effects of external variables on behavioral intentions seem to have been mediated by attitudinal and normative considerations. Similar findings emerged in an experiment by Ajzen and Fishbein (1974), in which three-person groups were to level a triangle board. This task was facilitated by spirit levels mounted on top of the triangle board in front of each group member. Two experimental conditions were created by varying the alignment of the spirit levels and thus affecting the information available to the group members. These variations had strong effects on behavioral intentions. In one condition, subjects intended to send an approximately equal number of communications to the other two group members, and each subject intended to comply with approximately the same proportion of the instructions he received from each group member. In the second condition, however, intentions were to send considerably more communications to one group member and to comply more with the other. Exactly the same pattern of results was observed with respect to the attitudinal and normative components. Attitudes toward the behavior and subjective norm were affected by the experimental manipulation in the same way as were intentions, indicating again that the theory's two components tend to mediate the effects of external variables, in this case a situational variable.

We have noted that a person's attitude toward some object (A_o) can be treated like any other variable external to the theory. That is, A_o is expected to predict intentions only to the extent that it is related to at least one of the theory's two components, and even then only if that component carries a significant weight in the regression equation.

Evidence for this claim has been obtained in several investigations. In the two studies employing the Prisoner's Dilemma game (Ajzen and Fishbein, 1970; Ajzen, 1971b), each subject was asked to evaluate his partner on four evaluative semantic differential scales. As expected, the correlations of this general measure of attitude toward the other player with intentions to cooperate with him (i.e., choose alternative X) were low and not always significant. In the first study, these correlations were .237 $(p < .05)$ and .091 (not significant) in the two Prisoner's Dilemma games played; in the second study, the correlation was .242 $(p < .05)$.

The role of the attitudinal and normative components in mediating these effects was explored by computing partial correlations between A_o and intentions, holding A_B and SN constant. Table 7.7 shows that whenever attitude toward the other player was correlated with intentions, it also correlated with the attitudinal and normative components of the theory. When these two components were held constant, the partial correlations between A_o and intentions were reduced to non-significance.

Table 7.7 Effects of Attitudes toward an Object (A_o) on Intentions (Adapted from Ajzen and Fishbein, 1973)

Study		Product-moment correlations			Partial correlations
		$A_o - I$	$A_o - A_B$	$A_o - b_i m_i$ ‡	$A_o - I$ §
Ajzen and Fishbein	Game 1	.237 *	.354 †	.262 *	−.126
(1970)	Game 2	.091	.239 *	.015	−.197
Ajzen (1971b)		.242 *	.257 *	.241 *	.092

* $p < .05$
† $p < .01$
‡ Only one referent was considered
§ A_B and $b_i m_i$ are held constant

Similar results were found in the triangle board study (Ajzen and Fishbein, 1974), in which the subject's attitudes toward his two coworkers were correlated with his intentions to send communications to them and to follow instructions from them. Although A_o was unrelated to intentions to communicate $(r = -.003)$, there was a low but significant correlation $(r = .279)$ with intentions to follow instructions. This correlation was again reduced to nonsignificance when the attitudinal and normative components were held constant. The relation between A_o and intentions to follow instructions seems to have been mediated by the relatively high correlation ($r = .418$, $p < .01$) between this general attitude toward the coworkers and the attitude toward following their instructions (A_B).

Although holding A_B and SN constant does not always completely eliminate the correlation between A_o and intentions (e.g., Darroch, 1971; Hornik, 1970), this correlation is always greatly attenuated. For example, Hornik measured subjects' attitudes toward their opponents in a two-person war game in which subjects could cooperate or compete by reducing or increasing the number of missiles they held. Hornik created three experimental conditions by varying the opponent's cooperative or competitive strategy. Correlations between attitudes toward the opponent and intentions to maintain a given number of missiles were found to be high and significant in two of the three conditions ($r = .771$, $.763$, and $-.085$, respectively). In the first two conditions high correlations were also found between A_o and the attitudinal and normative components of the theory. Holding these two components constant reduced the correlation between A_o and I to nonsignificance in the first condition ($r = .294$) and greatly attenuated it in the second condition ($r = .444$; $p < .05$).

Generally speaking, then, the results of several investigations indicate that the inconsistent attitude-intention relationship can largely be attributed to variations in the degree to which the general attitude measure (A_o) is related to the two determinants of intentions (A_B and SN).

VARIATIONS IN ELEMENTS OF INTENTIONS

The discussion above provides empirical evidence in support of Fishbein's model for the prediction of intentions. Most other research in this area has studied the effects of various factors on intentions by manipulating one or more of the four elements constituting the intention: behavior, target, situation, and time. Variations in any of these elements change the nature of the intention and are thus likely to influence responses. Other things being constant, a person may intend to perform one behavior but not another. Of greater interest, characteristics of the target may influence intentions. For example, a person may be willing to marry someone of his own but not of a different religion, of his own but not of a different race, etc. Similarly, variations in the situations are likely to influence intentions. A person may intend to drink iced tea on a hot day but not on a cold day, or to drink wine with dinner but not with breakfast. Finally, time may be an important determinant of intentions. Most people intend to go to sleep at night and not in the morning, to go to church on Sunday but not during the week, etc. Much of the research on factors influencing intentions has dealt with characteristics of the target; less attention has been paid to situational and behavioral variations; and the time dimension has usually not been considered. In addition, investigators have examined effects of individual differences among subjects (such as their sex, religiosity, and prejudice), and some studies have been concerned with the possible influence of social norms on intentions.

Effects of Target and Behavior

Although a distinction has been made between cognition, affect, and conation, the "conative component of attitude" had been submitted to little empirical investigation until the pioneering work of Triandis and his associates. We noted early in this chapter that Triandis (1964) measured a large set of intentions with respect to 34 different stimulus persons. In this fashion it was possible to systematically investigate the effects of the stimulus person's characteristics and of the type of behavior on the subjects' intentions. Specifically, Triandis varied the stimulus person in terms of race (Negro–white), sex (male–female), age (20–50 years), occupation (physician–soda fountain clerk), and religion (Protestant–Roman Catholic–Jewish). Although all possible combinations of the variables would require 48 stimulus persons ($2 \times 2 \times 2 \times 2 \times 3$), Triandis eliminated unlikely combinations that might antagonize subjects (e.g., Jewish Negroes, 20-year-old physicians). Each of the remaining 34 stimulus persons was rated on 64 behavioral intentions. These responses were factor-analyzed, and five factors were obtained (see Table 7.2).

Using an analysis of variance, Triandis found that the five stimulus characteristics had different effects on the five types of general intentions obtained in the factor analysis. Table 7.8 shows the percentage of variance accounted for by the five stimulus characteristics. The percentage of variance accounted for by a given stimulus factor (race, religion, etc.) may be viewed as an estimate of that factor's relative importance in determining subjects' responses. For example, although race accounted for 38 percent of the variance in intentions to show

Table 7.8 Relative Importance of Stimulus Characteristics for Five Types of Intention (Adapted from Triandis, 1964)

Stimulus characteristic	Formal social acceptance	Marital acceptance	Friendship acceptance	Social distance	Subordination-superordination
Age (A)	2.5 *	16.2	8.8	21.0	2.5
Sex (S)	—	17.9	51.0	—	—
Religion (Re)	4.4	1.4	4.4	10.0	5.4
Race (Ra)	38.4	23.6	3.3	—	—
Occupation (O)	37.8	—	—	—	10.2
A × S	—	8.2	3.1	5.3	—
A × Re	—	—	1.8	3.9	—
A × Ra	.9	7.9	3.0	7.9	—
S × Re	1.1	—	—	—	14.1
S × Ra	.6	9.2	—	—	—
Re × O	1.5	—	1.8	3.1	—

* Percent of variance accounted for by significant effects.

formal social acceptance and 24 percent of the variance in intentions to show marital acceptance, it accounted only for 3 percent of the variance in intentions to show friendship acceptance and for none of the variance in the remaining two intentional factors (social distance and subordination).

The results shown in Table 7.8 indicate that a subject's intentions are influenced by variations in the intention's target element, as well as by variations in its behavioral element. This finding supports our argument that different intentions represent different probability dimensions, and results obtained with respect to one intention will not necessarily hold with respect to some other intention.

Subsequent investigations by Triandis and his associates (Triandis, 1967; Triandis and Davis, 1965; Davis and Grobstein, 1966) have also shown that variations in the characteristics of the stimulus persons influence the five general intentions in different ways. Unfortunately, the results have not always been consistent. For example, in the study reported above, Triandis (1964) found that formal social acceptance was influenced most strongly by race, followed by occupation and religion; for marital acceptance race was found to be most important, followed by sex and age. In contrast, Davis and Grobstein (1966) found that formal social acceptance was most influenced by occupation, followed by religion and race, and that sex was more important than race in determining marital acceptance. For a review of studies using the behavioral differential to investigate the effects of target variations on different types of intentions, see Triandis (1967).

Race versus belief similarity. Triandis's interest in the effects of stimulus characteristics on intentions grew out of his work on the determinants of racial prejudice. Triandis and Triandis (1960) argued that previous research on prejudice had produced ambiguous results since the basis for discrimination was unclear. "When an American white subject indicates much social distance toward Negroes, it is difficult to know whether he rejects them because of their physical type or their probable lower class background. Or, to take another example, when an American shows social distance toward Irishmen, does he object to their nationality or to their probable religion (Roman Catholic)?" (Triandis and Triandis, 1965, p. 208) In order to answer these questions, Triandis and Triandis (1960) constructed 16 stimulus persons who varied in terms of *race* (black–white), *religion* (same as–different from subject's religion), *nationality* (high status: English, Swedish, French–low status: Portuguese, Italian, Greek), and *social class* (high status: physician, banker, civil engineer–low status: unskilled worker, coal miner, truck driver). All possible combinations of these characteristics formed the 16 stimulus persons in a $2 \times 2 \times 2 \times 2$ analysis-of-variance design. To give an example, one stimulus person was described as "Negro, different religion, Portuguese, physician," another as "Swedish, physician, white, same religion."

To measure prejudice with respect to each of these 16 stimulus persons, Triandis and Triandis developed a 15-item Thurstone scale, using intentional items such as "I would accept this person as an intimate friend," "I would accept this person as a neighbor," and "I would not permit this person's attendance of our universities." Subjects were asked to check the statements they agreed with, and a single "social distance" score was obtained. Thus, although the items on the questionnaire represent individual intentions, the dependent variable in the study can best be viewed as a measure of global intention or attitude.

An analysis of variance showed that global intentions toward the stimulus persons were influenced by all four characteristics. Race was found to be the most important factor, accounting for 77 percent of the variance in the dependent variable, followed by social class (17 percent), religion (5 percent), and nationality (1 percent). The interactions between these factors were not significant.[9]

In contrast to this conclusion that race is the most important determinant of prejudice, Rokeach's (1960) theory of dogmatism and prejudice led him to propose that "what appears at first glance to be discriminations among men on the basis of race or ethnic group may turn out upon closer analysis to be discriminations on the basis of belief congruence over specific issues" (Rokeach, Smith, and Evans, 1960, p. 135). To test this hypothesis, the investigators described stimulus persons as Negro or white and as taking a pro or con stand on eight issues, such as socialized medicine, communism, and desegregation. Descriptions of stimulus persons were presented in pairs, such as the following.

1. a) A white person who believes in God.
   b) A Negro who believes in God.

2. a) A white person who is for socialized medicine.
   b) A white person who is against socialized medicine.

3. a) A white person who is a communist.
   b) A Negro who is anti-communist.

Since the subject's stand on each issue was assessed at the beginning of the experiment, it was possible to classify these descriptions as dealing with a black or white person who agreed or disagreed with the subject. Each stimulus person was rated on a nine-point scale varying from "I *can't* see myself being friends with such a person" to "I can *very easily* see myself being friends with such a person." Although the design and analysis of the study make it difficult to draw unequivocal conclusions,[10] Rokeach, Smith, and Evans (1960) argued that the findings sup-

---

9. The reader will note the similarity of this study to research on impression formation. Stimulus characteristics replace trait descriptions, and the results are again consistent with a linear model in that they show no significant interaction effects.

10. The hypothesis of this study could have been tested in a simple 2 × 2 factorial design with main effects of race (white versus black) and belief similarity (similar versus different); the eight different issues could have been considered another factor in the design. In contrast to this simple analysis, Rokeach, Smith and Evans constructed 48 pairs of stimulus persons, computed differences between attitudes toward the members of each pair, and then counted the number of subjects who preferred one member over the other.

ported their hypothesis in showing that belief similarity was a more important determinant of "prejudice" than was race per se.

Responding to this study, Triandis (1961) took issue with the dependent measure of "prejudice" employed. He suggested that friendship choice involves only one level of social distance, and that a more appropriate measure of general prejudice (such as his own social distance scale, described above) would show the importance of race as a determinant of prejudice.[11] Using the same procedure as in the Triandis and Triandis (1960) study, he constructed 16 stimulus persons varying in terms of race (Negro–white), religion (same–different), occupation (bank manager–coal miner), and belief similarity (same–different philosophy of life). The 15-item social distance scale served again as a measure of attitude toward each stimulus person. The results of an analysis of variance showed that all four factors significantly influenced attitudes, and that the interactions were not significant. In support of Triandis's hypothesis, race was the most important determinant of prejudice (accounting for 59 percent of the variance), followed by occupation (18 percent), philosophy (16 percent), and religion (5 percent).

Rokeach (1961) criticized the study by Triandis and argued that the different results had nothing to do with the dependent measure of prejudice but could instead be attributed to differences in the manipulation of belief similarity. Whereas Rokeach and his associates had used specific belief items (such as belief in God), Triandis had varied stimulus persons in terms of same versus different philosophy of life, a general and rather vague concept.

Perhaps a more adequate manipulation of belief similarity was provided by Byrne and Wong (1962), who used Byrne's attraction paradigm (see Chapter 6) to construct a hypothetical stranger, who was described either as Negro or white, and who either agreed or disagreed with the subject on 26 opinion items. Attitudes toward the stranger were measured on Byrne's Interpersonal Judgment Scale. The two items measuring attraction showed a significant effect of belief similarity, as well as a significant interaction between belief similarity and race. No significant main effect of race was obtained. Byrne and Wong concluded that belief similarity is a more important determinant of prejudice than is race of the stimulus person.

Stein, Hardyck, and Smith (1965) tried to resolve the belief versus race controversy by using Byrne's procedure to manipulate belief similarity and by measuring "prejudice" in ways similar to both those of Rokeach, Smith, and Evans (1960) and Triandis (1961). Their teenage subjects were shown a questionnaire ostensibly filled out by a black or white person. The stranger's similarity to the subject was manipulated by varying his responses to 25 opinion items dealing with behavior of teenagers. Two measures of prejudice were obtained. The first, similar to the one used by Rokeach et al., was a five-point scale ranging from

---

11. Although Triandis (1961) clearly employed a measure of global intention or attitude, it is not clear to what extent Rokeach, Smith, and Evans's (1960) measure of "friendship choice" is related to the evaluative dimension.

"I would feel quite friendly" to "I would feel quite unfriendly"; it was designed to measure the subject's immediate reaction to the stranger. The second measure, a modified version of Triandis's (1961) social distance scale, consisted of 11 intentions suitable for use with teenage subjects, and the sum over these scales served as a measure of prejudice.

Consistent with the results of Rokeach, Smith, and Evans (1960) and Byrne and Wong (1962), both measures showed that belief similarity was a more important determinant of prejudice, although the effect of race was also significant. Thus there appeared to be considerable evidence that belief similarity, rather than race per se, was the more important determinant of "prejudice" toward another person. Note, however, that all results discussed thus far have been concerned with the effects of race versus belief similarity on *attitudes* or global intentions with respect to the stimulus persons, and it is not clear that the same results would obtain for measures of specific intentions. In fact, Stein, Hardyck, and Smith (1965) also reported separate analyses for each of the 11 behavioral intentions on their social distance scale. They found that although belief similarity was more important than race on nine of these intentions, the reverse was true for intentions to "invite the stimulus person home to dinner" and to "have the stimulus person date my sister (brother)."

It was at this stage that Triandis (1964) developed his behavioral differential and found that variations in stimulus characteristics tend to have different effects on different kinds of intentions. On the basis of these findings, Triandis and Davis (1965) argued that part of the confusion in previous discussions of the controversy concerning race versus belief similarity stems from the assumption that prejudice is a unidimensional construct. They suggested that conflicting findings are to be expected since the results of any given study will depend on the kind of dependent measure involved. To test these notions, Triandis and Davis constructed eight stimulus persons varying in sex (male–female), race (Negro–white) and opinion on civil rights (favorable toward strong civil rights legislation–opposed to major changes in status quo on civil rights). Subjects were asked to rate each person on a semantic differential measure of attitude as well as on a 15-item form of Triandis's behavioral differential measure containing three items representing each of the five intentional factors obtained in the study by Triandis (1964; see Table 7.2). Thus, with respect to each stimulus person, Triandis and Davis had a measure of attitude and a score for each of five general intentions.

The results of the study are summarized in Table 7.9. Consistent with the earlier studies by Rokeach, Smith, and Evans (1960), Byrne and Wong (1962), and Stein, Hardyck, and Smith (1965), attitudes toward the stimulus person were found to be influenced most strongly by belief, followed by race and sex. The same results were obtained for the first intentional factor (formal social acceptance), which, as indicated earlier, can best be viewed as an evaluative dimension and thus constitutes another measure of attitude. As might be expected, sex was found to be most important for marital intentions, followed by race and beliefs. Finally, consistent with the argument that race is more important than belief in

Table 7.9 Relative Importance of Race, Belief, and Sex as Determinants of Attitudes and Intentions (Triandis and Davis, 1965).

Order of importance	Attitude	Intentions				
		Formal social acceptance	Marital acceptance	Friendship acceptance	Social distance	Subordination
First	belief	belief	sex	race	race	race
Second	race	race	race	belief	belief	belief
Third	sex	sex	belief	sex	sex	sex

determining some aspects of prejudice, race was found to be the most important determinant of the remaining three intentions (friendship acceptance, social distance, and subordination).[12]

The race versus belief similarity controversy in reference to prejudice is thus resolved in part once it is realized that race and belief similarity have different effects on different measures of "prejudice," i.e., on attitudes and on different dimensions of behavioral intentions. Several problems still remain unresolved. For instance, in his initial study Triandis (1961) found race to be a more important determinant of global intention or attitude than belief similarity whereas later studies have consistently found the reverse effects. These inconsistent findings with respect to the effects of stimulus characteristics on attitudes are not unlike the inconsistent findings concerning the effects of stimulus characteristics on different intentional factors. Results of this kind indicate that although characteristics of the target person influence attitudes and intentions, the process by which these characteristics exert their influence is unclear.

Analysis of Variations in Target Characteristics

The studies discussed above are not unlike the research on impression formation and on interpersonal attraction in that subjects are given information about a stimulus person and are asked to evaluate the person or to judge the likelihood that they would perform various behaviors with respect to the person. In previous chapters we have seen that the information provided to the subject allows him to form descriptive and inferential beliefs about the stimulus person. These beliefs

---

12. Note, however, that this study did not manipulate belief *similarity* but instead examined the effects of the stimulus person's civil rights position irrespective of the subject's own stand on that issue. If belief *similarity*, rather than belief per se, had been manipulated, it is possible that belief similarity would always have had a stronger effect on intentions than race. Several more recent studies, however, have manipulated belief similarity and have provided some more direct support for the Triandis and Davis hypothesis (Insko and Robinson, 1967; Robinson and Insko, 1969).

may have several effects. First, they may influence the subject's attitude toward the stimulus person. In order to understand these effects on attitudes, it is necessary to measure belief strength and attribute evaluations. Without such measures, results may appear contradictory. In fact, we have seen that although attitudes or global intentions tend to be influenced by variations in target characteristics, the results have been somewhat inconsistent.[13]

A second possibility is that the beliefs formed about the target person may influence attitudes toward specific behaviors with respect to the person (A_B) or subjective norms (SN). From the point of view of our model for the prediction of intentions, inconsistent effects of stimulus variations on specific intentions are not unexpected. Variations in these characteristics may influence attitudes toward performing some behaviors with respect to the target person but not others. Further, for some behaviors the attitude may become more favorable, and for others it may become less favorable. The same can be said for the effects of variations in target characteristics on the normative component. Again, these effects on the normative component may differ with respect to different behaviors. To exemplify, consider the effects of a race manipulation on two intentions: the subject's intention to admit the stimulus person (black or white) to his tennis club and his intention to admit the person to his golf club. Suppose that the subject intends to admit the white stimulus person, rather than the black stimulus person, to his tennis club but intends to admit the black rather than the white person to his golf club. The apparent inconsistency can be resolved by considering the determinants of the intentions involved. Most obviously, the subject may hold different subjective norms concerning the two behaviors. He may believe that most important others think he should not admit blacks to the tennis club, but he may believe that these same referents think he should admit blacks to the golf club.

Alternatively, the race variable's locus of effect may be in the attitudinal component. The subject might believe, for example, that admitting a black to the tennis club would lead to more negative consequences than admitting a white person. With respect to the golf club, however, he may believe that admitting a black would lead to more positive consequences than admitting a white. The subject would therefore have a more favorable attitude toward admitting the white rather than the black person to the tennis club, whereas the reverse would be true with respect to the golf club.

Thus variations in characteristics of the stimulus person may or may not influence attitudes toward the behavior in question and may or may not influence the corresponding subjective norms. Further, some behavioral intentions may be primarily under attitudinal control, and others may be primarily determined by the normative component. Without knowledge of the relative weights of the two components and the loci of effect of a given manipulation, it is impossible to gain

---

13. Even if consistent results are obtained, effects on attitudes toward the target person may be unrelated to intentions to perform specific behaviors with respect to that person.

a clear understanding of the influence of that manipulation on behavioral intentions.

Relative Importance of Intentional Elements

Although most investigators recognize the importance of the situation, the studies discussed above have made no attempts to examine the effects of situational variations on behavioral intentions. The relative importance of situational variations on intentions has been investigated intensively by Sandell (1968) and Bishop and Witt (1970). Sandell studied the effects of situational and target elements on the intention to drink. The targets were 10 beverages, such as coffee, liquor, water, and wine. Situations were varied by asking subjects to indicate, on a seven-point scale, whether they would "willingly" or "unwillingly" drink each of the 10 beverages, in seven different situations. The situations included "when really thirsty," "when alone," "with a really delicious piece of meat," etc. Each subject, then, made 70 judgments in the 10×7 analysis of variance design. "Subjects" was included as an additional factor in the data analysis in order to determine the extent to which intentions were influenced by individual differences among subjects. Used in this manner, the analysis of variance allows the investigator to estimate the amount of variance in drinking intentions attributable to individual differences, type of drink (target), and situational variations.

In a similar fashion Bishop and Witt (1970) investigated effects of behavioral and situational or time variations on intentions to engage in different leisure-time activities. Their subjects were asked to indicate on a five-point scale whether they would or would not perform each of 13 leisure-time activities, such as "watch television," "visit a friend," "spend time in the out-of-doors walking or hiking," and "find a quiet place to sit and relax by myself." Subjects indicated their intentions to perform these activities in each of ten situation-time combinations, including the following.

1. You have just gotten results from the biggest exam of the year and you have either failed or not done as well as you expected to do.

2. Today you got up full of energy and never really wanted to go to class. As a result, the long hours of sitting in lectures has made you very restless. It is now afternoon and you have finished your last class.

3. You get back from the library where you have had a great deal of trouble studying due to the incessant noise.

In this study, then, each subject made 130 judgments in a 10×13 analysis of variance design; a subject factor was again included. The analysis of variance thus permitted estimates of the amount of variance in intentions to perform leisure-time activities accounted for by individual differences, the type of activity (behavior), and situational or time variations. Table 7.10 summarizes the results of the studies by Sandell (1968) and by Bishop and Witt (1970).

The first thing to note in Table 7.10 is that situational variations in and of themselves account for relatively little variance in intentions. In fact, in both

Table 7.10 Amount of Variance in Intentions Attributable to Individual Differences, Situational Variations, and Target or Behavior (Adapted from Sandell, 1968, and Bishop and Witt, 1970)

Source of variation	Variance, %	
	Sandell	Bishop and Witt (male Kentucky sample)
Individual differences (A)	.5	6.4
Situational variations (B)	2.7	3.3
Target or behavior (C)	14.6	9.3
A × B	2.7	5.4
A × C	11.8	21.2
B × C	39.8	7.7
A × B × C	27.8	46.7

studies over 80 percent of the variance is attributable to the interactions rather than to the main effects.[14] The Sandell study shows that among the three variables studied, the type of drink (target) had the strongest effect on intentions. This indicates that subjects intended to drink some beverages and not others, irrespective of the situation. The greatest amount of variance, however, was due to the interaction between situation and target. Not too surprisingly, subjects indicated that they would drink certain beverages in some situations but not in others. The large triple interaction indicates that even here, however, there exist considerable individual differences.

The Bishop and Witt study shows that some leisure-time activities are pursued more than others, irrespective of the situation. The interaction between leisure-time activities and individual differences indicates that subjects differ in their intentions to perform various behaviors. However, the largest effect is the triple interaction, suggesting that these individual differences in intentions depend in large part on the situation.

The results of these two studies, then, clearly indicate that variations in any of the four aspects of intentions (behavior, target, situation, and time) will influence the likelihood that a person will intend to perform the behavior in question. Further, the studies show that these four aspects of intentions are not independent and that the effect of variations in one aspect depends in part on the other aspects. Finally, these studies also provide evidence that individual differences can influence behavioral intentions.

Individual Difference Variables

Although there seems to be little question that different people hold different intentions, the studies by Sandell (1968) and by Bishop and Witt (1970) do not

---

14. Note that these findings cannot be accounted for by a linear model.

identify the dimensions along which individuals differ. Most of the studies discussed earlier that have dealt with effects of target characteristics on intentions have also obtained measures of various individual difference variables and have examined their effects on intentions. For example, Triandis (1964) performed separate factor analyses for Catholic, Protestant, and Jewish subjects, for male and female subjects, and for subjects high or low on authoritarianism. Although there was some similarity in the intentional factors that emerged for these samples of subjects, several important differences were also observed. For example, five factors emerged for low authoritarian subjects, but only three emerged for subjects high in authoritarianism. Similarly, the stimulus person's age was the most important determinant of social distance for Protestant males, but for Catholic males it was the stimulus person's sex. Many cross-cultural studies have found that the subject's nationality influences his intentions (cf. Triandis, 1967). With respect to friendship acceptance, for example, the religion of the stimulus person was most important for Japanese males, the sex for Indian males, and the age for American males.

There can be little doubt, then, that individual difference variables are related to behavioral intentions. The results, however, do not seem to reveal any systematic pattern. The same conclusion emerges from a study by Posavac and Triandis (1968), who reported an intensive investigation of the relation between various personality variables and intentional patterns. Using factor analysis, they identified four types of subjects differing in their patterns of behavioral intentions with respect to 16 stimulus persons.[15] The different personality variables were found to be unrelated to these subject types, indicating that subjects who differ greatly in terms of their intentions do not seem to differ systematically in terms of their personalities.

Situational Variations and Social Norms

One individual difference variable that has received considerable attention is the subject's racial prejudice. The usual assumption has been that highly prejudiced subjects will discriminate against blacks, whereas race will be of little importance for the intentions of nonprejudiced subjects. Earlier in this chapter we reviewed a number of studies dealing with intentions to be photographed with a black person under various conditions. We noted that there was little evidence for a relation between attitudes toward blacks and intentions to be photographed with blacks.

In order to explain their rather low relation between attitudes and intentions, DeFleur and Westie (1958) proposed that "the act of signing the photograph agreement involves a conscious consideration of reference groups" (p. 671). In order to test this notion, they asked their subjects if there was any particular person or group of people who came to mind when they decided to sign (or re-

---

15. These types of subjects were identified in the same way that N. Wiggins, Hoffman, and Taber (1969) isolated their types of judges (see Chapter 5).

fused to sign) the photographic release agreements, and whether there were any people who the subjects felt would approve or disapprove of their signing the agreements. On the basis of responses to these questions, DeFleur and Westie concluded that subjects make "significant use of their beliefs concerning possible approval or disapproval of reference groups as guides for behavior" (1958, p. 672). The low relation between attitudes and intentions was thus explained by assuming that perceived pressures of reference groups induce subjects to "behave" in ways inconsistent with their attitudes.

Linn (1965) conducted a postexperimental interview with his subjects in order to further examine the influence of perceived social pressures or norms, and like DeFleur and Westie, he concluded that the low relation between attitudes and intentions in his study could be due to these factors. His interviews suggested that other variables may also have to be considered: amount of anticipated interaction with the attitude object, the degree of visibility of this interaction, the people who may view it, and the consequences (positive or negative) that might arise.

Some of these factors have been examined in later studies. For example, J. A. Green (1972) manipulated two situational factors: the intimacy of the relationship expressed in the picture for which subjects were asked to pose and the amount of exposure each picture would get. Intentions to pose for the picture declined significantly with degree of intimacy; that is, subjects were less willing to pose for a photograph if it was to involve a high degree of intimacy with a black person. Contrary to expectations, degree of exposure did not significantly influence willingness to pose for the photograph.[16]

A study by Warner and DeFleur (1969), however, reported an effect of exposure on various intentions. These investigators sent letters through the mail asking students to sign a pledge to perform a certain behavior, or to indicate their disapproval of the behavior. Among the eight behaviors used were "contributing money to a civil rights organization," "attending a dinner to welcome ten Negro students to campus," and "endorsing an appeal to seek out qualified Negro candidates for public office." For half the subjects, the letter indicated that their responses would be completely anonymous; the other half were told that their pledges would be publicized in the student newspaper. Although anticipated exposure had little effect on responses of nonprejudiced students, students with negative attitudes toward blacks were found to be more willing to pledge performance of behaviors when their pledges would not be publicized.

In a study by Bronfenbrenner (1970) children were given descriptions of hypothetical situations in which they had to decide whether or not to go along with their friends. In one situation, for example, they had to decide whether they would go to a movie recommended by friends but disapproved by parents. Subjects' intentions to go along with their friends were measured on a six-point scale ranging from *absolutely certain I would refuse* to *absolutely certain I would go along*

---

16. The exposure × intimacy interaction was significant but difficult to interpret.

with my friends. The children were assigned to one of three experimental conditions of exposure: (1) No one except the investigator would see their responses. (2) Their parents as well as the parents of other children would see their responses. (3) The other children in the class would see their responses. The results indicated that these situational variations influenced behavioral intentions. American children were most likely to intend to go along with their friends in the third condition and least likely to do so in the second condition. Although children in the Soviet Union were also least likely to indicate that they would go along with their friends in the second condition, they were most likely to do so in the first condition.

All these studies, then, provide further support that situational variations influence a person's intentions. They also suggest that situational variations may influence perceived social norms and reference group pressures. Note, however, that the studies discussed so far have not measured perceived social pressures directly but have merely assumed that variations in degree of exposure influence the extent to which social norms are operative in a given situation.

The influence of perceived social pressures on intentions has been studied more directly by Mezei (1971), who constructed four stimulus persons varying in race (black–white) and belief similarity (pro-Communism–anti-Communism). Subjects indicated, on a seven-point scale, their intentions to perform each of 10 behaviors with respect to these stimulus persons. In addition, they also indicated whether their parents and friends would engage in each of these behaviors, on the same seven-point scales. The results reported by Mezei show that a subject's own intentions to perform various behaviors are strongly related to his perception of the intentions of his family and friends.[17]

Goldstein and Davis (1972) also examined normative influences by asking subjects to indicate the extent to which their parents and friends would approve or disapprove of their engaging in each of three interracial behaviors varying in intimacy (eat with, go on a trip with, and introduce to a relative as a blind date). The more intimate the behavior, the more subjects believed that their parents and friends would disapprove of it. This finding may explain the lower intentions for intimate behaviors found in some studies.

Analysis of Variations in Intentional Elements and Individual Differences

In this section we have seen evidence that variations in target, behavior, situation, and time influence the person's willingness to perform the behavior in question. For example, subjects were found to be willing to drink one kind of beverage but

---

17. Mezei (1971) was primarily interested in differences between intentions with respect to stimulus persons varying in race and belief similarity. He thus reported only correlations between difference scores, which are not readily interpretable and which make it impossible to determine the relative influence of social pressures on different types of intentions.

not another, to drink a given beverage in one situation but not another, to perform a certain leisure-time activity under some conditions but not others, and to be photographed with a black person in a nonintimate rather than an intimate situation.

From our point of view, such variations introduce changes in the nature of the intention, and different results are to be expected. When a person is asked whether he would perform a given behavior with respect to one person as opposed to another, or in one situation rather than another, it is our point of view that different intentions are being assessed. Although it is usually acknowledged that variations in an intention's behavioral element result in different intentions, it is often not recognized that the same is true for variations in the intention's target, situational, and time elements. We have repeatedly argued that different intentions represent different probability dimensions, and results obtained with respect to one intention may not generalize to other intentions.

Most research efforts in this area have been primarily descriptive attempts to explore effects of variations in target, behavior, situation, and time on one or more measures of intentions. From our point of view, these effects can be understood only when the processes intervening between stimulus and response variables are explicated. Like variations in target characteristics discussed earlier, variations in any other element constituting the intention may influence attitudes toward the behavior and subjective norms. It seems clear that situations may, but need not always, influence the perceived consequences of (and hence attitude toward) performance of a given behavior. Similarly, some of the studies reviewed suggested that variations in intentional elements can influence subjective norms. If the effects of variations in intentional elements on the attitudinal and normative components were assessed, it would be possible to understand their effects on a given intention.

These considerations also apply to individual difference variables, such as the subject's sex, religion, attitude toward the stimulus person, etc. For example, it appears reasonable to assume that Catholics and Protestants have different beliefs about (and hence attitudes toward) using birth control pills; but they may not differ in their beliefs about the consequences of attending church services regularly. The same may be true for the normative beliefs of Catholics and Protestants. Thus both groups of people may believe that their respective churches expect them to attend services regularly—but only Catholics may see their church as condemning the use of birth control pills. Finally, these two intentions may be primarily determined by normative considerations for Catholics, and primarily by attitudinal considerations for Protestants. In fact, many individual difference variables may affect intentions by influencing the relative weights of the two components. With respect to some intentions, men and women, people of different nationalities, and people differing in personality (e.g., authoritarianism) may place differential weights on the attitudinal and normative components. With respect to other intentions, there may be no differences between these groups of people in the weights they place on the two components. It follows that individual difference variables (like variations in intentional elements) may be related to some behavioral intentions but not to others.

CONCLUSION

In this chapter we have considered factors influencing the formation of behavioral intentions. The interest in behavioral intentions as a focus of investigation is only of relatively recent origin. Although social psychologists have often drawn a conceptual distinction between cognitive, affective, and conative components of attitude, this distinction has been neglected in most empirical research. Measures of beliefs, attitudes, and intentions have often been used interchangeably, on the assumption that these measures all serve as indicants of a person's "attitude." Consistent with this view is the general assumption that if a person likes some object he should also hold favorable beliefs about the object, and he should intend to perform and actually perform favorable behaviors with respect to it. In the two preceding chapters we tried to show that the assumption of a close link between attitudes, beliefs, and intentions is justified only at a very global level. In Chapter 6 we saw that although a person's attitude toward some object is a function of his salient beliefs about the object's attributes (and his evaluations of those attributes), and although that attitude is related to the totality of his beliefs, there is no necessary correspondence between attitude and any given belief. Similarly, the present chapter has made it clear that attitude toward an object is related to the totality of a person's intentions with respect to the object (taking the intentions' evaluative implications into account), but it may be unrelated to any given intention.

Given the inconsistent relation between attitude toward an object and specific intentions with respect to that object, it is obvious that traditional measures of attitude are usually not a sufficient basis for predicting intentions. In contrast to this traditional attitudinal approach, we described a theory which specifies the immediate determinants of an individual's intention to engage in a given behavior and thus provides the means for predicting such intentions. On the basis of Dulany's (1968) theory, Fishbein (1967b) proposed that a person's intention to perform a given behavior is a function of two basic determinants, one attitudinal and the other normative. The attitudinal component refers to the person's attitude toward performing the behavior in question; the normative component (i.e., the subjective norm) is related to the person's beliefs that relevant referents think he should or should not perform the behavior and his motivation to comply with the referents. Thus the formation of a given intention depends on the prior formation of a particular attitude (i.e., attitude toward the behavior in question) and of a particular belief (i.e., subjective norm). In previous chapters we have shown that different processes underlie the formation of beliefs and attitudes. The present chapter demonstrates that still different processes are involved in the formation of intentions. These considerations again emphasize the necessity for treating beliefs, attitudes, and intentions as different concepts instead of including them under the general label of "attitude." Research concerning race versus belief similarity as determinants of prejudice supports this argument by showing that variations in these stimulus characteristics may have differential effects on attitudes and various types of intentions.

In an attempt to understand the determinants of intentions, it is important to take their level of specificity into account. We showed that different degrees of specificity may be involved with respect to each of the four elements of an intention: behavior, target, situation, and time. According to the theory of intentions discussed in this chapter, intentions at any level of specificity are determined by attitude toward the behavior in question (A_B) and subjective norm (SN). Accurate prediction of a given intention, however, can be expected only when the attitudinal and normative components of the model are measured at the same level of specificity as is the intention.

In addition to providing a means for the prediction of intentions, the theory also suggests an explanation for the apparently inconsistent findings concerning effects of various experimental manipulations on intentions. We have reviewed different lines of research showing that although variations in target characteristics, behaviors, and situations, as well as individual differences, are often related to one intention or another, these effects have been inconsistent and have not led to a systematically integrated body of knowledge concerning the determinants of intentions. The most that can be said is that various factors influence intentions, but the basis for their effects is not well understood, and it is usually impossible to tell in advance what, if anything, the effect of a given variable will be. For example, investigators have found that differences in intentions to perform behaviors with respect to black and white stimulus persons sometimes favor blacks, sometimes whites, and sometimes no significant difference is obtained. These apparently inconsistent results can be explained by examining the effects of race on the attitudinal and normative components of the theory. Variations in race will affect the attitudinal component only to the extent that subjects hold different beliefs about the consequences of performing the behavior in question with respect to blacks as opposed to whites, or that they evaluate the consequences differently. Similarly, variations in race will influence the normative component only to the extent that subjects hold different normative beliefs about performing the behavior with respect to blacks and whites, or that their motivation to comply with relevant referents differs when the target person is black rather than white. Since race of the target person may or may not influence beliefs about the consequences of performing a given behavior with respect to the target person, and since it may or may not influence the normative component, the relation between race and intentions will be inconsistent. The same reasoning can be applied to explain the inconsistent relations between other variables and intentions. Thus this chapter also made it clear that there is no necessary relation between traditional measures of attitude toward some object and intentions to perform any given behavior with respect to that object.

Figure 7.2 summarizes our conceptual framework for an understanding of the formation of intentions. The reader can see that we are again advocating an approach which explicates the processes intervening between stimulus and response variables. The figure shows that intentions are determined by two intervening variables, A_B and SN. Consistent with our discussion in Chapter 6, attitude toward the behavior is a function of beliefs about the behavior's consequences and evaluations of those consequences. To understand the formation of A_B, one must examine the effects of stimulus conditions on the beliefs and evaluations. Figure 7.2 also shows that subjective norm is a function of normative beliefs and motivation to comply, which are in turn based on the information a person has about his relevant referents. We have discussed several processes whereby the person may use this information to infer normative beliefs concerning a given referent. We have tentatively suggested that his beliefs about the referent's power and his beliefs about the consequences of complying with the referent may influence his motivation to comply. A complete understanding of the ways in which the normative component is formed would require first that the relation between the informational base and this component be specified, and second that we examine the effects of stimulus conditions on the informational base. To account for the effects of a given variable on intentions, however, it is sufficient to know the variable's effects on the attitudinal and normative components. Since it is possible to obtain direct measures of A_B and SN, it is possible to study the effects of a given variable on the two components and to use this information to predict behavioral intentions.

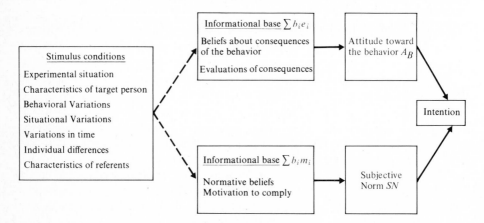

Fig. 7.2 Schematic representation of effects of stimulus variables on intentions.

Chapter 8

Prediction
of
Behavior

In the preceding chapters we have attempted to specify the determinants of beliefs, attitudes, and intentions. Some important problems are clearly still unexplored. Yet even assuming that we have a satisfactory understanding of the ways in which beliefs, attitudes, and intentions are formed, we are still faced with a question of greater practical significance, namely, the relation between these variables and a person's actual behavior. We have defined overt behavior as observable acts that are studied in their own right. Despite the commitment of the social sciences to the study of human behavior, relatively little research in the attitude area has investigated overt behavior as such. Instead, most studies have used observable acts to infer beliefs, attitudes, or intentions. Until very recently, empirical investigations have rarely concerned themselves with the relation of these variables to overt behavior.

It has usually been assumed that a person's behavior with respect to an object is in large part determined by his attitude toward that object. In this chapter we shall first review some of the research that has examined the attitude-behavior relation. We shall see that there is little evidence for a systematic relation between these variables. From the point of view of our conceptual framework, this is not unexpected. We have argued that a person's behavior is determined by his intention to perform that behavior. Although a person's attitude toward an object should be related to the totality of his behaviors with respect to the object, it is not necessarily related to any given behavior.

In order to gain a better understanding of the attitude-behavior relation, we shall examine the nature of different behavioral criteria. We shall see that, like intentions, behaviors can vary in terms of their specificity. The attitude-behavior relation will then be reexamined in light of the distinctions between behavioral criteria. We shall discuss alternative explanations for the low relation between at-

335

titude and behavior and analyze them within our conceptual framework. Finally, we shall consider the relation between intentions and behaviors and review some of the relevant research.

ATTITUDES AND BEHAVIOR

The relative neglect of the relation between attitude and behavior can in large part be attributed to the widespread acceptance of the assumption that there is a close correspondence between the ways in which a person behaves toward some object and his beliefs, feelings, and intentions with respect to that object. In fact, the term "attitude" was introduced in social psychology as an explanatory device in an attempt to understand human behavior. As we noted in Chapter 1, most investigators would agree with the definition of attitude as a learned *predisposition to respond* to an object in a consistently favorable or unfavorable manner. This definition implies a strong link between attitude and behavior, and the traditional view has been that any stimulus object comes to elicit an attitude which mediates or determines all responses to the object. It follows that if one could measure this attitude, one would be able to explain and predict a person's behavior.

The first step in this direction was to develop instruments or techniques that could be used to measure attitudes. These efforts eventually resulted in the development of the standard attitude scales discussed in Chapter 3. Much of the early research attempted to demonstrate the utility of the attitude concept by showing that people who behave in different ways also differ in their attitudes. Thus investigators found that union members have more favorable attitudes toward labor unions than management does, that pacifists have more negative attitudes toward war than nonpacifists do, that northerners are more favorable toward blacks than southerners are, etc. However, since the attitude scales used in these studies were developed in a way that almost ensured that they would distinguish between the comparison groups, these findings cannot be taken as evidence for a relation between attitude and behavior. Furthermore, the "behavioral" criterion in these studies can best be viewed as a behavioral syndrome rather than as a specific behavior toward the stimulus object. The finding that groups known to differ in their behaviors also differed in their measured attitudes nevertheless was taken as evidence confirming the assumption of a close link between attitude and behavior. Most investigators thus turned their attention to more controlled laboratory studies concerned with the determinants of attitude and attitude change. Studies of this kind continue to dominate research in the attitude area.

From time to time, however, studies were reported in which an attempt was made to examine the relation between attitude and behavior. In a review of this research Wicker (1969) was able to identify a relatively small number of studies in which "at least one attitudinal measure and one overt behavioral measure toward the same object [were] obtained for each subject" (p. 48). Table 8.1 presents Wicker's summary of research on the attitude-behavior relationship. On the basis of his consideration of these studies, Wicker concluded that "it is con-

Table 8.1 Summary of Studies of Attitude-Behavior Relationships (From Wicker, 1969)

Investigator(s)	Subjects	Attitude object	Overt behavior	n	Strength of relationship *
A. Jobs, industrial organizations and work groups					
Vroom (1964) (Review of 15 studies)	employees	one's job	job performance	range: 40–890	median r = .14 range .68 to −.03
Bernberg (1952)	aircraft plant employees	one's job	job absences	890	r = .01
Vroom (1962)	oil company employees	one's job	job absences	489	r = −.07
Weitz and Nuckols (1953)	insurance agents	one's job	job resignations	480	biserial r = .20, .05
Webb and Hollander (1956)	Air Force cadets	flight training program	dropping out of program	210	Kendall's *tau* = .22, .11
Sagi, Olmstead and Atelsek (1955)	college students	student activity groups	dropping out of group	123	(†)
B. Members of minority groups					
LaPiere (1934)	hotel and restaurant proprietors	Chinese	providing service to Chinese	128	9%
Kutner, Wilkins and Yarrow (1952)	restaurant and tavern proprietors	Negroes	providing service to a Negro	11	45%, 0%
DeFleur and Westie (1958)	college students	Negroes	willingness to have picture taken with a Negro and widely distributed	46	70%
Linn (1965)	college students	Negroes	willingness to have picture taken with a Negro and widely distributed	34	65%, 41%
Green [1972]	college students	Negroes	willingness to have picture taken with a Negro and widely distributed	44	r = .43
Fendrich (1967)	college students	Negroes	participation in group discussion on race relations	46	*gamma* = .69, .12

Investigator(s)	Subjects	Attitude object	Overt behavior	n	Strength of relationship *
Warner and DeFleur (1969)	college students	Negroes	signed agreement or disagreement to a request to engage in behaviors involving Negroes	123	63%
Mann (1959)	college students	Negroes	rated prejudice shown in discussion group	102	$r = .51, .22$
Katz and Benjamin (1960)	college students	Negroes	observed behaviors in racially mixed groups	32	(‡)
Rokeach and Mezei (1966)	college students	Negroes	choice of group members with whom to have coffee	68	54%
Kamenetsky, Burgess and Rowan (1956)	college students	Negroes	signing a petition for fair employment	100	biserial $r = .61, .59, .58, .54$
Himmelstein and Moore (1963)	college students	Negroes	imitation of Negro model's petition signing	51	47%
Bray (1950)	college students	Negroes, Jews	conforming to Negro's or Jew's autokinetic movement judgements	50 per group	$r = .15$ (Jewish condit.) $r = .11$ (Negro condit.)
Berg (1966)	college students	Negroes	conforming to Negro's autokinetic movement judgements	60	$r = -.10, -.14, -.21$
Malof and Lott (1962)	college students	Negroes	conforming to Negro's judgements in Asch-type conformity situation	60	67%
Smith and Dixon (1968)	college students	Negroes	being conditioned by a Negro E in a Taffel verbal conditioning procedure	80	(§)
C. Miscellaneous objects					
Carr and Roberts (1965)	Negro college students	civil rights activities	participation in civil rights activities	332	range of r: .29 to .10
Dean (1958)	industrial employees	local labor union	attendance at local labor union meetings	248	25%

Cattell, Heist, Heist and Stewart (1950); Cattell, Maxwell, Light and Unger (1950)	male college students and businessmen	football, movies, subject's chosen career, sleep	daily log of time and/or money spent	40	range of r: .26 to −.09
Corey (1937)	college students	cheating	cheating on self-graded exam	67	$r = .02$
Freeman and Ataov (1960)	college students	cheating	cheating on self-graded exam	38	range of Kendall's *tau*: .10 to −.19
Tittle and Hill (1967)	college students	student political activity	voting in student election	301	range of *gamma*: .50 to .29
Bellin and Kriesberg (1967)	mothers of families eligible for public housing	public housing	applying for public housing	79	60%
Newton and Newton (1950)	maternity ward patients	breast feeding	'success' of breast-feeding judged from amount of breast milk taken by infant	91	74%
Potter and Klein (1957)	maternity ward patients	breast feeding	observed affection toward infant and efforts to facilitate feeding at time of nursing	25	$r = .65$
[Wicker and Pomazal, 1971]	college students	participating as a subject in psychological research	commitment to participate and actual participation as a subject in psychological research	257	$r = .17$

* Statistics of association are shown when reported; otherwise, the figure is the percentage of subjects whose verbal attitudes were consistent with their overt behaviors.

† Group members who remained had more favorable attitudes toward their groups than those who dropped out.

‡ An inverse relationship was found between attitudes and behaviors: the more prejudiced white subjects were more accepting of suggestions by Negroes than were the less prejudiced white subjects.

§ Neither high nor low-prejudice subjects showed significant conditioning effects with the Negro experimenters; when compared to appropriate controls, high-prejudice subjects showed significantly greater conditioning with white experimenters than with Negro experimenters.

siderably more likely that attitudes will be unrelated or only slightly related to overt behaviors than that attitudes will be closely related to actions" (p. 65). Despite repeated failures to demonstrate a strong relation between attitude and behavior, the basic assumption that human behavior is determined by attitudes continued to persist.

Multicomponent View of Attitude

Until recently, most textbooks of social psychology either completely ignored the attitude-behavior question or made sweeping statements to the effect that "Man's social actions—whether the actions involve religious behavior, ways of earning a living, political activity, or buying and selling goods—are directed by his attitudes" (Krech, Crutchfield, and Ballachey, 1962, p. 139). Attitudes were viewed as complex systems comprising the person's beliefs about the object, his feelings toward the object, and his action tendencies with respect to the object. Given this inclusive view of attitude as encompassing all the person's experiences with respect to the object, it would be difficult to assume anything other than a strong relation between attitude and behavior. At the same time, however, this multi-component view of attitude was used to explain the low empirical relations between measures of attitude and overt behavior.

Figure 8.1 shows Rosenberg and Hovland's (1960) schematic representation of the three-component view of attitude. Note that all responses to a stimulus object are mediated by the person's attitude toward that object. The different responses, however, are classified into three categories: cognitive (perceptual responses and verbal statements of belief), affective (sympathetic nervous responses and verbal statements of affect), and behavioral or conative (overt actions

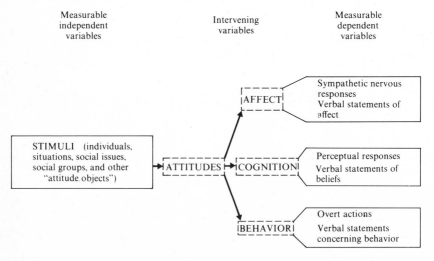

Fig. 8.1 Schematic conception of attitudes. (From Rosenberg and Hovland, 1960.)

and verbal statements concerning behavior). Corresponding to each of these response classes is one component of attitude.

According to this view, any response can be used to infer a person's attitude. It is perhaps for this reason that most research in the attitude area has treated very different response measures as equivalent or alternative indices of the same underlying attitude. Figure 8.1 also indicates, however, that certain responses are most indicative of the cognitive component, others of the affective component, and still others of the conative component. Since the assumption is that measures of these different components are not always highly related, a *complete* description of attitude requires that all three components of attitude be assessed by obtaining measures of all three response classes. It follows that measures of attitude based on only one or two response classes are incomplete and that use of such incomplete measures to predict overt behavior does not represent a fair test of the relation between attitude and behavior. The repeated finding of a low relation between attitude and behavior was explained by arguing that most measures of attitude merely assess the affective component. To obtain a complete measure of attitude, the cognitive and conative components would also have to be assessed.

On closer examination, however, we can see that this multicomponent view of attitude cannot provide an adequate explanation for the low attitude-behavior relation. First note that it is not clear whether the multicomponent view suggests that behavior is determined by attitude as a whole or merely by its conative component. The former interpretation implies that all three components need to be assessed whereas according to the latter interpretation it would be sufficient to obtain an index of the conative component alone. More important, we have discussed considerable evidence to show that indices based on a person's beliefs about an object ($\Sigma\,b_i e_i$), or on his intentions with respect to the object ($\Sigma\,I_i e_i$), constitute measures of the individual's attitude toward that object (A). In fact, we have seen that most measures of attitude are based either on beliefs or on intentions and that these measures are highly correlated with each other and with direct measures of evaluation. Later in this chapter we shall see that indices based on a person's behaviors (B) with respect to an object, taking each behavior's evaluative implication into account, are also highly related to his attitude toward the object in question (that is, $A = \Sigma\,B_i e_i$). These arguments can be summarized as follows:

Cognitive component		*Affective component*		*Conative component*
$\Sigma\,b_i e_i$	$=$	A	$=$	$\Sigma\,I_i e_i = \Sigma\,B_i e_i.$

From our point of view, measures of the cognitive, affective, or conative components are alternative ways of assessing the person's attitude. It follows that separate assessment of all three components is unlikely to lead to improved behavioral prediction.

Support for this position can be found in a study by Ostrom (1969), who attempted to obtain independent measures of cognition, affect, and conation and to examine the relations of these components to overt behavior. A sample of judges were asked to classify a large number of verbal statements about the church into the three response classes defined by Rosenberg and Hovland (1960; see Fig. 8.1), i.e., into verbal statements of belief, affect, or behavior. On the basis of each set of statements, three attitude scales were constructed: a Thurstone scale, a Likert scale, and a Guttman scale resulting in three different measures of each of the three attitudinal components. In addition, the following self-rating scales were constructed to measure each component.

Affective component

| I feel strong liking for the church. | | I feel strong disliking for the church. |

Cognitive component

| I believe the church has extremely desirable qualities. | | I believe the church has extremely undesirable qualities. |

Conative component

| I act strongly supportive toward the church. | | I act strongly hostile toward the church. |

Before we consider Ostrom's findings it is worth examining this procedure from a theoretical and methodological point of view. As we have noted in the preceding chapters, a measure of attitude should correlate highly with a global measure of intention to perform positive or negative acts, and both of these measures should be correlated with beliefs linking the object to various attributes and evaluations of those attributes. The three self-rating scales used by Ostrom should therefore be highly intercorrelated.

As to the standard attitude scales, if they are properly constructed, they should provide indices of the subject's location on the evaluative dimension regardless of whether "cognitive," "affective," or "conative" items were used to construct the scales. For example, the Thurstone scaling procedure makes use of judges to obtain estimates of each item's evaluative implications. So long as two sets of items, each representing the entire evaluative dimension, meet Thurstone's criteria of ambiguity and irrelevance, they constitute *by definition* parallel forms of the same test and therefore must yield the same results. Thus, irrespective of the kind of items used, if the standard attitude scales are properly constructed, they should all be highly intercorrelated. Ostrom's results support this analysis.

By using four methods for measuring each of the three attitudinal components, Ostrom was able to construct a multitrait-multimethod matrix.[1] The results indicated high convergent validity in that all four different types of attitude scales were found to be highly intercorrelated. In opposition to a multicomponent approach, there was little evidence for any discriminant validity. Measures of the

---

1. See Chapter 4 for a discussion of the multitrait-multimethod matrix.

three different attitudinal components were highly intercorrelated, demonstrating that indices based on the cognitive, affective, and conative response classes are best viewed as alternative measures of the same underlying evaluative dimension. With respect to the Likert scale, for example, cognition and affect correlated .79, cognition and conation .81, and a correlation of .79 was found between affect and conation. For the self-rating scale, these correlations were .77, .68, and .76, respectively.

In addition, Ostrom obtained seven self-reports of church-relevant behaviors, including days of church attendance per year, amount of money donated per year, whether or not the subject had even studied for the ministry, etc. At the end, the subject was given the opportunity to indicate his willingness to attend a future discussion by leaving his name and address with the experimenter. Each of the 12 attitude scales was correlated with each of the eight behavioral measures; thus there were 96 attitude-behavior correlations. They ranged from −.06 to .68, and most correlations were below .30. The only behavior that could be predicted with reasonable accuracy from the attitude scales was church attendance. More important, there were no appreciable differences in the predictive abilities of the three attitudinal components, and taking all three components into account would not improve prediction of behavior.[2] Thus the three-component view of attitude cannot provide a viable explanation for the low empirical relation between attitude and behavior.

"Other Variables" Approach

Despite the failure of the multicomponent view of attitude to account for low attitude-behavior relations, most investigators continue to regard attitudes as composed of cognitive, affective, and conative components. Further, attitudes continue to be regarded as primary determinants of a person's responses to the object, and any of these responses is assumed to provide an index of the person's attitude. At the same time, however, there is a growing recognition among investigators that there is no one-to-one correspondence between attitude and any given behavior. The most popular current views seems to be that

> . . . attitudes always produce pressure to behave consistently with them, but external pressures and extraneous considerations can cause people to behave incon-

---

2. In a more recent study, Kothandapani (1971) essentially replicated Ostrom's procedure, using birth control as his attitude object, and reported some evidence for the discriminant validity of scales measuring the three attitudinal components, as well as evidence that measures of the conative component were better predictors of the use of birth control methods than were measures of the cognitive and affective components. Although Kothandapani's results appear to contradict the position we have taken, it is worth observing that most discriminant validity was obtained with the Thurstone scale, a finding which is, by definition, impossible. Since most research in this area is inconsistent with Kothandapani's findings, we prefer to defer judgment until his results have been replicated.

sistently with their attitudes. Any attitude or change in attitude tends to produce behavior that corresponds with it. However, this correspondence often does not appear because of other factors that are involved in the situation. (Freedman, Carlsmith, and Sears, 1970 pp. 385–386)

Generally speaking, the "other variables" approach implies that attitude is only one of a number of variables that influence behavior and that the other variables must also be taken into account. Two interpretations can be given to this position.

Moderating effects of other variables. The first interpretation implies that the relation between attitude and behavior is *moderated* by other variables. For example, a high attitude-behavior relation might be found when subjects have the skills required to perform the behavior in question and a low relation when they lack the necessary skills. In this case, ability is viewed as a variable that *interacts* with attitude in determining behavior.

Independent effects of other variables. The second interpretation implies that other variables act in conjunction with attitude to determine behavior. That is, the other variables make an *independent* contribution to the prediction of behavior. For example, irrespective of their attitudes, high-ability subjects may be more likely to perform a given behavior than low-ability subjects. According to this view, other variables do not interact with attitude but instead they have *direct* effects on behavior.[3] Most investigators appear to assume that other variables have both moderating and independent effects on behavior.

A large array of "other variables" have been proposed to account for the inconsistent relation between attitude and behavior (see Ehrlich, 1969, and Wicker, 1969, for reviews of these variables). Among the variables suggested are other attitudes, competing motives, verbal, intellectual, and social abilities, individual differences, actual or considered presence of other people, normative prescriptions of proper behavior, alternative behaviors available, expected and/or actual consequences of various acts, and unforeseen extraneous events. However, as Wicker has pointed out, most of these factors have not been systematically studied, and there is surprisingly little research on the influence of any of these variables on behavior. "Often these factors are mentioned in discussion sections by investigators who failed to demonstrate attitude-behavior consistency. . . . The arguments for the significance of each factor are often plausible anecdotes and *post-hoc* explanations." (Wicker, 1969, p. 67)

Of the few studies that have explicitly attempted to test the other-variables explanation, most have employed a measure of intention rather than behavior as their criterion. Some were reviewed in the preceding chapter. These studies attempted to demonstrate the *moderating* effect of degree of exposure (Warner and DeFleur, 1969; Green, 1972) and intimacy (Green, 1972) on the attitude-behavior relation. As we have seen, these variables had no consistent independent

---

3. In an analysis of variance, the other variables (as well as attitude) would have main effects but would not need to interact with attitude.

effects on intentions, and they usually did not interact with attitude. Tarter (1969) studied the influence of an individual difference variable (individualistic versus collectivistic orientation) on the relation between attitude and "behavior." Again using intentions to release interracial photographs as the behavioral criterion, he found no evidence for the moderating effect of orientation on the relation between attitude and intention. In sum, then, not only have these studies used intentions rather than behaviors as their criterion measures, but the finding that "other variables" sometimes do and sometimes do not have independent and moderating effects on intentions contributes little to our understanding of the relation between attitude and behavior.

Wicker (1971) studied the independent effects of attitude toward the church and other variables on three religious behaviors. Each subject's attitude toward his own church was measured on five evaluative semantic differential scales. Three behaviors were to be predicted: (1) the number of Sundays the subject attended church during a 39-week period; (2) the amount of money contributed by the subject's family in the course of one year; and (3) the number of times the subject participated as a worker or a leader in the organized activities which occurred in the subject's church during a 3½ month period.

Three "other variables" were used as predictors in addition to attitude: perceived consequences of the behavior, evaluation of the behavior, and judged influence of extraneous events on the behavior. Nine presumably desirable consequences were specified, such as "setting a good example for one's children," "providing inspiration and help in coping with problems," and "making one more respected by the church pastor." Subjects indicated whether *regular attendance at Sunday worship service, regular contributions to the church,* and *taking an active part in church activities* did or did not lead to each of the nine consequences. Affirmative responses were given a score of +2, "uncertain" a score of +1, and a negative response was scored 0. The sum over the nine responses served as an index of perceived consequences for each of the three behaviors.

Evaluation of each behavior was assessed by computing complex indices which essentially represented the subject's attitudes toward *attending worship service every Sunday, contributing one month's income annually to the church,* and *spending more than 30 hours a week in church activities.*

To measure judged influence of extraneous events, Wicker constructed eight hypothetical situations for each of the three behaviors in which an unplanned extraneous event occurred. Subjects were asked to indicate the degree to which their church behaviors would be affected by the event. "For example, what would be the effect of a subject's worship service attendance if he had weekend guests who did not regularly attend church? How would a subject's contributions be affected if the congregation voted to spend funds on a project of which he disapproved?" (Wicker, 1971, p. 21) Subjects responded to each question on a four-point scale ranging from "the event almost certainly would not influence the behavior" (scored +4) to "the event almost certainly would reduce the likelihood of the behavior" (scored +1). The sum over the eight hypothetical events served as an index of the judged influence of extraneous events with respect to each of the three behaviors.

The results of the study are summarized in Table 8.2. The first four columns of figures show the correlations of attitude and the three other variables with each of the three behaviors. The last column represents the combined predictive power of all four variables. Consistent with previous findings, the relation between attitude and behavior is low and inconsistent. The correlations are low but significant for church attendance and contributions, and nonsignificant for participation in church activities. In fact, none of the four predictors is significantly related to all three behaviors. With respect to church attendance and contributions, judged influence of extraneous events was found to be the best predictor, and adding the other variables did not improve the multiple correlations with behavior.[4] The prediction of participation in church activities was largely unsuccessful.

Table 8.2 Prediction of Church Behaviors from Attitude and Other Variables (Adapted from Wicker, 1971)

Behavior	Product-moment correlations				Multiple correlation
	Attitude toward own church	Perceived consequences of behavior	Evaluation of behavior	Judged influence of extraneous events	
Attendance	.31 †	.19 *	.31 †	.42 †	.50 †
Contributions	.22 †	.05	.37 †	.45 †	.53 †
Participation	.11	.20 *	.06	.14	.23

* $p < .05$
† $p < .01$

Overall, then, these results again indicate that attitudes and other variables may or may not be related to a given behavior. So far as our understanding of the attitude-behavior relation is concerned, little information has been gained. Without some theoretical framework that specifies the "other variables" that are relevant for the prediction of a given behavior, continued search for additional variables can only serve to confound the problem. Clearly, if a sufficient number of "other variables" are measured, it is always possible to find one or two variables that are related to some of the behaviors under consideration. Such an approach fails to advance our understanding of the relation between attitude and behavior, however.

---

4. Indeed, the multiple-regression analysis showed that only the judged influence of extraneous events carried a significant regression weight in the prediction of church attendance and that this variable, as well as evaluation of the behavior, had significant weights in the prediction of contributions. None of the four variables had significant regression weights in the prediction of participation in church activities.

Wicker selected some of the variables that had been suggested by other investigators as possible additional determinants of behavior. However, Rokeach (1968; Rokeach and Kliejunas, 1972) has argued that the low attitude-behavior relationships "suggest the need for a clearer conceptualization of the attitude concept and of the relationships between attitudes and behavior." More specifically, he has proposed that "behavior-with-respect-to-an-object-within-a-situation (B_{os}) is always a function (f) of at least two interacting attitudes: attitude-toward-object (A_o) and attitude-toward-situation (A_s)" (Rokeach and Kliejunas, 1972; p. 195). According to Rokeach, attitude toward the situation has to be considered in addition to the traditional measure of attitude toward the object in order to predict behaviors with respect to the object in the situation. The attitudes are weighted for their subjective importance, as in Eq. 8.1.

$$B_{os} = f(A_o A_s) = (w) A_o + (1\text{-}w) A_s. \tag{8.1}$$

Rokeach and Kliejunas (1972) argued that A_o and A_s are independent and that each will reliably predict behavior to at least some extent.

To test this model, Rokeach and Kliejunas attempted to predict students' self-reports of the number of times they had cut a given class when the cut was not caused by "illness, accident, unusual weather conditions, etc." Attitudes toward the professor or instructor teaching the class (A_o) were measured on a nine-point scale ranging from *I liked* to *I disliked the instructor very much*. Subjects indicated their attitudes toward the situation (A_s) by rating "the importance or unimportance of attending class" on a nine-point scale ranging from *somewhat important to me* to *very important to me*. Finally, the relative importance of the two attitudes was assessed by asking subjects to indicate the extent to which "the frequency of attendance or the frequency of cuts in this course [were] determined by (a) their feelings about the professor and (b) their general feelings of the importance or unimportance of attending class." Subjects responded to questions (a) and (b) by stating percentages that indicated the perceived contributions of the two factors, and the two percentages had to sum to 100. For example, a subject could indicate that his cuts were determined 60 percent by his feelings about the professor and 40 percent by his feelings about the importance of attending class.

Consistent with expectations, Rokeach and Kliejunas found that over all courses and all subjects, A_o and A_s were uncorrelated, and A_s correlated significantly ($r = .46$) with behavior. Contrary to expectations, however, the A_o-behavior relation was not significant, and the multiple correlation, with both A_o and A_s used as predictors of behavior, was only slightly higher ($r = .49$) than the correlation for A_s alone. With the use of subjective weights to predict behavior on the basis of Eq. 8.1, a correlation of .61 was obtained. However, this correlation did not differ s'gnificantly from the multiple correlation. Thus, although the results seemed to indicate that behavior could be predicted from attitude toward the situation, attitude toward the object was largely unrelated to behavior.

Analysis of "other variables" research. We have described two studies showing that such variables as evaluation of the behavior, attitude toward the situation, perceived consequences of the behavior, and judged influence of extraneous events are sometimes related to behavior. It may be instructive to examine these findings from the point of view of our conceptual framework. Our orientation suggests that the immediate determinant of a person's behavior is his intention to perform the behavior in question. In the preceding chapter we saw that a person's intention to perform a given behavior is determined by his attitude toward the behavior (A_B) and by his subjective norm (SN). If a strong relation between intention and behavior can be assumed, these two components should also be predictive of the overt behavior. Further, "other variables" not included in the model are expected to influence intentions (and hence behaviors) only to the extent that they have an effect on A_B, SN, or the relative weights of these two components.

Let us now take a closer look at the "other variables" studied by Wicker (1971) and Rokeach and Kliejunas (1972). Clearly, Wicker's measures of "evaluation of the behavior" and "perceived consequences of the behavior" can be viewed as measures of the subject's attitude toward the behavior (A_B). Neither of Wicker's two indices, however, is a very satisfactory measure of A_B. The first index, evaluation of the behavior, was derived from a consideration of discrepancies between attitudes toward six related behaviors, namely six levels of the behavior in question (e.g., attitude toward attending worship service every Sunday, missing once or twice a year, . . . , missing more than twice a month). The higher the score, the more likely the subject felt that only high levels of behavior were acceptable (Wicker, 1971).

Wicker's index concerning perceived consequences is also an imperfect measure of attitude toward the behavior. Recall that attitude toward the behavior is a function of the person's beliefs about the behavior's consequences and his evaluations of the consequences ($A_B = \Sigma b_i e_i$). Wicker obtained beliefs about consequences presumed to be desirable, but he had no direct measures of their desirability. Thus, although the two indices may be interpreted as measures of attitude toward the behavior, they represent only approximations to the attitude in question.

Wicker's measure of judged influence of extraneous events can best be viewed as the subject's intention to perform the behavior. The subject was essentially asked whether he would or would not engage in the behavior in a variety of hypothetical situations. The index based on the subject's responses thus represents a general intention to perform the behavior in question. In sum, Wicker obtained two imperfect measures of attitude toward the behavior and a measure of behavioral intention, in addition to his measure of attitude toward the church.

In a consideration of the relations between these variables, it is important to note that they have not always been measured at the same level of specificity. Table 8.3 summarizes the different measures obtained by Wicker. The first two rows show that the two measures of attitude toward the behavior are not identical. Clearly, a person's attitude toward "making regular contributions to the

Table 8.3 Description of Measures in Wicker's Study

Variable	Attendance	Contributions	Participation
Perceived consequences $[\sim\Sigma b_i e_i]$	Regular attendance at Sunday worship service	Regular contributions to the church	Taking an active part in church activities
Evaluation of behavior $[\sim A_B]$	Attending worship service every Sunday	Contributing one month's income to the church	Spending more than 30 hours a week in church activities
Judged influence of extraneous events $[\sim I]$	Intention to attend worship service	Intention to contribute to church	Intention to participate in church activities
Behavior $[B]$	Number of Sundays subject attended church	Amount of money contributed to church	Number of times subject participated as worker or leader

church" may be very different from his attitude toward "contributing one month's income to the church." Further, intentions and behaviors are also measured at different levels of specificity. A person's intention to "participate in church activities," for example, may differ greatly from his intention to "participate as a worker or leader." By the same token, the behavior of participating as a worker or leader is measured at a more specific level than is the general intention to participate in church activities. Finally, the attitudes toward the behavior are measured at different levels of specificity than is either the intention or the behavior.

The discrepancies in levels of specificity are especially apparent with respect to participation in church activities (see the last column in Table 8.3). Considerably greater correspondence in levels of specificity is found with respect to contributions and church attendance.

As we pointed out in the preceding chapter, the degree of relationship between two variables should decrease to the extent that these levels of specificity fail to correspond. The results reported by Wicker are consistent with this analysis. Overall, intercorrelations among attitudes, intentions, and behavior were low, ranging from −.04 to .45. The low correlations reflect not only discrepancies in levels of specificity but also the above-mentioned problems concerning measurement of the two "attitude toward the behavior" indices. Thus, even when levels of specificity were somewhat comparable, these two indices were not highly correlated. For church attendance, a low but significant correlation of .26 was found between evaluation of attending worship service every Sunday and perceived consequences of attending Sunday worship service regularly. When the levels of specificity were highly discrepant, the correlation was even lower. For example, for participation in church activities, a nonsignificant correlation of −.04 was obtained between perceived attitude toward taking an active part in church activities and evaluation of spending more than 30 hours a week in church activities.

In similar fashion, correlations between intention and behavior were higher when the levels of specificity tended to correspond than when they did not. Thus, for church attendance and monetary contributions (where levels of specificity tended to correspond), intentions and behavior correlated .42 and .45, respectively. A nonsignificant correlation of .14 was obtained between intention to participate in church activities and the number of times a subject participated in the role of worker or leader.

As mentioned earlier, Wicker's main finding was that "judged influence of extraneous events" (an intention) was the best predictor of attendance and contributions whereas participation was not predictable from any of the variables considered. Our reanalysis suggests that a person's intention may be a good predictor of his behavior but only when these two variables are measured at the same level of specificity. We shall return to this point below.

A reexamination of the measure of "attitude toward the situation" employed by Rokeach and Kliejunas (1972) reveals that it is not a measure of attitude, nor is it directed at the situation in which the behavior is performed. A measure of attitude toward the situation would have been obtained by asking subjects to evaluate "the classroom situation." Instead, Rokeach and Kliejunas obtained a measure of the perceived importance of attending class. As such, it is perhaps more similar to an attitude toward the behavior than to an attitude toward the situation. However, we have noted that measures of importance may not be highly related to attitude. In fact, perceived importance of attending class may also reflect a person's normative belief as to whether he is supposed to attend class.

The results reported by Rokeach and Kliejunas indicated that cutting class could be predicted with greater accuracy by considering perceived importance of attending class than by considering attitude toward the professor. These results can be interpreted as showing that attitude toward the behavior and/or normative beliefs are better predictors of behavior than is attitude toward the target of the behavior. Although the importance of attending class was found to be uncorrelated with attitude toward the professor, this finding should not be taken as evidence that attitude toward a behavior (A_B) and attitude toward the object of the behavior (A_o) will *always* be uncorrelated. In the preceding chapter we reported some empirical findings showing high and significant correlations between A_B and A_o.

In sum, the "other variables" interpretation of the lack of consistent attitude-behavior relations is not incompatible with our conceptual framework. We have proposed that variables external to our model can influence behavior indirectly by affecting the determinants of behavioral intentions. This approach suggests that neither the attitude toward an object nor any other external variable will always be related to behavior. The "other variables" approach is based on the assumption that such attitudes *are* related to behavior, but that additional variables have to be considered in order to predict behavior accurately. Our analysis of research on the effects of "other variables" has revealed several methodological problems, and it may therefore be useful to reexamine the nature of research on the attitude-behavior relationship.

ATTITUDINAL PREDICTORS AND BEHAVIORAL CRITERIA

In our discussion above we noted the lack of correspondence between the labels that investigators apply to their variables and the measures they actually obtain. Variables assumed to be nonattitudinal (e.g., perceived consequences) may in fact be attitudinal in nature, and variables labeled "attitudes" may in fact be measures of other variables (e.g., importance). This recurring labeling problem in the attitude area calls into question the conclusion reached by an increasing number of investigators to the effect that empirical research shows little or no relation between "attitude and behavior." We have noted repeatedly that very different measures have all been labeled "attitude." We have also seen that there is some ambiguity in use of the term "behavior"—several studies dealing with the attitude-behavior relation have actually obtained measures of intention. Moreover, behavioral criteria may vary in terms of their level of specificity. In fact, the nature of the behavioral criteria has been largely neglected in studies concerned with attitudinal prediction of behavior (Ehrlich, 1969; Fishbein, 1967b, 1973). It may thus be instructive to examine the "attitudinal" predictors and "behavioral" criteria in more detail. Such an analysis demonstrates that appropriate measures of attitude *are* related to appropriate measures of behavior and that the results obtained in different studies are not so inconsistent as they initially appear.

Behavioral Criteria

Throughout the book we have distinguished among beliefs, attitudes, and intentions, and we have demonstrated the importance of this distinction. It should be clear by now that these variables may differ greatly in their relations to some overt behavior. An analysis of the literature suggests that it is also important to make some distinctions among different types of behavioral criteria. Although most investigators have taken behavior as a given, and some (e.g., Deutscher, 1969) have even argued that direct observation of behavior is "the ultimate evidence of validity," it is necessary to realize that behavioral observations are nothing more or less than one kind of data utilized by a behavioral scientist. Like any other measure, records of overt behavior may be unreliable or invalid and may be given inappropriate labels. Fishbein (1967b) has noted that, at least in the attitude area, behavioral criteria have seldom, if ever, been subjected to the same rigorous analyses to which verbal attitude measures have been subjected. He argued that such analyses are an essential first step for an understanding of the relation between attitude and behavior.

Consistent with this argument, Fishbein (1973) has distinguished between several types of behavioral criteria that have been employed in studies of the attitude-behavior relationship. One frequently used criterion is the single observation of a *single act*. Recording of the behavior may be either dichotomous (e.g., the subject does or does not contribute money to charity) or continuous (e.g., the amount of money contributed). Another criterion in frequent use is an index based on *repeated observations* of the same single act (e.g., behavior across several trials in an experiment). Here a distinction can be made between repeated observations under homogeneous or heterogeneous conditions. A third type of criterion, in less frequent use, is an index based on single or repeated observations of different behaviors, i.e., a *multiple-act* criterion.

Basic to this classification scheme is the *single-act criterion*. The behavioral measure here indicates whether or not the person performed the behavior in question. As in the case of behavioral intentions, a single-act criterion can be viewed as consisting of four elements: behavior, target, situation, and time. Unlike the situation with regard to intentions, however, a single-act criterion is always specific in that it involves a directly observable response to a certain target, in a given situation, at a given point in time. In the first empirical investigation of the attitude-behavior relation, for example, LaPiere (1934) measured acceptance of Orientals in hotels and restaurants by observing whether or not a particular

Chinese couple (target) was or was not served or admitted (behavior) at a given establishment (situation) at a given point in time.

In contrast to the single-act criterion, repeated-observation and multiple-act criteria vary in terms of their specificity with respect to at least one element of the behavior. A *repeated-observation criterion* can be obtained by observing the same specific behavior directed at different targets, in different situations, or at different times. These repeated observations are in some way combined, and the resulting index is the repeated-observation criterion. Repeated-observation criteria thus represent generalizations across targets, across situations, or across time. For example, if LaPiere had wanted to generalize across targets, he could have observed whether a given respondent admitted *different* people in the same establishment at approximately the same point in time.[5] At a less general level of target specificity, he could have observed the respondent's behavior with respect to different Orientals. From this point of view, the distinction between repeated observations under homogeneous or heterogeneous conditions refers to the behavior's level of specificity in target, situation, or time. The greater the variation in a given element, the more general the repeated observation criterion with respect to that element.

A *multiple-act criterion* generalizes across the fourth element, namely, the specific behavior under consideration. A multiple-act criterion is obtained by computing some index across observations of different behaviors. By viewing the single-act criterion as a cell in a two-dimensional table that has repeated observations as columns and different behaviors as rows, the multiple-act criterion can be described as an index based on the entries in the cells of a given column. Table 8.4 shows that a multiple-act criterion is based on observation of several behaviors with respect to a given target, in a given situation, at approximately the same point in time.

Table 8.4 summarizes our discussion up to this point. The cell entries in the table represent single-act criteria; row marginals represent repeated-observation criteria; and column marginals represent multiple-act criteria. The entry in each cell will be an observation of an act that may be either dichotomous or continuous. In the dichotomous case, the entries will be either 1 or 0 (e.g., a subject does or does not donate money); in the continuous case, they can take on many different values (e.g., the amount of money donated). The entries in a given row represent the same continuous or dichotomous act with respect to different targets, in different situations, or at different points in time.

In our description of repeated observation and multiple-act criteria, we made no mention of the ways in which observations are combined to yield these criteria. Entries in the cells of a given row or column may be summed, averaged, scaled, etc., and each of these procedures may yield a different criterion score. Therefore

---

5. Needless to say, repeated observations can never be taken at exactly the same point in time.

Table 8.4 The Four Major Types of Behavioral Criteria
(Adapted from Fishbein, 1973)

		Observations						
		1	2	3	... j ...	n	
	1	$B_{1,1}$	$B_{1,2}$	$B_{1,3}$	... $B_{1,j}$ ...	$B_{1,n}$	$R_1 = f(B_1.)$
	2	$B_{2,1}$	$B_{2,2}$	$B_{2,3}$	... $B_{2,j}$ ...	$B_{2,n}$	$R_2 = f(B_2.)$
	3	$B_{3,1}$	$B_{3,2}$	$B_{3,3}$	... $B_{3,j}$ ...	$B_{3,n}$	$R_3 = f(B_3.)$
Behaviors	⋮	⋮	⋮	⋮	⋮	⋮	⋮
	i	$B_{i,1}$	$B_{i,2}$	$B_{i,3}$	... $B_{i,j}$ ...	$B_{i,n}$	$R_i = f(B_i.)$
	⋮	⋮	⋮	⋮	⋮	⋮	⋮
	m	$B_{m,1}$	$B_{m,2}$	$B_{m,3}$	... $B_{m,j}$	$B_{m,n}$	$R_m = f(B_m.)$
		$M_1 = f(B._1)$	$M_2 = f(B._2)$	$M_3 = f(B._3)$	... $M_j = f(B._j)$ ...	$M_n = f(B._n)$	$MR_a = f(R_m)$ $MR_b = f(M_n)$ $MR_c = f(B_{m,n})$

$B_{m,n}$ = single observation of a single behavior
R_m = repeated observations of a single behavior
M_n = single observations of multiple behaviors
MR = repeated observations of multiple behaviors

an index based on a consideration of all row marginals may differ greatly from one based on all column marginals, and both may differ from a criterion score based on a consideration of the total set of cell entries. Finally, all indices based on repeated observations of more than one behavior can be viewed as composing a fourth type of behavioral criteria, namely *multiple-act, repeated-observation* criteria. As with behavioral intentions, this fourth criterion can vary in levels of specificity with respect to any of the four elements: behavior, target, situation, and time.

Constructing behavioral indices. Consider an investigator who has obtained a set of behavioral observations and who is now confronted with the task of constructing a repeated-observation or multiple-act criterion. Different problems are involved in constructing these two kinds of indices. Since the *repeated-observation criterion* deals with the *same behavior,* the investigator may be justified in simply summing or averaging the repeated observations. For example, if observations were taken of the amount of money a person contributed to his church on 52 consecutive Sundays, the sum would represent his total contributions in the course of a year, and the mean would provide a measure of the average contribution made each week. A different index could be obtained by counting the number of Sundays on which the person made some contribution.

A simple sum or mean across *different* behaviors, however, may not yield a very meaningful *multiple-act criterion*. Such a procedure may amount to adding apples and oranges. Generally speaking, the problems involved in obtained a multiple-act criterion score are identical to those encountered in obtaining a pencil-and-paper measure of attitude. Indeed, when properly constructed, multiple-act criteria are really nothing more than attitude scores that are based on behavioral observations rather than on verbal statements. In order to clarify this point, consider the parallels between an investigator who is constructing a Likert scale for measuring attitude toward the church and an investigator who wants to obtain a measure of religious behavior. The latter would simply identify a set of behaviors *which he believed were related to religiosity* (or to the individual's attitude toward the church). He would then go out and observe whether or not the individuals in his sample performed these behaviors or the degree to which they engaged in them. For example, the investigator might observe the number of times an individual attended church during a certain time interval, the amount of money he contributed to the church during this time interval, whether or not he attended a particular social event sponsored by the church, whether or not he owned a copy of the Bible, and so on.[6] The investigator now has a set of numbers (i.e., observations) for each respondent, and he is faced with the task of combining these numbers into a single index of "religious behavior."

So far, this investigator's procedure has been very similar to that of one who is constructing a Likert scale for measuring attitudes toward the church or toward religiosity. The behavioral observer first had to identify a set of behaviors (i.e., items) that he believed were related to religiosity. In a similar manner, the attitude scale constructor must first identify a set of opinion statements (i.e., items) that *he believes are related to attitudes toward the church* (or toward religiosity). He may, for example, select statements like, "One should attend church regularly," "People should be willing to support their church financially as well as morally," "A home without a Bible is a home without God," etc.[7]

---

6. Note that some of these behaviors would be classified as single-act criteria and others as repeated-observation criteria. For this reason we do not present a separate discussion of multiple-act–single-observation criteria and of multiple-act–repeated-observation criteria.

7. The attitude scale constructor will also try to select opinion statements that indicate antireligiousness (i.e., if an individual agrees with this statement he is less religious—has a more negative attitude toward the church—than if he disagrees). Although items of this type have seldom been utilized by behavioral observers, there is no reason to ignore them. For example, one can observe whether or not an individual signs a petition or votes for a political candidate who opposes the use of state funds for parochial schools or the tax-free status of religious organizations.

Once the attitude scale constructor has selected his set of opinion statements, he, like the behavioral observer, goes out and observes whether the individuals in his sample agree or disagree with his statements. The respondent may be asked to simply agree or disagree (i.e., be forced to make a dichotomous choice), or he may be asked to indicate the degree of his agreement (e.g., to respond on a five- or seven-place *agree–disagree* scale). At this stage, then, the attitude scale constructor, like the behavioral observer, has before him a set of numbers assumed to imply something about an individual's religiosity. Unfortunately, it is here that the similarity between these two types of investigators usually ends. Whereas the attitude scale constructor will test his assumptions by performing an item analysis, the behavioral observer will usually just accept his assumptions and decide on some arbitrary way of combining his numbers to arrive at a behavioral criterion score.[8] For example, he may first decide that people who have contributed more than $50 should be given a score of 5, that those who have contributed more than $25 but less than $50 should be given a score of 4, and so on. If he does this for each of his continuous variables, he can then simply sum his set of numbers and arrive at his multiple-act criterion.

In contrast, the attitude scale constructor first submits his items to a standard scaling procedure. As noted in Chapter 3, if using a Likert scale, he eliminates those items that fail to discriminate between subjects with favorable and unfavorable attitudes toward the church, or items that do not correlate with this attitude. In a sense, then, the investigator recognizes that some of the opinion items he selected do not serve as good indicants of the particular attitude he is measuring. Clearly, if the behavioral observer were to follow the same procedure, he too might find that some of the behaviors he has observed do not covary with the underlying dimension of religiosity. To put it a bit more bluntly, he might find that some of the behaviors he chose to observe have little to do with the degree of an individual's religiosity.

Two important conclusions can be drawn on the basis of these considerations. The first should be obvious: Not every behavior with respect to some object is related to the attitude toward that object. An investigator usually chooses to observe a given behavior because he assumes that it is relevant to the attitude under consideration. What we have tried to show is that an investigator's intuition can be wrong. Tests of the relation between attitude and a given behavior, therefore, can to a large extent be viewed as tests of the investigator's intuition. Given the assumption that attitude toward an object determines *all* responses to that object, an investigator is clearly free to choose any response to the object in testing the attitude-behavior relation. The considerations above indicate that this assumption is definitely invalid.

---

8. Frequently, the behavioral observer will not even try to construct a multiple-act criterion score but will merely treat each of his single-act observations as a different criterion. This procedure is as inappropriate as treating each item on a Likert scale or each bipolar adjective pair on a semantic differential as a separate dependent variable.

The second conclusion to emerge from our discussion is that a multiple-act criterion based on appropriately selected behaviors represents a measure of attitude and will be highly correlated with any other measure of the same attitude. Indeed, multiple-act criteria can be constructed by using any of the standard attitude scaling procedures: Guttman scaling, Likert scaling, and Thurstone scaling (see Chapter 3).[9]

When the multiple-act criterion is based on the entries in a given column of Table 8.3, it represents a measure of attitude toward a given object, in a given situation, at a given point in time. When it is based on observations of different behaviors with respect to a given object performed in different situations (i.e., on entries in different columns hetergeneous with respect to situation), it represents a general measure of attitude toward the object in question. A standard scaling procedure can also be applied in constructing repeated-observation criteria by combining the observations in a given row of Table 8.4. The resulting score would represent a person's attitude toward the behavior in question. If only time of observation was varied, the repeated-observation criterion would represent attitude toward performing the behavior with respect to a given target in a given situation. More general measures of attitude toward the behavior would be obtained if the columns represented variations in target, situation, and time.

Behavioral observations as indicants of attitude. In the preceding discussion we have suggested that behavioral observations can be used to measure the person's attitude. However, not every behavioral criterion can serve as a valid indicant of attitude. The most specific behavioral observation is the single-act criterion. It consists of a single observation concerning the performance (or nonperformance) of a particular behavior, with respect to a specified target, in a given situation, at a given point in time. Under the assumption of a strong relation between intention and behavior, such a specific behavior is determined by the actor's attitude toward performing the behavior (under the specified conditions) and his subjective norm with respect to this behavior. It follows that such a specific behavior may not even be indicative of the attitude toward the behavior since the behavior may be primarily determined by the subjective norm.

In contrast, multiple-act and repeated-observation criteria—when properly constructed on the basis of a standard scaling procedure—can serve as indicants of attitude. We have suggested that a properly constructed multiple-act criterion may be viewed as an index of attitude toward an object. By using a standard scaling procedure, the investigator ensures that each behavioral observation is related to the evaluative dimension with respect to the target object. When a given behav-

---

9. Although multiple-act criteria can also be constructed by arbitrarily combining behavioral observations, the validity of such criteria as attitude measures is an empirical question. So long as minimal care is taken in constructing a multiple-act criterion, however, the validity of the scale increases with the number of observations on which it is based.

ior is determined primarily by variables other than the attitude toward the object in question (variables such as subjective norms or competing attitudes), it is likely to be eliminated from the multiple-act criterion.

With respect to repeated-observation criteria, we have argued that such indices are indicative of a person's attitude toward performing a given behavior on different occasions. Use of a standard scaling procedure to construct the repeated-observation criterion again ensures that only observations relevant to this attitude are included. If on a given occasion the behavior is determined primarily by other variables, it will be eliminated from the repeated-observation criterion.

In conclusion, we have seen that attitude toward an object may be related to some single-act criteria but may be unrelated to others. Attitude toward an object, however, should correlate with a multiple-act criterion. Similarly, attitude toward a behavior is expected to be related to a repeated-observation criterion. These conclusions must again be qualified by considerations of correspondence in levels of specificity. Consider the relation between attitude toward an object and a multiple-act criterion. The particular behavioral criterion selected by the investigator determines the level of specificity of each of its four elements. For example, if a multiple-act criterion is based on all entries in a given column of Table 8.4, it represents a person's attitude toward a specific target in a given situation and at a given point in time. A verbal measure of attitude at this same level of specificity would correlate better with the multiple-act criterion than would a general measure of attitude toward the same target (without specification of situation and time). By the same token, lack of correspondence in levels of specificity of the target will also reduce correlations. For example, lack of correspondence is exhibited when a verbal measure of attitude toward a group of people (e.g., blacks, Orientals) is correlated with a multiple-act criterion based on behaviors with respect to a single specific member of the group. These same considerations also apply to the relation between attitude toward a behavior and a repeated-observation criterion.

Although investigators have not paid a great deal of attention to their behavioral criteria and have rarely distinguished between attitudes toward objects and attitudes toward behaviors, the notion that measures of attitude toward an object are related to the person's *pattern* of behaviors rather than to any single behavior is not new (cf. Thurstone, 1931; Doob, 1947; D. T. Campbell, 1963; Tittle and Hill, 1967). For example, as early as 1931, Thurstone pointed out that two persons may hold the same attitude toward some object but that "their overt actions [may] take quite different forms which have one thing in common, namely, that they are about equally favorable toward the object" (p. 262). Doob (1947) arrived at essentially the same conclusion on the basis of his behavior-theory analysis of attitudes. A given attitude may elicit any of a number of responses consistent with the attitude. The particular response selected by the individual will depend on his reinforcement history. For example, a large number of different behaviors may express liking for another person. Although two persons may like a third person equally well, the particular ways in which they express their liking will depend on their prior reinforcement histories. Again, however, their behaviors will be similar in that, taken as a whole, they will indicate the same degree of liking for the third person. These arguments are consistent with our conceptual framework, which suggests that although traditional measures of attitude toward an object will be related to multiple-act criteria, they will not necessarily be related to a given behavior and thus may not predict single-act or repeated-observation criteria.

Reanalysis of Research on "Attitude-Behavior" Relationships

The conclusions reached in the preceding section are consistent with the majority of studies on the attitude-behavior relationship. To demonstrate this consistency it is necessary to reexamine the studies that have usually been viewed as tests of the relation between attitude and behavior (see Table 8.1). Specifically, it is necessary to consider the nature of both the attitudinal predictors and the behavioral criteria. Closer examination of these studies shows that the "attitudinal" predictor frequently does not constitute a measure of attitude, as defined in this book. In his classic study, for example, LaPiere (1934) did not obtain a measure of attitude. Instead, he measured behavioral intentions by asking his subjects whether they would "accept members of the Chinese race as guests in [their] establishments." A similar measure of intentions was used by Kutner, Wilkins, and Yarrow (1952) to predict behavior. Newton and Newton (1950) measured mothers' intentions or desires to breast-feed their babies and used that measure as their "attitudinal" predictor. Other investigators have used personality tests as their measures of "attitude." For example, Katz and Benjamin (1960) obtained a measure of authoritarianism, and J. H. Mann (1959) used the patriotism subscale from a measure of ethnocentrism. Freeman and Ataov's (1960) "attitudinal" predictor was an assessment of the degree to which subjects perceived that others were cheating in hypothetical situations.

When the predictor variable was a measure of attitude, sometimes the attitude was toward a behavior, but more often it was toward an object. For example, Tittle and Hill (1967) assessed attitude toward "personal participation in student political activity." Another measure of attitude toward a behavior is Kamenetsky, Burgess, and Rowan's (1956) assessment of attitude toward using legislative measures to abolish discrimination against Negroes in employment matters. Attitudes toward objects have usually been measured at intermediate levels of target specificity, such as attitudes toward Negroes (Berg, 1966; Bray, 1950; Smith and Dixon, 1968) or the church (Wicker, 1971; Ostrom, 1969; Fishbein and Ajzen, 1974). Occasionally the attitude object is somewhat more specific, such as "Negro college students who take part in civil rights demonstrations" (Carr and Roberts, 1965).

Just as these studies vary considerably in terms of their predictor variables, they also vary considerably in behavioral criteria. As noted earlier, many studies (e.g., DeFleur and Westie, 1958; Linn, 1965; J. A. Green, 1972) have had no behavioral criterion but have measured intentions instead. Most investigations have used either a single-act criterion or a repeated-observation criterion. La-Piere's (1934) single-act criterion concerning acceptance of a Chinese couple in hotels and restaurants was described earlier. Tittle and Hill (1967) observed whether students did or did not vote in a student body election. Another single-act criterion was reported by Himmelstein and Moore (1963), who observed whether students did or did not sign a petition to extend library hours.

Repeated observations of a given behavior usually represent repeated trials in an experiment and thus are obtained under maximally homogeneous conditions. Smith and Dixon (1968), for example, recorded the number of trials on which the subject elicited the reinforced response in a verbal conditioning experiment. Similarly, Malof and Lott (1962) observed the number of trials on which the subject conformed with the incorrect judgments made by confederates. A somewhat different repeated-observation criterion was used by Bray (1950), who computed the discrepancy between judgments made by subjects and confederates over 50 trials. Newton and Newton (1950) recorded the average amount (in grams) of milk intake of a child on six occasions during the fourth day after birth. A somewhat more heterogeneous repeated-observation criterion was used by Tittle and Hill (1967), who obtained self-reports of the number of times a student voted in the last four student body elections.

Although multiple-act criteria are infrequently used, a few investigators have obtained them. Good examples are Tittle and Hill's (1967) indices based on self-reports of participation in 10 different political activities. Among the activities were frequency of participation in meetings of a student assembly, frequency of reading of the platforms of candidates for student political office, and frequency of voting over the last four elections. When these observations were submitted to Likert and Guttman scaling procedures, two different behavioral indices resulted. Since repeated observations of different behaviors were used, the obtained indices represent multiple-act, repeated-observation criteria. Another multiple-act criterion was constructed by Potter and Klein (1957), who recorded behavior of mothers during two nursing periods. Each recorded behavior was rated on a five-point scale ranging from "little or no effort to achieve successful nursing" to "manifestations of tenderness or affection." The multiple-act criterion was the mean rating of all behaviors performed by a given mother.

This analysis shows that many of the studies which have typically been viewed as testing the relation between attitude and behavior are actually of little relevance to that question. Of those studies that have obtained some measure of attitude and a behavioral criterion, most have attempted to predict a single-act or repeated-observation criterion from a traditional measure of attitude toward an object. As might be expected, these studies have met with little success. Although a few low but significant relations have been reported (e.g., Ostrom, 1969; Ajzen and Fishbein, 1970), most of these studies have found no relation between attitude and behavior (e.g., Berg, 1966; Bray, 1950; Smith and Dixon, 1968; Malof and Lott, 1962; Himmelstein and Moore, 1963).

In contrast, when attitude toward a behavior, rather than an object, has been used to predict single-act or repeated-observation criteria, significant findings have usually been obtained [10] (e.g., Tittle and Hill, 1967; Kamenetsky, Burgess, and Rowan, 1956; Ajzen and Fishbein, 1970; Ajzen, 1971b, Fishbein *et al.,* 1970). Further, it appears that the magnitude of the relationship varied with the degree of correspondence between levels of attitudinal-behavioral specificity. Finally, also consistent with expectations, whenever multiple-act criteria have been used, significant relations with attitude toward an object have been reported (e.g., Carr and Roberts, 1965; Bandura, Blanchard, and Ritter, 1969).

A Test of the Relations between Attitude toward an Object
and Behavioral Criteria

In order to directly test the notion that traditional attitudes are related to multiple-act criteria but have no consistent relation with single-act criteria, Fishbein and Ajzen (1974) constructed a set of 70 behaviors dealing with matters of religion. Included were the following items: pray before or after meals, take a religious course for credit, attend nonreligious wedding ceremonies, donate money to a religious institution, date a person against parents' wishes, etc. Thirty items were repeated in a refusal format, e.g., refuse to donate money to a religious institution, refuse to state a religious preference during university registration. Sixty-two subjects were asked to check those behaviors they had performed. In addition, they completed five traditional scales measuring attitude toward religion. The first, a Guilford self-rating scale, asked subjects to indicate their attitude toward being religious by checking an 11-point scale ranging from *extremely favorable* to *extremely unfavorable.* The second measure, a form of the semantic differential, consisted of five 11-point evaluative bipolar scales with the following endpoints: *good–bad, harmful–beneficial, wise–foolish, pleasant–unpleasant,* and *sick–healthy.* The concept rated was "being religious," and the sum across all five scales was taken as an index of attitude toward religiosity. The other three attitude measures were standard religiosity scales based on opinion items. One was a Likert scale (Bardis, 1961), the second was a scale of Guttman format (Faulkner and DeJong, 1969), and the third was a Thurstone scale (Poppleton and Pilkington, 1963).

In order to obtain a multiple-act criterion, Fishbein and Ajzen employed an independent sample of 37 judges to provide Thurstone-type judgments for each of the 100 behaviors. That is, the judges rated on an 11-point scale the degree to which performance of the behavior was indicative of a favorable or unfavorable attitude toward being religious.[11] Items were scored negatively or positively on

---

10. The relation between attitude toward a behavior (A_B) and a single-act criterion depends on the relative importance of the attitudinal component in determining the person's intention to perform and actual performance of the behavior in question.
11. These subjects also made the same judgments for nonperformance of each of the 70 basic behaviors.

the basis of these judgments. Performance of a positive behavior and non-performance of a negative behavior were given a score of 1, and the remaining alternatives were scored 0. Finally, a multiple-act criterion was obtained by summing over the 100 self-reports of behavior.

Table 8.5 presents correlations among the five verbal attitude scales, their correlations with the multiple-act criterion, and their mean correlations with the 100 single-act criteria. The table shows a high degree of convergent validity among the five verbal attitude scales. Further, consistent with expectations, all attitude scales correlated highly with the multiple-act criterion, whereas the prediction of single-act criteria tended to be low and nonsignificant. These results support our argument that an index based on a large number of behaviors can be viewed essentially as an alternative attitude-measurement procedure.

Table 8.5 Correlations of Verbal Attitude Measures with Multiple- and Single-Act Criteria (Adapted from Fishbein and Ajzen, 1974)

		Verbal attitude scales				
		SR	SD	G	L	T
Verbal attitude scales						
Self-report	(SR)	—				
Semantic differential	(SD)	.800	—			
Guttman	(G)	.519	.644	—		
Likert	(L)	.762	.762	.790	—	
Thurstone	(T)	.584	.685	.744	.785	—
Multiple-act criterion Correlation with sum over 100 behaviors		.640	.714	.608	.684	.628
Single-act criteria Average correlation with 100 single behaviors		.137	.149	.121	.142	.131

$r_{.05} = .250$
$r_{.01} = .325$

To provide further support for the notion that multiple-act criteria can be viewed as behavioral attitude scales, the investigators used the 100 behavioral items described above to construct three multiple-act criteria meeting the requirements of Guttman, Likert, and Thurstone scaling procedures, respectively. Before we turn to the findings, it is of interest to note that the majority of items were rejected by all three scaling procedures. Further, even though very different selection procedures were involved, some items were found to meet the criteria of more than one scaling technique and were thus included in more than one type of scale. The implications of these results will be discussed shortly.

Consistent with expectations, the data presented in Table 8.6 show considerable convergent validity between the three types of multiple act criteria. Further, all three of the scaled multiple-act criteria were highly correlated with all five of the verbal attitude scales, providing further support for the argument that multiple-act criteria can best be viewed as behavioral attitude scores. The correlations between the three scaled multiple-act criteria and the 100 single-act criteria were again low and mostly nonsignificant.

Table 8.6 Intercorrelations of Multiple-Act Criteria and Verbal Attitude Scales (Adapted from Fishbein and Ajzen, 1974)

		Multiple-act criteria		
		G	L	T
Multiple-act criteria				
Guttman	(G)	—		
Likert	(L)	.776	—	
Thurstone	(T)	.631	.792	—
Sum over 100 behaviors		.699	.898	.789
Single-act criteria				
Mean correlation with				
100 single behaviors		.143	.178	.156
Verbal attitude scales				
Self-report		.451	.582	.701
Semantic differential		.591	.688	.727
Guttman		.531	.647	.570
Likert		.660	.656	.611
Thurstone		.575	.624	.542

$r_{.05} = .250$
$r_{.01} = .325$

Attitudes toward objects and single-act criteria. The empirical evidence discussed above indicates that traditional measures of attitude toward an object can be used to predict properly constructed multiple-act criteria. Further, Fishbein and Ajzen (1974) found that even without application of a standard scaling procedure, a multiple-act criterion obtained by summing over 100 behaviors (scored in terms of their evaluative implications) correlated highly with verbal measures of attitude.

In contrast, traditional measures of attitude were not found to be consistently related to *single-act criteria.* Of the 100 single-act criteria considered by Fishbein and Ajzen (1974), only 39 were significantly related to at least one of the five verbal attitude measures; very few were related to all five attitude scales; and even these correlations tended to be relatively low. Further, these behaviors did not differ in any obvious way from those that could not be predicted. We are thus left with the unfortunate conclusion that traditional measures of attitude toward an object do not provide an adequate basis for the prediction of specific behaviors with respect to that object.

Conceptualizing multiple-act criteria as behavioral measures of attitude suggests one possible solution to this problem. This conceptualization indicates that the individual behaviors that constitute the multiple-act criterion score are essentially equivalent to items on an attitude scale. The question of the relationship between attitude and single-act criteria can then be restated in terms of the relationship between the multiple-act criterion (i.e., the behavioral attitude score) and the single behaviors of which it is comprised. Clearly this relationship depends on the particular manner in which single behaviors are combined to construct the multiple-act criterion.

Use of a standard attitude scaling procedure is one way of ensuring that the single-act criteria are in some way related to the attitude under consideration—i.e., that they constitute valid indicants of the attitude in question. However, this does not mean that performance or nonperformance of such a valid behavior will be *correlated* (i.e., linearly related) with the person's attitude. In Chapter 3 we saw that use of a standardized scaling procedure makes it possible to specify the theoretical relationship between the scaled behavioral attitude score and the individual behaviors that contribute to the score This relationship is indicated by the tracelines or operating characteristics which differ for items that meet the criteria of the different attitude scaling procedures. The hypothetical tracelines of behavioral items meeting Guttman, Likert, and Thurstone criteria are summarized in Fig. 8.2. Of course, little can be said about the prediction of single behaviors from attitude before the behavior's operating characteristic has been examined.

Figure 8.2 indicates that the traceline of a behavior in a Guttman scale is assumed to be a step function of the behavioral Guttman score. So long as a person's score is lower than the behavior's position on the scale, he will not perform the behavior, whereas a person whose score exceeds this position is expected

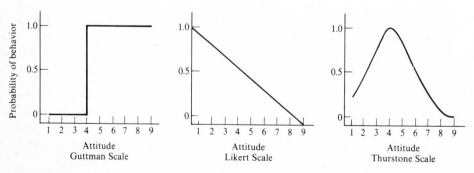

Fig. 8.2 Hypothetical tracelines of Guttman, Likert, and Thurstone scales for a behavior with a scale value of 4.

to perform it. For a perfect behavioral Guttman scale, it should therefore be possible to accurately predict all individual behaviors on the scale from a person's scale score. Thus, although *correlations* between a Guttman multiple-act criterion and the individual behaviors of which it is comprised may be low, one should be able to predict the behaviors from the scale scores by taking the traceline into account.

A behavior that has stood the test of Likert's internal consistency criterion is assumed to have a linear relation to the behavioral Likert score. Thus each behavior the scale comprises is expected to correlate highly with the multiple-act criterion.

Finally, behaviors meeting Thurstone's criterion of irrelevance are assumed to have nonmonotonic tracelines. Persons with behavioral Thurstone scores of the same favorability as the scale value of the behavior should be most likely to perform the behavior. Persons with less favorable or more favorable scores should be less likely to do so. The relationship between behavioral Thurstone scores and single-act criteria meeting Thurstone's criterion of irrelevance is therefore expected to be of an inverted U-shape. Thus, although *correlations* between a Thurstone multiple-act criterion and the individual behaviors of which it is comprised may be low, one should be able to predict the behaviors by taking the nonlinear traceline into account.

Since multiple-act criteria can be viewed as measures of attitude, the theoretical relations described above are applicable to any measure of attitude. Therefore one can argue that even when a single-act criterion is a valid indicant of the attitude under consideration, it may not *correlate* with the attitude since it may have a nonlinear traceline. It is interesting to note that most tests of the attitude-behavior relation are based on the assumption of a linear relation. That is, most investigators test whether individuals with favorable attitudes are more likely to perform a positive behavior than are individuals with unfavorable attitudes (or vice versa for a negative behavior) by computing correlations, *t*-tests, or similar indices. We have tried to show that this assumption may be wrong even when the behavior is a valid indicant of attitude. Although behaviors meeting Guttman or Thurstone criteria can be predicted from the behavioral attitude score by taking their tracelines into account, there is no simple way of predicting these behaviors from a verbal attitude score. Predicting behaviors that meet Guttman or Thurstone criteria involves a comparison between the locations of a person's behavioral attitude score and the location of the behavior on the same quantitative evaluative dimension. To make such predictions from verbal attitude scores would involve similar comparisons and would thus require that the verbal attitude scores be mapped onto the same quantitative dimension. Even with a high correlation between multiple-act criterion and verbal attitude score, a good mapping is not easy to achieve (cf. Fishbein and Ajzen, 1974).[12] These issues pose little difficulty

---

12. One possible exception concerns the relation between verbal and behavioral Thurstone scores which are assumed to involve the same quantitative dimension.

for single-act criteria that meet the requirements of Likert scaling. These behaviors are expected to correlate with the behavioral attitude score; they should therefore also correlate with any other measure of attitude.

In sum, it is theoretically possible to predict any valid single-act crite-rion from a verbal measure of attitude by taking its traceline into account, but from a practical point of view, it appears that verbal measures of attitudes toward objects can be used only to predict single-act criteria meeting the requirements of Likert scaling (i.e., only behaviors with approximately linear tracelines).

Some evidence for the hypothesis that single-act criteria can be predicted from traditional measures of attitude if the criteria have tracelines that approach linearity was reported by Fishbein and Ajzen (1974). Of the 100 religious be-haviors considered in that study, 32 were found to meet Likert scaling require-ments in that they correlated significantly with the total score over all 100 behav-iors. Most of these 32 single-act criteria also correlated significantly with the verbal attitude scales; only five could not be predicted from at least one of the scales. In contrast, of the remaining 68 behaviors, 56 did not correlate significantly with any of the five verbal attitude scales. It thus appears indeed possible to predict single-act criteria meeting Likert scaling requirements.

The reader should realize that this conclusion is problematic from a practical point of view. In order to ascertain that a given behavior indeed has a linear trace-line, one must observe a large number of behaviors in the same domain. Behaviors with linear tracelines are identified by high correlations with the total behavioral score. Without first observing the behavior, as well as a large number of other behaviors, one cannot specify in advance whether a given single-act criterion should correlate with traditional measures of attitude.

Linearity of single-act criteria. To solve this problem, let us examine the charac-teristics of behavioral items that meet or do not meet Likert scaling requirements. A single-act criterion is excluded from a behavioral Likert scale because perfor-mance or nonperformance of the behavior does not discriminate between people with high and low multiple-act criterion scores, i.e., between people with favorable and unfavorable attitudes. A behavior may fail to discriminate for at least two reasons. First, its evaluative implications may be unclear. Individuals with posi-tive attitudes may perform it because they believe it has favorable implications, but individuals with negative attitudes may also perform it because they believe it has unfavorable implications. There are also some behaviors that have neither favorable nor unfavorable implications. Such a behavior might be performed by individuals with high as well as low attitudes. More important, even behaviors with clear evaluative implications may fail to discriminate. Clearly, there are some behaviors that are likely to be performed (or not performed) by most members of a given population, irrespective of their attitudes. For example, irrespective of a person's attitude toward the church, he is unlikely to throw stones at church windows, and he will usually return the greetings of a minister or priest. Behaviors with such high (or low) *base rates* cannot be predicted from attitudes. Although it has long been recognized that restriction of range in criterion scores reduces correlation coefficients, the problem of high or low behavioral base rates has been largely neglected in studies of the attitude-behavior relationship.[13]

To reiterate, the problem that confronts us is the identification of behavioral items that distinguish people with favorable and unfavorable attitudes. One possible solution is to develop some independent index of linearity. It may be argued that a positive behavior has a traceline that approaches linearity to the extent that the probability of its performance is high for people with favorable attitudes *and* low for people with unfavorable attitudes. The opposite should be true for negative behaviors.[14] Note that this definition is closely related to Likert's criterion of internal consistency. One can perhaps best express these notions in terms of conditional probabilities, where $p(B|A+)$ is the probability of the behavior, given a positive attitude, and $p(B|A-)$ is the probability of the behavior, given a negative attitude. Fishbein and Ajzen (1974) proposed that the greater the absolute difference between these two conditional probabilities, the more the behavior's traceline approaches linearity.

The implication is that the higher this *linearity index,* the stronger should be the correlation between a measure of attitude and the behavior in question. To test these notions, Fishbein and Ajzen had two independent samples of subjects provide estimates of conditional probabilities for their 100 behaviors. They asked the first sample to think of 100 *religious* students and to indicate how many of these students perform each of 50 behaviors. The subjects were then asked to think of 100 *nonreligious* students and to indicate how many of these students perform each of the remaining 50 behaviors. For the second sample of subjects, the two sets of behaviors were exchanged. Thus, for each of the 100 behaviors, estimates of $p(B|A+)$ and $p(B|A-)$ were obtained. A third sample of subjects were asked to think of 100 *typical* students (without reference to religiosity) and to indicate how many of these students perform each of the 100 behaviors, providing a measure of the behavior's prior probability or base rate, $p(B)$.

These measures of $p(B|A+)$, $p(B|A-)$, and $p(B)$, as well as the linearity index $|p(B|A+) - p(B|A-)|$, were correlated with the correlations between each behavior and the five verbal attitude scales. The results are presented in Table 8.7. Consistent with expectations, the linearity index provided significant predictions of the strength of attitude-behavior relationships, irrespective of the attitude scale employed. Further, these predictions were superior to predictions based on either one of the two conditional probabilities or on the prior probability of the behavior.

---

13. The inclusion of habit in "other variable" explanations of the attitude-behavior relationship may be viewed as one attempt to recognize the importance of behavioral base rates (cf. Triandis, 1967, 1971).

14. In fact, most investigators select behavioral criteria that they assume have these characteristics. More often than not, unfortunately, their intuition appears to be misleading.

Table 8.7 Prediction of Attitude-Behavior Correlations from the Linearity Index (Adapted from Fishbein and Ajzen, 1974)

Verbal attitude scales	$p(B\|A+)$	$p(B\|A-)$	Linearity index	$p(B)$
SR	.074	−.113	.409	−.040
SD	.152	−.116	.455	−.002
G	.319	.170	.466	.262
L	.146	.017	.432	.084
T	.166	.068	.399	.130

$r_{.05} = .195$
$r_{.01} = .259$
SR = self-report scale; SD = semantic differential; G = Guttman scale; L = Likert scale; T = Thurstone scale

Thus the linearity index appears to allow the investigator to specify in advance whether the traceline of a given single-act criterion approaches linearity with respect to a given attitudinal dimension, and it provides some indication of the degree to which the behavior will be related to a measure of that attitude.[15] Essentially, then, the linearity index provides a means for an investigator to check his intuition that a given single-act criterion will be related to some measure of attitude. When the linearity index is high, attitude should be correlated with single-act criteria. In general, however, most single-act criteria have low linearity indices, and they cannot be predicted from traditional measures of attitude toward the object. Further, even behaviors with high linearity indices tend to have relatively low correlations with attitude. These considerations suggest that traditional measures of attitude toward an object cannot be relied on to predict single-act criteria with respect to the object.

INTENTIONS AND SINGLE-ACT CRITERIA

Our conceptual framework suggests an alternative approach to the prediction of single-act criteria. According to our approach there should be a high relation between a person's intention to perform a particular behavior and his actual performance of that behavior. Essentially, then, we are suggesting that single-act

---

15. Linearity indices can be obtained not only with respect to attitude but also with respect to any other stable disposition, such as personality variables or demographic characteristics. (See Jaccard, 1974, for an application of the linearity index to the prediction of single-act criteria from personality variables.) Conceptualizing the linearity index in terms of conditional probabilities also makes it possible to apply Bayes's theorem in an attempt to further understand the factors that determine linearity of relationships between a given disposition and a single-act criterion. (See Fishbein and Ajzen, 1974, for a more detailed discussion.)

criteria are really not very difficult to predict. If one wants to know whether or not an individual will perform a given behavior, the simplest and probably most efficient thing that one can do is to ask the individual whether he intends to perform that behavior. Since much of human behavior appears to be under volitional control (Ryan, 1970), the best single predictor of an individual's behavior will be a measure of his intention to perform that behavior. This does not mean that a measure of intention will always correlate perfectly with a single-act criterion; there are several factors that influence the size of any given intention-behavior relationship.

Three major factors can be identified that influence the magnitude of the relationship between intention and behavior: the degree to which intention and behavior correspond in their levels of specificity; stability of the intention; and the degree to which carrying out the intention is completely under the person's volitional control.

Correspondence in levels of specificity. Perhaps the most important factor influencing the size of the intention-behavior relation is the degree to which the intention is measured at the same level of specificity as the behavior to be predicted. Recall that specificity of intentions and behaviors can vary in terms of the behavior itself, the target, the situation, and time. The greater the correspondence in levels of specificity, the higher should be the correlation between intention and behavior. Suppose, for example, that today's date is Thursday, July 19, 1974 and that you are attending class at Omega University, which is situated in a small town that, among other things, has three movie theaters. Further, suppose that one of the theaters, the Rialto, is showing a rerun of "Casablanca" at 7:30 and 9:30 p.m. Suppose that it is important for you to predict whether or not another student will attend the 7:30 showing at the Rialto. It seems fairly obvious that the best prediction that you can make will be based on a measure of his intention to perform that particular behavior. That is, the best single predictor will be an item like the following.

I intend to go to the 7:30 showing of "Casablanca" at the Rialto Theater on the night of July 19, 1974

probable ____|____|____|____|____|____|____ improbable

Further, it should be clear that this item will lead to better prediction than

I intend to go to the Rialto Theater on the night of July 19, 1974

or

I intend to go to the movies on the night of July 19, 1974;

which, in turn, will be better predictors than

I intend to go to the Rialto Theater

or

I intend to go to the movies.

It would be possible to continue with these examples, but the point should be clear: the lower the correspondence between the intention's and the behavior's levels of specificity, the poorer the prediction will be.

Given that intention and behavior are measured at the same level of specificity, one expects a high relation between these variables. In other words, our conceptual framework suggests that a person's performance of some behavior at a given point in time is determined by his intention to perform the behavior at that point in time.

Stability of the intention. Clearly, a person's intention may change over time. It follows that a measure of intention taken some time prior to observation of the behavior may differ from the person's intention at the time that his behavior is observed. The longer the time interval between measurement of intention and observation of behavior, the greater the probability that the individual may obtain new information or that certain events will occur which will change his intention. Thus the longer the time interval, the lower the correlation between intention and behavior.

Very often, the behavior under consideration can occur only after some sequence of previous behaviors has been performed. For example, although a high school sophomore may intend to go to college, he will be able to carry out this intention only after he has performed other behaviors (graduated from high school, passed the college entrance exams, etc.). The greater the number of intervening steps, the lower the intention-behavior correlation will be. Here again, the problem is primarily one of the stability of the intention, rather than of its relation to behavior per se. The greater the number of intervening steps, the higher the probability that the completion of (or failure to complete) any single step will result in new information which may produce a change in the individual's intention.[16]

A somewhat similar problem concerns the degree to which carrying out the intention is dependent on other people or events. The higher the dependency, the lower the intention-behavior correlation is likely to be. If a person's intention is based on the expectation that another person will behave in a certain way, or on the expectation that some event will occur, and the expectation is not confirmed, this information may well lead to a change in intention.

It thus appears that in the interval between measurement of intention and observation of behavior, certain events can occur that may produce changes in an individual's intentions. To predict the behavior from the initial measure of intention, it may be necessary to consider other variables in addition to the intention. This will be particularly true when (a) there is a long time interval between the

---

16. It would be possible to consider the individual's intentions to perform each of the intervening behaviors, and the consideration of this set of intentions may lead to a better prediction of the ultimate behavior than the intention to perform that behavior per se.

measure of intention and the observation of behavior; (b) the behavior can occur only following some other sequence of behaviors; and (c) the performance of the behavior is dependent on other people or events. However, if one can obtain a measure of the intention immediately before the performance of the behavior, these additional variables will have already been taken into account, and the intention will accurately predict the behavior.

We are not here implying that the problems discussed above are unimportant. Indeed, one is often concerned with predicting future behaviors, and sometimes it is helpful or necessary to make these predictions months or years in advance of the actual behavioral act. Under such circumstances, one cannot rely solely on a measure of intention; one must also consider other variables. In Chapter 7 we showed that a person's intention to perform a given behavior is determined by his attitude toward performing that behavior and by his subjective norm concerning the behavior. It may thus be argued that the factors which have to be considered are those factors that are likely to influence one or both of these variables.

Volitional control. So far we have assumed that the behavior in question is under the actor's volitional control. In the preceding section we noted that performance of a behavior may depend on other people or on the occurrence of certain events. Therefore a person may be unable to carry out his intention. If performance of the behavior requires certain abilities or resources that the individual does not possess, or if it depends on the cooperation of another person, he may be unable to perform the behavior even if he intends to. A case in point is the person who intends to stop smoking, drinking, or using drugs but is unable to do so. The person's intention will influence what he *tries* to do by leading him to initiate certain preparatory acts; the behavior in question, however, is not performed. Once the person realizes that he is unable to perform the behavior, he is likely to change his intention. The new intention should be predictive of his future behavior.

Another possible breakdown in the intention-behavior relation may be due to a person's *habits*. Although a person may intend to do one thing, by "force of habit" he does something else. Before leaving home, a person may intend to try a new route to his office, but later he finds himself driving along the same route he takes every day. In fact, many well-learned skills (e.g., playing the piano, driving a car) are performed almost automatically without much conscious effort. Most behaviors of interest to social scientists, however, do not involve such automatic sequences of motor responses. Instead, investigators attempt to predict a person's decisions, participation in various activities, purchasing behavior, voting for political candidates, and interactions with other people. We have argued that these kinds of behaviors are under volitional control and thus can be predicted from the person's intentions.

Lack of ability, then, appears to be the only factor that may lead to a breakdown of the relation between intention and a behavior that is under volitional control. For the most part, however, people do not intend to perform behaviors that they realize are beyond their ability, and thus a person's intention, when appropriately measured, will usually predict his behavior.

Research on the Intention-Behavior Relation

Within our conceptual framework we assume that behavioral intentions are the immediate determinants of the corresponding overt behaviors. The discussion above has made it clear, however, that many factors may influence the magnitude of the intention-behavior relation. Only when the intention is measured at the same level of specificity as the behavior and has not changed between time of measurement and observation of the behavior, will it be highly predictive of the behavior in question. The wide range of intention-behavior relations that can be obtained is illustrated in an unpublished study by Ajzen, who asked students to indicate their intentions to perform each of 24 behaviors "in the foreseeable future." Intentions to take a psychology course for credit, to write letters home regularly, to go home for Christmas, to attend basketball games, to write fan mail to movie actors, etc., were measured on seven-point scales ranging from *I will* to *I will not*. About three months later, the students were contacted by telephone and asked whether or not they had performed each of the 24 behaviors since the time they had participated in the initial experiment. Although the majority of correlations were significant, they ranged from 0 to .77, with an average correlation of .34.

Many factors may have contributed to this great variation in the magnitude of intention-behavior relations. One problem is purely methodological and has to do with the behavior's base rate. Suppose that there is a perfect relation between intention and behavior, but because of measurement error, a perfect correspondence between these variables is obtained for only 99 percent of the subjects. To simplify computations, assume that intentions, like behaviors, are dichotomous (i.e., a person either intends or does not intend to perform the behavior). Now consider two behaviors, one with a very high base rate (everyone performs this behavior) and one with an intermediate base rate (50 percent of all people perform this behavior). Table 8.8 shows 2×2 contingency tables and the correlations between intentions and the high and low base rate behaviors. When the base rate is very extreme, a single exception to the correspondence between intention and behavior can reduce the correlation from 1 to 0. On the other hand, a single exception has little effect on the correlation when the behavior has a moderate base rate. Clearly, the behavioral base rate can greatly affect the size of the intention-behavior correlation. When correlations are used to estimate the strength of the intention-behavior relation, the behavioral base rate must be taken into consideration. Many of the low correlations in Ajzen's study were associated with extremely high or low base rate behaviors, such as attending meetings of Zero Population Growth, writing fan mail to movie actors, and going to movies regularly.

Table 8.8 Influence of Base Rates on Intention-Behavior Relation

High Base Rate

			Perfect correspondence							One exception		
			Intention							Intention		
			Yes	No						Yes	No	
			a	*b*						*a*	*b*	
	Behavior	Yes	99	0	99		Behavior	Yes		99	0	99
			c	*d*						*c*	*d*	
		No	0	1	1			No		0	1	1
			99	1						100	0	
			*r = 1.00							*r = .00		

Moderate Base Rate

			Perfect correspondence							One exception		
			Intention							Intention		
			Yes	No						Yes	No	
			a	*b*						*a*	*b*	
	Behavior	Yes	50	0	50		Behavior	Yes		50	0	50
			c	*d*						*c*	*d*	
		No	0	50	50			No		1	49	50
			50	50						51	49	
			*r = 1.00							*r = .98		

$$*r = \frac{ad - bc}{\sqrt{(a+b)\ (c+d)\ (a+c)\ (b+d)}}$$

Other low correlations may have been due to lack of opportunity on the part of some subjects to perform a given behavior they intended to perform or to unforeseen events, such as unexpected invitations to join friends at a basketball game, unexpected visitors, lack of financial resources, etc. Since these factors were not controlled, they may have changed the intentions of some subjects, thereby reducing the observed relation between the initial intentions and overt behaviors.

In contrast, several experiments have shown that when such factors are controlled, and when intentions and behaviors are measured at the same levels of specificity, high intention-behavior correlations are obtained. In Chapter 7 we discussed several studies dealing with the prediction of intentions on the basis of attitude toward the behavior and normative beliefs. Many of these studies have also included a measure of overt behavior. In the two studies using the Prisoner's Dilemma game (Ajzen and Fishbein, 1970; Ajzen, 1971b), the number of times subjects chose the cooperative alternative (i.e., alternative X) was predicted from their intentions to choose that alternative. In the three games played, the correlations over all subjects were .841, .897, and .822. Hornik (1970) asked subjects in his two-person war game how many missiles they intended to maintain to the end of the next trial, and he used this measure of intention to predict the number of missiles actually maintained. Correlations between intention and behavior were high. For example, the correlation between intentions measured after trial 25 correlated .867 with actual behavior on trial 26.

A different kind of behavior was predicted by Holman (1956), who presented students with a list of football games and for each game asked them to indicate whether they would or would not attend. After the football season was over, subjects were asked to report the games they had attended. A correlation of .80 was found between number of games attended and number of games subjects said they would attend.

A high intention-behavior correlation was also obtained by McArdle (1972). Patients at a V.A. hospital who were diagnosed as having a drinking problem indicated whether they intended to sign up for the hospital's Alcoholic Treatment Unit (ATU) by placing a check mark on a seven-point *likely–unlikely* scale. This question was part of a long questionnaire. Immediately following administration of the questionnaire, the patients were given a sign-up sheet for admission to the ATU. Intentions to sign up and actual signing behavior were found to correlate .76.

Finally, there is considerable evidence that people's intentions to vote for a given candidate are highly correlated with their self-reported voting behaviors (e.g., Fishbein and Coombs, 1974; Feldman and Fishbein, 1963b; A. Campbell *et al.*, 1960; Lazarsfeld, Berelson, and Gaudet, 1944). For example, Fishbein and Coombs (1974) found that correlations between intentions to vote and actual voting in the 1964 presidential election were .888 for Goldwater and .785 for Johnson.

Levels of specificity. The results presented so far indicate that high correlations can be obtained between appropriate measures of behavioral intentions and corresponding overt behavior. As we have noted earlier, one factor that may reduce the intention-behavior relation is lack of correspondence in levels of specificity. A case in point is LaPiere's (1934) study in which intentions to accept Chinese as guests in hotels and restaurants were compared with the actual acceptance of a particular Chinese couple at those establishments. Approximately six months after traveling with a Chinese couple throughout the United States, LaPiere sent a letter to each establishment they had visited asking the respondents whether "they would accept members of the Chinese race as guests in their establishments." With only one exception, the 250 establishments visited had accepted the Chinese couple; but of the 128 establishments that replied to LaPiere's letter, only one indicated that it would accept Chinese. However, Ajzen *et al.* (1970) have noted that the description of the attitude object and the situation is sufficiently incomplete and ambiguous in the letter-questionnaire that it probably constituted a very different stimulus from the actual Chinese couple. The relationship LaPiere found might have been different if the question had been worded, "Would you accept a young, well-dressed, well-spoken, pleasant, self-confident, well-to-do Chinese couple accompanied by a mature, well-dressed, well-spoken . . . educated European gentleman as guests in your establishment?" (p. 270)[17]

Fishbein (1966) reported some data showing the effects of variations in correspondence between levels of specificity in his study dealing with premarital sexual intercourse (PSI) among undergraduates. In this study, female subjects rated their general intentions to engage in PSI on a seven-point bipolar scale. On a second such scale they rated their intentions to engage in PSI *this semester*. The behavioral criterion was a self-report of sexual behavior during the course of the semester, obtained at the end of the semester. The general intention to engage in premarital sexual intercourse and self-reported behavior correlated .564. The more specific intention to engage in this behavior in the course of the semester showed a stronger relationship with behavior: The correlation was .676. Thus, as expected, the intention-behavior correlation increased with the degree of correspondence in levels of specificity. The reason that even the specific intention-behavior correlation was relatively low may in part have been that a whole semester had intervened between the measurement of these two variables. Many uncontrolled factors may have produced changes in the intention.

Stability of intentions. That behavioral intentions may change over time has been repeatedly demonstrated by political polls. For example, early in 1972 only 32 percent of the respondents in a national poll indicated that they would vote for McGovern if he ran against Nixon. Immediately prior to his nomination as the Democratic candidate for President, 41 percent indicated that they would vote for him. Following the Eagleton affair, this figure dropped to 34 percent. In the week prior to the election the figure had increased to 36 percent. McGovern actually received 38 percent of the popular vote. Not only do these data indicate that intentions change over time but, more important, that intentions measured immediately prior to the behavior tend to be better predictors than intentions measured some time in advance.

Although these data were based on group means, similar results were reported by Fishbein and Coombs (1974) for individual subjects. Intentions to vote for Goldwater in the 1964 presidential election correlated .796 with self-

---

17. Ajzen *et al.* (1970) also pointed out that "many of the respondents may have regarded the questionnaire not as an opportunity to speculate on what they would do in such a situation but as a convenient opportunity to avoid any possible trouble. Thus, the responses may not be honest expressions of intention. In addition, LaPiere had no way to determine if the person who responded to the questionnaire was the same person who had served him and the Chinese couple in the actual situation. Particularly in larger establishments, the person serving the Chinese couple and the person who responded to the questionnaire may not have been the same. Further, there may have been a number of changes in personnel during the six months between the observations of behavior and the questionnaire." (p. 270)

reported voting behavior when the intention was measured one month prior to the election and .888 when it was measured during the week preceding the election.

Further support for the notion that many intentions may change over time and thus lead to lowered correlations with behavior comes from Hornik's (1970) study, in which subjects played a two-person war game against a simulated partner. In the game, the players can convert "missiles" into "factories" or reconvert factories into missiles (see Pilisuk and Skolnick, 1968). The simulated partner played either a HAWK strategy (deceptive play, retaining all or most of his missiles on each trial), a GRIT strategy (taking small unilateral initiatives toward disarmament), or an RPM strategy (reward, punish, or match response to maximize the subject's disarmament). The measure of intention asked subjects to state how many missiles they intended to maintain till the end of the next trial. Overt behavior was the number of missiles actually maintained. Measures of intention were obtained at the beginning and after each block of five trials. In the GRIT and RPM conditions, in which the simulated confederate followed systematic cooperative strategies, the subjects' intentions became consistently and significantly more cooperative over trials. In the HAWK condition, in which the simulated confederate played six competitive response patterns in a random fashion, there was no systematic change in the mean number of missiles the subjects intended to maintain from trial to trial, although these intentions were not consistent (i.e., stable) over time. Further, it was predicted that the correlation between behavioral intention and game behavior would be highest when the intention is measured in close proximity to the behavior that serves as the criterion, and that this correlation would decline with increasing amounts of interaction between the measurement of intention and the observation of behavior. Hornik's data strongly supported these predictions. For example, behavior on trials 11 through 35 was highly related to intentions on trial 25; the mean correlation across conditions was .866 ($p < .001$). The average correlation between intentions on trial 10 and the same behavioral criterion was only .387 ($p < .05$), and intention at the beginning of the experiment (before trial 1) showed a nonsignificant correlation of .277 with the criterion.

It thus appears that the best measure of intentions for the prediction of a given behavior is one that is taken in close temporal proximity to the behavior that is to be predicted. Hornik's study also demonstrates that changes in intentions are affected by the nature of the events that intervene between measurement of intention and observation of behavior. Evidence for this notion also comes from a study by Darroch (1971), who employed a modified version of the DeFleur and Westie (1958) photographic-release technique. Polaroid pictures were taken of the subject with a black or a white confederate. Subjects were shown the photographs and asked to release them for a variety of purposes by signing appropriate release forms. Approximately one month prior to the picture-taking session, measures of specific behavioral intentions (as well as of other variables) had been obtained. Correlations between the number of releases signed and behavioral intentions varied from .262 to .584 for the different pictures taken, with an average of .462. (The subject was photographed with confederates varying in race and sex.)

A number of reasons may be suggested for these relatively low correlations. Variance in the predictor (intention) and the criterion (behavior) was found to be low; many subjects intended to sign and actually signed most release forms (i.e., base rates were high). In addition, approximately four weeks intervened between measurement of intentions and behavior. Moreover, at the beginning of the second session, a persuasive communication was introduced in an attempt to influence the subjects' normative beliefs. Unfortunately, no assessment was made of the effects of this manipulation on intentions. However, following the manipulation, measures were obtained of the subject's felt comfort in each picture, the degree of pleasure he would feel if his parents saw each picture, his perception of his friends' willingness to appear in a similar picture, and his judgment of the quality of each picture. On the assumption that these measures reflect to some degree the normative manipulation, as well as any other changes that may have occurred in the time interval, it should be possible to improve the prediction of behavior by considering these variables in addition to intentions. This expectation was confirmed by multiple correlations which ranged from .590 to .767, with an average multiple correlation of .735.

In her study of alcoholics, McArdle (1972) also investigated the effects of persuasive communications on behavior. As noted earlier, in the initial interview subjects expressed their intentions to sign up for the Alcoholic Treatment Unit and were given the opportunity to actually sign up. Three days later they were exposed to one of several persuasive communications designed to increase their sign-up rates and were then again given the opportunity to sign. Although the correlation between intention and the first measure of behavior was .76, that correlation was reduced to .63 following the persuasive communication.

We have argued that if Darroch or McArdle had obtained a measure of intention *after* exposing subjects to the persuasive communications, the intervening events would have been taken into account, and these posterior intentions would have predicted behavior more accurately. Although McArdle did not obtain a direct measure of posterior intention, she had an indirect estimate of this intention based on attitude toward the behavior and normative beliefs (see Chapter 7). Consistent with expectations, this estimate correlated .77 with behavior.

A more direct test of this hypothesis was reported by Ajzen and Fishbein (1974), who conducted a series of three studies in which the task of three-person groups was to balance a board in the shape of an equilateral triangle by raising or lowering their respective corners of the board.[18] On each trial the group members were permitted to send a written communication to one of their coworkers instructing him to raise or lower his corner. Two behavioral measures were taken:

---

18. A detailed description of the apparatus can be found in Raven and Eachus (1963), Raven and Shaw (1970), and Fishbein *et al.* (1970).

the number of instructions the subject sent to each coworker (communicative behavior) and the proportion of instructions from each coworker with which the subject complied (compliance behavior). Differences between the two coworkers on these two measures were used as the dependent variables. Similarly, differences were computed between the intentions to communicate with the two coworkers and between the intentions to comply with them, measured immediately prior to the first trial.

The correlation between intentions and communicative behavior was reasonably high ($r = .690$; $p < .01$); the correlation with compliance was much lower, though still significant ($r = .211$; $p < .01$). There is reason to suspect that the subjects changed their behavioral intentions as a result of their interactions on the task. First, with regard to communication, a person may initially intend to send instructions to one of his coworkers. But if he learns in the course of the interaction that this group member tends not to comply with his instructions, he is likely to change his evaluation regarding communication to this member, and he will modify his behavioral intentions accordingly. In support of this argument, a significant correlation of .528 was obtained between compliance by a given partner and the subject's communicative behavior toward that partner.

Second, concerning the subject's compliance behavior, it appears reasonable that his intention to comply with a given coworker will be influenced by the nature of the instruction he receives from the coworker. This argument is supported by the significant negative correlation ($r = -.456$) of compliance behavior with the absolute discrepancy between the instructions received by a subject and his own perception of the best course of action. That is, compliance decreased as the perceived unreasonableness of the instruction increased.

We expect addition of these mediating factors to the initial measures of behavioral intentions to improve the prediction of overt behavior. As Table 8.9 shows, this expectation was confirmed when the subject's intention to communicate and the coworker's compliance were regressed on communicative behavior. The regression weight of compliance by the coworker was .390 ($p < .01$), and the multiple correlation was .777. Similarly, a multiple correlation was computed with intention to comply and the above-mentioned index of discrepancy as predictors, and with compliance behavior as the criterion. The regression weight of the index of discrepancy was $-.431$ ($p < .01$), and the multiple correlation with behavior was .464. Thus the mediating variables made significant contributions to the prediction of overt behavior, independent of the specific intention measured at the *beginning* of the interaction.

More important, it is to be expected that the subject's intentions toward the *end* of the experiment will have been affected by these processes. In the study under consideration, posttest measures of behavioral intentions were obtained. When these posttest measures were used in multiple correlations on behavior, the regression weights of the mediating variables dropped to nonsignificance. The regression weight of compliance by coworkers in "postdicting" communications was .140, and the weight of the index of discrepancy was .122 in the postdiction of

Table 8.9 Correlations, Regression Coefficients, and Multiple Correlations of Behavioral Intentions (I), Perceived Percentage of Compliance (PPC), and Incompatibility Index (II) on Behavior (Communications and Compliance) (Adapted from Ajzen and Fishbein, 1974)

Behavior	Correlation coefficients		Regression coefficients		Multiple correlations
	I	PPC	I	PPC	
Communications					
Pretest	.690*	.605*	.532*	.390*	.777*
Posttest	.883*	.605*	.801*	.140	.890*
	I	II	I	II	R
Compliance					
Pretest	.211*	−.456*	.086	−.431*	.464*
Posttest	.502*	−.146	.560*	.122	.513*

* $p < .01$

compliance. The multiple postdictions of behavior were thus almost entirely due to the posttest behavioral intentions. The posttest correlations between intentions and behavior were .883 for instructions and .502 for compliance.

These findings provide some support for the notion that processes intervening between the measurement of intention and the observation of behavior will tend to reduce the relationship between these two variables by changing behavioral intentions. Prediction of behavior can be improved by either measuring the intentions after these changes have occurred or by taking the intervening events into account.

Volitional control. We have seen that when properly measured, intentions are highly predictive of corresponding overt behaviors. It can be shown, however, that the intention-behavior relation may break down if performance of the behavior depends on certain abilities or resources that the actor does not possess or if it depends on the cooperation of other people. For example, in Fishbein's (1966) study of premarital sexual intercourse among undergraduates, it was found that intentions were better predictors of behavior for females ($r = .676$; $p < .01$) than for males ($r = .394$; n.s.). This finding is consistent with the argument that lack of ability or opportunity may lower the correspondence between behavioral intentions and behavior. Clearly, females in our society may meet fewer obstacles than males when they attempt to execute their intentions to engage in premarital sexual intercourse. The reason that the correlation between intention and behavior was only .676 even for females can most likely be found in the fact that a whole semester intervened between the measurement of these two variables. Many uncontrolled factors may have produced changes in behavioral intentions.

Sometimes even behaviors that are apparently not under volitional control seem nevertheless to be related to intentions. In a study by Newton and Newton (1950) expectant mothers were classified as having positive, negative, or doubtful intentions to breast-feed their babies. After delivery, all mothers were told and encouraged to breast-feed. Milk supply on the fifth day following delivery was used to classify the mothers into three behavioral categories: successful (enough milk so that supplementary formulas were not necessary after the fourth hospital day), unsuccessful (continued breast-feeding, but supplementary formulas were necessary after the fourth day), and abortive (ceased efforts to breast-feed). The results of the study, presented in Table 8.10, show that breast-feeding behavior became more successful as intentions became more positive. Computing a measure of association[19] between intention and behavior results in a significant coefficient of .48. Thus, for example, mothers with positive intentions supplied more milk (an average of 59 grams per feeding on the fourth day) than did those with doubtful (42 grams) or negative (35 grams) intentions. Clearly, however, milk supply was not completely under volitional control. Even with positive intentions, some mothers were unable to supply a sufficient amount of milk for their babies.

Table 8.10 Relation Between Intention and Breast-feeding Behavior (Adapted from Newton and Newton, 1950)

Behavior	Intentions Positive		Doubtful		Negative	
Successful	74%	(38)	35%	(6)	26%	(6)
Unsuccessful	24%	(12)	47%	(8)	44%	(10)
Abortive	2%	(1)	18%	(3)	30%	(7)

Number of subjects in parentheses

To summarize briefly, we have tried to show that prediction of single-act criteria is not only possible but that it is relatively easy. Since much human behavior is under volitional control, most behaviors can be accurately predicted from an appropriate measure of the individual's intention to perform the behavior in question. For a high correlation between intention and behavior to obtain, however, two prerequisites have to be met. First, the intention has to be measured at the same level of specificity as the behavioral criterion, and second, the measure of intention must reflect the person's intention at the time he performs the behavior. Since intentions are usually measured some time prior to performance of the behavior, intervening events may change the behavioral intention and thus reduce its relation to behavior. Prediction of behavior can be improved by taking these intervening events into account. Although several factors may influence the size of any given intention-behavior relation, an investigator should usually be able to identify and appropriately measure an intention that will be highly correlated with the particular behavior he would like to predict.

---

19. A Phi coefficient was computed on Newton and Newton's (1950) data.

Given a high degree of correspondence between a person's intention and his actual behavior, one would expect the factors determining intentions also to be closely related to behavior. In Chapter 7 we discussed a theory for the prediction of intentions, and we showed that behavioral intentions are predictable from the attitudinal and normative components of the theory. It follows that whenever a high intention-behavior relation is observed, the behavior in question should also be predictable from attitude toward the behavior (A_B) and subjective norm (SN). Conversely, even when the two components accurately predict the intention, they will not predict the behavior if the intention measured is itself inappropriate for prediction of the behavior in question. We have already seen that A_B and SN can predict behavior with a high degree of accuracy. McArdle (1972) did not obtain a direct measure of intention but instead measured these two components. The multiple correlation of the two components with behavior was .77.

Additional evidence for these notions comes from several of the studies discussed earlier. We have discussed a number of studies that found a high correlation between intention and behavior, and in the preceding chapter we showed that many of the same intentions could be predicted with high accuracy from the attitudinal and normative components. As would be expected, these studies also showed that the two components were highly predictive of overt behavior. For example, in their study using two Prisoner's Dilemma games, Fishbein and Ajzen (1970) found multiple correlations of .732 and .793 between the two components of the model and strategy choices in the two games. In fact, owing to the high intention-behavior correlations, whatever factors were found to have significant effects on intentions were also found to have the same effects on the corresponding behaviors.

CONCLUSION

In this chapter we have discussed the prediction of overt behavior. We have seen that behavior can be measured at different levels of specificity and that it is important to distinguish between different types of behavioral criteria. Three major behavioral criteria were identified: single-act, repeated-observation, and multiple-act criteria. We showed that when properly constructed, repeated-observation criteria are essentially behavioral measures of attitudes toward behaviors, and multiple-act criteria are behavioral measures of attitudes toward objects.

We have argued that the best predictor of a person's behavior is his intention to perform the behavior, irrespective of the nature of the behavioral criterion. Intentions and behaviors were both shown to vary in terms of behavior, target, situation, and time. Whereas repeated-observation criteria represent behavioral measures across targets, situations, or time, multiple-act criteria represent measures across different behaviors. An appropriate measure of intention corresponds in its level of specificity to the behavior that is to be predicted. Thus, to predict such a single-act criterion as a person's attendance at the 7 A.M. Mass at St. Mary's Cathedral on the coming Sunday morning, the measure of intention has to

refer to exactly the same behavior. That is, the person's intention to attend the
7 A.M. Mass at St. Mary's Cathedral this coming Sunday has to be measured.
Similarly, the repeated-observation criterion "number of worship services at St.
Mary's Cathedral attended in the course of one year" requires a measure of intention such as "How many worship services at St. Mary's Cathedral do you intend
to attend during the coming year?" To predict a multiple-act criterion, it is usually
necessary to obtain an even more general measure of intention. A multiple-act
criterion based, for example, on observation of several religious behaviors at St.
Mary's Cathedral (e.g., number of worship services attended, amount of money
contributed, singing in the church choir, and teaching Sunday school) could be
predicted from the following measure of intention: "I intend/do not intend to
act supportive toward St. Mary's Cathedral."

Within our conceptual framework, intentions are viewed as the immediate
antecedents of corresponding overt behaviors. The apparent simplicity of this notion is somewhat deceptive, however. Since it is often impossible or impractical
to measure a person's intention immediately prior to his performance of the behavior, the measure of intention obtained may not be representative of the person's intention at the time of the behavioral observation. Intervening events that
may lead to changes in intentions will therefore also have to be taken into consideration. For example, if a person intends to buy a car three months hence, any
change in his financial position, the price of the car, or the availability of gasoline
may influence his intention and must therefore be taken into account if accurate
behavioral prediction is to be achieved. Barring such changes in intentions,
an appropriate measure of intention will usually allow accurate prediction of
behavior.

Understanding a person's behavior, however, requires more than just knowledge of his intention. It is not very illuminating to discover that people usually do
what they intend to do. If behavioral *prediction* is the primary objective, the
simplest and probably most efficient way to accomplish this is to obtain an appropriate measure of the person's intention. If *understanding* his behavior is the
primary objective, the factors determining his intention must be specified. Chapter
7 was devoted to a discussion of these factors. We presented a theoretical model
which specifies two major determinants of intentions: attitudes toward the behavior and subjective norms. These two components must be measured at the
same level of specificity as the intention. Given high correspondence between intention and behavior, one can also view the attitudinal and normative components
as the determinants of the behavior. In fact, when intention and behavior are
highly related, everything we have said about the factors influencing intentions
can also be applied to an understanding of the determinants of behavior. Thus,
it should not be surprising to find that attitude toward the behavior is often related to performance of the behavior.

In contrast, traditional measures of attitude toward an object can influence a
given behavior only indirectly, and thus low and inconsistent relations between
these attitudes and single-act or repeated-observation criteria are to be expected.

Unlike most traditional approaches, therefore, our approach has been to suggest that attitude toward an object will usually have at best a low relation to any given behavior with respect to that object. As would be predicted on the basis of our analysis of behavioral criteria, however, attitudes toward objects are found to be related to multiple-act criteria which may be viewed as behavioral measures of these same attitudes.

Part III

Changing Beliefs, Attitudes, Intentions and Behaviors

Chapter 9

Principles
of
Change

Of all the issues studied by investigators in the attitude area, the question of *attitude change* has undoubtedly received the most widespread attention. The usual assumption is that by means of changing the attitudes of individuals it is possible to influence their behavior, to improve social relations, or to produce social change. Thus, if it is possible to influence attitudes toward products, politicians, or minority groups, changes in consumer behavior, voting decisions, or interracial relations may follow. Reflecting the great interest in this issue, most previous books and reviews of the attitude area have dealt almost exclusively with processes of attitude change (e.g., Kiesler, Collins, and Miller, 1969; Insko, 1967; McGuire, 1969; Rosnow and Robinson, 1967; Greenwald, Brock, and Ostrom, 1968; Zimbardo and Ebbesen, 1969; Abelson *et al.,* 1968; Himmelfarb and Eagly, 1974a).

This book has devoted more than the usual amount of space to processes underlying the formation of beliefs, attitudes, and intentions, as well as to the prediction of behavior. Part III demonstrates the relevance of these processes for an understanding of the problems associated with attempts to bring about change. Chapter 9 develops some fundamental principles of change. We shall see that attempts to bring about change invariably involve exposure to new information about some object, behavior, issue, or event. Changes in beliefs resulting from such exposure to new information provide the foundation on which rests the ultimate effectiveness of any influence attempt. We will try to show that attempts to induce change in a given belief, attitude, intention, or behavior must take into account the relation between the variable that is to be changed and the beliefs that are affected most immediately by the influence attempt. Studies attempting to produce change in a given variable can only lead to inconsistent findings if the beliefs underlying that variable are not well understood. In Chapter 10 we shall discuss active participation on the part of the subject as a strategy for providing him with new information by means of direct observation. Chapter 11 will take up persuasive communication as the second major strategy of change; this strategy uses an outside source to provide the subject with new information.

Most investigations of attitude change have dealt with the effects of some experimental manipulation on a given dependent variable. Studies on the effects of a persuasive communication are not usually concerned with the amount of change produced by the communication itself; instead, they may examine the relative effectiveness of, say, attributing the message to a high as opposed to a low prestige communicator. Similarly, studies dealing with the effects of active participation are usually not concerned with the amount of change produced by the participation experience, but rather with the relative effectiveness of, for example, paying the person different amounts of money for his participation. Over the years, a large number of such variables have been manipulated in attempts to identify the most effective means of producing change. Almost without exception, these variables have not been found to have a systematic effect on the amount of change produced. In the following discussion we shall outline some basic principles of change that may help to explain these inconsistent findings.

THE ROLE OF BELEFS IN THE INFLUENCE PROCESS

Throughout this book we have made it clear that the notion of *belief* occupies a central role in our conceptual structure. A person's belief about an object was described as the perceived probabilistic relation between that object and some attribute.[1] We showed that the formation of one belief may lead to the development of other inferential beliefs; that a person's attitude is determined by his salient beliefs about the attitude object; and that beliefs about a given behavior and about the expectations of relevant others vis-à-vis that behavior determine a person's intention to perform the behavior and thus also influence the overt behavior itself.

This conceptualization makes it clear that an influence attempt, in the final analysis, must always be directed at one or more of the individual's beliefs. Our discussion in Chapter 5 suggested two ways in which a belief can be *directly* influenced. First, a person can be placed in a situation where he can personally observe that an object has a given attribute; and second, the person may be told by an outside source that the object has the attribute in question. These two alternative ways of directly influencing beliefs correspond to the two basic strategies used in attempts to produce change, namely, active participation and persuasive communication. Since a person rarely questions information received through his own sense organs, the major problem in active participation is to ensure that the

---

1. The terms "object" and "attribute" are used in the generic sense to refer to any discriminable aspects of the individual's world. Thus a physical object, a person, an institution, a behavior, a policy, an outcome, a trait, etc., may all constitute either the "object" of a belief or its attribute.

participant perceives the desired object-attribute association. In contrast, with persuasive communications, the major problem is to ensure that the receiver accepts (i.e., believes) the communication which attempts to link the object and the attribute.

Every object-attribute association to which an individual is exposed may be viewed as an "informational item." The individual's belief directly corresponding to an informational item will be termed a *proximal belief*. For example, the receiver of a persuasive communication may be exposed to such a statement as "The United States Constitution guarantees freedom of speech." This informational item links the object "United States Constitution" to the attribute "guarantees freedom of speech." The corresponding proximal belief is the receiver's initial (preexposure) subjective probability concerning this object-attribute link. In the case of active participation, the actor may observe a link between an object (such as a person) and an attribute (such as the person's hair color). The proximal belief corresponding to the observation that the person has black hair is the prior subjective probability concerning this object-attribute link.

In many instances, the proximal belief that is directly attacked by an informational item does not serve as the dependent variable of interest. Instead, some other belief, an attitude, an intention, or a behavior is the dependent variable that is to be changed. In fact, inferential beliefs, attitudes, intentions, and behaviors can be influenced only indirectly by changing one or more beliefs that serve as the primary determinants of these variables. One of the fundamental problems in any influence attempt, therefore, is the identification of those beliefs that need to be changed in order to influence the dependent variable under investigation. Such beliefs, which serve as the fundamental determinants of the dependent variable, will be termed *primary beliefs*. When the dependent variable is the attitude toward an institution, for example, beliefs about that institution's attributes or characteristics are some of the primary beliefs at which the influence attempt can be directed. When the dependent variable is attitude toward a behavior, primary beliefs associate the behavior with attributes such as costs or consequences. Much of the present chapter is devoted to an examination of the different kinds of primary beliefs that are appropriate for influence attempts designed to change inferential beliefs, attitudes, intentions, or behaviors.

Knowingly or unknowingly, an investigator makes the assumption that if certain beliefs are changed, a change in the dependent variable will follow. The beliefs which the investigator is attempting to change will be called *target beliefs*. Clearly, if the influence attempt is designed to change target beliefs that are unrelated to the dependent variable's primary beliefs, the influence attempt cannot be very effective. That is, a change in target beliefs will have little effect on the dependent variable unless the target beliefs selected by the investigator are themselves primary beliefs or are related to the primary beliefs.

To summarize our discussion thus far, an influence attempt is designed to change some dependent variable, whether it is a belief, an attitude, an intention, or a behavior. Closer examination reveals that the influence attempt is directed at certain target beliefs that are assumed to be the primary determinants of the dependent variable in question. Clearly, changing target beliefs will influence the dependent variable only when this assumption is met, that is, when the investigator's target beliefs are themselves primary or are related to the primary beliefs underlying his dependent variable. To produce the desired changes in his target beliefs, the investigator somehow exposes his subjects to a set of informational items. Resulting changes in the receiver's proximal beliefs may initiate a chain of effects, ultimately leading to a change in the dependent variable.

However, an influence attempt may also have an effect on *external beliefs,* that is, on beliefs that do not correspond to any of the informational items provided. Changes in external beliefs resulting from an influence attempt will be termed *impact effects.* Like direct effects on proximal beliefs, these indirect impact effects will influence the dependent variable only if the external beliefs affected serve as primary beliefs or if they are related to the primary beliefs.

Figure 9.1 illustrates some possible links between informational items and a dependent variable. We can see that primary beliefs serve as the fundamental determinant of the dependant variable. Informational items included in an influence attempt may produce changes in the receiver's proximal beliefs corresponding to the informational items or in some external beliefs. These proximal or external beliefs may themselves be primary beliefs (one-step chain), they may be directly related to the primary beliefs (two-step chain), or they may influence intervening external beliefs that are related to the primary beliefs (multiple-step chain). Some, all, or none of the beliefs in Fig. 9.1 may serve as target beliefs for the investigator. An influence attempt may fail to affect the dependent variable for at least three reasons. First, it may not produce the desired change in proximal be-

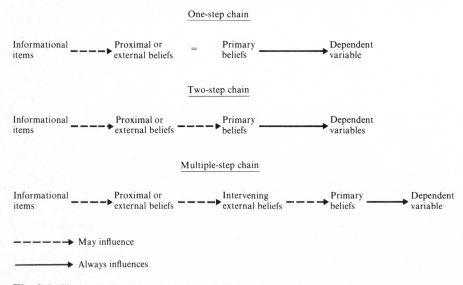

Fig. 9.1 Chain of effects involved in an influence attempt.

liefs. Second, even when changes in proximal beliefs occur, these changes may have no effect on the primary beliefs. Third, the influence attempt may have unexpected and undesirable impact effects on external beliefs, which can also influence the primary beliefs.

In Part II of this book we discussed the formation of inferential beliefs, attitudes, intentions, and behaviors, and we saw that these variables are influenced by (i.e., are functionally related to) different types of primary beliefs. We can now build on our previous analyses to provide some general principles of change.

Changing Inferential Beliefs

We have repeatedly noted that a person may form a belief directly by observing an object-attribute relation or accepting information to the effect that the object has the attribute, or he may form a belief indirectly by means of some inference process. Inferential beliefs are formed on the basis of other beliefs that the individual holds. Change in an inferential belief can therefore be brought about by changing some or all of the relevant (or primary) beliefs that provide the basis for the inference process.

We saw in Chapter 5 that an individual may arrive at a given belief in various ways. As an example, consider the belief "John is honest." Since honesty cannot be directly observed, the only way a person can acquire this belief directly is by accepting information from some outside source indicating that John is honest. However, there are numerous inference processes whereby he may arrive at the same belief. For example, the person may first form the belief that John returned a lost wallet, either by directly observing the event or by accepting information that the event occurred. In an attempt to find a causal explanation for John's behavior, he may make the attribution that John is honest. Alternatively, he may reach this inference on the basis of syllogistic reasoning. If we assume that he held the prior belief that people who return lost objects are honest, he might reason as follows: John returned a lost wallet; people who return lost wallets are honest; therefore John is honest. A different way of arriving at this inferential belief involves activation of an implicative structure of trait relations. Thus, if the person formed the belief that John was trustworthy, he might also infer that he was honest.

The ultimate purpose of an influence attempt, then, may be to change an inferential belief of this kind. To do so, one must induce changes in primary beliefs that are probabilistically related to and thus relevant for the inferential belief. In fact, the dependent inferential belief may be the end product of a chain of prior inferences (see Fig. 9.1). The investigator's choice of informational items and target beliefs should be guided by considerations of the underlying inference process. That is to say, he should be able to specify the probabilistic relations assumed to link the informational items to the dependent inferential belief. Such considerations should also permit the investigator to specify at least some of the relevant external beliefs.

Some evidence for these arguments can be found in several studies based on McGuire's (1960a, b, c) model of logical consistency (see Chapter 5). Recall that according to McGuire's model, acceptance of the conclusion in a logical syllogism is a function of the degree to which major and minor premises are accepted. McGuire (1960c) first attempted to show that by increasing a person's subjective probability that the minor premise (a primary belief) is true, one can increase the person's subjective probability that the related conclusion (the dependent inferential belief) is true. To test this hypothesis, McGuire constructed persuasive communications designed to increase beliefs in the minor premises of eight syllogisms. The minor premises thus served as his target beliefs. The messages were found to be quite effective; subjective probabilities associated with the eight minor premises increased, on the average, by 19.01 points on a 100-point probability scale. In addition, although conclusions were not mentioned in the persuasive messages, subjective probabilities for them also increased significantly. The average change for conclusions was 6.42 points. Similar results have been obtained in several other investigations (e.g., Holt and Watts, 1969; Dillehay, Insko, and Smith, 1966; Holt, 1970). Clearly, then, change in a target belief can produce change in a logically related belief, even though the inferential belief is never explicitly mentioned in the persuasive communication.

However, closer examination of these studies shows that the amount of change in the inferential belief (the conclusion) is *not* predictable from the amount of change in the target belief (the minor premise). Table 9.1 presents obtained changes in the eight minor premises, as well as changes in the eight conclusions, as reported by McGuire (1960c). Note that there is no systematic relation between amount of change in target belief and amount of change in the inferential belief. In one case, increased acceptance of the minor premise actually led to a significant *decrease* in the subjective probability associated with the con-

Table 9.1 Change in an Unmentioned Conclusion Produced by Change in a Minor Premise (Adapted from McGuire, 1960c)

Syllogism	Mean change in minor premise (target belief)	Mean change in conclusion (inferential belief)
3	7.14	12.14
2	11.07	4.29
5	18.56	9.64
1	18.56	14.63
4	20.71	13.56
8	22.85	−15.35
7	26.06	0.35
6	27.13	12.14

clusion, and in other cases, large increases in the minor premises were followed by small changes in the conclusions.

Viewed in terms of McGuire's logical consistency model, these results are not unexpected. Equation 9.1 is a formal statement of McGuire's model for the prediction of change in a conclusion,

$$\Delta p(c) = p(a) \, \Delta p(b) + \Delta p(a)p(b) + \Delta p(a) \, \Delta p(b) \qquad (9.1)$$

where a and b are the major and minor premises, c is the conclusion, Δp represents a change in the subjective probability that a premise or a conclusion is true, and p stands for the initial (precommunication) probability. It is apparent that change in the dependent inferential belief (the conclusion) is determined not only by change in the target belief (the minor premise) but also by a possible impact effect on an external belief not mentioned in the communication (i.e., change in the major premise).

If one takes into account impact effects on the major premise, in addition to change in the minor premise, it should be possible to improve prediction of change in the conclusion. Consistent with this argument, McGuire (1960c) measured amount of change in the two premises and used Eq. 9.1 to predict change in the conclusion. As expected, predicted and obtained changes in subjective probabilities associated with the conclusions were highly related. On the average, however, the obtained change (6.42) was significantly smaller than the change predicted by the model (12.85). Further, accuracy of prediction varied considerably among syllogisms. In some cases, the obtained change was greater, in others smaller, than the predicted change. Although some investigators (e.g., Dillehay, Insko, and Smith, 1966) have found no significant differences between predicted and obtained changes, the most common finding is that, even though considerations of changes in external beliefs (major premises) as well as target beliefs (minor premises) increases accuracy of prediction, there are significant differences between predicted and obtained changes in the dependent inferential beliefs (the conclusions).

McGuire (1960a, b, c) has attributed these differences to "wishful thinking," and he has shown that obtained changes in the conclusions are *smaller* than predicted changes when the conclusions are undesirable, and they are *larger* than predicted changes when the conclusions are desirable. An alternative explanation is possible, however. Looking at Eq. 9.1, we can see that according to McGuire's model, change in the conclusion of a logical syllogism is *completely* determined by changes in the major and minor premises. That is, the two premises are assumed to constitute the complete set of primary beliefs underlying the dependent variable. In contrast, McGuire's basic model of logical consistency (see Chapter 5) recognized that other beliefs might also influence the probability that a given conclusion is true, and thus change in the conclusion may also be due to changes in these other (external) beliefs. Further, although Eq. 9.1 assumes a deterministic relation between premises and conclusion, there is no reason to assume that subjects perceive such a strong relation between these variables; the degree of relationship between any two (or more) beliefs is an empirical question. If one takes the strength of this relationship into account, it should be possible to improve prediction of change in an inferential belief due to change in a target belief.

Considerable support for this argument comes from work based on Wyer's conditional consistency model (Wyer, 1970a, Wyer and Goldberg, 1970; see Chapter 5). According to this model, the amount of change in an inferential belief B is a function of the amount of change in some target belief A; the conditional probability of B, given A; and the conditional probability of B, given not-A. The two conditional probabilities attempt to take into account the relation between target belief and inferential dependent belief; further, the conditional probability $p(B|\overline{A})$ refers in part to relevant external beliefs that may also influence the inferential belief. Wyer's model is given in Eq. 9.2.

$$\Delta\, p(B) = \Delta\, [\, p(B|A)p(A) + p(B|\overline{A})p(\overline{A})\,]. \tag{9.2}$$

To test this model Wyer (1970a) first described nine hypothetical situations involving two central beliefs and the relation between these beliefs. The probability of the target belief, $p(A)$, was initially set at a low level. In one situation, for example, the probability that Governor Smith would be reelected was said to be low. The description also varied the relation of the target belief to an inferential belief (B), the conclusion, by manipulating the conditional probability that B would occur if A occurred $[p(B|A)]$, as well as the conditional probability that B would occur if A did not occur $[p(B|\overline{A})]$. For example, the probability that state aid to education would be increased, given that Governor Smith was (or was not) reelected, was set at a high, medium, or low level. Each of the nine situations represented a different combination of $p(B|A)$ and $p(B|\overline{A})$ in a 3 × 3 design.

Each subject read all nine situations, and after each description, measures of $p(A)$, $p(B)$, $p(B|A)$, and $p(B|\overline{A})$ were obtained; these measures demonstrated that the desired initial probability levels had been established. After providing probability judgments for a given situation, subjects read a message designed to increase $p(A)$, the probability of the target belief. A change in $p(A)$ was expected to influence the inferential belief $p(B)$ to the extent that beliefs A and B were related.

Consistent with expectations, the persuasive message produced considerable changes in the target belief as well as in the inferential belief; the amount of change in the inferential belief, however, varied from situation to situation. In some situations its probability increased, in others it remained about the same, and in some it decreased. On the average, Wyer found a change of .005 in the probability of the inferential beliefs. In comparison, the average amount of change in the probabilities of the target beliefs was found to be .417. Clearly, changes in the dependent variable could not be predicted from changes in the target belief. This is not unexpected since changes in the inferential belief depend not only on the amount of change in the target belief but also on the degree of relation between target and inferential beliefs.

Results presented in Table 9.2 show that the amount and direction of change in the inferential belief depended largely on its relation to the target belief. When that relation was strong and positive [that is, $p(B|A)$ was high and $p(B|\overline{A})$ was low], the greatest increase in the inferential belief was observed. When the relationship was low (the two conditional probabilities were about equal), little change was found. Finally, when there was a strong negative relation [$p(B|A)$ was low and $p(B|\overline{A})$ was high], the greatest decrease in the inference was observed.

Table 9.2 Change in Dependent Belief as a Function of Change in Target Belief and Relation between Target and Dependent Beliefs (Adapted from Wyer, 1970a)

	Low $p(B|\overline{A})$	Medium $p(B|\overline{A})$	High $p(B|\overline{A})$
High $p(B|A)$			
Change in target belief	.459	.296	.469
Change in dependent belief	.488	.151	.102
Medium $p(B|A)$			
Change in target belief	.441	.284	.575
Change in dependent belief	.165	−.027	−.351
Low $p(B|A)$			
Change in target belief	.304	.427	.496
Change in dependent belief	.247	−.182	−.545

By taking both amount of change in target beliefs and conditional probabilities into account, Wyer was able to predict (using Eq. 9.2) obtained changes in the inferential beliefs with considerable accuracy. Figure 9.2 shows the relation between predicted and obtained changes in the inferential dependent belief for the nine hypothetical situations. The average discrepancy between predicted and obtained changes was only .003.

In conclusion, the studies by McGuire (1960a, b, c), Wyer (1970a), Wyer and Goldberg (1970) and others have shown that an inferential belief can be influenced by changing a target belief. However, change in the target belief does not always influence the inferential belief. The amount of change in an inferential belief depends on many factors. First, it depends on the strength of the relationship between target and inferential beliefs. That is, the target belief selected by the investigator must itself be a primary belief or be related to one or more primary beliefs. Given some degree of relationship, amount of change in inferential belief is a function of the amount of change in target belief. Second, impact effects on external primary beliefs (i.e., primary beliefs not serving as target beliefs) have to be taken into consideration. Again, the effect on the inferential belief should increase with the amount of change in the external primary beliefs and with the

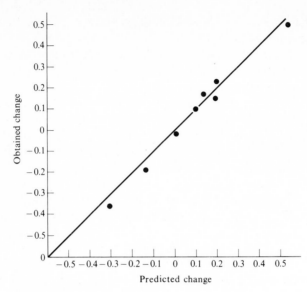

Fig. 9.2 Predicted and obtained changes in dependent beliefs. (From Wyer, 1970a.)

strength of the relationship between these primary beliefs and the dependent variable.

Changing Attitudes

We saw in Chapter 6 that attitude toward an object is determined by a person's salient beliefs that the object possesses certain attributes and by his evaluations of those attributes. Thus attitudes can be changed by changing one or more of the existing salient beliefs, by introducing new salient beliefs, or by changing the person's evaluations of the attributes. Beliefs about the object and attribute evaluations can therefore be viewed as two different determinants of attitude at which an influence attempt can be directed.

Changing beliefs about an object. The problems involved in changing beliefs were discussed in the preceding section. Inferential beliefs that were treated as dependent variables in the discussion of belief change may now be viewed as target beliefs in an attitude-change situation. An investigator typically assumes that if he can change certain beliefs that the subject holds, there will follow a change in the subject's attitude toward an object, person, concept, or behavior.

The first major problem consists in identifying the primary beliefs for a given attitude. Within our conceptual framework this problem is quite easily resolved. Any belief that associates the attitude object with some other object, concept, or property and that is part of the person's *salient* belief hierarchy constitutes a primary belief. It is important to note that the object of the primary beliefs is exactly the same as the object of the attitude which is to be changed. Consider, for example, an influence attempt designed to change attitudes toward communism. Salient beliefs linking *communism* to such attributes as totalitarian government, socialism, lack of freedom, etc., are primary beliefs and would therefore constitute appropriate target beliefs. If these same attributes were associated with a particular communist country, say Russia, we would obtain beliefs about *Russia,* such as "Russia has a totalitarian government" or "Russia practices socialism." Although these associations may constitute appropriate target beliefs for changing attitudes toward Russia, they do not serve as primary beliefs with respect to attitudes toward communism. In fact, they may be completely unrelated to the primary beliefs about communism. Similarly, if the cited attributes of totalitarian government, socialism, etc., were said to be consequences of a behavior such as *trading with communist countries,* we would be dealing with beliefs about this particular behavior, which may also be completely irrelevant for attitude toward communism.

It is unfortunate that these kinds of considerations have usually not guided selection of target beliefs, with the result that inappropriate target beliefs have often been attacked in attempts to influence attitudes. For example, attempts have been made to change attitudes toward minority groups by attacking beliefs about particular members of those groups or by attacking beliefs about the consequences of performing one or more behaviors with respect to certain group members.

Attitude change is expected only if the target beliefs are initially part of the subject's *salient* belief hierarchy, or if they become salient as a result of the influence attempt. Evidence indicating that an influence attempt can introduce new beliefs into the salient belief hierarchy was presented by Thomas and Tuck (in press). In this study, a sample of subjects were first asked to elicit their beliefs about Sweden. Three weeks later they were given a persuasive communication containing several (target) belief statements about Sweden that were not part of the initial set of salient beliefs. Immediately following exposure to this message, subjects were again asked to elicit their beliefs about Sweden. Some of the initially salient beliefs were no longer listed whereas a few of the target beliefs had entered the salient belief hierarchy. These effects were found to persist one week later when subjects were again asked to elicit their beliefs about Sweden. In comparison, control subjects who received no persuasive communication retained the same set of salient beliefs throughout the experiment.

Note that even appropriate target beliefs may represent only part of the primary beliefs determining a given attitude. The influence attempt may have an effect not only on target beliefs but also on other primary beliefs about the attitude object, and these impact effects may be responsible in part for the obtained attitude change. Similarly, the influence attempt may have impact effects on the evaluation of attributes associated with the primary beliefs, which may also influence the amount of attitude change obtained.

Some of the issues raised by directing an influence attempt at beliefs about the attitude object are illustrated in a study by Lutz (1973), who examined the effects of manipulating different kinds of target beliefs on attitude toward using a hypothetical laundry detergent. First, Lutz obtained a list of modal salient or primary beliefs by means of a free-elicitation procedure. Employing four experimental conditions, he then attempted to increase or decrease one of these primary beliefs that linked using the detergent with either a positive or negative outcome. Depending on their initial beliefs, subjects were told either that the detergent could or that it could not be used at all temperatures (positive outcome); in the remaining two conditions, subjects were told that using the detergent was or was not costly (negative outcome).

In addition to assessing the influence attempt's effect on the target belief, Lutz also measured its impact on nine other (primary) external beliefs about using the detergent. He found that attitude change could be predicted by considering changes in target and external beliefs. In all four conditions, the influence attempt produced the desired change in target belief. This change in target belief, taking into account attribute evaluation, showed a correlation of .415 with change in attitude toward using the detergent. However, the influence attempt was also found to have a significant impact effect on some of the primary external beliefs or on their attribute evaluations. When this impact effect was considered in addition to the change in target belief, the correlation with attitude change was raised to .572. As expected, the direction of attitude change was a function of both the direction of belief change and of attribute evaluation. Increasing a person's belief that the detergent can be used at all temperatures or decreasing his belief that using the detergent was costly led to a more favorable attitude whereas changing those beliefs in the opposite direction produced less favorable attitudes.

Changing attribute evaluations. Instead of attacking a person's beliefs that an object has certain attributes, the investigator may attempt to change the evaluations of some of those attributes. Recall that a person's evaluation of an attribute represents his attitude toward that attribute. It follows that changing his evaluation of a given attribute requires changing his primary beliefs about that attribute's characteristics or his evaluations of those characteristics. Since the latter evaluations again represent attitudes, this line of reasoning can be continued indefinitely. The main point is that, in the final analysis, attitude change involves changing a person's beliefs, whether they are beliefs about the object or beliefs about its attributes.

A full understanding of an influence attempt directed at attribute evaluations, therefore, requires consideration of the beliefs about the attribute that were changed by the influence attempt. However, in order to understand its effects on the dependent measure of attitude, it will often be sufficient to assess the influence attempt's effects on the attribute evaluations. In addition, it will be necessary to examine possible impact effects on evaluations of other attributes or on primary beliefs about the attitude object.

The study by Lutz (1973) described earlier also attempted to change attitude by attacking attribute evaluations. As noted, attribute evaluation can be changed only indirectly by influencing beliefs about the attribute. Lutz provided information about one outcome of using the hypothetical laundry detergent, namely, its suds production. One persuasive communication linked high suds production to three positive consequences (e.g., low wear and tear on the washing machine and clothing), and a second communication linked this attribute to three negative consequences (e.g., high wear and tear on the washing machine and clothing). These messages were found to influence the initial relatively neutral attribute evaluation as expected: subjects who received the first message now had a positive evaluation of sudsiness, and subjects who received the second message evaluated sudsiness negatively. In addition, the messages had significant impact effects. These changes in attribute evaluations and impact effects influenced attitude toward using the laundry detergent in the expected direction, although the change in attitude did not reach statistical significance. Subjects who believed that using the detergent produced a large amount of suds tended to increase their attitudes toward using the detergent when their evaluation of sudsiness was raised, whereas a decrease in attitudes was recorded when their evaluation of sudsiness was lowered. The two persuasive communications tended to have opposite effects for subjects who believed that using the detergent produced few suds.

In sum, attitudes can be changed by attacking beliefs that the object has certain attributes, or by influencing evaluations of those attributes. Irrespective of the strategy used, in order to understand the effects of an influence attempt on a dependent measure of attitude, one must know its effects on the person's salient belief hierarchy. Within our conceptual framework, attitude (A) is viewed as determined by the sum of the person's salient beliefs about an object's attributes (b) multiplied by his evaluations (e) of these attributes, as shown in Eq. 9.3.

$$A = \Sigma \ b_i e_i. \tag{9.3}$$

It follows that attitude change will be obtained only when the influence attempt succeeds in changing the sum of the cross-products $(\Sigma \ b_i e_i)$. In other words, to produce attitude change requires first and foremost a change in the informational base underlying the attitude.

The most common strategy is to direct the influence attempt at target beliefs which are assumed to be primary determinants of the attitude. These target beliefs may correspond directly to the informational items used in the influence attempt, or they may be attacked indirectly through impact effects. Changes in target beliefs, however, even when they are primary, may not be sufficient to bring about change in attitude. For example, if the belief affected linked the attitude object to a neutrally evaluated attribute, $\Sigma \ b_i e_i$ would remain unaltered and no change in attitude would result. Alternatively, if the influence attempt increased two of the individual's beliefs, one with a positive attribute and the other with a negative attribute, these effects would cancel each other, again leaving the attitude unchanged. Similarly, if the two attributes had the same evaluations, but one belief was increased and the other reduced, no change would be expected. Finally, if a target belief entered the salient belief hierarchy at the expense of an old belief with equivalent strength and attribute evaluation, $\Sigma b_i e_i$ would remain the same and no change in attitude would occur.

Similar considerations apply when attribute evaluations are to be changed. Even when the influence attempt produces a change in the evaluation of an attribute, this may have no effect on the attitude. Clearly, the attribute attacked must be associated with a salient belief about the attitude object; changing the evaluation of one attribute may have impact effects on the evaluations of other attributes, as well as on the strength of the primary beliefs about the object; changes in the evaluations of more than one attribute may cancel each other; and the amount and direction of attitude change will depend not only on the amount and direction of change in attribute evaluations but also on the strength of beliefs about the attitude object. In short, attitude change depends on the effects of the influence attempt on the total informational base underlying the attitude.

Changing Intentions

It is usually assumed that changing certain beliefs or attitudes will have an effect on a person's intention to perform a given behavior. Thus investigators have sometimes attacked beliefs about performing the behavior, attitudes toward the object of the behavior, or attitudes toward the situation in which the behavior is to occur. The problem is to identify the attitudes and beliefs relevant for a given intention. Our conceptual framework also provides an answer to this problem.

In Chapter 7 we saw that a person's intention to perform a given behavior is determined by his attitude toward the behavior and his subjective norm with respect to the behavior. Our model for predicting intentions is presented in Eq. 9.4.

$$I = [A_B]w_1 + [SN]w_2. \tag{9.4}$$

Attitude toward the behavior and the subjective norm thus represent the two immediate determinants of intentions. The effects of an attempt to influence intentions depend on its effects on these attitudinal and normative components; the amount of change in intention produced by a change in one of the components is a function of the component's relative weight in determining the intention. An influence attempt directed at any other variable will be effective in changing an intention only to the extent that it influences one or the other of the two components that serve as the determinants of that intention.

Recall that an intention is composed of four elements—the behavior, its target, the situation, and time—and that the intention can vary in terms of its specificity with respect to each of these four elements. In an attempt to change intention, it is important to ensure that A_B and SN are attacked at precisely the same level of specificity as the intention under consideration.

Changing attitude toward the behavior. In the preceding section we discussed the problems involved in changing attitudes. We saw that attitude toward a behavior can be influenced by changing salient beliefs about the behavior or by changing evaluations associated with these beliefs. A complete analysis of the influence attempt's effects on the attitudinal component, therefore, requires examination of its effects on the determinants of the attitude. However, when A_B is attacked in an attempt to produce change in intentions, it will often be sufficient to obtain a direct measure of the attitude toward the behavior.

Changing subjective norms. A person's subjective norm is his belief that important others think he should or should not perform a given behavior. A belief of this kind can be attacked either directly by providing information that most important others hold a given expectation or indirectly by changing some other beliefs. We noted that many different inference processes can lead to the formation of a given inferential belief. Thus a person may learn that most important others perform the behavior under consideration, and he may then infer that these important referents think he should perform the behavior.

Many different inference processes may be involved, but we considered one formulation in Chapter 7 that appears to be of particular importance. A person's subjective norm was viewed as a function of his normative beliefs that particular referents, relevant for the behavior in question, think he should or should not perform that behavior, weighted by his motivation to comply with each referent. This formulation implies that the subjective norm can be changed by attacking either the specific normative beliefs or the motivation to comply with a given referent. We saw in Chapter 7 that normative beliefs constitute inferences based on other beliefs about the referent individuals or groups. Earlier we discussed the principles involved in changing beliefs, and these principles can again be applied directly to normative beliefs. We noted in Chapter 7, however, that the processes underlying formation of motivation to comply are not well understood. It was suggested that motivation to comply may be related to beliefs about the referent's power or to intentions to comply with the referent. Thus, in order to change motivation to comply, in the final analysis it will again be necessary to change certain beliefs.

As in the case of the attitudinal component, it will usually be sufficient to assess the effectiveness of the influence attempt by obtaining a direct measure of the subjective norm, i.e., of the person's belief as to what important others think he should do. For a fuller understanding of the effects of an influence attempt on the normative component, however, normative beliefs and motivation to comply with respect to particular referents may have to be considered. As in the case of attitudes, a change with respect to one normative belief or a change in motivation to comply with a given referent may or may not influence subjective norms. Only when the weighted sum of normative beliefs times motivation to comply changes will a change in the subjective norm follow.

We have noted that attempts to change either the attitudinal or the normative component must, in the final analysis, be directed at certain primary beliefs. When attitude toward the behavior is to be changed, these beliefs are concerned with the kinds of outcomes produced by the behavior or with the characteristics of those outcomes. In the case of subjective norm, the primary beliefs may be the norm itself, or they may be beliefs about the expectations of relevant referents, their attitudes, their behavior, or their power. A complete analysis of an attempt to influence intentions may thus have to assess its effects on these different kinds of primary beliefs.

Impact effects on intentions. Not only may an item of information to which a person is exposed during an influence attempt affect one of the determinants of the intention—say, the attitude toward the behavior—but it may also have an impact on the second determinant of intention, the subjective norm. Consider, for example, a person who observes that his best friend receives $5 for tutoring a student. Formation of this descriptive belief may lead him to infer that tutoring a student is financially rewarding, and this belief may in turn increase his attitude toward tutoring a student. At the same time, the descriptive belief may also lead the person to infer that his best friend thinks he should tutor a student. This inferential belief may increase the subjective norm that most important others think he should tutor a student. Alternatively, once the person has changed his attitude in a favorable direction, he may infer that most important others also hold a favorable attitude toward tutoring a student and then make the further inference that these referents think he should perform this behavior. An influence attempt can thus have an impact effect even if it provides information that is directly relevant for only one determinant of intentions. The strength and direction of this kind of impact effect will depend on the extent to which the two components are related and the direction of the relationship.

The role of relative weights in changing intentions. Our discussion above indicated that intentions could be changed by attacking either attitudes toward the behavior or subjective norms. No consideration was given to the relative effectiveness of the two strategies. The model presented in Eq. 9.4 suggests that the two determinants may not be equally relevant for the intention under consideration. Even when successful in changing one of the determinants, an influence attempt may have little effect on intention if the component attacked does not carry a significant weight. The relative weights of the attitudinal and normative components may be influenced by variations in any one of the intention's four elements (behavior, object, situation, and time) and by individual-difference variables. Further, the influence attempt itself may affect the relative importance placed on the two components.

Two recent studies illustrate how intentions can be changed by influencing attitudes toward the behavior or subjective norms. They also demonstrate the importance of taking the relative weights of these two components into account. In the first study, Ajzen and Fishbein (1972) attempted to change behavioral intentions in a hypothetical decision situation involving some risk. The decision involved an investment of $1000 in a building project (see Chapter 7 for a description of the situation). In a pretest, the subject's estimate of the project's chances of success was set at 70 percent. Furthermore, his close family and friends with whom the subject was said to have discussed the issue also had a 70 percent subjective probability of success. The subject's intention to invest the money was measured, as were his attitude toward the behavior and his normative beliefs (i.e., the perceived expectations of his close family and friends). Computing the multiple correlation of attitude toward the behavior and normative beliefs on behavioral intentions showed that the attitudinal component was highly related to intention ($r = .841$) and that it carried most of the weight in the prediction ($w_1 = .833$). The regression coefficient of the normative component was nonsignificant ($w_2 = .019$). The investigators therefore predicted that change in the attitudinal component would be reflected in corresponding change of intentions, whereas intentions would be relatively unaffected by change in the normative component.

Following an unrelated intervening activity, subjects received a message designed to influence one of two target beliefs. In one condition, the subject was told that he had obtained new information which had lowered his own subjective probability of success to 30 percent (*attitudinal message*). In a second condition, he was told that his close family and friends had obtained new information which had lowered their subjective probability of the project's success to 30 percent (*normative message*).

Immediately following this communication, the subject's intention to invest the money, his attitude toward that behavior, and his normative beliefs were again measured. The persuasive communication had the expected effects on the components: The attitudinal message lowered the subject's attitude toward investing the money, and the normative message lowered his normative belief that his close family and friends thought he should invest the money. Intentions, however, were affected very little by the shift in normative beliefs, whereas the reduction in attitude toward the behavior was accompanied by a strong decrease in behavioral intentions.

This study demonstrates that changes in subjective norms will not produce changes in behavioral intentions when the normative component has little predictive power. The second study by Ajzen (1971b) supported the same principle with respect to changes both in attitude toward the behavior and in normative beliefs. The experiment involved a Prisoner's Dilemma game played under a cooperative or a competitive motivational orientation. As mentioned in Chapter 7, in the prediction of intentions the normative component is of greater importance than the attitudinal component in the cooperative condition, but the reverse is true for the competitive condition. Shifts in intentions resulting from changes in the subjective norm should thus be more pronounced in the cooperative condition than in the competitive condition. Conversely, changes in attitude toward the behavior should influence intentions more under competition than under cooperation.

To effect changes in the two components, half of the subjects in each motivational condition were given an attitudinal message, and the other half were given a normative message. The attitudinal message was designed to make the attitude

toward cooperation either more favorable or less favorable by changing the subject's beliefs about the consequences of cooperating or competing. The normative
message stressed that the other player expected the subject to cooperate or compete. As Fig. 9.3 shows, the results strongly supported the prediction. A highly
significant motivational orientation by message-type interaction was found: The
attitudinal message changed intentions under competition, and the normative
message was most effective under cooperation.

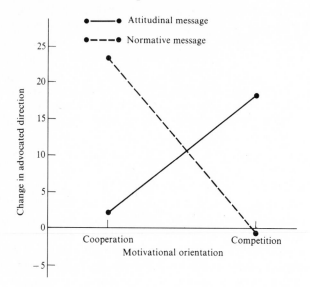

Fig. 9.3 Effects of attitudinal and normative messages
on intentions in a Prisoner's Dilemma game. (Adapted
from Ajzen, 1971b.)

These studies show that intention can be influenced by changing either the
attitudinal or the normative component. The effectiveness of an influence attempt
designed to change intention depends on the component that is attacked. Messages
directed at the attitudinal component are effective only if that component carries
a significant weight in the prediction of intentions. The same holds true for a
message directed at the normative component. If one of the components is of little
importance in the prediction of intentions, then any attempt to change it, even if
successful, cannot be expected to have a strong effect on intentions.

Another problem is that an influence attempt directed at one component may
have an unanticipated impact effect on the second component. This impact effect
may produce undesirable changes in intentions. Further, the influence attempt
may also have an effect on the relative weights of the two components. For example, if the subject's attention is called to normative considerations, the normative component may take on added weight. These effects may again produce
unexpected changes in intentions. These considerations suggest that change in

intentions can be expected only when the weighted sum of the two components [that is, $(A_B)w_1 + (SN)w_2$] is affected by the influence attempt.

Changing Behavior

We saw in Chapter 8 that many different variables have been proposed as possible determinants of overt behavior, and attempts to change behavior have been directed at one or more of these variables. Within our conceptual framework, however, the immediate determinant of a given behavior is the intention to perform that behavior. To change a person's behavior, it is therefore necessary to change his intention to perform the behavior, a process which was discussed in the preceding section. If an influence attempt fails to produce a change in intention, no change in behavior can be expected. A complete understanding of an influence attempt's effects on behavior, however, would require not only examination of its effects on intention but also its effects on all determinants of that intention.

That a change in intentions can produce behavioral change was shown by Ajzen (1971b) in the study using the Prisoner's Dilemma game. As noted, the persuasive communications led to the desired changes in intentions. Immediately following reception of the persuasive messages and assessment of intentions, subjects played the game for a total of 20 trials. Changes in intentions were found to produce corresponding changes in behavior.

An influence attempt that succeeds in changing intentions may not always lead to behavioral change, however. Recall that the specificity of behavioral criteria can vary with respect to behavior, target, situation, and time (see Chapter 8). Selection of a behavioral criterion determines the level of specificity for each of these four elements. Clearly, to be maximally effective in changing a behavior (or behavioral index), an influence attempt must be directed at the intention to perform that very behavior or behavioral pattern. That is, the intention and the behavioral criterion should correspond exactly in terms of their levels of specificity. For example, if the change in behavior is to be observed in a given situation at some point in the future, the intention at which the influence attempt is directed should be the person's intention to perform the behavior in question in that situation and at the specified point in time. The lower the correspondence, the less a change in intention can be expected to affect overt behavior.

A second consideration refers to events that may intervene between the change in intention brought about by the influence attempt (at time 1) and actual performance of the behavior (at time 2). These intervening events may produce additional unexpected changes in intention which may prevent the desired behavioral change. To increase the likelihood of the influence attempt's success, the investigator has three options. First, he can select a behavioral criterion which is likely to be associated with a stable intention. For example, there may be fewer events interfering with a general intention to "help other people" than with the more specific intention to "stop at the scene of a traffic accident." On the assumption that this is true, the attempt to change a multiple-act criterion based on several helping behaviors is more likely to succeed than the attempt to change a single-act criterion, such as stopping at the scene of a traffic accident. Second, the investigator can try to prevent the occurrence of intervening events. One way of accomplishing this is to change the actor's intention immediately prior to the time at which the behavior will be observed. The less time that elapses between the influence attempt and the behavior, the fewer events are likely to intervene. The third possibility is for the investigator to try to counteract the intervening event when it cannot be prevented. Imagine a television salesman who has succeeded in raising a person's intention to buy a color television set within the next two weeks and who knows that the prices for such sets will go down in about a month. Since the potential buyer may hear about the forthcoming price reduction, the salesman may try to counteract the possible interference by telling the buyer that although prices may go down in the future, the reduction in price will be accompanied by a reduction in the set's warranty and thus an increase in the cost of repairs.

BASIC GUIDELINES FOR CHANGE

Our discussion up to this point has made it clear that the distinction between belief, attitude, intention, and behavior is essential for an analysis of the influence process. This distinction is necessary since different factors serve as the immediate determinants of these variables. Moreover, what serves as a determinant in one situation may represent the dependent variable in another, resulting in a chain of influence effects that ranges from beliefs to behavior. Thus, in order to change behavior, an influence attempt should be directed at the intention to perform that behavior. To change that intention, however, it will be necessary to focus on attitude toward the behavior or subjective norms. Attitude toward the behavior, or any other attitude, can be changed by influencing primary beliefs about the attitude object or the evaluations of its attributes. The latter variable, however, is also determined by beliefs, namely, primary beliefs about the attributes. Similarly, if subjective norms were to be changed, the determinants would be primary normative beliefs and motivation to comply. Changing the latter variable again requires that certain primary beliefs be attacked. This chain of effects is illustrated in Fig. 9.4.

It is apparent that, irrespective of the dependent variable under consideration, to be effective an influence attempt must first produce changes in primary beliefs. These considerations lead us to the formulation of our first principle of change.

1. *The effects of an influence attempt on change in a dependent variable depend on its effects on the primary beliefs underlying that variable.*

This principle emphasizes the need for careful selection of informational items and target beliefs. By selecting target beliefs that constitute primary beliefs or that are related to the primary beliefs, the investigator increases the likelihood that a

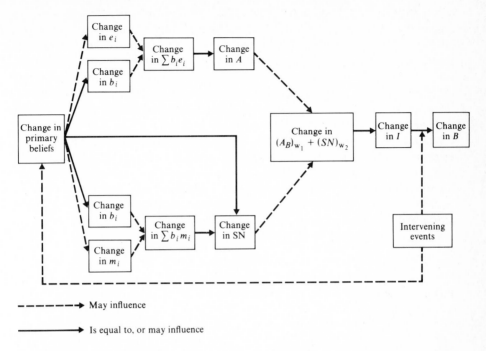

Fig. 9.4 Relations between change in primary beliefs and change in different dependent variables.

change in target beliefs will have the desired effects on the immediate determinants of the dependent variable and hence on the dependent variable itself.

To produce the desired changes in primary belief, the influencing agent provides informational items which may lead to changes in the receiver's corresponding proximal beliefs. Changes in these proximal beliefs are expected to influence certain target beliefs that are assumed to be directly or indirectly related to the dependent variable. In addition, the influence attempt may also have impact effects on external beliefs. For the influence attempt to be successful, the changes in proximal and external beliefs must lead to changes in primary beliefs. The changes in proximal and external beliefs, therefore, are ultimately responsible for any changes in the dependent variable (see Fig. 9.1).

This discussion suggests an additional principle of change.

2. *The effects of an influence attempt on change in a dependent variable are ultimately the result of changes in proximal beliefs and of impact effects.*

Even though an investigator may make inappropriate assumptions about the determinants of his dependent variable, his influence attempt may produce changes in proximal or external beliefs that are related to primary beliefs. For example, in order to change a person's intention to perform a given behavior, the investigator may attempt to change the attitude toward the object of the behavior. The informational items contained in the influence attempt, however, might correspond to beliefs about the consequences of performing the behavior with respect to the object. Although a change in these proximal beliefs about the behavior may have no effect on attitude toward the object, it may influence attitude toward the behavior and may thus have the desired effect on intention.

Our discussion has made it clear that many different processes intervene between an influence attempt and change in some dependent variable. The number of links involved varies from one dependent variable to another. Our third general principle of change deals with this chain of events.

3. *The effects of an influence attempt on change in beliefs, attitudes, intentions, and behaviors depend, in that order, on an increasing number of intervening processes.*

The smallest number of steps intervene between an influence attempt and change in proximal beliefs. The number of intervening steps increase when the dependent measure of change involves an inferential belief. As Fig. 9.4 shows, additional steps are necessary as one moves from belief change to changes in attitude and change in intention. The largest number of processes intervenes between an influence attempt and behavioral change.

EFFECTS OF EXPERIMENTAL MANIPULATIONS

An influence attempt exposes subjects to information that may produce changes in their beliefs. So far we have been concerned only with the effects of the information itself. Most studies of change not only expose subjects to some information but also manipulate one or more independent variables and measure the effects of the manipulations on the amount of change in the dependent variable. For example, in a study of persuasive communication, subjects may receive a message that is ultimately designed to change their attitudes toward family planning. In one condition the message may be attributed to the National Institute of Mental Health (high-credibility source) whereas in a second condition the same message may be attributed to a prison inmate (low-credibility source). The purpose of the experiment is to show that with variation of communicator credibility, the same message will produce different amounts of attitude change.

We have seen that the effect of an influence attempt on a dependent variable is the result of its immediate influence on proximal and external beliefs. If an experimental manipulation influences the amount of change in a dependent variable, it must have produced differential amounts of change in that variable's immediate determinants, and such effects can be due only to differential change in primary beliefs. In terms of the example above, this means that the message attributed to the high-credibility source must have produced more change in beliefs about family planning than did the message attributed to the low-credibility source. Changes in these primary beliefs must themselves be due to changes in proximal and external beliefs. Our final principle of change follows directly from these considerations.

4. *An experimental manipulation can affect amount of change in a dependent variable only to the extent that it influences amount of change in proximal and external beliefs.*

An influence attempt exposes subjects to a set of informational items. Experimental manipulations will influence amount of change in proximal and external beliefs to the extent that they affect observation of this information or its acceptance. Figure 9.5 illustrates the processes intervening between presentation of

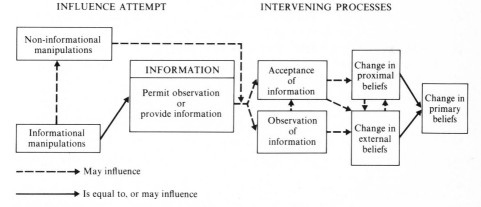

Fig. 9.5 Processes intervening between presentation of information and change in primary beliefs.

information and change in primary beliefs. Note that experimental manipulations may have direct effects on the kind and amount of information to which subjects are exposed. In addition, they may influence the degree to which these informational items are perceived and accepted, thereby affecting amount of change in proximal and external beliefs. Even when a manipulation does affect the amount of change in relevant proximal or external beliefs, there is no guarantee that this effect will be carried over to the dependent variable. Many links intervene between changes in proximal or external beliefs and changes in the dependent variable; the further removed the dependent variable from the proximal and external beliefs, the greater the number of possibilities of a breakdown in the effect (see Figs. 9.4 and 9.5). Manipulations designed to influence change in a dependent variable therefore cannot be expected to have any simple systematic effects on change in inferential beliefs, attitudes, intentions, or behaviors.

CONCLUSION

In this chapter we have discussed some of the basic principles of change, which are summarized in Figs. 9.4 and 9.5. An influence attempt is designed to change a given dependent variable by providing informational items that correspond to and may affect certain proximal beliefs. Figure 9.5 shows that the influence attempt will produce change in these proximal beliefs if the informational items are perceived and accepted. Even if not accepted, the informational items may produce changes in external beliefs. Changes in proximal and external beliefs are expected to influence certain primary beliefs which constitute or are related to the immediate determinants of the dependent variable under consideration (see Fig. 9.4). To understand the effects of an influence attempt on some dependent variable, it may be sufficient to examine its effects on the immediate determinants of that variable. For example, to study change in intention, it will often be sufficient to assess the effects of the influence attempt on the weighted sum of attitude toward the behavior and subjective norm. A complete understanding of the influence process, however, would require an examination of the total sequence leading from the informational items presented to the dependent variable.

Similar considerations apply to an understanding of the effects of experimental manipulations on the dependent variable. To influence the amount of change in the dependent variable, the manipulation must first have an effect on the amount of change in proximal and external beliefs. The manipulation may itself introduce informational items into the situation, or it may influence the perception and acceptance of the information. Its ultimate effect on the dependent variable will again depend on the processes intervening between the presentation of information and the dependent variable.

As we shall see in the following chapters, little attention has been paid to problems of specifying proximal, external, and primary beliefs or to the processes mediating between these beliefs and the dependent variable. Most studies of "attitude change" have manipulated some independent variable and have simply measured some dependent variable. It is therefore hardly surprising that research in this area has led to a large body of inconsistent and inconclusive findings. Given this state of affairs, there is little to be gained from a detailed review of the literature.[2] Instead we shall try to analyze the two major research paradigms used in studies of change in terms of the concepts and orientation developed in this chapter. We shall see that application of our approach to persuasive communication is relatively straightforward. Analysis of active participation and its effects on beliefs, attitudes, intentions, and behaviors is more difficult since it is often impossible to specify either the target or the proximal beliefs attacked in this kind of influence attempt.

---

2. Readers interested in a traditional and detailed review of research in this area are directed to McGuire's (1969) chapter in the *Handbook of Social Psychology*.

Chapter 10

Strategies of Change: Active Participation

Use of active participation as a means of bringing about change has taken many different forms, such as contact and interaction with other people, choice between several alternatives, a public speech in favor of some position, or performance of some other behavior. It is usually expected that experiences of this kind will produce changes in beliefs, attitudes, intentions, and behavior.

The notion that active participation is more effective as a means of bringing about change than passive exposure to information has been investigated in many different areas of social psychology. Perhaps the best-known example is Lewin's (1947) pioneering work in which certain methods of group decision were compared to lecturing and individual treatment as a means of changing social behavior. Although Pelz (1955) later showed that active participation was not a factor responsible for the superiority of group decisions, the facilitating effects of active participation in group discussions continue to be studied by investigators interested in group processes. Much of this research falls outside the realm of the attitude area; readers interested in problems of group process and decision making are referred to Cartright and Zander (1968), Collins and Guetzkow (1964), Davis (1969), and Steiner (1972).

Most studies have been concerned with the factors that influence the amount of change produced by active participation. Numerous variables have at one time or another been proposed, and the degree to which they mediate the effectiveness of active participation has been investigated. For example, it has been suggested that the effects of interpersonal contact on racial prejudice depend on the relative status of the different ethnic groups involved, on the intimacy of contact, on the degree to which the contact is pleasant or rewarding, and on the importance of the interaction (see Amir, 1969). Similarly, it has been suggested that the persuasive effects of performing a behavior in apparent contradiction to one's own attitude or belief are mediated by the amount of reward anticipated, by the degree of commitment to the act, and by the extent to which the behavior was performed voluntarily (e.g., Festinger and Carlsmith, 1959; Holmes and Strickland, 1970).

Implicit in this strategy of change is the assumption that active participation provides the actor with an opportunity to acquire new information. The participation experience thus provides the basis for change in "attitudes" (opinions, prejudice, intention, or interpersonal actions). It is worth noting that certain manipulations (status of the participants, intimacy of the relations, etc.) may influence not only the extent to which the interaction produces change, but also the nature of the interaction itself. Our conceptual framework suggests a similar but somewhat more complex process.

An Alternative Model of Active Participation

An interaction experience allows the participant to directly observe various objects, people, and events. The situation entails a large number of informational items, i.e., a large number of object-attribute links. Each informational item corresponds to a *proximal belief*. Since a person rarely questions his own observations, the participation experience is likely to produce changes in many of these proximal beliefs, although the person can obviously not observe each and every item of information to which he is exposed. In most active participation situations, the individual will perceive that certain people and objects are present in the environment, and he may observe that they possess certain attributes; he may also observe some of the behaviors performed by individuals in the situation, including his own behavior; further, he may perceive contingencies between these behaviors and certain outcomes. It can thus be argued that the actor, by virtue of his participation in the behavioral situation, acquires new descriptive beliefs about himself, about other people, about the consequences of his own or others' behaviors, and about his environment—or that he changes some of his existing descriptive beliefs.

The effect of these changes on any particular dependent variable, however, is an empirical question. As we saw in Chapter 9, the proximal beliefs attacked in an influence attempt need not be related to the dependent variable under investigation. That is, changing proximal beliefs may fail to produce changes in primary beliefs. Moreover, changes in proximal beliefs may have impact effects on relevant external beliefs, thereby producing unexpected changes in primary beliefs and dependent variables.

Figure 10.1 applies our general model of an influence attempt (see Fig. 9.5) to the active participation strategy. The effects of active participation on a primary belief can be traced through a number of mediating processes. As noted, a participant observes some of the informational items contained in the situation, and since he usually accepts his own observations, this leads to changes in certain proximal beliefs. Through various inference processes, changes in external beliefs may also occur. These changes in proximal and external beliefs may then influence

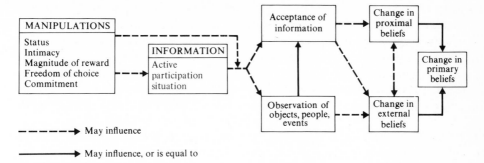

Fig. 10.1 Schematic presentation of active participation process.

primary beliefs. As a result, the desired change in the dependent variable should occur.[1] (See Fig. 9.4.)

Figure 10.1 also illustrates the possible effects of an experimental manipulation. The broken arrow leading to information indicates that certain manipulations may change the nature of the interaction itself, thereby exposing subjects in different conditions to different items of information. In addition, the manipulation may direct the participant's attention to some items of information rather than others, and it thus may influence amount of change in proximal and external beliefs. The manipulation may also provide information that is not part of the active participation situation. For example, prior to entering the situation, the participant may be promised a $5 reward in one condition and a $1 reward in another. Alternatively, some subjects may be led to believe that they are freely choosing to participate, and others may be led to believe that they have no decision freedom with respect to participation. The beliefs formed on the basis of the manipulation have often been treated as target beliefs in investigations of active participation. For example, the belief "I performed the experimental task voluntarily" has served as a target belief assumed to lead to the inference "I enjoyed the task" or "The task was interesting."

Controlling information and specifying target beliefs. In terms of the paradigm developed above, an influence attempt using active participation would ideally begin by specifying the *target beliefs* that are assumed to directly or indirectly influence the dependent variables. The next step would be to identify a set of *proximal beliefs* which, if changed, would produce the desired effects on target beliefs. At this stage the investigator is confronted with the difficult task of devising a situation in which the participant is exposed to informational items that directly attack the relevant proximal beliefs.

The reason this task is often very difficult is that the investigator may not

---

1. Although active participation may produce changes in *irrelevant* proximal and external beliefs, we have deleted these effects from the diagram for ease of presentation. Further, recall that any belief in this sequence may serve as a target belief.

have sufficient control over the ongoing interaction to ensure that participants will be exposed to the desired information. Thus, if the investigator studies the effects of interracial contact in a natural setting, such as a public housing project, the participants may never be exposed to certain informational items needed to produce changes in selected proximal beliefs. Further, various events may occur in the course of interracial interactions that expose participants to information which either prevents the desired changes or produces undesired changes in proximal beliefs. Moreover, even though the participants may be exposed to the desired information, there is no assurance that they will observe each relevant item of information. Clearly, then, it may sometimes be difficult to ensure that the active participation experience will result in observations producing change in the desired proximal beliefs, or even to specify the proximal beliefs that are directly attacked by the information to which participants *are* exposed.

At a minimum, however, the investigator should always be able to identify the target beliefs assumed to directly or indirectly influence the dependent variables that are to be changed, and to assess the effects of the active participation experience on these target beliefs and on the immediate determinants of the dependent variable. Unfortunately, in most studies not only is it difficult to identify the informational items to which subjects are exposed, but it is also impossible to specify the beliefs that were selected as target beliefs by the investigator.

The problem of influencing a specified set of target or proximal beliefs is related to the degree to which the investigator has control over the situation. Whenever he has less than complete control over the situation, subjects within the same experimental condition may be exposed to markedly different items of information. Indeed, the four main lines of investigation employing an active participation strategy are characterized by different degrees of control over the information presented. The amount of control increases as one moves from interpersonal contact to role playing, to counterattitudinal behavior, and finally, to choice situations.

INTERPERSONAL CONTACT

It is often assumed that interpersonal contact tends to produce more favorable interpersonal relations. Interaction between members of different races, for example, is expected to lead to a reduction in prejudice. "This view, which seems to be held rather commonly, is exemplified in the explicit or tacit objectives of various international exchange programs: student exchanges or those of professional people, organized tours and visits to foreign countries, . . . international seminars, international conferences and exhibitions, Olympic games—all these—are often thought to be effective because of the opportunities for contact they afford." (Amir, 1969, p. 320) The increased popularity in recent years of sensitivity training and encounter groups also seems to be based on the premise that interactions of this kind will reduce interpersonal tensions and generally lead to improved interpersonal relations.

In a review of research on the contact hypothesis in racial relations, Amir (1969) concluded that contact between members of different ethnic groups tends to produce some change in attitudes. However, interracial contact does not always have an effect; and if it does have an effect, it does not always serve to improve relations. Instead, contact is often found to increase rather than decrease prejudice (cf. Fishbein and Ajzen, 1972). "The direction of the change depends largely on the conditions under which contact has taken place; 'favorable' conditions tend to reduce prejudice, 'unfavorable' ones may increase prejudice and intergroup tension." (Amir, 1969, p. 338)

From our point of view this conclusion is of course not unexpected. In studies on the effects of interracial contact on prejudice, subjects are usually exposed to a wide range of interpersonal experiences over which the investigator has relatively little control. Since subjects in a given study are exposed to different items of information, it is difficult, if not impossible, to identify the proximal beliefs that are influenced by the contact experience. It is not at all clear what new beliefs the subject may be expected to form or which of his existing beliefs are likely to change. There is no assurance, therefore, that interracial contact will produce changes in primary beliefs that are related to the dependent variable under investigation. Further, since the investigator has little direct control over the kind of information his subjects receive, it is possible for these primary beliefs to change in an undesirable direction. Thus a moderately prejudiced person may actually come to hold an even more negative attitude toward a given minority group if in the course of interpersonal contacts with members of the group in question he acquires unfavorable beliefs about them.

Clearly, then, some contact situations favor the development of positive beliefs, and others lead to the formation of negative beliefs. When these beliefs are related to the dependent variables under investigation, favorable or unfavorable effects may be observed. Consider, for example, a white person who is induced to interact with blacks. Various kinds of descriptive and inferential beliefs may be formed as a result of this interaction. Depending on the social status, education, and personality characteristics of the particular blacks with whom he interacts, the white may come to believe that these blacks are intelligent or stupid, polite or rude, cooperative or uncooperative, educated or uneducated, etc. As discussed in Chapter 6, formation of such beliefs about the black persons in the interaction situation will then lead to more favorable or more unfavorable attitudes toward these black individuals.

By the same token, the white person may develop new beliefs about the consequences of certain behaviors with respect to these particular blacks and about the expectations of other people, i.e., normative beliefs. Thus he may learn that interacting with some blacks leads to favorable or unfavorable consequences in the immediate situation. He may also learn that his friends or his family approve or disapprove of such contacts. We saw that changes in beliefs about the consequences of a behavior may influence the person's attitude toward the behavior. Since behavioral intentions are determined by attitude toward the behavior and by subjective norm (see Chapter 7), interpersonal contact may either increase or reduce intentions to continue to interact with the black persons in question.

It is unfortunate that studies on the effects of interpersonal contact have not systematically investigated the immediate influence of such contact on a person's beliefs about the other participants, about the consequences of his own behavior, or about the expectations of relevant reference groups. To illustrate the importance of paying more attention to the formation and change of such beliefs, it may be instructive to examine in some detail one of the few controlled laboratory investigations concerned with the effects of contact on racial attitudes.

Cook (1970) recruited female college students for what they believed would be a part-time job. The students were first given various tests, including three measures of attitude toward Negroes. On the basis of this pretest, 23 subjects were selected who consistently expressed an anti-Negro attitude on all three instruments. The subjects were then asked to work two hours a day for a month on a simulated management game involving an imaginary railroad system. Each subject interacted with two female confederates, one white and the other black. At the end of the month subjects were given some further experience with blacks when they were asked to interview five students (including two blacks) who were ostensibly applying for the same job the subject had just completed. One to three months later, subjects were again asked to respond to three instruments measuring general attitudes toward Negroes; scores on the three measures were summed, and the sum served as the major dependent variable. The results showed that only eight of the 23 subjects (35 percent) changed their attitudes toward blacks in a favorable direction. One subject became more unfavorable, and the remainder exhibited no appreciable change.

It is of interest to note that in this study Cook attempted to create conditions that would be optimal for attitude change as a result of the contact experience. Consistent with conclusions reached by other investigators (e.g., Allport, 1954; Amir, 1969), Cook attempted to make sure that the following conditions were met: (1) The role of the black confederate in the simulated game provided her with a status equal to that of the white subject. (2) The participants were mutually interdependent in attempting to attain the task goal. (3) The black confederate (as well as the two black "interviewees") behaved in a friendly, able, ambitious, and self-respecting manner. (4) During breaks, subjects received rather intimate information about the black confederate. (5) The white confederate expressed sympathy for the black coworker, thereby providing normative support for favorable attitude change. The data reported by Cook fail to explain the fact that in spite of the great care taken to optimize the conditions of contact, the majority of the subjects did not change their attitudes toward Negroes.

An analysis of this experiment from our perspective suggests a number of possible explanations. Perhaps the most serious problem concerns the relevance of the contact experience for the dependent variable under investigation. The expressed purpose of the study was to change attitudes toward blacks, and the dependent variable was indeed a measure of attitude toward blacks in general. The appropriate target beliefs for such an influence attempt would be beliefs that blacks possess certain attributes and beliefs about those attributes. Thus the active participation experience should have provided information that could directly or indirectly produce changes in such beliefs. Had Cook measured changes in these primary beliefs, he might have found that for most subjects the contact experience did not have the desired effects. The interracial contact in this experiment exposed participants to considerable information about one particular black person (the confederate) and to limited information about two other blacks (the interviewees), but it did not provide any direct information about blacks in general. Thus the proximal beliefs attacked by the contact experience were for the most part beliefs about three particular black individuals. Had the dependent variables been measures of attitudes toward the specific black persons with whom the subject interacted, significant changes might have been obtained, even though the general attitude measure showed no effects. In other words, for many subjects the proximal beliefs addressed by the interpersonal contact experience may have been unrelated to the primary beliefs underlying their attitudes toward blacks in general. The fact that at least some subjects indicated a change in general attitude toward blacks indicates the presence of inference processes linking beliefs about a given member of a class to the class in general. The results of the experiment suggest that relatively few subjects made such inferences. It appears that in this study there was a low probabilistic relation between beliefs about specific individuals and beliefs about the class to which they belong.

These considerations imply that interpersonal contact is likely to produce change in beliefs, attitudes, intentions, and behaviors with respect to an ethnic, religious, or national group only when participants come in contact with a relatively large number of individuals who are clearly identified as members of that group. Unfortunately, these are precisely the kinds of situations in which the investigator has little control over the information available to participants and in which undesired as well as desired changes therefore tend to occur.

ROLE PLAYING

Interpersonal contact is often assumed to produce attitude change and improve relations because it provides individuals with an opportunity to get to know each other, to appreciate and perhaps to accept the other's point of view. On the basis of the same premise, it has also been argued that a person would be likely to exhibit attitude change if he was induced to play the role of someone holding opinions which do not correspond to his own. Perhaps the first use of role playing as a means of bringing about change is associated with Moreno's (1946) therapeutic approach known as psychodrama. Moreno's patients were asked to recreate problem situations in their lives by acting out their own roles or those of other people in those situations. The role playing experience was assumed to provide deeper insight into one's own motives, feelings, projections, and thoughts. As a result, the role player's beliefs, attitudes, and behaviors were expected to change. Because of its assumed therapeutic value, role playing was later used in a variety of other settings. For example, the technique is still very popular in management training programs, where supervisory personnel are asked to take the roles of workers or union leaders. These experiences are expected to alter the manager's perception of himself and his subordinates and therefore to improve management-labor relations (cf. Maier, 1952). In another application, Sarason (1968) has developed a program of role playing therapy for juvenile offenders. Despite the widespread interest in role playing, J. S. Wiggins *et al.* (1971) noted that "data from well-controlled studies on the success of role playing as a therapeutic method are as yet unavailable" (p. 428).

Since it is assumed that enacting the role of another person facilitates changes in an individual's views of himself, other people, and events, role playing has attracted the interest of investigators studying attitude change. A good example of this approach is a recent study by Clore and Jeffery (1972), who asked subjects to play the role of a handicapped student. A subject was seated in a wheelchair, instructed to wheel himself across campus to the student union, where he was to get a cup of coffee, and then to return to the laboratory. Subjects in a second group were told to follow and observe the role players. For purposes of control, a third group of subjects spent an equivalent amount of time walking on the campus. Immediately following their experience, subjects responded to a 12-item questionnaire about disabled students and rehabilitation; the sum over the 12 responses served as the dependent measure of "attitude toward disabled students." [2] At the end of the study, each subject was asked to provide the experimenter's supervisor with a confidential report about various aspects of the experiment. Included in this report were three evaluative items assessing the subject's attitude toward the experimenter (who appeared to be confined to a wheelchair).

The results showed that after their experience, role players held significantly more favorable attitudes toward disabled students and toward the experimenter than did the control subjects. The attitudes of the observers did not differ significantly from those of the role players. These results persisted four months later (in telephone interviews) when, among other alternatives, subjects were asked whether they would favor spending leftover funds to increase facilities for disabled students. In contrast, these results were not obtained with respect to a measure of intentions. One month after the experiment subjects were phoned and asked whether they would volunteer to show handicapped students around campus. No significant differences between conditions were obtained.

As in many active participation situations, the proximal beliefs in this study are not easily identifiable. Generally speaking, they corresponded to the items of

---

2. Since the items dealt not only with disabled students but also with issues such as the role of the rehabilitation center, the content of introductory psychology lectures, and preference for scholarship recipients, it is not clear whether this instrument provided an unambiguous measure of attitude toward disabled students.

information to which subjects were exposed while performing their respective experimental tasks. It stands to reason that the active role players and the observers were exposed to much the same information. Although the former may have been more aware that they had to expend considerable energy to move their wheelchairs, both could have increased their beliefs that handicapped people have difficulties in moving around, that there are too few facilities for handicapped students, etc. Since such beliefs were unlikely to change for control subjects, it is not surprising to find that role players and observers were more in favor of spending funds to increase facilities for disabled students.

With reference to the dependent measure of attitude toward handicapped students, the primary beliefs are beliefs about handicapped students. Some of those primary beliefs were likely to have changed for both role players and observers. Since role players and observers were exposed to virtually identical items of information, there was no reason to expect these groups to show differential changes in proximal beliefs. Therefore there should also have been little difference between these groups in terms of primary beliefs or the dependent measure of attitude. In contrast, the informational items available to control subjects were not likely to have changed proximal beliefs related to the primary beliefs and little change in attitude would have been expected. The findings concerning attitudes toward handicapped students are consistent with these considerations.

With reference to the second measure of attitude, the primary beliefs are beliefs about the apparently handicapped experimenter. Here the same items of information were available to all subjects, and hence the same proximal beliefs should have changed. It might therefore appear that there should have been no differences between experimental conditions in attitudes toward the experimenter. Two explanations may be offered for the finding that role players and observers held more favorable attitudes toward the experimenter than did control subjects. Clearly, all subjects were likely to have formed the belief that the experimenter was handicapped (or that she was a handicapped student). One explanation relies on the prior finding that attitudes toward handicapped students (the attribute of this belief) were more favorable for role players and observers than for control subjects. This difference in attribute evaluation may account for the difference in attitude toward the experimenter. Another possibility is that role players and observers, who formed more favorable beliefs about handicapped students in general than did control subjects, may have attributed some of those beliefs to the handicapped experimenter. Both explanations suggest that attitudes toward the experimenter were affected more indirectly than attitudes toward handicapped students, and this notion is supported by the finding that the experimental manipulation accounted for 25 percent of the variance in attitudes toward handicapped students but only for 11 percent of the variance in attitudes toward the experimenter.

As in other studies we have encountered, the results obtained with respect to attitudes did not generalize to intentions. The experimental manipulation apparently had no effect on amount of change in the primary beliefs relevant for the intention to show handicapped students around campus. In fact, there was no reason to expect subjects in the three conditions to hold different beliefs about the consequences of performing this behavior or about the expectations of relevant others. Thus there should have been little difference in the immediate determinants of the intention, i.e., attitude toward the behavior and subjective norm, and in the intention itself. The findings of this study again demonstrate that changing attitudes toward an object may have little or no effect on intentions to perform specific behaviors with respect to that object.

A unique feature of the Clore and Jeffery (1972) experiment is that the proximal beliefs of both role players and observers were attacked by means of direct observation. In most other studies the active participant plays the role of a person advocating a certain position on an issue while control subjects serve as passive observers. For example, in one of the first laboratory experiments investigating the effects of role playing on attitude, Culbertson (1957) asked subjects in three-person groups to discuss the adoption of an educational program to facilitate racial integration. Each subject was assigned the role of a person advocating a specific theme for the educational program. Three observers listened to the discussion, and each one was instructed to associate himself with an assigned role player.

Two weeks prior to the role playing session and again seven to ten days following the discussion, role players and observers indicated their attitudes toward "allowing Negroes to move into white neighborhoods," as well as their attitudes toward Negroes in general.[3] At equivalent points in time, an untreated control group merely provided measures of the same attitudes.

Table 10.1 reports the percentage of subjects in each condition who changed their attitudes in a favorable direction. Although no information concerning *degree* of change was reported, a significantly greater proportion of role players and observers than of the control subjects changed their attitudes on both measures in a favorable direction. Moreover, in contrast to the Clore and Jeffery (1972) findings, significantly more role players than observers showed favorable change on both attitude measures. The latter finding is consistent with Culbertson's hypothesis that "the closer the person is to a role—for example as a participant

Table 10.1 Percentage of Subjects Changing Attitudes in Favorable Direction (Adapted from Culbertson, 1957)

Attitude toward	Role players	Observers	Control
"Allowing Negroes to move into white neighborhoods"	67	43	11
Negroes in general	74	57	21

3. The first measure was based on the ranking of six opinion items, and the second measure was a standard Likert scale.

rather than an observer—the more likely are his cognitive and motivational dispositions to be affected by the experience" (1957, p. 230). Although she failed to elaborate on the psychological mechanism underlying this presumed effect, Culbertson did mention that role players, in comparison with observers, reported significantly more association with the assigned role, spending more time attending to the role and experiencing more emotional involvement with it.[4] Note that this explanation is inconsistent with the lack of significant differences between role players and observers reported by Clore and Jeffery (1972). Analysis of Culbertson's study in terms of our conceptual framework may suggest some reasons for the inconsistent findings.

As is often true in an active participation situation, the investigator had relatively little control over the kinds of arguments brought up in the course of the discussion. Nevertheless, it is possible to identify some of the proximal beliefs in this situation. Each statement voiced by a participant may be viewed as an informational item directed at a corresponding proximal belief. Depending on the relevance of these proximal beliefs for the primary beliefs, a change in proximal beliefs may or may not influence the dependent variable.

Generating versus Receiving Information

As in the Clore and Jeffery study, role players and observers in the Culbertson experiment were exposed to virtually identical information, and at first glance it might therefore appear that their attitudes should have changed to the same extent. However, in marked contrast to the Clore and Jeffery study, the Culbertson role players actively generated the information, and the observers were passively exposed to it. This difference between role players and observers may affect attitude change in at least two ways. First, it may influence the amount of change in proximal beliefs, and second, it may affect the perceived relevance of proximal beliefs for primary beliefs and dependent variables.[5]

Differential changes in proximal beliefs. As an illustration, consider a prejudiced role player who is confronted with the task of generating arguments in favor of letting blacks move into white neighborhoods (integration). At the outset, the subject has a hierarchy of beliefs linking integration to positive or negative attributes. The first belief coming to his mind might be "integration increases interracial conflict." Since his task is to argue in favor of integration, he may either reverse this belief and argue that integration reduces interracial conflict or reject it and consider the next belief in his hierarchy. As this process continues, the

---

4. These data are based on a questionnaire administered immediately after the discussion; the questionnaire was not described in detail.

5. It has often been argued that active role playing produces more change than passive exposure because active role players are more likely to accept the arguments they generate. This implies that role players and observers may be viewed as recipients of a persuasive communication. Factors influencing acceptance of informational items contained in a persuasive communication will be discussed in Chapter 11.

role player comes to elicit beliefs that were initially not part of his salient belief hierarchy.

In a series of experiments, Maltzman and his associates (Maltzman, 1960; Maltzman *et al.,* 1960; Maltzman, Bogartz, and Breger, 1958) have found that the mere elicitation of nonsalient beliefs tends to increase their probability of elicitation in the future. In a procedure called "originality training" Maltzman's subjects are asked to elicit different responses to repeated presentations of the same stimulus list. This procedure forces subjects to go further down in their belief hierarchies on each successive presentation. The training not only increases the salience of the low-probability responses but also increases the likelihood that low-probability or "original" responses will be elicited by other stimulus objects.

The role playing experience may thus serve to at least temporarily introduce previously nonsalient beliefs favorable to integration into the person's salient belief hierarchy. The observer's position differs greatly in that he is not forced to actively search through his own belief hierarchy. Some proximal beliefs may therefore become salient for the role players but not for the observers. Such differential changes in proximal beliefs could account for greater change in the dependent variable among role players than among observers. Indirect evidence for this argument can be found in a study by Greenwald and Albert (1968), who showed that subjects were better able to recall the arguments they had generated themselves than arguments produced by another person.

Differences in perceived relevance. Even when proximal beliefs do not show differential change, role players and observers may still differ in terms of the dependent variable. A role player who is instructed to adopt a given position develops arguments that he perceives to be relevant to and supportive of the position in question. The observer, however, may not perceive any relation between these beliefs and the dependent variable. For example, in an attempt to support racial integration, the role player might argue that since blacks have served their country well in the armed forces, they should be allowed to move into white neighborhoods. Unlike the role player, the observer may not see any connection between military service and racial integration. Although both role player and observer may increase their beliefs that blacks have served their country well in the armed forces, only the former would exhibit a more favorable attitude toward racial integration.

In conclusion, active role playing may indeed produce more change than passive exposure. This is expected to happen when the role player, in contrast to the observer, is forced to actively search through his belief system in order to find arguments in favor of the position he has been assigned. When the role playing procedure does not involve this active search for nonsalient beliefs, no differences between role players and observers are to be expected.

A similar conclusion was reached by King and Janis (1956) on the basis of two studies in which role players were asked to present oral arguments in support of an assigned position. In one of the first laboratory investigations of the persuasive effects of role playing, Janis and King (1954) investigated "the effects of one type of demand that is frequently made upon a person when he is induced to play a social role, namely, the requirement that he overtly verbalize to others various opinions which may not correspond to his inner convictions" (p. 211). Thus, in contrast to the Culbertson study, in which subjects were assigned a position with which they may have agreed, Janis and King asked subjects to give a short talk advocating a position which differed greatly from their own.[6]

About four weeks prior to the experiment, subjects completed a questionnaire containing, among other items, the following three questions.

1. How many commercial movie theaters do you think will be in business three years from now?

2. What is your personal estimate about the total supply of meat that will be available for the civilian population of the United States during the year 1953? (Subjects indicated the "percent of what it is at present," i.e., in the year during which the experiment was conducted).

3. How many years do you think it will be before a completely effective cure for the common cold is discovered?

Subjects participated in groups of three; each subject gave an informal talk on one of the topics and listened passively to the presentations of the other two members on the remaining topics. Thus each subject served as an "active participant" for one topic and as a "passive control" for two topics. More specifically, three minutes prior to each presentation, all group members were given an outline prepared by the experimenter. The outline advocated a position considerably lower than any of the three subjects' initial estimates. In addition to stating the conclusion, the outline summarized the main arguments to be presented. Role players as well as observers retained the outlines during the role player's informal talk. Immediately after the last talk all subjects completed a second questionnaire, which also included the three belief items listed above.

The outline given to the subjects essentially constituted a persuasive communication. Each statement in the outline was an informational item that could produce changes in the corresponding proximal beliefs of the role players and observers. Moreover, since prepared arguments were available to role players, it is not clear to what extent they had to search through their own belief systems in order to present their informal talks. Thus, not only may role players and observ-

---

6. Another difference between these two studies is that in the Janis and King experiment, role players did not discuss the issue in question among themselves. Most subsequent studies have followed the Janis and King procedure, which avoids the problem of exposing the role player to information about the issue generated by other participants.

ers have been exposed to the same information, but all this information may have been provided by an outside source (the experimenters).

Janis and King (1954) analyzed their data in terms of "net change scores," i.e., in terms of the percentage of subjects changing in the advocated direction minus the percentage changing in the opposite direction. They found that on each topic, subjects lowered their estimates significantly whether they served as active participants or as passive controls. Contrary to the experimental hypothesis, however, the net change index showed no significant differences between active participants and passive controls. Thus active role playing did not appear to be much more persuasive than passive exposure to the same arguments. This finding is quite consistent with our general conclusion that role playing will facilitate change only to the extent that the role player is forced to actively search through his own belief system. When he is provided with a set of arguments by the experimenter, the role player may or may not elicit previously nonsalient beliefs.[7]

In an attempt to further explore the role playing hypothesis, the investigators compared active participants and passive controls in terms of *sizable* changes. For the first topic (movie theaters) a sizable change was defined as an estimate increased or decreased by at least 5000 theaters; for the second topic (meat supply) a sizable change was 25 percent or more; and for the third topic (cure for the common cold) it was five years or more. In terms of "net sizable change" on the first two topics, active participants were influenced significantly more than passive controls. However, the difference was again nonsignificant on the third topic. Janis and King concluded that, at least under certain conditions, role playing is more effective in bringing about change than is passive exposure to the same information.

Although the results of this study are clearly far from conclusive, they have frequently been cited as evidence for an increased persuasive effect due to active role playing. In order to explore possible mediating factors underlying the gain in opinion change, Janis and King compared the conditions in which active participation produced more change than passive exposure (topics 1 and 2) with the condition in which it did not (topic 3). In general, they found that active participants discussing topics 1 and 2 seemed to improvise more and to be more satisfied with their own performance than active participants discussing topic 3. This suggested two possible explanations for the advantage of active role playing.

---

7. A series of recent studies by Greenwald (1969, 1970) suggests that role playing may produce more change than passive exposure even when it does not involve active search through the belief hierarchy. Greenwald found that subjects expecting to defend one side of an issue judged arguments in favor of that side to be valid more than did subjects expecting to defend the opposite side of the issue. This finding suggests that information provided by the experimenter is more likely to be accepted by role players than by passive control subjects. However, the study by Janis and King does not support this line of reasoning. In any case, Greenwald's findings are perhaps more relevant to studies on the effects of persuasive communication than to studies concerned with the effects of role playing.

1. *Improvisation.* This factor suggests that "the gain from role playing may occur primarily because the active participant tends to be impressed by his own cogent arguments, clarifying illustrations, and convincing appeals which he is stimulated to think up in order to do a good job of 'selling' the idea to others."

2. *Satisfaction.* The alternative explanation suggests that "the rewarding effects of the individual's sense of achievement or feelings of satisfaction with his performance in the role of active participant" may be responsible for the gain from role playing (Janis and King, 1954, p. 218).

King and Janis (1956) attempted to test these alternative explanations in a subsequent experiment. Several months prior to the experiment, male college students completed a questionnaire that included five items related to military service and the draft. Subjects were asked to estimate the following items.

1. The required length of service for draftees

2. The percentage of college students who will be deferred

3. The percentage of college students who will become officers

4. Their personal expectations of length of military service

5. Their personal expectations of being drafted

At the beginning of the experiment itself, all subjects read a persuasive communication dealing with the prospects of military service for college students. The communication argued in support of two main conclusions: (1) that over 90 percent of college students would be drafted within one year of their graduation, and (2) that the majority of college students would be required to serve at least three years in the military service. These conclusions represented positions significantly higher than the estimates made by the students.

The nature of the role playing task was varied by creating three experimental conditions. Subjects in the *improvisation* condition presented a talk in favor of the assigned positions shortly after reading the script but without the benefit of having it present during the talk. In the *nonimprovisation* condition, subjects were asked simply to read the persuasive communication aloud. Finally, control subjects merely read the script silently. This manipulation was designed to assess the effects of active participation with and without improvisation in comparison with a passive control group.

At the conclusion of the experiment, subjects again indicated their estimates for the five items listed above, and they also provided self-ratings of their satisfaction with their own performance. The main dependent variable in this study was the percentage of subjects who changed in the advocated direction on at least three of the five opinion items. The obtained percentages were 87.5 in the improvisation condition, 54.5 in the nonimprovisation condition, and 65.0 in the control group. The percentage of change in the improvisation group was significantly greater than the change in either of the other two groups, which did not differ significantly from each other.[8]

It thus appeared that improvisation was a necessary condition for active participation to increase amount of change. However, there was still the possibility that this effect was due to increased satisfaction resulting from improvisation. This possibility was ruled out by the finding that subjects in the nonimprovisation condition were significantly *more* satisfied with their own performance than were subjects in the improvisation condition. On the basis of this finding and some supplementary data to be discussed later, King and Janis concluded that the facilitating effect of active participation is due to the improvisation often required of role players, rather than to their greater satisfaction with their performance. This conclusion is consistent with our earlier argument that active participation facilitates change only when it requires searching through one's own belief hierarchy.

Analysis of role-playing research. Although a distinction is usually not made, the role playing studies discussed in this section involve procedural variations that influence the extent to which active participants are forced to elicit previously nonsalient beliefs. The role playing variations employed in these studies can be ordered with reference to the required amount of improvisation, as follows: (1) Since role players in the Clore and Jeffrey experiment did not engage in discussion but merely wheeled themselves across campus, they were obviously not required to improvise. Similarly, no improvisation was required of those subjects who merely read a prepared script in the King and Janis study. (2) When subjects were asked to give an informal talk on the basis of an available outline (Janis and King), or when they gave a talk on the basis of a previously read but no longer available script (King and Janis), some improvisation may have but need not have taken place. (3) Improvisation was clearly required only of subjects in the Culbertson study, who argued in favor of an assigned position without receiving prior information. The active participation procedure should thus have had a clear advantage over passive exposure only in the Culbertson study; it could have but need not have facilitated change in the Janis and King experiment or in the "improvisation" condition of the study by King and Janis. As we saw above, the results of the different studies were entirely consistent with this analysis.

Availability of information. The degree to which an active participant is forced to improvise depends in large measure on the kind and amount of information provided by the experimenter. This information essentially represents a persuasive communication that may produce changes in certain proximal beliefs. By the same

---

8. If the analysis had been performed on *net* changes rather than changes in the advocated direction only, the tests of significance might have shown different results. In fact, the results in terms of net changes differed greatly from item to item. Use of an index based on favorable changes in at least three of the five items is comparable to an analysis of *sizable* changes, which may show a significant effect when an analysis of all changes does not (see Janis and King, 1954).

token, studies vary in terms of the amount of information given to passive control subjects. In addition, passive controls may or may not be allowed to observe the role player or listen to his presentation. Thus the passive subject may actually receive two persuasive communications, one from the experimenter and the other from the active participant. Depending upon the amount and kind of information available, active participants may change more or less than passive controls. For example, subjects in the two conditions may receive the same persuasive communication from the experimenter (e.g., a prepared script), but the passive controls may not be permitted to listen to the role player's improvised talk based on the script (King and Janis, 1956). Since the role player's improvisation may generate items of information not included in the experimenter's communication, passive controls may exhibit less change on the dependent variable than active participants.

By way of contrast, providing passive controls with a prepared script not available to the role players may expose the passive controls to a greater number of informational items relevant for the dependent variable. This argument receives support from a number of studies in which passive reading of a communication was found to be more effective in bringing about change than was active role playing (see McGuire, 1969; Matefy, 1972). A person may frequently be unable to come up with relevant arguments in favor of a position that disagrees with his own, whereas the passive subjects may be exposed to a number of such arguments prepared by the experimenter. As a result, the role player's presentation may have less effect on the dependent variable than passive exposure has. McGuire (1964; McGuire and Papageorgis, 1961) presented some indirect evidence in support of this notion. He found that writing an essay without any guidance in support of one's own position was much less effective in producing *resistance* to a subsequent persuasive communication than was passively reading a supportive essay prepared by the experimenter. It appears that the experimenter is sometimes able to provide a greater number of relevant arguments in favor of the subject's position than is the subject himself (especially since the subject has only limited time at his disposal).

These considerations emphasize the crucial importance of the information made available to active participants and passive controls. When role players and observers are not exposed to identical items of information—whatever the source of the information—differences in proximal beliefs are to be expected, and hence, obtained differences in the dependent variable may be due to factors other than active participation. The potential confounding effect of providing different information to role players and observers is illustrated in a study by Janis and Mann (1965). In this study, moderate and heavy smokers played the role of a patient who had just been told by her doctor (played by the experimenter) that she had cancer. Our analysis suggests that this situation should facilitate change since it requires that the subject engage in active improvisation using arguments that are normally not part of her salient belief system. Further, these arguments, as well as those voiced by the "doctor," were directed at proximal beliefs that appeared to be relevant for the study's dependent variables. The results reported by Janis and Mann indeed showed that active participants changed more than passive controls. However, this finding is not unequivocal, since all control subjects were exposed to the same tape recording of a single role playing session selected for its "exceptionally dramatic and emotional quality." Thus the information available in the control condition was not identical to that available in the role playing condition.[9] In fact, had a different role playing session been recorded, it might have contained information that would have produced the same or even more change among passive controls than that obtained among the active role players.

The importance of providing subjects in different experimental conditions with identical items of information is further illustrated in Mann's (1967) follow-up of the Janis and Mann study. In an attempt to test the hypothesis that the effectiveness of role playing is due to emotional involvement, Mann compared two types of emotional role playing with a nonemotional technique. A *fear-emotional* condition was identical to that used by Janis and Mann. In a *shame-emotional* condition, smokers played the role of patients who, though found to be physically fit, were chided by their doctors for their lack of self-control. The third condition involved a nonemotional *cognitive* role playing procedure in which the subject played a debater and the experimenter played the coach of the debating team. With the help of the coach, the role player prepared to advocate "that smokers should quit smoking."

Clearly, subjects in the different role playing conditions were exposed to widely different items of information. Further, these informational items may have been directed at proximal beliefs that were not equally relevant for the dependent variables under investigation. The differences in the available information may in and of themselves have produced different degrees of change in the dependent variables. Obtained differences between role playing conditions, therefore, may have little to do with the degree of emotional involvement. In other words, type of role playing is confounded with informational content in this study, and no unequivocal conclusions can be derived from its data. Although Mann's results appear to indicate that emotional role playing was more effective than cognitive role playing, the results of the Clore and Jeffery (1972) study discussed above contradict this conclusion. In the Clore and Jeffery study informational content was not confounded with type of role playing, since the same information was available to the role players (who were put in wheelchairs) and active observers, who were not emotionally involved. Under these conditions, emotional involvement did not increase the effectiveness of role playing.

So far we have discussed studies that have attempted to demonstrate that

---

9. A more appropriate procedure would have been to permit each control subject to observe the role playing session of a *different* active participant (yoked controls). This procedure would also have equalized the availability of nonverbal informational items in the situation.

some types of active participation in the form of role playing are superior to passive exposure in bringing about change. In most studies the role player has been called on to adopt a certain position on an issue and defend it publicly. This task often requires the role player to generate and verbalize arguments that may not correspond to his privately held beliefs. The investigator's first consideration must be to ensure that the informational items available to control subjects are identical to those available to the role players. Any advantage of active participation over passive exposure must then be the result of either greater changes in proximal beliefs or greater perceived relevance of these proximal beliefs for primary beliefs and hence for the dependent variable in question. We have noted that such effects are likely to occur only when the role player is forced to actively search through his own belief system. To gain a full understanding of obtained differences between active participants and passive controls, it is therefore necessary to identify the relevant proximal beliefs and trace changes in these beliefs to changes in primary beliefs, to changes in the immediate determinants of the dependent variable, and to changes in the dependent variable itself. Unlike active participation in the form of interpersonal contact, the role playing situation does permit the investigator to identify at least those proximal beliefs that correspond to the informational items presented by the experimenter and by the role player himself. A relatively complete analysis of the influence process should thus be possible in most role playing situations.

COUNTERATTITUDINAL BEHAVIOR

The studies discussed thus far have compared role playing with passive exposure; it seems clear that the kind and amount of information available in the role playing situation determines the amount of change in the dependent variable. We now turn to an examination of studies that — without questioning the importance of the information available to subjects — have focused on other factors that may be of relevance. Two important features distinguish the research discussed in this section from traditional role playing experiments. First, the active participant is induced to adopt a position contrary to his own, and this counterattitudinal behavior is assumed to be one of the reasons for the effectiveness of role playing. Studies in this area have therefore focused on the counterattitudinal aspect of the subject's behavior, and various means other than developing arguments in support of a given position have been used to bring about such counterattitudinal behavior. The second distinguishing characteristic of this research is its manipulation of variables that may facilitate or inhibit the amount of change produced by the performance of counterattitudinal behavior.

For example, the King and Janis (1956) study described earlier included a manipulation designed to influence the effectiveness of a counterattitudinal role playing experience. Arguing that the effects of active participation may be mediated by satisfaction with own performance, the investigators provided subjects in the improvisation condition with favorable, unfavorable, or no ratings on their speaking performance. Although this manipulation had a significant effect on self-ratings of satisfaction, its effect on the dependent variable was reported to be non-significant.[10]

Effects of Reinforcement

A study directly concerned with the effects of positive and negative reinforcement for advocating a counterattitudinal position was conducted by Scott (1957). Subjects in pairs were asked to debate one of three issues in front of a student audience. The issues were concerned with universal military training, night hours for women students, and de-emphasis of football in college. Altogether Scott used 18 different audiences, each hearing two debates on one of the three issues.[11] On the basis of a pretest, role players with extreme positions on these issues were selected. For purposes of the debate and unknown to the audience, subjects with pro opinions were assigned the con side of the issue and vice versa. Following the two debates, each lasting ten minutes (five minutes for each side), the audience was asked to cast two ballots for the role players who in their opinion had done a better job in presenting their sides of the issue. Actually, subjects were given false feedback concerning these audience reactions such that the person advocating the pro position in one debate and the person advocating the con position in the other debate were said to have "won." This manipulation was supposed to express either group approval (positive reinforcement) or group disapproval (negative reinforcement) for the performance.

Two weeks prior to the debate and again immediately after the announcement of "winners" and "losers," the debaters as well as members of the audience were asked to respond to an open-ended question concerning the issue debated. Two members from each audience, one initially pro and one initially con, were selected to serve as control subjects. Responses were coded on seven-point scales ranging from *very pro* to *very con* on the issue in question. A pretest-to-posttest change score was computed for each subject, and the finding was that "winners" changed by a significantly greater amount in the direction of their adopted positions than either "losers" or controls. The difference between "losers" and controls was non-significant.

Consistent with a reinforcement theory of attitude change, Scott concluded that approval for the subject's performance positively reinforced his expressed beliefs, and disapproval provided negative reinforcement. Similar results were reported in a subsequent replication and extension of this study (Scott, 1959). These investigations suggest that reinforcement can influence the effectiveness of

---

10. This conclusion must be regarded with caution since the results are based on a small sample (about 10 subjects per condition) and the investigators provided little detail as to the dependent variable or data analysis.

11. Actually, 19 different classes were used, but because of administrative difficulties, two of the classes were exposed to only one debate each.

role playing by increasing the likelihood that the role player will believe his own counterattitudinal arguments. Subsequent investigations, however, have not always been able to demonstrate the facilitating effect of social approval or reinforcement. For example, Sarbin and Allen (1964) had an audience give positive reinforcement (e.g., smiles) or negative reinforcement (e.g., frowns) while the subject made a counterattitudinal speech. Contrary to a reinforcement hypothesis, no significant differences were found between the two conditions.

Complementing the reinforcement hypothesis, other investigators have argued that the mere knowledge of potential reinforcement can itself be an important factor influencing change. For example, according to incentive theory, the *prospect* of being evaluated by an audience or of receiving some other type of reward or punishment provides the subject with an added incentive to devise convincing arguments in favor of the adopted position (Janis and Gilmore, 1965; Rosenberg, 1965b). We would argue, however, that anticipated reward or punishment should serve as an incentive only to the extent to which it is perceived to be contingent upon quality of performance. The greater the incentive (i.e., the greater the expected magnitude of reward to be obtained or punishment to be avoided), the more change should result. For example, subjects who believe that a high monetary reward is contingent upon good performance of their role playing task may be expected to produce better arguments and thus to exhibit more "attitude" change than subjects who are promised a relatively small monetary reward for good performance or subjects who do not expect to be rewarded at all.[12]

Forced Compliance

An added incentive for role playing a position other than one's own or for engaging in some other counterattitudinal behavior is expected to have a completely different effect on attitude change, according to Festinger's (1957) dissonance theory. The "forced-compliance" paradigm in dissonance theory suggests that the greater the promised reward or threatened punishment, the more pressure is put on the individual to perform the counterattitudinal behavior and the more justified he should feel in performing this behavior. Increasing the magnitude of reward should thus lead to a reduction in dissonance. Since the amount of attitude change is assumed to vary directly with the magnitude of dissonance, promising a person a high reward for his counterattitudinal behavior should result in less attitude change than promising him a low reward for performing the same behavior (see Chapter 2).

---

12. Even when not contingent upon quality of performance, expectation of high reward may sometimes serve as a greater incentive than expectation of a low reward. This effect might occur when subjects feel obliged to work harder in order to justify a large reward, as would be predicted by equity theory (see J. S. Adams, 1965; Walster, Berscheid, and Walster, 1973). Moreover, many incentive theorists would argue not only that a reward may serve as an incentive but that its administration may also reinforce the performance, thereby increasing attitude change.

Studies formulated within the incentive theory framework have manipulated reward magnitude in an attempt to influence the quality of arguments produced. In addition both incentive theory and a reinforcement position suggest that reward magnitude also influences the degree to which the active participant believes his own arguments. In contrast, studies conducted within the forced compliance paradigm of dissonance theory have manipulated reward magnitude as one means of varying justification for the counterattitudinal behavior. Many other variables have also been manipulated in attempts to provide differential degrees of justification for a given behavior. Among these variables are the number of reasons the subject is given to induce him to perform the behavior; the degree to which the subject perceives that his decision to engage in the behavior was his own (freedom of choice); the amount of effort expended in performing the behavior (the lower the effort, the less the behavior has to be justified); and the prestige, status, or attraction of the person requesting performance of the behavior. The first direct test of the forced compliance paradigm is the now classic study by Festinger and Carlsmith (1959), to which we have already referred several times. It may now be instructive to examine this study in some detail.

Male undergraduates participated in an experiment described as dealing with "measures of performance." They performed two repetitive and boring manual tasks for about a half hour each while the experimenter appeared to measure their performance, using a stopwatch and making notations on a sheet of paper. Subjects were led to believe that working on these tasks constituted the total experiment. Actually, there was much more to come. After the subject had completed the second task, the experimenter explained that the major purpose of the experiment was to compare performance of individuals under two different conditions and that the subject had served in one of these conditions. They were further told that while the participants in the other condition were waiting for the experiment to begin, a confederate (ostensibly another student who had just taken part in the experiment) had told them that "the experiment was very interesting and enjoyable, I had a lot of fun, I enjoyed myself, it was very interesting, it was intriguing, it was exciting."

Up to this point all subjects had received exactly the same treatment. They were now divided into one control and two experimental conditions. Control subjects were at this point led to another room, where a person other than the experimenter interviewed them under the pretext of a departmental survey unrelated to the present study.

In the experimental conditions the experimenter explained that his assistant could not come today and that another student was already waiting to take part in the experiment. He then proposed to hire the subject to perform the role of the assistant on this occasion and in the future should the regular assistant be again unavailable. In one experimental condition subjects were offered payment of one dollar, and subjects in the second experimental condition were to receive twenty dollars.

Once a subject had agreed, he was led to the waiting room, where a female student (presumably a subject but actually the experimenter's assistant) was waiting. The experimenter introduced them, and in accordance with instructions, the subject attempted to convince the "new subject" that the experimental tasks she was going to work on were interesting and enjoyable. As in the control condition, the subject was then interviewed in an unrelated context.

The interview consisted of the following four questions, to which the subjects responded on 11-point scales.

1. Were the tasks interesting and enjoyable?
2. Did the experiment give you the opportunity to learn about your own ability to perform these tasks?
3. Would you say the experiment was measuring anything important?
4. Would you have any desire to participate in another similar experiment?

To summarize, subjects in the one-dollar condition were hired to tell a waiting subject that tasks which were rather boring were interesting and enjoyable; subjects in the twenty-dollar condition were hired to do the same for twenty dollars; and subjects in the control condition did not tell the waiting student that the tasks had been enjoyable.

Two features of this experiment are worth noting. First, the study involves an elaborate cover story, and the subjects are deceived in various ways. This is quite typical of research using the forced-compliance paradigm. Second, although the investigators realized that the four questions asked in the interview "varied in how directly relevant they were to what the subject had told the girl" (Festinger and Carlsmith, 1959, p. 206), they are all considered measures of attitude toward the experimental tasks or the experiment itself. From our point of view, of course, the first three questions appear to measure different beliefs, and the fourth an intention.

The results of the study are summarized in Table 10.2. A significant difference between the one-dollar and twenty-dollar conditions was found only with respect to the first question. Subjects in the one-dollar condition rated the tasks as more interesting and enjoyable than did subjects in the twenty-dollar condition. This difference supports the predicted dissonance effect. In comparison with subjects in the control condition, who rated the tasks as mildly uninteresting and unenjoyable, the amount of change was inversely related to reward magnitude. No significant differences were obtained with respect to the remaining three items; for two items the results were in the predicted direction, and the remaining item showed a tendency in the opposite direction.

Although the results of this study did not fully support the dissonance theory prediction, the conclusion that reward magnitude is inversely related to amount of change created considerable interest. As noted, this conclusion appeared to contradict the generally accepted reinforcement position, as well as an incentive hypothesis, both of which predict that amount of change should increase with magnitude of reward. Many subsequent experiments have therefore attempted to

Table 10.2 Average Ratings of Interview Questions for Each Condition
(From Festinger and Carlsmith, 1959)

Question on interview	Experimental condition		
	Control condition (N = 20)	One-dollar condition (N = 20)	Twenty-dollar condition (N = 20)
How enjoyable tasks were (rated from −5 to +5)	−.45	1.35	−.05
How much they learned (rated from 0 to 10)	3.08	2.80	3.15
Scientific importance (rated from 0 to 10)	5.60	6.45	5.18
Participate in similar experiment (rated from −5 to +5)	−.62	1.20	−.25

confirm the "counterintuitive" dissonance hypothesis by varying magnitude of reward for counterattitudinal behavior.

In an early attempt to confirm the Festinger and Carlsmith findings, Cohen (1962) asked his student subjects to write an essay justifying police actions in a campus disturbance for a reward of ten dollars, five dollars, one dollar, or fifty cents. Actually, the students were very much opposed to the police action. After writing the essay, subjects were asked to indicate whether the police action had been justified, on a 31-point scale ranging from *not at all justified* to *completely justified*. Consistent with dissonance theory, the perceived justification of the police action decreased as a function of reward magnitude. That is, the less money a subject received for writing the essay, the more he changed his belief in the direction of the adopted position.

One interesting implication of dissonance theory is that change in the dependent variable can be brought about even without actual performance of the counterattitudinal behavior. According to Brehm and Cohen (1962), the mere fact that a person commits himself to engage in a counterattitudinal behavior should be sufficient to arouse dissonance and hence produce "attitude" change. In a study designed to test this hypothesis, Rabbie, Brehm, and Cohen (1959) asked college students to write an essay supporting the elimination of intercollegiate athletics. Justification for this counterattitudinal behavior was manipulated not by varying magnitude of reward but instead by providing either many or few reasons for performing the behavior. After agreeing to write the essay, half the subjects completed a questionnaire measuring their attitudes toward elimination of intercollegiate athletics on a seven-point scale ranging from *extremely like* to *extremely dislike* and then wrote the essay; the remaining subjects first wrote the essay and then completed the questionnaire. Consistent with dissonance theory, more change in the direction advocated was found under low than under high justification. Further, consistent with the argument that commitment to engage in counterattitudinal behavior is sufficient to produce dissonance and consequent attitude change, this effect was significant even when attitudes were measured prior to the writing of the essay. In fact, the results for the two conditions were quite similar.

A large number of subsequent studies, however, attest to the difficulty of obtaining the dissonance effect consistently. For example, also using an essay-writing task, Janis and Gilmore (1965) offered students one dollar or twenty dollars for writing a short essay in favor of the proposition that a year of physics and a year of mathematics should be added as a requirement for all college students. Although care was taken not to pressure subjects into consenting to this request, all subjects agreed to write the essay, and they were immediately paid the money promised.[13] As in the Rabbie, Brehm, and Cohen (1959) study, half the subjects then completed a posttest questionnaire. The remaining subjects were given 10 minutes to write the essay, and only then did they complete the same questionnaire. The questionnaire consisted of five objective items (not specified) and an open-ended question, all assessing the subject's "present attitude" toward the proposed policy. The two dependent variables of this study were two measures of the same attitude, one obtained by summing over the five objective items and the other based on responses to the open-ended question.[14] Contrary to the dissonance hypothesis, whether or not subjects actually wrote the essay, magnitude of reward had no significant effects on either of the two measures of attitude. In fact, subjects in the twenty-dollar condition tended to have somewhat more favorable (or less unfavorable) attitudes than subjects in the one-dollar condition.

Partly in response to the difficulty of obtaining a consistent dissonance effect when magnitude of reward is manipulated, many investigators have turned to other variables that could also influence justification for performing the counterattitudinal behavior. These variables were expected to interact with reward magnitude and thus mediate the dissonance effect. For example, in addition to manipulating reward magnitude, studies using counterattitudinal essays have looked at such factors as freedom to participate (Holmes and Strickland, 1970; Sherman, 1970a, b), time of payment (Rossomando and Weiss, 1970; Sherman, 1970b), audience position (Nel, Helmreich, and Aronson, 1969), audience awareness that the subject is not presenting his own views (Helmreich and Collins, 1968; Steiner and Field, 1960), reason given for the assigned task (Collins and Helmreich, 1970; Janis and Gilmore, 1965; Elms and Janis, 1965), and time of dependent variable measurement (Crano and Messé, 1970). To be sure, some of these variables were found to interact with reward magnitude. For example, the three studies cited above which manipulated the subject's freedom to participate, in ad-

---

13. The students were contacted at their residences, and about 10 percent refused to talk to the experimenter and thus were never even asked whether they would be willing to write the essay.

14. The number of arguments unfavorable toward the proposed policy was subtracted from the number of favorable arguments expressed in response to the open-ended question.

dition to varying reward magnitude, reported the same significant interaction: A negative relationship between reward magnitude and change (i.e., a dissonance effect) was found in the choice condition, whereas a positive relationship (i.e., an incentive effect) was found in the no-choice condition. Unfortunately, this cannot be taken as an indication that dissonance effects will always be obtained under high-choice conditions (e.g., see Calder, Ross, and Insko, 1973). In fact, most studies on forced compliance attempt to convince the subject that his participation is voluntary. Yet these studies often do not produce the predicted effect of reward magnitude. For example, in the Janis and Gilmore (1965) study described above, every effort was made to ensure a high degree of decision freedom. Nevertheless, we saw that reward magnitude had no effect on the amount of attitude change produced by a counterattitudinal essay (cf. Collins and Helmreich, 1970; Collins, *et al.,* 1970; Nel, Helmreich and Aronson, 1969).

Much the same conclusions are reached with respect to research on other variables that were expected to interact with reward magnitude. Indeed, Collins and his associates (Collins *et al.,* 1970; Helmreich and Collins, 1968) have performed a large number of experiments dealing with forced compliance and have found it all but impossible to develop a paradigm that will consistently produce a negative relationship between reward magnitude and amount of change, irrespective of the kind of counterattitudinal behavior involved (see also Calder, Ross, and Insko, 1973).

Our discussion so far has centered on the effects of reward magnitude on changes produced by counterattitudinal behavior. As indicated above, many other variables that were assumed to influence justification have also been investigated. For example, not only has perceived freedom to participate been viewed as a factor interacting with reward magnitude, but it has also been studied in its own right. Similarly, the effects of varying the number of reasons given for the assigned task, time of dependent variable measurement, etc., have also been studied independent of reward magnitude. These manipulations have sometimes supported dissonance theory predictions, but they have usually been found to produce neither a main effect nor an interaction with other variables. The overall pattern of results is thus ambiguous and inconclusive.

This state of affairs has led to an ever increasing list of requirements, each of which is assumed to be a necessary but not sufficient condition for the arousal of dissonance. At last count, in order for the dissonance effect to be obtained, subjects must commit themselves to perform the counterattitudinal behavior in full awareness of the kind of behavior they will be asked to perform and the amount of reward they are to receive; they must commit themselves voluntarily with a maximum of subjective decision freedom; they must feel personally responsible for the aversive consequences of their behavior; the behavior to be performed must violate an expectancy related to the self-concept; and it must be impossible for subjects to justify their counterattitudinal behavior on any other grounds. The assumption is that in the absence of these conditions little dissonance is created, and hence no change in the dependent variable is to be expected. Unfortunately,

even when investigators have attempted to meet all these conditions, the dissonance effect has not always been observed. More important, if all these requirements were accepted as necessary conditions for the arousal of dissonance, it is
doubtful that any situation could be found in which dissonance plays an important role in determining social behavior.

Analysis of Counterattitudinal Behavior

We have noted earlier that the kind and amount of information generated within
an active participation situation are crucial factors in determining amount of
change. In our analysis of role playing studies we have discussed the ways in
which the informational items generated by the role player or provided by the
experimenter can influence proximal beliefs and related dependent variables. Dissonance theory suggests, however, that factors other than the information generated by the counterattitudinal behavior may be of primary importance in bringing
about change. That the information generated by counterattitudinal behavior is
accorded little importance is demonstrated by the fact that actual performance of
the behavior is not considered to be a necessary condition for change; the subject's commitment to perform the behavior is assumed to be sufficient to produce
dissonance and consequent change in the dependent variable.

Justification, incentive, and reinforcement. We saw above that studies of forced
compliance have usually manipulated magnitude of reward in an attempt to influence justification for performance of a counterattitudinal behavior. We have
also noted, however, that a reward may sometimes act as an incentive and that
it may have reinforcing properties. Which of these effects will be most pronounced
depends on three aspects of the reward manipulation: (1) The person may or
may not know in advance that performance of the counterattitudinal behavior will
be rewarded. (2) The reward may or may not be made contingent upon the quality of the person's performance. (3) The reward may or may not be administered
prior to measurement of the dependent variable.

When reward is neither expected nor administered, no reward manipulation
has taken place, and reward magnitude is irrelevant. When a reward is not expected but is nevertheless administered, it should provide neither incentive nor
justification for performing the behavior; its sole effect should be to reinforce the
behavior that has occurred. The four remaining ways of manipulating reward magnitude in the forced-compliance situation are shown in Table 10.3. In each of the
four possibilities, variations in reward magnitude influence *justification*. That is,
whenever a person performing a counterattitudinal behavior expects to be rewarded, the reward can serve to justify his behavior. The greater the expected
reward, the greater the justification. The *reinforcement* value of a reward also increases with its magnitude. However, for this variation in reinforcement value to
have an effect on a dependent variable, the reward must actually be administered,
and it must be administered prior to assessment of the dependent variable. Finally,
variations in reward magnitude also affect the reward's *incentive* value. However,

Table 10.3 Effects of Reward Magnitude When Reward Is Expected

Reward contingent upon quality of performance	Reward administered after counterattitudinal behavior but prior to dependent variable measurement	
	Yes	No
Yes	(1) Incentive Reinforcement Justification	(2) Incentive Justification
No	(3) Reinforcement Justification	(4) Justification

our analysis suggests that a reward will serve as an incentive only to the extent that it is made contingent upon the quality of performance. It follows that increasing the magnitude of a reward will not raise its incentive value when the reward is administered prior to performance of the counterattitudinal behavior or when the subject expects to obtain a given reward irrespective of the quality of his performance.

Table 10.3 shows that it may be impossible to predict the effects of variations in reward magnitude in many forced compliance situations. Consider, for example, an experiment employing the following procedure. All subjects are promised a reward if they write a counterattitudinal essay of high quality. In one condition they are told that the amount of money each can earn is $1 whereas in a second condition the amount of money each can earn is $10. All subjects then write the counterattitudinal essay and are given their respective rewards. Following administration of the reward, the dependent variables are assessed. In this situation (Cell 1 in Table 10.3) the variation in reward magnitude will have incentive and reinforcement, as well as justification or dissonance effects.

The main point to be made is that reinforcement and incentive effects on the one hand and dissonance effects on the other, need not be viewed as mutually exclusive. Instead, two or all three of these effects may be operative, sometimes canceling each other and at other times leading to either a positive or a negative relation between magnitude of reward and amount of change. A clear dissonance effect can theoretically be obtained in two ways. One is to administer the reward prior to performance of the counterattitudinal behavior. The second is to promise the reward irrespective of quality of performance and to measure the dependent variable before the reward is administered. Under these conditions reinforcement and incentive effects are not expected, and reward should serve only to justify the behavior. Note that a test of incentive predictions versus dissonance predictions would be inappropriate under these circumstances. Nevertheless, many studies have used precisely these procedures to test the competing hypotheses. For example, subjects have often been paid immediately after agreeing to perform the counterattitudinal behavior (e.g., Carlsmith, Collins, and Helmreich, 1966; Elms and Janis, 1965). In other studies (e.g., Linder, Cooper, and Jones, 1967) subjects were not paid prior to assessment of the dependent variables, but their rewards were not explicitly made contingent upon quality of performance. In fact, we have not been able to find a single study in which the incentive effect should have been clearly operative. Most studies fall into Cell 4 of Table 10.3, and a few studies fall into Cell 3. From the point of view of our analysis, therefore, studies using the forced compliance paradigm have not provided a crucial test between dissonance and incentive theories. Moreover, even under the conditions most favorable to the dissonance hypothesis (Cell 4), the predicted inverse relation between reward magnitude and amount of change has not been consistently obtained.

The forced compliance situation. In order to understand why conflicting results have been obtained in the forced compliance paradigm, it may be instructive to examine a situation which should maximize the likelihood of demonstrating the dissonance effect. Not only must this situation ensure that reward has no incentive or reinforcement effects, but it should also eliminate the possibility that the dissonance effect will be confounded with the informational items generated during performance of the counterattitudinal behavior. Let us therefore consider the situation in which subjects commit themselves to perform a counterattitudinal behavior for a given reward, and the dependent variable is assessed immediately after commitment. Thus, although expecting a reward, at the time of measurement the subject has neither performed the behavior nor received the reward.

According to Festinger's (1957) dissonance theory, a forced compliance situation of this kind involves two basic cognitive elements: (1) I committed myself to perform behavior X, and (2) I believe Y. Dissonance is assumed to exist when X is the "obverse" of Y, i.e., when "not-X follows from Y." For example, the belief "I agreed to write an essay in favor of eliminating intercollegiate athletics" is assumed to be dissonant with the belief "I am opposed to eliminating intercollegiate athletics." In practice, therefore, the investigator selects a behavior which, if performed, would be dissonant with the subject's position on the dependent variable. The magnitude of dissonance associated with the cognitive element K "I committed myself to perform behavior X" increases with the number and importance of all other cognitive elements that are dissonant with element K (e.g., "I believe Y") relative to the total number and importance of relevant cognitions (see Chapter 2). Equation 10.1 is a more formal statement of this definition, where D_K is

$$D_K = \frac{\Sigma I_d}{\Sigma I_d + \Sigma I_c}, \tag{10.1}$$

the magnitude of dissonance associated with element K, I_d is the importance of a dissonant element d, and I_c is the importance of a consonant element c. Equation 10.1 suggests that any cognitive element consonant with the commitment to perform a counterattitudinal behavior (element K) should reduce the magnitude of dissonance associated with that commitment. The belief "I was promised \$X for performing the behavior" is viewed as one such consonant element. Increasing magnitude of the promised reward is assumed to increase its importance and thus to lower the overall amount of dissonance. The growing list of conditions necessary for dissonance arousal mentioned above can be viewed as an attempt to specify other cognitions that may be consonant with the commitment. If these conditions are not met, consonant cognitions may be formed and may serve to reduce or eliminate the dissonance associated with commitment to perform the counterattitudinal behavior. For example, if a person did not believe that he agreed freely to perform the behavior, the cognitive element "I was forced to agree to perform the behavior" could reduce his dissonance. According to dissonance theory, if dissonance has been aroused, the person should try to reduce his dissonance by changing one or more of the dissonant elements. The difficulty encountered by most dissonance research is the need to ensure that no dissonant element other than the element corresponding to the dependent variable can change.

From the point of view of dissonance theory, then, there are a number of target beliefs in the forced compliance situation. The first is the person's belief that he has committed himself to perform (or actually has performed) a given behavior. All other beliefs that are consonant or dissonant with this knowledge are also considered to be target beliefs. The experimental manipulation is designed to attack certain target beliefs either directly (e.g., "I was promised \$10") or indirectly (e.g., "I had free choice"). Other target beliefs are directly or indirectly attacked by elaborate cover stories that often accompany forced compliance experiments. For example, subjects may be told that they are taking part in an undergraduate's pilot study for a term paper. A change in this proximal belief may increase the belief that "the experiment has no scientific value," a target belief which is assumed to be dissonant with the behavior. In fact, cover stories are frequently used in an attempt to ensure that all target beliefs, with the exception of those attacked by the manipulations, will be dissonant with the commitment to perform the behavior in question.

The almost unlimited number of potential target beliefs in the forced compliance situation has been recognized as one of the major problems in dissonance research since it is always possible to argue that one or more (unidentified) target beliefs are consonant with the counterattitudinal behavior. This argument can therefore always be used as a post hoc explanation whenever the dissonance effect is not obtained.

The dependent variable in a forced compliance situation is either a belief, an attitude, or an intention that is assumed to be dissonant with the target belief "I committed myself to perform behavior X." As we saw in Chapter 2, the original definition of a dissonant relation led to some confusion since investigators could not always agree that "the obverse" of performing a given behavior would follow from the person's initial belief or attitude. Aronson's (1968) rule of thumb that dissonance exists only when an expectation has been violated, i.e., when a person holding a given attitude would not be expected to perform the behavior, has thus far relied on the investigator's intuition. Not only can investigators disagree with respect to an attitude-behavior relation, but as we saw in Chapter 8, an investigator's intuition that some attitudes should be related to a given behavior is often fallacious.

We noted in Chapter 2 that dissonance theory deals exclusively with cognitive elements, i.e., beliefs. It may therefore be argued that the most appropriate dependent variable in any dissonance study is a measure of belief. Within the forced compliance paradigm, the relevant belief is the person's subjective probability that he holds a certain belief, attitude, or intention (i.e., that he has some disposition, D), given that he has committed himself to perform (or has actually performed) a behavior, B. This description of the dependent variable can be expressed as the conditional probability $p(D|B)$. However, dissonance theory is primarily concerned with the change from some prior belief, $p(D)$, to the posterior belief $p(D|B)$.

Although there has been some confusion concerning the definition of a dissonant relation, it is possible to translate Festinger's (1957) original statement into a conditional probability. Festinger stated that cognitive elements A and B are dissonant if not-B follows from A. Consider, for example, a person who has a negative attitude toward legalization of marijuana ($A-$) and who is induced to write an essay in favor of legalizing it ($B+$). Dissonance may be defined by the conditional probability $p(B+|A-)$.[15] This implies that we can define *degrees* of dissonance rather than merely stating that two cognitive elements are dissonant or consonant. Specifically, dissonance should be an inverse function of $p(B+|A-)$; the lower the probability of writing an essay in favor of legalizing marijuana ($B+$), given a negative attitude toward legalization ($A-$), the more dissonance should be aroused by commitment to perform (or actual performance of) this counterattitudinal behavior.

Another difficulty confronting dissonance theory is the concern that unidentified beliefs may be consonant with commitment to perform the behavior. This problem can also be analyzed in terms of the conditional probability $p(B+|A-)$. Each of the consonant beliefs could serve as an additional reason for commitment, thus increasing the probability that the person would commit himself to perform the behavior ($B+$) even if he had a negative attitude ($A-$). That is, factors which may serve to "justify" commitment to perform a behavior should increase the conditional probability $p(B+|A-)$, thereby reducing amount of dissonance.

---

15. Festinger's definition of dissonance as "not-X follows from Y" can also be translated into the conditional probabilities $p(B-|A+)$, $p(A-|B+)$, and $p(A+|B-)$. This illustrates the unclarity associated with Festinger's definition since these conditional probabilities are not equivalent. We could have selected $p(B-|A+)$ as a definition of dissonance in the forced compliance situation; the conclusions would be the same.

The definition of dissonance in terms of a conditional probability makes it possible to employ Bayes's theorem (described in Chapter 5) to further examine the forced compliance situation. When applied to this situation, Bayes's theorem can be stated as follows:

$$\frac{p(A+|B+)}{p(A-|B+)} = \frac{p(B+|A+)}{p(B+|A-)} \cdot \frac{p(A+)}{p(A-)}. \tag{10.2}$$

The amount of revision in beliefs favoring the hypothesis that the actor holds a positive attitude increases with the diagnostic value of the counterattitudinal behavior $B+$, that is, with the likelihood ratio $p(B+|A+)/p(B+|A-)$. The amount of change in belief produced by committing one's self to perform this behavior should therefore increase with the diagnostic value of the commitment. This implies that the conditional probability $p(B+|A-)$, which defines dissonance, is only one factor involved in the forced compliance situation. Not only must this conditional probability be low, but the conditional probability $p(B+|A+)$ should be relatively high. To return to our example, the probability of writing an essay in support of legalization of marijuana should be high, given that the person has a positive attitude toward legalization. In other words, the belief, attitude, or intention which constitutes the dependent variable must be relevant for the behavior under consideration. The notion that active participation in a forced compliance situation must involve a behavior that is clearly counterattitudinal corresponds to this requirement.[16]

In Chapter 5 we described the process of self-attribution in terms of Bayes's theorem, and we discussed various factors that can influence the likelihood ratio. These factors include perceived decision freedom, the behavior's utility or desirability, and consistency of behavior across objects, actors, and occasions. We also saw that the greater the number of plausible causes for the behavior, the lower its diagnostic value. This interpretation is similar to the self-attribution approach adopted by Bem (1965, 1967, 1972), Steiner (1970), and Trope (1973).

In terms of a Bayesian analysis, then, there are only two primary beliefs in a forced compliance situation, namely, the two conditional probabilities that make up the likelihood ratio. A given manipulation should influence amount of change in the dependent variable only if it affects this ratio. For a large revision to occur, $p(B+|A+)$ should be high and $p(B+|A-)$ low. Although the manipulation may influence the extent to which a given behavior allows an inference to be made with

---

16. The requirement that the behavior be counterattitudinal implies not only that it should be dissonant with the actor's own position $(A-)$, but that it should also be consonant with a position contrary to the actor's position $(A+)$. Thus dissonance theory also implies that revision in an actor's beliefs will be maximal when $p(B+|A+)$ is high and $p(B+|A-)$ is low.

respect to one dependent belief, the manipulation may have little effect on the behavior's diagnostic value for some other belief. Thus telling another person that the experiment was interesting may have diagnostic value for the the belief "The experiment was interesting," but it may not influence the belief "I liked the experiment" or the intention "I would participate in similar experiments in the future." [17]

The advantage of a Bayesian analysis, therefore, is that it specifies the two primary beliefs that should serve as the target beliefs beliefs in an attempt to influence a given dependent variable. The next step in the analysis concerns the extent to which changes in proximal beliefs will influence these primary beliefs. Earlier we reviewed some of the proximal beliefs that are attacked in the forced compliance paradigm. These proximal beliefs correspond to informational items provided by the manipulation and the cover story. As we saw, the informational items provided are primarily directed at proximal beliefs that are assumed to be related to $p(B+|A-)$. Thus offering a reward is assumed to increase the likelihood that the person will commit himself to perform the behavior even if he does not have the appropriate disposition. When $p(B+|A-)$ is relatively low, an experimental manipulation (such as varying reward magnitude) may raise this primary belief to varying degrees, and it may thus have an effect on the likelihood ratio. However, if $p(B+|A-)$ is high to begin with, the manipulation will have little effect. Indeed, Steiner (1970) has argued that subjects in a laboratory investigation of forced compliance never feel really free to decline participation. This implies that $p(B+|A-)$ will usually be high, and the experimental manipulation which is designed to increase this probability can have little effect on the likelihood ratio. In fact, it may be argued that there are few if any situations in which a person cannot find one or more external justifications for his counterattitudinal behavior. The likelihood ratio will therefore usually be close to 1, and little revision in dispositional probabilities can be expected.

To make matters worse, even when circumstances are such that a given manipulation can influence the likelihood ratio, not only may it affect proximal beliefs but it may also have impact effects on relevant external beliefs. For example, offering a person a $10 reward may lead not only to the proximal belief "I was promised $10" but also the inference "I am being bribed" (cf. M. J. Rosen-

---

17. Unipolar belief measures should therefore reflect changes in beliefs for which commitment to perform a counterattitudinal behavior has diagnostic value. The dependent measure, however, is usually a bipolar scale. So long as one of the endpoints on this bipolar scale defines one of the relevant beliefs, change in the belief should also be reflected in responses to the bipolar scale. When the dependent variable is measured by summing across a set of items, however, the resulting index may not reflect changes in the belief. For this reason, measures of attitude other than a single bipolar evaluative scale may be inappropriate dependent variables in a dissonance or attribution experiment.

berg, 1965b). Instead of increasing $p(B+|A-)$, the inference produced by the reward may lower this conditional probability.[18] Contrary to its intended effect, a high reward may thus serve to raise, rather than lower, the likelihood ratio (i.e., the dissonance).

From our point of view, then, it is highly unlikely that any situation can be found in which the mere commitment to perform a counterattitudinal behavior for some reward will have *consistent* effects on the likelihood ratio. Since it is impossible to specify in advance the effects, if any, of a given manipulation on the commitment's diagnostic value, inconsistent findings are to be expected.

So far we have discussed only the basic forced compliance situation in which a person commits himself to perform a counterattitudinal behavior as a result of a certain degree of pressure. Since conflicting findings are to be expected even in this relatively simple situation, introduction of additional factors will obviously serve to further confound the issue. As we have noted earlier, subjects may actually be asked to perform the counterattitudinal behavior. Making the reward contingent upon quality of performance may serve as an incentive and thus influence the performance; administration of the reward may then reinforce the behavior; and the nature of the informational items generated during performance may themselves be responsible for increases or decreases in the dependent variable, irrespective of the reward manipulation. In these forced compliance situations, therefore, no clear predictions can be made about the effects of any given manipulation. It appears that research within the forced compliance paradigm is unlikely to uncover any systematic relations between a manipulation and changes in beliefs, attitudes, or intentions.

This state of affairs is perhaps again attributable to the fact that intervening processes have received little systematic treatment. The experimental manipulations, the cover story, and performance of the counterattitudinal behavior itself provide informational items that may influence proximal beliefs. Changes in these proximal beliefs may have impact effects on external beliefs. The effect of forced compliance, including the manipulation, will depend on the degree to which changes in relevant proximal and external beliefs produce a chain of effects ranging from primary beliefs through the immediate determinant of the dependent variable to the dependent variable itself. As we have repeatedly pointed out, when these intervening processes are not taken into account, apparently conflicting findings are unavoidable.

Before we attempt to provide an overall evaluation of research generated by dissonance theory, it may be useful to examine the fourth active participation situation in which a person is confronted with a choice between two or more alternatives.

---

18. The inference might also lower $p(B+|A+)$ since a person who feels he is being bribed may refuse to perform the behavior $B+$ even if he has the appropriate attitude $A+$. This would constitute an impact effect consistent with the intended purpose of the reward manipulation.

CHOICE BEHAVIOR

The forced compliance paradigm discussed above can be viewed as a special case of a choice situation, in which the person chooses to perform or not to perform a counterattitudinal behavior. Whereas early research on choice behavior was concerned primarily with factors influencing a person's decision, dissonance theory drew attention to the possible effects of the choice on the person's beliefs, attitudes, and intentions. In Chapter 2 we noted that whenever a person makes a choice between two or more alternatives, dissonance is assumed to be aroused: Knowledge that the chosen alternative has some unfavorable aspects and that the unchosen alternatives have some favorable aspects is presumed to be dissonant with knowledge of the choice. The theory predicts that the person can reduce his dissonance by increasing his evaluation of the chosen alternative, decreasing his evaluation of the unchosen alternatives, or both.[19] "Since the dissonance exists in the first place because there were cognitive elements corresponding to favorable characteristics of the unchosen alternative and also cognitive elements corresponding to unfavorable characteristics of the chosen alternative, it can be materially reduced by eliminating some of these elements or by adding new ones that are consonant with the knowledge of the action taken." (Festinger, 1957; p. 44)

In a typical experiment on postdecision dissonance, subjects first rate the attractiveness of several objects or alternatives. They are then given a choice between two of the alternatives, such as two household products (Brehm, 1956), two records (Harris, 1969; Brehm and Jones, 1970), two Papermate pens of different colors (Gordon and Glass, 1970), or two swimming suits (Mittelstaedt, 1969). In the high-dissonance condition, subjects are asked to choose between two alternatives of approximately equal attractiveness. In the low-dissonance condition, one option is highly attractive, and the other is low in attractiveness. After making their choices, subjects again rate the attractiveness of the different alternatives. An increase in the attractiveness of the chosen option, and/or a decrease in that of the unchosen option, are taken as evidence in favor of the dissonance hypothesis.[20]

For example, in the first investigation of postdecisional dissonance reduction Brehm (1956) asked female subjects to rate eight articles (automatic toaster, stopwatch, portable radio, etc.) on an eight-point scale ranging from *definitely not*

---

19. Two additional ways of reducing postdecision dissonance have been suggested by Festinger: The person may psychologically change or revoke his decision, or he may establish cognitive overlap among the alternatives involved in the choice, thereby making the alternatives more similar.

20. Oshikawa (1968) has pointed out that this paradigm entails methodological problems since differential regression effects are to be expected in the high- and low-dissonance conditions. Thus changes in evaluations that have been taken as indications of dissonance reduction or of postdecisional regret may be confounded with regression effects, especially when changes in both alternatives are combined into a single index.

at all desirable to *extremely desirable*. Subjects were then told that as compensation for participating in the research, they could choose between two of the articles rated. One of these alternatives had been rated as desirable (that is, 5, 6, or 7 on the eight-point scale). For a condition of high dissonance, the other alternative offered was between ½ and 1½ scale points lower in desirability; in the low-dissonance condition, the second alternative was between 2 and 3 scale points less desirable than the first. After choosing, subjects again rated the desirability of all eight articles on the eight-point desirability scale described above.[21] The dependent variable in this study was an index of dissonance reduction obtained by subtracting changes in the unchosen alternative from changes in the chosen alternative. Although the results were in the predicted direction, the amount of dissonance reduction was not significantly greater in the high- than in the low-dissonance condition.

Although some later studies have reported significant changes in attitudes toward chosen and unchosen alternatives (e.g., Brehm and Cohen, 1959; Festinger, 1964), others have not been able to obtain the effects predicted by dissonance theory. For example, in addition to varying the *relative* attractiveness of choice alternatives, investigators have looked at variables such as the *absolute* attractiveness of choice alternatives (e.g., H. J. Greenwald, 1969), similarity of alternatives (Brehm and Cohen, 1959), involvement (Gordon and Glass, 1970), confidence (Greenwald, 1969), time of reevaluation measurement (Brehm and Wicklund, 1970), "salience" (i.e., leaving or removing photos of the choice alternatives during rating—Brehm and Wicklund, 1970), and telling or not telling subjects that a reward was contingent upon their choice and actually rewarding or not rewarding them (Brehm and Jones, 1970). Some of these studies have compared postdecisional dissonance reduction with predecisional changes (Davidson and Kiesler, 1964) or with changes due to postdecisional regret (Festinger and Walster, 1964; Brehm and Wicklund, 1970). Generally speaking, studies dealing with changes following a decision have found neither consistent nor significant effects, although auxiliary data analyses sometimes have led to apparently significant findings. In a systematic investigation of choice processes, Harris (1969) concluded that there was very little evidence in his data for postdecisional dissonance reduction. In fact, he found no significant differences between subjects who made repeated choices between pairs of records and a no-choice control group.

Analysis of Choice Behavior

Viewed within our conceptual framework, these inconsistent findings are again not unexpected. As in the forced compliance situation, research on postdecisional changes has tended to neglect the processes intervening between the choice and the dependent variable. Here, perhaps more than in other areas of research, the distinction between target beliefs and dependent variable is clearly revealed. As

---

21. In two additional conditions not considered here, subjects received some information about the articles following their choices but prior to the second rating.

we saw at the beginning of this section, Festinger argued that postdecision dissonance exists whenever the person believes that the chosen alternative has negative attributes and/or the unchosen alternative has positive attributes. According to the theory, dissonance can be reduced by "reevaluating the alternatives"; i.e., the person can reduce dissonance by eliminating some of these dissonant beliefs or by adding new consonant beliefs.[22] Similar to our conceptual framework, dissonance theory thus appears to suggest that attitude toward (or evaluation of) a given object is a function of the person's beliefs linking the object to positive and negative attributes. The appropriate target beliefs for a study on postdecisional attitude change, therefore, are the person's primary beliefs about the chosen and unchosen alternatives. In order to understand the effects of a given (dissonance) manipulation on attitude, one must assess its effects on these primary beliefs. Yet we know of no study in this area that has actually examined changes in the person's beliefs about the alternatives involved in the choice.

Our approach suggests, that in order to study changes in attitudes due to a choice between alternatives, one must assess the person's beliefs about each alternative.[23] This can be done at various stages of the experiment: (1) before the subjects see the alternatives; (2) after being exposed to the alternatives but before being told that they would have to choose; (3) after receiving this information but prior to making the decision; (4) immediately after choosing; and (5) after obtaining and in some way interacting with the chosen alternative. Consider, for example, a child who is offered a choice between a stuffed animal and a toy car. He can be asked to elicit his beliefs about "stuffed animals" and about "toy cars." These beliefs may differ greatly from the beliefs he would elicit after having a chance to examine a particular stuffed animal and a particular toy car. By being able to observe the objects, he may gain new information about them, thus changing some of his prior beliefs or adding new beliefs about the objects. After being told that he can choose one of the toys, he may reexamine both toys in a more critical fashion, and further changes in beliefs may result. According to dissonance theory, after the decision—but prior to interaction with the toy—additional revisions in beliefs should occur in an attempt to reduce postdecision dissonance. Finally, the child may acquire additional information about the chosen toy after he has had a chance to play with it.

Measuring the person's attitudes toward the choice alternatives at different stages in the decision process may yield different results. The appropriate com-

---

22. We noted previously (Chapters 2 and 5) that Bem (1965, 1967) has suggested a self-attribution explanation to account for attitudes following a choice, as well as other dissonance phenomena. According to this explanation, a person uses his own choice to infer that he must like the chosen alternative more than the unchosen alternatives. We saw in Chapter 5 that this view is consistent with a Bayesian analysis of self-attribution processes.

23. It would be desirable to use a free-elicitation procedure; alternatively, a standard set of modal salient beliefs might be obtained in a pilot study.

parison for a test of dissonance theory is between attitudes immediately prior to the choice (in full awareness that a choice will be made—Stage 3) and after the choice has been made but prior to interaction (Stage 4).[24] Any other comparison confounds the effects of dissonance with other processes. For example, most studies obtain their first measure of attitudes at Stage 1 or Stage 2 (prior to knowledge that a choice is called for). A postdecisional measurement (at Stage 4) may then reflect changes due to reexamination of the alternatives (at Stage 3) rather than a dissonance effect. It may however be extremely difficult to obtain an uncontaminated measure of attitude at Stage 3 (immediately prior to the decision) since one cannot be sure that the person has not already made an implicit choice prior to the measurement (cf. Festinger, 1964). Procedural variations with respect to time of measurement are therefore likely to produce apparently inconsistent findings.

To make matters worse, the dependent variables in studies on postdecision changes have not been primary beliefs about the alternatives; rather, they have been attitudes, preferences, intentions, or actual choice of an alternative on some future occasion. We have noted repeatedly that even if postdecision changes in primary beliefs do occur, there is no guarantee that changes in any of these variables will follow. Indeed, one repeated problem in studies of postdecision dissonance is that a large proportion of subjects have to be eliminated because they fail to choose the alternative they rated as more attractive on the pretest. This finding indicates that attitudes toward alternatives may be unrelated to choice between them. Clearly, then, many inconsistent findings may be due to differences in the dependent variables measured in different studies.

General Comments about Dissonance Research

Since the early 1960s, a large body of research has been generated in an attempt to provide support for the major dissonance principle according to which any treatment that produces dissonance between two cognitions will lead to attempts to reduce the dissonance. We have briefly considered the two most frequently studied paradigms: forced compliance and decisions between alternatives. The findings have been largely inconsistent and disappointing.

Part of the problem is that many dissonance studies are basically attempts to account for previously obtained inconsistent or negative findings. Many of the independent variables introduced in dissonance research were studied in attempts to account for failures to support the dissonance hypothesis. Although studies of this kind may sometimes be useful and necessary, it is unfortunate that they all too often result in an accumulation of reactive studies that are much more concerned with methodological details than with theoretical issues. Indeed, recent

---

24. The measurement at Stage 4 should probably be performed after a short interval since it has been argued that immediately following the choice, "postdecisional regret" may actually work against the dissonance hypothesis (cf. Festinger, 1964; Walster, 1964).

research investigating the effects of active participation on beliefs, attitudes, or intentions within the dissonance framework has not significantly advanced our understanding of the conditions under which such effects will be observed. This state of affairs may reflect shortcomings of dissonance theory, the reactive nature of much of the research, or the unusually weak methodology that has tended to characterize this body of research. It is perhaps in this area, more than anywhere else, that one encounters misuse of statistics, incomplete experimental designs, conclusions based on nonsignificant findings, partial and internal data analyses, etc. Although it is doubtful that greater methodological rigor would make up for the general shortcomings of reactive research, such an approach might at least serve to eliminate some of the apparent inconsistencies.

CONCLUSION

We have seen that active participation can sometimes be an effective strategy of change. The active participant is exposed to a variety of informational items, and direct experience of this kind tends to produce changes in corresponding proximal beliefs. The problem is to ensure that changes in proximal beliefs will have the desired effects on the dependent variable. To this end, it is first necessary to identify the primary beliefs that provide the immediate informational foundation for the dependent variable in question. These primary beliefs should serve as the targets of the influence attempt. The informational items to which active participants are exposed should either directly attack some of these target beliefs, or they should attack other proximal beliefs that are functionally related to the target beliefs. Since they are assumed to serve as primary beliefs, changes in target beliefs should be reflected in the dependent variable.

Most investigators, however, have not undertaken such a detailed analysis of their active participation situations. Usually, target beliefs are not made explicit, nor are changes in these beliefs assessed. Further, no attempts are made to identify the proximal beliefs in the situation, or to examine the relations between proximal and target beliefs. In fact, in some active participation situations, particularly in the interpersonal contact situation, the investigator has only limited control over the items of information to which participants are exposed. Clearly, when the proximal beliefs are neglected or not under the investigator's control, the effects of active participation on some dependent variable cannot be anticipated. Sometimes it may produce the desired change, but at other times it may have undesirable effects or no effects at all.

In many situations involving active participation, however, the proximal beliefs attacked can and should be identified. We have seen that this is true for many role playing situations, for studies using the forced compliance paradigm, as well as for research on the effects of choosing between available alternatives. The failure to explicate target beliefs, to identify proximal beliefs, and to consider the relations between proximal and target beliefs has led to largely inconsistent findings in these areas of investigation. Our analysis suggests that neither forced compliance nor choice between behavioral alternatives is likely to have strong and systematic effects on the dependent variables measured. In contrast, there is reason to believe that active role playing can greatly facilitate change. In comparison with a passive observer, the active role player is often forced to search through his own belief hierarchy in order to produce arguments in favor of the assigned position. This active search may increase, at least temporarily, the strength with which the previously nonsalient beliefs are held. Moreover, the role player is likely to perceive these beliefs as related to the primary beliefs and the dependent variable.

Much research on active participation has been concerned with the effects of independent variable manipulations. The assumption is that such manipulations will influence the amount of change produced by an active participation experience. There can be little doubt that manipulations do at times affect amount of change in a given dependent variable, but empirical findings have been far from consistent, and little systematic knowledge of such effects has accumulated. Two reasons for this failure may be suggested. First, we have just noted that the active participation situation has usually not been subjected to a careful analysis in terms of the information available to participants. Proximal beliefs have not been identified, and their relations to target beliefs and dependent variables have been left unspecified. Clearly, if the assumed relation between active participation and change in the dependent variable is not well understood, manipulations of factors designed to influence the strength of this relation cannot be expected to have systematic effects. Second, our analysis suggests that the active participation experience itself may not have a consistently facilitating effect because of the investigator's incomplete control over the situation. It follows that in these situations, manipulating an independent variable can produce only inconsistent findings.

We can thus conclude that the search for factors that systematically affect the amount of change due to active participation can be successful only when two conditions are met: First, the processes intervening between active participation and change in the dependent variable must be well understood; and second, the investigator must be able to exercise sufficient control over the items of information to which subjects are exposed, so that the active participation experience will consistently facilitate the desired change in the dependent variable under investigation.

Chapter 11

Strategies of Change: Persuasive Communication

The preceding chapter has considered active participation as one major strategy to bring about change in beliefs, attitudes, intentions, and behaviors. The present chapter deals with the second major strategy of change, namely, persuasive communication. In contrast to active participation, where the individual may gain information by observing objects, people, and events in a given situation, when the person receives a persuasive communication, he is provided with items of information by some outside source. Every day of their lives people are exposed to persuasive communications designed to influence their beliefs, attitudes, intentions, or behaviors: The boy is told to wash his hands; the potential consumer reads the description of a product; the senator is handed a petition; the potential voter attends a political rally; the person reads a textbook; the student attends a lecture; etc. Since persuasive communication has always been viewed as the major strategy of influencing people, it has held the interest of scholars and practitioners alike. Much of the impetus to controlled research on communication and persuasion, however, has come from the Yale Communication Research Program under the direction of Carl I. Hovland (cf. Hovland, Janis, and Kelley, 1953; Hovland, 1957; Hovland and Janis, 1959; Hovland and Rosenberg, 1960; Sherif and Hovland, 1961).

YALE COMMUNICATION RESEARCH PROGRAM

In their extended research program, Hovland and his associates attempted to investigate factors influencing the effectiveness of persuasive communication. Defining communication as "the process by which an individual (the communicator) transmits stimuli (usually verbal) to modify the behavior of other individuals (the audience)," they viewed their research task as the investigation of *who* says *what*

451

to *whom* with *what effect*. To study the effects of the *source* of a communication (the "who"), the investigators manipulate various characteristics of the communicator, such as his trustworthiness, expertise, status, likability, etc. An identical message may thus be attributed to two different sources, one with high credibility and one with low credibility. *Message* characteristics (the "what") have been manipulated in attempts to study effects of different types of communications. For example, one-sided messages have been compared with two-sided messages, messages with explicit conclusions have been contrasted with messages in which the conclusion is left implicit, emotional messages have been compared with logical messages, high-fear appeals with low-fear appeals, and the order of arguments in the message has been varied. Another line of research has dealt with *audience* variables or individual differences (the "whom") in terms of general persuasibility, initial opinions, intelligence, self-esteem, cognitive complexity, and various personality traits. In attempts to assess the effects of source, message, and audience variables, several types of responses have been obtained, including judgments of the degree to which the communicator was fair in presenting the facts, the degree to which the information presented justified the conclusion, recall of the communication's content, and changes in beliefs, attitudes, intentions, or behavior.

One basic assumption underlying this research is that the effect of a given communication depends on the extent to which it is *attended* to, *comprehended*, and *accepted*. Figure 11.1 summarizes the major factors identified by Hovland and his associates in their analysis of the communication and persuasion process. Note that primary concern is with "attitude change," but many different variables are subsumed under this label. The effects of source, message, and audience factors on attitude change are assumed to be mediated by attention, comprehension, and acceptance. One implication of this conceptualization is that a given manipulation may both facilitate and inhibit attitude change. A two-sided message, for example, may increase attention but reduce comprehension. Similarly, a high-fear appeal may reduce attention but increase acceptance.

McGuire's two-factor model. According to the Yale approach, "attention and comprehension determine what the recipient will *learn* concerning the content of the communicator's message; other processes, involving changes in motivation, are assumed to determine whether or not he will accept or adopt what he learns" (Hovland and Janis, 1959, p. 5). The effects of a communication, then, depend on two factors: learning of message content and acceptance of what is learned. Consistent with this approach, McGuire (1968) developed a two-factor model of persuasion which combines attention and comprehension into a single factor of reception. According to McGuire's model, the process of persuasion involves two basic steps: "reception of the message content and yielding to what is comprehended." In its simplest form, McGuire's model can be written symbolically as in Eq. 11.1,

$$p(O) = p(R)p(Y), \tag{11.1}$$

Independent
variables

Internal mediating
processes

Observable
communication
effects

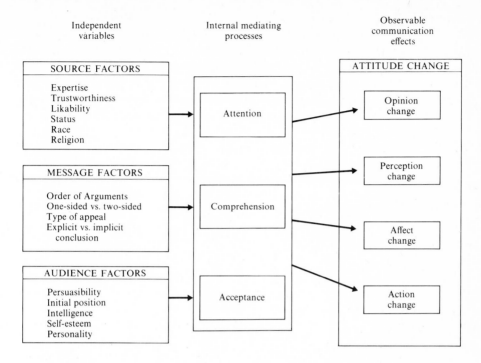

Fig. 11.1 Yale approach to communication and persuasion. (Based on Janis and Hovland, 1959.)

where $p(O)$ is the probability of opinion change; $p(R)$ is the probability of effective reception; and $p(Y)$ is the probability of yielding to what is received. McGuire suggested that the reception mediator can be measured directly, as can opinion change. According to McGuire, the yielding mediator is not measured directly; it is estimated on the basis of the degree to which the message was received and the amount of opinion change it produced. Consider, for example, a message that was well received but produced little opinion change. According to McGuire's model, lack of persuasion must then have been due to a low degree of yielding.

McGuire (1968) used this model to account for inconsistent findings concerning the effects of various individual difference variables on persuasion. We saw earlier that a given variable may have different effects on reception and yielding. McGuire suggested, for example, that reception may increase, but yielding decrease, with the receiver's intelligence. Since opinion change is assumed to be a positive function of both reception and yielding, there will be no simple relation between intelligence and opinion change. Specifically, according to the reception mediator, opinion change should increase with intelligence whereas, according to the yielding mediator, it should decrease with intelligence. McGuire's model (see Eq. 11.1) posits a multiplicative effect of reception and yielding on opinion change; the predicted nonmonotonic relation between intelligence and opinion change is given in Fig. 11.2. The greatest amount of opinion change will be predicted for recipients of medium intelligence, whereas subjects of high or low intelligence will change less. The observed relation between intelligence and opinion change will thus depend on the range of intelligence under consideration. A study using subjects with low to moderate intelligence would find a positive relation, and a study using moderately to highly intelligent subjects would find a negative relation. McGuire (1968) presented similar analyses for other individual difference variables, such as self-esteem, sex, and anxiety.

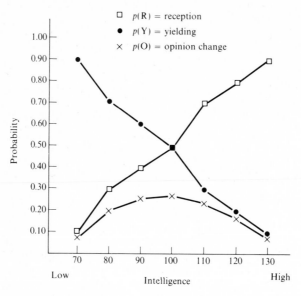

Fig. 11.2 Probability of reception, yielding, and opinion change as a function of intelligence.

More important, McGuire showed how additional factors might influence the relation between a given individual difference variable and opinion change. To return to our example, consider what would happen if an investigator used a very easy message that could be comprehended (i.e., received) by virtually every recipient. The predicted relation between intelligence and opinion change is given in Fig. 11.3. In this case, reception has relatively little effect, and opinion change varies directly with yielding. Thus, in contrast to Fig. 11.2, where intelligence had a curvilinear relation to opinion change, an easy message would result in a fairly linear negative relation.

Although concentrating on reception (attention and comprehension) and yielding, McGuire (1968, 1969) suggested two additional steps in the persuasion process: *retention* of the position agreed with and *action* in accordance with the retained agreement. Persuasion is thus regarded as a process involving five steps:

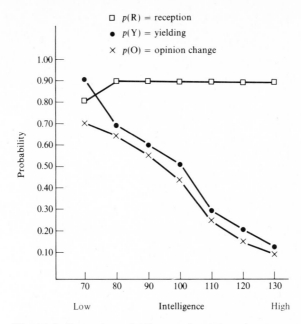

Fig. 11.3 Reception, yielding, and opinion change as a function of intelligence, using an easy message.

attention, comprehension, yielding, retention, and *action.* "The receiver must go through each of these steps if communication is to have an ultimate persuasive impact, and each depends on the occurrence of the preceding step." (McGuire, 1969, p. 173) Each step is viewed as a possible dependent measure of "attitude change" in a communication and persuasion study. These *destination* variables constitute one component of the communication process. The remaining components in McGuire's analysis are *source, message, channel,* and *receiver.* Thus, following Laswell (1948) and using a method similar to the earlier Yale analysis, he conceptualized the communication process in terms of who (source) says what (message) to whom (receiver) how (channel) and with what effect (destination). This approach is summarized in a matrix of persuasive communication (Fig. 11.4).

Most research on communication and persuasion has examined the effects of variations in source, message, or receiver on one or more destination variables. The major dependent variable in most studies is some measure of "attitude change," that is, change in a given belief, attitude, or intention. Relatively little attention has been paid to changes in actual behavior or to the retention of persuasive effects. Those studies that have dealt with retention have examined immediate effects versus delayed effects of a given manipulation or resistance to subsequent persuasive communications. All these persuasive effects are assumed to be mediated by reception and acceptance or yielding. Many studies have obtained some measure of reception, usually in the form of a multiple-choice or

Who? Source	What? Message	How? Channel	To whom? Receiver	With what effect? Destination
				Attention ⎫ Comprehension ⎬ Reception ⎭
				Acceptance or yielding
				(Attitude change)
				Retention
				Action

Fig. 11.4 Matrix of persuasive communication. (Adapted from McGuire, 1969.)

recall test dealing with the content of the message. The second mediating factor, acceptance or yielding, has not been directly measured. Instead, the usual argument is that in the absence of differences in reception, the effect of a given manipulation on persuasion is due to its effect on acceptance.

Social judgment theory. Sherif and his associates (Sherif and Hovland, 1961; Sherif, Sherif, and Nebergall, 1965) have attempted to study the two mediators in greater detail. Their social judgment theory deals with an ordered series of positions along any dimension. As we saw in Chapter 3, a person's own position and all other positions acceptable to him constitute his *latitude of acceptance;* all positions to which he objects define his *latitude of rejection;* the remaining positions constitute his *latitude of noncommitment.* Generally speaking, the more discrepant a given position from the person's own stand, the less likely it is to fall within his latitude of acceptance. With respect to acceptance or rejection of a given persuasive communication, the recipient's perception of the position advocated in the message becomes a crucial factor. If he perceives it to fall within his latitude of acceptance (or perhaps within his latitude of noncommitment), he will accept the communication. If the communication's perceived position falls within his latitude of rejection, acceptance should not occur. It follows that acceptance should be inversely related to the discrepancy between a person's own position and that advocated by a communicator.

In social judgment theory, a persuasive communication is assumed to put pressure on the recipient to change his position; the greater its perceived discrepancy from his own position, the more pressure it should exert. These considerations lead to the prediction that amount of change in position should *increase* with discrepancy so long as the advocated position is not perceived to fall within the latitude of rejection. When it does fall within the latitude of rejection, change in position should *decrease* with discrepancy.

Social judgment theory attempts to identify the factors that influence reception (by displacing perception of the advocated position) and that affect *acceptance* (by modifying the latitudes of acceptance, noncommitment, and rejection). Drawing an analogy to psychophysical judgments, Sherif and Hovland suggested that the person's position serves as an "anchor" or point of reference in his perception of the advocated position. It is expected that the recipient will *assimilate* positions close to his own stand (i.e., he will perceive positions falling within his latitude of acceptance as more similar to his own position than they really are), and that he will *contrast* positions discrepant from his own stand (i.e., he will perceive positions falling within his latitude of rejection as more dissimilar than they really are). It is not quite clear how positions falling within his latitude of noncommitment will be perceived.

According to social judgment theory, the more *ego-involved* the person is with the issue, the more his own position serves as an anchor for his judgments. Involvement should therefore affect reception by increasing assimilation and contrast effects. Further, involvement was originally expected to influence acceptance by narrowing the latitude of acceptance and by widening the latitude of rejection. Empirical research suggested, however, that involvement served primarily to widen the latitude of rejection (by narrowing the latitude of noncommitment).

The expected effects of involvement on amount of change in position are illustrated in Fig. 11.5. The amount of change is expected to be a curvilinear function of perceived discrepancy; the inflection point of this curve approaches the person's own position as involvement increases. Note that change is plotted against *perceived* discrepancy. Since the receiver may displace the position advocated by a persuasive communication, it is difficult, if not impossible, to specify the relation between *actual* discrepancy and amount of change. For example, two receivers with identical initial positions and latitudes who are given a message representing a position within the latitude of noncommitment may displace in different ways. If the advocated position is assimilated into the latitude of acceptance, change should occur, whereas little change should result if it is contrasted into the latitude of rejection.

In sum, Sherif and Hovland assumed that certain positions along an attitudinal dimension are acceptable and others are not. The closer the advocated position is perceived to be to the receiver's own stand, the more likely it is to fall within his latitude of acceptance. Involvement is expected to influence reception by displacing the advocated position and to influence acceptance by widening the latitude of rejection. Factors other than involvement have also been assumed to influence reception or acceptance. For example, it has been suggested that a highly credible communicator may increase change via the reception mediator by increasing the pressure to assimilate the advocated position into the latitude of acceptance (Sherif, Sherif, and Nebergall, 1965) or via the acceptance mediator by widening the latitude of acceptance (Himmelfarb and Eagly, 1974b).

AN ALTERNATIVE MODEL OF PERSUASIVE COMMUNICATION

Our emphasis on the mediating role of proximal beliefs in the influence process suggests a model that differs considerably from the traditional approach to persuasive communication. We have argued that in order to be successful, an influ-

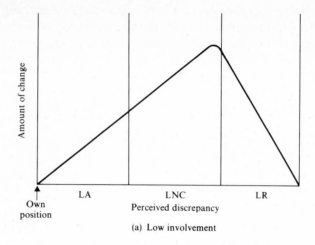

(a) Low involvement

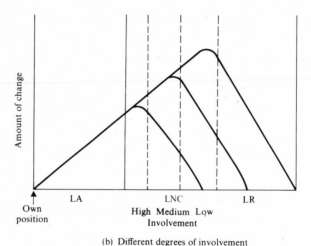

(b) Different degrees of involvement

Fig. 11.5 Change as a function of perceived discrepancy, involvement, and latitudes of acceptance (LA), noncommitment (LNC), and rejection (LR).

ence attempt must at the very least produce changes in proximal or external beliefs. In the preceding two chapters we have seen that attempts to produce change in a dependent variable involve exposing the subject to information that is designed to produce the desired change. Under the strategy of persuasive communication, this information is provided in the form of a written or oral message.

The persuasive communication. A message can be described as consisting primarily of a series of belief statements, each linking some object to an attribute, such as another object, a concept, an event, or a goal. The following example of a persuasive communication is an excerpt from one of the messages used by McGuire (1964) in his research program on resistance to persuasion. This particular message attacks the widely held belief that one should visit his physician annually for thorough medical checkups even in the absence of any particular symptoms.

> One bad effect of visiting a doctor's office at a regular interval even when one is in the best of health comes from the effect such visits have on the patient's peace of mind. In general, most people are already too preoccupied with worries about their health. . . . Routine visits to the physician's office could only serve to increase the person's preoccupation with the sickness since they would keep him thinking about illness and bring him into contact with hospitals and doctor's office and other anxiety provoking stimuli even when he is in the best of health.

> Medical authorities have argued against routine physical checkups once each year also because of the great expense involved and the liklihood that the money spent might be diverted more usefully to other activities promoting health. . . . Therefore, although medical authorities are unanimous in advising the person to see his physician at the first signs of any ailment, they advise against routine checkups at fixed periods, which practice they view as giving only very questionable benefits and doing some unquestionable harm.

A persuasive communication of this kind consists of a number of statements provided by a source, each corresponding to one or more beliefs. In the present example, 12 belief statements can be identified.

1. Visiting a doctor's office at a regular interval . . . has a bad effect on the patient's peace of mind.
2. Most people are already too preoccupied with worries about their health.
3. Routine visits to the physician's office increase a person's preoccupation with his sickness.
4. Routine visits to the physician's office keep a person thinking about illness.
5. Routine visits to the physician's office bring a person in contact with hospitals, doctor's office, and other anxiety provoking stimuli.[1]
6. Medical authorities have argued against routine physical checkups once each year.
7. Medical authorities have argued that routine physical checkups involve great expense.
8. Medical authorities have argued that it is likely that the money spent on routine medical checkups might be diverted more usefully to other activities promoting health.

---

1. This belief statement could be further broken down into three separate beliefs linking routine visits to the physician's office to (1) contact with hospitals, (2) doctor's office, and (3) other anxiety provoking stimuli.

9. Medical authorities are unanimous in advising the person to see his physician at the first signs of any ailment.

10. Medical authorities advise against routine general checkups at fixed periods.

11. Medical authorities view routine general checkups . . . as giving only very questionable benefits.

12. Medical authorities view routine general checkups as doing some unquestionable harm.

From our point of view, each of these 12 belief statements links an object to some attribute with a probability of 1.0. The second statement, for example, establishes a link between "most people" and "already too preoccupied with worries about their health." In terms of belief strength, this statement implies a probability of 1.0 that "most people" are "already too preoccupied. . . ."

Each of the 12 statements above is thus an informational item that represents a *source belief* or *source probability*. Corresponding to each source belief is the receiver's proximal belief or subjective probability that the object has the attribute specified in the message (the *proximal belief* or *proximal probability*). For example, a receiver might initially hold a .30 probability that "most people are already too preoccupied with worries about their health."

McGuire's message could have been designed to increase the receiver's subjective probability that annual checkups are unnecessary, to lower his attitude toward annual checkups, to reduce his intention to obtain annual checkups, or to persuade him to cancel a forthcoming appointment for an annual checkup. Implicitly or explicitly, the investigator views certain beliefs as targets since he assumes that changes in those beliefs will produce a change in the dependent variable.[2] For example, in order to raise the subjective probability that annual checkups are unnecessary (the dependent variable), he may attempt to change the belief that "medical authorities advise against routine general checkups at fixed periods" by including this informational item in his communication (belief 10 above). In order to increase the likelihood of obtaining a change in this target belief, he may provide supportive evidence. The source belief that "medical authorities view routine general checkups . . . as doing some unquestionable harm" may serve as a *supportive belief* for the target belief.

In sum, a persuasive communication comprises for the most part a set of belief statements. Each statement corresponds to a proximal belief held by the receiver. Some of these proximal beliefs may serve as dependent beliefs, others as target beliefs, and still others as beliefs that are assumed to support the target beliefs. Associated with each belief statement in the message are two probabilities, one representing the strength of the source's belief (source probability) and the other the strength of the receiver's initial belief (proximal probability).

In Chapter 9 we saw that various processes may intervene between changes

---

2. These beliefs may or may not be the primary beliefs for the dependent variable in question.

in proximal beliefs and change in the dependent variable. Whatever these intervening processes, however, in order to be effective, a message must first produce changes in proximal beliefs. The question of crucial importance, therefore, is how the message produces changes in the proximal beliefs. Unfortunately, since a message comprises many different belief statements, and since change in one proximal belief may produce change in another, the message may have a multitude of effects which cannot be easily isolated. To study effects of a persuasive communication on proximal beliefs, it may therefore be instructive to consider a message that consists of a single statement. Consider, for example, the persuasive communication comprising such a statement as "There is an 80 percent chance that the President is seriously ill." The source probability in this case is .80. Following a person's exposure to this message, two questions may be asked. The first concerns the degree to which the person is likely to *accept* the source belief. Complete acceptance of a source belief occurs when the receiver's postexposure probability corresponds exactly to the source probability. In the example above, complete acceptance occurs when the person indicates a subjective probability of .80 that "the President is seriously ill." Alternatively, acceptance may be measured in terms of the receiver's subjective probability that "there is an 80 percent chance that the President is seriously ill." With this measure, complete acceptance is indicated by a probability of 1.0.

The second question concerns the amount of *change* in proximal belief that is to be expected. A change in belief involves a revision in the proximal probability following exposure to the source probability. In the example above, if the person shifted his subjective probability from .70 to .80, a change of .10 would be recorded. It should be clear that acceptance of source belief and change in proximal belief are not the same. A person may exhibit complete acceptance of the source belief. Nevertheless, if prior to exposure he already held the same belief, no change would be expected. Although this may appear to be a trivial point, we noted in Chapter 5 that investigators frequently measure only posterior probabilities and ignore the prior probabilities. Such a procedure does not always allow the investigator to determine whether any change has taken place.

Acceptance of Source Beliefs

One factor that should clearly influence the probability that a source belief will be accepted is the *discrepancy* between the probability implied by the source belief, i.e., the source probability (p_s), and the receiver's proximal probability, (p_r). The greater this discrepancy, the lower should be the probability of acceptance. Although the exact nature of the relation between acceptance and discrepancy is unknown, for the sake of simplicity let us tentatively assume an inverse linear relation, as expressed in Eq. 11.2,

$$p(a) = 1 - D, \tag{11.2}$$

where $p(a)$ is the probability of acceptance and D is the absolute discrepancy between source and proximal probabilities. This negative relation between $p(a)$ and

D is shown graphically in Fig. 11.6, where the line, called the *acceptance gradient,* represents probability of acceptance as a function of discrepancy.

To take a numerical example, consider a person whose subjective probability is .70 that "heavy drinkers have serious marital problems." The probability that he would accept a source belief of .75 that "heavy drinkers have serious marital problems" can be computed as follows: Since $D = |p_s - p_r|$, $p(a) = 1 - |p_s - p_r|$ $= 1 - .05 = .95$. In comparison, for a receiver with an initial proximal belief of .40, the probability of acceptance would be $1 - .35 = .65$.

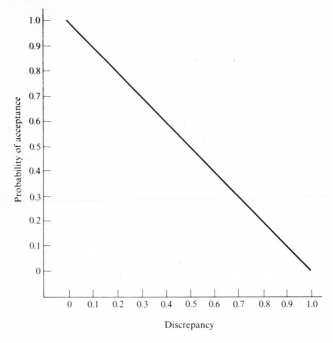

Fig. 11.6 Acceptance gradient: $p(a) = 1 - D$.

Facilitating Factors

Clearly, many factors other than discrepancy may influence probability of acceptance. Generally speaking, these factors can have one or both of two effects. They can influence the person's confidence in his own belief, that is, in his proximal probability and they can influence the person's judgment that the source probability is correct. These facilitating (or inhibiting) factors have traditionally been classified as source, message, and receiver variables.[3]

Source variables are characteristics associated with the communicator, such as his credibility, expertise, trustworthiness, attractiveness, sincerity, status, etc. It

---

3. Channel factors have received relatively little attention.

has usually been assumed that factors of this kind influence the receiver's confidence in the source belief and thus affect probability of acceptance.

In contrast, receiver variables have typically been viewed as influencing the person's confidence in his own belief. Receiver variables include relatively stable individual difference variables, such as general persuasibility, chronic anxiety, self-esteem, sex, intelligence, etc., as well as situational and topic-related factors, such as acute anxiety, involvement, extremity of own position, uncertainty, and the receiver's information about or knowledge of the topic.

Finally, message factors have been viewed as influencing the receiver's confidence associated either with his own belief or with the source belief. For example, order of presentation, validity of supportive arguments, and emotional versus rational appeals have often been assumed to affect confidence in the source belief. In contrast, high- versus low-fear appeals are assumed to influence acute anxiety (a receiver variable) and thus to affect confidence in the receiver's own belief.

For our purposes, this classification is not particularly useful. First, manipulation of a given facilitating factor will often influence both types of confidence. It seems reasonable to assume that as confidence in a proximal belief increases, confidence in the source belief will decline. More important, many of the factors listed above tend to have different facilitating effects at different levels of discrepancy (i.e., these factors may interact with discrepancy). For example, the perceived characteristics of a communicator often depend on discrepancy; a person advocating a discrepant position will tend to be judged as less of an expert, as less trustworthy, and perhaps as less attractive. Similarly, the perceived validity of an argument in support of a source belief may depend on the proximal probability corresponding to that source belief: The greater the discrepancy between source and proximal probabilities, the less valid an argument supporting the source belief may appear to be.[4] In addition, the various facilitating factors may interact with each other. Thus presentation of an emotional argument may lower the communicator's perceived credibility. It is apparent that it will usually be impossible to study the effects of these variables in an uncontaminated fashion. This may be one reason for the inconsistent findings obtained in studies of persuasive communication.

To summarize briefly, several factors may influence probability of acceptance of a given source belief. Generally speaking, it has been assumed that probability of acceptance will be high when the receiver has low self-esteem and high general persuasibility, when he receives a source belief from a highly credible communicator on an unimportant, noninvolving topic, and when the receiver is uncertain with respect to his initial (proximal) belief. Although it is true that this set of conditions could be viewed as maximizing the receiver's confidence in the source belief and minimizing his confidence in his own proximal belief, we prefer a somewhat different approach.

---

4. Obviously, when the same argument is used in support of different source probabilities, its perceived validity is likely to vary.

Although we are not committed to any specific formulation, it seems reasonable to assume that the different types of facilitating factors combine in some fashion to produce an overall level of general facilitation. The letter f will be used to denote this overall facilitation present in the situation.

We noted earlier that probability of acceptance will tend to be inversely related to discrepancy (see Fig. 11.6). It seems reasonable to assume that facilitating factors will influence this acceptance gradient. Specifically, when overall facilitation is low, probability of acceptance should decline rapidly as a function of discrepancy. Thus, if a receiver is extremely confident in his belief and the communicator is not particularly credible, the source belief is unlikely to be accepted even at very low discrepancy levels. Conversely, when the receiver has extremely low confidence and the communicator is highly credible (high overall facilitation), probability of acceptance should be high even at very great discrepancies. Thus overall facilitation may serve to moderate the relation between discrepancy and probability of acceptance. Consistent with the approach taken in other areas of psychological research (e.g., psychophysical judgment), probability of acceptance may be tentatively viewed as an exponential function of discrepancy, as expressed in Eq. 11.3.

$$p(a) = (1 - D)^{1/f} \; ; f > 0. \tag{11.3}$$

This equation generates the family of acceptance gradients shown in Fig. 11.7.

Equation 11.2, presented earlier, is a special case of Eq. 11.3, namely, the case when $f = 1$. The acceptance gradient for $f = 1$ in Fig. 11.7 is identical to the acceptance gradient in Fig. 11.6. As overall facilitation declines, probability of acceptance decreases rapidly with discrepancy. Conversely, as f exceeds 1, probability of acceptance remains relatively high even at large discrepancy levels.

Figure 11.7 also shows that the manipulation of any facilitating factor cannot be expected to have consistent effects on probability of acceptance. Clearly, if overall facilitation is at a high level to begin with, a manipulation designed to increase facilitation will not have much effect on the acceptance gradient. For example, when the receivers are not involved with the issue and when they are highly uncertain with respect to their own beliefs, the initial level of overall facilitation will be very high. The acceptance gradient will therefore remain relatively unchanged, whether the communicator has high or low credibility. To take a numerical example, if the f levels in the low and high credibility conditions are 50 and 100, respectively, little change in the acceptance gradient will result (see Fig. 11.7).

Further, even when initial level of overall facilitation is low, the effect of a manipulation such as communciator credibility will depend on the degree of discrepancy. Assume, for example, that attributing a source belief to a highly credible communicator raises f to 10, whereas attributing it to a source of low credibility results in a .50 level of overall facilitation. Table 11.1 shows the effects of the communicator credibility manipulation on probability of acceptance at three discrepancy levels. Variations in communicator credibility may have a large or small effect on probability of acceptance, depending on the discrepancy level.

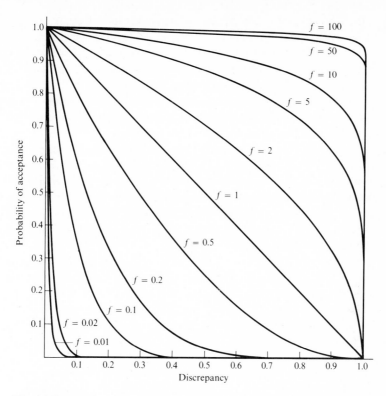

Fig. 11.7 Family of acceptance gradients for different degrees of facilitation: $p(a) = (1 - D)^{1/f}$.

To summarize briefly, we have suggested that probability of acceptance, $p(a)$, is an inverse function of discrepancy, D, and that the relation between $p(a)$ and D is influenced by facilitating factors, f. Generally speaking, as f increases, probability of acceptance should also increase. Although it seems reasonable to

Table 11.1 Hypothetical Probabilities of Acceptance as a Function of Communicator Credibility and Level of Discrepancy

Discrepancy	Communicator credibility		Effects due to communicator credibility
	High $f = 10$	Low $f = .50$	
High: $D = .90$	.79	.01	.78
Medium: $D = .50$	.93	.25	.68
Low: $D = .20$	.98	.64	.34

assume that there are systematic relations between probability of acceptance on the one hand and D and f on the other, the exact form of these relationships is not known at the present time. We started with the simplifying assumption of an inverse linear relation between $p(a)$ and D, and by making certain additional assumptions about the effects of facilitating factors on this relation, we arrived at Eq. 11.3, which represents one possible specification of the relations involved. We must emphasize that the particular statement of the relationships described by Eq. 11.3 is based largely on speculation and should therefore be regarded as highly tentative.[5] Future research may provide information leading to a more precise delineation of the ways in which facilitating factors influence the relationship between D and $p(a)$. For example, it may be necessary to replace the single f parameter with several parameters corresponding to different types of facilitating factors. Irrespective of the precise function, however, discrepancy and facilitation may reasonably be assumed to have the general effects on probability of acceptance shown in Fig. 11.7.

Our discussion suggests several important implications for the persuasion process. We have suggested that probability of acceptance is determined by two variables: discrepancy between source and proximal beliefs and various facilitating factors. If the exact function relating D and f to $p(a)$ were known, it would be possible to predict $p(a)$ on the basis of these determinants. Whether this function is the one specified in Eq. 11.3 or some other function, our analysis suggests that the effect of varying one of the two determinants will depend on the value of the other. An experimental manipulation can therefore not be expected to have a simple systematic effect on probability of acceptance. Most manipulations may be viewed as attempts to establish different levels of facilitation. A manipulation of communicator credibility, for example, may be designed to create high facilitation in one experimental condition and low facilitation in another. The precise values of f in the two conditions of credibility, however, may vary greatly, depending on the levels of other facilitating factors present in the situation. Even when successful, a manipulation of communicator credibility may have a strong effect in one study but little or no effect in another study. We saw, for example, that when the initial level of f is high, even large variations in f will leave the acceptance gradient relatively unchanged.

We also saw that the effect of a given manipulation on probability of acceptance will depend on the discrepancy level involved. This again implies that experimental manipulations will not be found to have very systematic effects on acceptance.

To further complicate matters, a belief statement by a given source may result in different source probabilities for different subjects. Consider the statement "Heavy drinkers have serious marital problems." So far we have assumed that this

---

5. In fact, it appears quite likely that the initial relation between $p(a)$ and D is not linear, but that it takes the form of an inverse ogive such that $p(a)$ declines slowly at first, more rapidly as D increases, and levels off as D becomes large.

statement implies a source probability of 1.0. However, if receivers were asked to estimate the source's probability that "heavy drinkers have serious marital problems," they might arrive at different estimates, such as .60, .70, or .80. It follows that the discrepancies between source and target beliefs may be affected by these differences in perceived source probabilities. This discussion implies that in order to obtain a value for the discrepancy variable, it may be necessary to measure not only the receiver's proximal belief but also his perception of the source belief. However, this problem may be of minor importance when the source probability is made explicit in a statement such as "There is an 80 percent chance that heavy drinkers have serious marital problems." Here the perceived source belief that "heavy drinkers have serious marital problems" should correspond closely to the objective source probability of .80. Nevertheless, the discrepancy (D) variable is best viewed in terms of two *subjective* probabilities—the proximal probability and the perceived source probability. Thus, just as a manipulation of communicator credibility may not always influence facilitation, a manipulation of source probability may have inconsistent effects on perceived discrepancy.

Even in the relatively simple case of a message consisting of a single source belief, attempts to find systematic relations between a manipulation of some independent variable and probability of acceptance are likely to produce only inconsistent results. Additional problems arise when change in a proximal belief, rather than the probability of accepting a source belief, is considered.

Change in Proximal Beliefs

As noted earlier, acceptance and change are not identical. To return to our previous example, assume a source belief of .75 that "heavy drinkers have serious marital problems" and two receivers who completely accept this source probability. Following exposure, the receivers will thus both have a .75 posterior probability. If one of these persons had an initial (proximal) probability of .30, he would have changed his belief more (.45) than the other person if the latter had a proximal probability of .70 (a change of .05). Thus, even though two receivers may accept a source belief to the same degree, they may show different amounts of change in their proximal beliefs.

Obviously, the *potential amount of change* in a proximal belief depends on its discrepancy from the source belief; the greater the absolute difference between source and proximal probabilities, the more room there is for change to occur. Actual change in the advocated direction, however, will depend not only on potential change but also on the probability of acceptance. Not only must there be room for change to occur, but the person exposed to the source belief must have at least some probability of accepting it. These ideas are expressed in Eq. 11.4,

$$C = p(a)D, \qquad (11.4)$$

which specifies the effects of discrepancy, D, and probability of acceptance, $p(a)$, on actual change in the advocated direction, C. The amount of change to be expected is thus a function of potential for change weighted by the probability that the discrepant information is accepted.

Figure 11.8 shows the effects of discrepancy on probability of acceptance, on potential change, and on actual change in the advocated direction. For ease of presentation, the acceptance gradient is based on Eq. 11.2, in which facilitation, f, is set at 1. Given this acceptance gradient, most change in the advocated direction is expected when discrepancy is at an intermediate level. When discrepancy is very low, potential change is minimal; when discrepancy is very high, probability of acceptance is low.

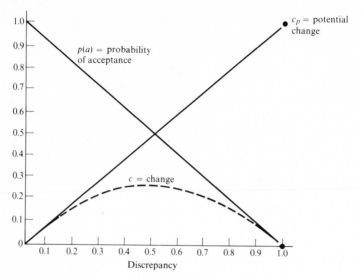

Fig. 11.8 Probability of acceptance, potential changes, and actual change as a function of absolute discrepancy.

Two points are worth noting. First, discrepancy is a necessary but not a sufficient condition for change. There can be no change in the advocated direction without some discrepancy between source and proximal beliefs. Second, since the amount of potential change is determined in advance by D, actual amount of change in the advocated direction is primarily determined by the acceptance gradient. We have seen earlier, however, that depending on the value of f, the acceptance gradient may take on very different forms. Figure 11.9 shows amount of change in the advocated direction as a function of discrepancy for some of the acceptance gradients depicted in Fig. 11.7. At a very high level of facilitation ($f \geqslant 100$) change always increases with discrepancy. When overall facilitation is very low ($f \leqslant .10$), little or no change is expected, irrespective of the discrepancy involved. At intermediate levels of f, the relation between D and C is curvilinear, such that change first increases and then decreases with discrepancy. We saw above that experimental manipulations cannot be expected to have simple systematic

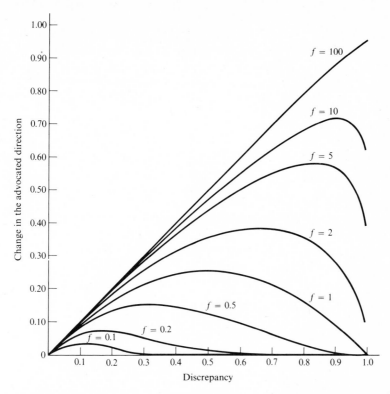

Fig. 11.9 Change in the advocated direction as a function of discrepancy and acceptance gradients with varying f values: $C = p(a)D$.

effects on probability of acceptance. We can now see that this is even more obvious in the case of change. Even if a manipulation does have a systematic effect on $p(a)$, it may or may not influence amount of change since change also depends on discrepancy.

Readers familiar with integration theory (discussed in Chapter 6) may detect the possibility of submitting the persuasion process to a treatment that differs from the approach taken here. It might be argued that the receiver's postexposure belief (P_{r1}) is a weighted linear function of his preexposure belief (P_{r0}) and of the source belief (P_s); that is, $P_{r1} = w_1 P_{r0} + w_2 P_s$. In this formulation, the weights could be interpreted as the levels of confidence with respect to the two beliefs. One way of investigating the effects of an experimental manipulation would be to assess the influence of the manipulation on the confidence levels, i.e., on the weights. To obtain estimates of the weights on the basis of the linear model, one has to assume that the weights and probabilities are independent. This assumption also implies a linear relation between discrepancy and change (i.e., between $|P_{r0} - P_s|$ and $|P_{r1} - P_{r0}|$). Our earlier discussion, however, indicated that confidence in source and proximal beliefs is not independent of the probability levels of these beliefs. Further, we also argued that there should be a curvilinear relation between discrepancy and change at intermediate levels of facilitation. From our point of view, therefore, little is to be gained by use of a linear model in this area.[6]

Boomerang effects. One other problem related to change may be worth noting. So far we have discussed change only in the advocated direction. Some studies, however, have reported "boomerang effects," i.e., shifts in the opposite direction. Findings of this kind appear to be inconsistent with our model since a significant change in the direction opposite to that advocated would imply a negative probability of accepting the source belief. However, an apparent boomerang effect may be due to inappropriate assumptions about the receiver's perception of the source belief. For example, a source who claims that "some cigarette smokers suffer from emphysema" may be viewed as having a source probability of .70 that "some cigarette smokers suffer from emphysema." If the receiver's initial target belief is .90 that this is true, an apparent boomerang effect might be reported. This example again shows that it may often be necessary to measure the perceived source belief in order to know its discrepancy from the target belief. Indeed, if the message consisted of a single source belief and if the perceived source probability were known, we would not expect boomerang effects to occur. Evidence directly relevant to this question is not available at present.

When the situation becomes more complex, however, boomerang effects— as well as many other unexpected effects—may very well be obtained. First, if the dependent variable is a measure of anything other than a proximal belief, a change in the proximal belief (even if in the advocated direction) may have no effect on the dependent variable or may even change it in the direction opposite to that intended. The "boomerang effect" in this case may be the result of an unjustified assumption linking the proximal belief to the dependent variable. Of equal importance, a persuasive communication usually comprises more than a single source belief. Let us therefore examine the effects of including additional items of information in a message.

Manipulations of Message Content

When a message consists of more than one statement, it is often convenient to view one (or more) of the source beliefs as the communication's target(s). To increase the likelihood that a given (target) source belief will be accepted, a communicator usually includes in his message additional belief statements that

---

6. In our model, interactions between facilitating factors and probability levels may influence the value of the f parameter. This parameter can be estimated in different ways. For example Eq. 11.3 can be expressed in logarithmic form:

$$\log p(a) = 1/f \log (1 - D).$$

Here, $\log p(a)$ is a linear function of $\log (1 - D)$, and f can be estimated by using a least-squares procedure.

are designed to provide supportive evidence for the target belief. Adding supportive belief statements provides new information, and this new information may influence the target belief. Let us now examine how a given supportive belief statement may increase acceptance of the target belief.

Supportive belief statements are included in a message under the assumption that if the supportive beliefs are accepted, the target belief is likely to change. In Chapter 9 we discussed some evidence that *change* in one belief may produce change in another belief. However, *acceptance* of supportive beliefs may or may not produce changes in these supportive beliefs; and even when the supportive beliefs do change, there is no guarantee that the target belief will change. Change in target belief is expected only when presenting a supportive belief produces a *change* in that supportive belief, when there is a probabilistic relation between supportive and target beliefs, and when there are no unexpected impact effects on relevant external beliefs.[7]

One effect of introducing supportive beliefs, then, may be to change the receiver's target probability even prior to the presentation of the (target) source belief. Consider a person with an initial probability of .40 that "the President is seriously ill." In a persuasive communication directed at this belief, the communicator may provide supportive evidence by arguing that "the President has not attended any diplomatic receptions for the last three months." Even prior to presentation of the source belief that "the President is seriously ill," acceptance of this supportive belief may itself lead the receiver to infer that the President must be seriously ill, raising his (target) probability to .70, say.

Another possible effect of introducing a supportive belief statement may be to influence the perceived source belief. If exposed only to the statement "the President is seriously ill," the receiver may estimate the source probability to be .70. After presentation of the supportive belief, his estimate of the source probability may increase to .80. In order to understand the effects of presenting a supportive belief on acceptance of a target belief statement, one must take into consideration the influence of supportive evidence on the receiver's target belief, as well as on the receiver's perception of the source belief. Specifically, presenting a supportive belief may affect the discrepancy between the source's and the receiver's probabilities that exists at the time of exposure to the target belief statement. In the example above, the initial discrepancy was .30 ($D = |p_s - p_r| = .70 - 40$). After presentation of the supportive belief, the discrepancy was reduced to $|.80 - .70| = .10$.

In addition, by changing the receiver's target probability from .40 to .70, the supportive belief may also have influenced the overall level of facilitation. For example, the receiver may be more certain of his new probability than he was of his initial probability. The amount of additional change produced by presenting

---

7. Even without change in supportive beliefs, presenting the supportive evidence may change the target belief by strengthening the perceived relations between supportive and target beliefs.

the target belief statement following the supportive belief will depend on the new levels of discrepancy and facilitation. Since a given belief may be supportive of one target belief but not another, its effects on acceptance of different target beliefs will be inconsistent. Similarly, when different belief statements are used to support the same target belief, the perceived relations between supportive and target beliefs may differ, again leading to inconsistent effects on probability of acceptance.

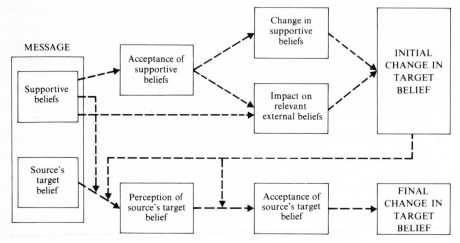

Fig. 11.10 Effects of supportive beliefs on change in a target belief.

This discussion is summarized in Fig. 11.10. Note that inclusion of supportive evidence in a message may have a variety of effects on acceptance of a target belief statement and on changes in the receiver's corresponding target belief. Attention has usually not been paid to the effects of presenting supportive arguments as such. Instead, investigators have often compared the effectiveness of different *types* of arguments by varying the nature of the supportive beliefs. However, we must recognize that message manipulations of this kind also affect the information to which receivers are exposed.[8] A "logical" or "rational" message involves different kinds of arguments than does an "emotional" message; a communication designed to produce a high degree of anxiety differs in content from one designed to create a low degree of anxiety, etc.[9]

---

8. One kind of message manipulation which does not affect message content is the order in which different arguments appear in the message. We have discussed order effects in the context of attitude formation (see Chapter 6), and we shall therefore disregard this message factor here.

9. By way of comparison, the exact same message can usually be attributed to sources varying in credibility or other characteristics; receivers of high and low self-esteem or of high and low intelligence can be exposed to the same information; and subjects can read or listen to identical arguments. When comparisons are made between a visual and an auditory channel, however, different information may again be involved.

We can thus see that message manipulations, in addition to any other effects, may have a direct influence on the content of the persuasive communication itself. It follows that the effects of a given message factor on persuasion cannot be unambiguously attributed to that factor alone; instead, they may be due to differences in information given to the receivers. For example, if a high-fear appeal was found to produce more (or less) change in a dependent variable than a low-fear appeal, the difference could be due to differences in anxiety or to differences in message content. It should be clear that, even more than for other kinds of manipulations, variations in message content cannot be expected to have any systematic effects on acceptance of source beliefs or change in target beliefs.

Figure 11.11 summarizes our discussion of the persuasive communication process. The reader may note that this diagram is essentially the same as Figs. 9.5 and 10.1, except that the subject is now the persuasive communication strategy. The heavy arrow indicates that message manipulations directly influence the nature of the persuasive communication. Such manipulations may at the same time influence characteristics of the source, channel, or receiver, as indicated by the broken arrow. For example, a message that presents a logical sequence of arguments may enhance the perceived credibility of the source. Similarly, inclusion of visual material in a message not only adds new information but also involves a manipulation of channel characteristics. Moreover, it may affect receivers by increasing their anxiety, interest, or involvement. Since message manipulations have

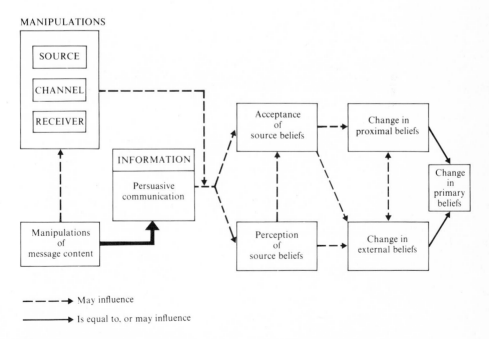

Fig. 11.11 Schematic presentation of persuasive communication process.

a direct effect on the information presented in the persuasive communication, they may influence the perception of source beliefs (see Fig. 11.10).

Noninformational manipulations of source, channel, and receiver variables can also influence perception of source beliefs as well as their acceptance. Perception and acceptance of the various source beliefs may produce changes in corresponding proximal beliefs and in relevant external beliefs. A proximal or external belief may itself constitute a primary belief, or it may be related to a primary belief. Change in proximal or relevant external beliefs may thus influence primary beliefs. Finally, in Chapter 9 we saw that different processes intervene between change in primary beliefs and change in different dependent variables.

In conclusion, our discussion indicates that many steps intervene between a given source, channel, audience, or message manipulation and change in a dependent variable. Without a consideration of these intervening processes it is impossible to understand the effects of such a manipulation on change in a belief, attitude, intention, or behavior. Further, given the complexity of the persuasion process, it is unlikely that any manipulation will have a consistent effect on change in a given dependent variable.

A COMPARISON OF THE TWO APPROACHES TO PERSUASION

It may be instructive to compare our model of the persuasion process with the traditional approach to communication and persuasion. According to the traditional approach, the effects of a persuasive communication on any dependent variable depend on reception of the message content and acceptance of (or yielding to) what is comprehended. Manipulations of source, message, channel, or receiver variables are expected to influence what is received and the extent to which this information is accepted. This approach suggests a research strategy in which some independent variable is manipulated, receivers are exposed to a persuasive communication, and change in some dependent variable is measured. Although most studies obtain a measure of reception, acceptance is not directly assessed. Instead, the assumption is that differences in the dependent variable that go beyond differences in reception must be due to differences in acceptance or yielding.

Our approach suggests that a persuasive communication is directed at one or more proximal beliefs, and via a series of intervening processes, changes in these proximal beliefs may produce change in the dependent variable. The crucial question concerns the factors that are responsible for change in the proximal beliefs. According to our approach, changes in proximal beliefs are determined primarily by the acceptance of source beliefs. Probability of acceptance is a function of two major factors: discrepancy between source and proximal beliefs and overall facilitation. Other things being equal, probability of acceptance decreases with discrepancy and increases with facilitation. For a number of reasons, no simple one-to-one relation between a manipulation and probability of acceptance (let alone any other dependent variable) is expected. First, the effect of the manipulation on overall facilitation will depend on the initial level of facilitation present in the situation. Second, the effect of variation in facilitation depends on the level of discrepancy, and vice versa. Our approach thus differs from the traditional analysis of persuasive communication in its treatment of acceptance, the role of reception, the expected effects of experimental manipulations, and concern with the nature of the dependent variable.

Acceptance. The term "acceptance" does not have the same significance in the two approaches. Within our model of the persuasion process, acceptance is viewed as equivalent to belief strength. That is, a person's acceptance of a belief is indicated by his subjective probability that the object-attribute relation in question is true. Thus, a person who has a subjective probability of .20 that "the President is ill" accepts this belief at a .20 level. This belief strength should not be confused with probability of acceptance. Depending on the perceived discrepancy and the presence of facilitating factors, the person may have a high, intermediate, or low probability of accepting a communicator's statement that "the President is ill." If probability of acceptance is high, after exposure to the message, the receiver may increase his subjective probability to .60, thus showing a new level of acceptance or belief strength.

A receiver may accept (i.e., believe) all, some, or none of the source beliefs contained in a persuasive communication. This is true whether or not the person is actually exposed to the source beliefs. Thus, even though a person may not have received the message stating that the President is ill, he may nevertheless hold this belief with a high probability and consequently accept it. Acceptance of any belief statement contained in a message can therefore be directly assessed by using some measure of belief strength. This measure of acceptance will remain the same, irrespective of the dependent variable under consideration. That is, acceptance of message content can be measured independently of assessing change in some dependent belief, attitude, intention, or behavior.

By way of contrast, we noted that acceptance is not directly assessed in the traditional approach. Instead, when reception remains constant, differences in the dependent variable are attributed to differences in acceptance or yielding. This implies that acceptance must refer to all processes involved in the persuasion process, with the exception of reception. From our point of view, then, acceptance in the traditional sense includes acceptance of target and supportive source beliefs, the relation between supportive and target beliefs, impact effects of the message, and the relation of all these effects to primary beliefs and the dependent variable.

Used in this way, the term "acceptance" does not contribute to our understanding of the persuasion process. For example, assume that the dependent variable does not correspond to a belief statement contained in the message but is instead some other belief, attitude, or intention. According to the traditional approach, change in any of these dependent variables is due to the degree to which the message was received and the degree to which the information received was accepted. Since we can assume that reception was the same, irrespective of the dependent variable, we can see that acceptance will take on different values (and thus must mean different things) whenever different dependent variables show different amounts of change. If the dependent belief changes a great deal, the attitude changes slightly, and no change in intention is observed, the traditional approach must assume that there is considerable, moderate, or no acceptance of the message received, depending on the respective dependent variable. Given that the message was identical in all cases, this approach can produce only inconsistent and ambiguous conclusions. We will reserve the term *acceptance* to refer only to acceptance of belief statements contained in the message, and following McGuire (1968), the term *yielding* will be used to refer to "acceptance" in the traditional sense.

Reception. The traditional approach has expended considerable effort to determine whether the statements contained in a message were received while at the same time paying little attention to acceptance of these statements. Further, as mentioned in Chapter 5, it is often impossible to tell whether a given learning or reception test is a measure of reception or acceptance. Since many "reception" tests are given in a multiple-choice or true-false format, subjects may respond either in terms of their recall of statements contained in the message (reception) or in terms of their agreement with those statements (acceptance). This ambiguity may be in part responsible for the inconsistent findings concerning the relation between reception and change in the dependent variable.

From our point of view, reception may be related to change in the dependent variable if it influences acceptance or impact effects. Indeed, we have noted that it may often be necessary to measure the receiver's perception of the source beliefs.[10] Thus reception may indeed influence the extent to which source beliefs are accepted, and a relation between reception and acceptance of source belief may often be found. However, there is no necessary relation between reception and acceptance. As noted above, a person may believe the informational items contained in a message (i.e., accept the message content) even without reception. Further, a person who receives a given belief statement may not accept it. A subject may believe that the communication said "Seventy-five percent of heavy drinkers have serious marital problems," but he may not believe that this statement is true. Since, according to our model, it is the *acceptance* of belief statements that may influence a dependent variable, not their reception, there seems to be little value in continuing to rely on measures of reception as the sole basis for understanding the persuasive effects of a communication.

The dependent variable. Although the traditional approach has, at best, made a gross distinction between "attitude change" on the one hand and "action change" on the other, we have repeatedly emphasized the necessity of distinguishing between beliefs, attitudes, intentions, and behaviors. Throughout this book we have

---

10. This measure should be an estimate of the source probability rather than a simple measure of recall or recognition.

tried to show that different processes underlie the formation of these variables and that they are determined by different antecedents.

The purpose of any persuasive communication is to produce change in some dependent variable, whether a belief, an attitude, an intention, or a behavior. Although the investigator usually does not make them explicit, he makes several assumptions linking the content of the message to the dependent variable in question. At the most general level, the assumption is that acceptance of the source belief statements contained in the message will lead to a change in the dependent variable. It may thus be argued that a message is *effective* to the extent that the receivers accept the source beliefs it contains. Change in the dependent variable requires that a number of additional assumptions be met. These assumptions link acceptance of source beliefs to change in the dependent variable. Failure to observe the predicted change in the dependent variable does not necessarily imply that the message was ineffective or that the manipulation employed had no effect. The source belief statements may have been accepted, and the manipulation may have influenced the degree of acceptance, as expected. The failure to produce the predicted changes in the dependent variable may be due to one or more fallacious assumptions linking acceptance of source beliefs to change in the dependent variable.

Effects of experimental manipulations. Perhaps the most important difference between the traditional approach and our approach concerns the effects of experimental manipulations on persuasion. The traditional approach has assumed that it will be possible to find simple systematic relations between a given variable and persuasion (i.e., *change* in a dependent variable). Thus in the research generated by this approach, investigators typically manipulated some source, message, channel, or audience variable and examined the effect of this manipulation on change in some dependent variable. Initially they assumed that manipulating a given variable would *always* have the same effect. For example, increasing the credibility of the source was expected always to increase persuasion. Indeed, if any manipulation was found to increase persuasion in one study, the assumption was that the same manipulation would increase persuasion in any other study. It soon became obvious that such systematic relations could not be obtained; McGuire's two-factor model was one attempt to account for some of these inconsistencies. More recent research in this tradition has therefore turned to investigation of interactions between independent variables. Nevertheless, the main purpose of such studies has been to discover consistent relations between independent variables and amount of "attitude" change.

In marked contrast, our approach suggests that such relations cannot be obtained and should not be expected. At the most basic level, we have tried to show that manipulations will not have simple systematic effects on probability of acceptance. Even when the manipulation does influence probability of acceptance, it may have no consistent effects on change in proximal beliefs, since such change is also dependent on discrepancy. Consequently, no systematic changes in the dependent variable can be expected. To be sure, an investigator usually attempts to construct messages that suggest a conclusion, attitude, or behavior that he assumes (or knows) is discrepant from the receiver's position. The problem is that the attempt to create some discrepancy is commonly concerned with the dependent variable and not with the source beliefs contained in the message. Receivers may strongly disagree with a communication's recommended action, for example, but they may have little quarrel with the source belief statements. In this case no chance in proximal beliefs is to be expected, and hence the manipulation is unlikely to affect change in intention or any other dependent variable.

At a more general level, even if the manipulation does have a consistent effect on proximal beliefs, changes in these beliefs may be unrelated to changes in primary beliefs or changes in the dependent variable. The greater the number of processes intervening between proximal beliefs and dependent variable, the more difficult it will be to obtain consistent relations between independent and dependent variables.

In support of this argument, the literature on communication and persuasion reveals virtually no consistent findings concerning the effects of any given manipulation on "attitude change." For example, communicator credibility has been found to increase persuasion in some studies but not in others. Studies on such message factors as fear appeals, order of presentation, and one-sided versus two-sided messages have yielded equally inconsistent results. As we saw in Chapter 6, variations in order of presentation sometimes produce recency effects, sometimes primacy effects, and sometimes no effects at all. A high-fear message is sometimes found to increase persuasion, sometimes to decrease persuasion, and sometimes to have the same effect as a low-fear message. The results are no more consistent when individual difference variables are considered. Chronic anxiety is sometimes found to have a positive relation, sometimes a negative relation, and sometimes no relation to the amount of persuasion. Other variables, such as distracting subjects or forewarning them that they will be exposed to a persuasive appeal, have also led to inconsistent and contradictory findings.

We have suggested that these inconsistent findings are unavoidable unless more attention is paid to the nature of the dependent variable being studied, to the assumptions that link the message with the dependent measure of persuasion, to acceptance of source beliefs and change in proximal belief, and to the impact effects of the persuasive communication on external beliefs. To clarify these problems, let us consider a few studies on communication and persuasion in some detail.

DISCREPANCY

Sherif and Hovland's (1961) social judgment theory, like our approach to persuasive communication, suggests that acceptance of a message is influenced by the discrepancy between the receiver's own position and the perceived position of the communicator. In one of the first systematic investigations of opinion change as a function of discrepancy, Hovland and Pritzker (1957) used 12 different belief statements, such as "All things considered, Washington was a greater president than Lincoln." Other statements concerned the likelihood of a cancer cure within five years, the adequacy of five hours' sleep per night, etc.

In a pretest, subjects indicated their degree of agreement with each statement on the following seven-point scale.

_____Agree strongly

_____Agree moderately

_____Agree slightly

_____Undecided

_____Disagree slightly

_____Disagree moderately

_____Disagree strongly

After indicating their beliefs, subjects were asked, "Of the following authorities, which group's opinion would you respect most in reference to this question?" The names of three or four possible authority groups relevant to the particular item were then listed. For the item concerning Washington and Lincoln, for example, teachers, historians, and parents were listed as possible referents.

Approximately one month later, subjects were again shown the 12 belief statements, this time accompanied by an indication of what was said to be the belief of the reference group selected by the subject as most authoritative for the item. In reality, these source beliefs were varied according to the subject's proximal belief. On each item, one-third of the subjects were given a source belief with an average difference of about 1.3 scale intervals from their own beliefs; for another third of the subjects, source and proximal beliefs had an average difference of about 2.6 scale intervals; and for the final third of the subjects, the discrepancy was about 3.9 intervals. For example, a subject in the largest discrepancy condition who initially indicated strong agreement with a given item was told that his most authoritative reference group disagreed slightly. After receiving this information, subjects were asked to restate their beliefs, using the same seven-point scale as on the pretest.

The results of the study are presented in Fig. 11.12, which shows the relation between discrepancy and the amount of change from pretest to posttest in the direction of the belief attributed to the reference group. Note that belief change increased directly with the amount of discrepancy. Other studies, however, have not always found increased "attitude" change with increases in discrepancy. In fact, we saw that according to social judgment theory, amount of change should *decrease* with discrepancy when the communicator's position is perceived to fall within the latitude of rejection.

To test this hypothesis, Hovland, Harvey, and Sherif (1957) conducted a study in Oklahoma in which they attempted to influence attitudes toward prohibi-

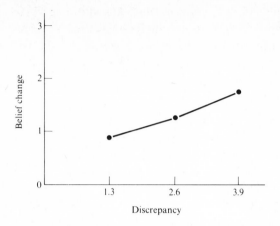

Fig. 11.12 Effect of discrepancy on belief change. (Adapted from Hovland and Pritzker, 1957.)

tion of alcohol. This issue was selected because a local referendum to eliminate prohibition had just failed by a narrow margin. Subjects were chosen to represent an extreme dry position (members of Women's Christian Temperance Union groups, the Salvation Army, and students of strict denominational colleges), an extreme wet position (25 persons with known antiprohibition positions), and a moderate position (a sample of college students).

The attitudinal dimension varied from pro- to antiprohibition, identified by the following nine positions.

1. Since alcohol is the curse of mankind, the sale and use of alcohol, including light beer, should be completely abolished.

2. Since alcohol is the main cause of corruption in public life, lawlessness, and immoral acts, its sale and use should be prohibited.

3. Since it is hard to stop at a reasonable moderation point in the use of alcohol, it is safer to discourage its use.

4. Alcohol should not be sold or used except as a remedy for snake bites, cramps, colds, fainting, and other aches and pains.

5. The arguments in favor of and against the sale and use of alcohol are nearly equal.

6. The sale of alcohol should be so regulated that it is available in limited quantities for special occasions.

7. The sale and use of alcohol should be permitted with proper state controls, so that the revenue from taxation may be used for the betterment of schools, highways, and other state institutions.

8. Since prohibition is a major cause of corruption in public life, lawlessness, immoral acts, and juvenile delinquency, the sale and use of alcohol should be legalized.

9. It has become evident that man cannot get along without alcohol; therefore there should be no restriction whatsoever on its sale and use.

On a pretest, all subjects were asked to indicate the one statement that came closest to their own point of view on the topic (i.e., their most preferred positions).[11] From one to three weeks later, subjects were exposed to one of three communications from an unidentified communicator. The three messages were of equal length, each requiring approximately 15 minutes for delivery. One communication supported an extremely dry position (represented by statement 2), the second a moderately wet position (statement 6), and the third an extremely wet position (statement 8). Following the communications, the questionnaire used on the pretest was again administered. Change in the most preferred position served as a measure of persuasion.

Changes in attitude as a function of discrepancy are presented in Fig. 11.13. Consistent with expectations, moderately discrepant messages produced more change than highly discrepant messages. Note, however, that in only one condition (moderate subjects receiving the wet communication) was the change significant, and even here it was quite small (.55 units out of the possible 2.9 units). The other four conditions showed no significant change, and they did not differ significantly from one another.

Although these results are consistent with the predictions derived from social judgment theory, the authors noted that the earlier study by Hovland and Pritzker (1957) reported findings that appeared to contradict the theory since in that study, attitude change increased even at maximal levels of discrepancy (see Fig. 11.12). They suggested two factors that might account for these conflicting findings: communicator credibility and involvement with the issue. Hovland and Pritzker attributed the message to reference groups selected by the subjects themselves as most authoritative on the issue. In other words, the source was highly credible. In contrast, the communicator in the Hovland, Harvey, and Sherif study was "an anonymous individual whose acceptability might be determined by the stand taken by him . . . if he differed greatly he would be regarded as incompetent and biased and fail to influence the subject's opinion" (Hovland, Harvey, and Sherif, 1957, p. 251). Thus, although a highly credible communicator may produce a great amount of change at a high discrepancy level, such a result is assumed to be unlikely when communicator credibility is low. In addition, subjects in the Hovland and Pritzker study were assumed to have been less involved in the issues than subjects in the prohibition study. According to social judgment the-

---

11. Latitudes of acceptance and rejection were also assessed.

● Moderate subjects receiving wet communication
□ Moderate subjects receiving dry communication
■ Dry subjects receiving moderately wet communication
✕ Dry subjects receiving wet communication
○ Wet subjects receiving dry communication

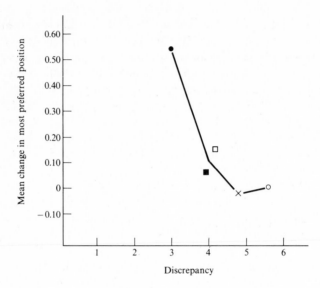

Note: Discrepancy is the absolute difference between average
initial positions of receivers and position advocated
by message.

Fig. 11.13 Change in most preferred position as a function of discrepancy in Hovland, Harvey, and Sherif
(1957) study.

ory, a highly discrepant position is likely to fall within the latitude of rejection for
involved subjects, but that need not be so for uninvolved receivers.

These considerations suggest that the effect of discrepancy on opinion change
should interact with involvement and communicator credibility. The difference in
opinion change under high and low involvement should be greater when discrepancy is high than when it is low. Similarly, a credibility manipulation should
have a stronger effect on amount of change at high than at low discrepancy levels.
A number of studies have attempted to test these predicted interaction effects.
Generally speaking, the research findings have been highly inconsistent. With respect to involvement, for example, Rhine and Severance (1970) obtained the
predicted interaction with discrepancy, whereas Rule and Renner (1968) failed
to find a significant interaction. (For a discussion of the effects of involvement,
see Kiesler, Collins and Miller, 1969, pp. 278–292.)

    Studying the effects of communicator credibility, Aronson, Turner, and Carl-smith (1963) and Bochner and Insko (1966) found the expected interaction with discrepancy. In contrast, Rhine and Severance (1970) and Eagly (1974) re-ported no significant interactions between discrepancy and communicator credibil-ity. To illustrate these conflicting findings, consider first the study by Bochner and Insko (1966). These investigators prepared a three-page essay "arguing, on the grounds of health and efficiency, for a reduction in the number of hours spent in sleep per night. . . . Discrepancy was manipulated by inserting the recom-mended hours of sleep (0, 1, 2, 3, 4, 5, 6, 7, or 8) into the persuasive communi-cation. The communication was identical at all discrepancy levels except for the hours recommendation." (pp. 615–616) Since an independent sample of subjects had indicated that approximately 8 hours of sleep were required, the experimental manipulation was viewed as creating discrepancies ranging from 0 to 8 hours. In addition to this discrepancy manipulation, source credibility was varied by attrib-uting the communication to either "Sir John Eccles, Nobel prize winning physiolo-gist" or to "Mr. Harry J. Olsen, director of the Fort Worth Y.M.C.A." Following the communication, subjects were asked to indicate the number of hours of sleep per night the average young adult should get for "maximum health and well being."

    Figure 11.14 shows the mean reduction (from 8 hours) in the number of re-quired hours of sleep produced by high and low credibility communicators at dif-ferent levels of discrepancy. As might be expected on the basis of social judgment

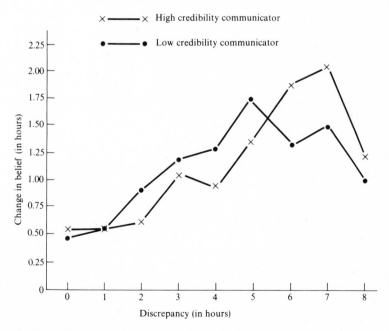

Fig. 11.14 Reduction in number of required hours of sleep as a func-tion of discrepancy. (Adapted from Bochner and Insko, 1966.)

theory, amount of change tended to increase up to a certain level of discrepancy, and to decrease after that level. More important, the point of maximal change occurred at a lower discrepancy level for the low- than for the high-credibility communicator. Since the differences between communicators were significant only at 6- and 7-hour discrepancies, Bochner and Insko concluded that the low- and high-credibility sources did not differ at low or moderate discrepancy levels, but that the high-credibility source was superior at extreme discrepancies.[12]

Unfortunately, Eagly (1974) was unable to replicate these findings in a series of three experiments primarily concerned with the effects of message comprehensibility. Like Bochner and Insko, she constructed a message designed to lower estimates of the required hours of sleep from 8 to 6, 4, or 2. In one experiment, the persuasive communication was attributed to a physiological psychologist doing research on sleep. Following exposure to the persuasive message, subjects indicated how many hours of sleep they "believed desirable for the average adult for maximum happiness, well being, and success in life." Although the message lowered the estimates significantly, the amount of change was unaffected by discrepancy. In another study, Eagly varied communicator credibility in addition to discrepancy. The persuasive communication advocated either 6 hours (low discrepancy) or 1 hour (high discrepancy) of sleep. In one condition it was attributed to the same source as in the previous study (high credibility), whereas in a second condition, it was attributed to a freshman psychology student who had researched the topic and written the lecture as part of a project for his introductory psychology class. The dependent measure in this study was an estimate of the number of hours of sleep the receiver thought *he* (rather than the average adult) should get. This measure was again found to be unaffected by discrepancy size. Further, credibility also had no significant effect on amount of change, nor did it interact with discrepancy.

Analysis of Discrepancy Research

According to our approach, the relation between discrepancy and change depends on probability of acceptance. For any given level of overall facilitation, there is one—and only one—acceptance gradient describing the relation between discrepancy and probability of acceptance (see Fig. 11.9). Generally speaking, unless facilitation is either very high or very low, probability of acceptance will tend to decrease with discrepancy. Whenever facilitation differs from one discrepancy level to another, different acceptance gradients may be operative at different levels of discrepancy.

As an example, consider the Hovland and Pritzker (1957) study described

---

12. At intermediate levels of discrepancy, the low-credibility source tended to be more effective than the highly credible source. These results were not predicted, and they appear to contradict the widely accepted notion that a high-credibility communicator should always be more effective than a communicator with medium or low credibility.

above. From our point of view this study is quite easy to interpret. The persuasive communication consisted of a single source belief, and the dependent variable was change in the corresponding proximal belief. The investigators attempted to establish a high degree of facilitation by attributing the source belief to a highly credible authority group. It may thus be expected that the acceptance gradient in this study would have tended to decrease only slightly with increasing discrepancy.

However, two difficulties related to facilitation are worth noting. First, involvement and confidence may have differed somewhat for the 12 beliefs employed in the study. Second, subjects varied in their initial target probabilities on each issue; discrepancy was manipulated by attributing varying probabilities to the appropriate reference group. Although this manipulation did create different discrepancy levels, the confidence associated with the proximal belief may have varied for different subjects at a given discrepancy level. For example, it is possible that at any given level of discrepancy, subjects who held initially moderate positions were less confident (and thus may have had a higher level of facilitation) than subjects whose initial positions were extreme. Fortunately, the investigators were careful to avoid confounding discrepancy with these potential differences in facilitation by essentially randomizing items and initial positions across the three discrepancy levels.

In sum, facilitation should have been high at all levels of discrepancy. It follows that probability of acceptance [$p(a)$] should have been relatively high irrespective of discrepancy level (D) and should have decreased only gradually with discrepancy. Since change in the advocated direction (C) is a function of $p(a)$ and D [that is, $C = p(a)D$], probability of acceptance can be estimated as follows:

$$p(a) = C/D. \tag{11.8}$$

Using Eq. 11.8 and the data supplied by Hovland and Pritzker, one obtains estimates for $p(a)$ of .68, .50, and .46 at low, medium, and high discrepancies, respectively. These levels of $p(a)$ are consistent with our discussion above.

Although the other studies concerning effects of discrepancy discussed earlier appear on the surface to be quite similar to the Hovland and Pritzker study, there are in fact a number of important differences. Perhaps of greatest importance is the question of correspondence between target belief and dependent variable. Consider, for example, the experiment reported by Bochner and Insko (1966), who attempted to persuade subjects that the average young adult needs a certain number of hours of sleep. In one condition the target source belief (which was part of the message) was that "the average young adult needs 5 hours of sleep"; in another condition it was that "the average young adult needs 2 hours of sleep." From our point of view, acceptance of these source beliefs may produce changes in the corresponding proximal beliefs. The most directly relevant dependent variable would be a measure of the receiver's probability that "the average young adult needs 5 (or 2) hours of sleep." Instead, the investigators asked subjects to indicate the number of hours of sleep they thought the average young adult should get (on a scale ranging from 0 to 10 hours).

In Chapter 3 we distinguished between belief position and belief strength. We noted that a subjective probability (belief strength) is associated with every position on a given content dimension. In terms of this distinction, the measure used by Bochner and Insko assesses the subject's *position* on the content dimension, rather than his belief strength with respect to that position (or any other position on the dimension). We must now note that change in the subjective probability associated with a given position (i.e., change in a proximal belief) may or may not influence the receiver's position on the content dimension. For example, a persuasive communication advocating 5 hours of sleep may in fact increase the subject's proximal probability that "the average young adult needs 5 hours of sleep" from, say, .20 to .40. This change may also result in a reduction from .90 to .70 in the subjective probability associated with the receiver's own position that the average young adult needs 8 hours of sleep. The receiver's position on the content dimension is nonetheless likely to remain the same despite the change in proximal probability. Indeed, the simplest way of viewing this issue is to treat each position on the content dimension as a different belief. As we saw in Chapter 9, change in one belief may or may not produce change in another belief, depending on the probabilistic relation between the beliefs. It follows that changes in the dependent variable measured by Bochner and Insko (as well as in the studies by Hovland, Harvey, and Sherif, 1957, and by Eagly, 1974) do not represent changes in proximal beliefs but rather are the result of impact effects produced by changes in the proximal beliefs.

To be sure, changes in subjective probabilities associated with a given position on a content dimension may sometimes be related to shifts in positions along that dimension.[13] This is particularly likely to be so whenever the content positions are to some extent mutually exclusive and when they form a unidimensional scale. Although such quantitative dimensions as number of hours of sleep or weight of an object appear to meet these conditions, the unidimensionality of a set of non-quantitative positions, such as those used by Hovland, Harvey, and Sherif (1957), must be established on the basis of one of the standard scaling techniques (see Chapter 3). However, even when the positions can be assumed (or are known) to form a unidimensional scale, the relation between changes in subjective probabilities at a given position and shifts from one position to another may be low. Further, if the proximal belief and the dependent variable represent markedly different content dimensions, the relation is likely to break down completely. For example, in one of Eagly's studies the proximal belief was that "the average adult needs 6 (or 1) hours of sleep," whereas the dependent variable was the receiver's estimate of the number of hours of sleep *he* should get. A dependent variable even further removed from the proximal belief might be a question such as "How many hours of sleep do you intend to get tonight?"

---

13. Wyer (1973) has shown that a subject's position on a content dimension is related to the expected value of his subjective probability distribution across the different positions on the content dimension.

We can now see that whereas Hovland and Pritzker manipulated discrepancy by varying the source probabilities associated with a *given* position, the investigators in the remaining studies manipulated discrepancy by varying the *position* of the source belief. From our point of view, whenever positions are varied, different proximal probabilities are involved, and change can be directly measured only in terms of these proximal probabilities. Thus the message might advocate 2, 4, or 6 hours of sleep, and its direct effects would be reflected by changes in the subjective probabilities associated with 2, 4, or 6 hours of sleep, respectively. Note, however, that in such a research paradigm, discrepancy would be confounded with facilitation. As noted earlier, receivers with different proximal beliefs may differ in terms of their confidence, and thus differences in facilitation may be involved. For example, a person who receives a message advocating 2 hours of sleep may have an initial proximal probability of .10, whereas a person exposed to the 6-hours message may have an initial proximal probability of .60. The first person may be more certain of his proximal probability than the second.

This example also demonstrates that the first person, who can move from .10 to 1.00 (complete acceptance), can change potentially more than the second person, who can change only by .40 units in the advocated direction from (.60 to 1.00).[14] Note that varying discrepancy in terms of positions is not the same as varying it in terms of the distance between source and proximal probabilities. Although in our hypothetical example, the larger discrepancy in positions was associated with the larger discrepancy between source and proximal beliefs, this need not be so. For example, the proximal beliefs of receivers with respect to 3, 2, and 1 hours of sleep might all be zero. In this case, although position discrepancy increases for messages advocating these different quantities of sleep, discrepancy between source and proximal beliefs remains the same.

In sum, discrepancy defined in terms of positions confounds discrepancy size with facilitation. Further, position discrepancy may be unrelated to discrepancy between source and proximal beliefs. Since a systematic relation between discrepancy and probability of acceptance (or change) is expected only when discrepancy is defined in terms of the distance between source and proximal probabilities and when facilitation is constant across these discrepancy levels, results with respect to position discrepancy are likely to be inconsistent. These problems may be responsible for some of the apparently contradictory findings in this area of research.

One way of avoiding these problems is to focus on a given position on the content dimension and to measure source and proximal beliefs with respect to that

---

14. Eagly (1974) essentially obtained a measure of initial proximal probabilities with respect to 1 and 6 hours of sleep. Consistent with the arguments above, these measures indicated that potential amount of change was .51 and .35, respectively. Computation of probability of acceptance shows the expected decrease with (estimated) discrepancy. In the 6-hours condition, $p(a) = .24$, and in the 1-hour condition, $p(a) = .08$.

position. This procedure was followed by Hovland and Pritzker. When the message is advocating different positions in different conditions, as in the hours of sleep experiments, the following procedure may be adopted. Subjects are first asked to indicate their probabilities with respect to a given position, such as 8 hours of sleep. They are then exposed to a source of belief advocating 7, 6, 5, 4, 3, 2, or 1 hours of sleep, and their probabilities with respect to 8 hours of sleep are again assessed. In addition, subjects in each condition are asked to estimate the communicator's probability that the average adult needs 8 hours of sleep. Thus proximal and perceived source probabilities correspond to the same position, and discrepancy can be determined. If one assumes a given level of overall facilitation, probability of acceptance and amount of change in proximal probabilities should be systematically related to this discrepancy.

So far we have considered only the problems concerning the relations between source beliefs, proximal beliefs, and dependent variable. Another complicating factor in the studies manipulating position discrepancy is that, unlike Hovland and Pritzker, the investigators introduced beliefs in support of the advocated position. In the Hovland, Harvey, and Sherif study, different source beliefs were used to support different positions on the pro–antiprohibition dimension, and the same source beliefs served as evidence for each of the different numbers of hours of sleep advocated in the remaining two studies. We have seen earlier how the introduction of supportive beliefs can lead to inconsistent findings concerning acceptance of a target source belief and change in the corresponding target belief. The conflicting findings reported by Bochner and Insko (1966) and by Eagly (1974) could be due to the fact that different sets of supportive arguments were used in these studies. Even when the same set of supportive arguments are used, however, these statements may be more supportive of one position than another. It follows that different amounts of change may occur at different positions, irrespective of the discrepancy involved, and thus no systematic relation between discrepancy and change can be expected.

In conclusion, despite their apparent similarities, studies investigating effects of discrepancy differ in a number of important respects. These differences in factors such as correspondence between source, proximal, and target beliefs and the dependent variable, use of different supportive arguments, the manipulation of discrepancy, etc., reduce the comparability of the studies and make apparently inconsistent findings unavoidable.

FACILITATING FACTORS

Most research on communication and persuasion has been concerned with the effects of various manipulations in source, message, or receiver on the amount of change produced by a persuasive message. In our terminology, these studies attempt to manipulate potential facilitating factors. In the following pages we shall examine a few representative studies in order to see why these attempts have been largely unsuccessful in finding manipulations that will *consistently* facilitate change in the dependent variable. Let us first examine some data on the effects of communicator credibility, a potential facilitating factor which is usually credited with producing the most consistent results of any manipulation designed to affect persuasion.

Communicator Credibility

In one of the first systematic studies on communication and persuasion, Hovland and Weiss (1951) examined the effects of communicator credibility on various responses of the audience. Opinions of college students concerning a variety of issues, as well as their judgments as to the trustworthiness of a long list of sources, were assessed in a pretest. Among the opinion items were the following four questions:

1. *Antihistamine drugs.* Should the antihistamine drugs continue to be sold without a doctor's prescription?
2. *Atomic submarines.* Can a practicable atomic-powered submarine be built at the present time?
3. *Steel shortage.* Is the steel industry to blame for the current shortage of steel?
4. *Future of movie theaters.* As the result of TV, will there be a decrease in the number of movie theaters in operation by 1955?

Subjects in the experiment read four different communications, one for each topic; the communications, represented as excerpts from magazine articles, took either an affirmative or a negative position. Each message was attributed to a high-credibility source for half of the subjects and to a low-credibility source for the other half. For example, the messages concerning the practicability of atomic submarines were attributed either to Robert Oppenheimer (high credibility) or to Pravda (low credibility). After reading the four articles, subjects were asked to indicate whether they considered each author fair in his presentation, to indicate whether they considered his conclusion justified by the facts he presented, and to restate their opinions on the four issues. In addition, subjects were given a "fact-quiz" consisting of 16 multiple-choice questions, four on each content area.

The results for these four dependent variables are presented in Table 11.2. Opinion change for high- and low-credibility communicators is shown in the first column. The investigators obtained a "net change" index by computing the percentage of subjects changing their opinions in the direction advocated in the communication minus the percentage of subjects changing their opinions in the opposite direction. On the average, the high-credibility communicator produced a greater net opinion change (23.0 percent) than did the low-credibility communicator (6.6 percent).

According to the traditional approach, this difference must be due to differences in reception or yielding. The multiple-choice "fact-quiz" was included in order to test whether there were any differences in reception. The results for the

Table 11.2 Effects of Communicator Credibility (Adapted from Hovland and Weiss, 1951)

Topic	Dependent variables							
	Net opinion change, %		Number of correct items on fact-quiz		"Fair" judgments, %		"Conclusion justified" judgments, %	
	High credibility	Low credibility	High credibility	Low credibility	High credibility	Low credibility	High credibility	Low credibility
Antihistamines	22.6	13.3	3.42	3.17	64.5	59.3	67.7	51.8
Atomic submarines	36.0*	0.0	3.48	3.72	96.0*	69.4	80.0*	44.4
Steel shortage	22.9*	−3.8	3.34	2.73	24.3	19.2	32.4	26.9
Future of movies	12.9	16.7	3.23	3.27	93.1*	63.7	58.6	42.4
Mean	23.0*	6.6	3.36	3.26	65.6	54.9	58.2*	41.8

* Significant difference between high and low credibility sources

multiple-choice test are shown in the second column of Table 11.2. On the average, the difference in reception was found to be nonsignificant (3.36 versus 3.26 items correctly received), and thus Hovland and Weiss concluded that the difference in opinion change was the result of greater yielding to the high- than to the low-credibility communicator.

Although yielding was not directly measured, results for the remaining two items were taken as providing some support for this argument. Columns 3 and 4 of Table 11.2 show that in comparison with the low-credibility source, the high-credibility source tended to be judged as more fair in his presentation of the facts, and his conclusion was seen as more justified by the facts he presented. These differences emerged despite the fact that the same messages were attributed to high- and low-credibility sources. Unfortunately, tests of significance were not reported.

This study has usually been taken as evidence that a message attributed to a high-credibility communicator produces more "attitude change" than does a message attributed to a low-credibility communicator. Further, the study has been taken as evidence that this effect is due to differences in yielding rather than reception. Closer examination of the data presented in Table 11.2, however, makes it clear that these conclusions are not warranted. First, the effect of communicator credibility on opinion change was not the same for the four different topics. A reanalysis of the data shows that although the high-credibility communicator produced greater opinion change than the low-credibility communicator on three topics, only two of the differences were significant. Further, for the fourth topic (the future of movie theaters), a nonsignificant difference in the opposite direction was observed, such that the low-credibility source tended to produce more change than did the high-credibility source.

A second problem related to the Hovland and Weiss (1951) study concerns the measure of reception. According to the authors, that test was designed to assess differences "in the amount of factual information acquired by the subjects" (p. 641). As in many other studies, it is not clear whether this measure reflects recognition of four belief statements contained in each message or acceptance of the belief statements. Assuming that this multiple-choice test represents a measure of reception, it is clear that reception is unrelated to opinion change. If this test is interpreted as a measure of acceptance, the results constitute evidence that there may be little relation between acceptance of beliefs contained in the message and opinion change. The finding reported by Hovland and Weiss can therefore be interpreted as demonstrating that communicator credibility has no effect on acceptance of belief statements, rather than as demonstrating that communicator credibility does not influence reception of the statements.

The data presented in Table 11.2 also show that the indirect measures of yielding (columns 3 and 4) cannot account for the differences in opinion change. Note that one of the largest differences in perceived fairness (29.4 percent) was found with respect to the future of movie theaters, the topic for which opinion change was in the opposite direction. Similarly, the smallest difference in perceived justification of the conclusion (5.5 percent) was associated with one of the largest differences in opinion change (steel shortage). Moreover, a reanalysis of the data shows that only a few of the differences in columns 3 and 4 of Table 11.2 are statistically significant.

Clearly, then, the findings of the Hovland and Weiss study are far from consistent, and they provide only limited support for the conclusion that a high-credibility source produces more opinion change, or that the effect of credibilty is due to increased yielding. A subsequent study by Hovland and Mandell (1952) also failed to provide support for this argument. In that study, subjects were given a communication in favor of devaluing American currency. The message was attributed either to an importer who would profit from devaluation (nontrustworthy source) or to an economist from a leading American university (trustworthy source). Although the trustworthy source was perceived to have done a better job of giving the facts on devaluation of currency and to have given a more fair and honest picture, he was not found to produce greater opinion change than the nontrustworthy source. Thus, not only were the indirect measures of yielding unrelated to opinion change, but the variation in source credibility was found to have no significant effect on opinion change.

Whereas the studies by Hovland and Weiss (1951) and Hovland and Mandell (1952) had *belief* change as their dependent variable, other experiments have examined the effect of communicator credibility on changes in *attitudes* and *intentions*. The results of these experiments have also been quite inconsistent. For example, Kelman and Hovland (1953) found that a highly credible and neutral source produced more change in attitude toward lenient treatment of juvenile delinquents than did a source of very low credibility. In contrast, Aronson and Golden (1962) found that attitudes toward arithmetic were influenced to the same extent by a message attributed to a white engineer or a white dishwasher. When the sources were black, however, the engineer produced significantly more change than did the dishwasher.

Analysis of Credibility Research

From the point of view of our analysis of the persuasive communication process, these conflicting findings are hardly surprising. According to our analysis, if a manipulation of such a factor as communicator credibility is effective, it influences facilitation; that is, it produces variations in the f parameter. Even when it is effective, however, a credibility manipulation may or may not influence probability of acceptance. Its effect on probability of acceptance depends on the initial level of overall facilitation, as well as on discrepancy size.

We have argued that a manipulation can be viewed as effective if it influences the degree to which the source beliefs are accepted. As we have also seen, however, a message which is effective in this basic sense may still have little effect on change in the dependent variable. In the case of a communicator credibility manipulation, receivers may be more willing to accept source beliefs coming from a highly credible communicator than beliefs originating from a low credibility source. However, if the decrepancy between source and target beliefs is small, little *change* in proximal beliefs can be expected in either condition. Even when the manipulation does produce differential change in proximal beliefs, it may have no effect on the primary beliefs or the dependent variable.

Of greater interest is the situation where proximal beliefs *are* related to the dependent variable. In this situation, if the credibility manipulation influences overall facilitation, it should also influence the dependent variable unless (1) the initial level of overall facilitation is high, (2) there is a small discrepancy between source and proximal beliefs, or (3) the message includes highly convincing supportive arguments that themselves produce changes in other proximal beliefs.

Some indirect support for the latter argument can be found in a study by McCroskey (1970), who attempted to change attitudes toward federal control of education. In one condition McCroskey provided strong supportive evidence for the target belief statements, and in another condition the target beliefs were stated with minimal supportive evidence. Variations in source credibility had a significant effect on attitude change only when minimal supportive evidence was presented. When the message contained strong supportive belief statements, equal amounts of attitude change were observed. It may be argued that in this condition subjects changed their target beliefs on the basis of the supportive evidence, irrespective of the source's credibility.

One way of testing this notion would be to assess the change in target beliefs produced by the supportive evidence, prior to actual presentation of the target belief statements. Another possibility would be to treat presentation of supportive evidence as a manipulation that may increase overall facilitation. Supportive evidence would thus function as any other facilitating factor in determining probability of acceptance and corresponding change.

Another interpretation of McCroskey's results is also possible. Even in the condition where minimal supportive evidence was provided, communicator credibility—although influencing f—may have had little effect on probability of acceptance. Instead, the observed effect of source credibility on attitudes may have been due to differential impact on external beliefs about the attitude object. Since McCroskey did not measure either acceptance of source beliefs, change in proximal beliefs, or impact effects, both interpretations are feasible. Like most investigators, McCroskey merely assessed changes in his dependent measure of attitude.

Some evidence for differential impact effects of high- and low-credibility sources was reported by Gorn and Tuck (1968). Subjects received a message designed to produce unfavorable attitudes toward abandoning nuclear overflights. The message was directed at six target beliefs that linked abandoning nuclear overflights with negative consequences. For example, one statement argued that "abandoning nuclear overflights is abandoning preparedness." The message was presented as an excerpt from a magazine article and was attributed to a high-credibility source (John F. Kennedy) or a low-credibility source (Barry Goldwater). A control group did not receive the message. The subjects' acceptance of these beliefs and their attitudes toward abandoning nuclear overflights were measured before and after the persuasive communication. At the same time, measures were also obtained of five salient external beliefs about abandoning nuclear overflights which did not appear in the message.

The results of this study are presented in Table 11.3. Note that the high-credibility source had a greater effect on attitude change than did the low-credibility source. Further, in comparison with the results for the control group, the message attributed to either communicator produced significant increases in acceptance of the belief statements it contained. However, changes in these target beliefs were no greater for the high- than for the low-credibility source. On the other hand, the message's impact on external beliefs was much greater for the high-credibility source. It thus appears that in this study the effect of communicator credibility on attitude change was due not to increased acceptance of a message coming from a high-credibility source but rather to its greater impact effect on relevant external beliefs.

Table 11.3 Effects of Source Credibility (From Gorn and Tuck, 1968)

Source	Attitude change	Change in target beliefs	Impact on external beliefs
High credibility	4.29	5.22	3.28
Low credibility	2.43	5.29	.39
Control	.93	2.22	1.29

Referent influence. Many of the problems above are lacking when a conclusion, recommendation, or attitude is simply attributed to a high- or low-credibility source without providing any supportive information. Even at this basic level, however, the results have been inconsistent. Although some of the conflicting findings may be due to the fact that, as before, many different dependent variables have been studied, two other problems appear to be primarily responsible. First, subjects may or may not accept the information that the particular source in question holds the belief or attitude attributed to him. Second, even if this information is accepted, the particular sources used may or may not be considered to be relevant referents for the topic under consideration. It follows that the credibility manipulation will not have any systematic effects on facilitation.

For example, in one of the first studies on referent influence, Lewis (1941) gave subjects a list of 10 political slogans, such as "Give me liberty or give me death!" and "Workers of the world, unite!" which were ranked in terms of their "authors' intelligence." The ranking was attributed to one of three sources: Roosevelt, Hoover, or Browder (at that time General Secretary of the Communist Party of the USA). For Roosevelt and Hoover, two conditions were created by reversing the rank order of the slogans. Subjects were asked to rank the slogans along four dimensions: compellingness to action, social significance, personal inspiration, and their own agreement or acceptance. A control group responded in the same fashion without receiving any referent information. The results showed no evidence of referent influence. Subjects' responses were influenced neither by the source of the referent information nor by the ranking attributed to him.

It appears that many subjects in this study rejected the claim that the source made the ranking attributed to him. In a postexperimental interview, one subject said indignantly, "Do you really expect me to believe that these are Browder's rankings?" Another said, "If Mr. Browder said that, he must have been misquoted by the newspapermen who reported him." Other subjects felt that the source was an irrelevant referent for the responses in question. In the words of one subject, "Mr. Hoover could influence the American Manufacturers Association, and I'm not a member."

The research on referent influence illustrates some of the problems related to manipulation of communicator characteristics. Even in this simple situation, it has been impossible to demonstrate a consistent effect of communicator credibility on amount of change. In this section we have discussed some of the reasons for the inconsistent findings. Let us now turn to a consideration of potential facilitating factors related to the message which have also received considerable attention in persuasion research.

Type of Appeal

We have seen that a persuasive communication may be quite effective in changing proximal beliefs, and that the amount of change in those beliefs may be influenced by the experimental manipulation, even though the effects may not be reflected in the dependent variable. The failure to separate acceptance of message content from change in the dependent variable and the failure to recognize that the relation between the two is largely an empirical question are perhaps the most basic problems in communication and persuasion research. These problems can be exemplified by considering some of the research that has dealt with the effects of varying the type of persuasive appeal.

Over the years investigators have examined the relative effectiveness of various types of persuasive appeals. The question that has frequently been raised is whether it is more effective to appeal to man's reason or to his emotions. Innumerable studies comparing "emotional" and "rational" messages have been conducted, and they have led to completely inconsistent results. Furthermore, Reuchelle (1958) found that experts in the area of speech and persuasive communication could not even agree among themselves whether a given appeal should be considered emotional or rational. It appears that rational and emotional appeals do not constitute opposite ends of a single continuum; rather, they are two relatively independent dimensions. Consequently, it is possible to construct messages that appear to be both rational and emotional.

There is some evidence to suggest that a message will be perceived as rational if it contains belief statements which the subject can accept; that is, if the subject agrees with the statements, he will tend to judge the message as rational or logical. If he does not accept the belief statements it contains, he will tend to judge the message as illogical or irrational. Fishbein, Platt, and Paluch[15] found a correlation of .775 between acceptance of belief statements in a message and judgments that the message was logical. In the same study, subjects were asked to evaluate the attribute associated with the objects of the belief statements, as well as to rate the communication's emotionality. Judgments of emotionality were found to correlate .683 with the polarity of attribute evaluations. Thus a message tends to be perceived as emotional if it contains belief statements that link objects to highly positive or highly negative attributes.

In research somewhat related to the comparison between emotional and rational appeals, a large number of studies have investigated the relative persuasive effects of messages designed to produce different levels of fear on the part of the receiver. Other studies have attempted to see whether it is more effective to present only one or both sides of an issue (the two-sided message contains not only all the arguments of the one-sided message but also presents and refutes the opposite point of view), or whether stating the conclusion is more effective than leaving it unstated. Finally, the effectiveness of messages varying in order of presentation has been compared. Order of presentation has been varied in two ways: by varying the order of arguments within a message or by switching the order in which two messages are presented. For example, the conclusion may be presented before or after the supportive belief statements, information may be presented in ascending ("climax") or descending ("anticlimax") orders of evaluation (see Chapter 6), or a pro message may precede or follow a con message.

We noted earlier that, except for order of presentation, all message variations directly influence the kind or amount of information to which subjects are exposed. Consider, for example, two messages designed to create different levels of fear concerning improper dental care. One message argues that improper dental care leads to cavities and discolored teeth, and the other claims that improper dental care leads to having teeth pulled, having cavities drilled, and getting mouth infections. Not only does the second message contain more belief statements than the first, but it also provides different information about improper dental care by linking this concept to different attributes or consequences. Clearly, these attributes differ not only in their denotative meaning but also in their evaluation. Thus any manipulation that varies the nature of a message involves variations in number or kind of belief statements presented, as well as in the evaluations of associated attributes.

It follows that variations in type of appeal, with the exception of order of presentation, are confounded with differences in the amount and kind of information provided. Thus, if a high-fear appeal is found to produce more change than a low-fear appeal, this effect may be due not to differential fear arousal but rather

---

15. Unpublished manuscript.

to the difference in information contained in the high- and low-fear messages. In fact, by carefully selecting belief statements, one should be able to construct a high-fear message that will be either more effective or less effective than a low-fear message. The same considerations apply to logical versus emotional appeals and one-sided versus two-sided messages. Clearly, then, comparing the relative persuasive effects of different types of appeal is rather meaningless, and only inconsistent findings can be expected. On the following pages we shall try to clarify these issues by discussing some studies of fear appeals.

Fear Appeals

In their now classic study, Janis and Feshbach (1953) conducted an experiment designed to investigate the consequences of using fear appeals in persuasive communication. According to these authors, "implicit in the use of fear appeals is the assumption that when emotional tension is aroused, the audience will become more highly motivated to accept the reassuring beliefs or recommendations advocated by the communicator" (p. 78). They also pointed out, however, that fear arousal may actually reduce the persuasive impact of a communication for at least three reasons. First, subjects may be motivated to avoid or not pay attention to a message that arouses fear and may thus fail to *receive* it. Second, if the communicator is perceived as being responsible for producing the fear, his statements may be rejected (i.e., the subject may fail to *yield* to the message). Finally, high fear may impair both reception and yielding if the receiver's "emotional tension is not readily reduced either by the reassurances contained in the communication or by self-delivered reassurance" (p. 78).

High school students were exposed to one of three illustrated lectures on dental hygiene designed to produce high, medium, and low levels of fear arousal. A fourth group, not exposed to a lecture on dental hygiene, served as a control group. All lectures contained information about causes of tooth decay, the "proper" type of toothbruth recommended by dental authorities, and five specific recommendations concerning oral hygiene practices. The five recommendations follow.

1. The teeth should be brushed with an up-and-down (vertical) stroke.
2. The inner surface of the teeth should be brushed as well as the outer surface.
3. The teeth should be brushed gently, using only a slight amount of force.
4. In order to cleanse the teeth adequately, one should spend about three minutes on each brushing.
5. In the morning, the teeth should be brushed after breakfast (rather than before).

The three lectures also presented information concerning the consequences of improper dental care. The three levels of fear arousal were created by varying the severity of the consequences associated with improper dental care, as well as by presenting slides varying in the degree to which they vividly portrayed tooth decay. The differences in the nonvisual information presented by the high-, medium-, and low-fear appeals are summarized in Table 11.4. The high-fear appeal not only linked improper dental care with a greater number of negative consequences, but also indicated that the consequences were more "severe" (i.e., evaluated more negatively).

Table 11.4 Information Contained in High-, Medium-, and Low-Fear Messages (Adapted from Janis and Feshbach, 1953)

Source beliefs: Consequences of improper dental care	Number of source beliefs		
	High fear	Medium fear	Low fear
Pain from toothaches	11	1	—
Cancer, paralysis, blindness	6	—	—
Having teeth pulled, cavities drilled	9	1	—
Having cavities filled, visit dentist	—	5	1
Mouth infections: sore, swollen, inflamed gums	18	16	2
Ugly or discolored teeth	4	2	—
"Decayed" teeth	14	12	6
"Cavities"	9	12	9
Total	71	49	18

One week prior to the lectures, all subjects completed a questionnaire represented as a general health survey. Subjects were asked, among other questions, to indicate how concerned or worried they felt about the possibility of developing diseased gums and decayed teeth, to indicate their beliefs about four characteristics of a "proper" toothbrush (e.g., "the brush should have three rows of bristles"), and to report their own oral hygiene practices. The latter questions were related to the five recommendations listed above, which were included in the subsequent communication. More specifically subjects were asked to "describe the way they were currently brushing their teeth: the type of stroke used, the amount of surface area cleansed, the amount of force applied, the length of time spent on brushing the teeth, and the time of day that the teeth were brushed" (Janis and Feshbach, 1953, p. 84).

Immediately after the lecture, subjects completed a second questionnaire designed to assess their reactions to the communication. This questionnaire again measured subjects' general concern about the possibility of developing diseased gums and decayed teeth, as well as their feelings of worry or concern evoked during the exposure to the communication. The subjects were also asked to evaluate the lecture in terms of its interest value, the degree to which it held their attention, and its overall quality. Finally, subjects responded to a 23-item "information test ... based on the factual assertions common to all three forms of the communication, including topics such as the anatomical structure of the teeth, the causes of cavities and of gum disease, the 'correct' technique of toothbrushing, and the type of toothbrush recommended by dental authorities" (Janis and Feshbach, 1953, p. 82).

Responses to this questionnaire revealed that the fear manipulation had been successful. Subjects in the high-fear condition showed a greater increase in their general concern about the possibility of developing diseased gums and decayed teeth than did subjects in the medium- and and low-fear conditions. Further, reported feelings of worry or concern evoked during the lecture were greatest in the high-fear condition, somewhat lower in the moderate-fear condition, and least in the low-fear condition. Despite the fact that the high-fear appeal led to greater arousal, it was judged of better quality, more interesting, and holding more attention than the medium- or low-fear appeals.

These reactions to the communications however were *not* reflected in the "information test." Although the three experimental groups had significantly higher scores on this test than the control group, they did not differ significantly from one another. These results were interpreted as indicating that different degrees of fear arousal did not interfere with *reception* of the message since subjects in all three experimental groups had acquired an equal amount of "factual information."

This questionnaire assessed affective reactions to and reception of the communication, but it did not assess the message's persuasive effects. One week after the lectures, therefore, a third questionnaire was administered. Subjects were again asked, among other items, to report their own oral hygiene practices by responding to the same five questions given on the pretest. Each student was given a score ranging from 0 to 5, representing the number of recommended practices to which he conformed. The pretest responses were scored in the same fashion, and the percentages of subjects showing increased, decreased, or unchanged conformity to recommended practices were computed. The major dependent variable in the study was the net change in self-reported behavior.

The effects of fear arousal on changes in self-reported behaviors are shown in Table 11.5. Note that the greatest net change in behavior was produced by the

Table 11.5 Effects of Fear Appeals on Reported Changes in Dental Hygiene Practices (Adapted from Janis and Feshbach, 1953)

	Fear appeal			
	High	Medium	Low	Control
Increased conformity, %	28	44	50	22
Decreased conformity, %	20	22	14	22
No change, %	52	34	36	56
Net change in conformity	+8	+22	+36 *	0

* Significantly greater than high-fear condition and control group ($N = 50$ per group, $p < .05$). No other differences between net changes are significant.

low-fear appeal; the medium- and high-fear appeals did not produce significantly greater behavior change than that which occurred without exposure to any message. Thus Janis and Feshbach (1953) concluded that "inclusion of fear-arousing material not only failed to increase the effectiveness of the communication, but actually interfered with its overall success" (p. 87). Since they found that the high-fear message did not interfere with reception, they argued that it must have produced less yielding than the low-fear message. Specifically, they reasoned that the strong emotions aroused by the high-fear appeal were not fully relieved by the recommendations contained in the message and that the subjects therefore became motivated to ignore or minimize the importance of the threat.

On the basis of these notions, Leventhal and Singer (1966) argued that if one were to provide recommendations that reduce fear more effectively, high-fear appeals should be more persuasive than low-fear appeals. To test this hypothesis, they exposed subjects to either a high- or low-fear appeal message linking improper dental care to severe or mild consequences, respectively. In one condition, no recommendations were given. In three other conditions, the message not only provided recommendations but included explicit statements designed to show how implementation of each recommended practice would reduce or prevent the kinds of consequences described in the message. On the assumption that the locations of the recommendations within the message might influence the degree to which they reduced fear, Leventhal and Singer placed the recommendations before, after, or between two parts of the message. In addition, one group of subjects was exposed only to the recommendations without a fear appeal, and a control group received no information at all.

Immediately after exposure to the messages, measures of fear arousal and intentions to follow each of the five recommended dental practices were obtained. Consistent with expectations, and in contrast to the Janis and Feshbach findings, the high-fear message resulted in significantly more acceptance of the recommended practices than did the low-fear message.

The greater effectiveness of the high-fear appeal, however, could not be attributed to the nature of the recommendations used in this study, since even in the condition in which no recommendations were provided, the high-fear appeal was more persuasive than the low-fear appeal. Clearly, the degree to which the recommendations permit fear reduction cannot be used to account for the conflicting findings of the two studies. Further, results concerning self-reports of arousal indicated that there was little relation between level of fear arousal and acceptance of recommended practices. Although placing the recommendations at the end of the high-fear appeal significantly reduced the amount of arousal reported, this manipulation had no significant effect on the degree to which the recommendations were accepted. Finally, the utility of using fear appeals is itself called into question by this study, since exposing subjects only to the recommendations produced as much acceptance as exposing them to the low- or high-fear appeals in addition to the recommendations.

These conflicting and inconclusive findings are typical of research on fear appeals. Some studies have reported a positive relation between fear arousal and persuasion, some a negative relation, and others no relation at all. In a review of 27 studies conducted between 1953 and 1968 in which fear levels were experimentally manipulated, Higbee (1969) concluded that this research "has yielded conflicting findings concerning the relative effectiveness of high versus low threat in persuasion. This research has also yielded some inconsistencies in attempting to determine what variable may interact with fear level to cause low fear to be more effective in some situations and high fear to be more effective in other situations." (p. 441) Although various attempts have been made to reconcile these conflicting findings (e.g., Janis, 1967; McGuire, 1968; Leventhal, 1970), no satisfactory explanation has yet emerged.

We have already discussed one of these explanations, namely McGuire's (1968) two-factor model, according to which anxiety or fear arousal reduces reception but increases yielding. A curvilinear relation between arousal and persuasion is predicted such that maximal persuasion should occur at moderate levels of arousal. By speculating about the amount of fear created by a given message and about the degree to which subjects received the message and yielded to it, one can provide a post hoc explanation for any given finding. One attempt to directly test this model (Millman, 1968) failed to provide any support for it, however. Indeed, from the perspective of our analysis of the persuasion process, explanations that rely on the traditional approach to communication and persuasion are unlikely to advance our understanding of the phenomena under consideration. Let us therefore consider the research on fear arousal from the perspective of our model of the persuasion process.

Analysis of research on fear appeals

Studies such as those described above attempt to manipulate an audience variable (anxiety) by varying message content. From our point of view the major purpose of a fear manipulation is to influence facilitation. The usual assumption is that high fear will facilitate acceptance of the message. We have noted earlier, however, that varying the content of a message may also affect overall facilitation. That is, some types of arguments may be more supportive of the target beliefs than others. It follows that differential persuasion may be attributable to differences in the information provided, rather than to different levels of fear arousal. Message content is thus confounded with level of fear, and even if increased change is obtained, it cannot be unambiguously attributed to a higher level of fear. Since little attention is usually paid to the differences in the information provided, inconsistent findings are to be expected. Moreover, the dependent variables in these studies have varied considerably, and manipulations of fear level have frequently been found to have different effects on beliefs, attitudes, intentions, and behaviors (e.g., Rogers and Thistlethwaite, 1970; Evans et al., 1970). Perhaps most important, little attention has been paid to the relations between the belief statements constituting a message and a given dependent variable.

Consider, for example, the Janis and Feshbach (1953) study. These investigators manipulated fear by linking "improper dental care" to severe, moderate, or mild consequences. From our point of view, even if it can be assumed that these source beliefs were accepted, their relation to the dependent variable (i.e., behavior change) is open to question. Changing a person's beliefs about the consequences of improper dental care may result in a change of his attitude toward improper dental care. Although the study does not provide direct evidence concerning these attitudes, the high-fear appeal should have resulted in more negative attitudes toward "improper dental care" than either the medium- or the low-fear appeals. A change in attitude toward "improper dental care," however, may have had little to do with the five behaviors that were investigated.

We have seen that in order to change a person's behavior (e.g., from brushing his teeth before breakfast to brushing his teeth after breakfast), it is necessary to increase his intention to perform that behavior (i.e., his intention to brush his teeth after breakfast). Changing this intention requires either increasing his attitude toward the behavior (i.e., his attitude toward brushing his teeth after breakfast) or his subjective norm concerning this behavior (i.e., his belief that important others think he should brush his teeth after breakfast). Clearly, changing this person's attitude toward *improper dental care* may have no effect on the determinants of this behavior.

In light of these considerations, it is possible to provide an alternative explanation for the finding reported by Janis and Feshbach. First, note that the "information test" used by these investigators may best be viewed as a measure of acceptance of certain source beliefs, rather than as a measure of reception. It appears unlikely that this test measured recall or recognition of message content; the same questions were asked of subjects in the control condition who were not exposed to any communication. Since there were no differences among the three experimental groups, it seems reasonable to assume that there was equal acceptance of the belief statements contained in the three fear messages and that fear level did not serve to facilitate acceptance.

Now consider a subject exposed to the high-fear appeal. He would tend to believe that improper dental care leads to having teeth pulled, to cancer, paralysis, blindness, and sore, swollen, and inflamed gums (see Table 11.4). Since it is unlikely that his own oral hygiene practices have resulted in any of these consequences, he would probably infer that he has been taking proper care of his teeth and thus he has no need to change his tooth-brushing behavior. The high-fear message may thus have had unexpected impact effects. In contrast, after exposure to the low-fear appeal, subjects would believe that improper dental care leads to having cavities and having to go to the dentist. Since most subjects have experienced these kinds of consequences, they would be likely to infer that they have *not* taken proper care of their teeth and thus that they should change their tooth-brushing behavior. Obviously, subjects in the low-fear appeal condition would be more likely to accept the specific recommendations concerning proper dental care presented in the lecture than would subjects in the high-fear appeal condition. Thus, although a subject may accept the message and believe that improper dental care leads to bad consequences, he may not believe that he is practicing improper dental care, or that his current method of dental hygiene will lead to those bad consequences. Further, even if he does believe that his current method of dental hygiene will lead to the bad consequences, he may not believe that abiding by the recommendations will prevent these undesirable consequences.

When it is made explicit that performance of the recommended practices will prevent the undesirable consequences (as was done in the Leventhal and Singer study), acceptance of this information may lead to a change in attitude toward the behavior in question. Since fear arousal is manipulated by varying the severity of the undesirable consequences, a high-fear appeal should produce a more positive attitude toward performing the recommended behaviors than a low-fear appeal. On the assumption that this attitude toward the behavior is related to intentions to perform the behavior, this would explain why, as in the Leventhal and Singer study, a high-fear appeal is sometimes more persuasive than a low-fear appeal.

The main point is that there are several assumptions underlying the expectation that acceptance of the belief statements contained in a persuasive message will lead to a change in a given dependent variable. These assumptions are usually not made explicit, they are seldom tested, and measures of acceptance of source beliefs, change in proximal beliefs, and impact effects are rarely obtained. A recent study demonstrates the importance of some of these assumptions. Rogers and Thistlethwaite (1970) found that smokers intended to smoke less only when they were led to believe that quitting or cutting down smoking reduces a smoker's susceptibility to lung cancer. When quitting or cutting down smoking was said to be an ineffective means for reducing the probability of lung cancer, smokers showed little change in intentions. Nonsmokers, whose behavior does not lead to the unpleasant consequences of lung cancer, were relatively unaffected by this belief manipulation.

A recent study by McArdle (1972) also illustrates some of these issues. Recall (see Chapter 8) that McArdle attempted to persuade alcoholics to sign up for the Alcoholic Treatment Unit (ATU) in a V.A. hospital. She first constructed a message representing a traditional *fear appeal,* which emphasized the short- and long-range negative consequences of continued drinking and then recommended that in order to avoid these consequences, subjects should sign up for the ATU. Specifically, the message contained 10 target beliefs linking "continued drinking" with 10 undesirable consequences, such as ruined physical and mental health, a poorer relationship with family and employer, less personal attention from the hospital staff, and less freedom to leave the hospital.

In contrast to this traditional approach, our model of the persuasion process suggests that in order to increase the likelihood that subjects will sign up for the ATU, their intentions to sign up must be increased. To accomplish this goal, an investigator must direct the message either at the attitude toward this behavior or at the subjective norm. In a pilot study McArdle found that intention to sign up for the ATU was primarily determined by the attitudinal component. Consequently, she constructed two additional messages, one designed to make attitudes toward the behavior of signing up for the ATU more favorable (*positive message*), the other designed to make attitudes toward not signing up for the ATU more unfavorable (*negative message*).

The negative message contained 10 belief statements linking "not signing up for the ATU" with the same 10 undesirable consequences used for the fear appeal. The positive message contained 10 belief statements linking "signing up for the ATU" with 10 desirable consequences, constructed by reversing the undesirable consequences. For example, signing up for the ATU was said to provide for improved physical and mental health, a better relationship with family and employer, etc. Thus the positive and negative messages were mirror images of each other, whereas the negative and fear-appeal messages differed only with respect to their attitude object ("not signing up for the ATU" versus "continued drinking"). The final paragraph in all three messages recommended that in order to avoid the negative consequences (or attain the positive consequences), subjects should sign up for the ATU.

The positive and negative messages, which were constructed in accordance with our model of the persuasion process, were directed at target beliefs that should be related to the dependent variable in question. That is, according to the model of behavioral intentions discussed in Chapter 7, if these messages were successful in changing beliefs about the consequences of *signing up for the ATU,* they should have influenced attitudes toward this behavior. These attitudinal changes should have been accompanied by changes in intentions and the corresponding behavior. In contrast, the traditional fear appeal was directed at target beliefs which, if accepted, would have led to more unfavorable attitudes toward *continued drinking.* Clearly, the effectiveness of this message depended on its impact on the immediate determinants of intentions to sign up for the ATU (i.e., the attitudinal and normative components). Our discussion of levels of specificity in Chapter 7 suggests that there may have been little relation between attitudes toward continued drinking and intentions to sign up for the ATU.

One to four days prior to receiving the persuasive communication, subjects were asked to fill out a questionnaire including measures of their intentions to continue drinking and their intentions to sign up for the ATU. In addition, measures of their attitudes toward continued drinking, toward signing up for the ATU, and toward not signing up for the ATU were obtained, along with measures of the normative component. Finally, subjects were given the opportunity to sign up for the ATU as a preliminary indication of their interest in taking part in the treatment program.

Subjects were assigned at random to one of four groups, such that each group contained 40 subjects, 20 of whom had indicated interest in signing up for the ATU and 20 of whom had not. The first three groups were exposed to one of the persuasive communications, and the fourth group served as a no-message control.

Immediately after exposure to the communication, a final sign-up sheet for admission to the ATU was passed to each subject. Control subjects received the sheet after they were told that they were candidates for the ATU.

Figure 11.15 shows the proportions of subjects who signed up for the ATU before and after the persuasive communications in the four experimental conditions. Although there was little change in rate of sign-up behavior of the control subjects, the positive and negative messages produced an *increase* and the fear appeal a *decrease* in the proportion of subjects who signed up for the ATU.

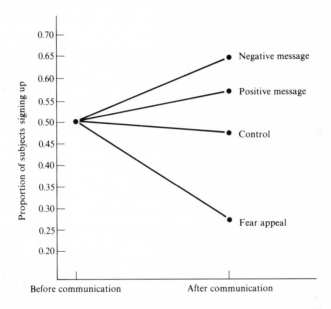

Fig. 11.15 Effects of various messages on sign-up behavior. (From McArdle, 1972.)

McArdle first showed that the traditional approach could not account for these results. After the communication, subjects reported the amount of arousal created by the message, and they were given a reception test in which they were asked whether the communication had contained each of 15 statements—the 10 that had actually been part of the communication they had received and five additional items. Greatest arousal was produced by the negative message, followed closely by the traditional fear appeal, and least arousal was produced by the positive message. The means were 3.98, 3.55, and 2.88, respectively, on a scale ranging from 0 to 9. Although the difference between the positive and negative messages was statistically significant, note that, in general, relatively low levels of arousal were created.

Message type also had a significant effect on reception, with the positive message producing most accurate reception (correct on 11.85 items out of the possible

15), followed by the fear appeal (11.10 correct) and the negative message (10.43 correct). Further, consistent with McGuire's (1968) two-factor model, there was a negative relation between arousal and reception ($r = -.26$; $p < .01$).

The differences in behavioral change, however, did not correspond to the differences in arousal or reception. Although the traditional fear appeal was intermediate in both arousal and reception, it had the least desirable persuasive effect. Since neither arousal nor reception can explain the obtained results, the traditional analysis must assume that the three messages had different effects on yielding. Specifically, it would have to be argued that the negative and positive messages produced more yielding than did the fear appeal. This explanation, however, contributes very little to our understanding of the processes underlying the effects of different types of appeals.

Explanation of the obtained results takes a completely different course following our model of persuasive communication. The first question concerns possible differences in acceptance of source beliefs and change in corresponding proximal beliefs addressed by the three messages. To answer this question, McArdle (1972) asked all subjects to indicate their agreement with each of the 30 belief statements contained in the three persuasive messages. Responses were made on five-point *strongly agree–strongly disagree* scales. Concerning *acceptance* of source beliefs, no significant differences were found for the 10 belief statements contained in the message to which a given subject was exposed. That is, subjects exposed to the positive message accepted the 10 belief statements in that message to the same extent that subjects exposed to the negative message or the fear appeal accepted the 10 belief statements in their respective messages.

Comparisons with the control group, however, revealed some interesting differences with respect to *change* in proximal beliefs. The positive and negative messages were quite effective in that they significantly increased agreement with the source beliefs. In contrast, subjects who were exposed to the traditional fear appeal dealing with the negative consequences of continued drinking were no more likely to accept belief statements arguing that continued drinking leads to unfavorable consequences than were subjects in the control group. Although belief statements in the fear appeal were accepted, this appeal produced little change in proximal beliefs.

The next question concerns the impact effects of the different messages. McArdle found that the three types of appeal had different impact effects on beliefs not contained in the message. Exposure to the positive message not only led to increased acceptance of the source belief statements contained in that message but also produced changes in external beliefs corresponding to the arguments contained in the negative message, and vice versa. For example, subjects who increased their belief (in comparison with the control group) that signing up for the ATU would improve physical and mental health also tended to increase their belief that not signing up for the ATU would ruin physical and mental health. The positive and negative messages had no impact effects on the 10 beliefs about the consequences of continued drinking contained in the fear appeal.

In marked contrast, the traditional fear-appeal message had large impact effects on beliefs about the consequences of signing up and not signing up for the ATU; subjects exposed to the fear appeal were *less* likely to believe that signing up leads to good consequences or that not signing up leads to bad consequences than were subjects in the control group.

These findings lead to the final and perhaps most important question in our analysis, namely, the extent to which changes in proximal and external beliefs may be expected to influence the dependent variable—in this study the behavior of signing up for the ATU. Since the positive and negative messages increased the perceived likelihood that signing up for the ATU leads to favorable consequences and that not signing up leads to unfavorable consequences, both of these messages should have increased attitudes toward signing behavior. The traditional fear appeal, however, had a negative impact effect, and this message should thus have reduced attitudes toward signing up for the ATU.

Direct measures of attitude toward signing up and not signing up for the ATU obtained after the persuasive communication provide evidence for these arguments. McArdle computed the difference between these two attitudes, and the results are shown in Fig. 11.16. Note that the positive and negative messages produced more favorable attitudes toward signing up, and the fear appeal reduced attitudes toward this behavior.

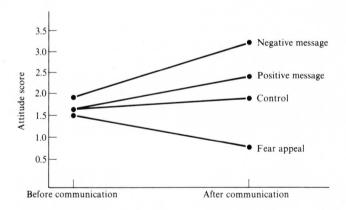

Fig. 11.16 Changes in attitude toward signing up for the ATU. (From McArdle, 1972.)

We reported in Chapter 8 that attitudes toward signing up for the ATU correlated highly with intentions to sign up ($r = .70$), which in turn were highly related ($r = .76$) to the overt act of signing up. Given these strong relations, it is to be expected that changes in behavior would have directly paralleled changes in attitude. Figure 11.15 supported this prediction.

Parenthetically, we note that intentions to continue drinking were unrelated ($r = .04$) to sign-up behavior, and thus, even if the traditional fear appeal had changed attitudes toward continued drinking, this result would have had little effect on the behavior in question.

The study by McArdle (1972) emphasizes the importance of considering acceptance of source beliefs, changes in proximal beliefs, and impact effects on external beliefs. Only by measuring these effects and by taking into account the relations of proximal and external beliefs to the dependent variable was it possible to explain the observed differential persuasiveness of the three messages. We have also seen that the traditional approach to communication and persuasion, relying on reception and yielding, could not account for the obtained results. Although the messages were found to produce differences in reception, the differences were not reflected in acceptance or in the overall persuasiveness of the messages.

CONCLUSION

This chapter has dealt with the most frequently used strategy of change, namely, persuasive communication. We have developed a model of persuasive communication and analyzed several lines of research by using this model in the context of our general conceptual framework. We compared our approach to persuasive communication with the traditional approach in this area and noted a number of important differences. In fact, the present chapter perhaps best illustrates the fundamental differences between the approach adopted in this book and prior analyses of attitudinal phenomena.

The emphasis in the traditional approach is on the manipulation of various independent variables. We have seen that these attempts to influence amount of change produced by a persuasive communication have not led to the discovery of consistent relations between independent and dependent variables. In contrast, our approach emphasizes a detailed analysis of the processes intervening between the manipulation and change in the dependent variable. We have shown that such an analysis requires the distinction between beliefs, attitudes, intentions, and behaviors. This emphasis on the dependent rather than independent variables also distinguishes our analysis from the traditional approach.

Perhaps the most fundamental principle underlying our entire approach to persuasion is our general assumption that man is basically a rational information processor whose beliefs, attitudes, intentions, and behaviors are influenced by the information available to him. This principle implies that any analysis of a persuasive attempt must begin with the items of information made available to subjects in the persuasive communication. The subject's processing of this information determines the effect of the communication on the dependent variable. The effects of an experimental manipulation can be understood only in conjunction with an informational analysis. At one extreme, when the information provided in the persuasive message is completely irrelevant to the dependent variable, no manipulation of source, message, channel, or receiver factor will produce different amounts of change. At the other extreme, if the information in and of itself produces maximal change in the dependent variable, a manipulation will again have little effect on amount of change. Between these extremes, the effects of an experimental manipulation on amount of change in a dependent variable are determined in part by the nature of the information contained in the message. It follows that attempts to find systematic relations between manipulations and change in dependent variables are meaningless without an accompanying informational analysis.

We saw that such an informational analysis involves specification of informational items or source beliefs, acceptance of these source beliefs, change in corresponding proximal beliefs, impact effects on external beliefs, and change in primary beliefs which provide the informational foundation for the dependent variable. Of course, it may not always be practical or necessary to examine each of these intervening processes. However, the investigator should always be able to specify his target source beliefs, other beliefs assumed to be primary, and the immediate determinants of his dependent variable. Effects of the manipulation on acceptance and change of target beliefs, impact on other primary beliefs, and changes in the immediate determinants of the dependent variable can be assessed. Such an analysis will often be sufficient for an understanding of the persuasion process. McArdle's (1972) study exemplifies how such an approach can be applied to research on the effects of fear appeals. We saw how this approach facilitated interpretation of the behavioral changes produced by the persuasive communications. It would have been impossible to understand these changes in behavior without the analysis of intervening processes. Indeed, we saw that a traditional analysis of these findings could not provide an explanation that would contribute to an understanding of the persuasion process.

Chapter 12

Conclusion

In the first part of this book we distinguished four major classes of variables: beliefs, attitudes, intentions, and behaviors. In contrast to most contemporary theory and research in the attitudes area, we have argued that these distinctions are an essential prerequisite for a systematic analysis of research findings in this area. In Chapters 3 and 4 we saw that it is possible to operationally distinguish between beliefs, attitudes, intentions, and behaviors, and to obtain reliable and valid measures of each of these constructs. We have also tried to show that the four major classes of variables are systematically related to one another. Toward the end of Chapter 1 we outlined a conceptual framework dealing with these interrelations. An analysis of contemporary theories of attitude formation and change in Chapter 2 showed that most of these theories are concerned primarily with the relations among beliefs and with the relations between beliefs and attitudes. At least at the conceptual level, relatively little attention has been paid to intentions and overt behavior.

Part II considered the determinants of beliefs, attitudes, intentions, and behaviors. We began our discussion in Chapter 5 with a consideration of processes underlying belief formation. Some beliefs are formed on the basis of direct observation, but most beliefs involve some inference on the part of the individual. This implies that most beliefs are based on or influenced by prior information available to the individual. Empirical evidence suggests that these inference processes reflect probabilistic rather than evaluative relationships among the beliefs a a person holds. His inferences appear to be based on rational considerations of these relationships and can be described quite adequately by formal probability models. For example, some inferential beliefs seem to be formed in accordance with laws of syllogistic reasoning, and others can be described by Bayes's theorem. The common denominator of these models is their suggestion that there are systematic relations among beliefs and that formation of new inferential beliefs is determined by the nature of these relationships. We reviewed studies of trait inferences, cue utilization, syllogistic reasoning, and formal probability models, which provided considerable evidence for the existence of such systematic and relatively stable relations among beliefs. In this context we showed that causal attributions to self and others are consistent with a Bayesian model of human inference processes.

Beliefs are the basic building blocks in our conceptual framework. In Chapter 6 we discussed the influence of a person's beliefs on his attitudes. A review of empirical research supported our conceptual framework by showing that a person's attitude toward any object, issue, behavior, or event is determined by his salient beliefs linking the object to various attributes and by his evaluations of those attributes. An expectancy-value formulation was found to account for research findings in such diverse areas as impression formation, interpersonal attraction, and classical conditioning of attitude. Also consistent with our general conceptual framework, a person's attitude was found to be related to the totality of his beliefs but not necessarily to any particular belief he holds. Similarly, in Chapter 7 we saw that a person's attitude is related to the totality of his intentions (weighted for their evaluative implications) but not necessarily to any given intention. We discussed a theoretical model for the prediction of intentions and presented evidence in support of this model. We found that intention to perform a given behavior is related to particular kinds of attitudes and beliefs, namely, attitudes toward the behavior and subjective norms concerning performance of the behavior.

Chapter 8 showed that when appropriately assessed (and barring unforeseen events), intentions serve as the primary determinants of overt behavior. Again we showed that although a person's attitude toward an object is related to the totality of his behaviors with respect to the object (a multiple-act criterion), it is not necessarily related to any given behavior (a single-act or repeated-observation criterion). This conclusion is in contrast to the recently emerging view that attitudes are unrelated to behavior. Our analysis suggests that the strength of this relation depends on the appropriateness of the attitudinal predictor to the behavioral criterion.

Part II demonstrated a sequence of systematic relations linking beliefs to attitudes, attitudes to intentions, and intentions to behaviors. We can now complete the cycle by realizing that in the final analysis a person can form new beliefs only by performing some behavior. To gain new information, he may read books, observe events, interact with other people, watch television, etc., and these activities provide the basis for the formation of descriptive and inferential beliefs. In a social interaction situation, for example, a person's behavior (and that of the other people involved) leads to the formation of beliefs about the attributes of objects in the environment, about the characteristics and reactions of other people, and about the consequences of the behavior. These beliefs provide the basis for the formation of attitudes toward the objects in the situation, toward the other people, and toward the behavior. In addition, they may also lead to the formation of normative beliefs concerning the behavior. Attitude toward the behavior and subjective norms in turn determine the person's intention to perform the behavior in the future, and this intention leads to performance or nonperformance of the behavior.

Part III was concerned with the ways in which beliefs, attitudes, intentions, and behaviors can be changed. Consistent with the discussion above, Chapter 9 showed that changes in these variables are initiated by exposing a person to information which produces changes in some of his beliefs. We reviewed research demonstrating that changing beliefs can produce changes in other beliefs as well as changes in attitudes, that changes in attitude toward a behavior or in subjective norms can lead to changes in intentions, and that changes in intentions can produce behavioral change.

Chapters 10 and 11 dealt with the two major strategies of change: active participation and persuasive communication. In each strategy, subjects are exposed to certain items of information which may produce changes in corresponding proximal beliefs and may also have an impact on external beliefs. The success of the influence attempt depends on the relation between these beliefs and the dependent variable. In Chapter 10 we showed how these considerations further our understanding of the diverse findings obtained in studies of interpersonal contact, role playing, counterattitudinal behavior, and decisions between alternatives. Chapter 11 presented a model for the acceptance of informational items provided by an outside source and change in corresponding proximal beliefs. According to the model, probability of acceptance decreases with discrepancy between source and proximal belief and increases with overall facilitation. Change in the advocated direction is predicted to be a function of probability of acceptance and potential change. Along with our general principles of change, this model allowed a systematic analysis of research on persuasive communication. A review of research on the effects of discrepancy, communicator credibility, and fear appeals showed that the results were generally consistent with the model. In contrast to the traditional approach to communication and persuasion, our analysis emphasizes the importance of distinguishing between beliefs, attitudes, intentions, and behaviors. Further, it suggests that experimental manipulations cannot be expected to have systematic effects on any one of these dependent variables. To understand the effects of experimental manipulations, it is necessary to examine their effects on proximal and external beliefs and to consider the relations of these beliefs to the dependent variable.

RESEARCH TRADITIONS IN THE ATTITUDE AREA

Much of the research on processes of change discussed in Chapters 10 and 11 can be classified as falling into two major research traditions, one associated with the Yale program of research on communication and persuasion under the direction of Carl Hovland, the other with Leon Festinger and his theory of cognitive dissonance. The explicit goal of the *Yale approach* was to identify the factors that influence persuasion. Its general research strategy was to manipulate independent variables that would influence the amount of "attitude" change. Since much of the research under the Yale approach has dealt with the effects of persuasive communication, the independent variables have included source credibility, type of appeal, order of arguments in the message, etc. Manipulations of these factors were assumed to influence amount of change to the extent that they affected two major intervening variables: reception (attention and comprehension) and acceptance or yielding. Thus the Yale approach was interested primarily in studying the ways in which "attitude" change can be brought about, and intervening processes were postulated in an attempt to understand the persuasion process.

In contrast, the *dissonance approach* concentrated not on an empirical phenomenon but rather on a hypothetical construct (dissonance) and proposed a broad theoretical hypothesis or principle, which can be stated as follows: Any treatment variable that produces dissonance between two cognitions will lead to attempts to reduce the dissonance. Much of the research has been conducted in order to support this general principle by looking at treatment variables that might produce dissonance and at dependent variables that might reflect the subject's attempt to reduce his dissonance. There was little interest in the effects of any particular independent variable on any specific dependent variable; that is, investigators were free to select any independent and dependent variables that allowed a test of the dissonance principle. Dissonance theory has been viewed as a theory dealing with attitude change, primarily because one class of dependent measures that are expected to reflect dissonance reduction are measures of attitudes or opinions.

Thus the Yale approach can be distinguished from the dissonance theory approach in terms of the phenomena that serve as the focus of research. Whereas the Yale program was interested in attitude change per se, research within the dissonance framework has studied attitude change primarily in an attempt to test the dissonance principle. One important implication of this difference in focus is that repeated failure to confirm a given experimental hypothesis in the Yale approach serves merely as evidence against the hypothesis and does not necessitate a change in research focus. In contrast, repeated failure to confirm an experimental hypothesis derived from the dissonance model raises doubt about the dissonance principle itself.[1]

EVALUATION OF ATTITUDE RESEARCH

At this stage it may be worth reflecting on the relevance of this research and examining the degree to which it has produced a cumulative, systematically integrated body of knowledge. According to Katz (1972),

> Of the thousands of experimental studies published in social psychology in the past 20 years, the number that supplies new information to a cumulative body of knowledge is surprisingly small. (p. 557)

---

1. This should not be taken as criticism of theory-based research; in such research, disconfirmation of a prediction may result merely in a modification of the theory. Research on dissonance "theory," however, has been concerned primarily with a single general principle.

An outside view is provided by the German psychologist Klaus Holzkamp (1970), who stated,

> When one considers the contents of experimental psychological research, rather than its methodology it can be argued that from a broader perspective, the kinds of questions being asked are more or less meaningless or trivial.[2]

Similar views of social-psychological research have been expressed by several American psychologists. For example, Lackenmeyer (1970) not only agreed with "the argument that many . . . social psychologists are investigating minutia and irrelevant problems" (p. 621); he also pointed out that the majority of this research is "used to verify isolated hypotheses: hypotheses not deduced from some general, deductive theory" (p. 620). In order to evaluate these criticisms, it is necessary to take a closer look at the research that has been conducted in the attitude area and, particularly, the research generated by the two major research traditions.

Dissonance approach. Although the dissonance approach started out with a general theoretical orientation, much of the research it has generated has tested hypotheses that have little theoretical significance. First, recall that the main focus of dissonance research is not a given empirical phenomenon but rather a single general dissonance principle.

> Instead of exploring the antecedent conditions that affected some standardized, reliable, and socially important dependent variable, experimenters in the Festinger tradition typically asked simple, direct, tailor-made questions . . . [which] were almost a casual afterthought. (Jones and Sigall, 1971, p. 350)

Initial studies attempted to test hypotheses derived from dissonance theory by employing some manipulation that was expected to produce different degrees of dissonance and then using the "tailor-made" questions to assess attempts at dissonance reduction. It soon became apparent that it was difficult to consistently demonstrate the operation of the dissonance principle, and studies with conflicting findings began to accumulate. Since most investigators were convinced of the validity of the dissonance principle, negative findings led not to the rejection of the hypothesis but rather to criticisms of the experimental procedures (see McGuire, 1973). Indeed, Aronson and Carlsmith (1968, p. 79) argued that "an experimenter can usually see weaknesses in his experiment; by making a few changes he can frequently strengthen his procedure and increase the probability of confirming a *true* hypothesis" (italics ours).

Studies disconfirming the dissonance hypothesis were carefully examined to discover procedural weaknesses in the manipulation of independent variables. Although research in the dissonance theory tradition has frequently been credited with "lavish[ing] great care on the independent variables being manipulated" (Jones and Sigall, 1971, p. 349; see also McGuire, 1969), it is apparent that the

---

2. Translated from the German article (Holzkamp, 1970, p. 6).

concern was really for the mechanics of manipulation rather than for the variable being manipulated. Perhaps it is characteristic of this state of affairs that Aronson and Carlsmith's (1968) "Experimentation in Social Psychology" places heavy emphasis on ways of deceiving and manipulating subjects. In that chapter we are told that some of the essential ingredients of a social-psychological experiment are of an "artistic, intuitive, ephemeral nature" (p. 1), and that "part of being a good experimental social psychologist involves learning to say 'whoops' convincingly" (p. 45). We are further told that "it is extremely important for all subjects to be brought to the identical point by the manipulation of the independent variable" (p. 46), even if different procedures are necessary to accomplish this.

Unfortunately, this approach to experimentation is quite characteristic of research in the dissonance tradition. It implies that instead of being a scientific undertaking, the social-psychological experiment is an artistic endeavor comparable to staging a theatrical drama. Like that of a director in the theater, the investigator's role is seen as one of moving and manipulating actors, settings, and props until he is intuitively satisfied with the effects of these manipulations. "Heavy attention is paid to dramatizing the experiment. This correctly reflects the imagination and ingenuity of the members of this school who seem at times to be frustrated playwrights." (Katz, 1971, p. 277). Needless to say, this approach is not only unscientific; it is actually detrimental to scientific progress since it violates one of the cardinal rules of scientific research, namely, that procedures used by one investigator be replicable by other investigators. Clearly, this can be achieved only if the manipulations employed are objective and communicable rather than "artistic, intuitive, and ephemeral."

This emphasis on the *mechanics* of independent variable manipulations has come at the expense of paying attention to what is being manipulated. Instead of studying the extent to which dissonance theory could account for some interesting phenomenon, investigators shifted the central focus of dissonance research to the effects of frequently minute and trivial variations in some specific manipulation. Thus, instead of being oriented toward furthering our understanding of some phenomenon, much dissonance research began to study quasi-methodological issues concerning the manipulation of some specific variable whose theoretical and practical significance did not go beyond the confines of a particular experimental situation.

Meehl (1967, p. 114) has characterized this state of affairs and its implications as follows:

> ... there exists among psychologists a fairly widespread tendency to report experimental findings with a liberal use of *ad hoc* explanations for those that didn't "pan out." This methodological sin is especially tempting in the "soft" fields of (personality and social) psychology, where the profession highly rewards a kind of "cuteness" or "cleverness" in experimental design, such as a hitherto untried method for inducing a desired emotional state, or a particularly "subtle" gimmick for detecting its influence upon behavioral output. The methodological price paid for this highly-valued "cuteness" is, of course, an unusual ease of escape

from [accepting negative findings and refuting the theory]. For, the logical structure of the "cute" component typically involves use of complex and rather dubious auxiliary assumptions, which are required to mediate the original prediction and are therefore readily available as (genuinely) plausible "outs" when the prediction fails. It is not unusual that this *ad hoc* challenging of auxiliary hypotheses is repeated in the course of a series of related experiments, in which the auxiliary hypothesis involved in Experiment 1 . . . becomes the focus of interest in Experiment 2, which in turn utilizes further plausible but easily challenged auxiliary hypotheses, and so forth. In this fashion a zealous and clever investigator can slowly wend his way through a tenuous nomological network, performing a long series of related experiments which appear to the uncritical reader as a fine example of "an integrated research program," *without ever once refuting or corroborating so much as a single strand of the network.* Meanwhile our eager-beaver researcher, undismayed by logic-of-science considerations and relying blissfully on the "exactitude" of modern statistical hypothesis-testing, has produced a long publication list and been promoted to a full professorship. In terms of his contribution to the enduring body of psychological knowledge, he has done hardly anything. His true position is that of a potent-but-sterile intellectual rake, who leaves in his merry path a long train of ravished maidens but no viable scientific offspring.[3]

Clearly, if attitude research is to reach the goal of providing a cumulative and systematically integrated body of knowledge concerning attitude phenomena, research must be more than quasi-methodological treatments of pseudo-problems created by conceptual ambiguities or procedural weaknesses. Another characteristic feature of research in the dissonance tradition has been its encouragement of counterintuitive or unexpected hypotheses. Despite our criticism of the intuitive approach, we are convinced that intuition and common sense play an important role in the formulation of hypotheses and the development of a theory. In fact, many commonsense hypotheses have found considerable support. For example, the notions that similarity leads to attraction and that a person's information about an object determines his attitude toward that object are clearly based on common-sense observations.

Our criticism is directed not so much at investigators who rely on common sense as at a particular use of intuition to *defeat* common-sense notions. For some

---

3. "Lest the reader wonder (quite appropriately) whether these impressions of the psychological literature ought perhaps to be dismissed as mere 'sour grapes' from an embittered, low-publication psychologist *manqué,* it may be stated that the author (a past president of the American Psychological Association) has published over 70 technical books or articles in both 'hard' and 'soft' fields of psychology, is a recipient of the Association's Distinguished Scientific Contributor Award, also of the Distinguished Contributor Award of the Division of Clinical Psychology, has been elected to Fellowship in the American Academy of Arts and Sciences, and is actively engaged in both theoretical and empirical research at the present time. He's not mad at anybody—but he is a bit distressed at the state of psychology" (Meehl, 1967, p. 114).

reason, many investigators seem to place a premium on being able to demonstrate the nonobvious. They select some reasonably well-established relationship (which is consistent with common sense) and then attempt to find some situation in which the relationship will not hold. It is almost as though an investigator says to himself, "Everybody thinks that if a person performs a commendable deed, liking for the person will increase. Wouldn't it be interesting if I could figure out some way to show that performing a commendable deed can actually *reduce* attraction?" The investigator then proceeds to search for some unique circumstances under which his counterintuitive hypothesis might be supported. At the same time, he speculates about possible intervening processes that can explain the counterintuitive phenomenon if it is substantiated. The theoretical relevance of the phenomenon and of the proposed intervening processes is of minor concern. Even if the investigator's intuition is supported, the results for the most part will be trivial, albeit unexpected. This should not be taken to mean that it is unimportant to identify the limits of a given phenomenon. What we are criticizing is the exclusive search for unexpected counterintuitive limitations of phenomena, limitations that can be demonstrated only under very special circumstances. As we have noted, most of these counterintuitive hypotheses have found little empirical support and have merely generated a wealth of inconsistent and inconclusive results.

It is unfortunate not only that research based on counterintuitive hypotheses has become acceptable but, as Meehl (1967) and Lackenmeyer (1970) have pointed out, that a premium is increasingly placed on the "cuteness" of experimental hypotheses and the sophistication and ingenuity of experimental procedures at the expense of theoretical and empirical relevance. This trend is illustrated by a passage from Aronson and Carlsmith's (1968) chapter on experimentation in social psychology. In discussing sources for hypotheses they state,

> Where the idea comes from is not terribly important. Indeed, ideas—even interesting ones—are cheap in social psychology. The important and difficult feat involves translating a conceptual notion into a tight, workable, credible, meaningful set of experimental operations." (p. 37)

To summarize briefly, there appear to be at least two reasons for the failure of the dissonance approach to generate a cumulative body of knowledge. First, in response to negative findings, much dissonance research has been distracted by tangential methodological issues that are of little relevance to the dissonance hypothesis. Second, the dissonance approach encouraged investigators to formulate counterintuitive and isolated hypotheses that do not contribute to a cumulative body of knowledge. It is unfortunate that this approach to experimentation appears to have been adopted by many investigators in the attitude area. For example, much of the currently fashionable research on interpersonal attraction (see Chapter 6) is characterized by "cute" intuitive hypotheses, inappropriate concern with methodological details, and a lack of theoretical perspective.

It has sometimes been suggested that the tendency to study relatively trivial issues and methodological details might be overcome by investigating socially relevant problems in field settings (McGuire, 1967; Katz, 1972). As noted in Chapter 4, however, there is no necessary relation between the way in which research is conducted and the setting in which these hypotheses are tested. It is just as easy to arrive at trivial ideas about socially relevant problems as it is to develop counterintuitive notions in laboratory settings. Indeed, a review of the literature shows that current field research is hardly more promising or fruitful than laboratory investigations. In a recent paper, McGuire (1973) reversed his position on the advantages of field research: "Recently I have come to recognize that this flight from the laboratory manipulational experiment to the field study, which I myself helped to instigate, is a tactical evasion which fails to meet the basic problem" (p. 449).

Yale approach. Research in the Yale tradition can be criticized neither for an excessive concern with pseudo-methodological problems nor for the testing of isolated, counterintuitive, or trivial hypotheses. The Yale approach has dealt for the most part with persuasion, an issue of considerable social relevance. Most hypotheses have relied on commonsense notions about the effects of source, message, and audience factors on the amount of "attitude" change produced by a persuasive communication. Nevertheless, this approach has also failed to produce a cumulative body of knowledge. The large volume of research generated by the Yale approach has not been able to demonstrate consistent effects of independent variable manipulations on persuasion.

In our opinion, this state of affairs is due in large part to the neglect of the nature of the dependent variable, a practice which the Yale approach shares with most other lines of research in the attitude area. Throughout this book we have demonstrated the importance of distinguishing between beliefs, attitudes, intentions, and behaviors. The major thrust of our argument has been that these variables have different determinants. When they are all treated as instances of a single construct, namely "attitude," the implicit assumption is made that they are all determined by the same antecedent variables. In fact, the Yale approach has assumed that persuasive effects, assessed by changes in beliefs, attitudes, intentions, or behaviors, are always a function of reception of message content and yielding to what is received. The fallacy of this approach becomes apparent whenever the same persuasive communication has different effects on different kinds of dependent variables. According to the Yale approach, reception and yielding occur with respect to the message. Since these processes are assumed to occur prior to the measurement of "attitude" change, they cannot be influenced by the nature of the particular measure used to assess such change. This implies that the same results should be obtained whether beliefs, attitudes, intentions, or behaviors serve as the dependent variable. The fact that different results are often obtained demonstrates that the conceptualization suggested by the Yale approach does not provide an adequate account of the persuasion process.

The conceptualization proposed by Hovland and his associates has a deceptive elegance. Since the yielding mediator is never directly assessed, it is always possible to account for any obtained result by making suitable post hoc assumptions about this mediator. The crucial test of this theory rests on the investigator's ability to demonstrate the consistency and validity of his assumptions concerning the yielding parameter. These problems are seen most clearly in McGuire's (1968) formal two-factor model:

$$p(O) = p(R)p(Y).$$

Probability of opinion change is viewed as a function of probability of reception and probability of yielding. If opinion change and reception are measured, it becomes possible to solve this equation and obtain a value for yielding. This procedure, however, adds little to our understanding of persuasion unless the estimated value is consistent with psychological theory.

Our discussion above concerning inconsistent results with respect to different dependent variables provides one example in which estimates of the yielding parameter would be incompatible with psychological theory. Specifically, such findings are inconsistent with the assumption that yielding is invariant with respect to the kind of dependent variable under consideration. A similar problem exists in relation to the effects of various independent variable manipulations. For example, to account for the inconsistent effects of high- and low-fear appeals, one would have to argue that fear arousal sometimes increases yielding and at other times reduces yielding. This argument is inconsistent with the assumption that a given manipulation, such as fear arousal, should have consistent effects on yielding.

These considerations apply whenever a theory is tested by estimating one or more of its major variables or parameters. Although such an approach is perfectly legitimate, it will contribute to a cumulative body of knowledge only if it is accompanied by a psychological theory that allows the investigator to derive testable hypotheses about the theory's parameters. The psychological assumptions linking independent variables to the parameters should not be changed arbitrarily from one study to another or changed to account post hoc for a given set of experimental findings. We have discussed some of these problems with respect to the application of Anderson's weighted averaging model to studies of information integration (see Chapters 5 and 6).

TOWARD A CUMULATIVE BODY OF KNOWLEDGE

We have adopted in this book an approach based on our conceptual framework which we hope will facilitate the accumulation of knowledge in the attitude area. This approach makes a clear distinction between beliefs, attitudes, intentions, and behaviors; it indicates how these variables can be measured; and it specifies the relations among them. This set of concepts and their specified interrelations provide a conceptual framework which can be used to analyze various phenomena and lines of research in a systematic and consistent fashion. We have seen that this approach leads to the formulation of hypotheses that are consistent with a wide array of empirical findings. At the same time, it provides explanations for the apparently inconsistent findings in different areas of investigation.

Most important, our approach permits the investigator to test his hypotheses about theoretical processes directly by obtaining measures of his explanatory constructs. Most studies are designed to test a hypothesis about the effects of some manipulation on a dependent variable. According to our approach, the influence of the manipulation on the dependent variable is mediated by its effects on certain beliefs and the direct or indirect relations of these beliefs to the dependent variable. Hypotheses about the effects of the manipulation on a given set of beliefs and about the exact nature of the relation between these beliefs and the dependent variable can be directly tested. This is done by first measuring the beliefs in question and examining whether the manipulation had the hypothesized effects. The links intervening between these beliefs and the dependent variable can also be assessed, allowing a test of the hypothesized relations.

Stated somewhat differently, adoption of our conceptual framework forces the investigator to make explicit assumptions about the processes intervening between his manipulation and the dependent variable. Moreover, our conceptual framework specifies the intervening processes appropriate for a given dependent variable. On the basis of this approach, an investigator studying the effects of communicator credibility on behavioral change might make the following assumptions: (1) Communicator credibility will influence acceptance of the statements contained in the message. (2) Differential acceptance of source beliefs will produce different amounts of change in the corresponding proximal beliefs. (3) Differential changes in proximal beliefs will influence amount of change in beliefs about performance of the behavior. (4) These changes will produce corresponding changes in attitude toward the behavior. (5) As a result, communicator credibility will affect intentions to perform the behavior. (6) The corresponding behavior will also be affected. Each variable in this sequence can be directly measured, and the hypothesized effects of communicator credibility can be tested. When communicator credibility fails to influence behavioral change, it is possible to discover where in this chain of effects the investigator made inappropriate assumptions. For example, the assumption that changes in beliefs about the consequences of performing the behavior will lead to change in attitude toward that behavior may not have been supported in this particular study.

We have seen that many of the contradictory and inconclusive findings in the attitude area appear to be attributable to such inappropriate assumptions about the relations between different kinds of variables. One clear example of such a fallacious assumption is the hypothesis that attitude toward an object is related to specific behaviors with respect to that object. It is our hope that by distinguishing between beliefs, attitudes, intentions, and behaviors and by specifying the determinants of these variables, our conceptual framework will contribute to the development of a cumulative body of knowledge in the attitude area.

References

Abelson, R. P., E. Aronson, W. J. McGuire, T. M. Newcomb, M. J. Rosenberg, and P. H. Tannenbaum (eds.). *Theories of Cognitive Consistency: A Sourcebook.* Chicago: Rand McNally, 1968.

Abelson, R. P., and D. E. Kanouse. Subjective acceptance of verbal generalizations. In S. Feldman (ed.), *Cognitive Consistency: Motivational Antecedents and Behavioral Consequents.* New York: Academic Press, 1966, pp. 171–197.

Abelson, R. P., and M. J. Rosenberg. Symbolic psycho-logic: A model of attitudinal cognition. *Behavioral Science,* 1958, **3,** 1–13.

Adams, J. A. *Human Memory.* New York: McGraw-Hill, 1967.

Adams, J. A., and N. W. Bray. A closed-loop theory of paired-associate verbal learning. *Psychological Review,* 1970, **77,** 385–405.

Adams, J. A., J. S. McIntyre, and H. I. Thorsheim. Response feedback and verbal retention. *Journal of Experimental Psychology,* 1969, **82,** 290–296.

Adams, J. S. Inequity in social exchange. In L. Berkowitz (ed.), *Advances in Experimental Social Psychology,* Vol. 2. New York: Academic Press, 1965, pp. 267–299.

Ajzen, I. Attribution of dispositions to an actor: Effects of perceived decision freedom and behavioral utilities. *Journal of Personality and Social Psychology,* 1971, **18,** 144–156. (a)

Ajzen, I. Attitudinal vs. normative messages: An investigation of the differential effects of persuasive communications on behavior. *Sociometry,* 1971, **34,** 263–280. (b)

Ajzen, I. Effects of information on interpersonal attraction: Similarity versus affective value. *Journal of Personality and Social Psychology*, 1974, **29,** 374–380.

Ajzen, I., R. K. Darroch, M. Fishbein, and J. A. Hornik. Looking backward revisited: A reply to Deutscher. *The American Sociologist*, 1970, **5,** 267–273.

Ajzen, I., and M. Fishbein. The prediction of behavioral intentions in a choice situation. *Journal of Experimental Social Psychology*, 1969, **5,** 400–416.

Ajzen, I., and M. Fishbein. The prediction of behavior from attitudinal and normative variables. *Journal of Experimental Social Psychology*, 1970, **6,** 466–487.

Ajzen, I., and M. Fishbein. Attitudes and normative beliefs as factors influencing behavioral intentions. *Journal of Personality and Social Psychology*, 1972, **21,** 1–9.

Ajzen, I., and M. Fishbein. Attitudinal and normative variables as predictors of specific behaviors. *Journal of Personality and Social Psychology*, 1973, **27,** 41–57.

Ajzen, I., and M. Fishbein. Factors influencing intentions and the intention-behavior relation. *Human Relations*, 1974, **27,** 1–15.

Ajzen, I., and W. H. Holmes. Uniqueness of behavioral effects on causal attribution. Unpublished manuscript, University of Massachusetts, 1974.

Allport, G. W. Attitudes. In C. Murchinson (ed.), *A Handbook of Social Psychology*. Worcester, Mass.: Clark University Press, 1935, pp. 798–844.

Allport, G. W. *The Nature of Prejudice*. Cambridge, Mass.: Addison-Wesley, 1954.

Allport, G. W. The historical background of modern social psychology. In G. Lindzey and E. Aronson (eds.), *The Handbook of Social Psychology,* 2nd ed., Vol. 1. Reading, Mass.: Addison-Wesley, 1968, pp. 1–80.

Amir, Y. Contact hypothesis in ethnic relations. *Psychological Bulletin*, 1969, **71,** 319–342.

Amster, H., and L. D. Glasman. Verbal repetition and connotative change. *Journal of Experimental Psychology*, 1966, **71,** 389–395.

Anderson, L. R. Prediction of negative attitude from congruity, summation, and logarithm formulae for the evaluation of complex stimuli. *Journal of Social Psychology*, 1970, **81,** 37–48.

Anderson, L. R., and M. Fishbein. Prediction of attitude from the number, strength, and evaluative aspect of beliefs about the attitude object: A comparison of summation and congruity theories. *Journal of Personality and Social Psychology*, 1965, **2,** 437–443.

Anderson, N. H. Test of a model for opinion change. *Journal of Abnormal and Social Psychology*, 1959, **59,** 371–381.

Anderson, N. H. Application of an additive model to impression formation. *Science*, 1962, **138,** 817–818.

Anderson, N. H. Averaging versus adding as a stimulus-combination rule in impression formation. *Journal of Experimental Psychology,* 1965, **70,** 394–400. (a)

Anderson, N. H. Primacy effects in personality impression formation using a generalized order effect paradigm. *Journal of Personality and Social Psychology.* 1965, **2,** 1–9. (b)

Anderson, N. H. Component ratings in impression formation. *Psychonomic Science,* 1966, **6,** 279–280.

Anderson, N. H. Averaging model analysis of set size effect in impression formation. *Journal of Experimental Psychology,* 1967, **75,** 158–165.

Anderson, N. H. Application of a linear-serial model to a personality-impression task using serial presentation. *Journal of Personality and Social Psychology,* 1968, **10,** 354–362. (a)

Anderson, N. H. Likableness ratings of 555 personality-trait words. *Journal of Personality and Social Psychology,* 1968, **9,** 272–279. (b)

Anderson, N. H. Functional measurement and psycho-physical judgment. *Psychological Review,* 1970, **77,** 153–170.

Anderson, N. H. Integration theory and attitude change. *Psychological Review* 1971, **78,** 171–206. (a)

Anderson, N. H. Two more tests against change of meaning in adjective combinations. *Journal of Verbal Learning and Verbal Behavior,* 1971, **10,** 75–85. (b)

Anderson, N. H., and G. R. Alexander. Choice test of the averaging hypothesis for information integration. *Cognitive Psychology,* 1971, **2,** 313–324.

Anderson, N. H., and A. A. Barrios. Primacy effects in personality impression formation. *Journal of Abnormal and Social Psychology,* 1961, **63,** 346–350.

Anderson, N. H., and S. Hubert. Effects of concomitant verbal recall on order effects in personality impression formation. *Journal of Verbal Learning and Verbal Behavior,* 1963, **2,** 379–391.

Anderson, N. H., and A. Jacobson. Effect of stimulus inconsistency and discounting instructions in personality impression formation. *Journal of Personality and Social Psychology,* 1965, **2,** 531–539.

Anderson, N. H., and A. K. Lampel. Effect of context on ratings of personality traits. *Psychonomic Science,* 1965, **3,** 433–434.

Anderson, N. H., and A. Norman. Order effects in impression formation in four classes of stimuli. *Journal of Abnormal and Social Psychology,* 1964, **69,** 467–471.

Aronson, E. Dissonance theory: Progress and problems. In R. P. Abelson *et al.* (eds.), *Theories of Cognitive Consistency: A Sourcebook.* Chicago: Rand McNally, 1968, pp. 3–27.

Aronson, E. Some antecedents of interpersonal attraction. In W. J. Arnold and D. Levine (eds.), *Nebraska Symposium on Motivation.* Lincoln: University of Nebraska Press, 1970, pp. 143–173.

Aronson, E., and J. M. Carlsmith. Experimentation in social psychology. In G. Lindzey and E. Aronson (eds.), *The Handbook of Social Psychology,* 2nd ed., Vol. 2. Reading, Mass.: Addison-Wesley, 1968, pp. 1–79.

Aronson, E., and V. Cope. My enemy's enemy is my friend. *Journal of Personality and Social Psychology,* 1968, **8,** 8–12.

Aronson, E., and B. W. Golden. The effect of relevant and irrelevant aspects of communicator credibility on opinion change. *Journal of Personality,* 1962, **30,** 135–146.

Aronson, E., and D. Linder. Gain and loss of esteem as determinants of interpersonal attractiveness. *Journal of Experimental Social Psychology,* 1965, **1,** 156–171.

Aronson, E., J. A. Turner, and J. M. Carlsmith. Communicator credibility and communication discrepancy as determinants of opinion change. *Journal of Abnormal and Social Psychology,* 1963, **67,** 31–36.

Aronson, E., B. Willerman, and J. Floyd. The effect of a pratfall on increasing interpersonal attractiveness. *Psychonomic Science,* 1966, **4,** 227–228.

Asch, S. E. Forming impressions of personality. *Journal of Abnormal and Social Psychology,* 1946, **41,** 258–290.

Atkinson, J. W. Motivational determinants of risk-taking behavior. *Psychological Review,* 1957, **64,** 359–372.

Azuma, H., and L. J. Cronbach. Cue-response correlations in the attainment of a scalar concept. *American Journal of Psychology,* 1966, **79,** 38–49.

Bahrick, H. P. The ebb of retention. *Psychological Review,* 1965, **72,** 60–73.

Bandura, A., E. B. Blanchard, and B. Ritter. Relative efficacy of desensitization and modeling approaches for inducing behavioral, affective, and attitudinal changes. *Journal of Personality and Social Psychology,* 1969, **13,** 173–199.

Barber, T. X., and M. J. Silver. Fact, fiction, and the experimenter bias effect. *Psychological Bulletin Monograph,* 1968, **70,** 1–29. (a)

Barber, T. X., and M. J. Silver. Pitfalls in data analysis and interpretation: A reply to Rosenthal. *Psychological Bulletin Monograph,* 1968, **70,** 48–62. (b)

Bardis, D. D. A religion scale. *Social Science,* 1961, **36,** 120–123.

Bass, F. M., and W. W. Talarzyk. An attitude model for the study of brand preferences. *Journal of Marketing Research,* 1972, **9,** 93–96.

Beach, L. R., and J. A. Wise. Subjective probability estimates and confidence ratings. *Journal of Experimental Psychology,* 1969, **79,** 438–444.

Becker, W. C. The matching of behavior ratings and questionnaire personality factors. *Psychological Bulletin*, 1960, **57,** 201–212.

Bem, D. J. An experimental analysis of self-persuasion. *Journal of Experimental Social Psychology*, 1965, **1,** 199–218.

Bem, D. J. Self-perception: An alternative interpretation of cognitive dissonance phenomena. *Psychological Review*, 1967, **74,** 183–200.

Bem, D. J. Attitudes as self-descriptions: Another look at the attitude-behavior link. In A. G. Greenwald, T. C. Brock, and T. M. Ostrom (eds.), *Psychological Foundations of Attitudes*. New York: Academic Press, 1968, pp. 197–215. (a)

Bem, D. J. The epistemological status of interpersonal simulations: A reply to Jones, Linder, Kiesler, Zanna, and Brehm. *Journal of Experimental Social Psychology*, 1968, **4,** 270–274. (b)

Bem, D. J. Self-perception theory. In L. Berkowitz (ed.), *Advances in Experimental Social Psychology,* Vol. 6. New York: Academic Press, 1972, pp. 1–62.

Bem, D. J., and H. K. McConnell. Testing the self-perception explanation of dissonance phenomena: On the salience of premanipulation attitudes. *Journal of Personality and Social Psychology*, 1970, **14,** 23–41.

Bellin, S. S. and L. Kriesberg. Relationship among attitudes, circumstances, and behavior: The case of applying for public housing. *Sociology and Social Research,* 1967, **51,** 453–469.

Berg, K. E. Ethnic attitudes and agreement with a Negro person. *Journal of Personality and Social Psychology*, 1966, **4,** 215–220.

Berkowitz, L. Resistance to improper dependency relationships. *Journal of Experimental Social Psychology*, 1969, **5,** 283–294.

Bernberg, R. E. Socio-psychological factors in industrial morale: I. The prediction of specific indicators. *Journal of Social Psychology*, 1952, **36,** 73–82.

Bishop, D. W., and R. A. Witt. Sources of behavioral variance during leisure time. *Journal of Personality and Social Psychology*, 1970, **16,** 352–360.

Bochner, S., and C. A. Insko. Communicator discrepancy, source credibility, and opinion change. *Journal of Personality and Social Psychology*, 1966, **4,** 614–621.

Bogardus, E. S. Measuring social distance. *Journal of Applied Sociology*, 1925, **9,** 299–308.

Bourne, L. E., Jr. Factors affecting strategies used in problems of concept-formation. *American Journal of Psychology*, 1963, **76,** 229–238.

Bourne, L. E., Jr. Learning and utilization of conceptual rules. In B. Kleinmuntz (ed.), *Concepts and the Structure of Memory*. New York: Wiley, 1967, pp. 1–32.

Bourne, L. E., Jr., B. R. Ekstrand, and R. L. Dominowski. *The Psychology of Thinking*. Englewood Cliffs, N.J.: Prentice-Hall, 1971.

Bray, D. W. The prediction of behavior from two attitudes scales. *Journal of Abnormal and Social Psychology*, 1950, **45,** 64–84.

Brehm, J. W. Post-decision changes in the desirability of alternatives. *Journal of Abnormal and Social Psychology*, 1956, **52,** 384–389.

Brehm, J. W., and A. R. Cohen. Re-evaluation of choice alternatives as a function of their number and qualitative similarity. *Journal of Abnormal and Social Psychology*, 1959, **58,** 373–378.

Brehm, J. W., and A. R. Cohen. *Explorations in Cognitive Dissonance.* New York: Wiley, 1962.

Brehm, J. W., and R. A. Jones. The effect on dissonance of surprise consequences. *Journal of Experimental Social Psychology*, 1970, **6,** 420–431.

Brehm, J. W., and R. A. Wicklund. Regret and dissonance reduction as a function of postdecision salience of dissonant information. *Journal of Personality and Social Psychology*, 1970, **14,** 1–7.

Brickman, P. Rational and nonrational elements in reactions to disconformation of performance expectancies. *Journal of Experimental Social Psychology*, 1972, **8,** 112–123.

Brickman, P., J. Redfield, A. A. Harrison, and R. Crandall. Drive and predisposition as factors in the attitudinal effects of mere exposure. *Journal of Experimental Social Psychology*, 1972, **8,** 31–44.

Brigham, J. C., and S. W. Cook. The influence of attitude on the recall of controversial material: A failure to confirm. *Journal of Experimental Social Psychology*, 1969, **5,** 240–243.

Brigham, J. C., and S. W. Cook. The influence of attitude and judgments of plausibility: A replication and extension. *Educational and Psychological Measurement,* 1970, **30,** 283–292.

Bronfenbrenner, U. Reaction to social pressure from adults vs. peers among Soviet day school and boarding school pupils in the perspective of an American sample. *Journal of Personality and Social Psychology*, 1970, **15,** 179–189.

Bruner, J. S. On going beyond the information given. In H. E. Gruber, K. R. Hammond, and R. Jessor (eds.), *Contemporary Approaches to Cognition.* Cambridge, Mass.: Harvard University Press, 1957, pp. 41–69.

Bruner, J. S., J. L. Goodnow, and G. A. Austin. *A Study of Thinking.* New York: Wiley, 1956.

Bruner, J. S., D. Shapiro, and R. Tagiuri. The meaning of traits in isolation and in combination. In R. Tagiuri and L. Petrullo (eds.), *Person Perception and Interpersonal Behavior.* Stanford, Cal.: Stanford University Press, 1958, pp. 277–288.

Bruner, J. S., and R. Tagiuri. The perception of people. In G. Lindzey (ed.), *Handbook of Social Psychology,* Vol. 2. Reading, Mass.: Addison-Wesley, 1954, pp. 634–654.

Brunswik, E. *The Conceptual Framework of Psychology.* Chicago: University of Chicago Press, 1952.

Brunswik, E. Representative design and probability theory in a functional psychology. *Psychological Review*, 1955, **62,** 193–217.

Brunswik, E. *Perception and the Representative Design of Experiments*. Berkeley: University of California Press, 1956.

Burgess, T. D. G. II, and S. M. Sales. Attitudinal effects of "mere exposure": A reevaluation. *Journal of Experimental Social Psychology*, 1971, **7,** 461–472.

Burke, R. C., and W. G. Bennis. Changes in perception of self and others during human relations training. *Human Relations*, 1961, **14,** 165–182.

Byrne, D. Interpersonal attraction and attitude similarity. *Journal of Abnormal and Social Psychology*, 1961, **62,** 713–715.

Byrne, D. Response to attitude similarity-dissimilarity as a function of affiliation need. *Journal of Personality*, 1962, **30,** 164–177.

Byrne, D. *An Introduction to Personality: A Research Approach*. Englewood Cliffs, N.J.: Prentice-Hall, 1966.

Byrne, D. Attitudes and attraction. In L. Berkowitz (ed.), *Advances in Experimental Social Psychology,* Vol. 4. New York: Academic Press, 1969, pp. 35–89.

Byrne, D. *The Attraction Paradigm*. New York: Academic Press, 1971.

Byrne, D., M. H. Bond, and H. J. Diamond. Response to political candidates as a function of attitude similarity-dissimilarity. *Human Relations*, 1969, **22,** 251–262.

Byrne, D., and G. L. Clore. A reinforcement model of evaluative responses. *Personality: An International Journal*, 1970, **1,** 103–128.

Byrne, D., G. L. Clore, W. Griffitt, J. Lamberth, and H. E. Mitchell. When research paradigms converge: Confrontation or integration? *Journal of Personality and Social Psychology*, 1973, **28,** 313–320.

Byrne, D., G. L. Clore, and P. Worchel. The effect of economic similarity-dissimilarity on interpersonal attraction. *Journal of Personality and Social Psychology,* 1966, **4,** 220–224.

Byrne, D., and C. R. Ervin. Attraction toward a Negro stranger as a function of prejudice, attitude similarity, and the stranger's evaluation of the subject. *Human Relations*, 1969, **22,** 397–404.

Byrne, D., and W. Griffitt. Similarity and awareness of similarity of personality characteristics as determinants of attraction. *Journal of Experimental Research in Personality*, 1969, **3,** 179–186.

Byrne, D., and J. Lamberth. Cognitive and reinforcement theories as complementary approaches to the study of attraction. In B. I. Murstein (ed.), *Theories of Attraction and Love*. New York: Springer, 1971, pp. 59–84.

Byrne, D., J. Lamberth, J. Palmer, and O. London. Sequential effects as a function of explicit and implicit interpolated attraction responses. *Journal of Personality and Social Psychology*, 1969, **13,** 70–78.

Byrne, D., and O. London. Primacy-recency and the sequential presentation of attitudinal stimuli. *Psychonomic Science*, 1966, **6,** 193–194.

Byrne, D., O. London, and W. Griffitt. The effect of topic importance and attitude similarity-dissimilarity on attraction in an intrastranger design. *Psychonomic Science*, 1968, **11,** 303–304.

Byrne, D., and D. Nelson. Attraction as a function of attitude similarity-dissimilarity: The effect of topic importance. *Psychonomic Science*, 1964, **1,** 93–94.

Byrne, D., and D. Nelson. Attraction as a linear function of proportion of positive reinforcements. *Journal of Personality and Social Psychology*, 1965, **1,** 659–663. (a)

Byrne, D., and D. Nelson. The effect of topic importance and attitude similarity-dissimilarity on attraction in a multistranger design. *Psychonomic Science,* 1965, **3,** 449–450. (b)

Byrne, D., and R. Rhamey. Magnitude of positive and negative reinforcement as a determinant of attraction. *Journal of Personality and Social Psychology,* 1965, **2,** 884–889.

Byrne, D., and T. J. Wong. Racial prejudice, interpersonal attraction, and assumed dissimilarity of attitudes. *Journal of Abnormal and Social Psychology*, 1962, **65,** 246–253.

Byrne, D., R. K. Young, and W. Griffitt. The reinforcement properties of attitude statements. *Journal of Experimental Research in Personality*, 1966, **1,** 266–276.

Calder, B. J., M. Ross, and C. A. Insko. Attitude change and attitude attribution: Effects of incentive, choice, and consequences. Journal of Personality and Social Psychology, 1973, **25,** 84–99.

Campbell, A., P. E. Converse, W. E. Miller, and D. E. Stokes. *The American Voter.* New York: Wiley, 1960.

Campbell, D. T. Factors relevant to the validity of experiments in social settings. *Psychological Bulletin,* 1957, **54,** 297–312.

Campbell, D. T. Social attitudes and other acquired behavioral dispositions. In S. Koch (ed.), *Psychology: A Study of a Science*, Vol. 6. New York: McGraw-Hill, 1963, pp. 94–172.

Campbell, D. T., and D. W. Fiske. Convergent and discriminant validation by the multitrait-multimethod matrix. *Psychological Bulletin,* 1959, **56,** 81–105.

Campbell, D. T., and J. C. Stanley. Experimental and quasi-experimental designs for research on teaching. In N. L. Gage (ed.), *Handbook of Research on Teaching.* Chicago: Rand McNally, 1963, pp. 171–246.

Carlsmith, J. M., B. E. Collins, and R. L. Helmreich. Studies of forced compliance: The effect of pressure for compliance on attitude change produced by face-to-face role playing and anonymous essay writing. *Journal of Personality and Social Psychology*, 1966, **4,** 1–13.

Carlson, A. R. The relationship between a behavioral intention, attitude toward the behavior and normative beliefs about the behavior. Unpublished doctoral dissertation, University of Illinois, 1968.

Carlson, E. R. Attitude change through modification of attitude structure. *Journal of Abnormal and Social Psychology*, 1956, **52**, 256–261.

Carr, L., and S. O. Roberts. Correlates of civil-rights participation. *Journal of Social Psychology*, 1965, **67**, 259–267.

Cartwright, D., and F. Harary. Structural balance: A generalization of Heider's theory. *Psychological Review*, 1956, **63**, 277–293.

Cartwright, D., and A. Zander (eds.). *Group Dynamics: Research and Theory*. New York: Harper and Row, 1968.

Cattell, R. B. *The Description and Measurement of Personality*. New York: World Book, 1946.

Cattell, R. B., A. B. Heist, P. A. Heist, and R. G. Stewart. The objective measurement of dynamic traits. *Educational and Psychological Measurement*, 1950, **10**, 224–248.

Cattell, R. B., E. F. Maxwell, B. F. Light, and M. P. Unger. The objective measurement of attitudes. *British Journal of Psychology*, 1950, **40**, 81–90.

Chaikin, A. L. The effects of four outcome schedules on persistence, liking for the task, and attributions of causality. *Journal of Personality*, 1971, **39**, 512–526.

Chalmers, D. K. Meanings, impressions, and attitudes: A model of the evaluation process. *Psychological Review*, 1969, **76**, 450–460.

Chapman, L. J., and J. P. Chapman. Atmosphere effect reexamined. *Journal of Experimental Psychology*, 1959, **58**, 220–226.

Chave, E. J. A new type scale for measuring attitudes. *Religious Education*, 1928, **23**, 364–369.

Chlebek, J., and R. L. Dominowski. The effect of practice on utilization of information from positive and negative instances in identifying disjunctive concepts. *Canadian Journal of Psychology*, 1970, **24**, 64–69.

Clore, G. L., and B. Baldridge. Interpersonal attraction: The role of agreement and topic interest. *Journal of Personality and Social Psychology*, 1968, **9**, 340–346.

Clore, G. L., and B. Baldridge. The behavior of item weights in attitude-attraction research. *Journal of Experimental Social Psychology*, 1970, **6**, 177–186.

Clore, G. L., and D. Byrne. A reinforcement-affect model of attraction. In T. L. Huston (ed.), *Perspectives on Interpersonal Attraction*. New York: Academic Press, 1974, pp. 143–170.

Clore, G. L., and K. M. Jeffery. Emotional role playing, attitude change, and attraction toward a disabled person. *Journal of Personality and Social Psychology*, 1972, **23**, 105–111.

Cohen, A. R. An experiment on small rewards for discrepant compliance and attitude change. In J. W. Brehm and A. R. Cohen, *Explorations in Cognitive Dissonance*. New York: Wiley, 1962, pp. 73–78.

Cohen, J. L. A Bayesian approach to impression formation. Unpublished doctoral dissertation, University of Illinois, 1973.

Collins, B. E., R. D. Ashmore, F. W. Hornbeck, and R. E. Whitney. Studies in forced compliance: XIII & XV. In search of a dissonance-producing forced compliance paradigm. *Representative Research in Social Psychology*, 1970, **1,** 11–23.

Collins, B. E., and H. Guetzkow. *A Social Psychology of Group Processes for Decision Making.* New York: Wiley, 1964.

Collins, B. E., and R. L. Helmreich. Studies in forced compliance: II. Contrasting mechanisms of attitude change produced by public-persuasive and private-true essays. *Journal of Social Psychology*, 1970, **81,** 253–264.

Cook, S. W. Motives in a conceptual analysis of attitude-related behavior. In W. J. Arnold and E. Levine (eds.), *Nebraska Symposium on Motivation, 1969.* Lincoln: University of Nebraska Press, 1970, pp. 179–231.

Corey, S. M. Professed attitudes and actual behavior. *Journal of Educational Psychology*, 1937, **28,** 271–280.

Crano, W. D., and L. A. Messé. When does dissonance fail? The time dimension in attitude measurement. *Journal of Personality*, 1970, **38,** 493–508.

Crespi, L. P. Quantitative variation of incentive and performance in the white rat. *American Journal of Psychology*, 1942, **55,** 467–517.

Cronbach, L. J. Response sets and test validity. *Educational and Psychological Measurement*, 1946, **6,** 475–494.

Cronbach, L. J. Further evidence on response sets and test design. *Educational and Psychological Measurement*, 1950, **10,** 3–31.

Cronbach, L. J. The two disciplines of scientific psychology. *American Psychologist*, 1957, **12,** 671–684.

Cronkhite, G. *Persuasion: Speech and Behavioral Change.* New York: Bobbs-Merrill, 1969.

Culbertson, F. M. Modification of an emotionally held attitude through role playing. *Journal of Abnormal and Social Psychology*, 1957, **54,** 230–233.

D'Andrade, R. G. Trait psychology and componential analysis. *American Anthropologist*, 1965, **67,** 215–228.

Darroch, R. K. Attitudinal variables and perceived group norms as predictors of behavioral intentions and behavior in the signing of photographic releases. Unpublished doctoral dissertation, University of Illinois, 1971.

Davidson, A. R. The prediction of family planning intentions. Unpublished doctoral dissertation, University of Illinois, 1973.

Davidson, J., and S. Kiesler. Cognitive behavior before and after decisions. In L. Festinger (ed.), *Conflict, Decision, and Dissonance*. Stanford, Cal.: Stanford University Press, 1964, pp. 10–19.

Davis, E. E., and N. Grobstein. Multimode factor analysis of interpersonal perceptions. Technical Report No. 36, Group Effectiveness Research Laboratory, University of Illinois, 1966.

Davis, J. H. *Group Performance*. Reading, Mass.: Addison-Wesley, 1969.

Dean, L. R. Interaction, reported and observed: The case of one local union. *Human Organization*, 1958, **17**, 36–44.

DeFleur, M. L., and F. R. Westie. Verbal attitudes and overt acts: An experiment on the salience of attitudes. *American Sociological Review*, 1958, **23**, 667–673.

DeNike, L. D., and M. P. Leibovitz. Accurate anticipation of reinforcement in verbal conditioning. *Journal of Personality*, 1969, **37**, 158–170.

Deutscher, I. Looking backward: Case studies on the progress of methodology in sociological research. *American Sociologist*, 1969, **4**, 35–41.

DeVries, D. L., and I. Ajzen. The relationship of attitudes and normative beliefs to cheating in college. *Journal of Social Psychology*, 1971, **83**, 199–207.

Dillehay, R. C., and M. L. Clayton. Forced-compliance studies, cognitive dissonance, and self-perception theory. *Journal of Experimental Social Psychology*, 1970, **6**, 458–465.

Dillehay, R. C., C. A. Insko, and M. B. Smith. Logical consistency and attitude change. *Journal of Personality and Social Psychology*, 1966, **3**, 646–654.

Doob, L. W. The behavior of attitudes. *Psychological Review*, 1947, **54**, 135–156.

Downey, J. E., and G. E. Knapp. The effect on a musical programme of familiarity and of sequence of selections. In M. Schoen (ed.), *The Effects of Music*. New York: Harcourt, Brace, 1927.

DuCharme, W. M. Response bias explanation of conservative human inference. *Journal of Experimental Psychology*, 1970. **85**, 66–74.

DuCharme, W. M., and C. R. Peterson. Proportion estimation as a function of proportion and sample size. *Journal of Experimental Psychology*, 1969, **81**, 536–541.

Dudycha, L. W., and J. C. Naylor. Characteristics of the human inference process in complex choice behavior situations. *Organizational Behavior and Human Performance*, 1966, **1**, 110–128.

Dulany, D. E. Hypotheses and habits in verbal "operant conditioning." *Journal of Abnormal and Social Psychology*, 1961, **63**, 251–263.

Dulany, D. E. The separable effects of the information conveyed by a reinforcer. Paper read at the Psychonomic Society meetings, 1964.

Dulany, D. E. Awareness, rules, and propositional control: A confrontation with S-R behavior theory. In D. Horton and T. Dixon (eds.), *Verbal Behavior and S-R Behavior Theory.* Englewood Cliffs, N.J.: Prentice-Hall, 1968, pp. 340–387.

Dulany, D. E., and D. C. O'Connell. Does partial reinforcement dissociate verbal rules and the behavior they might be presumed to control? *Journal of Verbal Learning and Verbal Behavior,* 1963, **2,** 361–372.

Dulany, D. E., S. Schwartz, and C. Walker. Why the informational and distributional parameters of reinforcement interact. Paper read at the Psychonomic Society meetings, 1965.

Dustin, D. S., and P. M. Baldwin. Redundancy in impression formation. *Journal of Personality and Social Psychology,* 1966, **3,** 500–506.

Eagly, A. H. The comprehensibility of persuasive arguments as a determinant of opinion change. *Journal of Personality and Social Psychology,* 1974, **29,** 758–773.

Edwards, A. L. Political frames of reference as a factor influencing recognition. *Journal of Abnormal and Social Psychology,* 1941, **36,** 34–61.

Edwards, A. L. *Techniques of Attitude Scale Construction.* New York: Appleton-Century-Crofts, 1957.

Edwards, A. L. Trait and evaluational consistency in self-description. *Educational and Psychological Measurement,* 1969, **29,** 737–752.

Edwards, A. L.. and K. C. Kenney. A comparison of the Thurstone and Likert techniques of attitude scale construction. *Journal of Applied Psychology,* 1946, **30,** 72–83.

Edwards, W. The theory of decision making. *Psychological Bulletin,* 1954, **51,** 380–417.

Edwards, W. Dynamic decision theory and probabilistic information processing. *Human Factors,* 1962, **4,** 59–73.

Edwards, W. Conservatism in human information processing. In B. Kleinmuntz (ed.), *Formal Representation of Human Judgment.* New York: Wiley, 1968, pp. 17–52.

Edwards, W., H. Lindman, and L. J. Savage. Bayesian statistical inference for psychological research. *Psychological Review,* 1963, **70,** 193–242.

Ehrlich, H. J. Attitudes, behavior, and the intervening variables. *American Sociologist,* 1969, **4,** 29–34.

Einhorn, H. J. The use of nonlinear, noncompensatory models in decision making. *Psychological Bulletin,* 1970, **73,** 221–230.

Elizur, D. *Adapting to Innovation.* Jerusalem: Jerusalem Academic Press, 1970.

Elms, A. C., and I. L. Janis. Counter-norm attitudes induced by consonant versus dissonant conditions of role-playing. *Journal of Experimental Research in Personality,* 1965, **1,** 50–60.

Estes, W. K. Probability learning. In A. W. Melton (ed.), *Categories of Human Learning*. New York: Academic Press, 1964, pp. 89–128.

Evans, R. I., R. M. Rozelle, T. M. Lasater, T. M. Dembroski, and B. P. Allen. Fear arousal, persuasion, and actual versus implied behavioral change: New perspective utilizing a real-life dental hygiene program. *Journal of Personality and Social Psychology*, 1970, **16**, 220–227.

Ewing, T. N. A study of certain factors involved in changes of opinion. *Journal of Social Psychology*, 1942, **16**, 63–88.

Faulkner, J. E., and G. F. DeJong. Religiosity in 5-D: An empirical analysis. In J. P. Robinson and P. R. Shaver (eds.), *Measures of Social Psychological Attitudes*. Ann Arbor: University of Michigan, Institute for Social Research, 1969.

Feather, N. T. Subjective probability and decision under uncertainty. *Psychological Review*, 1959, **66**, 150–164.

Feather, N. T. A structural balance model of communication effects. *Psychological Review*, 1964, **71**, 291–313. (a)

Feather, N. T. Acceptance and rejection of arguments in relation to attitude strength, critical ability, and intolerance of inconsistency. *Journal of Abnormal and Social Psychology*, 1964, **69**, 127–136. (b)

Feather, N. T. Attribution of responsibility and valence of success and failure in relation to initial confidence and task performance. *Journal of Personality and Social Psychology*, 1969, **13**, 129–144.

Feather, N. T. Organization and discrepancy in cognitive structures. *Psychological Review*, 1971, **78**, 355–379.

Feather, N. T., and J. G. Simon. Attribution of responsibility and valence of outcome in relation to initial confidence and success and failure of self and other. *Journal of Personality and Social Psychology*, 1971, **18**, 173–188. (a)

Feather, N. T., and J. G. Simon. Causal attribution for success and failure in relation to expectations of success based upon selective or manipulative control. *Journal of Personality*, 1971, **39**, 527–541. (b)

Feldman, S., and M. Fishbein. Social psychological studies in voting behavior: II. Factor analyses of attitudes towards, and the perceived importance of, campaign issues. Paper presented at the Midwestern Psychological Association meetings, May 1963. (a)

Feldman, S., and M. Fishbein. Social psychological studies in voting behavior: III. Party affiliation and beliefs about candidates. *American Psychologist*, 1963, **18**, 374–375 (abstract). (b)

Felipe, A. I. Evaluative versus descriptive consistency in trait inferences. *Journal of Personality and Social Psychology*, 1970, **16**, 627–638.

Fendrich, J. M. A study of the association among verbal attitudes, commitment, and overt behavior in different experimental situations. *Social Forces*, 1967, **45,** 347–355.

Festinger, L. Informal social communication. *Psychological Review*, 1950, **57,** 271–282.

Festinger, L. A theory of social comparison processes. *Human Relations*, 1954, **7,** 117–140.

Festinger, L. *A Theory of Cognitive Dissonance.* Evanston, Ill.: Row, Peterson, 1957.

Festinger, L. (ed.), *Conflict, Decision, and Dissonance.* Stanford, Cal.: Stanford University Press, 1964.

Festinger, L., and J. M. Carlsmith. Cognitive consequences of forced compliance. *Journal of Abnormal and Social Psychology*, 1959, **58,** 203–210.

Festinger, L., and E. Walster. Post-decision regret and decision reversal. In L. Festinger (ed.), *Conflict, Decision, and Dissonance.* Stanford, Cal.: Stanford University Press, 1964, 100–112.

Fishbein, M. An investigation of the relationships between beliefs about an object and the attitude toward that object. *Human Relations*, 1963, **16,** 233–240.

Fishbein, M. The relationship of the behavioral differential to other attitude instruments. *American Psychologist*, 1964, **19,** 540 (reference).

Fishbein, M. Sexual behavior and propositional control. Paper read at the Psychonomic Society meetings, 1966.

Fishbein, M. (ed.). *Readings in Attitude Theory and Measurement.* New York: Wiley, 1967. (a)

Fishbein, M. Attitude and the prediction of behavior. In M. Fishbein (1967a), pp. 477–492. (b)

Fishbein, M. A behavior theory approach to the relations between beliefs about an object and the attitude toward the object. In M. Fishbein (1967a), pp. 389–400. (c)

Fishbein, M. A consideration of beliefs and their role in attitude measurement. In M. Fishbein (1967a), pp. 257–266. (d)

Fishbein, M. The prediction of behavior from attitudinal variables. In C. D. Mortensen and K. K. Sereno (eds.), *Advances in Communication Research.* New York: Harper and Row, 1973, pp. 3–31.

Fishbein, M., and I. Ajzen. Attitudes and opinions. *Annual Review of Psychology*, 1972, **23,** 487–544.

Fishbein, M., and I. Ajzen. Attitudes toward objects as predictors of single and multiple behavioral criteria. *Psychological Review*, 1974, **81,** 59–74.

Fishbein, M., I. Ajzen, E. Landy, and L. R. Anderson. Attitudinal variables and behavior: Three empirical studies and a theoretical reanalysis. Technical Report

No. 70-9, ARPA Order 454, Contract 177-473 N00014-67-A0103-0013, Seattle: University of Washington, 1970.

Fishbein, M., and F. S. Coombs. Basis for decision: An attitudinal analysis of voting behavior. *Journal of Applied Social Psychology*, 1974, **4,** 95–124.

Fishbein, M., and S. Feldman. Social psychological studies in voting behavior: I. Theoretical and methodological considerations. *American Psychologist*, 1963, **18,** 388 (reference).

Fishbein, M., and R. Hunter. Summation versus balance in attitude organization and change. *Journal of Abnormal and Social Psychology*, 1964, **69,** 505–510.

Fishbein, M., E. Landy, and G. Hatch. Some determinants of an individual's esteem for his least preferred co-worker. *Human Relations*, 1969, **22,** 173–188.

Fishbein, M., and B. H. Raven. The AB scales: An operational definition of belief and attitude. *Human Relations*, 1962, **15,** 35–44.

Fleming, D. Attitude: The history of a concept. *Perspectives in American History*, 1967, **1,** 287–365.

Freedman, J. L., J. M. Carlsmith, and D. O. Sears. *Social Psychology*. Englewood Cliffs, N. J.: Prentice-Hall, 1970.

Freeman, L. C., and T. Ataov. Invalidity of indirect and direct measures of attitude toward cheating. *Journal of Personality*, 1960, **28,** 444–447.

Freibergs, V., and E. Tulving. The effect of practice on utilization of information from positive and negative instances in concept identification. *Canadian Journal of Psychology*, 1961, **15,** 101–106.

French, J. P. R., Jr., and B. H. Raven. The bases of social power. In D. Cartwright (ed.), *Studies in Social Power*. Ann Arbor: University of Michigan Press, 1959, pp. 150–167.

Friedman, P. H., R. Buck, and V. L. Allen. Arousal, anxiety, aggression, and attitude change. *Journal of Social Psychology*, 1970, **82,** 99–108.

Frieze, I., and B. Weiner. Cue utilization and attributional judgments for success and failure. *Journal of Personality*, 1971, **39,** 591–605.

Fromkin, H. L. Effects of experimentally aroused feelings of undistinctiveness upon evaluation of scarce and novel experiences. *Journal of Personality and Social Psychology*, 1970, **16,** 521–529.

Gallo, P. S., Jr., and I. A. Dale. Experimenter bias in the prisoner's dilemma game. *Psychonomic Science*, 1968, **13,** 340.

Gilson, C., and R. P. Abelson. The subjective use of inductive evidence. *Journal of Personality and Social Psychology*, 1965, **2,** 301–310.

Glassman, M. The effects of personality and demographic factors on the formation of attitudes toward convenience goods. Unpublished master's thesis, University of Illinois, 1971.

Glassman, M., and M. Birchmore. The relationship between subjective norms and normative beliefs. Unpublished manuscript, University of Illinois, 1974.

Glinski, R. J., B. C. Glinski, and G. T. Slatin. Nonnaivety contamination in conformity experiments: Sources, effects, and implications for control. *Journal of Personality and Social Psychology*, 1970, **16**, 478–485.

Goldberg, L. R. Simple models or simple processes? Some research on clinical judgments. *American Psychologist*, 1968, **23**, 483–496.

Goldberg L. R. Man versus model of man: A rationale, plus some evidence, for a method of improving on clinical inferences. *Psychological Bulletin*, 1970, **73**, 422–432.

Goldstein, M., and E. E. Davis. Race and belief: A further analysis of the social determinants of behavioral intentions. *Journal of Personality and Social Psychology*, 1972, **22**, 346–355.

Golightly, C., and D. Byrne. Attitude statements as positive and negative reinforcements. *Science*, 1964, **146**, 798–799.

Gollob, H. F. Impression formation and word combination in sentences. *Journal of Personality and Social Psychology*, 1968, **10**, 341–353.

Gordon, A., and D. C. Glass. Choice ambiguity, dissonance, and defensiveness. *Journal of Personality*, 1970, **38**, 264–272.

Gormly, J., A. Gormly, and C. Johnson. Interpersonal attraction: Competence motivation and reinforcement theory. *Journal of Personality and Social Psychology*, 1971, **19**, 375–380.

Gorn, G., and M. Tuck. The locus of effect of communicator prestige. Unpublished master's research project, London School of Economics and Political Science, 1968.

Green, B. F. Attitude measurement. In G. Lindzey (ed.), *Handbook of Social Psychology*, Vol. 1. Reading, Mass.: Addison-Wesley, 1954, pp. 335–369.

Green, J. A. Attitudinal and situational determinants of intended behavior toward blacks. *Journal of Personality and Social Psychology*, 1972, **22**, 13–17.

Greenwald, A. G. On defining attitude and attitude theory. In A. G. Greenwald, T. C. Brock, and T. M. Ostrom (eds.), *Psychological Foundations of Attitudes*. New York: Academic Press, 1968, pp. 361–388.

Greenwald, A. G. The open-mindedness of the counterattitudinal role player. *Journal of Experimental Social Psychology*, 1969, **5**, 375–388.

Greenwald, A. G. When does role playing produce attitude change? Toward an answer. *Journal of Personality and Social Psychology*, 1970, **16**, 214–219.

Greenwald, A. G., and R. D. Albert. Acceptance and recall of improvised arguments. *Journal of Personality and Social Psychology*, 1968, **8**, 31–34.

Greenwald, A. G., T. C. Brock, and T. M. Ostrom (eds.). *Psychological Foundations of Attitudes*. New York: Academic Press, 1968.

Greenwald, H. J. Dissonance and relative versus absolute attractiveness of decision alternatives. *Journal of Personality and Social Psychology*, 1969, **11,** 328–333.

Grush, J. E. Limitations of the mere exposure hypothesis and an alternative mediational process in the frequency-affect relationship. Unpublished doctoral dissertation, University of Illinois, 1974.

Guilford, J. P. *Psychometric Methods*, 2nd ed. New York: McGraw-Hill, 1954.

Guttman, L. A basis for scaling qualitative data. *American Sociological Review*, 1944, **9,** 139–150.

Haaland, G. A., and M. Venkatesan. Resistance to persuasive communications: An examination of the distraction hypothesis. *Journal of Personality and Social Psychology*, 1968, **9,** 167–170.

Hackman, J. R., and L. R. Anderson. The strength, relevance, and source of beliefs about an object in Fishbein's attitude theory. *Journal of Social Psychology*, 1968, **76,** 55–67.

Hakel, M. Significance of implicit personality theories for personality research and theory. *Proceedings of the American Psychological Association*, 1969.

Hallworth, H. J. Dimensions of personality and meaning. *British Journal of Social and Clinical Psychology*, 1965, **4,** 161–168.

Hammond, K. R. Measuring attitudes by error-choice: An indirect method. *Journal of Abnormal and Social Psychology*, 1948, **43,** 38–48.

Hammond, K. R., C. J. Hursch, and F. J. Todd. Analyzing the components of clinical inference. *Psychological Review*, 1964, **71,** 438–456.

Hammond, K. R., and D. A. Summers. Cognitive control. *Psychological Review*, 1972, **79,** 58–67.

Hansen, F. Consumer choice behavior: An experimental approach. *Journal of Marketing Research*, 1969, **6,** 436–443.

Harris, R. J. Dissonance or sour grapes? Post-"decision" changes in ratings and choice frequencies. *Journal of Personality and Social Psychology*, 1969, **11,** 334–344.

Harrison, A. A. Response competition, frequency, exploratory behavior, and liking. *Journal of Personality and Social Psychology*, 1968, **10,** 363–368.

Harvey, O. J., D. E. Hunt, and H. M. Schroeder. *Conceptual Systems and Personality Organization*. New York: Wiley, 1961.

Heider, F. Social perception and phenomenal causality. *Psychological Review*, 1944, **51,** 358–374.

Heider, F. Attitudes and cognitive organization. *Journal of Psychology*, 1946, **21,** 107–112.

Heider, F. *The Psychology of Interpersonal Relations.* New York: Wiley, 1958.

Heise, D. R. Affectual dynamics in simple sentences. *Journal of Personality and Social Psychology,* 1969, **11,** 204–213.

Heise, D. R. Potency dynamics in simple sentences. *Journal of Personality and Social Psychology,* 1970, **16,** 48–54.

Helmreich, R., E. Aronson, and J. LeFan. To err is humanizing—sometimes: Effects of self-esteem, competence, and a pratfall on interpersonal attraction. *Journal of Personality and Social Psychology,* 1970, **16,** 259–264.

Helmreich, R., and B. E. Collins. Studies in forced compliance: Commitment and magnitude of inducement to comply as determinants of opinion change. *Journal of Personality and Social Psychology,* 1968, **10,** 75–81.

Hendrick, C., and A. F. Costantini. Effects of varying trait inconsistency and response requirements on the primacy effect in impression formation. *Journal of Personality and Social Psychology,* 1970, **15,** 158–167.

Hendrick, C., and D. R. Shaffer. Effects of arousal and credibility on learning and persuasion. *Psychonomic Science,* 1970, **20,** 241–243.

Hess, E. H. Attitude and pupil size. *Scientific American,* 1965, **212,** 46–54.

Hewitt, J. Liking and the proportion of favorable evaluations. *Journal of Personality and Social Psychology,* 1972, **22,** 231–235.

Higbee, K. L. Fifteen years of fear arousal: Research on threat appeals: 1953–1968. *Psychological Bulletin,* 1969, **72,** 426–444.

Himmelfarb, S., and A. H. Eagly (eds.). *Readings in Attitude Change.* New York: Wiley, 1974. (a)

Himmelfarb, S. and A. H. Eagly. Orientations to the study of attitudes and their change. In S. Himmelfarb and A. H. Eagly (eds.), *Readings in Attitude Change.* New York: Wiley, 1974, pp. 2–49. (b)

Himmelfarb, S., and D. J. Senn. Forming impressions of social class: Two tests of an averaging model. *Journal of Personality and Social Psychology,* 1969, **12,** 38–51.

Himmelstein, P., and J. C. Moore. Racial attitudes and the action of Negro- and white-background figures as factors in petition signing. *Journal of Social Psychology,* 1963, **61,** 267–272.

Hoepfl, R. T., and G. P. Huber. A study of self-explicated utility models. *Behavioral Science,* 1970, **15,** 408–414.

Hoffman, P. J. The paramorphic representation of clinical judgment. *Psychological Bulletin,* 1960, **47,** 116–131.

Holman, P. A. Validation of an attitude scale as a device for predicting behavior. *Journal of Applied Psychology,* 1956, **40,** 347–349.

Holmes, D. S., and A. S. Appelbaum. Nature of prior experimental experience as a determinant of performance in a subsequent experiment. *Journal of Personality and Social Psychology*, 1970, **14**, 195–202.

Holmes, J. G., and L. H. Strickland. Choice freedom and confirmation of incentive expectancy as determinants of attitude change. *Journal of Personality and Social Psychology*, 1970, **14**, 39–45.

Holt, L. E. Resistance to persuasion on explicit beliefs as a function of commitment to and desirability of logically related beliefs. *Journal of Personality and Social Psychology*, 1970, **16**, 583–591.

Holt, L. E., and W. A. Watts. Salience of logical relationships among beliefs as a factor in persuasion. *Journal of Personality and Social Psychology*, 1969, **11**, 193–203.

Holzkamp, K. Wissenschaftstheoretische Voraussetzungen kritischemanzipatorischer Psychologie (Teil 1). *Zeitschrift fuer Sozialpsychologie*, 1970, **1**, 5–21.

Hornik, J. A. Two approaches to individual differences in an expanded prisoner's dilemma game. Unpublished master's thesis, University of Illinois, 1970.

Horowitz, I. A. Effects of volunteering, fear arousal, and number of communications on attitude change. *Journal of Personality and Social Psychology*, 1969, **11**, 34–37.

Hovland, C. I. Experimental studies in rote-learning theory, II. Reminiscence with varying speeds of syllable presentation. *Journal of Experimental Psychology*, 1938, **22**, 338–353.

Hovland, C. I. (ed.). *The Order of Presentation in Persuasion*. New Haven: Yale University Press, 1957.

Hovland, C. I., O. J. Harvey, and M. Sherif. Assimilation and contrast effects in reactions to communication and attitude change. *Journal of Abnormal and Social Psychology*, 1957, **55**, 244–252.

Hovland, C. I., and I. L. Janis (eds.). *Personality and Persuasibility*. New Haven: Yale University Press, 1959.

Hovland, C. I., I. L. Janis, and H. H. Kelley. *Communication and Persuasion*. New Haven: Yale University Press, 1953.

Hovland, C. I., and W. Mandell. An experimental comparison of conclusion-drawing by the communicator and by the audience. *Journal of Abnormal and Social Psychology*, 1952, **47**, 581–588.

Hovland, C. I., and H. A. Pritzker. Extent of opinion change as a function of amount of change advocated. *Journal of Abnormal and Social Psychology*, 1957, **34**, 257–261.

Hovland, C. I., and M. J. Rosenberg (eds.). *Attitude Organization and Change*. New Haven: Yale University Press, 1960.

Hovland, C. I., and W. Weiss. The influence of source credibility on communication effectiveness. *Public Opinion Quarterly*, 1951, **15,** 635–650.

Hovland, C. I., and W. Weiss. Transmission of information concerning concepts through positive and negative instances. *Journal of Experimental Psychology*, 1953, **45,** 175–182.

Hull, C. L. *The Principles of Behavior*. New York: Appleton-Century-Crofts, 1943.

Hull, C. L. *Essentials of Behavior*. New Haven: Yale University Press, 1951.

Humphreys, L. Acquisition and extinction of verbal expectations in a situation analogous to conditioning. *Journal of Experimental Psychology*, 1939, **25,** 294–301.

Huttenlocker, J. How certain formal reasoning problems are solved. *Journal of Verbal Learning and Verbal Behavior*, 1967, **6,** 802–808.

Insko, C. A. Verbal reinforcement of attitude. *Journal of Personality and Social Psychology*, 1965, **2,** 621–623.

Insko, C. A. *Theories of Attitude Change*. New York: Appleton-Century-Crofts, 1967.

Insko, C. A., R. R. Blake, R. B. Cialdini, and S. A. Mulaik. Attitude toward birth control and cognitive consistency: Theoretical and practical implications of survey data. *Journal of Personality and Social Psychology*, 1970, **16,** 228–237.

Insko, C. A., and R. B. Cialdini. A test of three interpretations of attitudinal verbal reinforcement. *Journal of Personality and Social Psychology*, 1969, **12,** 333–341.

Insko, C. A., and J. E. Robinson. Belief similarity versus race as determinants of reactions to Negroes by Southern white adolescents: A further test of Rokeach's theory. *Journal of Personality and Social Psychology*, 1967, **7,** 216–221.

Jaccard, J. J. Predicting social behavior from personality traits. *Journal of Experimental Research in Personality*, 1974, **7,** 358–367.

Jaccard, J. J., and A. R. Davidson. Toward an understanding of family planning behaviors: An initial investigation. *Journal of Applied Social Psychology*, 1972, **2,** 228–235.

Jaccard, J. J., and M. Fishbein. Inferential beliefs and order effects in personality impression formation. *Journal of Personality and Social Psychology*, 1975, in press.

Janis, I. L. Effects of fear arousal on attitude change: Recent developments in theory and experimental research. In L. Berkowitz (ed.), *Advances in Experimental Social Psychology* Vol. 3. New York: Academic Press, 1967, pp. 166–224.

Janis, I. L., and S. Feshbach. Effects of fear-arousing communications. *Journal of Abnormal and Social Psychology*, 1953, **48,** 78–92.

Janis, I. L., and F. Frick. The relationship between attitudes toward conclusions and errors in judging logical validity of syllogisms. *Journal of Experimental Psychology*, 1943, **33,** 73–77.

Janis, I. L., and J. B. Gilmore. The influence of incentive conditions on the success of role playing in modifying attitudes. *Journal of Personality and Social Psychology*, 1965, **1,** 17–27.

Janis, I. L., and C. I. Hovland. An overview of persuasibility research. In C. I. Hovland and I. L. Janis (eds.), *Personality and Persuasibility*. New Haven: Yale University Press, 1959, pp. 1–26.

Janis, I. L., and B. T. King. The influence of role playing on opinion change. *Journal of Abnormal and Social Psychology*, 1954, **49,** 211–218.

Janis, I. L., and L. Mann. Effectiveness of emotional role-playing in modifying smoking habits and attitudes. *Journal of Experimental Research in Personality*, 1965, **1,** 84–90.

Jersild, A. Primacy, recency, frequency, and vividness. *Journal of Experimental Psychology*, 1929, **12,** 58–70.

Johnson, D. M. *A Systematic Introduction to the Psychology of Thinking.* New York: Harper and Row, 1972.

Johnson, H. H., and J. A. Scileppi. Effects of ego-involvement conditions on attitude change to high and low credibility communicators. *Journal of Personality and Social Psychology*, 1969, **13,** 31–36.

Johnson, N. B., M. R. Middleton, and H. Tajfel. The relationship between children's preferences for and knowledge about other nations. *British Journal of Social and Clinical Psychology*, 1970, **9,** 232–240.

Johnson, R. C., C. W. Thomas, and G. Frinke. Word values, word frequency, and visual duration thresholds. *Psychological Review*, 1960, **67,** 332–342.

Johnson, T. J., R. Feigenbaum, and M. Weiby. Some determinants and consequences of the teacher's perception of causation. *Journal of Educational Psychology*, 1964, **55,** 237–246.

Jones, E. E., and J. Aneshansel. The learning and utilization of contravaluent material. *Journal of Abnormal and Social Psychology*, 1956, **53,** 27–33.

Jones, E. E., and K. E. Davis. From acts to dispositions: The attribution process in person perception. In L. Berkowitz (ed.), *Advances in Experimental Social Psychology*, Vol. 2. New York: Academic Press, 1965, pp. 219–266.

Jones, E. E., K. E. Davis, and K. J. Gergen. Role playing variations and their informational value for person perception. *Journal of Abnormal and Social Psychology*, 1961, **63,** 302–310.

Jones, E. E., and R. deCharms. Changes in social perception as a function of the personal relevance of behavior. *Sociometry*, 1957, **20,** 75–85.

Jones, E. E., and H. B. Gerard. *Foundations of Social Psychology.* New York: Wiley, 1967.

Jones, E. E., and V. A. Harris. The attribution of attitudes. *Journal of Experimental Social Psychology*, 1967, **3,** 1–24.

Jones, E. E., and R. Kohler. The effects of plausibility on the learning of controversial statements. *Journal of Abnormal and Social Psychology*, 1958, **57,** 315–320.

Jones, E. E., and R. E. Nisbett. *The Actor and the Observer: Divergent Perceptions of the Causes of Behavior.* New York: General Learning Press, 1971.

Jones, E. E., L. Rock, K. G. Shaver, G. R. Goethals, and L. M. Ward. Pattern of performance and ability attribution: An unexpected primacy effect. *Journal of Personality and Social Psychology*, 1968, **10,** 317–340.

Jones, E. E., and H. Sigall. The bogus pipeline: A new paradigm for measuring affect and attitude. *Psychological Bulletin*, 1971, **76,** 349–364.

Jones, E. E., S. Worchel, G. R. Goethals, and J. F. Grumet. Prior expectancy and behavioral extremity as determinants of attitude attribution. *Journal of Experimental Social Psychology*, 1971, **7,** 59–80.

Jones, R. A., D. E. Linder, C. A. Kiesler, M. Zanna, and J. W. Brehm. Internal states or external stimuli: Observers' attitude judgments and the dissonance-theory self-persuasion controversy. *Journal of Experimental Social Psychology*, 1968, **4,** 247–269.

Kahneman, D., and A. Tversky. Subjective probability: A judgment of representativeness. *Cognitive Psychology*, 1972, **3,** 430–454.

Kamenetsky, J., G. G. Burgess, and T. Rowan. The relative effectiveness of four attitude assessment techniques in predicting a criterion. *Educational and Psychological Measurement*, 1956, **16,** 187–194.

Kanouse, D. E. *Language, Labeling, and Attribution.* New York: General Learning Press, 1971.

Kaplan, K. J. On the ambivalence-indifference problem in attitude theory and measurement: A suggested modification of the semantic differential technique. *Psychological Bulletin*, 1972, **77,** 361–372.

Kaplan, K. J., and M. Fishbein. The source of beliefs, their saliency, and prediction of attitude. *Journal of Social Psychology*, 1969, **78,** 63–74.

Kaplan, M. F. Context effects in impression formation: The weighted average versus the meaning-change formulation. *Journal of Personality and Social Psychology*, 1971, **19,** 92–99.

Kaplan, M. F., and N. H. Anderson. Information integration theory and rein-forcement theory as approaches to interpersonal attraction. *Journal of Personality and Social Psychology*, 1973, **28**, 301–312.

Katz, D. The functional approach to the study of attitudes. *Public Opinion Quarterly*, 1960, **24**, 163–204.

Katz, D. Social psychology: Comprehensive and massive. *Contemporary Psychology*, 1971, **16**, 273–282.

Katz, D. Some final considerations about experimentation in social psychology. In C. G. McClintock (ed.), *Experimental Social Psychology*. New York: Holt, 1972, pp. 549–561.

Katz I., and L. Benjamin. Effects of white authoritarianism in biracial work groups. *Journal of Abnormal and Social Psychology*, 1960, **61**, 448–456.

Kelley, H. H. Attribution theory in social psychology. In D. Levine (ed.), *Nebraska Symposium on Motivation*. Lincoln: University of Nebraska Press, 1967, pp. 192–238.

Kelley, H. H. *Attribution in Social Interaction*. New York: General Learning Press, 1971.

Kelley, H. H. *Causal Schemata and the Attribution Process*. New York: General Learning Press, 1972.

Kelley, H. H. The processes of causal attribution. *American Psychologist*, 1973, **28**, 107–128.

Kelley, H. H., and A. J. Stahelski. The inference of intentions from moves in the prisoner's dilemma game. *Journal of Experimental Social Psychology*, 1970, **6**, 401–419.

Kelman, H. C., and C. I. Hovland. "Reinstatement" of the communicator in delayed measurement of opinion change. *Journal of Abnormal and Social Psychology,* 1953, **48**, 327–335.

Kidder, L. H., and D. T. Campbell. The indirect testing of social attitudes. In G. F. Summers (ed.), *Attitude Measurement*. Chicago: Rand McNally, 1970, pp. 333–385.

Kiesler, C. A., B. E. Collins, and N. Miller. *Attitude Change*. New York: Wiley, 1969.

Kiesler, C. A., and G. N. Goldberg. Multi-dimensional approach to the experimental study of interpersonal attraction: Effect of a blunder on the attractiveness of a competent other. *Psychological Reports*, 1968, **22**, 693–705.

Kimble, G. A. *Hilgard & Marquis' Conditioning and Learning*. New York: Appleton-Century-Crofts, 1961.

King, B. T., and I. L. Janis. Comparison of the effectiveness of improvised versus nonimprovised role-playing in producing opinion change. *Human Relations*, 1956, **9**, 177–186.

King, G. W., and J. J. Jaccard. The relation between behavioral intention and attitudinal and normative variables. Paper presented at the Speech Communication Association, New York, 1973.

Kothandapani, V. Validation of feeling, belief, and intention to act as three components of attitude and their contribution to prediction of contraceptive behavior. *Journal of Personality and Social Psychology*, 1971, **19**, 321–333.

Krech, D., and R. S. Crutchfield. *Theory and Problems in Social Psychology*. New York: McGraw-Hill, 1948.

Krech, D., R. S. Crutchfield, and E. L. Ballachey, *Individual in Society*. New York: McGraw-Hill, 1962.

Kruglanski, A. W. Much ado about the "volunteer artifacts." *Journal of Personality and Social Psychology*, 1973, **28**, 348–354.

Kruglanski, A. W. The human subject in the psychological experiment: Fact and artifact. In L. Berkowitz (ed.), *Advances in Experimental Social Psychology*, Vol. 8. New York: Academic Press, in press.

Kutner, B., C. Wilkins, and P. R. Yarrow. Verbal attitudes and overt behavior involving racial prejudice. *Journal of Abnormal and Social Psychology*, 1952, **47**, 649–652.

Lackenmeyer, C. W. Experimentation—A misunderstood methodology in psychological and social-psychological research. *American Psychologist*, 1970, **25**, 617–624.

Landy, D., and E. Aronson. Liking for an evaluator as a function of his discernment. *Journal of Personality and Social Psychology*, 1968, **9**, 133–141.

Landy, D., and E. Aronson. The influence of the character of the criminal and his victim on the decisions of simulated jurors. *Journal of Experimental Social Psychology*, 1969, **5**, 141–152.

LaPiere, R. T. Attitudes vs. actions. *Social Forces*, 1934, **13**, 230–237.

Laswell, H. D. The structure and function of communication in society. In L. Bryson (ed.), *The Communication of Ideas*. New York: Harper, 1948, pp. 37–51.

Laughlin, P. R. Selection strategies in concept attainment as a function of number of persons and stimulus display. *Journal of Experimental Psychology*, 1965, **70**, 323–327.

Laughlin, P. R. Selection strategies in concept attainment as a function of number of relevant problem attributes. *Journal of Experimental Psychology*, 1966, **71**, 773–777.

Laughlin, P. R., and R. M. Jordan. Selection strategies in conjunctive, disjunctive and biconditional concept attainment. *Journal of Experimental Psychology*, 1967, **75**, 188–193.

Lazarsfeld, P. F., B. Berelson, and H. Gaudet. *The People's Choice: How the Voter Makes Up His Mind in a Presidential Campaign.* New York: Columbia University Press, 1944.

Lee, J. C., and R. B. Tucker. An investigation of clinical judgment: A study in method. *Journal of Abnormal and Social Psychology*, 1962, **64**, 272–280.

Lefford, A. The influence of emotional subject matter on logical reasoning. *Journal of General Psychology*, 1946, **34**, 127–151.

Leventhal, H. Findings and theory in the study of fear communications. In L. Berkowitz (ed.), *Advances in Experimental Social Psychology*, Vol. 5. New York: Academic Press, 1970, pp. 119–186.

Leventhal, H., and R. P. Singer. Affect arousal and positioning of recommendations in persuasive communications. *Journal of Personality and Social Psychology*, 1966, **4**, 137–146.

Levine, J. M., and G. Murphy. The learning and forgetting of controversial material. *Journal of Abnormal and Social Psychology*, 1943, **38**, 507–517.

Levine, M. Hypothesis behavior by humans during discrimination learning. *Journal of Experimental Psychology*, 1966, **71**, 331–336.

Levinger, G. Little sandbox and big quarry: Comment on Byrne's paradigmatic spade for research on interpersonal attraction. *Representative Research in Social Psychology*, 1972, **3**, 3–18.

Lewin, K. Group decision and social change. In E. E. Maccoby, T. M. Newcomb, and E. L. Hartley (eds.), *Readings in Social Psychology*. New York: Holt, 1947, pp. 197–211.

Lewis, H. B. Studies in the principles of judgments and attitudes: IV. The operation of "prestige suggestion." *Journal of Social Psychology*, 1941, **14**, 229–256.

Lewit, D. W., and P. J. Shanley. Prejudice and the learning of biracial influence structures. *Psychonomic Science*, 1969, **17**, 93–95.

Lichtenstein, E., and W. H. Craine. The importance of subjective evaluation of reinforcement in verbal conditioning. *Journal of Experimental Research in Personality*, 1969, **3**, 214–220.

Likert, R. A technique for the measurement of attitudes. *Archives of Psychology*, 1932, No. 140.

Linder, D. E., J. Cooper, and E. E. Jones. Decision freedom as a determinant of the role of incentive magnitude in attitude change. *Journal of Personality and Social Psychology*, 1967, **6**, 245–254.

Linn, L. S. Verbal attitudes and overt behavior: A study of racial discrimination. *Social Forces*, 1965, **44**, 353–364.

Lopes, L. L. A unified integration model for "prior expectancy and behavioral extremity as determinants of attitude attribution." *Journal of Experimental Social Psychology*, 1972, **8**, 156–160.

Lott, A. J., and B. E. Lott. A learning theory approach to interpersonal attitudes. In A. G. Greenwald, T. C. Brock, and T. M. Ostrom (eds.), *Psychological Foundations of Attitudes.* New York: Academic Press, 1968, pp. 67–88.

Lott, A. J., B. E. Lott, and M. L. Walsh. Learning of paired associates relevant to differentially liked persons. *Journal of Personality and Social Psychology*, 1970, **16**, 274–283.

Lott, B. E. Attitude formation: The development of a color-preference response through mediated generalization. *Journal of Abnormal and Social Psychology*, 1955, **50**, 321–326.

Lowe, C. A., and J. W. Goldstein. Reciprocal liking and attributions of ability: Mediating effects of perceived intent and personal involvement. *Journal of Personality and Social Psychology*, 1970, **16**, 291–297.

Lutz, R. J. Cognitive change and attitude change: A validation study. Unpublished doctoral dissertation, University of Illinois, 1973.

Maier, N.R.F. *Principles of Human Relations.* New York: Wiley, 1952.

Malof, M., and A. J. Lott. Ethnocentrism and the acceptance of Negro support in a group pressure situation. *Journal of Abnormal and Social Psychology*, 1962, **65**, 254–258.

Malpass, R. S. Effects of attitude on learning and memory: The influence of instruction-induced sets. *Journal of Experimental Social Psychology*, 1969, **5**, 441–453.

Maltzman, I. On the training of originality. *Psychological Review*, 1960, **67**, 229–242.

Maltzman, I., W. Bogartz, and L. Breger. A procedure for increasing word association originality and its transfer effects. *Journal of Experimental Psychology*, 1958, **56**, 392–398.

Maltzman, I., I. Simon, D. Raskin, and L. Licht. Experimental studies in the training of originality. *Psychological Monographs*, 1960, **74**, 5, Whole No. 493.

Mandler, G. Verbal learning. In T. M. Newcomb (ed.), *New Directions in Psychology*, Vol. 3. New York: Holt, 1967, pp. 1–50.

Mann, J. H. The relationship between cognitive, affective, and behavioral aspects of racial prejudice. *Journal of Social Psychology*, 1959, **49**, 223–228.

Mann, L. The effects of emotional role playing on smoking attitudes and behavior. *Journal of Experimental Social Psychology*, 1967, **3**, 334–348.

Mascaro, G. F. Correspondence between evaluative expectations and attitudes. *Australian Journal of Psychology*, 1970, **22**, 115–125.

Mascaro, G. F., and J. A. Lopez. The effect of delayed judgmental similarity on evaluative attraction. *Psychonomic Science*, 1970, **19**, 229–230.

Matefy, R. E. Attitude change induced by role playing as a function of improvisation and role-taking skill. *Journal of Personality and Social Psychology*, 1972, **24,** 343–350.

Matlin, M. W. Response competition as a mediating factor in the frequency-affect relationship. *Journal of Personality and Social Psychology*, 1970, **16,** 536–552.

McArdle, J. B. Positive and negative communications and subsequent attitude and behavior change in alcoholics. Unpublished doctoral dissertation, University of Illinois, 1972.

McArthur, L. A. The how and what of why: Some determinants and consequences of causal attribution. *Journal of Personality and Social Psychology*, 1972, **22,** 171–193.

McCroskey, J. C. The effects of evidence as an inhibitor of counter persuasion. *Speech Monographs*, 1970, **37,** 188–194.

McEwen, W. J., and B. S. Greenberg. Effects of communication assertion intensity. *Journal of Communication*, 1969, **19,** 257–265.

McEwen, W. J., and B. S. Greenberg. The effects of message intensity on receiver evaluations of source, message, and topic. *Journal of Communication*, 1970, **20,** 340–350.

McGuire, W. J. Cognitive consistency and attitude change. *Journal of Abnormal and Social Psychology*, 1960, **60,** 345–353. (a)

McGuire, W. J. Direct and indirect persuasive effects of dissonance producing messages. *Journal of Abnormal and Social Psychology*, 1960, **60,** 354–358. (b)

McGuire, W. J. A syllogistic analysis of cognitive relationships. In C. I. Hovland and M. J. Rosenberg (eds.), *Attitude Organization and Change*. New Haven: Yale University Press, 1960, pp. 65–111. (c)

McGuire, W. J. Inducing resistance to persuasion: Some contemporary approaches. In L. Berkowitz (ed.), *Advances in Experimental Social Psychology*, Vol. 1. New York: Academic Press, 1964, pp. 191–229.

McGuire, W. J. Some impending reorientations in social psychology. *Journal of Experimental Social Psychology*, 1967, **3,** 124–139.

McGuire, W. J. Personality and susceptibility to social influence. In E. F. Borgatta and W. W. Lambert (eds.), *Handbook of Personality Theory and Research*. Chicago: Rand NcNally, 1968, pp. 1130–1187.

McGuire, W. J. The nature of attitudes and attitude change. In G. Lindzey and E. Aronson (eds.), *The Handbook of Social Psychology*, 2nd ed., Vol. 3. Reading, Mass.: Addison-Wesley, 1969, pp. 136–314.

McGuire, W. J. The yin and yang of progress in social psychology: Seven koan. *Journal of Personality and Social Psychology*, 1973, **26,** 446–456.

McGuire, W. J., and D. Papageorgis. The relative efficacy of various types of prior belief-defense in producing immunity against persuasion. *Journal of Abnormal and Social Psychology*, 1961, **62**, 327–337.

McLaughlin, B. Similarity, recall, and appraisal of others. *Journal of Personality*, 1970, **38**, 106–116.

McLaughlin, B. Effects of similarity and likableness on attraction and recall. *Journal of Personality and Social Psychology*, 1971, **20**, 65–69.

McNeel, S. P., and D. M. Messick. A Bayesian analysis of subjective probabilities of interpersonal relationships. *Acta Psychologica*, 1970, **34**, 311–321.

Meehl, P. E. A comparison of clinicians with five statistical methods of identifying psychotic MMPI profiles. *Journal of Counseling Psychology*, 1959, **6**, 102–109.

Meehl, P. E. Theory testing in psychology and physics: A methodological paradox. *Philosophy of Science*, 1967, **34**, 103–115.

Mettee, D. R. Changes in liking as a function of the magnitude and affect of sequential evaluations. *Journal of Experimental Social Psychology*, 1971, **7**, 157–172.

Mettee, D. R., and P. C. Wilkins. When similarity "hurts": The effects of perceived ability and a humorous blunder upon interpersonal attractiveness. *Journal of Personality and Social Psychology*, 1972, **22**, 246–258.

Meyer, M. Experimental studies in the psychology of music. *American Journal of Psychology*, 1903, **14**, 456–476.

Mezei, L. Perceived social pressure as an explanation of shifts in the relative influence of race and belief on prejudice across social situations. *Journal of Personality and Social Psychology*, 1971, **19**, 69–81.

Miller, A. G. Role of physical attractiveness in impression formation. *Psychonomic Science*, 1970, **19**, 241–243.

Miller, A. G. (ed.). *The Social Psychology of Psychological Research*. New York: The Free Press, 1972.

Miller, G. A. The magical number seven; plus or minus two: Some limits on our capacity for processing information. *Psychological Review*, 1956, **63**, 81–97.

Millman, S. Anxiety, comprehension, and susceptibility to social influence. *Journal of Personality and Social Psychology*, 1968, **9**, 251–256.

Minard, R. D. Race relations in the Pocahontas Coal Field. *Journal of Social Issues*, 1952, **8**, 29–44.

Mittelstaedt, R. A dissonance approach to repeat purchasing behavior. *Journal of Marketing Research*, 1969, **6**, 444–446.

Moore, H. T., and A. R. Gilliland. The immediate and long time effects of classical and popular phonograph selections. *Journal of Applied Psychology*, 1924, **8**, 309–323.

Moreno, J. L. *Psychodrama*, Vol. 1. New York: Beacon House, 1946.

Morgan, W. J., and J. T. Morton. The distortion of syllogistic reasoning produced by personal convictions. *Journal of Social Psychology*, 1944, **20**, 39–59.

Nel, E., R. Helmreich, and E. Aronson. Opinion change in the advocate as a function of the persuasibility of his audience: A clarification of the meaning of dissonance. *Journal of Personality and Social Psychology*, 1969, **12**, 117–124.

Nelson, E. Attitudes. *Journal of General Psychology*, 1939, **21**, 367–436.

Nemeth, C. Effects of free versus constrained behavior on attraction between people. *Journal of Personality and Social Psychology*, 1970, **15**, 302–311.

Newcomb, T. M. An approach to the study of communicative acts. *Psychological Review*, 1953, **60**, 393–404.

Newcomb, T. M. The prediction of interpersonal attraction. *American Psychologist*, 1956, **11**, 575–586.

Newton, N., and M. Newton. Relationship of ability to breast feed and maternal attitudes toward breast feeding. *Pediatrics*, 1950, **5**, 869–875.

Norman, W. T. Toward an adequate taxonomy of personality attributes: Replicated factor structure in peer nomination personality ratings. *Journal of Abnormal and Social Psychology*, 1963, **66**, 574–583.

Novak, D. W., and M. J. Lerner. Rejection as a consequence of perceived similarity. *Journal of Personality and Social Psychology*, 1968, **9**, 147–152.

Orne, M. T. On the social psychology of the psychological experiment: With particular reference to demand characteristics and their implications. *American Psychologist*, 1962, **17**, 776–783

Orne, M. T. Demand characteristics and the concept of quasi-controls. In R. Rosenthal and R. L. Rosnow (eds.), *Artifact in Behavioral Research*. New York: Academic Press, 1969, pp. 143–179.

Osgood, C. E. The nature and measurement of meaning. *Psychological Bulletin*, 1952, **49**, 197–237.

Osgood, C. E., and D. C. Ferguson. The semantic effects of word combination. Reported in C. E. Osgood, G. J. Suci, and P. H. Tannenbaum, *The Measurement of Meaning*. Urbana: University of Illinois Press, 1957, pp. 275–284.

Osgood, C. E., G. J. Suci, and P. H. Tannenbaum. *The Measurement of Meaning*. Urbana: University of Illinois Press, 1957.

Osgood, C. E., and P. H. Tannenbaum. The principle of congruity in the prediction of attitude change. *Psychological Review*, 1955, **62**, 42–55.

Oshikawa, S. The theory of cognitive dissonance and experimental research. *Journal of Marketing Research*, 1968, **5**, 429–430.

Oskamp, S. How clinicians make decisions from the MMPI: An empirical study. Paper presented at the American Psychological Association, St. Louis, 1962.

Osterhouse, R. A., and T. C. Brock. Distraction increases yielding to propaganda by inhibiting counter-arguing. *Journal of Personality and Social Psychology*, 1970, **15,** 344–358.

Ostrom, T. M. The emergence of attitude theory: 1930–1950. In A. G. Greenwald, T. C. Brock, and T. M. Ostrom (eds.), *Psychological Foundations of Attitudes.* New York: Academic Press, 1968, pp. 1–32.

Ostrom, T. M. The relationship between the affective, behavioral, and cognitive components of attitude. *Journal of Experimental Social Psychology*, 1969, **5,** 12–30.

Page, M. M. Social psychology of a classical conditioning of attitudes experiment. *Journal of Personality and Social Psychology*, 1969, **11,** 177–186.

Page, M. M. Role of demand awareness in the communicator credibility effect. *Journal of Social Psychology*, 1970, **82,** 57–66. (a)

Page, M. M. Demand awareness, subject sophistication, and the effectiveness of a verbal "reinforcement." *Journal of Personality*, 1970, **38,** 287–301. (b)

Page, M. M., and R. J. Scheidt. The elusive weapons effect: Demand awareness, evaluation apprehension, and slightly sophisticated subjects. *Journal of Personality and Social Psychology*, 1971, **20,** 304–318.

Passini, F. T., and W. T. Norman. A universal conception of personality structure? *Journal of Personality and Social Psychology*, 1966, **4,** 44–49.

Peabody, D. Trait inferences: Evaluative and descriptive aspects. *Journal of Personality and Social Psychology Monograph*, 1967, **7,** Whole No. 644.

Peabody, D. Evaluative and descriptive aspects in personality perception: A reappraisal. *Journal of Personality and Social Psychology*, 1970, **16,** 639–646.

Pelz, E. B. Discussion, decision, commitment and consensus in "group decision." *Human Relations*, 1955, **8,** 251–274.

Peterson, C. R., and L. R. Beach. Man as an intuitive statistician. *Psychological Bulletin*, 1967, **68,** 29–46.

Peterson, C. R., and A. J. Miller. Sensitivity of subjective probability revision. *Journal of Experimental Psychology*, 1965, **70,** 117–121.

Peterson, C. R., Z. J. Ulehla, A. J. Miller, L. E. Bourne, Jr., and D. W. Stilson. Internal consistency of subjective probabilities. *Journal of Experimental Psychology*, 1965, **70,** 526–533.

Peterson, D. R. Scope and generality of verbally defined personality factors. *Psychological Review*, 1965, **72,** 48–59.

Phillips, L. D. Some components of probabilistic inference. Unpublished doctoral dissertation, University of Michigan, 1966.

Phillips, L. D., and W. Edwards. Conservatism in a simple probability inference task. *Journal of Experimental Psychology*, 1966, **72,** 346–354.

Piaget, J. *The Moral Judgment of the Child.* New York: Harcourt, Brace, 1932.

Piliavin, J. A., I. M. Piliavin, E. P. Loewenton, C. McCauley, and P. Hammond. An observer's reproductions of dissonance effects: The right answers for the wrong reason? *Journal of Personality and Social Psychology*, 1969, **13,** 98–106.

Pilisuk, M., and P. Skolnick. Inducing trust: A test of the Osgood proposal. *Journal of Personality and Social Psychology*, 1968, **8,** 121–133.

Pollack, I. Action selection and the Yntema-Torgerson worth function. In E. Bennett (ed.), *Information System Science and Engineering: Proceedings of the First Congress on the Informational Systems Sciences.* New York: McGraw-Hill, 1964.

Poppleton, P., and G. Pilkington. The measurement of religious attitudes in a university population. *British Journal of Social and Clinical Psychology*, 1963, **2,** 20–36.

Posavac, E. J., and H. C. Triandis. Personality characteristics, race and grades as determinants of interpersonal attitudes. *Journal of Social Psychology*, 1968, **76,** 227–242.

Postman, L., W. O. Jenkins, and D. L. Postman. An experimental comparison of active recall and recognition. *American Journal of Psychology*, 1948, **61,** 511–519.

Potter, H. W., and H. R. Klein. On nursing behavior. *Psychiatry*, 1957, **20,** 39–46.

Press, A. N., W. H. Crockett, and P. S. Rosenkrantz. Cognitive complexity and the learning of balanced and unbalanced social structures. *Journal of Personality*, 1970, **37,** 541–553.

Rabbie, J. M., J. W. Brehm, and A. R. Cohen. Verbalization and reactions to cognitive dissonance. *Journal of Personality*, 1959, **27,** 404–417.

Raven, B. H., and H. T. Eachus. Cooperation and competition in means-independent triads. *Journal of Abnormal and Social Psychology*, 1963, **67,** 307–316.

Raven, B. H., and J. I. Shaw. Interdependence and group problem-solving in the triad. *Journal of Personality and Social Psychology*, 1970, **14,** 157–165.

Reuchelle, R. C. An experimental study of audience recognition of emotional and intellectual appeals in persuasion. *Speech Monographs*, 1958, **25,** 49–58.

Rhine, R. J. A concept-formation approach to attitude acquisition. *Psychological Review*, 1958, **65,** 362–370.

Rhine, R. J., and L. J. Severance. Ego-involvement, discrepancy, source credibility, and attitude change. *Journal of Personality and Social Psychology*, 1970, **16,** 175–190.

Roberge, J. J. A reexamination of the interpretations of errors in formal syllogistic reasoning. *Psychonomic Science,* 1970, **19,** 331–333.

Robinson, J. E., and C. A. Insko. Attributed belief similarity-dissimilarity versus race as determinants of prejudice: A further test of Rokeach's theory. *Journal of Experimental Research in Personality,* 1969, **4,** 72–77.

Robinson, J. P., and P. R. Shaver. *Measures of Social Psychological Attitudes.* Ann Arbor, Mich.: Institute for Social Research, 1969.

Rogers, R. W., and D. L. Thistlethwaite. Effects of fear arousal and reassurance on attitude change. *Journal of Personality and Social Psychology,* 1970, **15,** 227–233.

Rokeach, M. (ed.). *The Open and Closed Mind.* New York: Basic Books, 1960.

Rokeach, M. Belief versus race as determinants of social distance: Comment on Triandis' paper. *Journal of Abnormal and Social Psychology,* 1961, **62,** 187–188.

Rokeach, M. *Beliefs, Attitudes, and Values.* San Francisco: Jossey-Bass, 1968.

Rokeach, M. and L. Mezei. Race and shared belief as factors in social choice. *Science,* 1966, **151,** 167–172.

Rokeach, M., and P. Kliejunas. Behavior as a function of attitude-toward-object and attitude-toward-situation. *Journal of Personality and Social Psychology,* 1972, **22,** 194–201.

Rokeach, M., P. W. Smith, and R. I. Evans. Two kinds of prejudice or one? In M. Rokeach (ed.), *The Open and Closed Mind.* New York: Basic Books, 1960, pp. 132–168.

Rosenberg, M. J. Cognitive structure and attitudinal affect. *Journal of Abnormal and Social Psychology,* 1956, **53,** 367–372.

Rosenberg, M. J. An analysis of affective-cognitive consistency. In C. I. Hovland and M. J. Rosenberg (eds.), *Attitude Organization and Change.* New Haven: Yale University Press, 1960, pp. 15–64.

Rosenberg, M. J. Inconsistency arousal and reduction in attitude change. In I. D. Steiner and M. Fishbein (eds.), *Current Studies in Social Psychology.* New York: Holt, 1965, pp. 121–134. (a)

Rosenberg, M. J. When dissonance fails: On eliminating evaluation apprehension from attitude measurement. *Journal of Personality and Social Psychology,* 1965, **1,** 28–42. (b)

Rosenberg, M. J. The conditions and consequences of evaluation apprehension. In R. Rosenthal and R. L. Rosnow (eds.), *Artifact in Behavioral Research.* New York: Academic Press, 1969, pp. 280–349.

Rosenberg, M. J. and C. I. Hovland. Cognitive, affective, and behavioral components of attitudes. In C. I. Hovland and M. J. Rosenberg (eds.), *Attitude Organization and Change.* New Haven: Yale University Press, 1960, pp. 1–14.

Rosenberg, S., C. Nelson, and P. S. Vivekananthan. A multi-dimensional approach to the structure of personality impressions. *Journal of Personality and Social Psychology*, 1968, **9**, 283–294.

Rosenberg, S., and K. Olshan. Evaluative and descriptive aspects in personality perception. *Journal of Personality and Social Psychology*, 1970, **16**, 619–626.

Rosenthal, R. *Experimenter Effects in Behavioral Research*. New York: Appleton-Century-Crofts, 1966.

Rosenthal, R. Experimenter expectancy and the reassuring nature of the null hypothesis decision procedure. *Psychological Bulletin Monograph*, 1968, **70**, 30–47.

Rosenthal, R. Interpersonal expectations: Effects of the experimenter's hypothesis. In R. Rosenthal and R. L. Rosnow (eds.), *Artifact in Behavioral Research*. New York: Academic Press, 1969, pp. 181–277.

Rosenthal, R., and R. L. Rosnow (eds.), *Artifact in Behavioral Research*. New York: Academic Press, 1969.

Rosnow, R. L., and E. J. Robinson (eds.). *Experiments in Persuasion*. New York: Academic Press, 1967.

Rosnow, R. L., and J. M. Suls. Reactive effects of pretesting in attitude research. *Journal of Personality and Social Psychology*, 1970, **15**, 338–343.

Rossomando, N. P., and W. Weiss. Attitude change effects of timing and amount of payment for counterattitudinal behavior. *Journal of Personality and Social Psychology*, 1970, **14**, 32–38.

Rotter, J. B. *Social Learning and Clinical Psychology*. Englewood Cliffs, N.J.: Prentice-Hall, 1954.

Rubin, Z., and R. B. Zajonc. Structural bias and generalization in the learning of social structures. *Journal of Personality*, 1969, **37**, 310–324.

Rule, B. G., and J. Renner. Involvement and group effects on opinion change. *Journal of Social Psychology*, 1968, **76**, 189–198.

Ryan, T. A. *Intentional Behavior: An Approach to Human Motivation*. New York: Ronald, 1970.

Sachs, D. H., and D. Byrne. Differential conditioning of evaluative responses to neutral stimuli through association with attitude statements. *Journal of Experimental Research in Personality*, 1970, **4**, 181–185.

Sagi, P. C., D. W. Olmstead, and F. Atelsek. Predicting maintenance of membership in small groups. *Journal of Abnormal and Social Psychology*, 1955, **51**, 308–311.

Sandell, R. G. Effects of attitudinal and situational factors on reported choice behavior. *Journal of Marketing Research*, 1968, **5**, 405–408.

Sarason, I. G. Verbal learning, modeling, and juvenile delinquency. *American Psychologist*, 1968, **23**, 245–266.

Sarbin, T. R., and V. L. Allen. Role enactment, audience feedback, and attitude change. *Sociometry*, 1964, **27**, 183–193.

Sarnoff, I. Psychoanalytic theory and social attitudes. *Public Opinion Quarterly*, 1960, **24**, 251–279.

Savage, L. J. *The Foundations of Statistics*. New York: Wiley, 1954.

Schachter, S. The interaction of cognitive and physiological determinants of emotional state. In L. Berkowitz (ed.), *Advances in Experimental Social Psychology*, Vol. 1. New York: Academic Press, 1964, pp. 49–80.

Schachter, S. Some extraordinary facts about obese humans and rats. *American Psychologist*, 1971, **26**, 129–144.

Scheibe, K. E. *Beliefs and Values*. New York: Holt, 1970.

Schmidt, C. F. Personality impression formation as a function of relatedness of information and length of set. *Journal of Personality and Social Psychology*, 1969, **12**, 6–11.

Schwartz, S. Trial-by-trial analysis of processes in simple and disjunctive concept attainment tasks. *Journal of Experimental Psychology*, 1966, **72**, 456–465.

Schwartz, S. H., and R. C. Tessler. A test of a model for reducing measured attitude-behavior discrepancies. *Journal of Personality and Social Psychology*, 1972, **24**, 225–236.

Scott, W. A. Attitude change through reward of verbal behavior. *Journal of Abnormal and Social Psychology*, 1957, **55**, 72–75.

Scott, W. A. Attitude change by response reinforcement: Replication and extension. *Sociometry*, 1959, **22**, 328–335.

Scott, W. A. Attitude measurement. In G. Lindzey and E. Aronson (eds.), *The Handbook of Social Psychology*, 2nd ed., Vol. 2. Reading, Mass.: Addison-Wesley, 1968, pp. 204–273.

Scott, W. A. Structure of natural cognitions. *Journal of Personality and Social Psychology*, 1969, **12**, 261–278.

Sechrest, L. Testing, measuring, and assessing people. In E. F. Borgatta and W. W. Lambert (eds.), *Handbook of Personality Theory and Research*. Chicago: Rand McNally, 1968, pp. 529–625.

Sereno, K. K., and C. D. Mortensen. The effects of ego-involved attitudes on conflict negotiation in dyads. *Speech Monographs*, 1969, **36**, 8–12.

Shaver, K. G. Defensive attribution: Effects of severity and relevance on the responsibility assigned for an accident. *Journal of Personality and Social Psychology*, 1970, **14**, 101–113. (a)

Shaver, K. G. Redress and conscientiousness in the attribution of responsibility for accidents. *Journal of Experimental Social Psychology*, 1970, **6**, 100–110. (b)

Shaw, J. I., and P. Skolnik. Attribution of responsibility for a happy accident. *Journal of Personality and Social Psychology*, 1971, **18**, 380–383.

Shaw, M. E., and H. T. Reitan. Attribution of responsibility as a basis for sanctioning behavior. *British Journal of Social and Clinical Psychology*, 1969, **8**, 217–226.

Shaw, M. E., and J. L. Sulzer. An empirical test of Heider's levels in attribution of responsibility. *Journal of Abnormal and Social Psychology*, 1964, **69**, 39–46.

Shaw, M. E., and J. M. Wright. *Scales for the Measurement of Attitudes*. New York: McGraw-Hill, 1967.

Shepherd, J. W., and A. J. Bagley. The effects of biographical information and order of presentation on the judgment of an aggressive action. *British Journal of Social and Clinical Psychology*, 1970, **9**, 177–179.

Sherif, C. W., M. Sherif, and R. E. Nebergall. *Attitude and Attitude Change: The Social Judgment-Involvement Approach*. Philadelphia: Saunders, 1965.

Sherif, M., and C. I. Hovland. *Social Judgment: Assimilation and Contrast Effects in Communication and Attitude Change*. New Haven: Yale University Press, 1961.

Sherif, M., and C. W. Sherif. The own categories procedure in attitude research. In M. Fishbein (ed.), *Readings in Attitude Theory and Measurement*. New York: Wiley, 1967, pp. 190–198.

Sherman, S. J. Effects of choice and incentive on attitude change in a discrepant behavior situation. *Journal of Personality and Social Psychology*, 1970, **15**, 245–252. (a)

Sherman, S. J. Attitudinal effects of unforeseen consequences. *Journal of Personality and Social Psychology*, 1970, **16**, 510–520. (b)

Sheth, J. N., and W. W. Talarzyk. Perceived instrumentality and value importance as determinants of attitudes. *Journal of Marketing Research*, 1972, **9**, 6–9.

Sigall, H. Effects of competence and consensual validation on a communicator's liking for the audience. *Journal of Personality and Social Psychology*, 1970, **16**, 251–258.

Sigall, H., and E. Aronson. Opinion change and the gain-loss model of interpersonal attraction. *Journal of Experimental Social Psychology*, 1967, **3**, 178–188.

Sigall, H., and E. Aronson. Liking for an evaluator as a function of her physical attractiveness and nature of the evaluations. *Journal of Experimental Social Psychology*, 1969, **5**, 93–100.

Silverman, I., and C. R. Regula. Evaluation apprehension, demand characteristics, and the effect of distraction on persuasibility. *Journal of Social Psychology*, 1968, **75**, 273–281.

Silverman, I., and A. D. Shulman. A conceptual model of artifact in attitude change studies. *Sociometry*, 1970, **33**, 97–107.

Singer, R. D. Verbal conditioning and generalization of prodemocratic responses. *Journal of Abnormal and Social Psychology*, 1961, **63**, 43–46.

Singer, S. Factors related to participant's memory of a conversation. *Journal of Personality*, 1969, **37**, 93–109.

Skinner, B. F. *Verbal Behavior*. New York: Appleton-Century-Crofts, 1957.

Slovic, P., D. Fleissner, and W. S. Bauman. Analyzing the use of information in investment decision making: A methodological proposal. *The Journal of Business*, 1972, **45**, 283–301.

Slovic, P., and S. Lichtenstein. Comparison of Bayesian and regression approaches to the study of information processing in judgment. *Organizational Behavior and Human Performance*, 1971, **6**, 649–744.

Smith, E. W. L., and T. R. Dixon. Verbal conditioning as a function of race of the experimenter and prejudice of the subject. *Journal of Experimental Social Psychology*, 1968, **4**, 285–301.

Smith, M. B., J. S. Bruner, and R. W. White. *Opinions and Personality*. New York: Wiley, 1956.

Spence, K. W. *Behavior Theory and Conditioning*. New Haven: Yale University Press, 1956.

Staats, A. W. Social behaviorism and human motivation: Principles of the attitude-reinforcer-discriminative system. In A. G. Greenwald, T. C. Brock, and T. M. Ostrom (eds.), *Psychological Foundations of Attitudes*. New York: Academic Press, 1968, pp. 33–66.

Staats, A. W., and C. K. Staats. Attitudes established by classical conditioning. *Journal of Abnormal and Social Psychology*, 1958, **57**, 37–40.

Staats, A. W., and C. K. Staats. Effect of number of trials on the language conditioning of meaning. *Journal of General Psychology*, 1959, **61**, 211–223.

Staats, C. K., and A. W. Staats. Meaning established by classical conditioning. *Journal of Experimental Psychology*, 1957, **54**, 74–80.

Staats, C. K., A. W. Staats, and W. G. Heard. Attitude development and ratio of reinforcement. *Sociometry*, 1960, **23**, 338–350.

Stalling, R. S. Personality similarity and evaluative meaning as conditioners of attraction. *Journal of Personality and Social Psychology*, 1970, **14**, 77–82.

Stein, D. D., J. A. Hardyck, and M. B. Smith. Race and belief: An open and shut case. *Journal of Personality and Social Psychology*, 1965, **1**, 281–290.

Steiner, I. D. Perceived freedom. In L. Berkowitz (ed.), *Advances in Experimental Social Psychology*, Vol. 5. New York: Academic Press, 1970, pp. 187–248.

Steiner, I. D. *Group Process and Productivity*. New York: Academic Press, 1972.

Steiner, I. D., and W. I. Field. Role assignment and interpersonal influence. *Journal of Abnormal and Social Psychology*, 1960, **61**, 239–245.

Stewart, R. H. Effect of continuous responding on the order effect in personality impression formation. *Journal of Personality and Social Psychology*, 1965, **1,** 161–165.

Storms, M. D., and R. E. Nisbett. Insomnia and the attribution process. *Journal of Personality and Social Psychology*, 1970, **16,** 319–328.

Streufert, S., and S. C. Streufert. Effects of conceptual structure, failure, and success on attribution of causality and interpersonal attitudes. *Journal of Personality and Social Psychology*, 1969, **11,** 138–147.

Stricker, L. J., S. Messick, and D. N. Jackson. Evaluating deception in psychological research. *Psychological Bulletin*, 1969, **71,** 343–351.

Suedfeld, P., Y. M. Epstein, E. Buchanan, and P. B. Landon. Effects of set on the "effects of mere exposure." *Journal of Personality and Social Psychology*, 1971, **17,** 121–123.

Summers, D. A., J. D. Taliaferro, and D. J. Fletcher. Subjective vs. objective description of judgment policy. *Psychonomic Science*, 1970, **18,** 249–250.

Summers, S. A. The learning of responses to multiple weighted cues. *Journal of Experimental Psychology*, 1962, **64,** 29–34.

Szalay, L. B., C. Windle, and D. A. Lysne. Attitude measurement by free verbal associations. *Journal of Social Psychology*, 1970, **82,** 43–55.

Tarter, D. E. Toward prediction of attitude-action discrepancy. *Social Forces*, 1969, **47,** 398–405.

Taylor, D. A., I. Altman, and R. Sorrentino. Interpersonal exchange as a function of rewards and costs and situational factors: Expectancy confirmation-disconfirmation. *Journal of Experimental Social Psychology*, 1969, **5,** 324–339.

Tesser, A. Trait similarity and trait evaluation as correlates of attraction. *Psychonomic Science*, 1969, **15,** 319–320.

Thomas, K., and M. Tuck. Some applications of Fishbein scaling. *European Journal of Social Psychology*, in press.

Thurstone, L. L. The measurement of attitudes. *Journal of Abnormal and Social Psychology*, 1931, **26,** 249–269.

Thurstone, L. L., and E. J. Chave. *The measurement of Attitude*. Chicago: University of Chicago Press, 1929.

Tittle, C. R., and R. J. Hill. Attitude measurement and prediction of behavior: An evaluation of conditions and measurement techniques. *Sociometry*, 1967, **30,** 199–213.

Tolman, E. C. *Purposive Behavior in Animals and Men*. New York: Appleton-Century-Crofts, 1932.

Triandis, H. C. A note on Rokeach's theory of prejudice. *Journal of Abnormal and Social Psychology*, 1961, **62,** 184–186.

Triandis, H. C. Exploratory factor analyses of the behavioral component of social attitudes. *Journal of Abnormal and Social Psychology*, 1964, **68**, 420–430.

Triandis, H. C. Towards an analysis of the components of interpersonal attitudes. In C. W. Sherif and M. Sherif (eds.), *Attitudes, Ego Involvement, and Change.* New York: Wiley, 1967, pp. 227–270.

Triandis, H. C. *Attitudes and Attitude Change.* New York: Wiley, 1971.

Triandis, H. C., and E. E. Davis. Race and belief as determinants of behavioral intentions. *Journal of Personality and Social Psychology*, 1965, **2**, 715–725.

Triandis, H. C., and M. Fishbein. Cognitive interaction in person perception. *Journal of Abnormal and Social Psychology*, 1963, **67**, 446–453.

Triandis, H. C., M. Fishbein, E. Hall, A. V. Shanmugam, and Y. Tanaka. Affect and behavioral intentions. In A. K. P. Sinha, H. K. Misra, A. K. Kanth, and K. S. Rao (eds.), *Contributions to Psychology.* New Delhi: Institute for Social and Psychological Research, 1968, pp. 28–52.

Triandis, H. C., R. S. Malpass, and A. R. Davidson. Cross-cultural psychology. In B. J. Siegel (ed.), *Biennial Review of Anthropology 1971.* Stanford, Cal.: Stanford University Press, 1972, pp. 1–84.

Triandis, H. C., Y. Tanaka, and A. V. Shanmugam. Interpersonal attitudes among American, Indian and Japanese students. *International Journal of Psychology*, 1966, **1**, 177–206.

Triandis, H. C., and L. M. Triandis. Race, social class, religion and nationality as determinants of social distance. *Journal of Abnormal and Social Psychology*, 1960, **61**, 110–118.

Triandis, H. C., and L. M. Triandis. Some studies of social distance. In I. D. Steiner and M. Fishbein (eds.), *Recent Studies in Social Psychology.* New York: Holt, 1965, pp. 207–217.

Trope, Y. The informational values of behaviors and social situations: A Bayesian analysis of attribution processes. Paper presented at the Midwestern Psychological Association meetings, 1973.

Trope, Y., and E. Burnstein. Processing the information contained in another's behavior. Unpublished manuscript, University of Michigan, 1973.

Tulving, E., and S. A. Madigan. Memory and verbal learning. *Annual Review of Psychology*, 1970, **21**, 437–484.

Tupes, E. C., and R. E. Christal. Recurrent personality factors based on trait ratings. *USAF ASD, Technical Report*, 1961, No. 61–97.

Tversky, A. Intransitivity of preferences. *Psychological Review*, 1969, **76**, 31–48.

Uleman, J. S. Awareness and motivation in generalized verbal conditioning. *Journal of Experimental Research in Personality*, 1971, **5**, 257–267.

Uleman, J. S., and G. R. VandenBos. Generalized verbal conditioning: Some effects of the meaning and delay of reinforcement on awareness and conditioning. *Journal of Experimental Research in Personality*, 1971, **5**, 49–56.

Valins, S. Cognitive effects of false heart-rate feedback. *Journal of Personality and Social Psychology*, 1966, **4**, 400–408.

Valins, S., and R. E. Nisbett. *Attributional Processes in the Development and Treatment of Emotional Disorders*. New York: General Learning Press, 1971.

Vroom, V. H. Ego-involvement, job satisfaction, and job performance. *Personnel Psychology*, 1962, **15**, 159–177.

Vroom, V. H. *Work and motivation*. New York: Wiley, 1964.

Wallace, W. P. Review of the historical, empirical, and theoretical status of the von Restorff phenomenon. *Psychological Bulletin*, 1965, **63**, 410–424.

Walster, E. The temporal sequence of post-decisional processes. In L. Festinger (ed.), *Conflict, Decision, and Dissonance*. Stanford, Cal.: Stanford University Press, 1964, pp. 112–127.

Walster, E. Assignment of reponsibility for an accident. *Journal of Personality and Social Psychology*, 1966, **3**, 73–79.

Walster, E. "Second-guessing" important events. *Human Relations*, 1967, **20**, 239–250.

Walster, E., V. Aronson, D. Abrahams, and L. Rottman. Importance of physical attractiveness in dating behavior. *Journal of Personality and Social Psychology*, 1966, **4**, 508–516.

Walster, E., E. Berscheid, and G. W. Walster. New directions in equity research. *Journal of Personality and Social Psychology*, 1973, **25**, 151–176.

Waly, P., and S. W. Cook. Effect of attitude on judgments of plausibility. *Journal of Personality and Social Psychology*, 1965, **2**, 745–749.

Warner, L. G., and M. L. DeFleur. Attitude as an interactional concept: Social constraint and social distance as intervening variables between attitudes and action. *American Sociological Review*, 1969, **34**, 153–169.

Warr, P. B., and J. S. Smith. Combining information about people: Comparisons between six models. *Journal of Personality and Social Psychology*, 1970, **16**, 55–65.

Watson, W. S., and G. W. Hartman. The rigidity of a basic attitudinal frame. *Journal of Abnormal and Social Psychology*, 1939, **34**, 314–335.

Watts, W. A., and L. E. Holt. Logical relationships among beliefs and timing as factors in persuasion. *Journal of Personality and Social Psychology*, 1970, **16**, 571–582.

Webb, W. B. and E. P. Hollander. Comparison of three morale measures: A survey, pooled group judgments, and self evaluations. *Journal of Applied Psychology*, 1956, **40**, 17–20.

Weber, S. J., and T. D. Cook. Subject effects in laboratory research: An examination of subject roles, demand characteristics, and valid inference. *Psychological Bulletin*, 1972, **77**, 273–295.

Weiner, B., I. Frieze, A. Kukla, L. Reed, and R. M. Rosenbaum. *Perceiving the Causes of Success and Failure*. New York: General Learning Press, 1971.

Weiner, B., and A. Kukla. An attribution analysis of achievement motivation. *Journal of Personality and Social Psychology*, 1970, **15**, 1–20.

Weiss, D. J., and N. H. Anderson. Subjective averaging of length with serial presentation. *Journal of Experimental Psychology*, 1969, **82**, 52–63.

Weitz, J. and R. C. Nuckols. The validity and direct and indirect questions in measuring job satisfaction. *Personnel Psychology*, 1953, **6**, 487–494.

Wickens, D. D. Encoding categories of words: An empirical approach to meaning. *Psychological Review*, 1970, **77**, 1–15.

Wicker, A. W. Attitudes vs. actions: The relationship of verbal and overt behavioral responses to attitude objects. *Journal of Social Issues*, 1969, **25**, 41–78.

Wicker, A. W. An examination of the "other variables" explanation of attitude-behavior inconsistency. *Journal of Personality and Social Psychology*, 1971, **19**, 18–30.

Wicker, A. W. and R. J. Pomazal. The relationship between attitudes and behavior as a function of specificity of attitude object and presence of a significant person during assessment conditions. *Representative Research in Social Psychology*, 1971, **2**, 26–31.

Wiggins, J. S. *Personality and Prediction: Principles of Personality Assessment*. Reading, Mass.: Addion-Wesley, 1973.

Wiggins, J. S., K. E. Renner, G. L. Clore, and R. J. Rose. *The Psychology of Personality*. Reading, Mass.: Addison-Wesley, 1971.

Wiggins, N. Individual differences in human judgment: A multivariate approach. In L. Rappaport and D. A. Summers (eds.), *Human Judgment and Social Interaction*. New York: Holt, 1973, pp. 110–142.

Wiggins, N., and P. J. Hoffman. Three models of clinical judgment. *Journal of Abnormal Psychology*, 1968, **73**, 70–77.

Wiggins, N., P. J. Hoffman, and T. Taber. Types of judges and cue utilization in judgments of intelligence. *Journal of Personality and Social Psychology*, 1969, **12**, 52–59.

Wishner, J. Reanalysis of "impressions of personality." *Psychological Review*, 1960, **67**, 96–112.

Woodmansee, J. J. The pupil response as a measure of social attitudes. In G. F. Summers (ed.), *Attitude Measurement*. Chicago: Rand McNally, 1970, pp. 514–533.

Woodmansee, J. J., and S. W. Cook. Dimensions of verbal racial attitudes: Their identification and measurement. *Journal of Personality and Social Psychology*, 1967, **7**, 240–250.

Woodworth, R. S., and H. Schlosberg. *Experimental Psychology*. New York: Holt, 1954.

Woodworth, R. S., and S. B. Sells. An atmosphere effect in formal syllogistic reasoning. *Journal of Experimental Psychology*, 1935, **18**, 451–460.

Wyer, R. S., Jr. The effects of information redundancy on evaluation of social stimuli. *Psychonomic Science*, 1968, **13**, 245–246.

Wyer, R. S., Jr. Quantitative prediction of belief and opinion change: A further test of a subjective probability model. *Journal of Personality and Social Psychology*, 1970, **16**, 559–570. (a)

Wyer, R. S., Jr. Information redundancy, inconsistency, and novelty and their role in impression formation. *Journal of Experimental Social Psychology*, 1970, **6**, 111–127. (b)

Wyer, R. S., Jr. The prediction of evaluations of social role occupants as a function of the favorableness, relevance and probability associated with attributes of these occupants. *Sociometry*, 1970, **33**, 79–96. (c)

Wyer, R. S., Jr. Category ratings as "subjective expected values": Implications for attitude formation and change. *Psychological Review*, 1973, **80**, 446–467.

Wyer, R. S., Jr., and M. Dermer. Effect of context and instructional set upon evaluations of personality-trait adjectives. *Journal of Personality and Social Psychology*, 1968, **9**, 7–14.

Wyer, R. S., Jr., and L. Goldberg. A probabilistic analysis of relationships among beliefs and attitudes. *Psychological Review*, 1970, **77**, 100–120.

Wyer, R. S., Jr., and J. D. Lyon. A test of cognitive balance theory implications for social inference processes. *Journal of Personality and Social Psychology*, 1970, **16**, 598–618.

Wyer, R. S., Jr., and S. F. Watson. Context effects in impression formation. *Journal of Personality and Social Psychology*, 1969, **12**, 22–33.

Zajonc, R. B. Structure of the cognitive field. Unpublished doctoral dissertation, University of Michigan, 1954.

Zajonc, R. B. The process of cognitive tuning in communication. *Journal of Abnormal and Social Psychology*, 1960, **61**, 159–164.

Zajonc, R. B. Cognitive theories in social psychology. In G. Lindzey and E. Aronson (eds.), *The Handbook of Social Psychology*, 2nd ed., Vol. 1. Reading, Mass.: Addison-Wesley, 1968, pp. 320–411. (a)

Zajonc, R. B. Attitudinal effects of mere exposure. *Journal of Personality and Social Psychology Monograph Supplement*, 1968, **9**, Part 2, 1–27. (b)

Zajonc, R. B., P. Shaver, C. Tavris, and D. Van Kreveld. Exposure, satiation, and stimulus discriminability. *Journal of Personality and Social Psychology*, 1972, **21,** 270–280.

Zajonc, R. B., W. C. Swap, A. A. Harrison, and P. Roberts. Limiting conditions of the exposure effect: Satiation and relativity. *Journal of Personality and Social Psychology*, 1971, **18,** 384–391.

Zeaman, D. Response latency as a function of the amount of reinforcement. *Journal of Experimental Psychology*, 1949, **39,** 466–483.

Zimbardo, P., and E. B. Ebbesen. *Influencing Attitudes and Changing Behavior.* Reading, Mass.: Addison-Wesley, 1969.

Zimbardo, P., M. Snyder, J. Thomas, A. Gold, and S. Gurwitz. Modifying the impact of persuasive communications with external distraction. *Journal of Personality and Social Psychology*, 1970, **16,** 669–680.

Author Index

563

Subject Index

Acceptance gradient, 462
Acceptance of a message, 452, 461–467, 475–476, 491
Action; *see* Behavior
Active participation, 411–450
Activity dimension, 76
Adding-averaging controversy, *see* Information integration
Affect, 7, 11–14, 28, 35, 38, 56; *see also* Attitude, Evaluation, Value
Affective component of attitude, 340–343
Aggressiveness, 7
Assimilation, 457
Attention decrement, 247
Attention to a message, 452
Attitude; *see also* Attitude theories, Measurement techniques, Research in the attitude area
and behavior, 2, 9, 26, 336–351
toward a behavior, 16, 31, 218, 301–302, 351, 400–401
change, 2, 35, 37–38, 41, 43, 51, 396–400
definition of, 1, 5–11
determinants of, 217–222
effects of behavior on, 35, 43
effects of information on, 51
formation, 14, 25, 35, 39, 50–51, 216–287

as a learned response, 9, 10
multicomponent view of, 340–343
toward an object, 14, 15, 16, 29, 35, 218, 347, 351
as a predisposition, 6, 8, 9, 10, 15, 336
relation to intention, 289–298, 317–318
as a residue of past experience, 10
single-response measures of, 56–58
toward a situation, 347
Attitude scales, *see* Measurement techniques, standard attitude scaling
Attitude theories, 21–52; *see also* names of specific theories
dynamic approach, 34, 42, 50–52
functional approach, 31
information-processing approach, 13, 14, 50, 52, 222–255
relations among beliefs, attitudes, intentions, and behavior, 14, 15, 16
Attraction, 1, 13, 255–277
similarity and, 255–270
Attribute, evaluation of, 14, 29, 31, 35, 60–62, 64, 81–86, 398–399
object-attribute association, 12–14, 28, 35, 54, 57, 131, 134
Attribution; *see also* Attribution theories, Beliefs, inferential
causal, 32, 45, 47, 49, 190–195

573